Cross-Domain Deterrence

Cross-Domain Deterrence

Strategy in an Era of Complexity

EDITED BY JON R. LINDSAY
and
ERIK GARTZKE

Oxford University Press is a department of the University of Oxford. It furthers the University's objective of excellence in research, scholarship, and education by publishing worldwide. Oxford is a registered trade mark of Oxford University Press in the UK and certain other countries.

Published in the United States of America by Oxford University Press
198 Madison Avenue, New York, NY 10016, United States of America.

© Oxford University Press 2019

All rights reserved. No part of this publication may be reproduced, stored in a retrieval system, or transmitted, in any form or by any means, without the prior permission in writing of Oxford University Press, or as expressly permitted by law, by license, or under terms agreed with the appropriate reproduction rights organization. Inquiries concerning reproduction outside the scope of the above should be sent to the Rights Department, Oxford University Press, at the address above.

You must not circulate this work in any other form
and you must impose this same condition on any acquirer.

Library of Congress Cataloging-in-Publication Data
Names: Lindsay, Jon R., editor of compilation. | Gartzke, Erik, editor of compilation.
Title: Cross-domain deterrence : strategy in an era of complexity / editors, Jon Lindsay and Erik Gartzke.
Description: 1st edition. | New York, NY : Oxford University Press, [2019]
Identifiers: LCCN 2018023972 (print) | LCCN 2018026312 (ebook) |
ISBN 9780190908669 (Universal PDF) | ISBN 9780190908676 (E-Pub) |
ISBN 9780190909604 (Oxford Scholarship Online) | ISBN 9780190908645 (hardcover: alk. paper) |
ISBN 9780190908652 (pbk. : alk. paper)
Subjects: LCSH: Deterrence (Strategy) | Asymmetric warfare. |
Military art and science—Technological innovations.
Classification: LCC U162.6 (ebook) | LCC U162.6 .C76 2019 (print) |
DDC 355.02—dc23
LC record available at https://lccn.loc.gov/2018023972

CONTENTS

Acknowledgments vii

1. Introduction: Cross-Domain Deterrence, from Practice to Theory 1
   JON R. LINDSAY AND ERIK GARTZKE

THE CONCEPT OF CROSS-DOMAIN DETERRENCE

2. Cross-Domain Deterrence in American Foreign Policy 27
   MICHAEL NACHT, PATRICIA SCHUSTER, AND EVA C. URIBE

3. The Past and Future of Deterrence Theory 50
   PATRICK M. MORGAN

4. Simplicity and Complexity in the Nth Nuclear Era 66
   RON LEHMAN

STRATEGIC IMPLICATIONS OF DIFFERENT MILITARY DOMAINS

5. Deterrence in and through Cyberspace 95
   JACQUELYN G. SCHNEIDER

6. Antisatellite Weapons and the Growing Instability of Deterrence 121
   BENJAMIN W. BAHNEY, JONATHAN PEARL, AND MICHAEL MARKEY

7. Air Power versus Ground Forces: Deterrence at the Operational Level of War 144
   PHIL HAUN

8. Sea Power versus Land Power: Cross-Domain Deterrence in the Peloponnesian War 163
JOSHUA ROVNER

COMMUNICATION AND CREDIBILITY ACROSS DOMAINS

9. International Law and the Common Knowledge Requirements of Cross-Domain Deterrence 187
JAMES D. MORROW

10. Signaling with Secrets: Evidence on Soviet Perceptions and Counterforce Developments in the Late Cold War 205
BRENDAN RITTENHOUSE GREEN AND AUSTIN G. LONG

11. Extended Deterrence and Assurance in Multiple Domains 234
RUPAL N. MEHTA

INTERACTIONS ACROSS MILITARY AND NONMILITARY DOMAINS

12. Asymmetric Advantage: Weaponizing People as Nonmilitary Instruments of Cross-Domain Coercion 259
KELLY M. GREENHILL

13. Linkage Politics: Managing the End of the Cold War 290
JOSHUA R. ITZKOWITZ SHIFRINSON

14. Beyond Military Deterrence: The Multidimensionality of International Relations in East Asia 317
CHIN-HAO HUANG AND DAVID C. KANG

15. Conclusion: The Analytic Potential of Cross-Domain Deterrence 335
JON R. LINDSAY AND ERIK GARTZKE

Contributor Biographies 373
Index 379

ACKNOWLEDGMENTS

The idea for this project emerged through conversations in 2013 with Michael Nacht, who had recently served in the first Obama administration as Assistant Secretary of Defense for Global Strategic Affairs (ASD-GSA). During his tenure Dr. Nacht managed a diverse policy portfolio of cyber, space, nuclear, and missile defense issues in the context of strategic challenges posed by China, Russia, Iran, North Korea, and the Al Qaeda network, among others. Grappling with what had by then come to be known as "cross-domain deterrence," he convened an eclectic group of scholars, futurists, and corporate leaders in 2010 for a series of meetings—the 21st Century Cross-Domain Deterrence Initiative—to discuss the strategic challenges of emerging technologies. Traditional deterrence theory did not seem to offer any simple answers.

The conversation has continued under the auspices of a research program on "Deterring Complex Threats" sponsored by the Department of Defense Minerva Initiative (administered through an Office of Naval Research grant [N00014-14-1-0071]) in collaboration with the Lawrence Livermore and Los Alamos National Laboratories. Several of the contributors to this book presented early drafts of their chapters at an academic conference held in November 2014 at the University of California, San Diego. The views expressed in the chapters of this book are those of the authors and do not necessarily reflect those of the DoD or its services. A subsequent workshop in May 2016 at George Washington University reconvened many of the original participants of the 2010 meeting hosted by ASD-GSA. Our 2016 workshop included some of the most eminent scholars of deterrence, including George Quester, Morton Halperin, Robert Jervis, and Richard Betts.

Most academic books develop over a long period of time and benefit from the efforts of many people, and this one is no exception. Jason Lopez has served as the administrative linchpin of our cross-domain deterrence project. Nothing would have happened without his tireless efforts. The students and research associates affiliated with the project and the UCSD Center for Peace and Security Studies (cPASS) have been a reliable source of feedback, criticism, and encouragement. Barry Posen offered helpful comments about the project in its early stages at a panel at the 2014 meeting of the International Studies Association. Christine Kerns and Beth Proznitz provided expert organization for the 2014 conference. J. Andres Gannon and Jason Lopez ensured that the 2016 workshop was a success. Jasmine Chorley Foster and Nicola Plummer both copyedited drafts of the entire text, which was vastly improved by their efforts. David McBride and the entire team at Oxford University Press shepherded the project through a lengthy review and production process. Most importantly, we are grateful to our families for their love and support all along the way.

We had the honor of dining with Thomas Schelling to discuss the evolving nature of deterrence just a few months before he passed away. His penetrating thought and lively prose are without equal in the canon of strategic studies. We dedicate this book to his memory.

Cross-Domain Deterrence

1

Introduction

Cross-Domain Deterrence, from Practice to Theory

JON R. LINDSAY AND ERIK GARTZKE

Political leaders since antiquity have made threats to dissuade others from harming their interests. "When there is mutual fear," as Thucydides observes, "men think twice before they make aggressions on one another."[1] Yet deterrence as a precise theoretical concept and a paramount element of national security policy only emerged in the nuclear era. Throughout most of human history, leaders could rely on the same military means to both threaten and wage war. So long as there were practical limits to the amount or rate of violence that armies and weapons could produce, war remained a real option for settling disagreements when threats failed. Military victory could also deliver real benefits such as arable acres, plunder, or extra pairs of hands to till the soil or work in the mines, while an army that was large and skilled enough could provide effective protection from attack. The calculus of war changed in the aftermath of Hiroshima, however. The United States and the Soviet Union fielded large arsenals of intercontinental missiles, bombers, and submarines, but even a single bomb might incinerate an entire city, and a general exchange appeared likely to make the planet inhospitable. Each of the superpowers sought ways to limit the horrific damage they might experience in a general nuclear exchange, yet the sheer number, mobility, and dispersion of launch platforms—located on land, in the air, and under the sea—made military defense nearly futile. Nuclear warfighting came to seem like a suicidal proposition, and victory in a nuclear war would be pyrrhic at best.

Yet if the idea of *winning* a nuclear war became meaningless, as Bernard Brodie famously pointed out, then for the same reason *threats* of nuclear war became especially useful for keeping the peace.[2] The superpowers both developed weapons they

---

[1] Benjamin Jowett, *Thucydides, Translated into English, to Which Is Prefixed an Essay on Inscriptions and a Note on the Geography of Thucydides*, 2nd ed. (Oxford: Clarendon Press, 1900), para. 4.62.

[2] Bernard Brodie et al., *The Absolute Weapon: Atomic Power and World Order* (New York: Harcourt, Brace, 1946), 75.

dared not use but needed in order to discourage aggression, or for occasional blackmail. The central paradox in both the theory and practice of deterrence was how to credibly threaten to use weapons for coercion (i.e., deterrence or compellence) that were too costly to use in war. While an intuition about threats may have sufficed in an earlier era, many desired something a bit more formal to underwrite decisions about Armageddon. A vast literature developed during the Cold War to explicate deterrence as a problem of high-stakes bargaining, including specialized elaborations on the credibility of nuclear guarantees to allies, the incentives for conventional war in the shadow of nuclear deterrence, the safety and reliability of nuclear command and control systems, and psychological and institutional deviations from rationalist assumptions. This work produced a rough consensus on the logic, if not the practice, of deterrence.[3]

The complexity of the twenty-first century's threat landscape contrasts markedly with the bilateral nuclear bargaining context envisioned by classical deterrence theory. Nuclear and conventional arsenals continue to develop alongside antisatellite programs, autonomous robotics or drones, cyber operations, biotechnology, and other innovations barely imagined in the early nuclear age. Some of these technologies may produce disruptive effects on a par with weapons of mass destruction, but many of them open up new options for low-intensity or even nonlethal effects. Some of these technologies are specialized for unique military applications (e.g., hypersonic cruise missiles), but many draw their aggressive potential from their utility and availability in the global economy (e.g., commercial software development platforms). Different types of actors may be able and motivated to exploit these capabilities in unexpected ways, from ambitious rising powers like China to dissatisfied regional powers like Russia or Iran, domestic factions of weak allies like Pakistan and Iraq, anarchist movements like Anonymous, terrorist groups like Islamic State (Daesh), and the list goes on.

---

[3] Lawrence Freedman, *Deterrence* (Cambridge: Polity Press, 2004), 117. Freedman notes "how complicated a theoretical tangle developed around deterrence even during the cold war, a period of unusual clarity and continuity in international affairs." Influential works include: Brodie et al., *The Absolute Weapon*; Albert Wohlstetter, *The Delicate Balance of Terror* (Santa Monica, CA: RAND Corporation, December 1958); Herman Kahn, *On Thermonuclear War* (Princeton, NJ: Princeton University Press, 1960); Glenn H. Snyder, *Deterrence and Defense: Toward a Theory of National Security* (Princeton, NJ: Princeton University Press, 1961); Thomas C. Schelling, *Arms and Influence: With a New Preface and Afterword* (New Haven, CT: Yale University Press, 2008); Robert Jervis, *The Meaning of the Nuclear Revolution: Statecraft and the Prospect of Armageddon* (Ithaca, NY: Cornell University Press, 1989); Robert Powell, *Nuclear Deterrence Theory: The Search for Credibility* (Cambridge: Cambridge University Press, 1990). For argument that Cold War nuclear policymaking departed significantly from strategic precepts, see: Francis J. Gavin, *Nuclear Statecraft: History and Strategy in America's Atomic Age* (Ithaca, NY: Cornell University Press, 2012); Austin Long and Brendan Rittenhouse Green, "Stalking the Secure Second Strike: Intelligence, Counterforce, and Nuclear Strategy," *Journal of Strategic Studies* 38, nos. 1–2 (2014): 38–73, https://doi.org/10.1080/01402390.2014.958150.

The term "cross-domain deterrence" (CDD) entered the defense lexicon near the end of the George W. Bush administration as policymakers and commanders grappled with these problems, and in particular the emerging challenges in space and cyberspace. The Pentagon now recognizes five operational environments or so-called domains: land, sea, air, space, and cyberspace. Across the entire spectrum of conflict, from disaster relief and counterterrorism on up to major combat operations and nuclear war, U.S. military power depends on carefully synchronized operations across all domains. While the term CDD as such (and related terms like "multidomain" or "full-spectrum" deterrence) has a peculiar American provenance, the strategic problem appears to be more general. The Chinese concept of "integrated strategic deterrence," for example, responds to similar challenges and opportunities created by the expanded diversity and interdependence across military technologies, stressing an imperative for coordinating nuclear, conventional, space, and cyber capabilities to achieve Chinese security objectives.[4] The Russian concept of "strategic deterrence" similarly aims to integrate nonnuclear, informational, and nuclear means to counteract the threat of Western "hybrid warfare."[5]

Many emerging technologies give rise to contradictory expectations. It is possible, and much feared in some circles, that weaker states and nonstate actors might exploit the technologies of globalization to undermine the conventional military advantages of great powers like the United States. Yet it is also possible that strong and wealthy states are better poised to integrate emerging capabilities to augment and enhance their power. Many fear that daunting complexity will result in higher levels of danger. Alternatively, global interdependence may provide new means for strategic actors to subvert the status quo without triggering war. Cross-domain operations and strategy pose urgent and difficult operational problems confronting most twenty-first-century militaries. They pose difficult intellectual problems as well.

The goal of this book is to problematize CDD as a theoretical concept. We ask whether CDD provides any additional analytical traction beyond classical notions of deterrence, as well as whether familiar concepts of political bargaining can be used to make sense of new and future domains. In conceptualizing CDD, we pay particular attention to the *means* of deterrence. Cross-domain deterrence posits

---

[4] Michael S. Chase and Arthur Chan, *China's Evolving Approach to "Integrated Strategic Deterrence"* (Santa Monica, CA: RAND Corporation, 2016), http://www.rand.org/pubs/research_reports/RR1366.html; M. Taylor Fravel, "Shifts in Warfare and Party Unity: Explaining China's Changes in Military Strategy," *International Security* 42, no. 3 (January 1, 2018): 37–83, https://doi.org/10.1162/ISEC_a_00304.

[5] Kristin Ven Bruusgaard, "Russian Strategic Deterrence," *Survival* 58, no. 4 (2016): 7–26, https://doi.org/10.1080/00396338.2016.1207945; Dima Adamsky, "From Moscow with Coercion: Russian Deterrence Theory and Strategic Culture," *Journal of Strategic Studies* 41, nos. 1–2 (2018): 33–60, https://doi.org/10.1080/01402390.2017.1347872. Western analysts sometimes misinterpret Russian concepts that describe the admixture of covert action and conventional warfare by *Western* states as a description of *Russian* doctrine.

that *how* actors choose to deter affects the quality of the deterrence they achieve. Classical deterrence theory says little formally about the particular instruments used to impose costs or deny benefits. The pressing problem of the Cold War was how to deter nuclear war with nuclear weapons, and thus deterrence theory dealt with "apples and apples." Yet deterrence in practice has always dealt with a diverse array of "apples and oranges," that is, different military services with different nuclear, conventional, and unconventional weapons, together with various diplomatic, economic, and cultural instruments of national power.

We define CDD as the use of threats of one type, or some combination of different types, to dissuade a target from taking actions of another type to attempt to change the status quo. More simply, CDD is the use of unlike technological means for the political ends of deterrence. States and other actors today have a large and growing portfolio of tools for coercion, warfighting, and influence. Domains of action and technological capabilities may differ markedly from each other in their geographical, material, organizational, and political characteristics. Thus policymakers may use air strikes to retaliate for terrorism, cyber operations to disable an adversary's command and control or to influence its electorate, targeted economic sanctions to punish a cyber intrusion, or even migration policy to coerce neighboring states. Indeed, nonmilitary options for exerting influence and extracting concessions are increasingly available right alongside novel weaponry. Sociotechnical complexity is the problem that gives rise to CDD, and complexity calls the feasibility of deterrence into question.

This introductory chapter offers some context on the historical development of CDD in practice and then pivots to a consideration of CDD in theory. The authors of all the chapters in this book probe the analytical utility of CDD by examining how differences across, and combinations of, different military and nonmilitary instruments affect choices and outcomes in coercive policy.

Cross-domain Deterrence in Historical Context

The U.S. military was without peer at the dawn of the twenty-first century. It was also expensive, thinly stretched, and highly dependent on vulnerable information networks. The notion of CDD first emerged in defense policy circles in the context of the strategic conundrums of cyberspace and outer space. These problems were particularly acute in the context of Chinese military modernization and the threat China posed to continued U.S. dominance in the western Pacific. Furthermore, Russian aggression in Estonia, Georgia, and Ukraine in the context of Russian nuclear modernization amplified concerns about American vulnerability. Meanwhile, the U.S. military remained engaged in protracted combat operations in Afghanistan and Iraq, complicated by Iranian covert intervention and efforts at nuclear proliferation.

The U.S. Joint Force combines capabilities from the Army, Navy, Air Force, Marine Corps, Coast Guard, Special Operations Command (SOCOM), and the fledgling Cyber Command (CYBERCOM), all linked together by globe-spanning networks for command, control, communication, and intelligence. Cyber and space systems enable powerful synergies, but by the same token, they also are attractive targets for U.S. adversaries. Chinese strategists, among others, believe that information and logistics systems are the Achilles heel of American military power.[6] Chinese military modernization, cyber espionage campaigns, and antisatellite weapons tests during the George W. Bush and Obama administrations dramatized the danger. Many feared that low-cost, plausibly deniable attacks on vital infrastructure on Earth or in orbit had the power to disrupt the United States' ability to project power and sustain intervention in an overseas contingency. American policymakers thus sought new ways and means to discourage attacks in cyberspace or outer space, perhaps by using instruments of national power in other military or even nonmilitary domains. This, in turn, raised difficult questions about how to issue threats and offer reassurances that were credible, proportional, affordable, and, above all, effective. American mastery of cross-domain *operations* thus came at the price of more complicated cross-domain *deterrence* problems.[7]

The Cyber Domain

The appearance of the term "domain" in the military lexicon is inextricably linked to the rise of cyberspace as a national security concern for the United States, and as a bureaucratic opportunity for its military services. The colloquial term "domain" has both geographical and functional connotations. According to the *Oxford Dictionary*, a domain is "an area of territory owned or controlled by a ruler or government" or "a specified sphere of activity or knowledge," while the term in computer science—"a distinct subset of the Internet with addresses sharing a common suffix or under the control of a particular organization or individual"—has a jurisdictional connotation

---

[6] Jacqueline Newmyer, "The Revolution in Military Affairs with Chinese Characteristics," *Journal of Strategic Studies* 33, no. 4 (2010): 483–504, https://doi.org/10.1080/01402390.2010.489706; Kevin Pollpeter, "Controlling the Information Domain: Space, Cyber, and Electronic Warfare," in *Strategic Asia 2012-13: China's Military Challenge*, edited by Ashley J. Tellis and Travis Tanner (Seattle: National Bureau of Asian Research, 2012): 163-194.

[7] Discussion of CDD by contemporaries include Shawn Brimley, "Promoting Security in Common Domains," *Washington Quarterly* 33, no. 3 (July 1, 2010): 119–132, https://doi.org/10.1080/0163660X.2010.492725; James A. Lewis, "Cross-Domain Deterrence and Credible Threats" (Washington, DC: Center for Strategic and International Studies, July 2010); Vincent Manzo, "Deterrence and Escalation in Cross-Domain Operations: Where Do Space and Cyberspace Fit?," (Washington, DC: Institute for National Strategic Studies, National Defense University, December 2011); Madelyn R. Creedon, "Space and Cyber: Shared Challenges, Shared Opportunities," *Strategic Studies Quarterly* 6, no. 1 (Spring 2012): 3–8, https://www.hsdl.org/?view&did=702266.

that draws on the geographic metaphor.[8] Cyberspace is best considered a domain in the functional rather than the geographic sense. The Internet is a heterogeneous assemblage of technical and institutional components that provide information and control services to diverse actors; these components and links are all physically located on land, under water, in the air, and in orbit. While the notion of "cyberspace" as some sort of virtual place can be quite misleading, the functional concept of domain has turned out to be useful in bureaucratic politics as the nascent U.S. cyber community seeks expanded budgets and authorities to "man, train, and equip" cyber forces.[9]

Throughout the 1990s and early 2000s, specialists in what was then known as the "information warfare" community worked to gain acceptance for the idea of cyberspace as a warfighting domain.[10] Just as strategic bombing doctrine aided the champions of an independent air force in the 1930s and 1940s, the notion of a new "fifth domain" had important budgetary and legal implications. A September 2006 briefing by the director of the U.S. Air Force Cyberspace Task Force promoted the new religion with "The Cyber Creed," which states: "cyber is a war-fighting domain. The electromagnetic spectrum is the maneuver space. Cyber is the United States' Center of Gravity—the hub of all power and movement, upon which everything else depends. It is the Nation's neural network. Cyber superiority is the prerequisite to effective operations across all strategic and operational domains—securing freedom from attack and freedom to attack."[11] The same briefing noted that "Cross-Domain Dominance = Sovereign Options." This is a modern variation on the classic air power theme that advanced technology creates strategic or "sovereign" alternatives to traditional fighting. The Air Force thus aimed to position itself as the service leader in three of the five domains, and it even adopted a new mission statement: "to fly, fight and win . . . in air, space and cyberspace." The Air Force was the first service to establish a major cyber warfare command, but the Navy and Army

---

[8] "Domain," *Oxford English Dictionary*, accessed 25 April 2018, https://en.oxforddictionaries.com/definition/us/domain.

[9] See Jacquelyn Schneider, chapter 5 here, and Jordan Branch, "Spatial Metaphors and the Territorialization of Cybersecurity," International Studies Association Annual Conference, San Francisco, April 4–7, 2018.

[10] On the professionalization of cyber warfare in the U.S. military, see: Gregory J. Rattray, *Strategic Warfare in Cyberspace* (Cambridge, MA: MIT Press, 2001), ch. 5; Michael Warner, "Cybersecurity: A Pre-history," *Intelligence and National Security* 27, no. 5 (2012): 781–799, https://doi.org/10.1080/02684527.2012.708530; Jason Healey, ed., *A Fierce Domain: Conflict in Cyberspace, 1986 to 2012* (Washington, DC: Cyber Conflict Studies Association, 2013), ch. 1; Fred Kaplan, *Dark Territory: The Secret History of Cyber War* (New York: Simon and Schuster, 2016).

[11] Lani Kass, "A Warfighting Domain" (Headquarters U.S. Air Force, AF Cyberspace Task Force, Washington, DC, September 26, 2006), http://www.au.af.mil/info-ops/usaf/cyberspace_taskforce_sep06.pdf.

were not about to turn over the digital future to the Air Force and thus created their own cyber units shortly thereafter.

Yet it was the National Security Agency (NSA), the signals intelligence (SIGINT) component of the U.S. intelligence community, that had most of the budget and technical expertise for covert computer network operations. In May 2010, the Pentagon consolidated service efforts under CYBERCOM as a subunified command under U.S. Strategic Command (STRATCOM), collocated with the NSA; General Keith Alexander, who was also Director of the NSA, became its first "dual hatted" commander. The acknowledgment by senior Defense leadership that cyberspace was a domain "just as critical to military operations as land, sea, air, and space" gave CYBERCOM a legitimacy and influence it might not otherwise have had.[12] The consolidation of U.S. nuclear, cyber, and space forces under the STRATCOM umbrella, moreover, provided an institutional locus of concern for the strategic interaction of these quite different but increasingly interdependent capabilities.[13]

The vulnerability of the cyber domain led naturally to concerns about CDD because computer networks connected and controlled all other military capabilities. A wave of distributed denial of service (DDoS) attacks hit Estonia in 2007, resulting in millions of dollars in lost productivity and remediation costs.[14] In 2008, Georgia was hit with a similar barrage of DDoS attacks, this time coinciding with the Russian land invasion of South Ossetia and naval blockade of Abkhazia.[15] Russian penetrations of Pentagon systems, including operations dubbed Moonlight Maze and Buckshot Yankee, raised serious concerns that the same cyber methods used for intelligence collection might one day be employed for disruptive attack. Indeed, STRATCOM had played a key role, together with the NSA and Israeli intelligence, in a major cyber campaign against Iran that was inadvertently compromised to the world in 2010. The Stuxnet operation was a cyber attack against an Iranian nuclear

---

[12] William J. Lynn III, "Defending a New Domain: The Pentagon's Cyberstrategy," *Foreign Affairs* (September/October 2010), https://www.foreignaffairs.com/articles/united-states/2010-09-01/defending-new-domain.

[13] STRATCOM's enduring focus on CDD is reflected in recent comments by its commander: "as we look back on the events of 2014, and the early part of 2015, we can see that today's threat environment is more diverse, complex and uncertain than it's ever been, against a backdrop of global security environment latent with multiple actors, operating across multiple domains. From under the sea to geosynchronous orbit, you have your Strategic Command focused on addressing existential threats and preserving our democratic values and way of life." Cecil Haney, "Department of Defense Press Briefing by Adm. Haney in the Pentagon Briefing Room," U.S. Department of Defense, 24 March 2015, accessed 25 April 2018, http://www.defense.gov/News/News-Transcripts/Transcript-View/Article/607027.

[14] Andreas Schmidt, "The Estonian Cyberattacks," in Healey, *A Fierce Domain*, 174–193.

[15] Ronald J. Deibert, Rafal Rohozinski, and Masashi Crete-Nishihata, "Cyclones in Cyberspace: Information Shaping and Denial in the 2008 Russia-Georgia War," *Security Dialogue* 43, no. 1 (2012): 3–24, https://doi.org/10.1177/0967010611431079.

facility in lieu of an Israeli airstrike, intended to both frustrate an adversary and reassure an ally; Michael Nacht and his coauthors in chapter 2 note that the case helped motivate policymaker thinking about CDD. Stuxnet also raised the specter that adversaries might employ similar methods to subvert U.S. deterrence.

Cyber espionage from China, meanwhile, had risen to epidemic levels by 2011. It was motivated mainly, although not exclusively, by nonmilitary objectives such as industrial modernization and domestic political censorship. While cyber futurists often invoked (and skeptics ridiculed)[16] the danger of a "digital Pearl Harbor," an alternative danger in the form of a gradual "death by a thousand cuts" via the erosion of U.S. military and economic competitiveness began to unfold. Defense planners still could not rule out a catastrophic Chinese cyber attack, in part because strategists in the People's Liberation Army (PLA) wrote enthusiastically about just such an eventuality. Chinese concepts of "unrestricted warfare" and "integrated network electronic warfare" elaborated on American ideas about the disruptiveness of the information revolution and extolled the asymmetric, low-cost, offense-dominant, and decisive potency of network warfare. Chinese doctrine for "limited war under conditions of informatization" thus imparted considerable urgency to American thinking about the problem of CDD. Notably, moreover, Chinese theorists have argued that information dominance depends, in turn, on control of the space domain.[17]

The Space Domain

Part of cyberspace is literally in outer space. Communication satellites broadcast content and relay data. Precision navigation and timing constellations like the Global Positioning System (GPS) synchronize global financial transactions and support commercial mapping applications. Remote sensing platforms collect images and signals for intelligence and commercial uses that can be combined with other data. Conversely, space capabilities rely on cyberspace because satellite computers in orbit connect to ground stations and to each other via radio data links. Space and cyberspace are inherently cross-domain because they host the information infrastructure for command, control, communication, computation,

---

[16] Erik Gartzke, "The Myth of Cyberwar: Bringing War in Cyberspace Back Down to Earth," *International Security* 38, no. 2 (2013): 41–73, https://doi.org/10.1162/ISEC_a_00136; Sean Lawson, "Beyond Cyber-Doom: Assessing the Limits of Hypothetical Scenarios in the Framing of Cyber-Threats," *Journal of Information Technology & Politics* 10, no. 1 (2013): 86–103, https://doi.org/10.1080/19331681.2012.759059.

[17] On Chinese cyber operations and policy, see: Jon R. Lindsay, Tai Ming Cheung, and Derek S. Reveron, eds., *China and Cybersecurity: Espionage, Strategy, and Politics in the Digital Domain* (New York: Oxford University Press, 2015). On China and space, see: Kevin Pollpeter, "Space, the New Domain: Space Operations and Chinese Military Reforms," *Journal of Strategic Studies* 39, nos. 5–6 (2016): 709–727, https://doi.org/10.1080/01402390.2016.1219946.

intelligence, surveillance, and reconnaissance (C4ISR). The two domains provide the global nervous system that enables and knits together operations in all of the other domains. Moreover, from a CDD perspective, the importance and vulnerability of informational functions creates some strategically salient similarities across these two domains: they are vital, vulnerable, global, and dependent on advanced technology. Space and cyberspace are thus often discussed together, and sometimes managed by the same bureaucratic agency (e.g., China's recently created Strategic Support Force).

Nevertheless, there are also some striking differences. Space is a physical environment, but cyberspace is an assemblage of human-constructed artifacts and institutions. From this perspective, the economic and operational characteristics of cyberspace and space are quite distinct. Millions of firms and individuals can own and design portions of cyberspace at relatively low cost. The pace of innovation in information technology is famously rapid, and the internet can accommodate a lot of inconsistent software. Countless civilians and military personnel in countries around the world have direct experience with cyberspace and even malicious hacking. By contrast, there are only a handful of spacefaring nations, and space operations are managed by a small (and secretive) cadre of technocratic experts. Heavy lift and ground control infrastructure is very expensive, and operating costs remain high even with the advent of commercial space. When satellites become damaged or derelict, it takes millions of dollars and years to replace them. Satellites travel at extremely high velocities, circling the Earth in as little as ninety minutes, and thus orbits must be carefully managed to avoid collisions with other satellites or debris. One irony is that while space is physically vast, its economic and operational characteristics make it surprisingly compact. These characteristics create challenges for deterrence that differ from other domains.[18]

The Bush administration released a space policy in August 2006 that asserted, "freedom of action in space is as important to the United States as air power and sea power," and directed the Pentagon to "develop capabilities, plans, and options to ensure freedom of action in space, and, if directed, deny such freedom of action to adversaries."[19] The new policy was put to the test in January 2007 when China tested a direct ascent anti-satellite (ASAT) kill vehicle, destroying its own *Fengyun-1C* satellite in low earth orbit (LEO) and creating the largest orbiting debris cloud in history. This incident highlighted not only the vulnerability of spacecraft in LEO (which includes many U.S. intelligence platforms) and the troubling debris potential of space warfare but also the specter of differing national opinions regarding the escalatory nature of ASATs. In February 2008, just weeks after China and Russia

---

[18] James Clay Moltz, *Crowded Orbits: Conflict and Cooperation in Space* (New York: Columbia University Press, 2014).

[19] Office of Science and Technology Policy, "U.S. National Space Policy," White House, 31 August 2006, accessed 25 April 2018, https://history.nasa.gov/ostp_space_policy06.pdf.

began advocating at the United Nations for a ban on space weapons, the United States launched a Standard Missile-3 (SM-3) from a *Ticonderoga*-class guided missile cruiser in the central Pacific. Although the SM-3 was designed as a ballistic missile interceptor, Operation Burnt Frost repurposed it as an ASAT weapon to destroy a derelict U.S. satellite. The stated purpose of the operation was to prevent the spillage of toxic hydrazine fuel from the deorbiting spacecraft, but its timing so soon after the Chinese ASAT test prompted considerable speculation that it was also a strategic signal from Washington warning Beijing and Moscow that they were vulnerable in space too. China proceeded with additional ASAT tests in the following years, but it took efforts to minimize the generation of debris in these subsequent tests. The vulnerability of vital space assets and the ambiguity of space signaling was, and remains, a serious CDD challenge.[20]

Contested Commons

Space is a key domain that enables the U.S. military to project power globally in other domains. U.S. military power, according to Barry Posen, depends on "command of the commons," which is the United States' ability to use the Earth's oceans, atmosphere, and outer space for military advantage while preventing opponents from doing the same. Posen cautions, however, that in terrestrial and littoral "contested zones," challengers can impose serious military costs on the United States. Abundant small arms, local nationalism, and limited strategic interests combine to turn most U.S. military adventures on foreign soil into costly quagmires. Areas that are uncontested might reflect either military predominance or the absence of a dispute. Thus, it is only where the United States lacks resolve, or the costs of U.S. intervention are high, that the military hegemon tends to be challenged.

Posen thus champions a grand strategy of "offshore balancing" (also known as "restraint") that would protect U.S. command of the commons but eschew intervention in contested zones where U.S. vital interests are not threatened.[21] In effect, offshore balancing is a strategy that leverages air and naval cross-domain capabilities to confront hegemonic challenges originating from the Eurasian landmass. While proponents intend offshore balancing to deter provocation, several chapters in this

---

[20] See chapter 6 here, as well as Michael Krepon and Julia Thompson, eds., *Anti-satellite Weapons, Deterrence and Sino-American Space Relations* (Washington, DC: Stimson Center, 2013); Brian Weeden, "Through a Glass, Darkly: Chinese, American, and Russian Anti-satellite Testing in Space," *Space Review* (17 March 2014), accessed 25 April 2018, http://www.thespacereview.com/article/2473/1.

[21] Barry R. Posen, "Command of the Commons: The Military Foundation of U.S. Hegemony," *International Security* 28, no. 1 (2003): 5–46, https://doi.org/10.1162/016228803322427965; Barry R. Posen, *Restraint: A New Foundation for U.S. Grand Strategy* (Ithaca, NY: Cornell University Press, 2014).

book (in particular those by Phil Haun and Rupal Mehta and our conclusion) imply that the very mobility and flexibility of air and naval forces, which make them so useful for military warfighting, actually undermine the predictability and credibility required for effective deterrence.

Two years after Posen's seminal article, the 2005 National Defense Strategy (NDS) asserted that "operating in the global commons" was one of America's "key operational capabilities" and was "critical to the direct defense of the United States and its partners."[22] The NDS (but not Posen) also included cyberspace alongside the sea, air, and space domains. Whereas Posen described contested zones simply as the limits of American military power, the new discourse construed them as illegitimate attempts to undermine the global liberal order safeguarded by the United States.[23] As the U.S. chief of naval operations, Admiral Jonathan Greenert, and the Air Force chief of staff, General Norton Schwartz, wrote in 2012, "free access to the ungoverned 'commons' of air, maritime, cyberspace and space is the foundation of the global marketplace. . . . But this interconnectedness also makes the global economy more susceptible to disruption. The fragility of chokepoints in air, space, cyberspace and on the sea enable an increasing number of entities, states and nonstate actors alike to disrupt the global economy with small numbers of well-placed, precise attacks."[24] Greenert and Schwartz continued with a barely concealed reference to China: "autocratic states and groups seeking to subvert the prevailing political and economic order are already leveraging their geographic advantages to employ armed coercion and political action to counter American presence and power projection, as well as to disrupt free access to key areas in the air and maritime commons. As these revisionist strategies advance, America's friends will increasingly seek the security and stability provided by comprehensive U.S. national power."[25] The phrase "command of the commons" struck a chord, ironically enough, among proponents of more muscular visions of U.S. grand strategy (i.e., "primacy" or "liberal hegemony") that seem at odds with Posen's vision. The grand strategies of "offshore balancing" and "restraint" advocated for strategic retrenchment in the face of expanding contested zones; by contrast, "primacy" aimed to prevent or even roll back the expansion. American analysts described China's military modernization

---

[22] "The National Defense Strategy of the United States of America," U.S. Department of Defense, March 2005, 15–16, accessed 25 April 2018, http://history.defense.gov/Portals/70/Documents/nds/2005_NDS.pdf?ver=2014-06-25-124535-143.

[23] E.g., Abraham M. Denmark and James Mulvenon, eds., *Contested Commons: The Future of American Power in a Multipolar World* (Washington, DC: Center for a New American Security, 2010); Scott Jasper, ed., *Securing Freedom in the Global Commons* (Stanford, CA: Stanford University Press, 2010).

[24] Jonathan W. Greenert and Norton A. Schwartz, "Air-Sea Battle," *American Interest*, 20 February 2012, accessed 25 April 2018, http://www.the-american-interest.com/2012/02/20/air-sea-battle.

[25] Ibid. The choice of the phrase "comprehensive U.S. national power" is notable given that "comprehensive national power" is the usual translation of the core Chinese concept of 综合国力.

as an "antia-acess/area-denial (A2/AD)" or "counter-intervention" strategy, even as Chinese doctrine never used these terms.[26] The U.S. military responded with operational concepts like "AirSea Battle," which it later renamed "Joint Access and Maneuver in the Global Commons."[27] These concepts, backed up by freedom-of-navigation operations conducted by the U.S. Navy, asserted a right of U.S. access to common areas and construed Chinese attempts at denial as revisionist provocation. Thus the "global commons" would remain open only as long as the military "domains" were controlled by the U.S. liberal hegemon. The semantic tension between the notion of a "commons" open to all and a "domain" under proprietary control went largely unmentioned. China, for its part, perceived real or threatened U.S. intervention in its "near seas" as aggressive interference in its sovereign interests.

The expanding contested zone in the western Pacific was, and remains, a major stimulus for thinking about CDD.[28] Chinese strategists highlight (correctly) that cyber and space systems are the key enabling components of U.S. military operations; accordingly, the PLA has developed capabilities to disrupt them. Chinese military modernization has produced long-range antiship missiles, advanced surface-to-air missiles, fifth-generation fighters, fast patrol craft, quiet diesel submarines, and space and counter-space capabilities, many of which remain veiled in secrecy. The PLA has also developed new doctrine and implemented sweeping institutional reforms to tie all these capabilities together. To counter Chinese A2/AD capabilities, the Pentagon has envisioned a "third offset" strategy to harness the innovative capacity of Silicon Valley and counter China with artificial intelligence, robotics, quantum computing, directed energy, microsatellites, and other technological fixes.[29] The concept of a third offset makes reference to

---

[26] On A2/AD, see: Evan Braden Montgomery, "Contested Primacy in the Western Pacific: China's Rise and the Future of U.S. Power Projection," *International Security* 38, no. 4 (2014): 115–149, https://doi.org/10.1162/ISEC_a_00160; Joe McReynolds, ed., *China's Evolving Military Strategy* (Washington, DC: Jamestown Foundation, 2016). On the absence of A2/AD or the purportedly Chinese term "counter-intervention" in Chinese doctrine, see: M. Taylor Fravel and Christopher P. Twomey, "Projecting Strategy: The Myth of Chinese Counter-intervention," *Washington Quarterly* 37, no. 4 (2015): 171–187, https://doi.org/10.1080/0163660X.2014.1002164.

[27] "Air-Sea Battle: Service Collaboration to Address Anti-access & Area Denial Challenges," U.S. Department of Defense, Air-Sea Battle Office, May 2013, accessed 25 April 2018, http://archive.defense.gov/pubs/ASB-ConceptImplementation-Summary-May-2013.pdf; Michael E. Hutchens et al., "Joint Concept for Access and Maneuver in the Global Commons: A New Joint Operational Concept," *Joint Force Quarterly* 84 (27 January 2017): 134–139, http://ndupress.ndu.edu/Media/News/Article/1038867/joint-concept-for-access-and-maneuver-in-the-global-commons-a-new-joint-operati/.

[28] Forrest E. Morgan et al., *Dangerous Thresholds* (Santa Monica, CA: RAND Corporation, 2008); James Scouras, Edward Smyth, and Thomas G. Mahnken, *Cross Domain Deterrence in U.S.-China Strategy*, workshop report (Laurel, MD: Johns Hopkins Applied Physics Laboratory, 2014).

[29] Bob Work, "The Third U.S. Offset Strategy and Its Implications for Partners and Allies," Speech hosted by the Center for a New American Security and the NATO Allied Command Transformation Willard InterContinental Hotel, Washington, DC, 28 January 2015, accessed 25 April 2018, https://

a supposed "first offset" in the early Cold War, when the United States fielded a nuclear arsenal to counter Soviet conventional power, and a "second offset" in the late Cold War, when the United States fielded advanced reconnaissance and precision strike weapons to counter Soviet material preponderance in Europe. All three offsets are, in effect, cross-domain strategies that shift and combine capabilities to counter an opponent's strengths, or in the Chinese case, counter the opponent's cross-domain counters. While the balance of power still favors the United States over China in most domains for most conceivable scenarios, China has been steadily narrowing the gap(s).[30] Any conflict between the United States and China would surely be costly in blood and treasure, as Joshua Rovner discusses in chapter 8.

Amid increasing worries about cyberspace, space, and China, the Bush administration initiated, and the Obama administration continued, a number of different studies of the problem of deterrence across domains. The intelligence community, national nuclear weapons laboratories, STRATCOM, and the Office of the Secretary of Defense all weighed in with concerns about CDD. One such study was the 21st Century Cross Domain Deterrence Initiative (CDDI), organized in early 2010 by Michael Nacht in his capacity as assistant secretary of defense for global strategic affairs. Nacht and his colleagues summarize some of the insights that emerged from that study in chapter 2 here. The CDDI and similar efforts produced a greater appreciation for the urgency and complexity of CDD. A new strategic consensus regarding the best way forward was elusive, however. The notion of CDD when it emerged was really more a description of the problem than a solution.

As a staff member in the office of the undersecretary of defense for policy observed in 2010, "cross-domain deterrence dynamics will constitute a core analytic issue for the U.S. defense, diplomatic, and intelligence community, particularly as shifts in the actual or perceived balance of power in sea, air, space, and cyberspace become more opaque."[31] If he is right, then security analysts and international relations scholars have an opportunity (and a challenge) to reevaluate the foundations of strategic thought. This book probes whether there is more to CDD than the faddish currents of Pentagon jargon or American paranoia about space, cyberspace, and China.

---

www.defense.gov/News/Speeches/Speech-View/Article/606641/the-third-us-offset-strategy-and-its-implications-for-partners-and-allies/.

[30] Eric Heginbotham et al., *The U.S.-China Military Scorecard* (Santa Monica, CA: RAND Corporation, 2015); Stephen Biddle and Ivan Oelrich, "Future Warfare in the Western Pacific: Chinese Antiaccess/Area Denial, U.S. AirSea Battle, and Command of the Commons in East Asia," *International Security* 41, no. 1 (Summer 2016): 7–48, https://doi.org/10.1162/ISEC_a_00249.

[31] Brimley, "Promoting Security in Common Domains," 129.

The Analytical Potential of Cross-Domain Deterrence

Deterrence is the use of threats to protect the status quo. Its offensive twin, *compellence*, is the use of threats to change (or restore) the status quo. Both are types of *coercion*, the use of threats of future harm to achieve a goal, which is distinct from brute force or operations, the inflicting of harm or shifting of benefits in the present. Coercive threats can inflict *punishment* or exercise *denial*; thus the prospects of retaliation or impenetrable defenses might deter an attack, and the prospects of unpleasant penalties or military conquest might compel concessions. These analytic distinctions can be ambiguous in practice. Denial can be punishing. A coercive strategy may employ some force in the present to enhance the credibility of threats of even more force in the future. Compellence may combine deterrent threats to demand concessions while preventing retaliation, the coercive analog of the shield protecting the sword; for example, the United States imposed a naval blockade to compel the Soviet Union to dismantle missile batteries on Cuba, combined with an implicit deterrent threat of U.S. nuclear retaliation. Actors may disagree about the status quo, so deterrence for one actor may look like compellence for the other; for example, consider an U.S. intervention to counter a Chinese invasion of Taiwan triggered by a declaration of independence from the mainland. Because there are rhetorical advantages to appearing to act in self-defense, many actors will use the term "deterrence" colloquially to describe their own acts of compellence.[32]

Deterrence itself has always been a *political* problem that depends on interests, power, information, and resolve. Yet deterrence theory arose historically in response to the *technological* problem of nuclear weapons. Technology, however, did not become an explicit part of deterrence theory because the enterprise assumed, implicitly, that the relevant means were nuclear. Traditional deterrence theorists focused on the challenge of credibility in the shadow of annihilation rather than the choice of means, and empirical scholars debated the applicability and scope of nuclear deterrence theory.[33] Much deterrence scholarship today still puts primary emphasis

---

[32] For a primer on coercion, see: Robert J. Art and Kelly M. Greenhill, "Coercion: An Analytical Overview," in *Coercion: The Power to Hurt in International Politics*, edited by Kelly M. Greenhill and Peter J. P. Krause (New York: Oxford University Press, 2018), 3–32.

[33] For a recent review of theoretical and empirical deterrence scholarship, see: Shannon Carcelli and Erik Gartzke, "The Diversification of Deterrence: New Data and Novel Realities," *Oxford Research Encyclopedia of Politics*, September 2017. Insightful reviews of the classical literature include: Fred Kaplan, *The Wizards of Armageddon* (New York: Simon and Schuster, 1986); Lawrence Freedman, "The First Two Generations of Nuclear Strategists," in *Makers of Modern Strategy: From Machiavelli to the Nuclear Age*, edited by Peter Paret (New York: Oxford, 1986), 735–778; Marc Trachtenberg, *History and Strategy* (Princeton, NJ: Princeton University Press, 1991), ch. 1.

on a putative "second nuclear age," a framework that is reasonable enough, given the dangers posed by North Korea and Iran, among others, but may also be limiting.[34]

The diversity of technological means was prominent in the practice of deterrence during the Cold War, of course, if not in theory. Military commanders and arms control negotiators worried obsessively about force structures and postures, including interactions between nuclear and conventional operations. The portfolio of options available for influence expanded despite, if not because of, the dangers of nuclear war. Throughout the Cold War, therefore, the superpowers jockeyed for advantage and participated in peripheral conflicts around the globe. The literature on the interaction between nuclear and conventional forces thus offers potentially useful insights about CDD, in particular the ideas that nuclear stability can incentivize limited or proxy wars (i.e., the "stability-instability paradox") or that limited conventional attacks might inadvertently escalate to nuclear war.[35] Likewise, conventional military strength today may incentivize cyber exploitation, covert infiltration, and other "gray zone" provocations that fall below clear thresholds of nuclear retaliation yet still risk escalation.[36]

Recent work has begun to tackle the complexity of modern deterrence by relaxing the classical focus on nuclear weapons, bilateral bargaining, and state actors to address problems of proliferation, terrorism, conventional war, and other forms of aggression.[37] In particular, there is an emerging literature that grapples

---

[34] Inter alia, T. V. Paul, Richard J. Harknett, and James J. Wirtz, eds., *The Absolute Weapon Revisited: Nuclear Arms and the Emerging International Order* (Ann Arbor: University of Michigan Press, 2000); Avery Goldstein, *Deterrence and Security in the 21st Century: China, Britain, France, and the Enduring Legacy of the Nuclear Revolution* (Stanford, CA: Stanford University Press, 2000); George P. Shultz, Sidney D. Drell, and James E. Goodby, *Deterrence: Its Past and Future—Papers Presented at Hoover Institution, November 2010* (Stanford, CA: Hoover Institution, 2011); Toshi Yoshihara and James R Holmes, eds., *Strategy in the Second Nuclear Age: Power, Ambition, and the Ultimate Weapon* (Washington, DC: Georgetown University Press, 2012); Vipin Narang, *Nuclear Strategy in the Modern Era: Regional Powers and International Conflict* (Princeton, NJ: Princeton University Press, 2014); Todd S. Sechser and Matthew Fuhrmann, *Nuclear Weapons and Coercive Diplomacy* (New York: Cambridge University Press, 2017).

[35] Inter alia, Glenn H. Snyder, "The Balance of Power and the Balance of Terror," in *The Balance of Power*, edited by Paul Seabury (San Francisco, CA: Chandler, 1965); Jervis, *The Meaning of the Nuclear Revolution*; Barry R. Posen, *Inadvertent Escalation: Conventional War and Nuclear Risks* (Ithaca, NY: Cornell University Press, 1991); Avery Goldstein, "First Things First: The Pressing Danger of Crisis Instability in U.S.-China Relations," *International Security* 37, no. 4 (2013): 49–89, https://doi.org/10.1162/ISEC_a_00114; Narang, *Nuclear Strategy in the Modern Era*.

[36] Michael Green et al., *Countering Coercion in Maritime Asia: The Theory and Practice of Gray Zone Deterrence* (Washington, DC: Center for Strategic and International Studies, May 2017), https://www.csis.org/analysis/countering-coercion-maritime-asia; Jon R. Lindsay and Erik Gartzke, "Coercion through Cyberspace: The Stability-Instability Paradox Revisited," in *Coercion: The Power to Hurt in International Politics*, edited by Kelly M. Greenhill and Peter Krause (New York: Oxford University Press, 2018), 179–203.

[37] Inter alia, Frank C. Zagare and D. Marc Kilgour, *Perfect Deterrence* (New York: Cambridge University Press, 2000); Patrick M. Morgan, *Deterrence Now* (New York: Cambridge University Press,

with the idiosyncratic challenges of deterrence in space and cyberspace.[38] Yet many open questions remain about the expanding menu of deterrent options and the interdependencies among them. Given that classic deterrence theory was itself a historical product of a particular technological innovation, one might ask about the theoretical implications of the emergence of new technologies.[39]

The concept of a "domain" in CDD arose in particular historical circumstances, as mentioned, but theorists can conceive it more generally. In this book we consider a *domain* to be any pathway or means for coercion that is different from other means in respect to its utility for political bargaining. Nuclear and conventional weapons can fruitfully be treated as different domains because of their profoundly different material and political characteristics, even as both types of forces are deployed in the land, sea, air, and space environments. The word "domain" thus might describe a discrete territory with clearly delineated boundaries, a legal or bureaucratic jurisdiction, an assertion of ownership, a division of labor, or an area of technical expertise. Any such distinction, if it marks out interesting variation in the potential for coercive bargaining, might enable analysts to compare interactions between political actors according to how like confronts like and, increasingly, how unlike confronts unlike. Cross-domain deterrence can thus be likened to a game of "rock, paper, scissors" where different capabilities have different relative strengths and weaknesses depending on the context of their use. Ontological debates about what is *really* a domain are not particularly useful or relevant.

The primary consideration for a theory of CDD is simply that domains differ from one another, however one wishes those differences to be defined for a specific application. The rough categorization of the five "warfighting domains" described in contemporary military discourse highlights quite different types of weapons and operational possibilities. The Pentagon's domains are sufficiently differentiated from one another that they offer a reasonable place to start looking for the deterrence implications of multiple means. Yet a theory of CDD does not have to end

---

2003); Timothy W. Crawford, *Pivotal Deterrence: Third-Party Statecraft and the Pursuit of Peace* (Ithaca, NY: Cornell University Press, 2003); T. V. Paul, Patrick M. Morgan, and James J. Wirtz, eds., *Complex Deterrence: Strategy in the Global Age* (Chicago: University of Chicago Press, 2009); Jeffrey W. Knopf, "The Fourth Wave in Deterrence Research," *Contemporary Security Policy* 31, no. 1 (2010): 1–33, https://doi.org/10.1080/13523261003640819; Anne E. Sartori, *Deterrence by Diplomacy* (Princeton, NJ: Princeton University Press, 2013); Greenhill and Krause, *Coercion*.

[38] For reviews, see chapters 5 and 6 here on cyberspace and space, respectively.

[39] The military innovation literature focuses more on the relationship between technology, doctrine, and military force structure and effectiveness than on the implications for deterrence. See: Adam Grissom, "The Future of Military Innovation Studies," *Journal of Strategic Studies* 29, no. 5 (2006): 905–934, https://doi.org/10.1080/01402390600901067; Michael C. Horowitz, *The Diffusion of Military Power: Causes and Consequences for International Politics* (Princeton, NJ: Princeton University Press, 2010); Stuart Griffin, "Military Innovation Studies: Multidisciplinary or Lacking Discipline?," *Journal of Strategic Studies* 40, nos. 1–2 (2017): 196–224, https://doi.org/10.1080/01402390.2016.1196358.

there. Our approach frees researchers and practitioners from arbitrary restrictions of geography, technology, or doctrinal convention, and it expands the historical applicability of the topic and its insights. It also opens up the way to considering nonmilitary means like economic sanctions, diplomatic inducements, or immigration policy as alternatives or complements to the range of forms of military force. Complex strategies can span, combine, or substitute domains.

Plan of the Book

The contributors to this book include scholars and practitioners with deep expertise in a range of areas related to specific technologies, international relations scholarship, or national security policy. Indeed, an interdisciplinary approach is required to understand whether and how different means affect coercion in theory and in practice. The chapters unfold in four parts. The first reflects broadly on the notion and utility of CDD in the context of deterrence theory and historical and contemporary challenges. The second examines the strategic implications of particular military domains, exploring the dynamics of deterrence in cyberspace, space, land, sea, and air. The third examines the central, and difficult, deterrence problems of communication and credibility in a CDD context. The fourth expands the aperture of CDD behaviors to examine interactions across military and nonmilitary domains. A thematic conclusion assesses the findings of the book and lays out some potential directions for future research.

The Concept of Cross-Domain Deterrence

One important theme that spans the book is that the emergence of CDD as a term postdates considerably the use of CDD in practice. Chapter 2, by Michael Nacht, Patricia Schuster, and Eva C. Uribe, shows that CDD is hardly new, even if our consciousness of it may be. Prominent cases from the Cold War, such as the Korean War and the Cuban Missile Crisis, can be interpreted through the lens of CDD and fruitfully compared with more contemporary cases, such as Stuxnet. These cases illustrate the variation across domains by the adversary and U.S. responses. The authors find that the United States generally responded to these crises by initially limiting itself to the domain where a crisis started and only later expanding into other domains. The United States has typically been cautious when shifting domains and has tried to escalate in ways that would not produce adversarial retaliation.

The subsequent two chapters present reflections on the notion of CDD by two men with a depth of expertise in the theory and practice of deterrence, respectively. In chapter 3, Patrick M. Morgan draws on decades of influential scholarship on deterrence—including several book projects examining the problems of complex deterrence after the Cold War—to evaluate the promises and pitfalls of CDD in the context of the historical evolution of deterrence theory. In chapter 4, Ron Lehman uses his experiences in a diverse set of senior positions at the U.S. Department of Defense, the Department of State, the White House, and the Lawrence Livermore National Laboratory to compare, contrast, and synthesize deterrence issues related to the emergence of new military technologies, with a special focus on what he describes as the complex geometries of escalation.

Strategic Implications of Different Military Domains

The second part of the book then transitions to an analysis of the deterrence implications of particular military technological capabilities, beginning with the inherently cross-domain problems of cyber and space warfare, which together were the primary motivations for policy interest in CDD. In chapter 5, Jacquelyn G. Schneider argues that most of the discussion of cyber deterrence has been "riddled with ambiguity, uncertainty, and a lack of empirical precedent, which has trickled down to policies that remain largely unformed or partially implemented." Schneider reviews debates about the definition of cyber operations and cyber deterrence, distinguishing the use of cyberspace to support deterrence in other domains and the deterrence of actions within cyberspace itself. She finds that uncertainty is a resounding theme in this literature, which poses both challenges and opportunities for CDD. Cyber-enabled military capabilities may both bolster U.S. deterrence policies and incentivize attack. In cyber as well as in space, the United States confronts a difficult paradox of enhanced capability *and* vulnerability.

In chapter 6, Benjamin W. Bahney, Jonathan Pearl, and Michael Markey, all from the Lawrence Livermore National Laboratory, articulate the logic of ASAT weapons employment in the post–Cold War era. During the Cold War, space reinforced nuclear deterrence because the superpowers relied on space to reinforce second-strike stability for nuclear weapons. ASAT technology was also immature. Today, the broader use of space for conventional power projection together with more mature target discrimination and ASAT technology create strong incentives for both the United States and its adversaries to conduct counter-space operations. United States military power projection is utterly dependent on space assets for command, control, communications, intelligence, and targeting, but these assets are increasingly vulnerable to ASAT capabilities, including not only direct attacks on satellites but also indirect cyber and electronic warfare interference. Several cross-domain options are available for deterrence, both by denial (the threat of effective defense) and by punishment (the threat of retaliation). Unfortunately, the lack of shared norms regarding space warfare has uncertain consequences for escalation dynamics, and similar to the cyber domain, space deterrence faces challenging issues of credibility and attribution.

In chapter 7, Phil Haun, Dean of Academics at the U.S. Naval War College and a former A-10 (Warthog) pilot, identifies the conditions under which air power is most lethal and therefore has the greatest effect on deterring ground forces. Classical deterrence concepts were developed to prevent nuclear war, for obvious reasons, and thus tend to focus on high-stakes crisis bargaining, or "chicken" games. Yet deterrence may operate in many different settings (i.e., different games) and with the repeated interaction of participants. This is especially the case in war itself, where many different platforms can be combined to constrain the battlefield choices of the enemy over the course of a campaign. Deterrence can operate at the operational level even when a state is defending or attacking at the strategic level. Drawing on a number of historical examples, Haun argues that command of the air over the battlefield deters ground forces from massing and maneuvering, which can benefit either offensive and defensive operations. The degree to which an air force can deter depends on various operational factors, including the degree of air superiority achieved over the battlefield, the capability of an air force to locate and target enemy ground forces, the composition of enemy forces, the presence of friendly ground forces, and environmental conditions.

To contest the idea that CDD is only relevant for advanced technology, chapter 8 features the domains of hoplites and triremes. Joshua Rovner asks whether the concept of CDD can shed any new light on one of the most famous wars in the history of international relations. Two millennia ago, Athens enjoyed unquestioned maritime superiority, and Sparta was the dominant land power in ancient Greece; both sides played to their competitive advantage. Rovner finds that CDD failed when both sides wanted it to succeed but, ironically, succeeded when both sides wanted it to fail. During the prewar crisis, the two sides believed they could overcome their asymmetric disadvantages through alliances and arms racing. The disastrous first few years of the war proved these beliefs to be wrong, and both sides grudgingly admitted that cross-domain asymmetries were facts of life. Neither side was able to lure the other side into a confrontation in its favored domain, which resulted in a protracted stalemate. This novel interpretation of a classic case challenges an existing consensus about CDD as rapid, dynamic, and destabilizing. Similar disparities at sea and on the continent in Asia, for example, could ensure that any conflict between China and the United States is longer, more costly, and less decisive than either side perhaps expects.

Communication and Credibility across Domains

The third part of the book turns to the complex communication and credibility problems associated with signaling across domains. Deterrence depends, among other things, on the clear communication of credible threats, which in turn assumes that the sender and the receiver share a context that allows for mutual interpretation. In chapter 9, James Morrow argues that the complexity of CDD is a major barrier to establishing coordinated expectations about violations and consequences. For a system of CDD to work, actors must understand what actions will trigger a response, what the response is likely to be, and how willing the respondent is to act. Any such system is likely to be less robust than Cold War nuclear deterrence because of the number of domains involved, constraints on revealing secret capabilities or even the identity of the challenger, and the availability of means for provocation that fall below some established threshold of response. Morrow recommends using an analogy to the law of war rather than nuclear deterrence to understand the possibilities of setting up a workable CDD regime, even as he is pessimistic that the complexity of CDD can be adequately managed by any collective regime. Morrow's analysis helps to explain why attention to the question of establishing norms for cyberspace and space has received so much attention in recent years.

Many CDD technologies, notably in space and cyberspace, rely on secrecy to be effective, but secrecy can undermine the effectiveness of deterrent signals. In chapter 10, Brendan Rittenhouse Green and Austin G. Long examine the problems of clandestine deterrence in the Cold War. They demonstrate that widespread strategic interaction across different domains with challenging secrecy constraints is not a new phenomenon. During the late Cold War, nuclear forces deterred conventional attack, theater nuclear forces deterred strategic nuclear escalation, and conventional threats to nuclear capabilities deterred conventional attack. Some of these capabilities, particularly intelligence collection and communication networks, depended on sensitive tactics and technologies that could not be revealed lest the enemy develop effective countermeasures. This raised uncertainty about the true balance of power, which might have made conflict more likely, according to rationalist theory. Green and Long show, however, that the United States was able to use several mechanisms to communicate its capabilities to the Soviet Union without thoroughly compromising the ability to use them. Leveraging historical evidence from senior Soviet leadership, they argue that American counterforce nuclear strategy influenced Soviet perceptions and affected Soviet policy across a variety of military and political domains.

An essential component of the implementation of any deterrence policy is the assurance of both allies and adversaries that one will indeed act as promised when a threshold is crossed. Assurance has received very little scholarly attention, in contrast to the use of threats, but the problem is as urgent as ever, given the multilateral complexity of modern CDD. In chapter 11, Rupal N. Mehta examines how the proliferation of domains might affect commitments to allies. She draws on the precedent of the U.S. nuclear triad, where the advent of intercontinental and submarine-launched ballistic missiles inadvertently undermined U.S. deterrence commitments in East Asia and Western Europe. Mehta argues that the plethora of capabilities emerging in the twenty-first century will enable allies and adversaries alike to engage in risky behavior while undermining American willingness to intervene overseas. She concludes with implications for the U.S. polity and that of its alliance partners, as well as predictions about the general evolution of extended deterrence strategies in an increasingly cross-domain system.

Interactions across Military and Nonmilitary Domains

The final part of the book moves to a discussion of the role of nonmilitary instruments and objectives in CDD. Some coercive means need not be military or technological at all. Moreover, they may have important advantages precisely because they are traditional and not cutting-edge. In chapter 12, Kelly M. Greenhill discusses coerced migration flows as an alternative to military influence, a tactic employed in particular by weaker illiberal states against more powerful democracies. The aims of coercive engineered migration vary tremendously and usually include political, military, and economic goals. A widely held belief in deterrence theory, first articulated by Thomas Schelling, is that compellence is harder than deterrence. Greenhill finds, however, that weak actors have often been able to successfully use coercive migration to compel stronger states to alter their policies. Initiators can use the strategy of "capacity swamping" to manipulate the target's physical ability to deal with migration or the strategy of "political agitation" to change the behavior of the target by stoking and exploiting its domestic politics. Greenhill finds that liberal democracies are especially vulnerable to this particular means of coercion, even as they have important advantages in other arenas. This novel example of compellence using a nonmilitary form of CDD shows convincingly that a difference in means in the right context can have a major differential effect on the success or failure of coercion.

If new and different means have a differential effect on the political ends of deterrence, then we should also expect variation in political ends to highlight newly salient features of existing means. In chapter 12, Joshua R. Itzkowitz Shifrinson asks whether shifts in a state's desired ends and available means carry different strategic risks. Political leaders often attempt to link different issues to offset the bargaining weaknesses in any one issue in isolation, but what happens when leaders experience a change in goals? Shifrinson draws on newly available archival evidence to examine this problem in the case of U.S. efforts to deter Soviet repression in Poland and East Germany at the end of the Cold War. In both cases, U.S. policymakers used diplomatic reassurance and threats of isolation to shape Soviet policy as the United States pressed its new-found political interests in Eastern Europe rather than emphasizing its traditional preoccupation with military affairs. Shifrinson finds that the very ambiguity of cross-domain actions, which Morrow and others highlight as a problem for deterrence, can in some situations benefit political actors. Complex CDD environments enable actors to probe intentions and assess risks, giving potential adversaries the opportunity to avoid confrontational meeting engagements by playing for time to clarify interests and choosing the means most suited to achieving new goals. A broader diplomatic conception of CDD, moreover, highlights the potential of using financial, institutional, or other nonmilitary actions that render the threat or use of force less attractive.

Cross-domain deterrence concerns have become acute during twenty-first-century globalization. While many authors stress the vulnerability and instability of interconnected infrastructure in space and cyberspace, by contrast, a long tradition of theorizing in international relations highlights the stabilizing effect of political and economic linkages.[40] In chapter 14, Chin-Hao Huang and David Kang argue that in some circumstances, it may be prudent to be aware of the multiplicity of domains in which a state interacts with another state. Situating the security domain alongside economic and social domains of interaction among countries is important for creating a full analysis of a state's priorities in a particular region, or with any particular other state. The U.S. policy of "pivoting to Asia," for example, showcases both the multidimensionality of U.S. preferences regarding China and the risk that priorities will be widely misunderstood. The pivot itself emphasized diplomacy first, followed by economic relations in the region and lifting pressure on the military dimension. However, the pivot increasingly came to be viewed as a purely military response to China's rise. Yet data on East Asian defense spending over twenty-five years appears to present a puzzle: by many measures, East Asian military expenditures have declined significantly over the past quarter century. This finding appears starkly at odds with the conventional wisdom that Chinese bellicosity, its expenditure on A2/AD, and the U.S. reallocation of forces are increasing tensions in the region. Failure to appreciate the nonmilitary dimensions of international relations in Asia can lead one to misdiagnose the prospects of conflict and cooperation, potentially leading to tragic spirals.

Conclusion

A basic challenge for the next era of deterrence research is to render the increasing complexity of domain-crossing coercion analytically tractable, even for technologies or domains that have yet to develop. Perhaps artificial intelligence, synthetic biology, or quantum computing have unique coercive implications we have barely imagined, or perhaps not. The chapters in this book suggest that CDD is indeed a useful concept that provides new insights for scholars and practitioners alike. It will certainly continue to be an important defense policy problem in the twenty-first century, as currently simmering crises on the Korean Peninsula, in Eastern Europe, and in the Middle East suggest. Analytical insights gleaned from CDD in past cases, moreover, have the potential to clarify and provide impetus for future thinking about grand strategy and military affairs.

---

[40] For a review of the interdependence literature, see: Erik Gartzke and Jiakun Jack Zhang, "Trade and War," in *The Oxford Handbook of the Political Economy of International Trade*, ed. Lisa L. Martin (New York: Oxford University Press, 2015).

Our concluding chapter provides an analytical summary of insights that emerge across the chapters, focusing in particular on the ways in which different means and combinations of means can improve or undermine deterrence. The intent of this book is not to provide a finished theory of CDD but to explore whether the concept of CDD provides any analytical insight into contemporary and historical cases. By and large, the contributors to this book find that it does. The notion of CDD can reveal novel choices and nuances across means that any general theory of deterrence should incorporate. Indeed, we should appreciate that deterrence in history has *often* occurred across domains, combining land and naval power as well as force, diplomacy, and economic statecraft. Deterrence theory as we know it, which has neglected the question of means in its focus on credibility, is quite likely just a specialized subset of what we are calling CDD, an account of deterrence that takes means as seriously as ends. Means matter because different tools and combinations of tools have different consequences for the costs, credibility, and consequences of deterrence.

THE CONCEPT OF CROSS-DOMAIN DETERRENCE

2

Cross-Domain Deterrence in American Foreign Policy

MICHAEL NACHT, PATRICIA SCHUSTER, AND EVA C. URIBE

Deterrence was the bedrock of U.S. strategic thought in the Cold War. Deterring a nuclear attack on the American homeland, a nuclear or conventional attack on U.S. allies in Europe and Northeast Asia, and reassuring these same allies of the credibility of U.S. security guarantees so that they did not acquire their own nuclear forces were all central to U.S. defense policy and strategy for several decades.

In the more than twenty-five years since the collapse of the Soviet Union, the security environment has become markedly more complex. Russia still possesses enough nuclear capabilities to easily destroy the United States; in that sense, it continues to pose an "existential threat." But Putin's aggressive actions in Ukraine and his frequent public references to use nuclear weapons, together with new Russian training and doctrine on "escalate to deescalate," suggests a redefined Russian strategy aimed at intimidating its neighbors and other North Atlantic Treaty Organization (NATO) members, and with the intent of expanding Russian influence in the states of the former Soviet Union and perhaps, in the longer term, inducing the disintegration of the NATO alliance. China, bent on expanding its influence in East Asia, has adopted what the U.S. terms an "anti-access/area-denial" (A2/AD) strategy that seeks to nullify the ability of the United States to project its military forces into the region in the event of a crisis in Taiwan, the South China Sea, or elsewhere. This approach focuses on areas of U.S. vulnerability that include aircraft carriers and space and cyber assets. North Korea and Iran—new or potential nuclear weapons states—seem motivated to acquire their own nuclear forces for regime maintenance, and to expand regional influence through intimidation, but also to deter the threat of U.S. conventional intervention to topple their regimes. In these cases, the United States is less the party seeking to deter action than the party being deterred. And the emergence of Islamic State, as well as al-Qaeda, both of which use suicide attacks as central to their strategy and tactics (and religious guarantees of the afterlife to motivate these attacks), pose highly capable threats for which deterrence calculations appear to have limited relevance.

While the United States was preoccupied in the first decade of the twenty-first century with responding to the 9/11 attacks with major military commitments in Afghanistan and Iraq, the emergence of new technologies began to change the strategic landscape. China's antisatellite test in January 2007 was a graphic illustration of its A2/AD strategy aimed at exposing the vulnerability of the United States' dependence on its space assets. Later in 2007 and in 2008, Russia used its emerging cyber capabilities in Estonia and Georgia, respectively. In the former, Russia launched distributed denial of service (DDoS) attacks to overload Estonian websites after the government in Tallinn sought to relocate a Soviet-era statue and war graves. In the latter, Russia attacked the website of Georgia's president, Mikheil Saakashvili, and then interrupted communication between government ministries and Georgian armed forces, shortly before sending its armored divisions into Georgia to occupy the renegade provinces of Abkhazia and South Ossetia.

The changing complexities of the international security environment were recognized early in the George W. Bush administration. Secretary of Defense Donald Rumsfeld instituted in the 2001 "Quadrennial Defense Review Report" the concept of "capabilities based planning." He noted that a "capabilities-based model [is] one that focuses more on how an adversary might fight than who an adversary might be and where a war might occur."[1] In Rumsfeld's accompanying "Nuclear Posture Review," he established a "New Triad" composed of offensive strike systems (nuclear and nonnuclear), defenses (active and passive), and a revitalized defense infrastructure "that will provide new capabilities in a timely fashion to meet emerging threats . . . bound together by enhanced command and control (C2) and intelligence systems."[2] This called for an enlargement of the deterrence concept beyond nuclear weapons.

In early 2007, the defense analyst Elaine Bunn posed an important question that had been considered in the Bush administration: "Can Deterrence Be Tailored?"[3] She noted the importance of cultural differences among U.S. adversaries, concluding that "the capabilities needed for tailored deterrence go beyond nuclear weapons and the strategic capabilities of the so-called New Triad, to the full range of military capabilities, presence, and cooperation, as well as diplomatic, informational, and economic instruments."[4] The point was to reject the "one size fits all" approach

---

[1] "Quadrennial Defense Review Report," Department of Defense, 30 September 2001, accessed 10 March 2018, http://archive.defense.gov/pubs/qdr2001.pdf.

[2] "Nuclear Posture Review Report," Department of Defense, 11 November 2001, accessed 10 March 2018, http://archive.defense.gov/news/Jan2002/d20020109npr.pdf.

[3] M. Elaine Bunn, "Can Deterrence Be Tailored?," *Strategic Forum*, no. 225, Institute for National Strategic Studies, National Defense University, January 2007, accessed 10 March 2018, https://www.hsdl.org/?view&did=481759.

[4] Bunn, "Can Deterrence Be Tailored?"

to deterrence derived from Cold War logic in favor of individualized deterrence postures taking into account the value systems of particular adversaries and the threats that would be most credible to them. Indeed, "tailored deterrence" was later endorsed in President Donald Trump's "Nuclear Posture Review."[5]

Capabilities based planning, the New Triad, and tailored deterrence were some of the key conceptual legacies inherited by the Obama administration when it took office in January 2009. During the Obama transition efforts prior to 20 January 2009, it was decided to create the post of assistant secretary of defense for global strategic affairs (ASD-GSA), focusing on nuclear weapons, ballistic missile defense, space policy, cyber policy, and countering the proliferation of weapons of mass destruction.

With the growing importance especially of cyber capabilities, it became increasingly clear that the existing intellectual basis for deterrence in this very complex environment needed still further rethinking. It was more than a need for better intelligence or revised plans. Could there be a path to integrate the diverse elements of the ASD-GSA portfolio into a coherent framework or strategy that included both functional and regional considerations, using the overarching theme of cross-domain deterrence (CDD)? In this case, "domain" referred to actions on land, in and under the sea, in the air, in space, and in the humanmade realm of "cyberspace." It was left for later to consider economic, diplomatic, and other "nonkinetic" measures. In particular, a pressing concern at the time was to identify the characteristics of a cyberattack on the United States that would likely necessitate a kinetic U.S. response.

To address these concerns, a group of prominent thinkers was convened by the Department of Defense in 2010 to address these issues. A subsequent publication reflects some of the questions and concerns posed by these discussions:[6]

1. Uncertainties over attribution and collateral damage reduce the ability to make a credible threat outside of armed conflict.
2. When is a cyber incident an act of war?
3. Deterrence is less credible in an environment where the United States has more to lose than its opponent.
4. Deterrence in space or "cyberspace" cannot be "domain limited" and will require threats in other domains.

---

[5] "Nuclear Posture Review," Department of Defense, February 2018, accessed 10 March 2018, https://media.defense.gov/2018/Feb/02/2001872886/-1/-1/1/2018-NUCLEAR-POSTURE-REVIEW-FINAL-REPORT.PDF. It endorsed "tailored strategies and flexible capabilities."

[6] James A. Lewis, "Cross-Domain Deterrence and Credible Threats," Center for Strategic and International Studies, July 2010, accessed 10 March 2018, https://csis-prod.s3.amazonaws.com/s3fs-public/legacy_files/files/publication/100701_Cross_Domain_Deterrence.pdf.

5. Religiously motivated opponents are much less likely than government leaders to be deterred by the threat of retaliation.
6. A credible threat by the United States to retaliate in some other domain brings a risk of escalation of the conflict.
7. Deterring some kinds of attacks may require "stigmatization"—creation of a credible international norm that such attacks (e.g., in space or cyberspace) run counter to acceptable international behavior.

Moreover, understanding foreign perceptions in such a complex security environment is especially important and demanding.

While the term "cross-domain deterrence" may be new,[7] the challenges associated with it are not. Taking a broader view of U.S. foreign policy during previous decades, we can see that many of the hard problems in CDD—new means, multiple means, ambiguous means, surprising actors—have appeared before. Strategy has always had the challenge of integrating ends, ways, and means.

This chapter understands CDD to be the act of deterring an action in one domain with a threat in another domain, where the "domains" are defined as land, under the land, at sea, under the sea, in the air, in space, and in cyberspace, plus economic sanctions and other diplomatic and political tools. "Deterrence" is defined as a threat intended to dissuade an adversary from doing something it was planning to do. Such threats are "if, then" propositions: if you do x then you will be punished with z. "Deterrence" is often confused with "compellence," defined as the act of persuading an adversary to stop an action it has already undertaken.[8] Compellence is far more difficult to implement than deterrence because in the case of deterrence, the adversary has already made the commitment to act. In the past several decades, "deterrence" and "compellence" have often been combined under the term "coercive diplomacy."[9] A noteworthy recent study based on a large number of case studies concludes that, despite widespread beliefs to the contrary, nuclear coercion has rarely been effective.[10]

---

[7] The term "cross-domain deterrence" has never been fully accepted by all parts of the U.S. government. Some claim that it does not mean anything new; others, such as the U.S. Strategic Command, claim that "integrated strategic deterrence" is more apt; still others assert that it is a hypothesis yet to be verified.

[8] Thomas Schelling notes: "the threat that compels rather than deters often requires that the punishment be administered *until* the other acts, rather than *if* he acts. This is because often the only way to become committed to an action is to initiate it." Thomas Schelling, *Arms and Influence*, 2nd ed. (New Haven, CT: Yale University Press, 2008), 70.

[9] Robert J. Art and Patrick M. Cronin, *The United States and Coercive Diplomacy* (Washington, DC: United States Institute of Peace Press, 2003).

[10] See Todd S. Sechser and Matthew Fuhrmann, *Nuclear Weapons and Coercive Diplomacy* (Cambridge: Cambridge University Press, 2017). For a discussion of ten myths about nuclear coercion, see 235–254.

Leaders want options and do not seek to be constrained by within-domain responses. Flexibility is a virtually universal aspiration before making decisions, even if responses are frequently within-domain.[11]

Examples from the Obama and George W. Bush Administrations

Cases arose early in the twenty-first century that illustrate the evolution of thinking about CDD. In reviewing these cases it is useful to focus on the following:

1. What major policy alternatives did U.S. policymakers consider? What were the constraints on each?
2. If U.S. policymakers were conscious of considering options across domains, did they consider the perceived trade-offs for each domain?

The Cyberattack on Iranian Uranium Centrifuges

Bilateral relations between the United States and Iran have been deeply adversarial since the 1979 Iranian Revolution that established the Islamic Republic of Iran. The United States and the United Kingdom had been implicated in the 1953 overthrow of Iranian prime minister Mohammad Mosaddegh, who was replaced by a military government. This government enabled the head of the country's monarchy, Shah Mohammad Reza Pahlavi, to rule Iran as an absolute monarch for a quarter century. The shah had a pro-Western foreign policy that supported U.S. interests in the Middle East. He sought to westernize Iranian society. He also suppressed critical Shi'a clerics and did not tolerate domestic dissent.

When the shah was overthrown, exiled Shi'a cleric Ayatollah Khomeini returned from Paris and was proclaimed supreme leader of the Islamic Republic of Iran. Bilateral relations with the United States deteriorated precipitously. On 4 November 1979, a group of pro-Islamic Iranian students seized the U.S. embassy in Tehran and held fifty-two U.S. diplomatic personnel hostage for 444 days. The day after the seizure, Khomeini described the United States as "the Great Satan," the principal source of imperialism and corruption in the world. From 1980 to 1988, Iran fought a bitter eight-year war with Iraq. The U.S. supported Iraq in this struggle, viewing Khomeini's Iran as posing a greater long-term threat. Consequently, no diplomatic relations have existed between Washington and Tehran since 1980.

---

[11] Tom Schelling points out that having options is often in tension with signaling commitment. Does CDD therefore complicate credibility by providing options? Does the adversary's perception of fewer options on our part increase the deterrent effect of the options available? See Schelling, *Arms and Influence*.

Strategically, the dominant issue between them for many years has been the Iranian nuclear energy program, which is intended to support a covert nuclear weapons development capability. These weapons activities had their origin under the shah, who dreamed of making Iran a global power. After a period of suspension, the nuclear weapons effort was restarted, probably in the mid-1980s.[12] The administration of President Bill Clinton supported the Iran Sanctions Act, passed by Congress in 1996, which is the basis for the United States' current comprehensive sanctions against Iran. The United States has also exerted pressure on Iran's trading partners to terminate economic relations with Iran and has, in some instances, imposed sanctions on third parties who conducted business with Iran, especially in the military sector. President George W. Bush used the term "Axis of Evil" in his 29 January 2002 State of the Union address to describe those states that supported terrorism and sought to acquire weapons of mass destruction. He cited Iran, Iraq, and North Korea explicitly. Since the United States invaded Iraq one year later, his policies may have accelerated the pace of Pyongyang's and Tehran's nuclear weapons activities and further motivated their aim of acquiring a credible nuclear deterrent against U.S. conventional force intervention.[13]

In January 2011, the *New York Times* reported that Israel had launched a cyberattack against the control systems of an Iranian uranium enrichment facility to delay the development of Iran's nuclear program. A more detailed account followed, in a book by David Sanger on Obama's use of American military power.[14] Sanger describes the operation, Operation Olympic Games, as "one of the most secret, compartmentalized programs inside the U.S. government."[15] He noted: "the fuller story will be filled in, likely in bits and pieces, in future years, as elements of the program are declassified."[16] A book by Kim Zetter is a major contribution to our understanding.[17]

According to Sanger, the idea of a cyberattack against uranium centrifuges began at U.S. Strategic Command in 2006, and the operation was initiated in 2008 "to throw a little sand in the gears" of the uranium centrifuges that were built to

---

[12] A large number of Iranian nuclear engineers received graduate training at MIT and other top-ranked nuclear engineering departments in the United States in the 1970s.

[13] A definitive causal relationship, however, cannot be demonstrated.

[14] William J. Broad, John Markoff, and David E. Sanger, "Israeli Test on Worm Called Crucial in Iran Nuclear Delay," *New York Times*, 15 January 2011, accessed 10 March 2018, http://www.nytimes.com/2011/01/16/world/middleeast/16stuxnet.html. The more complete account is in David E. Sanger, *Confront and Conceal: Obama's Secret Wars and Surprising Use of American Power* (New York: Crown, 2012). See ch. 8, "Olympic Games," 188–225. Neither the United States nor Israel has acknowledged any aspect of Olympic Games. Iran also has said nothing.

[15] Sanger, *Confront and Conceal*, 190.

[16] Ibid., 450.

[17] See Kim Zetter, *Countdown to Zero Day: Stuxnet and the Launch of the World's First Digital Weapon* (New York: Crown Books, 2014).

stockpile weapons-grade material for Iranian nuclear weapons.[18] In other words, it was viewed as a delaying tactic rather than an explicit effort to "compel" Iran to halt its program, and U.S. policymakers were not very optimistic that it would have a significant impact on the pace of Tehran's program.

Sanger claims that the Israelis were brought in for three reasons: their technical cyber skills; their intelligence of the Natanz fuel enrichment plant; and to persuade Israeli decision-makers that the United States was making serious efforts to degrade the Iranian nuclear program. The last objective, in turn, was intended to dissuade Israel from launching air strikes on the Iranian nuclear complex that could precipitate a wider war in the Middle East.[19] Thus, Olympic Games was an effort not to deter Iran from furthering its clandestine nuclear program but to deter Israel from launching what the United States viewed as a premature, preemptive strike on Iranian nuclear facilities, in order to allow diplomatic alternatives to succeed. Sanger quotes Michael Hayden, former CIA director, as stating that "this is the first attack of a major nature in which a cyberattack was used to effect physical destruction . . . you can't help but describe it as an attack on critical infrastructure."[20]

When president-elect Obama was briefed on the program by outgoing President Bush, he agreed to continue it but had numerous questions:

1. Could the source of the attacks be attributed to the United States?
2. Would there be collateral damage as a result of the attacks (e.g., hospital electricity interrupted)?
3. If the Iranians discovered the source, what would be their options for retaliation?
4. Bush had approved a small number of limited attacks to determine feasibility and effectiveness. How expansive should the attacks be?

The core idea behind Olympic Games was to introduce a computer worm through infected USB flash drives that would attack programmable logic controllers. The worm was designed to target Siemens supervisory control and data acquisition systems that controlled and monitored the centrifuges. Five different facilities were targeted, and about 20 percent of Iran's centrifuges were destroyed.[21]

---

[18] Zetter, *Countdown to Zero Day*, 192.

[19] The Natanz plant, a vast facility covering 100,000 square meters, is built eight meters underground and is protected by a wall two and a half meters thick. It is estimated to contain 7,000 centrifuges, with 5,000 producing low enriched uranium. Many of the Iranian nuclear facilities are buried deep underground.

[20] Sanger, *Confront and Conceal*, 200.

[21] Zetter highlights the importance of work done at Oak Ridge National Laboratory on how the Iranian centrifuges worked and how cyberattacks could disrupt their operations. See Zetter, *Countdown to Zero Day*, 317–327.

When a more advanced worm with limited testing was deployed to target a large array of centrifuges at Natanz, the worm infected the Internet, and various malfunctions unrelated to the centrifuges led to its discovery.[22] Civilian cybersecurity researchers named the malware "Stuxnet," a combination of key words found in the software code.

What major policy alternatives did U.S. policymakers consider, and what were the constraints? The United States had already implemented virtually all options available short of conventional military force: diplomatic isolation and, more recently, nuclear diplomacy and formal negotiations; increasingly severe economic sanctions; and, finally, cyber-attack. The main constraint was not to risk actions that would provoke an escalation leading to widespread armed conflict.

Were U.S. policymakers aware that they were considering options across different domains, and if so, what were the perceived trade-offs recognized for each domain? The Olympic Games cyberattack was part of a larger suite of options and alternatives pursued by U.S. policymakers to prevent further progression of Iran's latent nuclear weapons capability. The utility of Olympic Games extended beyond the damage to Iran's uranium enrichment program. The Department of Defense and intelligence agencies estimated that the operation delayed Iran's pathway to building a nuclear weapon by one to three years, and the International Atomic Energy Agency estimated that Iran's enrichment output was not significantly damaged.[23] The attack bought time for the United States to follow through with other nonmilitary, primarily economic means to pressure Iran to abandon its nuclear weapons ambitions. These, of course, culminated in the completion of the Joint Comprehensive Plan of Action between the P5 + 1 (the United States, Russia, China, the United Kingdom and France, plus Germany), which went into effect in January 2016.

Olympic Games did not preclude the United States and Iran from reaching an agreement in which Iran committed to reduce significantly its nuclear activities. Such an agreement, which would later be realized as the Joint Comprehensive Plan of Action, would almost certainly not have been possible had the United States or Israel conducted an air strike against one or more of Iran's nuclear facilities. Cyber warfare allowed the United States to buy time and temper its ally, all while leaving the door open for negotiations on an agreement that could thwart Iran's ability to manufacture a nuclear weapon. As one official told Sanger: "we told the Israelis that if you bomb Natanz, it will take the Iranians two years to replace it . . . and you'll make them want the bomb even more. But if you do it this way, they won't see it, and the longer we can go before you have to bomb it."[24]

---

[22] Sanger, *Confront and Conceal*, 204–205.
[23] Ibid., 207.
[24] Ibid., 190.

The cyber operation also put Iran in the unique position of downplaying its effectiveness in the media. Olympic Games was designed to exploit the insecurities of the scientists running the enrichment facilities. In a latent period, the worm first recorded the state of normal operations: the typical speeds at which the centrifuges spun and the normal rates at which they were sped up and slowed down. It then fed these "normal" signals back to the control room while it changed the actual speeds and acceleration rates, causing the centrifuges to break apart. For a long time, the scientists in charge could not find the cause, and several of them were fired. "The intent was that the failures should make them feel they were stupid, which is what happened," one participant explained. Once the Iranian Atomic Energy Organization learned of the worm, they publicly denied that it had had any significant effect. To admit otherwise would be to acknowledge technical incompetence. The Iranians had isolated computers and controllers from the Internet, but the worm was snuck in on a thumb drive that was plugged into one of the controllers by an engineer working at the facility, without knowing what he was doing.[25] Thus, the United States' deniability of the operation was enhanced by Iran's embarrassment of its failure to enforce a simple "air gap"—a physical separation between networks that would have inhibited the automatic propagation of code.

In this case, use of a weapon in the cyberspace domain allowed policymakers to balance two objectives: that of reassuring a key ally by participating in a destructive, but not kinetic, attack and that of extending nonescalation for as long as possible to allow diplomatic alternatives to succeed in resolving the conflict. Cross-domain actions are thus not just about deterrence but extend across the coercive diplomacy spectrum.

Space Policy in the George W. Bush Administration

Space operations are almost sure to be included in the repertoire of cross-domain responses in future crises. In one of the only space-related cases to date, China surprised the West by testing an antisatellite weapon in January 2007, the first known successful satellite intercept test since 1985. This test demonstrated a potential Chinese capability to threaten U.S. space assets that are vital for early warning, tracking, weather forecasting, timing, intelligence, surveillance, reconnaissance, and other essential functions of effective military operations. The public debate that ensued in the U.S. national security community focused predominantly on countermeasures in space and diplomatic initiatives related to international control of space

---

[25] Ibid., 199, 206, 196.

operations.[26] The Bush administration did not choose to respond explicitly to the Chinese test, either within-domain or cross-domain.

Global trends point inexorably toward an international security environment marked by a proliferation of state and nonstate adversaries; growth in the number of weapons available to these adversaries; a more demanding task of maintaining alliance cohesion because of competing interests among states; and an enlargement of the number of nonkinetic forms of coercive diplomacy that could resolve conflicts short of major war.[27]

Pre–Nuclear Deterrence Thinking

Two major features of what came to be the Cold War deterrence paradigm developed with the advent not of nuclear weapons but of heavy bomber aircraft. The first was the use of counter-value strikes to inflict pain on civilian populations. The second was offense advantage, or the advantage of conducting a preemptive, disabling first strike. While these tactics may have existed previously,[28] they became highly accessible to military strategists with the development of air power, which allowed a nation to inflict serious damage on an enemy's territory without having to defeat its land forces.

Air power counter-value strategies (that held politically valuable targets like cities at risk as contrasted with counter-force strategies that targeted military forces) were established in the 1920s and 1930s. At first, the idea of targeting civilian populations was considered unethical and not useful militarily, having "no place in the armament of a nation which has a National Policy of good will and a Military Policy of protection, not aggression."[29] The theoretical distinction between counter-force and counter-value operations was made early. However, practical limitations in technology rendered this distinction as an overlapping spectrum. Escalation was often unintentional. For both the Allied and Axis powers, the targets of bombing raids evolved steadily from isolated counter-force targets to those near industrial centers and then to entirely counter-value targets.[30] When the United States entered World

---

[26] The United States did consult extensively with its allies and admonished China's ambassador to the United States, but no publicly known further action was taken. Source: senior Bush administration official, conversation with one of this article's authors, 29 January 2015.

[27] Precisely targeted economic sanctions against the adversary's leadership and key components of its economy are increasingly the first weapon of choice adopted by Washington. See Juan Zarate, *Treasury's War: The Unleashing of a New Era of Financial Warfare* (New York: Public Affairs, 2013).

[28] Schelling, *Arms and Influence*, 70.

[29] George Quester, *Deterrence before Hiroshima* (Baltimore: Johns Hopkins University Press, 1966), 127.

[30] Quester observes that Churchill's August 1940 bombing of Berlin was an attempt to induce Hitler to retaliate against London, which would draw the Luftwaffe away from the RAF. Ibid., 117.

War II, it focused on counter-force strikes, while the Royal Air Force had moved to nighttime, counter-value "area attacks."[31] There is evidence that the United States' counter-force strikes were more damaging to Germany than Britain's counter-value strikes.[32]

The second deterrence paradigm that matured with the advent of air power was offense advantage. Before air power, defensive forces were thought to have the advantage of fighting on their home territory. Military strategists soon realized that conducting bombing raids was easy compared to defending against them.

George Quester notes that Japan's fear that the United States was developing a "terror-bombing" capacity in the Pacific motivated their "preemptive" attack at Pearl Harbor.[33] This fear was captured by Kinoaki Matsuo's 1942 book *The Three Power Alliance and a United States–Japanese War*: "Once the enemy succeeds in making an air raid on a large scale upon the Japanese cities, which are mostly of wooden houses, it is feared that all the cities will be reduced to ashes."[34]

In the Cold War decades, the language of "counter-value" strikes and "offense advantage" became common parlance in nuclear deterrence, the new domain born out of World War II. Yet the origins of these concepts was in cross-domain thinking that became most useful to strategists prior to the bombings of Hiroshima and Nagasaki.

Nuclear Perspectives from the Cold War

Nuclear weapons may appear somewhat difficult to fit conceptually into CDD as defined above. They can be used on land, on or under the sea, in the air, or in space (though outlawed by the Outer Space Treaty, which entered into force in 1967). Employment of nuclear weapons constitutes a use of military force across domains, but of such destructive power that they have played a singular role diplomatically, psychologically, and politically without ever having been used since 1945. Thus, they might reasonably be considered a functionally unique domain, even if not geographically distinct.

---

[31] Ibid., 145, 154.

[32] Albert Speer, in charge of German industrialization, wrote: "the American attacks, which followed a definite system of assault on industrial targets, *were by far the most dangerous. It was in fact these attacks that caused the breakdown of the German armaments industry*. The night attacks did not succeed in breaking the will to work of the civilian population." Ibid., 154.

[33] Ibid., 133.

[34] Kinoaki Matsuo, *The Three Power Alliance and a United States–Japanese War* (London: George G. Harrap, 1940).

Table 2.1 **Characteristics of Cases of Cross-Domain Deterrence (Chronological Order)**

Case	Adversary's domain	Domain of U.S. response	Deterrence or compellence	Were U.S. objectives achieved?
Korean War	Conventional forces; diplomatic	Nuclear threat	Compellence	Yes
Berlin Crisis	Conventional forces	Nuclear threat/ conventional	Deterrence	Yes
Cuban Missile Crisis	Nuclear missiles	Nuclear threat	Deterrence	Yes and no
		Naval blockade; threatened land invasion; diplomacy	Compellence	
Yom Kippur War	Ground troop deployments	Nuclear alert	Deterrence	Yes
Olympic Games	Nuclear weapons (Iran)	Cyber	Neither? Deter Israel attack on Iran	Yes?

We will review four cases from the Cold War that highlight the role of nuclear weapons within a cross-domain context. These cases are illustrative of instances where U.S. policymakers specifically considered responding or chose to respond outside the domain from which the threat originated. We use primary sources in each case to document key points. Table 2.1 compares key characteristics of these cases as well as the more modern Olympic Games (Stuxnet) case.

The Korean War, 1953

On 25 June 1950, North Korea invaded South Korea, initiating the Korean War. After U.S./UN/Republic of Korea forces repelled and destroyed much of the North Korean army, moving deep into North Korea in October 1950, Chinese forces intervened, and a bitter, protracted conflict ensued.

From the start, the U.S. nuclear arsenal was in the background as a potential military option. Although it does not appear that President Harry S. Truman seriously considered the trade-offs of using nuclear weapons, the threat of use was implied several times, presumably in the hope that this would lead to a negotiated settlement and would deter China and the Soviet Union from widening the war. In November 1950, Truman promised that the United States would take "whatever steps are necessary" to deter Chinese aggression and warned that the use of nuclear weapons had been considered.

The United States' policy options were constrained because neither Truman nor, subsequently, President Dwight D. Eisenhower wished to provoke a general war with the Soviet Union or China. The United States was in the process of implementing a limited war strategy: limited objectives (produce the status quo ante, removing North Korean troops from South Korea); limited means (threaten but do not use nuclear weapons); and limited territory (sustaining the conflict on the Korean peninsula without extension into Chinese territory).

After Joseph Stalin died in March 1953, the Communist side proposed resuming talks, abruptly becoming somewhat more conciliatory. Policymakers in the United States remained skeptical, however, after three years of fighting.[35] Many U.S. policymakers felt that the Communist bloc was trying to dupe the Americans into pursuing peace while they themselves prepared for the next offensive operation.[36]

To break the deadlock, the Eisenhower administration contemplated introducing atomic weapons on the Korean battlefield. But there were important arguments against such a move: Eisenhower was concerned about Soviet nuclear retaliatory capability; he and Secretary of State John Foster Dulles did not have a plan for the use of nuclear weapons, which were not easily deployable; and the use of U.S. nuclear weapons on another Asian people after Hiroshima and Nagasaki ran the risk of condemnation from allied and neutral states and from American critics as well.[37] Dulles may well have been prone to use nuclear weapons against North Korea whether or not he considered carefully the consequences of their use. Eisenhower, much more risk averse, realized the danger, in that such use could precipitate a general war with both the Soviet Union and China, and chose conventional forces and diplomacy as the preferred alternative. Regardless of whether nuclear weapons would realistically have been introduced, nuclear threats were believed to be a cheaper solution to the stalemate in Korea than conventional war.[38]

In a visit to New Delhi in May 1953, Dulles told India's prime minister, Jawaharlal Nehru, known to have close ties to China, that the United States would use "stronger rather than lesser" military means if armistice talks collapsed. Indeed, in February 1953 Eisenhower "expressed the view that we should consider the use of tactical

---

[35] Sheila Miyoshi Jager, *Brothers at War: The Unending Conflict in Korea* (New York: Norton, 2014) 277. President Eisenhower wanted to take advantage of the shift in the Communist attitude and gave a speech titled "The Chance for Peace."

[36] Jager, *Brothers at War*, 276.

[37] Thomas Allen, "No Winners, Many Losers: The End of the Korean War," in *Security in Korea: War, Stalemate, and Negotiation*, edited by Phil Williams, Donald M. Goldstein, and Henry L. Andrews (Boulder, CO: Westview Press, 1994), 107.

[38] Michael J. Mazarr, *North Korea and the Bomb: A Case Study in Nonproliferation* (New York: St. Martin's Press, 1997), 16. Eisenhower presented this argument in a National Security Council meeting on 15 May 1953. It became the theme of the administration's "New Look" policy, in which the United States used its nuclear weapons as a substitute for matching the adversary's conventional power.

nuclear weapons on the Kaesong area, which provided a good target for this type of weapon."[39] In May, the chair of the Joint Chiefs of Staff recommended "the extensive strategical and tactical use of atomic bombs."[40] Within two weeks of this conversation, Dulles received word that the North Koreans had started negotiating seriously.[41] Ultimately, the Armistice was signed on 27 July 1953, establishing the Korean demilitarized zone, initiating a ceasefire, and finalizing the exchange of prisoners of war.

After the war ended, both Dulles and Eisenhower claimed that the threat of introducing nuclear weapons had played a major role in completing the agreement that ended the war. In Dulles's words, "the principle of using methods of our choice was ready to be invoked, and it helped to stop the war which the enemy had begun and had pursued on the theory that it would be a limited war, at places and by means of its choosing."[42] However, it is not clear that the threat of nuclear retaliation was decisive. The severe losses that North Korea had suffered, the economic hardship in the People's Republic of China, and the expectation of reduced Soviet support in the war effort following Stalin's death seemed at the time to be more influential.[43] In particular, China made important concessions on prisoner of war exchanges after Stalin's death. Georgy Malenkov, Stalin's initial successor, had taken a much softer line on the war, beginning with a "peace offensive" speech at Stalin's funeral. Moreover, several previous U.S. references to nuclear weapon use by both Truman and Eisenhower had seemingly no effect on Chinese or North Korean aggressive policies. A scholar of Chinese archives claims that the Communist Party leadership in Beijing paid no attention to possible U.S. use of nuclear weapons.[44]

In sum, there is no strong evidence that nuclear weapons compellence by the United States was influential on the Chinese leadership. The armistice ending the Korean War in July 1953 resulted from other, nonnuclear considerations.

---

[39] Cited from White House meeting notes in Sechser and Fuhrmann, *Nuclear Weapons and Coercive Diplomacy*, 175.

[40] Ibid., 175.

[41] James Shepley, "How Dulles Averted War," *Life*, 16 January 1956, 70–72. The author implies a connection between Dulles's implied threats to Nehru and the negotiations.

[42] John Foster Dulles, "Policy for Security and Peace," *Foreign Affairs* 32, no. 3 (April 1954): 353–364, accessed 10 March 2018, https://www.foreignaffairs.com/articles/united-states/1954-04-01/policy-security-and-peace.

[43] Allen, "No Winners, Many Losers," 102. There was also domestic political pressure on the United States to bring the war to a close; Jager, *Brothers at War*, 274. There is additional information that implies that the shift in policy was a direct result of Stalin's death. In August and September 1952, Stalin and China's premier, Zhou Enlai, met to discuss the war. Zhou was eager to end the war, since it was Chinese, not Soviet, forces who were dying in Korea, but his request for flexibility was met by an adamant Stalin. After Stalin's death, the new Soviet leadership ushered in a "striking shift in foreign policy," announcing a peace initiative and discontinuing anti-American propaganda. On 19 March, a review of Soviet policy in Korea indicated Moscow's desire to end the Korean War.

[44] Sechser and Fuhrmann, *Nuclear Weapons and Coercive Diplomacy*, 180.

The Berlin Crisis, 1961

The Berlin Crisis is one of the most well-studied episodes of the Cold War, but it can be viewed afresh through a CDD lens. In 1948, Stalin imposed a blockade of Berlin that Truman broke with an airlift. Truman's resolve solidified a perception that Berlin was an enduring symbol of resistance to the encroachment of Communism, that its protection was central to the NATO alliance, and that the United States was willing to put American lives on the front lines to defend it.[45] The conflict over Berlin was perceived as a contest for the fate of Europe, in which the Soviet Union fought to maintain and strengthen the position it believed had been granted to it as a victor of World War II.[46]

After World War II, the Soviet Union had a large conventional superiority concentrated in East Germany and Berlin. NATO based its defense policy on two assumptions: (1) that the greatest threat to Europe was invasion by Soviet conventional forces, and (2) that the best way to counter this threat was use of the U.S. nuclear deterrent.[47]

In August 1961, the Soviets and East Germans erected a wall extending around all of West Berlin to prohibit movement of East Germans to West Germany through Berlin. Khrushchev wanted to eliminate the influence of Berlin as a Western outpost in East Germany[48] and to reduce the number of East Germans fleeing the country through West Berlin, which threatened to cripple East Germany's economy.[49] Berlin's location within East Germany provided the Soviet Union with an asymmetrical advantage that may have motivated Soviet policymakers to initiate the threat. In this case, the *threat* of closing Berlin, which incited division among the Allies, was more valuable to Khrushchev than any actual military action, which would have united them.[50]

The Berlin crises spanned both the Eisenhower and Kennedy presidencies. President John F. Kennedy ran for office on a platform that included closing the missile gap by rapidly building up U.S. strategic nuclear forces and weaning NATO from reliance on strategic nuclear weapons by increasing the number of conventional

---

[45] Alexander L. George and Richard Smoke, *Deterrence in American Foreign Policy: Theory and Practice* (New York: Columbia University Press, 1974), 392.

[46] Ibid., 116–117.

[47] William W. Kaufmann, *The McNamara Strategy* (New York: Harper and Row, 1964), 103.

[48] George and Smoke, *Deterrence in American Foreign Policy*, 395. Khrushchev viewed West Berlin as an "unhealthy tumor," a breeding ground for subversive activities. See: Sergei Khrushchev, ed., *Memoirs of Nikita Khrushchev*, vol. 3, *Statesman (1953–1964)*, trans. George Shriver (University Park: Pennsylvania State University Press, 2007), 320.

[49] By the autumn of 1958, 10,000 East Germans were fleeing through West Berlin every month. George and Smoke, *Deterrence in American Foreign Policy*, 395. By early 1961, that number rose to 1,000 per day. Moscow could not tolerate the collapse of East Germany's economy; 420.

[50] Ibid., 399, 417–418.

forces in Europe. He argued that "main but not sole reliance" on nuclear weapons restricted the president's options: "the only choice is all or nothing at all, world devastation or submission—a choice that necessarily causes us to hesitate on the brink and leaves the initiative in the hands of our enemies."[51] He charged his secretary of defense, Robert McNamara, to search for alternatives to massive retaliation that could be used to respond to Soviet threats below the threshold of nuclear war—in particular, the threat of seizing Berlin using conventional forces.

One major constraint McNamara faced was resistance by the European allies, who feared that a buildup of U.S. conventional forces in Europe meant that Kennedy was less willing to use nuclear weapons to deter the Soviets. But McNamara argued that a more *flexible response* with a suite of conventional and nuclear capabilities would increase the credibility of the strategic nuclear deterrent. He wrote: "if we have shown ourselves able and ready to engage in large-scale non-nuclear warfare in response to a Communist provocation, the Soviets can hardly misconstrue two things: first that we regard this provocation as a challenge to our vital interests; and second, that we will use nuclear weapons to prevail, if this becomes necessary."[52]

Though key policymakers did not explicitly refer to the nuclear and conventional realms as separate *domains*, it is clear that they considered them as separate categories, and that they grappled with how to properly distribute the U.S. deterrence posture between them. As the Soviet Union began to achieve the perception of parity in the new nuclear domain, U.S. policymakers found themselves facing the uncomfortable reality "that every pinprick must be met by nuclear war."[53] That was not a credible deterrent to the Soviets; perhaps more important, nor was it a credible assurance to the allies.

The Cuban Missile Crisis, 1962

A CDD perspective also freshly illuminates the Cuban Missile Crisis of October 1962 by revealing how U.S. decisionmakers weighed various military options across different domains during the foremost nuclear crisis of the Cold War. Ultimately, the United States deployed a naval quarantine to combat a Soviet nuclear missile threat in Cuba, though the actual response involved every domain available to Kennedy.[54] The cross-domain response was chosen because they believed it would

---

[51] Kaufmann, *The McNamara Strategy*, 40, 44. Kennedy felt this dichotomy acutely during the Cuban Missile Crisis, saying: "there's bound to be a reprisal from the Soviet Union, there always is—of their just going in and taking Berlin by force at some point. Which leaves me only one alternative, which is to fire nuclear weapons—which is a hell of an alternative." Ernest R. May and Philip D. Zelikow, eds., *The Kennedy Tapes: Inside the White House during the Cuban Missile Crisis* (New York: Norton, 2002), 112.

[52] Kaufmann, *The McNamara Strategy*, 76.

[53] Ibid., 131.

[54] May and Zelikow, *The Kennedy Tapes*.

prevent the full operationalization of the missile sites under construction in Cuba, while minimizing the likelihood of Soviet reprisal in Berlin.

Following the discovery of medium- and intermediate-range ballistic missile (MRBM and IRBM, respectively) construction sites on 14 and 17 October,[55] Kennedy assembled an Executive Committee tasked with considering all options for responding to the threat. While the primary objective was to remove the missiles, the committee's discussion also focused on an important secondary objective: to minimize negative impact on the United States' allies in Europe. The forty-two MRBMs and estimated twenty-four to thirty-two IRBMs, if fully operationalized, would increase by half the ability of the Soviet Union to strike the United States from Cuba.[56] Kennedy had drawn a line at introduction of ground-to-ground missiles in Cuba during a 4 September public address, and failing to respond would therefore compromise Americans' confidence in him as president.[57] Those closest to the president, however, saw that the primary challenge lay not in removing the missiles but in preserving the NATO alliance. McNamara explained: "it is not a military problem that we're facing. It's a political problem. It's a problem of holding the alliance together. It's a problem of properly conditioning Khrushchev for our future moves ... all require action that, in my opinion, the shift in military balance does not require."[58]

The Executive Committee considered several policy options, including not acting, pursuing international diplomatic routes at the UN, conducting a limited air strike on select targets, conducting a naval blockade, and carrying out a comprehensive air strike and invasion of Cuba. Both the "do nothing" and international diplomacy alternatives would prevent escalation to a degree acceptable to the allies but would not remove the threat to the United States caused by the simple presence of the missiles in Cuba. Furthermore, intelligence revealed that some of the missile sites had become operational, so the limited air strike option was ruled out because of the danger that Soviet missiles that survived a U.S. disarming first strike would be fired in retaliation before being destroyed.[59]

A naval blockade allowed the president to respond militarily but to avoid or delay taking aggressive action that could further escalate the crisis. McNamara listed the advantages of a blockade as follows:[60]

---

[55] MRBMs have a range of about 1,100 miles and can carry two to three megaton weapons. IRBMs have a range of about 2,200 miles and can carry about five megaton weapons.
[56] George and Richard Smoke, *Deterrence in American Foreign Policy*, 461.
[57] Ibid., 468–469.
[58] May and Zelikow, *The Kennedy Tapes*, 84.
[59] As Kennedy explained to congressional leadership: "if we go into Cuba we have to all realize that we are taking a chance that these missiles, which are ready to fire, won't be fired. So, is that really a gamble we should take? In any case we are preparing to take it. I think, fact is, that is one hell of a gamble." Ibid., 176.
[60] Ibid., 128.

1. It would cause us the least trouble with our allies.
2. It avoids any surprise air attack on Cuba, which is contrary to our tradition.
3. It is the only military course of action compatible with our position as a leader of the free world.
4. It avoids a sudden military move which might provoke a response from the USSR which could result in escalating actions leading to general war.

Kennedy publicly announced the naval quarantine on 22 October and stated that the United States would regard any nuclear missile launched from Cuba against any nation in the Western Hemisphere as "an attack by the Soviet Union on the United States, requiring a full retaliatory response upon the Soviet Union." This action was combined with mobilization for a massive air strike and invasion of Cuba, as well as an escalation of military readiness to Defense Condition III (DEFCON III), which indicates an increase in force readiness above that required for normal readiness and is considered the highest alert level in peacetime. Moreover, Strategic Air Command escalated the readiness level to DEFCON II, the level just below imminent nuclear war. On 26 October, Kennedy received a private letter from Khrushchev with an offer to remove the missiles if the United States pledged never to invade Cuba. Roughly twelve hours later, Khrushchev made a different offer, broadcast over public radio: the Soviet Union would withdraw its missiles from Cuba if the United States agreed to withdraw its Jupiter missiles from Turkey.[61]

Kennedy's carefully crafted response contained two key components. The first was a public acceptance of Khrushchev's first offer, in which the U.S. promised not to invade Cuba in exchange for withdrawal of Soviet missiles. The second was a private message delivered by U.S. attorney general Robert Kennedy to ambassador Anatoly Dobrynin that a massive air strike and invasion of Cuba were imminent unless the Soviets ceased construction immediately, and that the president intended to remove the Jupiter missiles from Turkey, but only as part of a separate negotiation.

The naval quarantine (with the threat of subsequent air strikes and land invasion) alternative was chosen specifically because it was a clear military response that kept two alternatives open: that of military escalation to remove the missiles by force if the Soviets did not retreat, as well as that of deescalation to avoid fracturing of NATO should Khrushchev seize Berlin. Thus, cross-domain deterrence *and* compellence were utilized to keep the option of crisis deescalation open for as

---

[61] Ibid., 186, 224, 299, 313. Kennedy was planning to replace the Jupiters with Polaris submarine-launched ballistic missiles based in the Mediterranean. Turkey, however, was strongly opposed to removal of the Jupiter missiles until the Polaris missiles were deployed. A senior Turkish diplomat informed one of this article's authors that Turkey's present-day uncertainty about the credibility of U.S. security guarantees stems from the removal of the Jupiter missiles decades ago. Nonattributable interview, 11 May 2011, Doha, Qatar.

long as possible. The primary motivation for deescalation was to preserve key allies' confidence in the United States' extended deterrence policy.

The Yom Kippur War, 1973

On 6 October 1973, the Yom Kippur War began when Egypt and Syria, supported by a coalition of other Arab states, launched a surprise attack on Israel. In the first few days of the war, Egyptian forces regained sectors of the Sinai Peninsula that had been lost to Israel in the 1967 Six-Day War, and Syrian forces threatened to regain the Golan Heights and enter Israeli territory. However, Israel mobilized within three days, stopped the Egyptian advance, pushed Syrian forces back, and launched a counter-offensive deep into Syria.

A UN resolution calling for a ceasefire in the war was adopted on 22 October. The ceasefire was quickly violated. Israelis encircled the Egyptian Third Army east of the Suez Canal, endangering Cairo, and advanced into Syria within artillery range of Damascus. Egyptian president Anwar Sadat called on the United States and the Soviet Union to send troops to the region to uphold the ceasefire and called for a UN Security Council meeting to discuss the crisis.

On 24 October, a message to President Richard Nixon arrived in which General Secretary Leonid Brezhnev stated: "I will say it straight that if you find it impossible to act jointly with us in this matter, we should be faced with the necessity urgently to consider the question of taking appropriate steps unilaterally."[62] In Nixon's words, this "scarcely veiled threat of unilateral Soviet intervention" contained "the most serious threat to U.S.-Soviet relations since the Cuban missile crisis eleven years before."[63] The crisis was further intensified by intelligence information that Soviet and East German forces were mobilizing. It is also alleged that a Soviet ship carrying nuclear weapons was anchored in Alexandria, Egypt.[64]

The first objective for U.S. policymakers was to prevent the Soviet Union from unilaterally deploying troops to the Middle East. The United States was "determined to resist by force if necessary the introduction of Soviet troops into the Middle East."[65] Another objective was to minimize international support of the introduction of U.S. and Soviet troops to the Middle East.[66] A third objective may have been

---

[62] The letter from Brezhnev to Nixon has been declassified and is available online; see: William Burr, ed., "The October War and U.S. Policy," National Security Archive, 7 October 2003, accessed 10 March 2018, https://nsarchive2.gwu.edu/NSAEBB/NSAEBB98/.

[63] Richard M. Nixon, *RN: The Memoirs of Richard Nixon* (New York: Simon and Schuster, 1990), 938. Although Richard Nixon was not a primary decisionmaker in this crisis, he reflects on the severity of the threat in his memoirs.

[64] Edgar O'Ballance, *No Victor, No Vanquished: The Yom Kippur War* (San Rafael, CA: Presidio Press, 1978), 175.

[65] Henry Kissinger, *Years of Upheaval* (Boston: Little Brown, 1982), 580.

[66] Ibid., 592.

to convince Israel of the absolute necessity to observe the ceasefire by making the threat of Soviet intervention appear credible.[67]

Kissinger called a meeting of principals to discuss the crisis.[68] The participants anticipated an airlift of Soviet materiel and possibly troops to Egypt to begin in a few hours. The participants agreed that the United States should proceed with a diplomatic course, aiming to slow down the Soviets' timetable with talks and undermine international support for the plan. However, it was believed that a U.S. reply would have no impact unless it was backed up with noticeable action that conveyed determination to resist unilateral moves.[69] The group quickly settled on alerting U.S. forces to DEFCON III, the highest military readiness stage for peacetime conditions. This was seen as the minimum alert level that would undeniably be noticed by the Soviets. This order was made immediately. Additional news of an imminent Soviet military move seemed to indicate that the Soviets might not have noticed the DEFCON III alert before they moved their forces, so additional alerts were conveyed.[70]

Meanwhile, the participants wrote a letter to Sadat in Nixon's name reiterating the rejection of a joint U.S.-Soviet force. It warned of the consequences to Egypt if the superpowers were to meet militarily on Egyptian soil. A reply to Brezhnev was sent in Nixon's name rejecting all Soviet demands. It did not refer to the military alert but offered U.S. approval of a UN truce supervisory force and restated that the United States would not accept unilateral action.[71]

The Politburo recognized the U.S. threat as credible, stating that the alert was an irresponsible overreaction and the conflict was heading toward a confrontation between the United States and the Soviet Union.[72] The Soviet Union did not respond to the alert, deciding that it was "not reasonable to become engaged in a war with the United States because of Egypt and Syria."[73]

---

[67] Ray Maghroori and Stephen M. Gorman, *The Yom Kippur War: A Case Study in Crisis Decision-Making in American Foreign Policy* (Washington, DC: University Press of America, 1981), 53. This does not appear as an objective in Kissinger's or Nixon's memoirs. It is speculated in many analyses, including that by Maghroori and Gorman.

[68] Kissinger, *Years of Upheaval*, 586.

[69] The necessity of backing up diplomatic moves with noticeable action is discussed in the memoirs of Nixon, *RN: The Memoirs of Richard Nixon*, 938, and Kissinger, *Years of Upheaval*, 587.

[70] Ibid., 588, 587, 589.

[71] The letter from Nixon to Brezhnev is available online; see Burr, "The October War and U.S. Policy."

[72] Victor Israelyan, *Inside the Kremlin during the Yom Kippur War* (University Park: Pennsylvania State Press, 2010), 179, 194. Many in the Politburo reveled in the Americans' panic, believing that the Americans' fear would make the rest of the world respect the Soviet Union more.

[73] Ibid., 180–182. The Soviet premier, Alexei Kosygin, made this statement in a meeting of the Politburo on 25 October. Kosygin was nominally second in command to Brezhnev.

Ultimately, the United States had effectively helped end the Yom Kippur War without deploying U.S. or Soviet troops to the region. Kissinger had written extensively on the effectiveness of nuclear weapons for deterrence, coercive diplomacy, and alliance reassurance and was intimately familiar with the tactic of nuclear signaling as a diplomatic tool. Although the concept of "cross-domain deterrence" was not explicitly mentioned, it appears that U.S. policymakers weighed carefully their military and diplomatic moves in an effort to constrain Israeli military action, deter Soviet military intervention, and produce a peaceful resolution to the crisis.

Conclusion

This chapter has examined five prominent cases of CDD in American foreign policy (table 2.1). In the Korean War case, the United States used the explicit or implicit threat to use nuclear weapons to bring hostilities to an end on more than one occasion. It is not clear that the United States would have actually used nuclear weapons had compellence failed. What is most difficult to determine, however, is the influence of these threats on China's and North Korea's decisionmaking. Stalin's death and North Korean and Chinese battlefield losses appear to have been far more significant determinants of their behavior.

The Berlin crises of 1958 and 1961 illustrate the U.S. employment of nuclear threats to avert an imminent conflict on the ground. A key distinction between the two crises is that in the 1958 one, an attack on the Soviet Union was implied, which Soviet policymakers may not have thought totally credible. In the 1961 one, the United States resorted to a more diverse and limited set of nuclear and conventional threats that probably were more readily believed in Moscow.

The Cuban Missile Crisis was the most complex and stressful for U.S. policymakers, as it called on them to use naval assets to *compel* withdrawal of the Soviet missiles, nuclear threats to *deter* their use, and extensive and subtle diplomatic maneuvering to resolve the crisis peacefully. Yet the United States still had to offer important concessions before agreement could be reached—to no longer threaten to invade Cuba and overthrow the Castro regime and to withdraw Jupiter MRBMs from Turkey. Providing Fidel Castro with a credible way out was also a top priority. In addition, the asymmetry of stakes (more important to Washington than to Moscow) probably was a highly determinant factor.

The 1973 U.S. nuclear alert during the Yom Kippur War demonstrated Washington's resort to a nuclear threat to deter the intervention of Soviet conventional forces in the Middle East. In this case, it was a change in operational readiness rather than a shift in declaratory policy that was intended to send a message to Moscow. Once again, the imbalance of interests—U.S. protection of Israel versus extending Soviet influence in the region—probably led to an outcome in the United States' favor.

In all four of these Cold War cases, the nuclear threat was the primary U.S. option besides conventional force deployments and diplomacy. These cases illustrate that CDD is not new and that major cases of deterrence in U.S. foreign policy are rife with cross-domain interactions. What is new is that the complexity of CDD today makes it more explicitly apparent in a way it was not before. Deterrence theory and practice may have been able to avoid appreciating its CDD aspect, but no longer.

In the post–Cold War cases, we have examined nonnuclear CDD interactions. Our brief discussion of the U.S. response to China's direct ascent antisatellite weapon test in 2007 illustrated that the initial inclination of U.S. decisionmakers and the bureaucratic process is to respond within-domain. Specialists on the technology (in this case space, in other cases cyber) or domain (maritime is often prevalent) often address the issue initially based on their areas of expertise. Only as the decisionmaking process expands do opportunities for cross-domain considerations present themselves.

Finally, Olympic Games is a harbinger of things to come. It demonstrates the use of an offensive cyber capability to destroy equipment that could assist Iran in its development of its nuclear arsenal. Use of cyber offensive operations had different objectives from those of the employment of nuclear threats in the Cold War cases: to *delay* progress of the program rather than to compel its closure, and to engage Israel's participation in order to *reassure* Jerusalem of the seriousness of U.S. intent and thus obviate the need for an Israeli air strike on the Iranian facilities. Could alliance reassurance thus be a central objective of future offensive cyber operations? Moreover, it may have been reasoned in Washington that inducing a significant program delay coupled with the imposition of severe economic sanctions would then compel Iran to seek a negotiated resolution of the issue. A combination of nonkinetic options may thus be a hallmark of future U.S. coercive diplomacy.

These cases illustrate that U.S. policymakers tend to move cautiously in a crisis; seek to have the widest number of available options for maximum flexibility; and seek to prevail and support U.S. national interests while minimizing the likelihood of adversary retaliatory escalation that could lead to armed conflict or to the use of nuclear weapons. In this environment, it makes sense for the policy community to raise explicitly at the outset of a crisis the benefits and risks of CDD. Future research should be conducted on the conditions in which CDD is escalatory rather than stabilizing, using both historical cases and quantitative modeling; on how the introduction of space weapons and biological weapons could affect cross-domain calculations; on the impact of CDD on adversary leadership with different cultural and religious values; and on whether the establishment of international norms or codified agreements could reduce the likelihood of the use of weapons that could do enormous harm to modern societies.

This chapter has examined cases from 1950 through the Obama administration, a period marked by what Nobel Prize–winner Thomas Schelling characterized as the "tradition of non-use of nuclear weapons."[74] With such a consistent reluctance to use these weapons of extraordinary destructive power, it is understandable that decisionmakers would search—sometimes systematically, sometimes impulsively—for nonnuclear alternatives to resolve conflicts and crises. And in the last decade, the availability of sophisticated space and cyberweapons has opened additional options for government leaders to consider.

There are, however, dark clouds on the strategic horizon that challenge assumptions that this tradition can be sustained. Some of these clouds stem from recent changes in Russian military doctrine that appear to call for "escalate to deescalate" measures in which, for example, a Russian conventional attack in the Baltics is followed by initial use of tactical nuclear weapons to deter NATO retaliation. Some measures cited in the Trump administration's 2018 "Nuclear Posture Review" are evidently meant to meet this threat.[75]

Moreover, the intense rivalry of regional nuclear powers has presented concerns about highly escalatory conditions in which nuclear weapons would in fact be used.[76] The dangers of these threatening developments increase the necessity of gaining a sophisticated appreciation of what cross domain measures could lead to crisis control and de-escalation. This requirement calls for adjustment of the U.S. policymaking process so that representatives of a full spectrum of technology and domain specialists are engaged at the outset to ensure that the broadest perspectives and options are highlighted for serious consideration.

---

[74] Thomas Schelling, "Prize Lecture: An Astonishing Sixty Years: The Legacy of Hiroshima," Beijersalen, Royal Swedish Academy of Sciences, Stockholm, 8 December 2005, accessed 10 March 2018, https://www.nobelprize.org/nobel_prizes/economic-sciences/laureates/2005/schelling-lecture.pdf.

[75] "Nuclear Posture Review," Department of Defense, February 2018, 20–22.

[76] One scenario that has received widespread attention is that of a repeat of the 2008 Pakistani terrorist attack in Mumbai, followed by Indian conventional force retaliation on Pakistani territory, which leads to Pakistan using tactical nuclear weapons on Indian forces deployed in Pakistan. Some surmise that this would invite a massive Indian nuclear response on Pakistan civilian and military targets.

3

The Past and Future of Deterrence Theory

PATRICK M. MORGAN

Serious attention to deterrence first emerged in the United Kingdom as World War II was approaching, and detailed study of it, particularly nuclear deterrence, began immediately after the war, driven in particular by the onset of the Cold War.[1] Preoccupation with deterrence in theory and practice was soon intense and continued until the end of the Cold War many years later. This event brought a significant relaxation of tensions among the great powers, sharp cuts in their nuclear arsenals, and shrinking great power defense budgets and forces, plus similar reductions in a number of other states. It also temporarily reduced attention to deterrence analytically and in practice.

A series of historical developments then revived attention to deterrence early in the twenty-first century. First, rising tensions and conflict reappeared among the great powers, alongside efforts by several other states seeking to become nuclear powers (i.e., Iran, North Korea). Second, terrorism increased in several areas of the world, along with continuing outbursts of conventional, asymmetrical, and various forms of guerrilla or other insurgent warfare. Third, an epidemic of widespread cyberattacks erupted, suggesting the prospect of future cyber warfare. Fourth, an array of new weapons and weapon systems, drawing on or deriving from new military and other technologies, has steadily increased and spread.

The revived interest in the theory and practice of deterrence includes investigation of elements largely ignored, marginalized, or underdeveloped during the Cold War. They include elements of deterrence by denial, deterrence by international collective actors, the changing nature, conduct, and role of general deterrence (as

---

[1] Actually, deterrence is older, but it really blossomed in theory and practice from the late 1930s on. On this and its development after World War II, see: Patrick Morgan and George Quester, "How History and the Geopolitical Context Shape Deterrence," in *Deterrence: Its Past and Future*, edited by George P. Shultz, Sidney D. Drell, and James E. Goodby (Stanford, CA: Hoover Institution Press, 2011), 1–45. The best introduction to deterrence, short yet highly instructive, is Lawrence Freedman, *Deterrence* (Cambridge: Polity Press, 2004).

contrasted with immediate or crisis deterrence) in sustaining international security and stability globally, and some erratic use of deterrence in interventions at the regional, state, and domestic levels by ad hoc groups of states seeking to sustain peace and security.[2]

The current interest in deterrence is notably conscious of the frequent failure of recent deterrence efforts to sustain security and stability in international politics. Efforts to deter, contain, and end conflict face frequent difficulty—whether terrorism, intrastate ethnic, religious and political fighting, and interstate fighting. There is increasing conflict and serious disarray in the East-West deterrence relationship again, with disturbing possibilities of outright conflict now being openly discussed among analysts and observers.

On Deterrence

Deterrence is a fundamental strategy and method for escalation control, in both international and intrastate conflict, intended by an actor to prevent an attack on itself or others that it wants to protect.[3] The general idea is hardly new, but the specific term and its modern-day components began to emerge as World War II approached, and it became a striking phenomenon after the use of atomic weapons in 1945. Deterrence and its close relative, compellence, are components of coercive diplomacy.[4] Deterrence quickly developed into a strategy because it seemed crucial for preventing another great war and any further use of nuclear weapons, making it of vast importance in managing security in the international system and a recourse for preventing wars between conflicting states. It became a key factor for shaping peace and security, as a tactic as well as a strategy, and a central driver in developing modern arms control. It could prevent ruinous wars, by eliminating the utility of cheap-victory strategies that encouraged them, and could manage peace without fighting by controlling threats by enemies to use unimaginably destructive weapons against one another.

Deterrence thinking eventually embraced two broad types of deterrence situations and two distinctive kinds of deterrence associated with them. One is

---

[2] This refers to deterrence via international bodies like the UN Security Council or ad hoc groups of states. See: Patrick Morgan, "Collective Actor Deterrence," in *Complex Deterrence: Strategy in the Global Age*, edited by T. V. Paul, Patrick Morgan, and James Wirtz (Chicago: University of Chicago Press, 2009), 158–182.

[3] Patrick Morgan, *Deterrence Now* (New York: Cambridge University Press, 2003), 105.

[4] See, for example, Peter Viggo Jakobsen, "The Strategy of Coercive Diplomacy: Refining Existing Theory to Post–Cold War Realities," in *Strategic Coercion, Concepts and Cases*, edited by Lawrence Freedman (New York: Oxford University Press, 1998), 61–85; Peter Viggo Jakobsen, "Coercive Diplomacy: Countering War-Threatening Crises and Armed Conflicts," in *Contemporary Security Studies*, 4th ed., edited by Alan Collins (Oxford: Oxford University Press, 2016), 280–293.

general deterrence: a state, or group of states, maintains a continuing military posture and forces intended to scare off potential attacks.[5] The other is *immediate deterrence*: a state is threatened with being attacked or otherwise seriously harmed and puts some or all of its forces and government on much higher alert.[6] General deterrence can operate almost indefinitely, being periodically adjusted to changes in the international system or a regional or local system. It can operate at a low level of salience and readiness, and is often somewhat vague. It is used this way in balance of power relationships and in stabilizing regional and global security management efforts in international politics. When effective, general deterrence can even build up considerable influence, lowering chances of serious conflict and war breaking out, to enhance stability in international relations.

In sharp contrast, immediate deterrence involves an intense crisis with an outbreak of fighting looming or even some limited fighting already under way. With such tension comes fear of irrationality or mistakes provoking death and destruction, which in turn incite strong emotions and last-minute efforts to dampen all this. Such a situation usually lasts only briefly—it is too tense and dangerous to sustain indefinitely—either abating or giving way to serious fighting. We have some experience in practice but no reliable theory on how to effectively manage an emerging shift from general to immediate deterrence, smoothly or safely and durably, and then reorienting in the opposite direction. More theory has been developed on shifting deterrence to effectively create or sustain a pluralistic security community, building a working collective security system, or developing a great power concert.

Backed by great powers' nuclear weapons and often their significant conventional forces, deterrence appears to have prevented large great power wars throughout the Cold War, helping to stabilize the core international system, but not without deep concerns and strenuous objections at times. Lesser wars occurred nonetheless, some dangerous enough to promote fears of escalation into nuclear war, and provoked or reinforced fear that the world was on the edge of disaster or Armageddon. After all, deterrence could be effective, but it was not certain to be perfect.

---

[5] For example, the United States, in general deterrence, has long maintained forces in and around Japan and the Republic of Korea for its own and selected others' protection. General deterrence varies greatly in intensity; in many places it is modest in presence and intensity, while for years the Republic of Korea, Japan, and U.S. forces have been kept on fairly high alert because a North Korean attack looks likely or at least quite possible, and the same is true for North Korea vis-à-vis the United States and the Republic of Korea. This is nicely discussed in Terrence Roehrig, "Reinforcing Deterrence: The U.S. Response to North Korean Provocations," in *Joint U.S.-Korean Academic Studies: Facing Reality in East Asia: Tough Decisions on Competition and Cooperation*, edited by Gilman Rozman (Washington, DC: Korea Economic Institute of America, 2015), 221–238.

[6] For example, North Korea's missile and nuclear weapons tests in 2016–2018 led to U.S. and South Korea forces being put on high alert, and vice versa.

Thus the end of the Cold War and sharp decline in great power conflict brought enormous relief and almost immediate steps back from that brink. However, enough remaining reliance on deterrence, plus mistrust, made it impossible to totally discard deterrence postures, including nuclear deterrence. And sure enough, great power disagreements soon reappeared. Threats and indications of continued or resumed reliance on nuclear weapons started reappearing, alongside escalating military spending, modernized missiles and nuclear warheads, and more military posturing at borders, at sea, or in the air. Meanwhile, numerous lower-level conflicts emerged or continued, many quite vicious and destructive, with familiar results: surges in numbers of refugees, vast social disruptions, terrific human rights burdens, worries over possible loss of control of weapons of mass destruction somewhere, and threats of complete disarray in places where various states and societies lost control of big portions of their territories and citizens. New threats have included direct invasions and fierce foreign-based terrorism by nonstate actors, with foreigners penetrating societies to mount devastating individual or small-group attacks, as well as startling domestic uprisings. The concept of deterrence was not designed for such eruptions, a plurality of actor types, for so many potential attack situations, or for having so many people facing grave situations as deterrence crumbled around them. Many people now suffer much harm and destruction without conventional wars, and this spreads fear about the potential for interstate—even nuclear—wars.

Attempts to deter effectively have therefore become more complex, difficult, even unpredictable and unmanageable at times, thus bringing the reliability of the very concept of deterrence for providing stability and security into question. This is reinforced by some noticeable decay in cooperation among major states—both allies and opponents—in conducting deterrence efforts. The United States is therefore immersed in problems in pursuing deterrence efforts in and with Europe, the Middle East, Northeast Asia, South Asia, and parts of Africa, problems approached from a largely global perspective, while numerous other states are practicing deterrence in their neighborhoods.

Conceptual Stretching in Deterrence

In part, some confusion arises because the concept of deterrence is being stretched to cover a greater variety of situations. Initially focused primarily on the nuclear threat and mounting a retaliatory nuclear threat to contain it, deterrence was later applied to major and minor conventional attacks and wars, with an eye on possible escalation to the nuclear level, as in the traditional deterrence problem; deterrence then increasingly also focused on protecting allies, improving or defending one's position in the international system, and providing assistance to strategically placed states, longtime friends, and diaspora communities. Thus the concept of deterrence was expanded to deal with even quite limited conflicts or to see that they end appropriately.

There has been interest in applying deterrence concepts to low-level threats with or among others, such as extensive low-level fighting, struggles with radical elements in the Middle East, or ethnic and religious anger directed at the West while also violently directed at neighbors. Outside parties respond, claiming they have vital stakes to sustain. Such widespread, often only partially cohesive, attacks or deterrence efforts often put lives and holdings at serious risk. It is especially difficult to target deterrence against cyberattacks and similar threats that seem almost random or self-organized, sometimes only partially supported by governments and including actively hostile religious groups, criminal elements, breakaway ethnic groups, and so on.[7] Terrorists can be very harmful, as demonstrated by the 9/11 attacks, Islamic State (Daesh) attacks, attacks by central African groups, and widespread violence that drives refugee flows. The dangers grow with the proliferation of low-cost, high-impact weapons, and thus so does interest in deterrence.[8]

Shifts from general to immediate deterrence situations can spring up almost instantly, as with 9/11. Moreover, the range and scale of possible attacks have been expanding. One implication is that to intervene to establish or repair deterrence outside actors may have to reach inside a country and society, not just confront its government, and do so by use of force, not just threats. There are more ways to pursue deterrence by nonmilitary steps, i.e., by supporting the citizens against the government, displacingor buying out anti-regime elements, and attacking the regime by sanctions, isolation, various disruptions, and so on.

A common Western practice now is deterrence by nonfatal or limited casualty steps, such as advanced weapons for precision attacks from long distance, cutting off flows of weapons to targeted actors, imposing financial and other sanctions via international organizations and agencies, incremental punishment (a common Israeli military practice), gradually escalated retaliation in the hope that the target will back down, and blending deterrence with arms control and other measures to stabilize a situation (like the 2015 deal on Iran's nuclear weapons program).[9]

Too little attention is paid to how the application of deterrence is now being stretched and bent by still other environmental aspects. For example, Vladimir Putin's efforts to restore Russia's great power status are military rearmament steps for protection that also tap into Russia's resentment over the West's supposed isolation of it. This justification enables Russia to make moves toward dominating its neighbors again, and thereby bolster Putin's domestic rule, via an expansionist, aggressive style

---

[7] On deterring many of these sorts of opponents, see: James H. Lebovic, *Deterring International Terrorism and Rogue States: US National Security Policy after 9/11* (New York: Routledge, 2007).

[8] An example, detailing the elaborate Islamic State arsenal at the time: "Taking Stock; The Arming of Islamic State," Amnesty International, December 2015, accessed 13 March 2018, https://www.es.amnesty.org/uploads/media/Taking_Stock_The_arming_of_IS.pdf.pdf.

[9] See: James M. Action, Edward Ifft, and John McLaughlin, "Arms Control and Deterrence," in Schultz et al., *Deterrence, Its Past and Its Future*, 279–324.

of deterrence. He sees opportunities for Russia in coercive interactions from a nationalist deterrence posture and perspective. Such deterrence-related efforts are hard on international interactions. The West perceives Russia as harsh and semi-isolationist, adopting expansionist leanings that recall Cold War attitudes and necessitate a revitalization of Western deterrence postures. This is likely to contribute to the further degradation of East-West relations.

China's interaction with other major powers and neighbors similarly stems from seeing the West as essentially expansionist, leading Beijing to a deterrence perspective that is deeply affected by cultural, historical, and fearful attitudes. Western responses are depicted as continuing efforts to alter contemporary China's regime, national structure, society, and culture. This has evoked a very tough deterrence posture, pushing outsiders' responses toward similar steps: strengthening deterrence postures and deterrence-oriented military preparations and associations around China, all of which reflect classic deterrence thinking applied to novel circumstances.

Domestic environments also deeply affect Western deterrence efforts. The aftereffects of the Great Recession of 2008, together with the unimpressive results of Western interventions in the Middle East, Africa, and Afghanistan, have eroded domestic support for foreign interventions to wage war in restive foreign societies at great expense in blood and treasure. This reticence undercuts the American and European image abroad and considerably reduces the credibility of deterrent threats to intervene.

Of course, the international environment shapes deterrence as well—and is also unevenly appreciated. Collective actor deterrence can be established by ad hoc collections of states on behalf of global or major regional groups' collective values for human rights, human welfare, peace and security, and so on. It can involve numerous kinds of deterrence efforts. The Security Council was supposed to supply a significant degree of deterrence, enough to manage international security. It has never reached its intended level of cooperation and success.

Deterrence today often involves threats of punishment that go beyond retaliation to encompass invasion or some other penetration with more than retaliation in mind. This way of curbing harmful behavior involves steps almost unheard of in classic deterrence thinking. It involves extended fighting at times and even more management and development and can run on for years. This is only partly deterrence because the focus is ultimately on achieving political/cultural change, not simply preventing change. Blending all this together can be difficult, even onerous, as when it requires incorporating national feeling, state rule, and multiple cultural sectors and religions, plus building political and economic cohesion, any or all of which can arouse widespread opposition. There is little or no appreciation of this in classical deterrence theory and only limited understanding of it among practitioners orchestrating the deterrence effort. Often failure in the broader objectives erodes much or all of any initial success. The results are on display in too many places in the world today.

Thus Western deterrence is often stretched thin—in capacities, the number of states involved, cohesion in supplying the military presence, and the interventions generated by the supplying states. Often it confronts not one opponent but several. As a result, the deterrence applied may lack coherence, a sound structure, cohesive policy, and even a potent pattern of action.

Classic deterrence conceptually and theoretically focused on threatening direct attacks and planning military postures to block them. General deterrence resources were available to readily support an immediate deterrence effort, sustaining interstate stability via understood theoretical principles. Today, this deterrence, often lacking well-established policy and less coherent in military and other action patterns, seems unmoored from a theory and field of study with sustained practices. The West has pursued new versions of it and faces others mounted by locals in retaliation. Those resisting want to scare the West out of invading or out of remaining once there, not unlike what the British confronted in the American Revolution. The intent is to block insertions of Western control, culture, ideals, and beliefs and to shorten and conclude the process. The results have been uneven, but the West has clearly lost considerable support along the way, at home and elsewhere.

An odd result is concern over lesser warfare situations while facing rising fears that standard wars might return, possibly from attacks without warning. Russian leaders talk about this; North Koreans have done so for some time. But lesser warfare is still predominant, with deterrence stretched to explain and confront lesser forms of conflict, including such outbreaks as: periodic armed responses to limited attacks (terrorist strikes); blockades, sanctions, and other interdictions; border military demonstrations or incursions; cyberattacks or retaliations; inserting military forces/resources into civil or terrorist wars; major human rights violations; and suppression of civil conflicts.

On Domains

How does the concept of domain in "cross-domain deterrence" (CDD) pertain to deterrence today? It is useful to examine the domains involved and the resulting links to, for instance, U.S. deterrence efforts. A domain is a relatively coherent integrated collection of knowledge, technology, practices, training, resulting capabilities, and focused objectives. For instance, in the U.S. armed forces the term identifies distinct clusters of knowledge, experience, objectives, preparation, responsibilities, and orderly cooperative action. Each armed service has its own domain, as may subsections or other components. Other sections of society also have relevant domains. A cross-domain situation occurs when one domain is significantly penetrated by, overlapped by, and interactive with another. While often complex and difficult, this may be also innovative and rewarding in improving outcomes through expanded perceptions, capacities, and flexibility.

Cross-domain deterrence can apply in and among services, and in interchanges between military/security and civilian sectors. Civilian/military-cross-domain interaction has a long history in the United States. Numerous civilian domains, rife with new ideas, products, and capacities, such as railroads, the telegraph, war bonds, and the development and manufacture of repeating rifles, were tapped hugely by the North in the Civil War. Cross-domain deterrence is about further upgrading this dimension in more pointed, rigorous, well-defined, and extended ways.

The introduction to this book defines a domain as "any pathway or means for coercion that is different from other means in respect to its utility for political bargaining" and thus "might enable analysts to compare interactions between political actors according to how like confronts like and, increasingly, how unlike confronts unlike." This applies to both nonmilitary and military domains, with many military units and their endeavors deeply affected by injections of nonmilitary units in training, cyber activities, communications, management, maintenance, healthcare, and so on. Modern forces are immersed in interactions with civilian activities, personnel, education, and even armed civilian personnel for selected operations and services. The distance between civilian and military is eroded in a wide spectrum of activities, making the concept of "domain" increasingly fluid and amorphous, complicating analysis of the nature and impact of CDD. U.S. forces increasingly incorporate civilians, and overseas operations involve civilians, many foreign—driving, medicating, protecting, feeding, translating, and so on. Can the concept of "domain" remain cohesive for analytical purposes as a result? All sorts of situations have been displayed in the Iraq and Afghanistan wars, particularly when U.S. and associated forces took over. In such situations, description and analysis of what goes on within and between domains can be difficult to keep coherent.

Cross-Domain Deterrence

Initial work on the CDD-national security connection has focused heavily on improving and exploiting security resources, particularly in new and emerging technologies, plus enhancing reconsideration and application of older domains and technologies, to facilitate preparation for and conduct of military operations as necessary.[10] This can readily enhance the conduct of deterrence (and compellence).

A neglected subject in recent, but not classical, deterrence theory is not just deterring attacks but preventing escalation of existing attacks to intolerable levels.

---

[10] A major forerunner was the Revolution in Military Affairs. For an overview of its relationship with deterrence, see: Michel Fortmann and Stefanie Von Hlatky, "The Revolution in Military Affairs: The Impact of Emerging Technologies on Deterrence," in Paul et al., *Complex Deterrence*, 304–319.

This was a huge preoccupation in the Cold War, of course, concerning the use of nuclear weapons (by either side) and avoiding nuclear retaliation for nasty lower-level attacks too. Recently threats to resort to such steps have been advanced by several governments (e.g., Moscow), which is very disturbing. On conventional forces, new kinds of threats meant to deter or curb fighting have consistently cropped up over clashes in the Middle East.

Other deterrence complications arise because states generate and deal with a wide variety of threats and by numerous ways that go well beyond simple threats to fight and harm if attacked. States employ numerous ways of designing and delivering threats for both general and immediate deterrence purposes, plus deterrence efforts as preparations or assertions for show or as a bluff.

Key to these threats' impact is credibility—being believed to possess the necessary forces and intent to use them or at least having them under development.[11] With little or no credibility, deterrence can readily collapse. A major problem is that credibility is not just created by the deterrer; it has to be perceived or otherwise believed by the target, and with a sufficient effect. And there are complications. What if the threat is credible but it is believed that the harm inflicted will be bearable, or the objective so vital that the harm must be borne anyway (as Kim Jong Un promises)? What if preparing to possibly impose that harm or defeat appears to the opponent as preparing to attack instead, provoking its attack as a result? But trying hard not to convey such an image might mean failing to make the threat look tough enough and thus credible enough. Any real deterrence policy is usually somewhat amorphous, almost naturally given the uncertain situations considered, and that is part of why it is not guaranteed to work.

This can be problematic for CDD contributions to deterrence, since the associated analyses of them cannot be guaranteed to fully comprehend and convey, especially in advance, all the results of added domains, their components, and their activities. Having a clear sense of how particular CDD efforts will shape officials' and analysts' grasp of deterring an opponent in a particular situation and time, and thus how best to conduct that effort, will be very valuable if attained, especially for the United States, which, for mounting or sustaining deterrence threats, frequently wrestles with multiple current or potential opponents on a large spectrum of behavior and perception patterns. Shaping such efforts properly depends on the adequacy and effective application of cross-domain resources. But further study will likely note the domains often clashing or competing in security activities. A common phenomenon in U.S. forces, defense industry sectors, and the like is clashing views, competitive struggles, and frequent displays of ideas in advance of adequate capabilities. Adding more domains will compound all this.

---

[11] On credibility in general deterrence, for example, see: Morgan, *Deterrence Now*, 101–105.

Opponents of Western deterrence policy (like Russia, China, and North Korea) will introduce their own versions of CDD, so monitoring developments in doctrine and force development is vital. A key to deterrence stability is the opponents' having a relatively clear understanding of each other's military capabilities and overall strategic perceptions and plans. This was vital in the Cold War between the superpowers, and the recent historiography uncovering the scale and nature of what they misunderstood about what each saw, planned, and feared, has been hair-raising! Can CDD analyses and uses offer enough necessary help in deterrence in the future in a practical, timely, and suitable fashion?

Familiar Complications

Some of the complications of CDD are familiar from previous experience with deterrence. It is reasonable to begin with the assumption that effective deterrence starts by sending a clear, credible message signaling a predictable outcome if the proscribed action is carried out by the target. This assumption seems logical but then confronts various complications. First, governments and leaders often resist fixed deterrence postures, understandable in general deterrence but often a poor fit in immediate deterrence efforts. They readily issue threats to prevent actions they oppose, with hints or other evidence of their intended responses to noncompliance. Specifically stating what they will do is rare, for obvious reasons—to avoid giving the opponent a better chance to fully prepare for what is coming, assess how harmful it will be, and probe it for flaws. Governments and leaders want multiple plans at least partially at hand for a crisis, given the uncertainty, plus backup plans and room to delay before having to act, plus last minute retreat options, and so on. Cross-domain deterrence could be considerably useful here, uncovering new or underappreciated alternative steps, if steered in this direction.

Sometimes, the more explicit the deterrence threat, the more it antagonizes the opponent, stiffening its determination, particularly if it is certain it is in the right and thus entitled to attack. The threat might be taken as further evidence of how improper and dangerous the deterrer's intent is, how arrogant or humiliating. The more explicit and public the threat, the more difficult it is domestically and internationally for one or both parties to be seen giving in, for fear that flexibility suggests weakness: believing that backing down will encourage intransigence in one's opponent.

Thus ambiguity is often a serious factor in such exchanges, especially when they are often immersed in private or third-party information about the situation and who is planning to do what. Thus a deterrence threat and response are seldom clear and simple. Complexity is often unavoidable, especially because misperceptions often crop up. Today's greater complexity in weapons, intentions, intragovernmental perceptions, and the like should add to the ambiguity, despite continued CDD escalation of information flows to try to offset it.

Next, threats, and deterrence threats in response, are typically bargaining maneuvers, bluffs, probes, and the like, adding more ambiguity. Even the government or its leaders often do not know exactly what they will do until getting very close to doing it. Usually the task of assembling a firm foreign or domestic coalition for an attack or responding to one is difficult, and the decisionmaking on what steps to take is always complicated. The exact nature of the situation may be difficult to ascertain until *after* an attack is launched or not. Officials on each side may have contingent plans rather than finely tuned ones.

It is not certain whether CDD elements will help to clarify such situations or not. As available information expands, available options and also estimates of possible outcomes probably will too. Will this make for more sophisticated deterrence strategies or designs that better fit conflict and crisis situations? Serious research to deal with all this will be necessary. Otherwise, the desires expressed in the project statement, to develop analytically rigorous but not overly complex theory, will likely be too ambitious.

Also notable is that while deterrence theory was initially associated mostly with arousing an opponent's rational decisionmaking, the accompanying fear now is about the irrationality detected in various situations. A good example is the tension that emerged between the United States and North Korea after the election of Donald Trump, with both sides alienating even close associates, deeply irritating each other, and seemingly poised to violate international norms as they approached the brink of war. There is no sign yet that CDD can enhance rationality via deterrence theory and in deterrence situations, whether nuclear weapons are involved or not.

Another substantial problem confronting CDD starts with it having been substantially involved in the physical components involved in deterrence—military actions, resources, technological capabilities, equipment enhancement (i.e., real people doing real things in real time). But a significant aspect of conducting deterrence remains psychological, exploiting not just an opponents' rational decisionmaking but their emotions, fears, thought processes, and understandings in a situation; for example, in how credibility is involved and perceived or is irrationality stimulated. Cross-domain deterrence should be evaluated as to how psychological considerations affect the conduct of deterrence through careful study and analysis.[12]

Another current complication is that use of deterrence, and military retaliation when it fails, must now be undertaken with awareness of the constraints of human rights considerations while confronting the human rights violations many of

---

[12] For examples of the study of psychological elements of deterrence, see: Robert Jervis, "Psychology and Security: Enduring Questions, Different Answers," *Yale Journal of International Affairs* 7, no. 2 (Summer 2012): 9–15; Janice Gross Stein, "Rational Deterrence against 'Irrational' Adversaries? No Common Knowledge," in Paul et al., *Complex Deterrence*, 58–82.

today's opponents (Islamic State, Syria, the Taliban) relish with indifference as part of deterring the United States and other western parties. A related element is that many are committed to accepting death, even to seeking it out, and thus are hard to overcome, take as prisoners, extract information from, and deter. This behavior appears irrational, and if so, there is no consistent way to effectively deter it.

Emerging Complications

Some complications with CDD are more novel. A recurring problem will be how public to make the development of new weapons, systems, or strategies in the fear that they will be copied, developed, and modified too rapidly and effectively. The United States suffers endless cyber- and other attacks seeking to steal technology, military capabilities, defense plans, and the like. This golden age of spying and theft is running at an ever-increasing pace.[13] Another problem is that deterrence requires that the necessary capabilities for retaliation and resistance not be overly hidden! A secret domain of combat or potent enhancements to it, so unfamiliar to the opponents that they have nothing comparable, may be fine for handicapping their next attack, but it does not help get them to avoid starting it.

Another complication is that opponents may overreact when shocked by a new capability, seeing it not as deterrence but as being poised for attack. This was how the Kremlin reacted almost immediately to the first U.S. nuclear weapons, and such overreaction is apparent both in the intensified Pyongyang nuclear weapons drive and in Russia's haste in preparing to be able to merge nuclear and conventional forces in a future military clash with the West.

Can CDD help here? Thus far, it is not easy to see how. Cross-domain deterrence developments almost never seem to effectively improve control over the increasing diffusion of new knowledge, technology, information, creation, and imitation. Many developments and much of the diffusion in and among domains are due to brilliant self-motivated experimenters on the edges of the domains, and word of the achievements often readily spreads, sometimes due to the lure of financial gain or patriotism.

If well-developed theory in CDD on all this remains difficult to construct, it will be better to concentrate on constantly updating strategy, training, and theory in expectation of technological and other domain changes and interactions with others doing the same. Hopefully, via CDD, accepting the pace of change and its effects will be matched by suspicions that initial grasp of oncoming developments will

---

[13] Studies of all this include: "Deterrence in Cyberspace," *The Military Balance 2016* (London: International Institute for Strategic Studies, 2016), 16–18; Myriam Dunn Cavelty, "Cyber-Security," in *Security Studies*, 4th ed., edited by Alan Collins (Oxford: Oxford University Press, 2016), 400–416.

typically be somewhat flimsy, with many unanticipated consequences. It is relatively easy to envision CDD expanding and complicating security matters, particularly deterrence, as new factors encompass a wider range of information, resources, invention, and technology. But this may expand difficulty in grasping security challenges and their surrounding intricacies, the resources needed, and how to effectively use them. Deterrence surrounded by such changes often comes with more intense pressure. Can CDD help to cope with this?

Probably. Much time and energy in pursuing and exploiting emerging domains, individually and in combination, is aimed at making many activities less complicated, and juggling more activities simultaneously is getting simpler via modern communications and other technologies in numerous cross-domains. We are on the edge of utilizing self-driving military vehicles. Many military activities using complex technology now exploit webs of domains to accurately deliver ordinance hundreds or thousands of miles away in a markedly simpler fashion. U.S. forces can be smaller and less expensive yet just as powerful or more so, because they do many things more simply and quickly. Intelligence agencies gather valuable information (secret and otherwise) about opponents or others at an unprecedented pace and scale, processing in unprecedented fashion.

Grasping cross-domain effects will require recognizing how often they make things simpler and more comprehensible, when complexity is expanding or retreating, and when and why simplicity or complexity matters the most, and in ways that go beyond just science and technology. Modern states are more complicated to operate. International collective actors, particularly NGOs, are more numerous and often more influential—operating them as governments want is often quite complicated, not just in the cross-domain elements involved but because the participants as actors are very difficult to organize. In combination, the North Atlantic Treaty Organization (NATO) and its associates' efforts have repeatedly demonstrated that effective cooperation and coordination are getting more difficult to achieve and sustain. The United States found this repeatedly in the war against Serbia and again in the war in Syria, often preferring, if possible, to do without others' assistance. Problems mount when relevant domains are unevenly employed or mismatched in participants' capabilities. Then willingness to use them can be very uneven and the parties' staying power inadequate.

Another likely CDD-incited complication is profound. More overlap between civilian and military activities means that policymakers and citizens alike had better prepare to confront domains not yet rooted or operating deeply in U.S. security affairs. This requires considering redesigning the entire range of contemporary security affairs—weapons, actions, capabilities, organization, and the like. Our security affairs will be almost completely reshaped eventually, perhaps rapidly, tracking similar developments taking place for some time in our media, other communications, medical care systems, and transportation. Why not also with our capacities for controlling warfare in the international system and within its members?

The Ultimate Concern Facing CDD Efforts

There has still not been a nuclear war since 1945, nor a major war of any sort between major powers, so perhaps deterrence deserves some credit. Yet for other types of conflict, the United States and its friends and allies have apparently been experiencing sharp declines in results from deterrence efforts because they have either failed or achieved only limited success. This is partly due to erosions in thinking about the nature of deterrence and its uses, impacting on the "stretching" of deterrence. This is important for the future of CDD in light of some relevant developments.

With less support for direct military operations, the United States now turns more to training, special operations, protection, and various selective attacks. Outright combat operations as in the World Wars were serious efforts, but there is now much less of this. The favored responses to states and armed groups ignoring U.S. deterrence pressure are less likely to involve inserting conventional ground forces and more likely to involve using aerial or drone attacks, special operations forays, together with displays of military threats and traditional verbal, diplomatic, economic, and other deterrence-related threats. Even fighting such as the United States experienced in Iraq and Afghanistan appears to be in stasis or decline in any large scale. Yet challenges from China and Russia give pause.

When deterrence efforts are unsuccessful, one path is to tolerate the failure but signal that the tolerance will end if the unacceptable behavior does not. Another is to mount alternative kinds of pressure or preparations for outright military action again—shifting to outright fighting of some sort and threats of escalation beyond—but this would be hard to install in today's domestic climate about fighting abroad. And if the United States is not effectively preventing attacks, it is no longer driving a deterrence effort, because preventing attacks is primarily what deterrence is meant to be about. Such alternatives involve containing the status quo on a limited scale in fighting for national security objectives because deterrence—including CDD—is somehow seriously overstretched.[14] Conducting such conflicts is very difficult. They arouse opposition domestically and often from other allies and associates. Friction with allies may be unavoidable as the United States finds that they are woefully inadequate for fighting or providing other sorts of support. Some friction at home comes from citizens who support the fighting and charge that it is being fought in too limited a fashion such that national security interests and commitments are insufficiently protected. If support falls off, U.S. national security objectives and

---

[14] On why such fighting often turns out badly for the United States and the West, see: Ivan Arreguin-Toft, "Unconventional Deterrence: How the Weak Deter the Strong," in Paul et al., *Complex Deterrence*, 204–221.

policies shrink, producing a corresponding shrinkage in U.S. stature and influence abroad.

The United States is not far from this sort of situation, in view of its ongoing but contained involvement in Syria, Iraq, and Afghanistan. It is on the edge of shifting in this direction in relations with parts of NATO and with some allies and associates on the North Korean situation. Disagreements with China could seriously strain U.S. deterrence in East Asia and Southeast Asia. The United States faces the revival of aspects of the Cold War with Russia that is already provoking expanded U.S. defense spending, military planning, force distributions, and readiness. There is considerable interest in restoring aspects of the Cold War, such as sharply upgrading nuclear weapons in the United States and military capabilities for deterrence purposes in Europe. This is still at a preliminary stage, including the associated capacities of CDD.

CDD-D?

Given the stretching of deterrence in theory and practice, the proper title for the CDD project may turn out to be CDD-D, or cross-domain deterrence and (national) defense. The concept and strategy of deterrence, originally and obviously meant to prevent attacks, now embraces a wide range of fighting, from real attacks involving extensive, perhaps very destructive, warfare to those primarily encompassing lesser threatening conflicts, some with no fighting at all. How the CDD concept has been applied thus far falls mainly within the scope of the original CDD objectives—delivery of ever more flexibility and innovation across the spectrum of national security, intelligence, military affairs, and related activities by exploiting emerging capabilities and developments in interactive, overlapping domains. But it is on the edge of or even somewhat beyond this already complex set of developments that CDD will have to be used, given the general weakening of deterrence and the broader security threat facing the West.

United States deterrence efforts are now either only barely satisfactory or seriously unsatisfactory, and thus frustrating for policymakers, and often dangerous for national security. Policymakers cannot be counted on to sufficiently embrace CDD and to sufficiently adapt in practice and action to meet changing conflict situations soundly. They also cannot be counted on to reliably accommodate necessary domestic conditions and reactions in the United States as either deterrer or target. Deterrence theory has not yet fully grasped the future of deterrence practices or fully anticipated the specific threats it will be necessary to confront. Global security conditions are too fluid and unpredictable, as are the domestic and international political conditions.

The ultimate example of the stretching of deterrence, and of having to face a potentially greater threat that it can pose, lies in the rapidly developing cyber world.

Major governments, especially the United States, have seriously focused in recent years on exploiting cyberspace in their ongoing rivalries. A cyber-related struggle has been under way for roughly fifteen years over major governments' information capacities, thefts of their secrets, how to damage each other's networks, and the crux of their operations and crucial civilian and military technologies should serious warfare break out, with each government seeking to be able to effectively disrupt the others' capacities first.

Most critical here is the application of cyber capabilities to many specific aspects of war and cyber warfare: disabling or defending against air and missile attacks (degrading or destroying the missiles and planes), disrupting or destroying military information operations, disabling or destroying political administration structures. Equally critical is the capacity to mount preventive or preemptive attacks, because cyber warfare can be initiated and applied almost instantly, and thus its crucial components must be delivered first. Acquiring necessary information on an oncoming attack is the key to performing the other steps—such as destruction of enemy nuclear command, control, and communication (NC3) and information resources. Thus the cyberattack threat is expanding, such attacks having been perceived for some time as serious candidates for crippling nuclear weapons capabilities, particularly missiles. Ahead is a possible clash of cyber capabilities at every level of international affairs in the cyber-dominated world.

Similar bursts of change in numerous other dimensions will deeply affect not only deterrence and military affairs but also many other components of the planet's environment. An example is the growing problem of space debris: the vast amount and variety of materials that have steadily been inserted over time in space, are still there, and are rapidly accumulating as more governments and private enterprises use outer space. This is why the United States must seriously undertake further development and application of CDD (or CDD-D) and why it needs more analysis, application, and refinement—as rapidly as possible. Global security management as a whole is clearly in need of repair, and cyber developments are reshaping the world, including vast changes that extend to security, military capabilities, and the capacities to protect national welfare, particularly via deterrence. They are simultaneously multiplying vulnerabilities for international systems occupants—not just attack vulnerabilities but deterrence vulnerabilities. There is much here to consider and much to be done.[15]

---

[15] On cyber developments and deterrence, surveying two important new books on the subject, see: Susan Hennessey, "Deterring Cyberattacks: How to Reduce Vulnerability," *Foreign Affairs* (November/December 2017): 39–46; Greg Austin and Pavel Sharikov, "'Pre-emption Is Victory': Aggravated Nuclear Instability of the Information Age," *Nonproliferation Review* 23, nos. 5–6 (2016): 691–704.

4

Simplicity and Complexity in the Nth Nuclear Era

RON LEHMAN

Because separate expert organizations with distinct cultures inform nuclear, cyber, space, and other special operations, perspectives often differ on strategy, capabilities, threats, and priorities. Thus, a comparative approach can provide interesting insights, analogies, and lessons learned, highlighting relative strengths and weaknesses. When confronted with the most challenging scenarios, however, an important defense policy goal is synergism between cross-domain and nuclear deterrence—a total deterrent greater than the sum of the parts. Unfortunately, new capabilities, notably in cyberspace and space, could instead undermine deterrence by adding complexity, reducing reaction times, and creating common failure modes, potentially eroding even the nuclear components of deterrence.

In discussions of CDD, imprecise language frequently multiplies the uncertainty. The confusion is built in. The word "domain" has several relevant definitions. It may refer to an area, region, or place, usually demarcated by a particular environment or governance. At the same time, "domain" may denote a "specified sphere of activity or knowledge."[1] Accordingly, "domain" often refers to the places where activities take place, the associated activities themselves, and more. For example, space operations take place in the "space domain" but also in the other domains, such as land, sea, and air. Cyber is especially confusing. In a sense, the entire physical "cyber domain" is located in all the other domains. Nevertheless, the emergent power of "cyber warfare" has prompted wide acceptance today of a formally designated cyber domain. The "electromagnetic spectrum," however, has not been officially delineated

---

[1] See: "Domain," *Oxford English Dictionary*, accessed 30 January 2018, https://en.oxforddictionaries.com/definition/domain; "Domain," *Merriam-Webster Dictionary*, accessed 30 January 2018, https://www.merriam-webster.com/dictionary/domain.

as a domain, and its overlap with cyberspace is unclear. Yet electromagnetic warfare long preceded "cyber" and still has a profound impact on all the domains.[2]

Nuclear weapons, and to a degree other weapons of mass destruction (WMD), are also historically "multidomain." Where nuclear weapons might explode is of the greatest importance. The over 2,000 recorded nuclear weapon detonations have taken place on the ground, underground, at sea, underwater, in the air, and in outer space.[3] Nuclear weapons also have cross-domain effects. For example, electromagnetic pulse effects from the 1962 Starfish Prime nuclear test in outer space impacted satellites in low-earth orbit, radios on aircraft, and electrical equipment on the ground in distant Hawaii.[4] Again, the distinctly destructive potential of nuclear war, however, has not resulted in the official designation of a "nuclear domain."

Delineation of military domains continues to morph, and where humanity enters a domain, warfare follows. War was initially confined to the land, but greater movement over larger bodies of water inevitably led to the advance of naval warfare. For each of these early domains of warfare—land and sea—strategies were developed, organizations created, and weapons procured—each increasingly tailored to the domain. As illustrated in history from the ancient Greek and Persian wars to modern times, however, each domain impacts the others even when strategy or tactics result in an emphasis on capabilities for one particular domain. Getting the balance right and coordinating operations is a challenge.[5]

The military forces of the United States were managed by two separate departments, War and Navy, until after World War II. The two domains overlapped and interacted, as illustrated by the emergence of an amphibious Marine Corps. Military matters continue to become ever more complex. The portent of new military domains could be seen in the Army Air Corps, the Artillery Branch, and the Signal Corps. Today we speak of land, sea, air, outer space, and cyber as the

---

[2] See: Mark Pomerleau, "What Would It Take to Declare the Electromagnetic Spectrum a Domain of Warfare?," *C4ISRNET*, 30 November 2016, accessed 30 January 2018, https://www.c4isrnet.com/c2-comms/2016/11/30/what-would-it-take-to-declare-the-electromagnetic-spectrum-a-domain-of-warfare/.

[3] Preparatory Commission for the Comprehensive Nuclear-Test-Ban Treaty Organization, "World Overview," *CTBTO.org*, accessed 30 January 2018, https://www.ctbto.org/nuclear-testing/history-of-nuclear-testing/world-overview/.

[4] Preparatory Commission for the Comprehensive Nuclear-Test-Ban Treaty Organization, "9 July 1962 'Starfish Prime', Outer Space," *CTBTO.org*, accessed 30 January 2018, https://www.ctbto.org/specials/testing-times/9-july-1962starfish-prime-outer-space.

[5] See, for example, such classics as Herodotus, *The History of Herodotus* [440 BCE], trans. George Rawlinson, http://classics.mit.edu/Herodotus/history.html; Thucydides, *The History of the Peloponnesian War* [431 BCE], trans. Richard Crawley, http://classics.mit.edu/Thucydides/pelopwar.html; Alfred Thayer Mahan, *The Influence of Sea Power upon History, 1660–1783* (1890), http://www.gutenberg.org/ebooks/13529; and H. J. Mackinder, "The Geographical Pivot of History," *Geographical Journal* 23, no. 4 (April 1904): 421–437, https://www.jstor.org/stable/1775498.

fundamental domains of conflict. Some would add unconventional warfare/special operations, undersea, and even underground as military domains. In the future, if warfare develops advanced means to target the internal mental and/or physical state of human combatants or autonomous machines, existing organizations that now focus on psychological/information operations, biosecurity, or artificial intelligence might point the way to designation of additional domains. We might then speak of the "noosphere"[6] or "genomic/proteomic warfare" or a "singularity battlefield" as additional military domains.[7]

Adapting organizations to integrate cross-domain operations continues. From 1879 to 1921, the Departments of State, War, and the Navy were collocated in a single building next to the White House that is now known as the Eisenhower Executive Office Building.[8] For a more complex world, the National Security Act of 1947 created the consolidated Department of Defense with a secretary of defense and the Joint Chiefs of Staff, the Central Intelligence Agency, and the National Security Council to integrate across domains and added the Air Force to give greater attention to a domain made highly strategic by the invention of the atomic bomb.[9] The launch of Sputnik I in 1957 highlighted the fact that outer space would become a vital domain, leading to the Air Force Space Command, then a unified command, and now a proposal for a Space Force as a sixth branch of the armed services.[10] In August 2017 the president ordered creation of a unified U.S. Cyber Command independent of STRATCOM, which became a reality in May 2018.[11] Some of the

---

[6] Per the *Oxford English Dictionary*, a noosphere is "a postulated sphere or stage of evolutionary development dominated by consciousness, the mind, and interpersonal relationships." See: "Noosphere," *Oxford English Dictionary*, accessed 30 January 2018, https://en.oxforddictionaries.com/definition/noosphere.

[7] Various concepts of a "singularity" invoke the specter that at some time in the future humanity will be overwhelmed and threatened by an exponential advance of technology, particularly if artificial intelligence could comprehend what humans could never comprehend. For a short guide to definitions and the literature, see: "17 Definitions of the Technological Singularity," *Singularity Weblog*, 18 April 2012, accessed 30 January 2018, https://www.singularityweblog.com/17-definitions-of-the-technological-singularity/; Peter Rejcek, "Can Futurists Predict the Singularity?," *SingularityHub*, 31 March 2017, accessed 30 January 2018, https://singularityhub.com/2017/03/31/can-futurists-predict-the-year-of-the-singularity/.

[8] See: Office of the Historian, "State, War, and Navy Building July 1875–April 1947," U.S. Department of State, accessed 30 January 2018, https://history.state.gov/departmenthistory/buildings/section27.

[9] See: Office of the Historian, "National Security Act of 1947," U.S. Department of State, accessed 30 January 2018, https://history.state.gov/milestones/1945-1952/national-security-act.

[10] See: "Chronology," U.S. Air Force Space Command, accessed 30 January 2018, http://www.afspc.af.mil/About-Us/Heritage/chronology/.

[11] See: Jim Garamone and Lisa Ferdinando, "DoD Initiates Process to Elevate U.S. Cyber Command to Unified Combatant Command," Department of Defense, 18 August 2017, accessed 30 January 2018, https://www.defense.gov/News/Article/Article/1283326/dod-initiates-process-to-elevate-us-cyber-command-to-unified-combatant-command/.

most important cross-domain questions involve cyber. Are cyberattacks commensurate with kinetic attacks or something different? Can cyber itself be a significant deterrent capability, or is cyber warfare's impact on deterrence primarily through an ability to degrade or enhance traditional deterrent forces? Integrating cyber and space operations continues to be highlighted in the National Security Strategy of the United States.[12]

Integration and optimization of operations across multiple domains remains vital in classic nuclear deterrence, but the emergence of "hybrid warfare" has also moved cross-domain operations to the center of conflicts at lower levels. Hybrid warfare is commonly defined today as the use of unconventional, irregular, or proxy forces supported by cyber and information warfare, often with external sanctuary support for logistics, air defense, and firepower, perhaps also accompanied by threats of vertical or horizontal escalation. This might include, in the case of the Russian Federation, threats of nuclear use at levels of escalation well below what the West would countenance as appropriate. Russian military operations in Ukraine (often described as "frozen conflicts") are the most visible examples of hybrid warfare cited today, but U.S. operations in Afghanistan in 2001 and certain operations by antagonists in the Vietnam War might also be examined as historical variations.

Exploring the theory and practice of classical deterrence provides insight into CDD. At the same time, examining space, cyber, and unconventional warfare across domains such as land, sea, air, or outer space highlights what may persist and what will change in traditional deterrence thinking, including its nuclear dimension. All components of deterrence—nuclear and conventional, offensive and defensive—are more closely linked to space, cyber, and unconventional operations than is widely recognized. All are becoming more salient, interactive, and intense at lower levels of the escalatory ladder. As the United States encounters more potential adversaries who think differently about these matters, all deterrence increases in complexity.

Challenges to deterrence created by diverse military operations across various domains by multiple players should be explored in the context of recent political and technological transformations, the renewed importance of regional deterrence, and an increasing diversity among adversaries and allies. Rapid change suggests a steep learning curve about deterrence under the new conditions. Meanwhile, decades of disinterest in nuclear matters have created a significant "forgetting curve" that is relevant to all deterrence in all domains.

Issues that we would call "cross-domain" predate even the Revolution in Military Affairs, but they seem more leveraging today as we enter yet another nuclear era.

---

[12] See: "National Security Strategy of the United States of America," White House, December 2017, accessed 30 January 2018, https://www.whitehouse.gov/wp-content/uploads/2017/12/NSS-Final-12-18-2017-0905.pdf.

The United States is not alone in revisiting the diverse, WMD/cross-domain/hybrid components of deterrence. Facing emerging, often asymmetrical threats, the United States needs innovation in strategy and capabilities to provide its own asymmetrical leverage.

Simplicity and Complexity

Is truth to be found more in simplicity or in complexity? This heuristic question shapes thinking in deterrence strategy just as it does in philosophy, science, public policy, and art. We define an "idea" but struggle with its many forms. We develop explanatory theories but trust them only with confirming data. We paint with a "minimalist" broad brush but explain from a "pointillist" perspective. We pursue uniform laws but then fear unwanted outcomes when particular circumstances change.

Nuclear deterrence also struggles with this simplicity/complexity dichotomy.[13] Doctrines are promulgated through simple ideas—superiority, sufficiency, flexible response, assured destruction, minimum deterrence, countervailing force, reduced reliance. Implementation, however, is more complex. In analytical studies, the implications of these fundamental concepts are tested against complicated simulations, gaming, and "big data" analysis, often looking for the unexpected, such as chaotic effects or emergent behavior. And in political-military operations, concise guidance is actualized through highly diverse forces deployed on land, at sea, through the air, under the oceans, underground, in outer space, and throughout the electromagnetic/cybersphere.

The difficulty of understanding the significance of the "simple" versus the "complex" still beleaguers decisionmaking two millennia after Archilochus of Paros famously said: "the fox knows many things, but the hedgehog knows one big thing."[14]

---

[13] For a recent compilation of essays exploring broad versus narrow approaches to deterrence theory, see: Elbridge A. Colby and Michael S. Gerson, eds., *Strategic Stability: Contending Interpretations* (Carlisle, PA: U.S. Army War College, 2013). The book cover design is drawn from Kazimir Malevich's *Black Cross*, an early twentieth-century painting in the Russian Museum in St. Petersburg expressing a bold, simple geometric pattern in black and white.

[14] Among those who have built on Archilochus's distinction is Isaiah Berlin, *The Hedgehog and the Fox: An Essay on Tolstoy's View of History*, 2nd. ed. (1953; reprint, Princeton, NJ: Princeton University Press, 2003). Berlin's work is often cited for its discussion of the strengths and weaknesses of hedgehogs and foxes and the potential for merging both. Earlier thinkers, such as Erasmus in 1500, favored the firm principle of the hedgehog; see: Desiderius Erasmus, *The Adages of Erasmus*, ed. William Watson Barker (Toronto: University of Toronto Press, 2001), 87. Others have continued the effort to integrate hedgehog and fox; see, for example, Steven Jay Gould, *The Hedgehog, the Fox, and the Magister's Pox: Mending the Gap between Science and the Humanities* (New York: Harmony Books, 2003). Others favor the fox; see, for example, Philip Tetlock, "Why Foxes Are Better Forecasters Than Hedgehogs," lecture at Long Now Foundation, 26 January 2007, http://longnow.org/seminars/02007/jan/26/why-foxes-are-better-forecasters-than-hedgehogs/.

Even in the twenty-first century, experts invoke "foxes" and "hedgehogs" to anchor nuclear strategy. The hedgehog understands the terrifying power of nuclear weapons. The fox knows that many other important matters may ultimately determine whether nuclear weapons are ever used again. In a world being transformed rapidly by politics and technology and increasingly "cross-domain," should we look more to the fox or to the hedgehog?

Deterrence, like disarmament, leans heavily on one big idea—fear should stimulate restraint. A credible approach to deterrence and arms restraint, however, requires attention to many ideas—different values, alternative priorities, conflicting interests, uneven strengths, unequal vulnerabilities, competing histories, diverse cultures, divergent norms, anomalous psychologies, asymmetrical strategies, and countervailing technologies. Geopolitical and technological changes continuously alter these factors.

We see this complexity expanding in today's discussions of CDD. National security operations using diverse capabilities at different levels of conflict across multiple domains are not new. Nevertheless, interconnected societies, global economies, and even advanced military forces feel increasingly vulnerable to loss of communications, data, transportation, infrastructure, energy, and even lives from attacks that can come in many forms from multiple sources. A common thread in all domains is fear of the destruction, denial, or abuse of information technology for strategic leverage. When defenses against such attacks prove weak, interest in deterrence grows.

Applying lessons from classical nuclear deterrence theory to cyber, space, and other cross-domain operations can be useful, especially if care is taken to consider what is different. Deterrent effects of diverse military capabilities across different domains vary greatly. Few are as stark as WMD, especially nuclear. Greater intellectual insight, however, might actually flow in the other direction, in that analysis of space, cyber, and hybrid warfare might improve our understanding of classical deterrence and its nuclear component. This additional insight might be gained partly by use of analogies but, more important, grows out of understanding how these factors interact. Again, sustaining deterrence while exploring restraint in this more complex nuclear era requires transforming decisionmaking to balance a wider range of considerations.

Changing Circumstances across the Strategic Landscape

In the immediate future, all aspects of deterrence face expanding challenges and complexity, developments that certainly tighten the linkage of nuclear deterrence to space, cyber, and even unconventional warfare. Each of these deserves some elaboration.

The Accelerated Advance and Spread of Latent, Strategic Dual Use Technologies

Advanced simulations, "big data," and artificial intelligence are so powerfully enabling theory and experimentation—the two traditional pillars of science—that experts have difficulty tracking real-world applications. This accelerates the rapid advance and spread of dual use technology, thus complicating deterrence calculations as more states and nonstate actors acquire latent or actualized WMD. Space, cyber, and advanced conventional technology have joined nuclear, chemical, biological, and radiological weapons in posing dangers to societies, economies, and militaries. Given that preventing their spread is problematic, greater emphasis is now being placed on ways to deter or defend against weapons that might result from latent capabilities in untrustworthy hands.

A New Nuclear Normal

At the end of the Cold War, nonproliferation seemed almost a consensus international norm. Wide agreement about nonproliferation was reflected at the first UN Security Council Summit in 1992;[15] and was embodied in the decisions by South Africa, Ukraine, Belarus, and Kazakhstan to give up their nuclear weapons and in the short-lived 1991 North-South Korean Denuclearization Agreement, in which both Seoul and Pyongyang gave up enrichment and reprocessing.

Today, the growing nuclear arsenals of North Korea, India, and Pakistan and the militantly latent nuclear program of Iran—each a different case—will test the impact of nuclear deterrence on stability. This "new normal" impacts other governments or blocs seeking greater security, status, or influence. Most governments will forgo the nuclear option, but many are already looking for other military enhancements with strategic impact, including various cross-domain capabilities. Hackers from Russia, China, North Korea, and Iran have already demonstrated considerable offensive cyber capability. The talent and interest to copy these cross-domain military capabilities exists in many troubled regions. A fresh look at deterrence in South Asia, for example, might help analysts escape perceptual bias, such as stereotyping or mirror imaging left over from the Cold War, not only for classical deterrence but also for cross-domain and hybrid approaches.

---

[15] On 31 January 1992, speaking as president of the UN Security Council Summit, then British prime minister John Major declared, on behalf of the Summit heads of State and governments: "the proliferation of all weapons of mass destruction constitutes a threat to international peace and security"—traditionally powerful UN language used when strong action, including possible military force, is to be endorsed. See: 1962 John Major, "United Nations: Security Council Summit Statement Concerning the Council's Responsibility in the Maintenance of International Peace and Security," *International Legal Materials* 31, no. 3 (May 1992): 762, http://www.jstor.org/stable/20693700.

Levers for Regime Interests and Survival

In many countries, latent or actualized weapons programs can increase a government's public support at home and political prestige abroad. Iran's latent weapons capability provided leverage in negotiations to remove sanctions and reduce isolation. North Korea has shown how a failing, pariah regime can buy decades of survival by manipulating its transition from latent to actualized nuclear weapons. Ukraine used nuclear weapons in its possession as bargaining chips in part for security assurances under the U.S.-Russia-Ukraine Trilateral Statement of January 1994. Belarus and Kazakhstan had already begun denuclearizing, but both states also insisted on security assurances under the Budapest Memorandum of 1994.[16]

With several former Soviet republics under pressure from a nuclear-armed Russia and with Russian troops occupying Crimea, opinion leaders in several countries are questioning the wisdom of forgoing nuclear options. The fall of Muammar Gaddafi, after Libya gave up its WMD programs, is often contrasted with the resilience of those regimes that have acquired WMD or kept the option near at hand. Indeed, Syria gave up its declared chemical weapons only in a context in which the survival of the regime of Bashar al-Assad might be prolonged. Space, cyber, and unconventional operations might increasingly become important elements of strategies to secure regime objectives. Cyber, in particular, is a tool for domestic control in authoritarian regimes that can readily become an international lever.

A Rising China and a Provocative Russia

Both Russia and China are now more provocative in asserting territory disputed with neighbors. Russia has occupied Crimea, inserted troops into eastern Ukraine, expanded its presence and expectations in the Arctic, and escalated its intervention in Syria. "Oil and gas" diplomacy and an extractive economy reinforce this behavior.

The interests of China and Russia often diverge. Their styles of rhetoric and diplomacy have important differences. Nevertheless, military and geopolitical cooperation between these two nuclear-armed, authoritarian regimes is increasing. Each has important asymmetrical military capabilities, including in space, cyber, and unconventional operations that are of concern to their neighbors, including U.S. allies. They are setting examples of cross-domain/hybrid operations that others might copy.

---

[16] United Nations General Assembly Security Council, "Letter dated 7 December 1994 from the Permanent Representatives of the Russian Federation, Ukraine, the United Kingdom of Great Britain and Northern Ireland and the United States of America to the United Nations addressed to the Secretary-General," S/1994/1399, 19 December 1994, accessed 15 September 2018, https://www.securitycouncilreport.org/atf/cf/%7B65BFCF9B-6D27-4E9C-8CD3-CF6E4FF96FF9%7D/s_1994_1399.pdf

The Backlash against "Western Values"

Renewed interest in nuclear geopolitics among countries in troubled regions coincides with their growing skepticism and even animosity toward Western values as reflected in openness, transparency, market economies, free trade, the rule of law, the sanctity of boundaries, nongovernmental organizations, and human rights. These political developments have important security implications. For example, confidence in military restraint, stability measures, arms reductions, and disarmament is based on norms creating open access and transparent behavior. Instead, these values and norms, associated with verifiable arms control and confidence-building, are increasingly a source of tension between states, especially as authoritarian regimes invoke nationalism and make ethnic or cultural identity a rationale for the control of information and travel.

Both the norms of restraint and the conditions for restraint are weakening. Does this portend more aggressive behavior? Consider, for example, that the pushback against libertarian approaches to the Internet coincides with wider exploitation of cyber operations. As more governments look to these means to deal with terrorism or political opposition, the capacity for cyber warfare will grow and with it the prospect for more cross-domain operations among many states, nonstate entities, and even individuals.

Strategic Effects at Lower Levels of Arms

At lower levels of deterrent forces, small changes in numbers or capabilities might have greater significance. This increases the importance of situational awareness. Many of the technologies that provide the necessary transparency for warning or verification, however, are also associated with cross-domain/multicapability military and intelligence operations and targeting. These can produce further challenges to confidence and stability.

Reductions in nuclear weapons are generally welcomed, but fear of vulnerability at low numbers might make some states providing nuclear umbrellas less willing or able to make credible commitments. This, in turn, could encourage other states to seek their own, independent deterrents through WMD or space, cyber, and unconventional capabilities.

Cross-Domain Asymmetrical Responses

For some governments, nuclear programs are asymmetric responses to deter larger military powers. Interest in cross-domain operations as asymmetrical responses is also growing and coincides with the recognition that advanced conventional munitions, cyberattacks, space warfare, and covert military operations might have strategic, even dramatic impact. This complicates escalation control measures, such as signaling and demonstrations of restraint, and becomes even more worrisome with the invocation by countries such as Russia and North Korea of nuclear threats in small, regional confrontations.

The fuzzy relationship between cross-domain operations and military escalation creates ambiguous thresholds, perhaps undermining strategic stability. A decision to employ nonkinetic, cross-domain capabilities, such as cyber operations, is easier than a decision to use conventional or nuclear weapons, in part because it might be more legally ambiguous.[17] Cyber operations begun in peacetime, however, might be viewed differently once conflict begins. If the consequences of soft-kill, cross-domain attacks rise, adversaries might respond with kinetic weapons.

More and Different Possibilities

Just as the "N-body problem" in celestial mechanics complicates predictability, so adding more powerful cross-domain capabilities to the quivers of an increasing number of diverse antagonists complicates risk assessment. For example, cyber warfare is not confined to the military. Cyber operations have already empowered state security affiliated organizations, criminal syndicates, and even malicious individuals to threaten harm to the financial and social health of great powers and to their military forces, including potentially early warning and command and control. Similar dependencies and vulnerabilities are increasing with respect to satellites and space operations.

The diversity of those who could exploit these different weapons may also be increasing. The intellectual history of deterrence is, in many ways, a history of logic trees and game theory. Still, a strict and common rationality does not explain all behavior. Differences in culture, personality, and training can alter outcomes. The growing, diverse pool of possible decisionmakers with tools applicable to many domains complicates understanding of what is already complex psychology. The social sciences, like the physical sciences, have developed many techniques to analyze complexity, but few of these have found their way into real-world decisionmaking.

"Learning Curves" and "Forgetting Curves"

During the Cold War, many of the finest military leaders, diplomats, technologists, and academics were steeped in the theory, policy, and operations related to nuclear deterrence, including air and missile defense, antisubmarine warfare, electronic countermeasures, space operations, and covert actions. A vast literature of analysis

---

[17] John Norton Moore, Guy B. Roberts, and Robert F. Turner, eds., *National Security Law*, 3rd ed. (Durham, NC: Carolina Academic Press, 2015). See especially: Paul Rosenzweig, "Law and Warfare in the Cyber Domain," in *National Security Law & Policy*, 3rd ed., edited by John Norton Moore, Guy B. Roberts, and Robert F. Turner (Durham, North Carolina: Carolina Academic Press, 2015), 537–562.

and lessons learned was produced. With the end of the Cold War, interest and understanding of deterrence declined.

As deterrence again rises in importance, new generations face both "learning curves" and "forgetting curves" as traditional deterrence language morphs into somewhat different meanings. What does "deterrence" mean when the source of an attack is difficult to attribute and may not be a government? What does "warfighting" mean when war is not declared and weapons are not kinetic? What is "unacceptable damage" when cyber "shrinkage" and the cost of prevention involves billions of dollars? How do we understand "escalation" when the next step is a soft, "functional kill" that might, or might not, have devastating secondary effects well into the range associated with kinetic or even nuclear weapons?

Yet Another Nuclear Era

From the perspective of the hedgehog and his one big idea, we live in a single, continuous nuclear age. The nuclear weapons age has a beginning. We do not know how or if it will end. Given widespread nuclear "know-how," we will live under the shadow of this big idea well into the future. From the perspective of the fox, however, with his many ideas, several nuclear ages, or perhaps eras, can be delineated. These eras may be defined by changes in potential adversaries, the military balance, opposing strategies, probabilities of conflict, the weapons involved, and the possible consequences of war. One could, for example, divide the nuclear age into approximate eras this way:

- U.S. Nuclear Monopoly (c. 1945–1949)
- U.S. Nuclear Superiority (c. 1950–1960)
- Bilateral Nuclear Balance (c. 1961–1991)
- U.S. Military Superiority (c. 1992–2008)
- Strategic Regional Complexity (c. 2009–2013)
- Peer and Pariah Asymmetrical Challenges (c. 2014–?)

Each such attempt to delineate different nuclear eras will have flaws, but clearly there has been a significant phase change in nuclear-related geopolitics.

Our world is disappointingly more dangerous now than was anticipated early in the post–Cold War years. The improving missile capabilities of North Korea to strike South Korea are being extended to reach Japan and the United States. The intense centrality of tactical nuclear forces for countries like Russia and Pakistan, especially in smaller, regional contexts, challenges assumptions about what is existential. The evolution of the basic nuclear forces of China, India, and Pakistan toward diversification on land, at sea, and in the air, reopens questions of sufficiency as diversity becomes more important to maintain stability. At the same time, the energetic renewal of Cold War symbols of first strike, such as the large, liquid-fueled, Russian intercontental ballistic missiles (ICBMs) with large numbers of multiple independently targetable reentry vehicles (MIRVs), which were prohibited in the Strategic Arms Reduction Treaty II, underscores different views of "strategic stability."

Potential adversaries explicitly acquire space, cyberspace, advanced conventional weapons, and "hybrid" capabilities to counter conventional U.S. force projection. The ultimate asymmetrical response, however, is the threat to use nuclear weapons even in those scenarios that the United States has sought to denuclearize. Russia, in particular, sees nuclear weapons as escalatory top cover for its cross-domain and hybrid operations. Both allies and potential adversaries of the United States are watching these developments closely. The interaction of all of these developments may not result in a disastrous "perfect storm," but major storm clouds are appearing that require new risk assessments and an update to U.S. strategic thinking.

Simplifying the Complex in a Cross-Domain Nuclear Age

"Thinking about the unthinkable," as the enterprise of deterrence was described during the Cold War, became unfashionable in the two decades after its end. Thinking deeply about the unthinkable, sadly, has again become a necessity. To help simplify the complex, three subjects deserve a deeper analysis: CDD, varieties of escalation, and the morphing of doctrinal deterrence concepts as the next nuclear age comes to fruition.

Cross-Domain Deterrence as a Priority

In the preface to a recent National Research Council study, the cochairs noted: "*nuclear* deterrence is not synonymous with *strategic* deterrence"; "all Air Force capabilities, including space, cyber, and conventional capabilities play a role in effective deterrence and provide options for decision makers"; "there does appear to be agreement within DoD [Department of Defense] and within the Air Force that *strategic* deterrence is *cross-domain* deterrence"; and there is "an emphasis on how the concept of *tailored* deterrence is evolving, the different mindsets of regional aggressors, controlling escalation in regional crises, the growing importance of missile defenses, and new dynamics for a concept that in the Cold War was called *extended* deterrence."[18]

---

[18] Gerald F. Perryman, Jr., and Allison Astorino-Courtois, preface to Committee on U.S. Air Force Strategic Deterrence Military Capabilities in the 21st Century Security Environment, Air Force Studies Board, Division on Engineering and Physical Sciences, *U.S. Air Force Strategic Deterrence Analytic Capabilities: An Assessment of Tools, Methods, and Approaches for the 21st Century Security Environment*

This clear statement that nuclear, space, cyber, and conventional capabilities are elements of both CDD and strategic deterrence is not new. Nor is the emphasis on tailoring deterrence to regional settings. What is new is the sense of urgency in dealing with these complex interactions with nuclear deterrence even at lower levels of escalation. Nuclear weapons are meant to be different from other weapons. They scream "Don't Tread on Me!" They delineate "bright-lines" not to be violated at higher levels of conflict,[19] even if they inevitably cast weaker shadows of warning that escalation is dangerous around redlines well below the nuclear threshold.

A clear line between nuclear and conventional strikes has important utility in escalation control—a goal potentially undermined by the emerging, fuzzy cross-domain environment. Space, cyber, and some nonconventional warfare operations might substitute for nuclear and conventional attacks but might be evaluated differently by diverse decisionmakers. This might make signaling more difficult and actions more dangerous.

Comparing, contrasting, and synthesizing these deterrence issues related to nuclear, conventional, unconventional, air and missile defense, electromagnetic, cyber, and space operations is an excellent exercise for promoting new thinking about deterrence in all its dimensions. Consider some of the following classic challenges.

Attribution and Accountability

During the bipolar Cold War, strategists worried that third parties might provoke catalytic war by conducting an anonymous nuclear strike that one superpower might think was perpetrated by the other. Today, space, cyber, and hybrid operations are presenting new difficulties, both technical and political, for attribution and the resulting inability to hold accountable those responsible. More cross-domain players, each with different escalatory dynamics, increase the prospects for such confusion. At lower levels of conflict or crime, this might be tolerable, but sudden, great violence, combined with confusion over responsibility, could result in a dangerously wrong response.

Asymmetrical Responses and Blowback Effects

Blowback against the advantages of one adversary often motivates others to exploit asymmetric responses, such as terrorism, guerrilla warfare, improvised explosives, landmines, and chemical weapons. Russian hybrid warfare, as conducted in Eastern

---

(Washington, DC: National Research Council, 2014), xii–xiii, https://www.nap.edu/read/18622/chapter/1. The author was a member of the committee.

[19] For the use of "bright-line" rules in jurisprudence to influence behavior, see: "Bright-Line Rule," Legal Information Institute, accessed 30 January 2018, https://www.law.cornell.edu/wex/bright-line_rule.

Europe and the Caucasus, involves an asymmetrical strategy that integrates cyber operations, covert deployments, proxy insurgents, and information warfare but adds threatening nuclear rhetoric. For countries like Russia and Pakistan, tactical nuclear weapons are asymmetrical responses to superior conventional power.

Russian success at cross-domain operations in local settings, including nuclear saber-rattling in the face of strong Western opposition, has not been lost on other countries. Iran, for example, has demonstrated extensive cyber, information, drone, and proxy warfare prowess while it sustains a latent nuclear capability and develops missile and space launch systems. The low cost of entry and different vulnerabilities make cyber operations a powerful equalizer. Low-earth orbit, with so many vital satellites, may yet be another realm where asymmetric dependencies invite asymmetric strategies.

The United States may be said to have its own asymmetrical strategy—one that emphasizes the "soft power" of political, cultural, and economic influence. Its asymmetrical "hard power" preferences have been conventional cruise missiles, no-fly zones, and fast-moving ground units supported by the "shock and awe" of high-technology weapons. For example, U.S. Special Forces deployed in small numbers with the Northern Alliance in Afghanistan conducted a U.S. form of hybrid warfare from horseback, supported by reconnaissance satellites, drones, and B-52 strategic bombers armed with conventional joint direct attack munitions. As more potential state or nonstate adversaries of the United States and its allies turn to space, cyber, information, and hybrid operations, the West will need to explore more asymmetrical options of its own, whether high-tech or otherwise and involving both hard and soft power.

Collateral Damage and Proportionality

United States policy and law requires that any use of force, from nonlethal to nuclear, must be targeted only against legitimate military objectives and proportionate to the military necessity. Civilian casualties and property damage inflicted incidentally to otherwise legal military operations, often termed "collateral damage," might be war crimes if they are excessive under the circumstances.[20]

Recent history suggests a disturbing trend: a greater proportion of civilian to military casualties even in small, local wars, particularly those involving nonstate actors and failed states. This derives primarily from the intense ethnic, religious, and linguistic divides that characterize those wars. Often this involves the explicit use of terror as a tool of influence and of civilians as both shields and

---

[20] Office of General Counsel of the Department of Defense, *Department of Defense Law of War Manual* (Washington, DC: Department of Defense, June 2015), 393–395, accessed 30 January 2018, http://www.defense.gov/Portals/1/Documents/pubs/Law-of-War-Manual-June-2015.pdf.

targets—developments increasing the risk of collateral damage when outsiders intervene.

Cross-domain technology plays a role also—in some cases improving the ability to distinguish civilians from combatants but in other cases placing them at risk. Greater urbanization has made populations more vulnerable to loss of power, water, sanitation, and other vital infrastructure. The prospect that space, cyber, and other cross-domain actions could result in great collateral damage by indirect means on urban populations has important implications for both deterrence and the laws of warfare.

Counterforce, Countervalue, Escalation, Deescalation

Cross-domain operations, such as space and cyber, can be aimed at military or industrial targets. These operations, however, face difficulties similar to those that kinetic weapons face in identifying or avoiding civilians. Escalation might make this even more difficult. Cyber warfare, for example, might be able to attack with great precision the control systems—known specifically as supervisory control and data acquisition (SCADA) systems—that manage electrical grids, gas pipelines, communications, water supplies, transportation, and industrial processes. Such nonkinetic attacks might or might not produce immediate casualties yet ultimately could result in massive loss of life. A major disconnect between what was intended and the resulting consequences could easily erase signals meant to show restraint.

Damage Assessment, Certainty, Uncertainty, and Sufficiency

In the kinetic world, both nuclear and conventional, many models exist for approximating expected damage to targets. Plans can then be designed to ensure that critical targets are destroyed and collateral damage reduced. In the actual fog of combat, however, implementation of attack plans and subsequent damage assessment are challenges at all levels of warfare. For example, tanks on a battlefield are often struck many times again after they were originally neutralized and their operators killed because the next forces to encounter them do not recognize that they had already been destroyed.

Nonkinetic cross-domain attacks have many of the same targeting and damage assessment challenges. In particular, "functional kill" can amplify uncertainties about the success of the attack or unintended effects. Likewise, determining requirements for force structures and capabilities is often linked to the confidence cobelligerents have in their estimates of the damage they can inflict or might suffer. Thus, uncertain effects might complicate calculating sufficiency, just as they complicate the psychological dynamics of escalation.

Decision Cycles, Response Times, and the "Fait Accompli"

Fear of the "fait accompli" has long been a preoccupation in deterrence theory. If one side believes that it faces ready and relevant responses, it might be deterred. If that party believes, however, that a delayed response will mean a weak response or none at all, it might strike. Thus, inadequate options, insufficient clarity, and unwieldy decisionmaking are weaknesses in deterrence that could be exacerbated and exploited by an effective cross-domain adversary. Space, cyber, and hybrid warfare can, as in the case of carefully orchestrated kinetic attacks, negate retaliatory capabilities, create uncertainty, and delay decisionmaking by destroying forces, denying communications and analysis, or altering the perceived context for a decision.

Like the "frog in the pot" phenomenon, living with extensive, unattributed cyber operations during a lengthy, preconflict phase could reduce responsiveness if an attack occurs later. Creation of such a mental fog about where on the escalatory ladder things stand could be destabilizing.

Measure/Countermeasure Dynamics and Defenses

In deterrence theory, the relationship of offensive forces to defensive forces in stability calculations is hotly debated. Would a party with confidence in its own missile defense, for example, be more likely to strike first, believing that its defenses would be even more effective against a depleted retaliation? On the other hand would an attacker risk a first strike if the missile defenses of the other side might prevent a disarming first strike or if overcoming those defenses requires such a massive attack that unacceptable countervalue retaliation would be an inevitable consequence?

The offense-defense relationship in strategy is but one example of measure/countermeasure dynamics, a process that is very intense in space, cyber, and other cross-domain endeavors. Significant instabilities seem to be associated with dependence on vulnerable assets without providing diverse and redundant backup. Modern military forces and societies have become dependent on space satellites and other vulnerable interconnected information technology. Deterrence has been the strategy of choice to prevent nation-state attacks on these assets, but the return of outlaw states and the rise of cyber hackers has shown the importance of also developing countermeasures and defenses. The ingenuity of cybercrime, however, illustrates how volatile confidence in countermeasures can be.

More work is needed to understand CDD and its implications for classical deterrence. A larger number of parameters must be considered as the complexity of all deterrence calculations increases due to various factors: linkage to economic and political sanctions, information warfare and propaganda, messaging and the "signal to noise" problem, nonnuclear WMD, "gray area" weapons that are difficult to categorize, and others.

Geometries of Escalation

Exploration of escalation dynamics can illuminate uncertainties in deterrence theory and might offer more integrated perspectives for deterrence decisionmaking in a world in which cross-domain operations interact more intensely with the totality of deterrence, including its nuclear dimensions.

Escalation as a Singularity

Crossing the nuclear threshold means generating a phase change in destructive potential. All calculations expand fundamentally at the point of nuclear use. The danger at this singularity is so great that many believe that a "taboo" militates strongly against the possibility of any "rational" nuclear first use. Fear of an all-or-nothing certainty of destruction is expected to reinforce the nuclear taboo and the logic of disarmament.

Unfortunately, the idea of a shared norm against any and all nuclear use faces real challenges. Nuclear saber-rattling from Pyongyang and Moscow intimidates by implying that these states are prepared to ignore the nuclear taboo in situations in which Western norms would not permit making nuclear threats. These states' rhetorical "nuclear brinksmanship" in contemporary crises suggests that they have some ideas about when actual nuclear use might serve their national interests.

The persistence of real-world nuclear-threat-mongering is a challenge to the single-point, zero-dimensional perspective that asserts that any nuclear use could only be all-or-nothing. Cross-domain operations continue the assault. Fundamentally, the history of space, cyber, and advanced conventional and unconventional warfare demonstrates that such operations are not at all confined to a single decision or circumstance. They escalate and deescalate continuously from the innocuous and preconflict phases all the way to total war, either in support roles or as weapons themselves. The danger is that nonkinetic and unconventional operations might inadvertently constitute an unacceptable escalation leading to major kinetic or even nuclear responses.

Escalation as Linear

The deterrence policies of most nuclear weapons states do not assume that all nuclear use is inevitably out of control. To be seen as "credible" by adversaries, by allies, and in their own minds, nuclear powers want options that can be limited. Traditionally, they speak of an "escalatory ladder," which is a linear, one-dimensional concept. The "ladder" links higher and lower levels of conflict with "rungs" or "steps," suggesting that escalation can be turned up, modulated, paused, even deescalated. Cross-domain operations are relevant to the one-dimensional nuclear escalatory ladder, both in support of the diverse nuclear forces that are required during movement up or down an escalatory ladder and because such operations themselves are often described as "tunable," opening up more dimensions for escalation response and control. Whether more tools and more data will ease or complicate escalation control remains uncertain, but more cross-domain tools and data are emerging in any case.

Escalation as Planar

In recent years, analysts have increasingly replaced the concept of the nuclear "escalatory ladder" with a cross-domain "escalatory lattice." Such two-dimensional, "planar" concepts reflect a view that cross-domain operations can themselves be powerful weapons, sometimes substituting for nuclear or conventional weapons. Cross-domain options have long been available. The prospect that operations in the space or cyber domains, to some degree, could impact other domains, inflicting high levels of counterforce or countervalue damage, compels consideration of this wider dimension. Escalation is not just from conventional to nuclear or to more of both. What has changed is the perception now that cross-domain operations can have highly leveraging or damaging effects on a scale once associated only with major escalation in kinetic conflict or even with limited nuclear strikes.

Escalation as Cubic

"Cross-domain" strategy also highlights a third dimension, "escalatory depth." Operations around the Earth, through the atmosphere, and in outer space involve allies, friends, and potential adversaries dispersed around the globe. The phrase "horizontal escalation," meaning escalation in a different geographical region, as opposed to "vertical escalation," meaning a higher level of violence, has always underscored the spatial aspects of deterrence. Such geographical strategies are again being seen, in part amplified by the inherent mobility of cross-domain operations. Cyber operations, for example, can move from one area to another quickly or can act globally, constantly keeping one antagonist or another off balance. In the age of modern cross-domain capabilities, confining conflict geographically will be problematic.

Escalation as Temporal

This agility of cross-domain warfare to move great distances reminds us also of yet another important dimension of escalation; namely, the temporal. Different elements of the nuclear triad operate and interact on different timelines. Likewise, cross-domain warfare can be inserted into the middle of timelines for decisionmaking concerning other military deployments. Such timely intervention provides considerable leverage. Timing gives us a fourth dimension in escalatory calculations, one that becomes even more important because military operations in the electromagnetic/cyber spectrum can take place at the speed of light.

Escalation as Nth Dimensional

How many dimensions of escalation are there? Many, undoubtedly, but not all are equal or even significant. Where do we draw the line? At least a fifth dimension seems necessary; namely, the role of human variety as reflected in different histories, cultures, and psychologies. We know enough about classical deterrence to suspect that rules-based logic is not sufficient to explain important strategic behavior.

In some ways, cross-domain operations make this human behavioral consideration even more important. The rules and logic of CDD are less well understood and universalized than those of classical nuclear deterrence, making decisions even more complicated by diverse cultures and psychologies. For example, the exploitation of information technology by criminals and terrorists points the way for nation-states both before and after conflict.

The Morphing of Deterrence Language

A major goal of deterrence is war prevention. This is frequently contrasted with warfighting or defense, options for when prevention presumably has failed. The language of deterrence relies heavily on such contrasting frames of reference to evaluate strategies, promulgate guidance, and set force requirements. These concepts, however, may not be so distant from each other. More often, the meanings change with circumstances and relocate along a continuum of possibilities that make them less distinct. The rise of cross-domain capabilities in the context of deterrence may reinforce tendencies for seemingly antagonistic categories in analysis or policy to converge, diverge, or overlap. An examination of key concepts is illuminating.

"Conflict" versus "Crisis"

International law has long recognized that absence of a formal declaration of war does not mean that there is no war. The laws of warfare apply under a wide range of conflicts. Likewise, nation-states find the boundary between preconflict and conflict fuzzy, given the historical use of espionage, agents of influence, propaganda, sanctions, demonstrations of force, and proxies. Cross-domain operations, such as cyber, might lie dormant or be active in this fuzzy region only to blow up into full-scale warfare. Even then, some confusion might exist as to whether a war is under way and how serious it is.

Cross-domain operations and even conventional strikes, however, might not "let slip the dogs of war." Conceivably, an electromagnetic pulse attack might fall in this category. Both the attacker and the attacked in a crisis might not want to escalate. Tactics like hybrid warfare might permit a very hot, simmering condition that avoids flame or an explosion. However, the risk of conflagration under such "nonwar" circumstances can be high, particularly when the adversaries have different thresholds of tolerance and might initiate actions that are misunderstood or have greater consequences than anticipated.

Space, cyber, and hybrid operations run particular risks because their potentially intense cross-domain activities range both well below and well above the fuzzy conceptual and physical boundaries that now define conflict or war. Unlike the demilitarized zone that divides the Korean peninsula, designed to keep major combatants clearly apart, cyber operations can extend the zone of confrontation to great distances inside sovereign boundaries even in times of peace. As long as the antagonists find these provocations tolerable, many acts that might constitute a casus belli might not lead to war. Attitudes can change quickly, however, perhaps triggered by a perceived change in the quality or quantity of cross-domain damage being inflicted or suffered. This volatile subjectivity complicates the managing of stability on the basis of rule-based logic.

"Deterrence" versus "Warfighting"

The contrast between deterrence and warfighting may be more theoretical than practical. For example, some ethicists argue that use of nuclear weapons could never be moral, legal, or rational. Ironically, a number of these same ethicists also argue that nuclear weapons should be retained during dangerous times, but only for their cautionary influence. At the far opposite end of the spectrum from this view was the expectation after World War II that nuclear weapons would routinely replace other weapons for combat use whenever they were more effective or affordable. Neither of these views is that of the U.S. government. For clear policy reasons, the United States long ago mandated that nuclear weaponry should not be regarded or treated as just another, cheaper version of bombs or bullets. If in dire circumstances no acceptable alternative exists, however, nuclear weapons could be used.[21]

A stark conceptual contrast between pure "deterrence" and pure "warfighting" provides a useful shorthand for discussion of policy and strategy. In the physical world, the distinction is less absolute. Indeed, major doubts exist about the wisdom of either policy in its purest form. Strategies of deterrence and of warfighting appear

---

[21] The view in Moscow, which is defended by nuclear-armed antiballistic missile systems, may be less clear. The Russian military seems interested in retaining nuclear warheads for several types of military missions that the United States has converted to conventional warheads. Part of the rationale seems to be greater cost-effectiveness.

more credible toward the middle of the continuum that runs between the two extremes. Along that continuum, there is considerable overlap. Deterrence is about preventing a war, not fighting one. Yet the credibility of deterrence rests on the prospect that proportionate retaliatory action can and will be taken.

To be proportionate, both in the just war tradition and in the practical military tradition of Clausewitz, such retaliation and any escalation must be purposeful, rational, and measured. Forces maintained for deterrence must impact military capabilities. Thus, for legal and military reasons, deterrence requires something like warfighting. Attempting to limit destruction though escalation control suggests a similar conclusion: nuclear weapons are too dangerous to be used except when absolutely necessary, but to reserve potential use only for massive retribution after all is lost might make that worst outcome more likely.

How do new cross-domain capabilities impact the distinction between "deterrence" and "warfighting"? Given that cyber operations in particular are used every day, one might assume that cross-domain operations would be little more than warfighting, even in circumstances other than war. On the other hand the ability of cyber and space warfare to damage or disrupt nuclear forces and their associated C4ISR,[22] in whatever domain in which forces have been deployed, places cross-domain operations at the heart of deterrence calculations because of the implications for strategic stability. Equally significant is the prospect that cross-domain strikes could inflict significant damage on civil infrastructure, resulting in massive indirect casualties. "Fuzzy deterrence" and "fuzzy warfighting" could become largely indistinguishable, increasing the importance of understanding what damage is being done.

"Countervalue" versus "Counterforce"

If deterrence is thought of as influence through the generation of fear, then which is feared more, destruction or defeat? Undoubtedly the answer depends on how the audience assesses the probabilities of either of these consequences. Still, this simple question defines the public debate between "countervalue" and "counterforce" targeting.

Countervalue targeting, such as strikes on civil infrastructure, is broader than its most extreme, illegal form, which would be deliberate attacks designed to maximize civilian casualties. Likewise, counterforce is broader than its most intuitive focus, defeat of uniformed military formations. Countervalue and counterforce overlap considerably when strikes are aimed at defense industries, communications nodes, power grids, and transportation systems. In theory, for both counterforce and

---

[22] The acronym C4ISR stands for command, control, communications, computers, intelligence, surveillance, and reconnaissance.

countervalue strategies, as escalation increases, the countervalue destruction grows, as does "collateral damage," such as civilian casualties. Do cross-domain operations follow the same escalatory path? Not necessarily. Several aspects of cross-domain escalation may be nonlinear in consequences and could increase uncertainty and danger.

First, space, cyber, and hybrid attacks might overlap conventional and nuclear weapons in functional effects and collateral damage. Consider, for example, how different cobelligerents might perceive attacks by various means that produce the same massive destruction or disruption to their electrical generation and distribution systems. The analysis of aerial bombing in World War II performed by the United States Strategic Bombing Survey suggested that the destruction of electrical power capacity would have significantly reduced German weapons production and concluded that electrical power was not effectively targeted.[23]

In the early days of the Cold War, experts wondered if a key element of deterrence should be the threat of massive nuclear explosive strikes along the Soviet electrical grid and on power plants. Years later, in 1962, the Starfish Prime nuclear weapons test demonstrated that the electromagnetic pulse from nuclear weapons could damage electrical and electronic systems without such weapons' heat, blast, or ionizing radiation extending near the surface of the Earth.[24]

During Operation Desert Storm, nonnuclear means were found to destroy electrical power generation and distribution through conventional air strikes and even nonexplosive means. In recent years, the Department of Homeland Security has expressed concern that cyber hackers might be able to bring down large segments of the U.S. electrical power grid. More recently, a well-planned sniper attack on a Pacific Gas and Electric transformer station near San Jose, California, reminded everyone that in an age of global terror, advanced societies have vulnerabilities to unconventional forces, insurgencies, criminals, and even inspired "lone wolves."[25] Exploring such common targets of cross-domain threats reminds us that weapons we perceive as very different—nuclear, electromagnetic pulse, conventional, cyber, "little green men"—can have similar functional effects operating across the domains.

Second, if various cobelligerents perceive the degree of escalation associated with these alternative means of warfare differently, then cross-domain escalation

---

[23] *The United States Strategic Bombing Survey Summary Report (European War)*, (Washington, DC: Government Printing Office, 1945).

[24] Office of the Deputy Assistant Secretary of Defense, "Appendix C: Basic Nuclear Physics and Weapons Effects," *Nuclear Matters Handbook 2016* (Washington, DC: Department of Defense, 2016), accessed 15 September 2018, https://www.acq.osd.mil/ncbdp/nm/NMHB/chapters/Appendix_C.htm.

[25] Matthew L. Wald, "California Power Substation Attacked in 2013 Is Struck Again," *New York Times*, 28 August 2014, accessed 30 January 2018, http://www.nytimes.com/2014/08/29/us/california-power-substation-attacked-in-2013-is-hit-again.html.

might further undermine predictability and stability. For example, consider a simple matrix of cyber, conventional, and nuclear attacks against cyber, conventional, and nuclear targets. One might easily expect a roughly linear progression in escalation logic from cyber-on-cyber attacks through conventional-on-conventional attacks to nuclear-on-nuclear attacks. Yet a cyberattack on cyber assets perceived by one antagonist as restrained might result in damage that another antagonist associates with major kinetic strikes or even electromagnetic pulse or nuclear. This might be worse when what is intended as a limited counterforce measure, such as an attack on electrical power, nevertheless is perceived as a major countervalue escalation because of the consequences for civilians.

Space and cyber operations might not be kinetic, or immediately lethal, yet their counterforce and/or countervalue impacts could be large and significant. Consider, for example, the "Manichaean" dilemma we face in our interconnected, all-seeing world: the once inconceivable "light" shed on everything by our digitally interconnected world could quickly become disastrously "dark." The same microelectronics revolution that permits global sharing of immense data for business, personal, and military applications can also be used to destroy or disrupt the ability to know what is happening and to communicate about it. Perhaps even worse is the advanced capability in the information age to deceive, distort, or mislead. Expectation of nearly total awareness might be comforting. Loss of C4ISR would be very stressing. Being confused might be deadly.

"Homeland Security" versus "Over There"

Extending a "nuclear umbrella" to allies has long been the ultimate sign that the security shared should be considered inseparable—that what happens in foreign lands matters at home. An attack on one is an attack on all. The problem, of course, is that the national security interests of states are no more identical than their economic and political interests are. Deterring an "existential" threat to the homeland might be the most universally agreed-on role for nuclear deterrence. But what is "existential" and whose "homeland"? At what intensity in the conflict should nuclear use be considered? In the nuclear realm, allies may differ on whether the escalatory ladder should be steep or flat. Views may change; states may even switch sides.

Differences among allies over where the nuclear threshold should be located are often managed by ambiguity about thresholds. In the case of cross-domain cyber and space operations, the ambiguity is less in the use than in the effects. Preconflict operations may seem small and local but can easily lead to large or global effects. The regional application of space assets involves exposing global operations to threats based far from the homeland. Similarly, cyber warfare not only blurs the boundary between nonconflict and conflict but also does not always require a regional presence or local logistics to attack. In short, cross-domain operations tend to link the fortunes of distant regions, even as their actual use might be less controversial among allies. Obviously, extended deterrence will remain a key element as CDD matures. Indeed, threats against the very space and cyber assets that many states vitally depend on might offer strong coupling effects in deterrence terms.

As we transition into a more intensely cross-domain view of deterrence, our concepts will likely morph to reflect further blurring of distinctions. Western policymakers continue to emphasize that nuclear weapons are different from other weapons, but more attention will have to be paid to what we mean and what others mean when they say those words. We will continue to find useful such shorthand as "counterforce," "countervalue," "warfighting," and "extended deterrence," but these will be even less exclusive categories than they are today. As conceptual categories of classical deterrence theory increasingly overlap with their opposites in this new multidisciplinary, cross-domain world, our living language must capture subtle but important changes in the meaning of our words. Yet our age will remain nuclear. And, as before, the nuclear specter does not mean the end of conflict, including wars that could escalate to use of nuclear weapons.

Along the way, Russia and China have demonstrated new asymmetrical and cross-domain capabilities for area denial and escalation dominance. The Russian invasion of Crimea, its hybrid warfare in Eastern Ukraine, and Moscow's invocation of nuclear weapons in smaller, regional crises spotlight the dangers. This new cross-domain/nuclear era will become even more dangerous if other players in troubled regions borrow from the Russian playbook.

Multidisciplinary Perspectives on Deterrence Today

Rethinking deterrence in our new nuclear/cross-domain era is vital. The timing is fortuitous. Multidisciplinary analysis of the complexities of recent developments may actually generate important new thinking. Our topic here, cross-domain and nuclear deterrence and the morphing of strategic concepts, confronts us with a steep "learning curve" even as we are likely to discover that we have been on a sizeable "forgetting curve." Hopefully, new thinkers looking at old data and old thinkers looking at new data can generate the deeper understandings that we now need.

Geopolitically, a quarter of a century after the end of the Cold War, we may feel like the protagonists in the motion picture *The Big Chill*.[26] We have left behind our youth and are discovering that we have not accomplished all that we had hoped. Our sense of vulnerability is great. We are in an age of angst. What do current political and technological changes portend? With deep reductions in nuclear weapons,

---

[26] *The Big Chill*, directed by Lawrence Kasdan (Columbia Pictures, 1983).

is the "unthinkable" becoming more "thinkable," and to whom? Do others think differently about goals, strategy, values? How can objective logic influence what appears to be highly subjective behavior? Is real deterrence local or global or an interaction of both?

We must be careful not to prejudge the outcomes of a fresh look at deterrence today. Undoubtedly, some fundamental truths will reassert themselves. Not all WMD are alike. Nothing is as comprehensively and instantaneously destructive as the blast, heat, and direct radiation of nuclear weapons. Biological weapons pose another plausible threat of mass destruction. Chemical, conventional, space, and even cyber warfare may nevertheless pose great threats to military operations and civilian lives. Recognition of these potential horrors should cast a shadow of caution. Fear alone, however, has not prevented wars from beginning and escalating.

For the United States, a major challenge to deterrence occurs when escalation takes place at levels well short of an immediate, existential threat to the American homeland. Given an expectation that Washington cares less about the Russian "Near Abroad" than does Moscow, the Kremlin may be sounding the nuclear klaxon in smaller, local conflicts such as Georgia or Ukraine precisely because the Russian leadership believes that Western powers would conclude that their interests do not warrant any nuclear risk. Certainly keeping local conflicts from becoming global or nuclear must be a main focus for the United States, but care must be taken not to create power vacuums into which others gain dangerous leverage for conventional, space, cyber, or unconventional operations precisely by threatening to go nuclear.

A number of hypotheses about contemporary deterrence are warranted. Basic deterrence principles seem enduring, but cross-domain developments such as cyber and space complicate deterrence calculations. This occurs at time when many assumptions about deterrence are already being challenged by changes in weapons, targets, geography, and players. At low nuclear weapons numbers and especially in the context of regional escalation dynamics, not only does the unthinkable require more thinking, but the entanglement and overlap of nuclear and nonnuclear may be very serious.

Like WMD, nonWMD cross-domain activities can be seen as asymmetric responses to the strengths of an adversary. Space, cyber, and unconventional operations blur boundaries such as those between conflict and crisis or between countervalue and countermilitary consequences by confusing attack assessments. Indeed, they may create gaps and creases to be exploited in escalation logic and behavior.

Cross-domain operations have important symbolic and operational linkages to nuclear deterrence. They may play more heavily as the unthinkable becomes more thinkable at lower levels of nuclear arms and with more nuclear and cross-domain antagonists. Intense space, cyber, and hybrid operations are here to stay, are increasingly "go-to" asymmetrical options for adversaries, allies, and ourselves, and have vital implications for deterrence. Across all domains, the United States should exploit more sophisticated technology, simulations, and gaming in support of analysis, training, planning, and evaluation of tactics, forces, weapons, networks, and systems.

STRATEGIC IMPLICATIONS
OF DIFFERENT MILITARY DOMAINS

5

Deterrence in and through Cyberspace

JACQUELYN G. SCHNEIDER

"Cyber deterrence" has become a buzzword for U.S. policymakers. Whether it is the use of cyber operations to deter actions within other domains or the deterrence of adversary cyberspace operations within the cyber domain, U.S. policymakers are increasingly concerned with deterrence and cyberspace. The 2015 U.S. Department of Defense (DoD) Cyberspace Strategy advocates a "comprehensive cyber deterrence strategy to deter key state and nonstate actors from conducting cyberattacks against U.S. interests";[1] initiative 10 of the U.S. "Comprehensive National Cybersecurity Initiative" directs the U.S. government to "define and develop enduring deterrence strategies and programs";[2] and the 2017 Executive Order on strengthening cybersecurity calls for "the Nation's strategic options for deterring adversaries."[3] Even the Department of State is preoccupied with deterrence in cyberspace, arguing that norms must be developed "in support of deterrence and de-escalation of cyberattacks."[4] These calls for cyber deterrence also clamor from outside of the executive branch, with increasingly vehement calls for cyber deterrence from Senate leaders and domestic constituencies.[5] Despite the resounding calls win U.S. policy

---

[1] U.S. Department of Defense, "DoD Cyber Strategy," April 2015, 10, accessed 25 January 2018, http://www.defense.gov/Portals/1/features/2015/0415_cyber-strategy/Final_2015_DoD_CYBER_STRATEGY_for_web.pdf.

[2] White House, "Comprehensive National Cybersecurity Initiative," 2009, 5, accessed 25 January 2018, https://obamawhitehouse.archives.gov/sites/default/files/cybersecurity.pdf.

[3] White House, "Presidential Executive Order on Strengthening the Cybersecurity of Federal Networks and Critical Infrastructure," 2017, accessed 25 January 2018, https://www.whitehouse.gov/presidential-actions/presidential-executive-order-strengthening-cybersecurity-federal-networks-critical-infrastructure/.

[4] U.S. State Department, "Final Report of the International Security Advisory Board (ISAB) on a Framework for International Cyber Stability," 2 July 2014, 5, accessed 25 January 2018, http://www.state.gov/documents/organization/229235.pdf.

[5] Scott Maucione, "McCain Presses Obama Administration on Cyber Deterrence," *Federal News Radio*, 20 November 2015, accessed 25 January 2018, http://federalnewsradio.com/defense/2015/11/mccain-presses-obama-administration-cyber-deterrence.

circles for comprehensive cyber deterrence policies, the vast majority of this discussion has been riddled with ambiguity, uncertainty about capabilities and effects, and a lack of empirical precedent, which has trickled down to policies that remain largely unformed or partially implemented.

These puzzling policy questions and uncertainty about deterrence and cyberspace extend beyond the U.S. government or foreign policy. There are significant implications for international relations theory, as well as potential solutions or frameworks that it can provide to help make progress in cyber deterrence policy. First, the revolutionary nature of cyber technologies—from the lack of geographic buffers to the time compression of cyber technology to the offensive effect of cyber operations on conventional warfare—poses new questions about international stability and deterrence effectiveness. Is this technology so fundamentally different that it challenges existing theories and hypotheses about deterrence? Second, international relations theory can provide frameworks and theories from which to derive and ultimately test hypotheses about cyber and deterrence, ultimately advancing cyber deterrence policies to increase the potential for international stability.

This chapter provides a primer on existing debates on both the role of cyber operations in cross-domain deterrence (CDD) and deterrence of cyber operations in cyberspace. These two are intimately connected because it is the difficulty of deterring cyber operations that has provided the catalyst for discussion about the role of cross-domain deterrence as a substitute for within-domain deterrence strategies. This chapter draws from existing literature on cyberspace operations and deterrence, theories of deterrence and signaling, and policy debates in order to ask the following questions. What are the major limitations and concerns for cyberspace deterrence? What are the potential opportunities for successful deterrence? What is the current state of U.S. deterrence policies? The chapter proceeds first with a definition of cyber and moves to an exploration of current U.S. government deterrence policies. The following section focuses on debates about CDD of cyberspace operations and then examines the use of cyberspace operations as a cross-domain alternative. The chapter concludes with a discussion about the role of uncertainty in cyberspace deterrence and implications for U.S. cyber deterrence policies.

What Is "Cyber"?

Defining "cyber" is a problematic and increasingly complicated part of the cyber deterrence problem. The lens through which we understand the word "cyber"—whether it is a domain, a platform, a system, or an adjective—shapes the implications these technologies and concepts have for deterrence. Not only does our understanding of what "cyber" is define who and what is to be deterred in cyberspace but also these definitions set the parameters for what CDD means for cyberspace.

Lieutenant General Brett Williams, former U.S. Cyber Command director of operations, argues that "cyber" is best understood as a descriptive prefix, an adjective conveying the digital or computer-like nature of the noun to which it is attached.[6] In this sense, "cyber" describes the character of an object or concept and flags the subsequent noun as something more automated and more likely to be digital and computer dependent. By the same token, while an opposite of "cyber" does not exist per se, the prefix "cyber" implies that a non-"cybered" noun is something less digitally advanced and more likely to operate off the network grid. For example, think of the difference between hard copy and soft copy, cash payments and digital transfers, or manual ticket generation and automated airline ticketing kiosks. "Cyber," as an adjective, therefore refers to the digital nature of an entity. As a prefix, it can be utilized so expansively as to apply to physical objects, virtual networks, software, operations conducted virtually, or effects bounded within a digital domain.

Also important to this discussion is defining the cyberspace realm in which digital, or cyber, technologies operate. While used prolifically, the term "cyberspace" is still a hotly debated concept. What are the physical limits of cyberspace? Where does cyberspace start and stop? What do these conceptual limitations mean for CDD? Perhaps most expansively, a 2009 definition of cyberspace by Daniel Keuhl not only included the electronic object and networks of the digital domain but also expanded cyberspace to include the electromagnetic sphere through which digital information passes: "a global domain within the information environment whose distinctive and unique character is framed by the use of electronics and the electromagnetic spectrum to create, store, modify, exchange, and exploit information via interdependent and interconnected networks using information-communication technologies."[7] The DoD's "Joint Publication 3-12" asserts a slightly more restrictive understanding of cyberspace as "the domain within the information environment that consists of the interdependent network of information technology (IT) infrastructures and resident data. It includes the Internet, telecommunications networks, computer systems, and embedded processors and controllers."[8] Regardless of whether cyberspace includes both the digital bits and the electromagnetic spectrum through which these digital bits are transmitted, most definitions of cyberspace include both the physical nodes of digital networks, the virtual uses

---

[6] Brett Williams, "The Joint Force Commander's Guide to Cyberspace Operations," *Joint Forces Quarterly* 73, no. 2 (2014): 12–19, http://ndupress.ndu.edu/JFQ/Joint-Force-Quarterly-73/Article/577499/the-joint-force-commanders-guide-to-cyberspace-operations/.

[7] Daniel T. Keuhl, "From Cyberspace to Cyberpower: Defining the Problem," in *Cyberpower and National Security*, edited by Franklin Kramer, Stuart H. Starr, and Larry Wentz (Dulles, VA: Potomac, 2009), ch. 2.

[8] U.S. Department of Defense, "Joint Publication 3-12: Cyberspace Operations," 8 June 2018, accessed 16 September 2018, http://www.jcs.mil/Portals/36/Documents/Doctrine/pubs/jp3_12.pdf?ver=2018-07-16-134954-150.

of software and digital information, and the individuals and organizations who operate these systems and objects. Cyberspace, therefore, is a virtual concept that includes physical elements and virtual operations that might create physical effects.

But if cyberspace is a virtual concept and its physical geography crosses nation-state and civilian/military divides, what are the administrative boundaries of cyberspace? Is cyberspace an infrastructure, a societal substrate, or a domain? Does it matter what we administratively bound cyberspace as? What is particularly important about both Keuhl's and the DoD's definitions is the qualification of cyberspace as a domain—an attribute that sets cyberspace apart from the conventional land, sea, and air warfighting domains and allows U.S. military planners to equip, train, plan, and fight independently of the existing physical domains.[9] This is particularly significant for a study of CDD, because the delegation of cyberspace as a domain makes cyber operations both a tool to use across conventional domains of warfare and a domain from which operations must be deterred. This is significantly different from a conception of cyberspace as an infrastructure through which other conventional domains facilitate operations.

Perhaps most significant, this conception of cyberspace as a domain is not necessarily how the rest of the U.S. government,[10] or U.S. civilian users of cyberspace, view cyberspace.[11] As Peter Dombrowski and Chris Demchak argue, "for security and military purposes cyberspace is not a domain but a substrate ... an underlying layer on which modern society is built. Cyberspace uniquely underpins all four other warfighting domains. This substrate has a topology that is largely and (surprisingly to some) territorial."[12] How do you deter actions that occur within a substrate?

---

[9] William J. Lynn III, "Defending a New Domain," *Foreign Affairs* 89, no. 5 (September/October 2010): 97–108, https://www.foreignaffairs.com/articles/united-states/2010-09-01/defending-new-domain.

[10] See, for example, "National Security Presidential Directive/NSPD-54/Homeland Security Presidential Directive/HSPD-23," which presents a definition of cyberspace that includes, "the interdependent network of information technology infrastructures, and includes the Internet, telecommunications networks, computer systems, and embedded processors and controllers in critical industries." White House, "National Security Presidential Directive/NSPD-54/Homeland Security Presidential Directive/HSPD-23," 8 January 2008, 3, accessed 25 January 2018, https://fas.org/irp/offdocs/nspd/nspd-54.pdf. The 2009 "U.S. Cyberspace Policy Review" builds on this definition to explain that "common usage of the term also refers to the virtual environment of information and interactions between people." White House, "U.S. Cyberspace Policy Review," 2009, accessed 24 April 2018, https://nsarchive2.gwu.edu/NSAEBB/NSAEBB424/docs/Cyber-028.pdf.

[11] Martin C. Libicki, *Crisis and Escalation in Cyberspace* (Santa Monica, CA: Rand Corporation, 2012); Martin C. Libicki, "Cyberspace Is Not a Warfighting Domain," *Journal of Law and Policy for the Information Society* 8 (2012): 321, https://www.rand.org/pubs/external_publications/EP51077.html; Peter Dombrowski and Chris C. Demchak, "Cyber War, Cybered Conflict, and the Maritime Domain," *Naval War College Review* 67, no. 2 (2014): 70–91, https://search.proquest.com/docview/1514370919.

[12] Dombrowski and Demchak, "Cyber War, Cybered Conflict, and the Maritime Domain," 75.

How do you use actions conducted within and through a societal topology to deter others from taking actions in conventional warfighting domains? It might be administratively cohesive to think of cyberspace as a domain and deterrence, therefore, as across and through the cyberspace domain. However, the interpretation of cyberspace as a societal infrastructure that connects not only warfighting domains but also civilian networks and functions significantly complicates the deterrence discussion. Cyberspace in this understanding becomes a target we must deter others from attacking, and the forces and technologies that are used in cyberspace act more as highways and lines of communication than weapons platforms. This has significant implications for cross-domain discussions. Imagine, for example, examining a tank's ability to deter land, sea, and air conventional operations versus a highway's ability to deter those same operations.

Further, these understandings of cyberspace are not necessarily the ways in which other international actors view cyberspace. For example, Russian and Chinese warfighting doctrine situates cyber and cyberspace within a larger information warfare and information space.[13] In fact, for Russia, cyberspace is far more inclusive than U.S. domain-specific understandings and extends to the use, manipulation, and operation of all virtual information. Conversely, the Chinese definition of cyberspace excludes the human and behavioral elements of U.S. definitions and focuses strictly on the "virtual host—no more than the necessary components for connecting a machine to a network for the specific purposes of communicating via protocols such as HTML, email and so on."[14] Therefore, U.S. concepts of deterring cyber operations or developing policy for cyberspace deterrence might not be appropriately tailored for adversaries that view the use of cyber operations or the concept of cyberspace in fundamentally different ways.

This short synopsis of a confusing and contradictory understanding of cyber and cyberspace demonstrates the challenges of discussing cyber and deterrence. Are we deterring cyber operations? Utilizing cyber tools to deter conventional or nuclear operations? Or operating solely in cyberspace to deter actions taken by physical entities to create virtual effects? In general, when the U.S. government discusses cyberspace deterrence, the focus is on deterring cyberspace attacks, which might have both physical and virtual effects. However, cyberspace operations[15] might also

---

[13] Keir Giles and William Hagestad, "Divided by a Common Language: Cyber Definitions in Chinese, Russian and English," paper presented at International Conference on Cyber Conflict, Tallinn, Estonia, 4–7 June 2013, http://www.ccdcoe.org/publications/2013proceedings/d3r1s1_giles.pdf.

[14] Ibid., 423.

[15] Cyberspace operations are defined as "the employment of cyberspace capabilities where the primary purpose is to achieve objectives in or through cyberspace ... [and which] comprise the military, intelligence, and ordinary business operations of DoD in and through cyberspace," U.S. Department of Defense, "Joint Publication 3-12," vii, x.

be used for deterrence in other domains. For the purpose of this analysis of CDD, I will examine two uses of the adjective "cyber" with the concept of deterrence: first, *cyber deterrence* refers to deterring cyber operations within the cyberspace domain that might create effects that are either virtual or physical in nature; second, *cyber* as a *tool of deterrence* examines how cyberspace tools and operations might be used to impact conventional or nuclear deterrence across domains. I will detail policies the United States is implementing for both understandings of cyber and deterrence and then move into theoretical exploration of challenges and opportunities for both cyberspace deterrence and deterrence using cyberspace alternatives.

U.S. Cyber and Deterrence: Current Policies and Practices

Debate about cyber and deterrence—deterrence both in cyberspace and utilizing cyber capabilities—is not happening in an intellectual vacuum or removed from policy decisions. Policymakers in the U.S. government are grappling with these definitional and more theoretical issues of deterrence effectiveness as they craft options for deterrence in and through cyberspace. A brief overview follows of how these debates are currently unfolding in the U.S. government.

United States cyberspace deterrence policy dates back to two foundational documents published by the Obama administration in 2009. The White House's "Comprehensive National Cybersecurity Initiative" and the "U.S. Cyberspace Policy Review" both identify cyberspace as an emerging national security concern for the United States and call on the U.S. government to develop deterrence policies for mitigating vulnerabilities to malicious cyberattack. In particular, Initiative number 10 of the "Comprehensive National Cybersecurity Initiative" calls explicitly for a whole-of-nation cyber deterrence strategy with a focus on deterrence-by-denial by means of "building an approach to cyber defense strategy that deters interference and attack in cyberspace by improving warning capabilities, articulating roles for private sector and international partners, and developing appropriate responses for both state and non-state actors."[16]

The calls for deterrence-by-denial policies in 2009 were augmented by a more articulate version of the threat and additional deterrence-by-punishment options in the Obama administration's 2011 International Strategy for Cyberspace. In the strategy, which devotes a significant section of text to deterrence, the Obama administration recognizes the increased threat from nonstate and criminal actors in cyberspace and escalates previous deterrence strategies by stating: "we reserve the right to use all necessary means—diplomatic, military, and economic—as appropriate

---

[16] White House, "Comprehensive National Cybersecurity Initiative," 5.

and consistent with applicable international law, in order to defend our Nation, our allies, our partners, and our interests."[17] In addition, the 2011 International Strategy for Cyberspace extended deterrence to allied nations and elaborated the role of collective defense and international partnerships in a successful deterrence policy.

From 2011 to 2015, the U.S. government expanded on the promised deterrence-by-punishment options referred to in the International Strategy for Cyberspace and developed a series of policy documents and official statements through the State Department, the Department of Defense, the Department of Homeland Security, and the Treasury Department. These statements and department-level policies specified authorities and tools within the U.S. government in order to provide more codified deterrence practices based on the guidance provided in the 2011 International Strategy for Cyberspace. First, Presidential Policy Directive 21 delineated U.S. critical infrastructure and laid out roles and responsibilities within the U.S. government for the protection of these capabilities. Perhaps most significantly for deterrence, this directive identified targets the United States valued sufficiently to deter cyber attacks. This order, together with an administrative delegation of authority and responsibility, also signaled to adversaries the difference between attacking military versus civilian targets in cyberspace.[18]

The United States extended its deterrence-by-punishment credibility in 2014 when it utilized Department of Justice tools to indict five Chinese hackers for economic espionage.[19] The indictments, while failing to bring these international actors into the United States for punishment, advanced U.S. deterrence policy in a series of ways. First, the indictments signaled to states that the United States viewed economic espionage as malicious cyber activity that the United States was willing to use punishment to deter. This increased the credibility of U.S. cyberspace espionage deterrence efforts. Second, by explicitly naming Chinese individuals and separating them from their official affiliation with the Chinese state and the People's Liberation Army, the United States tailored its deterrence to specific actions and individuals.

The year 2015 saw a further expansion of deterrence-by-punishment tools. Partly in response to the Sony cyberattacks, the United States went further to equip itself with punishment options in Executive Order 13694, which gave the Treasury Department the authority and capability to execute sanctions against malicious

---

[17] White House, "International Strategy for Cyberspace," May 2011, 13, accessed 25 January 2018, https://obamawhitehouse.archives.gov/sites/default/files/rss_viewer/international_strategy_for_cyberspace.pdf.

[18] White House, "Presidential Policy Directive—Critical Infrastructure Security and Resilience," 12 February 2013, accessed 25 January 2018, https://obamawhitehouse.archives.gov/the-press-office/2013/02/12/presidential-policy-directive-critical-infrastructure-security-and-resil.

[19] U.S. Department of Justice, "U.S. Charges Five Chinese Military Hackers with Cyber Espionage against U.S. Corporations and a Labor Organization for Commercial Advantage," 19 May 2014, accessed 25 January 2018, https://www.justice.gov/usao-wdpa/pr/us-charges-five-chinese-military-hackers-cyber-espionage-against-us-corporations-and.

cyber activity, including both attacks on critical infrastructure and intellectual property theft and extending to both state and nonstate actors.[20] Finally, building on this focus on deterrence of critical infrastructure attacks, the Department of State in May 2015 issued a series of norms meant to bolster the credibility of U.S. deterrence and more clearly laid out the sorts of cyberspace attacks the United States aims to deter:

> First, no country should conduct or knowingly support online activity that intentionally damages or impedes the use of another country's critical infrastructure. Second, no country should seek either to prevent emergency teams from responding to a cybersecurity incident, or allow its own teams to cause harm. Third, no country should conduct or support cyber-enabled theft of intellectual property, trade secrets, or other confidential business information for commercial gain. Fourth, every country should mitigate malicious cyber activity emanating from its soil, and they should do so in a transparent, accountable and cooperative way. And fifth, every country should do what it can to help states that are victimized by a [cyberattack].[21]

Finally, the DoD issued two documents that together provide the foundation of the United States' military approach to its cyber deterrence policy. The first, "Joint Publication 3-12: Cyberspace Operations," first published in 2013, identifies capabilities and authorities the DoD may utilize in cyberspace—including both defensive-responsive actions and offensive cyber operations. By detailing these capabilities and delineating the authority to conduct these operations, "Joint Publication 3-12" provides a credible signal to adversaries that the United States is prepared to put the full force of a multibillion-dollar warfighting institution behind both deterrence-by-denial and deterrence-by-punishment methods.[22] The document does not go so far as to detail a deterrence plan, but the 2015 DoD Cyber Strategy explicitly links these cyber capabilities to deterrence and lays out specific elements of a military deterrence policy as including "declaratory policy, substantial indications and warning capabilities, defensive posture, effective response procedures, and the overall resiliency of U.S. networks and systems,"[23] to be used

---

[20] White House, "Executive Order—Blocking the Property of Certain Persons Engaging in Significant Malicious Cyber-Enabled Activities," 1 April 2015, accessed 25 January 2018, https://obamawhitehouse.archives.gov/the-press-office/2015/04/01/executive-order-blocking-property-certain-persons-engaging-significant-m.

[21] John Kerry, "An Open and Secure Internet: We Must Have Both," remarks, Korea University, Seoul, 18 May 2015, accessed 25 January 2018, https://2009-2017.state.gov/secretary/remarks/2015/05/242553.htm.

[22] U.S. Department of Defense, "Joint Publication 3-12."

[23] U.S. Department of Defense, "DoD Cyber Strategy," 10.

"to deter or defeat strategic threats in other domains,"[24] as well as in the cyberspace domain, from both state and nonstate actors. The DoD Cyber Strategy also links cyber deterrence to response, including response to offensive cyber operations, and emphasizes the use not only of military options to deter actors in other domains but also of cross-domain options to deter actions in cyberspace.

Based on these policy documents and official statements, what does the United States want to deter in cyberspace? Despite significant rhetoric about the potentially calamitous use of Pearl Harbor–esque attacks in cyberspace, the vast majority of current policy progress on cyber deterrence focuses on a much more rudimentary (and unmilitarized) level. This includes deterrence of intellectual property theft and attacks on the supply chain but also escalates to deterrence against attacks on critical infrastructure.[25] In addition, implicit in "Joint Publication 3-12" and the 2015 DoD Cyber Strategy is a concern about strategic threats to military effectiveness. Though these concerns have been less explicit than many of the policies articulated by the Department of Justice or the Treasury Department about economic espionage or critical infrastructure attacks (for instance, does the DoD care more about deterring attacks to military operational command and control structures than attacks on weapons platforms?), they are certainly implicit in discussions of deterrence and operational effectiveness in both "Joint Publication 3-12" and the 2015 DoD Cyber Strategy.

What do these existing plans reveal about how the United States intends to deter in cyberspace? While the U.S. government still lacks an overall cyber deterrence strategy policy, department-level policies and official statements from the executive are shaping what appears to be a cyber deterrence strategy that focuses mainly on deterrence-by-denial but is increasingly seeking creative ways to implement deterrence-by-punishment across domains. These punishment tools include sanctions, Department of Justice prosecution, offensive cyber operations, defensive actions supporting the .gov and .com domains through the Department of Homeland Security, and defensive actions through the DoD. Some elements of these denial and punishment strategies are clearly articulated (for instance, economic espionage can be punished with economic sanctions); authorities have been delegated and resources allocated for capability development. However, there is still significant ambiguity about potential responses to a host of different types of malicious cyber activity, and questions about proportionality, capability, and credibility continue to constitute large challenges for the successful implementation of cyber deterrence policy in the United States. The difficulty of calibrating responses to the Petya ransomware incident and the Russian electoral hacking of 2016 and the

---

[24] Ibid., 5.

[25] Interestingly, prior to the 2016 U.S. election, the electoral system was not included as a critical infrastructure sector.

WannaCry ransomware incident of 2017 highlight the limited maturity of many of these policies.

These policy challenges reflect existing debates in international relations and security studies about the effects of cyberspace technology on deterrence. An introduction to these debates and assumptions that inform U.S. deterrence policy challenges follows.

Cross-Domain Deterrence of Cyberspace Operations

Cross-domain deterrence *of* cyber operations involves the use of punishment and denial across domains of warfighting and foreign policy in order to deter adversaries from utilizing cyber operations to create virtual or physical effects. In general, the major underlying debate for all arguments about cyberspace and deterrence is whether or not cyberspace is unique to conventional and nuclear models of deterrence. Advocates of cyberspace's unique characteristics argue that the technical qualities of cyberspace affect attribution, signaling, capabilities, and actors in a way that fundamentally negates the way we have traditionally viewed successful deterrence. These authors argue that it is uniquely difficult to attribute responsibility for cyber attacks in a timely fashion, to signal capabilities overtly, to anticipate cyberspace effects, to use cyberspace weapons repeatedly, and to limit the amount of actors you need to deter. Taken in conjunction with the unique interdependence of military and civilian cyber infrastructures, the perceived asymmetries in vulnerabilities between the United States and its enemies, and the lack of existing norms, these critics argue that the United States cannot rely on retaliatory deterrence strategies or mutually assured vulnerability for effective deterrence of cyber operations. Those who hold that cyberspace has unique qualities recommend policies that are strategically ambiguous, that are focused on defense and resiliency, and that invest in attribution technologies over retaliatory measures.

Those who argue that cyberspace is not unique to traditional models of deterrence point to a series of analogies in conventional and even nuclear domains.[26] For

---

[26] Patrick M. Morgan, "Applicability of Traditional Deterrence Concepts and Theory to the Cyber Realm," in *Proceedings of a Workshop on Deterring Cyberattacks: Informing Strategies and Developing Options for U.S. Policy* (Washington, DC: National Academies Press, 2010), 55–76; Charles Glaser, "Deterrence of Cyber Attacks and U.S. National Security," Cyber Security Policy Research Institute (Washington, DC: George Washington University, 1 June 2011), https://cspri.seas.gwu.edu/sites/g/files/zaxdzs1446/f/downloads/2011-5_cyber_deterrence_and_security_glaser_0.pdf; Dorothy Denning, "Rethinking the Cyber Domain and Deterrence," *Joint Forces Quarterly* 77 (2015): 8–16, http://ndupress.ndu.edu/Portals/68/Documents/jfq/jfq-77/jfq-77_8-15_Denning.pdf; Joseph S. Nye, Jr., "Deterrence and Dissuasion in Cyberspace," *International Security* 41, no. 3 (Winter 2016/17): 44–71, https://doi.org/10.1162/ISEC_a_00266; Department of Defense, Defense Science

these scholars, the human aspect of conflict and the fundamental logic of deterrence are not uniquely affected by the technological characteristics of the cyber domain. First, while these scholars recognize that attribution is an issue, they do not believe that it is fundamentally unique to cyberspace or an unsolvable problem.[27] As Charles Glaser notes, most strategic cyberattacks would not occur in a vacuum and instead would be tied to political signals. Indeed, in his case study of three cyber events, Will Goodman finds that attribution becomes less difficult and less tied to technical capabilities when it is coupled with conventional conflict. Further, these authors proffer a solution to the proliferation of actors in the cyberspace domain, arguing that higher thresholds for deterrence and tailored responses for the most dangerous actors (for example, states like China, Russia, North Korea, and Iran) can increase the chance that cyberspace deterrence succeeds. These thresholds need to be coupled with clear declaratory policies about what actions and what actors the United States is concerned about in cyberspace. In general, scholars who argue that cyberspace is not unique recommend policies that include declaratory statements, realistic thresholds for action, and a mix of deterrence-by-denial (investments in resiliency and defense) and cross-domain deterrence-by-punishment.

Next I will walk through these existing debates about CDD of cyber operations by examining three fundamental questions of deterrence: Whom to deter? What to deter? And how to deter?

Whom to Deter?

One of the fundamental questions in the cyberspace deterrence debate is whether the actors we are deterring in cyberspace are fundamentally different from those in other domains. In fact, this question of actors in cyberspace represents one of the largest problems for cyberspace deterrence in general. Can we attribute cyberspace attacks? And without timely attribution, is it possible to deter cyberspace attacks? Cyber deterrence skeptics argue that attribution in the cyberspace realm is technically more difficult than in other domains. This is partly because of the rapid rate of change for weapons and tactics in cyberspace, partly because of the inherently secretive nature of the domain, and partly because cyberspace offers a variety of ways to hide identities that do not have clear analogs in the physical realm. Further, without any existing arms control arrangements or norms of use, few institutions exist that are designed specifically to attribute cyberattacks. And while it is not technically

Board, "Task Force on Cyber Deterrence," February 2017, accessed 25 January 2018, https://www.acq.osd.mil/dsb/reports/2010s/DSB-CyberDeterrenceReport_02-28-17_Final.pdf.

[27] Thomas Rid and Ben Buchanan, "Attributing Cyber Attacks," *Journal of Strategic Studies* 38, nos. 1–2 (2015): 4–37, https://doi.org/10.1080/01402390.2014.977382; Will Goodman, "Cyber Deterrence: Tougher in Theory Than in Practice?," *Strategic Studies Quarterly* (2010): 102–136, http://www.dtic.mil/dtic/tr/fulltext/u2/a528033.pdf.

impossible to attribute a cyberattack, the time it might take to reach an attribution conclusion could significantly affect the calculus of a potential attacker and pose serious problems for deterrence-by-punishment credibility. As Martin Libicki puts it,

> how low can the odds of attribution fall without destroying the empirical basis for deterrence? The raw calculus of deterrence is fairly straightforward: The lower the odds of getting caught, the higher the penalty required to convince potential attackers that what they might achieve is not worth the cost. Unfortunately, the higher the penalty for any one [cyberattack], the greater the odds that the punishment will be viewed as disproportionate—at least by third parties (who will not know what the attacker did get away with) and perhaps even by the attacker. In other domains with low catch rates (e.g., traffic violations, marijuana possession), the accused at least know that they were caught because they were guilty.[28]

However, as other scholars note, these attribution problems are not necessarily unique to cyberspace, and conventional deterrence often grapples with the problem of attribution when designing effective deterrence strategies. In fact, part of the error with cynical perspectives on the attribution problem is the reliance on the nuclear analogy over analogies in the conventional domain (for example, electromagnetic jamming or covert operations). Certainly it is easier to attribute a ballistic missile launch or even a nuclear test than a cyberspace attack, and the physical characteristics of nuclear material provide biological attribution clues that are not present in the virtual cyber realm. However, states often have problems with nonnuclear attribution in the conventional realm. Case studies from covert action in the Korean War, Angola, Afghanistan, and the recent MH-17 shoot-down highlight successes states have had signaling deterrent policies by manipulating uncertainty around attribution.[29] Therefore, not only is the attribution problem not unique to cyberspace but also it might be manipulated to augment deterrence.

In addition, strategic cyberspace attacks will likely not take place in a vacuum. These attacks are often tied to geopolitical realities that make the technical problem

---

[28] Libicki, *Cyberdeterrence and Cyberwar*, 43.

[29] MH-17, Malaysia Airlines Flight 17, was a commercial flight shot down in 2014 over eastern Ukraine. Austin Carson, "Did Russian Personnel Help Take Down MH17?," *Washington Post*, 22 July 2014, accessed 25 January 2018, https://www.washingtonpost.com/news/monkey-cage/wp/2014/07/22/did-russian-personnel-help-take-down-mh17; Austin Carson, "Facing Off and Saving Face: Covert Intervention and Escalation Management in the Korean War," *International Organization* 70, no. 1 (Winter 2016): 103–131, https://doi.org/10.1017/S0020818315000284; Austin Carson and Keren Yarhi-Milo, "Covert Communication: The Intelligibility and Credibility of Signaling in Secret," paper presented at the annual meeting of the International Studies Association, New Orleans, Louisiana, 18–21 February 2015.

of attribution less important when placed in a larger context.[30] Further, a finding from a series of case studies of cyberattacks indicated that attribution was not a fundamental problem for a series of cyber incidents. Instead, the unwillingness to utilize punishment techniques was a greater issue for credible deterrence.[31] As Thomas Rid and Ben Buchanan argue in their analysis of the attribution problem in cyberspace, "attribution is what states make of it." Not only do they list a series of multidomain clues to the cyberspace attribution problem (intimating the technical problem is not as insurmountable as previously thought) but also they make the important point that attribution always has some uncertainty. It is the stakes a state perceives for attribution and the risk that it associates with that attributional uncertainty that is the larger challenge for cyberspace attribution.

Another complication to the attribution problem and the question of whom we are deterring in cyberspace is the vast quantity of actors in cyberspace. Certainly the barriers to entry in cyberspace are considerably lower than those in the nuclear domain, making attribution a major problem for cyber deterrence but not for nuclear deterrence (or at least nuclear deterrence theory). As opposed to great power nuclear deterrence or even nuclear proliferation deterrence, cyber deterrence involves a host of state and nonstate actors with almost no way of cordoning out actors with arms control agreements or technological barriers. Especially for low-level, unsophisticated attacks and data exploitation, hackers from across the globe with limited expertise and facing very few physical risks have almost no barriers to entry into the cyber fight.[32] However, if we compare these barriers to entry to those to more conventional forms of warfighting and, in particular, low-level kinetic conflict and terrorism, we find that the range of actors who may need to be deterred in cyberspace is not as unique as some cyber deterrence theorists claim. Indeed, the decentralized, remote nature of the Internet and the asymmetric cost of attack bear remarkable resemblance to challenges in deterring terrorism. Further, if states raise the threshold for deterrence to deterring cyber operations that are equivalent to strategic conventional attack, then the technical capacity to conduct these attacks becomes a much larger hurdle for new actors to overcome. While an operational cyber capacity might not require the same research and development or investment as a fifth-generation fighter or aircraft carrier, it often does require a nation-state to have significant intelligence capabilities to gain access for more complicated "advanced persistent threat" attacks on strategic nodes. This then makes cyberspace deterrence more analogous to conventional deterrence between peer and near-peer adversaries.

---

[30] Glaser, "Deterrence of Cyber Attacks and U.S. National Security."

[31] Goodman, "Cyber Deterrence: Tougher in Theory than in Practice?"

[32] Dorothy Denning, "Barriers to Entry," *IO Journal* (April 2009): 7–10, http://faculty.nps.edu/dedennin/publications/Denning-BarriersToEntry.pdf.

What might, however, be strikingly unique about the quantity and type of actors in the cyberspace domain is the lack of perceived risk. Without the deterrent of physical risk that is prominent in any manned physical attack, actors are more likely to operate in the cyberspace virtual domain than they would be to operate in other physical warfighting domains. This is partly because individuals are rarely, if ever, at physical risk when conducting cyberattacks. However, there might be a more fundamental difference between physical and cyberattacks, because there is also a perception that cyberattacks are qualitatively different—less harmful, less escalatory—than their physical, kinetic counterparts.[33] As Dorothy Denning argues, "many cyber attacks such as web defacements and low-level DoS [denial of service] attacks are perceived to be relatively harmless. Nobody dies and damages are not usually permanent. Defaced websites are quickly restored and normal traffic flow resumed when DoS attacks stop. Consequently, there may be less psychological aversion to conducting a cyber attack than a kinetic one, especially one that employs lethal weapons."[34] It is useful here to look at cyber crime as an analogy. A hacker who steals funds virtually from a bank might be at risk of jail if caught, but he does not run the risk of physical harm or physically harming others. So, while we know that stealing funds virtually or physically is illegal, there is a much greater risk barrier to stealing funds physically than virtually. Therefore, there are more actors using cyberspace to conduct financial crime than old-school bank robbers. This becomes a prickly problem for cyberspace deterrence because it might be hard to qualitatively change perceptions of risk in this domain.

What to Deter?

Whom to deter is only one of the questions pivotal to cyberspace deterrence. What a state wants to deter in cyberspace will also affect the appropriate strategy and probability of success. First, there is an important difference between what popular media might sometimes call an attack and what a state views as cyberattacks or even what cyber actions it wants to deter. The vast majority of cyber activity, including the hack into the U.S. Office of Personnel Management publicized in 2015, does not meet the criteria of cyberattack but instead is better characterized as cyber network exploitation (CNE), which includes both the downloading of information and the accessing of networks. It might even include the dissemination of information retrieved illegally by hacking into another entities' networks. The important characteristic of CNE is that it is gathering information, not manipulating or deleting information. Cyber network exploitation is prolific and can be accomplished by both unsophisticated actors and highly sophisticated states. Because CNE is so

---

[33] Kenneth Geers, *Strategic Cyber Security* (Tallinn, Estonia: CCDCOE, 2011).
[34] Denning, "Rethinking the Cyber Domain and Deterrence," 8.

technically varied, is so prolific, and falls below the threshold of armed conflict, it is very difficult to deter. Therefore, while states and publics might be alarmed at the rising scope and intensity of CNE, their ability to deter CNE might be greatly limited.

Why then would a state want to expend finite resources to deter CNE? First, CNE can be a precursor to a military operation, including a conventional kinetic or cyberspace attack. Indeed, the first step in a cyberattack is establishing accesses within an adversary's networks or systems. The separation between CNE and attack can be a few seconds and a few keystrokes. This elevates spying to potentially a short-fuse national security challenge. Further, CNE includes the theft of intellectual property, including military trade secrets held by the defense industrial base, and could include the exploitation of networks related to a state's critical infrastructure (for instance, civilian nuclear energy, dams, or financial institutions). Therefore, many states, despite the prolific and ubiquitous nature of CNE, might want to design cyber deterrence strategies that encompass not only cyberattacks but also certain kinds of cyber network exploitation.[35] For example, the recent U.S. executive order authorizing sanctions for cyberspace actions includes "the receipt or use for commercial or competitive advantage or private financial gain, or by a commercial entity, outside the United States of trade secrets misappropriated through cyber-enabled means, knowing they have been misappropriated, where the misappropriation of such trade secrets is reasonably likely to result in, or has materially contributed to, a significant threat to the national security, foreign policy, or economic health or financial stability of the United States."[36]

In addition, ongoing discussions between the United States and China about the cyber theft of intellectual property demonstrate the very palpable concern about CNE as a national security challenge. Finally, CNE might reach such a magnitude that it surpasses the limits of what states are able to defend against or willing to accept. This might be especially applicable in a time of big data, when vast quantities of information can be stolen at once. Over 21.5 million individuals' private information was stolen in the Office of Personnel Management hack, including over 5 million fingerprints and sensitive information about U.S. spies, defense personnel, and diplomats.[37] Another increasingly prolific use of cyberspace is the use of

---

[35] Eric Lorber and Jacquelyn Schneider, "Sanctioning to Deter: Implications for Cyberspace and Beyond," *War on the Rocks*, 14 April 2015, accessed 25 January 2018, https://warontherocks.com/2015/04/sanctioning-to-deter-implications-for-cyberspace-russia-and-beyond/.

[36] White House, "Executive Order—Blocking the Property of Certain Persons Engaging in Significant Malicious Cyber-Enabled Activities."

[37] Marina Koren, "About Those Fingerprints Stolen in the OPM Hack," *Atlantic*, 23 September 2015, accessed 25 January 2018, http://www.theatlantic.com/technology/archive/2015/09/opm-hack-fingerprints/406900/; James Eng, "OPM Hack: Government Finally Starts Identifying 21.5 Million Victims," *NBC News*, 1 October 2015, accessed 25 January 2018, http://www.nbcnews.com/tech/security/opm-hack-government-finally-starts-notifying-21-5-million-victims-n437126.

cyber exploitation, coupled with social media and other digital media, to influence states' behaviors. The extensive Russian information operations targeting the 2016 U.S. presidential election and the 2017 French election—brazen provocations even if the effects on the outcome of the elections were marginal at best—highlights the potential power of utilizing CNE as a tool of state power.[38] While this was a powerful tool, Russia's activities combined traditional CNE with legal use of U.S. commercial social media platforms. These actions, which resemble counterintelligence and not kinetic conflict, beg questions about the role of government in regulating U.S. commercial interests as well as the aforementioned difficulty previously in deterring CNE.

Based on the challenges to deterring CNE and cyber-enabled information operations, states might choose to limit their deterrence strategies to cyberattack. What then constitutes a cyberattack? According to the DoD, cyber operations elevate beyond theft or spying to the level of a cyberattack when cyberspace actions "create various direct denial effects in cyberspace (i.e., degradation, disruption, or destruction) and manipulation that leads to denial that is hidden or that manifests in the physical domains."[39] Therefore, a cyberattack must create an effect. Those effects might be virtual, such as the deletion or manipulation of data or the distributed denial of service (DDoS) of a website. They might be physical; for example, the Stuxnet attack used a cyberspace operation to create a physical effect at the Iranian nuclear facility.[40] These effects might impact military or civilian targets. They might be aimed at a noncritical aspect of a state's civilian networks, or they might be targeted at key nodes of critical infrastructure. And while not as prolific as CNE, cyberattacks—especially low-level DDoS attacks—are increasingly prevalent parts of the cyber landscape. Therefore, some states might determine that even deterring low-level cyberattacks is not possible and instead might develop more tailored deterrence policies that aim to deter a specific type of cyberattack or a specific threshold of effects from cyberattack.

For instance, a large part of the conversation about cyberspace deterrence revolves around the deterrence of "strategic" or "significant" cyberattacks.[41] The Obama administration's executive order on cyberspace sanctions, for example, places the bar for action at a "significant threat to the national security, foreign

---

[38] Kevin Mandia, "Senate Intelligence Committee: Russia and 2016 Election," written statement for testimony before the U.S. Senate Intelligence Committee on 30 March 2017, *Fireeye.com*, accessed 25 January 2018, https://www.fireeye.com/content/dam/fireeye-www/solutions/pdfs/st-senate-intel-committee-russia-election.pdf; Laura Daniels, "How Russia Hacked the French Election," *Politico*, 23 April 2017, accessed 25 January 2018, https://www.politico.eu/article/france-election-2017-russia-hacked-cyberattacks/.

[39] U.S. Department of Defense, "Joint Publication 3-12."

[40] Jon R. Lindsay, "Stuxnet and the Limits of Cyber Warfare," *Security Studies* 22, no. 3 (2013): 365–404, https://doi.org/10.1080/09636412.2013.816122.

[41] David Elliott, "Deterring Strategic Cyberattack," *IEEE Security & Privacy* 9, no. 5 (2011): 36–40.

policy, or economic health, or financial stability of the United States." Meanwhile, the 2015 DoD Cyberspace Strategy identifies its purpose as deterring "specific state and nonstate actors from conducting [cyberattacks] of significant consequence on the U.S. homeland and against U.S. interests, including loss of life, significant destruction of property, or significant impact on U.S. foreign and economic policy interests."[42] Both conceptions of "significant" attack include both physical and virtual effects caused by cyberattack and are broad enough to include both attacks on national security capabilities and attacks on the economic instruments of national prosperity and power (though they might have been vague enough to leave out information operations against electoral processes). The bar, then, for reaching a strategic or significant attack seems to be based on a state's perception at the time of the attack. This allows for significant ambiguity in a deterrence policy—something that can be both a challenge and an opportunity for successful deterrence.

This discussion about what to deter leads to two important policy ramifications. First, what do these debates mean for general versus tailored deterrence policies? If a state seeks to deter general "malicious" cyberspace activity—including CNE, cyber-enabled information operations, low-scale attacks, and significant attacks—then it might call for a deterrence strategy that is largely ambiguous, focuses on deterrence-by-denial, and reserves the right to conduct deterrence-by-punishment against a wide variety of actions in cyberspace.[43] However, if a state chooses to focus on specific types of actions to deter, for example significant cyberattacks rather than CNE, then deterrence policies would need to be more declaratory and more explicitly linked to deterrence-by-punishment. Perhaps most significant, what states choose to deter will impact the ways deterrence success is gauged. A deterrence strategy that calls for deterrence against low-sophistication, highly prolific activities might allow for some level of malicious activity to occur, and effectiveness might be based more on achieving a percentage of success than on a binary success-or-failure measure. On the other hand a tailored deterrence policy that focuses on high-sophistication, low-occurrence events might require a binary interpretation of effectiveness.

Second, what norms exist that might guide the success or failure of these deterrence strategies? Norms that set magnitude thresholds for acceptable levels of intellectual property theft or CNE might help mitigate ambiguity problems in deterring these highly prolific threats. Meanwhile, a significant cyberattack taboo could augment deterrence strategies against larger scale cyberattacks. These norms are still in formation and might benefit later deterrence policies but cyber deterrence policy planners today have little explicit normative guidance.

---

[42] U.S. Department of Defense, "DoD Cyber Strategy."
[43] White House, "International Strategy for Cyberspace."

How to Deter?

In general, deterrence involves a combination of deterrence-by-denial and deterrence-by-punishment. What is the appropriate mix of denial and punishment in cyberspace? What are the challenges and opportunities posed by each type of deterrence strategy? First, the limited literature on cyberspace deterrence suggests that deterrence-by-denial, including focusing on resiliency and defense, would seriously augment both tailored and general deterrence. Because defense does not require high thresholds for attribution, can be generalized for a wide variety of threats and actors, and does not require political will to be utilized, deterrence-by-denial is a logical policy recommendation for any state seeking to deter actions in cyberspace. Further, there is an important divergence between cyber and nuclear deterrence strategy that makes deterrence-by-denial a more feasible option than during the Cold War. While cyber activities might be difficult to defend against, cyberattacks are in general a much more defendable threat than a nuclear attack (especially on the scale of what the United States was devising nuclear strategy for during the Cold War).

Deterrence-by-denial, therefore, is more a question of technical capability than political feasibility. Can you deny actions in cyberspace? While cyberspace is generally accepted as an offense-dominated domain, there are still actions that states can take to defeat the vast majority of low-scale and high-magnitude cyber activity. First, states can establish baseline information security hygiene requirements about passwords and access restrictions. These simple requirements, as well as educating individuals about spearphishing[44] and system security updates, can defend against a large proportion of malicious cyber activity. Second, building information technology systems that are hardened against attack and have redundant components in case attacks are successful allows for limited access and resiliency in the case of attack. Further, training individuals in critical infrastructures and national security command and control to operate in degraded cyberspace environments decreases the potential benefit to attackers while also reducing the overall vulnerability to cyberspace attacks. Building institutions that bridge the public-private gap in cyberspace to share information about cyber threats and effective defense can also significantly augment states' deterrence-by-denial successes. Institutionalizing threat reporting and information sharing not only augments the technical capacity to respond to emerging threats but also increases the chance of responding to attacks in a concerted way.

Finally, deterrence-by-denial might be augmented by cross-domain capability. A significant portion of deterrence-by-denial in the cyberspace domain

---

[44] "Phishing" is a "social engineering" technique that uses fraudulent email to trick a user into clicking on a malicious link or opening an infected file. "Spearphishing" uses targeted personal information to make the fraud more believable for a specific victim.

is securing the supply chain and physical infrastructure of both civilian and military networks. Supply chain defense could include economic or diplomatic measures, while securing physical nodes of civilian and military networks could include conventional military defense. For instance, both space-based satellite and undersea fiber-optic networks provide the backbone of communication, navigation, and intelligence for modern networked warfare.[45] Defending satellites and cables requires cross-domain conventional capability, for example submarine patrols, unmanned underwater systems, and antisatellite ballistic missile countermeasures.[46]

All that said, deterrence-by-denial by itself might not be able to credibly or effectively deter both low-scale malicious cyberspace activity and more significant cyberattacks. Despite generally effective defensive strategies, the sheer quantity of cyber probes and attack attempts makes it unlikely that any state would be able to effectively combat all cyber threats. This inability to perfectly defend, coupled with the low cost of entry into the threat space, makes it highly unlikely that a state can credibly deter all low-level actions in cyberspace. Further, highly sophisticated cyberattacks—like those that states conduct against strategic assets—will likely be able to circumvent the vast majority of the defenses that states design for highly prolific low-level attacks. This leaves states that are devising deterrence policies that are solely reliant on deterrence-by-denial strategies uncertain about their ability to deter a portion of the small-scale activities and the few but highly capable sophisticated and significant threats.

What then are the challenges and opportunities for denial-by-punishment? Despite increasing calls for denial-by-punishment to address cyberspace deterrence shortfalls, significant hurdles remain for both within-domain and cross-domain deterrence in cyberspace.[47] Challenges to deterrence-by-punishment include within-domain concerns to create repeatable, predictable retaliatory effects and cross-domain concerns about proportionality. All of these critiques tie into a larger concern about the credibility of punishment for cyberspace attacks. Finally, significant debate exists about the escalatory effects of retaliating against cyberspace

---

[45] David Sanger and Eric Schmitt, "Russian Ships near Data Cables Are Too Close for U.S. Comfort," *New York Times*, 25 October 2015, accessed 25 January 2018, http://www.nytimes.com/2015/10/26/world/europe/russian-presence-near-undersea-cables-concerns-us.html.

[46] David Larter, "Navy Grapples with Russian Threats to Undersea Cables," *Navy Times*, 30 October 2015, accessed 25 January 2018, http://www.navytimes.com/story/military/2015/10/30/uuvs-protecting-undersea-cables-russia-darpa/74823926.

[47] Glaser, "Deterrence of Cyber Attacks and U.S. National Security"; Franklin Kramer and Melanie Teplinsky, "Cybersecurity and Tailored Deterrence," *Atlantic Council Issue Brief*, 3 January 2014, accessed 25 January 2018, http://www.atlanticcouncil.org/publications/issue-briefs/cybersecurity-and-tailored-deterrence.

actions, which might cause states to question deterrence strategies built around deterrence-by-punishment.[48]

Perhaps the most proportional deterrence-by-denial response to a cyberspace attack is a similar cyberspace attack. However, there are significant problems with tit-for-tat response strategies strictly within the cyber domain. Because cyberspace attacks (especially the most sophisticated) often require accesses that are time-sensitive and difficult to obtain, states might be unwilling to "burn" a cyberspace access simply in order to deter another state.[49] In addition, sensitive tradecraft techniques might be revealed by utilizing a cyberspace attack. While the attack might initially succeed, showing the adversary one's technical capabilities allows it to quickly respond and change its defenses so that they are less likely to be affected by the punishment strategy in the future. Further, most cyberattacks must be conducted with significant uncertainty about their extent, scale, and effectiveness. Therefore, it might be difficult to gauge before the punishment is inflicted whether or not the attack will create proportional effects on the adversary (or even whether it has been successful after it has been conducted). Finally, the inherently secretive nature of cyberspace might cause states to misperceive a cyberspace attack as an internal technical problem or even to misattribute the actor. While this could help diffuse potential escalation, it also makes signaling with cyberspace punishment more complicated.

Because of these challenges, calls for CDD-by-punishment strategies are increasing. Fewer cyberspace options are available than cross-domain ones, which are generally more perceptible and therefore send stronger signals and have greater levels of certainty about their overall effectiveness. However, cross-domain punishment for cyberspace deterrence invokes a very significant concern about proportionality. In 2014, when the Sony cyberattacks were attributed to North Korea, President Obama promised to "respond proportionally" at a time and place of his choosing. The question became—what is a proportional response to a cyberspace attack? The most obvious proportional response is an attack in kind on an adversary's cyber infrastructure. In this case, however, the adversary offered limited cyber targets of opportunity. Certainly North Korea had no equivalent private corporate target like Sony nor any valuable intellectual property or trade secret emails to steal and reveal. Shortly after the attacks, Obama signed the executive order allowing for sanctions against cyberspace attacks (as had been employed in response to North Korea's hack of Sony Pictures Entertainment in late 2014), indicating that the Obama administration felt that economic sanctions were appropriate proportional punishment options for many types of cyberspace attacks.

---

[48] Jacquelyn Schneider, "The Information Revolution and International Stability: A Multi-article Exploration of Computing, Cyber, and Incentives for Conflict" (PhD diss., George Washington University, 2017).

[49] Libicki, *Cyberdeterrence and Cyberwar*.

A state's CDD-by-punishment strategy is more likely to be viewed as credible if it has a set of responses to draw from that are deemed proportional and legitimate. Without previous cases to draw from or arms control agreements, legal precedent, or norms, proportionality (especially across domains) becomes a significant credibility issue for deterrence-by-punishment strategies. Proportionality could start with a discussion of effects-based proportionality. This is more likely to work when a cyberspace attack creates a kinetic effect that can be replicated with conventional kinetic punishment. For example, a cyberspace attack that caused a radar system to cease functioning could be punished with an electromagnetic jamming attack with little concern for inappropriate proportionality. However, if a cyberspace attack causes a financial institution to lose resources, what are the most appropriate noncyber proportional responses? And what about attacks with inherently virtual effects—for instance taking down a command and control node? Would a similar attack that physically destroyed a command and control node (say, for example, with a bomb) be considered proportional? There are significant cognitive differences between the virtual effects of cyberspace attacks and the concreteness of a similar physical attack that produces first-order damage to life or limb.[50]

Despite the concerns about proportionality for cross-domain cyberspace deterrence strategies, academics seem to agree that in order for retaliatory deterrence to succeed in cyberspace, policymakers must explore punishment methods across domains. While this could include conventional kinetic options, scholars also advocate the use of economic sanctions, diplomatic actions, trade embargoes, and judiciary punishments.[51]

Deterrence across Domains Utilizing Cyberspace Tools

The previous discussion delved into issues related to deterrence of cyberspace actions. However, states might also be interested in using cyberspace tools and operations across domains to bolster conventional deterrence. Here I will detail arguments about the effectiveness of cyber operations to deter across other domains. I focus on two sets of issues commonly discussed in debates about the effectiveness of cyber operations as a tool for CDD: first, signaling and secrecy, and second, escalation dominance and control.

---

[50] Henry Farrell and Charles L. Glaser, "The Role of Effects, Saliencies and Norms in US Cyberwar Doctrine," *Journal of Cybersecurity* 33, no. 1 (2017): 7–17, https://doi.org/10.1093/cybsec/tyw015.

[51] Jonathan Solomon, "Cyberdeterrence between Nation-States: Plausible Strategy or a Pipe Dream," *Strategic Studies Quarterly* (2011): 1–25, http://www.au.af.mil/au/ssq/2011/spring/solomon.pdf; Lorber and Schneider, "Sanctioning to Deter."

Signaling and Secrecy

Critics of cyber tools for conventional deterrence argue that the inherently secretive nature of cyber operations might make cyber punishments difficult signals for deterrence. First, because cyber operations are generally covert and often difficult to attribute, they might not be perceptible enough for adversaries to factor into their action calculus.[52] Second, cyber operations, which often operate below the threshold of armed conflict, might not be salient enough to deter conventional conflict. Finally, cyber tools, even if they are perceived appropriately and cause significant harm, might not offer credible future punishment threats for deterrence-by-punishment strategies because they lack previously demonstrated effects.[53] There are no air shows for cyber operations, nor can an information warfare squadron visibly signal a state's intentions and capability in the same visceral way as the transit of an aircraft carrier near adversary territory. Critics argue that the huge amount of uncertainty surrounding cyber operations—a product of its secretive and virtual nature—serves as a hindrance to the utilization of cyber operations for deterrence. Perhaps more fundamental to these critics' concern about utilizing cyber operations as a means of signaling deterrence credibility is the inability of covert and secret actions to tie the hands of states to deterrence-by-punishment strategies. This is a concern that resonates with international relations scholarship that argues that the most credible signals are those that publicly tie domestic constituencies with leaders' punishment strategies.[54] How can nonattributable actions taken in cyberspace, especially those that do not explicitly link a state to a cyberspace operation, convey credible punishment signals?

Studies of covert operations—which also have issues with signal perceptibility—reveal some potential opportunities to utilize cyber operations as credible signals of deterrence across domains. First, utilizing covert methods to signal a threat might

---

[52] Erica D. Borghard and Shawn W. Lonergan, "The Logic of Coercion in Cyberspace," *Security Studies* 26, no. 3 (2017): 452–481, https://doi.org/10.1080/09636412.2017.1306396; Brandon Valeriano and Ryan C. Maness, *Cyber War versus Cyber Realities: Cyber Conflict in the International System* (Oxford: Oxford University Press, 2015).

[53] Libicki, *Cyberdeterrence and Cyberwar*; Solomon, "Cyberdeterrence between Nation-States"; Elliott, "Deterring Strategic Cyberattack"; Richard J. Harknett, John Callaghan, and Rudi Kauffman, "Leaving Deterrence Behind: War-Fighting and National Cybersecurity," *Journal of Homeland Security and Emergency Management* 7, no. 1 (2010): 1547–7355, https://doi.org/10.2202/1547-7355.1636; Richard A. Clarke and Robert K. Knake, *Cyber War: The Next Threat to National Security and What to Do about It* (New York: Harper Collins, 2010).

[54] James Fearon, "Domestic Political Audiences and the Escalation of International Disputes," *American Political Science Review* 88, no. 3 (1995): 577–592, https://doi.org/10.2307/2944796; James Fearon, "Signaling Foreign Policy Interests: Tying Hands versus Sinking Costs," *Journal of Conflict Resolution* 41, no. 1 (1997): 68–90, https://doi.org/10.1177/0022002797041001004; Kenneth Schultz, "Domestic Opposition and Signaling in International Crises," *American Political Science Review* 92, no. 4 (1998): 829–844, https://doi.org/10.2307/2586306.

give a state the ability to back down without losing domestic face. As Austin Carson points out in his study of covert operations and signaling, "making threats privately . . . reduces the domestic audience costs for an opponent's capitulation and makes a bargain short of war more likely."[55] Further, in a series of case studies, Carson and Keren Yarhi-Milo find that "if states engage in covert military coercion, local allies and strategic adversaries often observe significant expenditure of resources and the willingness to run counter-escalation and exposure risks. This imbues covert action with informational power previous scholars have overlooked even as secrecy preserves a degree of leader flexibility."[56] Carson and Yarhi-Milo point to the tailored nature of covert operations as a way for leaders to convey credible signals to targeted audiences, offering policymakers a new option for tailored deterrence in cyberspace and for extending deterrence to allies in a more credible way. Therefore, cyber operations might provide policymakers with a first-step, less escalatory, and more targeted way to establish deterrence in conventional war domains—especially in cases in which states are seeking to limit conflict, keep it within manageable boundaries, and avoid escalation to general conventional warfare.

An additional assumption made by critics of cyber operations as a tool of deterrence in other domains is the belief that uncertainty and secrecy are fixed characteristics of cyber tools. This might not necessarily be true. First, the obsession with covert operations in cyberspace might be a product of the bureaucratic incentives of the institutions from which cyber operations evolved. Therefore, this covert bias in cyber operations is not necessarily a characteristic of all states' cyber operations. For the United States, the United Kingdom, and even Russia, the state's cyber capabilities have derived both institutionally and technically from intelligence organizations (the National Security Agency in the United States, Government Communications Headquarters in the United Kingdom, and the Komitet Gosudarstvennoy Bezopasnosti in Russia).[57] Intelligence organizations are incentivized to hide their capabilities and are willing to sacrifice military operational objectives in order to retain intelligence access and attributional anonymity. In nations where cyber capabilities reside in or started from intelligence organizations, the "intel gain-loss" calculation (or the access that must be sacrificed for an operation) will skew toward intelligence gains and prioritizes covert operations over the type of overt military demonstrations that a typical military operational unit would

---

[55] Carson, "Facing Off and Saving Face," 6.
[56] Carson and Yarhi-Milo, "Covert Communication," 1.
[57] Tony Romm, "NSA Chief Defends Dual Roles," *Politico*, 12 June 2013, accessed 25 January 2018, http://www.politico.com/story/2013/06/nsa-chief-keith-alexander-defends-092676; Defence Committee, "MoD Networks, Assets, and Capabilities," Parliament of the United Kingdom, 9 January 2013, accessed 25 January 2018. http://www.publications.parliament.uk/pa/cm201213/cmselect/cmdfence/106/10605.htm; Ryan Maness and Brandon Valeriano, *Russia's Coercive Diplomacy: Energy, Cyber, and Maritime Policy as New Sources of Power* (New York: Palgrave Macmillan, 2015).

prioritize. True to form, we see that nations like the United States and Russia typically utilize covert cyber operations, while countries like China, in which cyber forces evolved institutionally from the People's Liberation Army, are more likely to take overt action in cyberspace.[58] Therefore, the institutional incentives of nation-states might make states more or less likely to experience similar problems with secrecy and signaling in their cyber operations as they do in other operations.

Second, the focus on covert operations for cyberspace effectiveness is often tied to the difficulty of obtaining and retaining accesses in order to infiltrate malicious code into a target network. Because cyber accesses are mutable and easy to lose, states are more likely to use covert operations and to obscure their activity in order to retain these accesses. This concern has been a constant for sophisticated cyberattacks (as opposed to brute force DDoS and webpage defacement) but might diminish if emerging research into cyber access via the electromagnetic spectrum moves from science fiction to reality.[59] This is an especially revolutionary advancement for the use of cyber operations as a tool of deterrence across domains, because the technology utilizes existing radio frequency weapons (for example, almost all radars, some data links, and communications equipment) as persistent accesses for cyberattacks. If states no longer have to worry about "burning" accesses for cyber operations, they can demonstrate cyber capabilities with much lower risk of losing their capability to continue operating. In addition, because the vast majority of modern weaponry relies on activity within the electromagnetic spectrum for modern, networked warfare, the existence of a persistent access cyberweapon might keep states from launching conventional attacks.

Escalation Dominance and Escalation Control

A corollary to CDD effectiveness is the impact deterrent policies have on controlling escalation from limited confrontation to full-scale conventional or nuclear conflict. Drawing on the previous arguments about secrecy and signaling, we can see that characteristics of cyber operations have potentially large implications within conflict deterrence. Some scholars argue that the use of cyber operations, which is ambiguous and below the threshold of declared armed conflict, allows for flexible options to limit escalation. Further, by demonstrating the will to take any

---

[58] Steve DeWeese, *Capability of the People's Republic of China (PRC) to Conduct Cyber Warfare and Computer Network Exploitation* (US-China Economic and Security Review Commission, 2009).

[59] Mordechai Guri, Gabi Kedma, Assaf Kachlon, and Yuval Elovici, "AirHopper: Bridging the Air-Gap between Isolated Networks and Mobile Phones Using Radio Frequencies," in 2014 9th International Conference on Malicious and Unwanted Software: The Americas (MALWARE), Fajardo, PR, 28–30 October 2014 (IEEE, 2014): 58–67, https://ieeexplore.ieee.org/document/6999418/; John Costello, "Bridging the Air Gap: The Coming 'Third Offset.'" *War on the Rocks*, 17 February 2015, accessed 25 January 2018, http://warontherocks.com/2015/02/bridging-the-air-gap-the-coming-third-offset/.

action, cyber operations provide a means to respond credibly to threats without creating kinetic responses. On the other hand scholars are concerned that extensive vulnerabilities and linkages to conventional operations and critical infrastructure might unwittingly escalate crises to conventional conflicts. These academics look at the increasing reliance on cyber capabilities to conduct warfighting and argue that attacks on military cyber targets—especially those that affect nuclear and conventional command and control—might create a first mover advantage that could create dangerous escalation effects.[60]

Contrary to both of these explanations, a growing body of work on behavioral explorations of cyberspace and escalation suggest that, at least for U.S. policymakers and domestic audiences, cyberspace operations have little to no effect on cyber escalation dynamics.[61] In fact, these games and experiments reveal a strong reticence both to use cyber operations in the offense and to respond to cyberattacks against the United States. Together, these studies suggest that cyber operations might not have the same saliency or emotional effect as conventional operations—even when they create the same physically destructive effects. Therefore, cyberspace sparring might take place outside or below the firebreak of traditional conflict escalation ladders.

Conclusion: Uncertainty, Cyber, and Deterrence and Implications for U.S. Cyber Deterrence Policies

A resounding theme in the existing debates about deterrence in and through cyberspace is the role that uncertainty will play in successful cyber deterrence; uncertainty about effects of cyberattacks, capabilities to create cyberattacks, actors conducting attacks, and responses to cyberattacks. The uncertainty is a technical

---

[60] Schneider, "The Information Revolution and International Stability"; Glaser, "Deterrence of Cyber Attacks and U.S. National Security"; Morgan, "The Applicability of Traditional Deterrence Concepts and Theory to the Cyber Realm"; Davis, Paul K. "Deterrence, Influence, Cyber Attack, and Cyberwar," *Journal of International Law and Politics* 47, no. 2 (2014): 327–355; David C. Gompert and Martin Libicki, "Cyber Warfare and Sino-American Crisis Instability," *Survival* 56, no. 4 (2014): 7–22, https://doi.org/10.1080/00396338.2014.941543; Jacquelyn Schneider, "Digitally-Enabled Warfare: The Capability-Vulnerability Paradox," (Washington, DC: Center for a New American Security, 29 August 2016), accessed 25 January 2018, https://www.cnas.org/publications/reports/digitally-enabled-warfare-the-capability-vulnerability-paradox.

[61] Schneider, "The Information Revolution and International Stability"; Sarah Kreps and Debak Das, "Warring from the Virtual to the Real: Assessing the Public's Threshold for War over Cyber Security," *Research & Politics* 4, no. 2 (2017): https://doi.org/10.1177/2053168017715930; Jacquelyn Schneider, "Cyber Attacks on Critical Infrastructure: Insights from War Gaming," *War on the Rocks*, 26 July 2017, accessed 25 January 2018, https://warontherocks.com/2017/07/cyber-attacks-on-critical-infrastructure-insights-from-war-gaming/.

characteristic of these operations but extends to the behavioral reaction to cyber operations. The competing hypotheses presented above indicate that this uncertainty poses opportunities and challenges for U.S. cyber deterrence policies. The United States can embrace the uncertainty of cyber technology, accept this uncertainty as a unique and immutable quality of the domain and operations, and focus on deterrence policies that manipulate this uncertainty for the Unites States' strategic benefit. These policies would remain largely ambiguous, focus on investments in defense, and shy away from CDD options that might inadvertently escalate crises. Meanwhile, the United States would use covert cyber operations as a tailored deterrence-by-punishment option to signal resolve in limited conflict and would focus its cyber tools of deterrence on crises in which U.S. foreign policy decisionmakers did not want to be beholden to domestic constituencies.

However, if the United States believes that cyber uncertainty is not fixed, it can take a series of steps to try to increase certainty within the domain. These decisions would also lead to divergent choices for cyber deterrence policies. For example, the United States could invest heavily in attribution technologies, focus on tailored high-threshold deterrence, and advocate declaratory punishment policies. At the same time, the United States would need to pursue overt cyber capabilities, potentially with persistent access through the electromagnetic spectrum. Meanwhile, the United States should try to increase certainty by advocating norms of behavior in cyberspace and entering into arms control and information-sharing agreements.

Regardless of whether the United States pursues policies that focus on manipulating uncertainty or creating certainty, this chapter has highlighted the unique complications of CDD from a cyber perspective. So far, literature in international relations has largely consisted of untested hypotheses about the impact of cyber technology on deterrence effectiveness. Further research and hypothesis testing—both empirical and logical—not only will greatly improve the state of our understanding about CDD theories but also will guide the development and implementation of U.S. cyber deterrence policies.

6

Antisatellite Weapons and the Growing Instability of Deterrence

BENJAMIN W. BAHNEY, JONATHAN PEARL, AND MICHAEL MARKEY

United States officials currently face two inescapable realities: Washington's unprecedented dependence on space systems for conventional military operations and a nascent threat that future opponents will use antisatellite (ASAT) weapons to offset U.S. conventional military advantages. In 2014 congressional testimony, U.S. Director of National Intelligence James Clapper told legislators that Russian and Chinese military leaders "understand the unique information advantages afforded by space systems and are developing capabilities to disrupt U.S. use of space in a conflict."[1] In 2015, then U.S. Assistant Secretary of State Frank Rose stated that "both Russia and China are developing ASAT capabilities to hold U.S. systems at risk."[2]

Spurred on by such warnings and a series of Chinese and Russian ASAT tests, U.S. policymakers have been responding. In the 2015 Defense Authorization Act, Congress mandated that the Department of Defense review its capabilities for space control, develop a strategy for space control and space superiority for national space assets, and review existing deterrence strategies relevant to space.[3] Also in 2015, the Department of Defense announced its plans to spend $5 billion over five years for space security and space control activities, the latter to be geared toward actively

---

[1] James Clapper, "Statement for the Record, Worldwide Threat Assessment of the U.S. Intelligence Community," Senate Select Committee on Intelligence, 29 January 2014, accessed 31 January 2018, https://www.dni.gov/index.php/newsroom/congressional-testimonies/congressional-testimonies-2014/item/1005-statement-for-the-record-worldwide-threat-assessment-of-the-us-intelligence-community.

[2] Sam Jones, "Satellite Wars," *Financial Times*, 20 November 2015, accessed 31 January 2018, http://www.ft.com/intl/cms/s/2/637bf054-8e34-11e5-8be4-3506bf20cc2b.html.

[3] See: H.R. 3979 Carl Levin and Howard P. "Buck" McKeon National Defense Authorization Act for Fiscal Year 2015, 113th Congress (2013-14), 19 December 2014, secs. 1606–1607, accessed 31 January 2018, https://www.gpo.gov/fdsys/pkg/PLAW-113publ291/pdf/PLAW-113publ291.pdf.

protecting U.S. space capabilities or denying an adversary's access to space systems.[4] The fiscal year 2016 defense budget included investments in key capabilities for space security, nuclear deterrence, power projection, and intelligence, surveillance, and reconnaissance (ISR) out through fiscal year 2020.[5] More recently, the Trump administration's National Security Strategy has called out space security as a major focus area for the United States, saying that "the United States must maintain our leadership and freedom of action in space. Communications and financial networks, military and intelligence systems, weather monitoring, navigation, and more have components in the space domain. As U.S. dependence on space has increased, other actors have gained access to space-based systems and information... Others believe that the ability to attack space assets offers an asymmetric advantage and as a result, are pursuing a range of antisatellite (ASAT) weapons."[6]

The threat from foreign ASAT capabilities is also capturing the attention of U.S. military commanders. General John Hyten, then commander of the U.S. Air Force Space Command, appeared on the national news program *60 Minutes* in early 2015 to discuss the threat posed to U.S. space systems by Russia and China and to assert the U.S. military's determination to respond.[7] Indeed, the military and the intelligence community have been setting the stage for a renewed focus on space security since at least 2011. That year, the U.S. Department of Defense and the Director of National Intelligence coauthored the first revision to the National Security Space Strategy in over a decade, proclaiming that space is now "congested" by satellites and debris from foreign nations; "competitive," in terms of the decline in Washington's technological advantage as both competing states and commercial firms become much more capable in space; and "contested" in all orbits by potential U.S. adversaries seeking ASAT weapons. As that document argued, "today space systems and their supporting infrastructure face a range of man-made threats that may deny, degrade, deceive, disrupt or destroy assets. Potential adversaries are seeking to exploit perceived space vulnerabilities. As more nations and nonstate actors develop counterspace capabilities over the next decade, threats to U.S. space systems and challenges to the stability and security of the space environment will increase. Irresponsible acts against space systems could have implications beyond

---

[4] Colin Clarke, "US Presses Russia, China on ASAT Tests; Space Control Spending Triples," *Breaking Defense*, 16 April 2015, accessed 31 January 2018, http://breakingdefense.com/2015/04/space-control-spending-triples.

[5] "Fiscal Year 2016 Budget of the U.S. Government," Office of Management and Budget, accessed 31 January 2018, https://www.gpo.gov/fdsys/pkg/BUDGET-2016-BUD/pdf/BUDGET-2016-BUD.pdf.

[6] "National Security Strategy of the United States of America," White House, December 2017, accessed 31 January 2018, https://www.whitehouse.gov/wp-content/uploads/2017/12/NSS-Final-12-18-2017-0905.pdf.

[7] David Martin, "The Battle Above," *60 Minutes*, CBS News, 26 April 2015, accessed 31 January 2018, http://www.cbsnews.com/news/rare-look-at-space-command-satellite-defense-60-minutes.

the space domain, disrupting worldwide services upon which the civil and commercial sectors depend."[8]

This chapter investigates why the U.S. military and its foreign counterparts are increasingly preparing for military action against national security space systems, explains the logic underlying such weapons and attacks, and examines the challenges that threats to space systems are likely to pose to deterrence and escalation control in the coming decades. It dissects how space security affects the two key aspects of strategic stability: arms race stability, or the incentives for fielding new weapons, and crisis stability, or the incentives each side may have to strike first or escalate a crisis. It begins by discussing the history and logic of space security during the Cold War, including the later years when the United States and the Soviet Union both developed space capabilities to support conventional military operations and—nearly simultaneously—began developing space control options to deny or destroy their opponents' space capabilities. It then describes how over the past decade, rising regional military powers have been developing their own space capabilities to support military operations as well as new ASAT capabilities to threaten their rivals' space infrastructure.

Next, this chapter sets forth the logic for space control operations—the use of military force to affect foreign space systems or to protect one's own—focusing in particular on conflicts between regional powers and power-projecting states. The chapter concludes by arguing that strategic competition between states that rely on space systems and states with the means to deny, damage, or destroy an adversary's space systems will have far-reaching consequences for crisis stability and escalation. Further, policymakers and military strategists do not yet have a shared understanding of the dynamics of space-related competition, including the impact of asymmetries on the onset and escalation of crises or conflicts. Accordingly, we lay out a series of questions for further social science research.

Finally, we argue that space systems provide militaries with unrivaled strategic reach and that ASAT weapons threaten to keep power-projecting states "grounded" by eliminating their ability to deliver force at a distance. Because of the increasingly contested space environment, the prospect of warfare extending into space must no longer be relegated to the pages of science fiction novels but instead treated as an emerging new domain of potential conflict against which to plan and prepare—one that will exert a strong shaping force on the future geopolitical environment and on the political, economic, and military fortunes of the United States and its allies.

---

[8] U.S. Department of Defense and Office of the Director of National Intelligence, "National Security Space Strategy: Unclassified Summary," January 2011, accessed 31 January 2018, https://www.dni.gov/index.php/newsroom/reports-publications/reports-publications-2011/item/620-national-security-space-strategy.

Space: A Historically Stable and Stabilizing Domain?

Policymakers in the United States, China, Russia, and Europe often warn of the dangers of an arms race and military conflict in the space domain. Their exhortations reflect a prevailing belief that ASAT weapon development and use would represent a significant and dangerous break from existing norms of behavior that have served to protect national security space systems from direct military threats. Against the backdrop of the 1967 Outer Space Treaty, which committed signatories not to station weapons of mass destruction in space or to establish military installations of any type on the moon or other celestial bodies,[9] many of these same policymakers are today debating the merit of introducing new diplomatic tools, such as a space code of conduct or an updated treaty, to head off future ASAT weapons development.

These debates tend to overlook the fact that the stable and stabilizing nature of space during the first half of the Cold War probably had more to do with the United States and the Soviet Union—the era's two primary space-enabled competitors—lacking attractive targets and weapons capable of conducting precision strikes against the other side's space systems than with any normative or legal proscription of space warfare. Indeed, aside from the basic observation that the United States and the Soviet Union were engaged in a cold rather than a hot war, Moscow and Washington perceived such attacks as disadvantageous during much of that era. That was because prior to the telecommunications satellite revolution in the 1970s and 1980s, U.S. and Soviet space systems primarily supported real-time nuclear warning and nuclear command and control (NC2) functions.[10] Attacking early warning or NC2 systems that served to underpin the nuclear deterrent in both nations could have potentially been interpreted by either side as a preparatory move for a nuclear strike. Consequently, the United States and the Soviet Union had a strong mutual disincentive during much of this period to develop broad counter-space capabilities or doctrine, except to hedge against the possibility of escalation to general nuclear war. In this light, space was a first-strike stable domain during the early Cold War, in large part because it enabled nuclear first-strike stability through early warning and C2 functions.

Moreover, ASAT capabilities during much of the Cold War were relatively crude.[11] At least until the 1970s, the immaturity of conventional precision strike

---

[9] U.S. Department of State, Bureau of Arms Control, Verification, and Compliance, "Treaty on Principles Governing the Activities of States in the Exploration and Use of Outer Space, Including the Moon and Other Celestial Bodies" (27 January 1967), accessed 31 January 2018, http://www.state.gov/t/isn/5181.htm.

[10] Forrest E. Morgan, *Deterrence and First-Strike Stability in Space, A Preliminary Assessment* (Santa Monica, CA: RAND, 2010), http://www.rand.org/pubs/monographs/MG916.html.

[11] Michael Krepon, "Space and Nuclear Deterrence," in *Anti-satellite Weapons, Deterrence and Sino-American Space Relations*, edited by Michael Krepon and Julia Thompson (Washington, DC: Stimson Center, September 2013), 16.

technologies like missile guidance and seekers meant that ASAT attacks would probably have to employ nuclear devices in order to reliably destroy their targets.[12] Using nuclear weapons to attack satellites that were intended to build transparency and enhance strategic stability would have been perverse in both intent and effect by crossing the nuclear firebreak, signaling potential nuclear escalation while degrading the other side's ability to confirm otherwise, and potentially risking the degradation of one's own space operations for a period of months to years through the spread of harmful radiation across broad swathes of the space environment.[13] The fact that few, if any, states other than the United States and the Soviet Union were capable during that period of reliably threatening an adversary's space assets using ground- or space-based technologies likely contributed to the space domain's relative stability, if for no other reason than that the number of potential belligerents was limited. Game theorists have long noted that an increase in the number of potential belligerents increases the risk of crisis and conflict escalation.

These disincentives to ASAT strikes—a shortage of both non-NC2 targets and nonnuclear ASAT weapons—began to erode in the 1970s. By the mid-1970s, the National Reconnaissance Office's Keyhole-11 satellites were providing imagery intelligence and reconnaissance in near real-time using relay satellites,[14] which theoretically could be used for military targeting. It was in this same time period that Soviet officials began to view U.S. satellites as viable targets that could be struck without risking nuclear escalation. The Soviets tested their coorbital system, called Istrebitel Sputnikov ("Satellite Killer"), in the early 1970s; despite its limitations and need for manual operation, it was declared operational in 1973.[15] The Soviets continued to update and test Istrebitel Sputnikov throughout the 1970s and, in particular, attempted to increase its operational range and to update its seeker systems for better precision guidance.[16]

United States National Security Council documents from the Ford and Carter administrations demonstrate that U.S. policymakers were similarly concerned in the mid- to-late 1970s about the development of Soviet space assets to enable long-range

---

[12] Morgan, *Deterrence and First-Strike Stability in Space, A Preliminary Assessment*; Bhupendra Jasani, ed., *Space Weapons and International Security* (New York: Oxford University Press, 1987), 15; "IS-A [Istrebitel Sputnik Antisatellite]," Encyclopedia Astronautica, accessed 31 January 2018, http://www.astronautix.com/i/is-a.html.

[13] Morgan, *Deterrence and First-Strike Stability in Space, A Preliminary Assessment*; David Wright, Laura Grego, and Lisbeth Gronlund, *The Physics of Space Security: A Reference Manual* (Cambridge, MA: American Academy of Arts and Sciences, 2005), 138–139.

[14] "50 Years of Vigilance from Above," National Reconnaissance Office, accessed 31 January 2018, http://www.nro.gov/about/50thanniv/50th-flyer.pdf.

[15] Laura Grego, "A History of Anti-satellite Programs," Union of Concerned Scientists, January 2012, accessed 31 January 2018, 3, https://www.ucsusa.org/sites/default/files/legacy/assets/documents/nwgs/a-history-of-ASAT-programs_lo-res.pdf.

[16] Ibid., 4.

standoff strikes. Both the Republican Ford and Democratic Carter administrations perceived Soviet Radar Ocean Reconnaissance Satellites (RORSATs) and Electronic Ocean Reconnaissance Satellites (EORSATs) as posing a threat to the United States' power projection because of their ability to find and target American naval assets in near real time for Soviet standoff missiles.[17] The nuclear-powered RORSATs were accepted into service in the Soviet arsenal in 1975, and the Soviet Union successfully added the EORSATs in 1978.[18] The geolocation capabilities of the RORSATs and EORSATs against U.S. Navy ships appear to have raised novel concerns for U.S. policymakers, as the United States approved ASAT programs in the late 1970s in order to have options for protecting forward deployed U.S. forces from Soviet precision strikes.[19] The United States finally initiated its program for a precision, air-launched kinetic kill ASAT in 1982, which culminated in the ASAT missile 135 (ASM-135) system.[20]

By the mid-1980s, both the United States and the Soviet Union had conducted ASAT tests, signaling that the space domain was fair game for military competition and confrontation between the superpowers.[21] In fact, the United States and the Soviet Union may have seen this eventuality coming a decade earlier, as they neglected to sign a treaty proscribing such developments during the 1960s and early 1970s. The carefully crafted 1967 Outer Space Treaty, for example, prohibited neither the use of weapons of mass destruction in space nor the deployment

---

[17] Asif Siddiqi, "Staring at the Sea: The Soviet RORSAT and EORSAT Programmes," *Journal of the British Interplanetary Society* 51, no. 11/12 (November/December 1999), http://faculty.fordham.edu/siddiqi/writings/p14_siddiqi_jbis_rorsat_1999.pdf.

[18] "US-A Space System," Encyclopedia Astronautica, accessed 31 January 2018, http://www.astronautix.com/u/us-a.html; "US-P Space System," Encyclopedia Astronautica, accessed 31 January 2018, http://www.astronautix.com/u/us-p.html.

[19] "Document 130. Memorandum from the President's Assistant for National Security Affairs (Scowcroft) to President Ford," "Document 137. Memorandum from the Deputy Chief of the Office of Assistant Director (Smith) to the President's Assistant for National Security Affairs (Scowcroft)," and "Document 141. Memorandum from the President's Assistant for National Security Affairs (Scowcroft) to President Ford," all in *Foreign Relations of the United States, 1969–1976*, vol. E-3, *Documents on Global Issues, 1973–1976*, Office of the Historian, U.S. Department of State, accessed 31 January 2018, http://history.state.gov/historicaldocuments/frus1969-76ve03/d130; http://history.state.gov/historicaldocuments/frus1969-76ve03/d137; http://history.state.gov/historicaldocuments/frus1969-76ve03/d141.

[20] Grego, "A History of Anti-satellite Programs," 4–5.

[21] U.S. Congress, Office of Technology Assessment, *Anti-satellite Weapons, Counter-measures, and Arms Control* (Washington, DC: U.S. Government Printing Office, 1 September 1985), ch. 5, accessed 31 January 2018, https://www.princeton.edu/~ota/disk2/1985/8502/850207.pdf; Krepon, "Space and Nuclear Deterrence," 16; Michael Krepon and Sonya Schoenberger, "Annex: A Comparison of Nuclear and Anti-satellite Testing, 1945–2013," in Krepon and Thompson, *Anti-satellite Weapons, Deterrence and Sino-American Space Relations*, pp. 131–137.

of earth-based, air-launched, or space-based non-nuclear ASAT weapons.[22] On the few rare occasions when Washington and Moscow agreed to binding restrictions on ASAT activities during the 1960s and early 1970s, as in the anti–ballistic missile treaty, the agreed language only covered niche elements of the other side's military space infrastructure that were seen as essential for protecting the Cold War nuclear deterrence balance, specifically national technical means reconnaissance satellites that both sides used for arms control verification.[23]

Indeed, Washington and Moscow's historical failure to reach agreement on an ASAT Treaty—negotiated in earnest during the late 1970s and proposed on several occasions into the 1980s—underscored both sides' historical reluctance to close off its ASAT strike options, especially during the final decades of the Cold War, when the number of potentially attractive targets was increasing and precision strike capabilities were emerging on both sides.[24]

The Revolution in Military Affairs and the Reemergence of ASAT Competition

The end of the Cold War largely halted ASAT weapons research and development in the United States and Russia, as well as strategic thinking about conflict in the space domain. With the collapse of its political and economic system, Moscow discontinued its real-time space-based ISR systems as well as its ASAT programs.[25] For Washington, the disappearance of its mortal adversary and peer competitor led it to mostly mothball its own ASAT programs.[26]

Yet the "unipolar moment" of the 1990s was also marked by a dramatically increasing U.S. reliance on space systems, including for conventional military operations. Most prominently, the information technology-enabled Revolution in Military Affairs (RMA) vastly deepened the cross-domain integration of

---

[22] U.S. Department of State, Bureau of Arms Control, Verification, and Compliance, "Treaty on Principles Governing the Activities of States in the Exploration and Use of Outer Space, Including the Moon and Other Celestial Bodies."

[23] U.S. Department of State, Bureau of Arms Control, Verification, and Compliance, "Treaty between the United States of America and the Union of Soviet Socialist Republics on the Limitation of Anti-ballistic Missile Systems" (26 May 1972), accessed 31 January 2018, https://www.state.gov/t/avc/trty/101888.htm; U.S. Department of State, Bureau of International Security and Nonproliferation, "Interim Agreement between the United States of America and the Union of Soviet Socialist Republics on Certain Measures with Respect to the Limitation of Strategic Offensive Arms" (26 May 1972), accessed 31 January 2018, https://www.state.gov/t/isn/4795.htm.

[24] U.S. Congress, Office of Technology Assessment, *Anti-satellite Weapons, Counter-measures, and Arms Control*, ch. 5; Krepon, "Space and Nuclear Deterrence," 16; Krepon and Schoenberger, "Annex."

[25] "US-A Space System"; "US-P Space System"; "IS-A."

[26] Grego, "A History of Anti-satellite programs," 6–8.

space-based C4ISR technology with military operations in the land, sea, and air domains.[27] This trend was spearheaded by the United States and, encouraged by perceptions of a relatively low post–Cold War threat environment in the space domain, the United States and partner nations developed high-cost and long-lifetime national security space systems, favoring exquisite capabilities over redundant and resilient ones that could survive military attack. In a positive feedback loop, the high cost and low resilience of these systems incentivized their owners—again, most notably the United States—to avoid the reemergence of ASAT competition that would have disproportionately threatened its space systems.

By the early 2000s, the unipolar moment had begun to fade, and a reemergent regional competition between the United States and aspiring powers was again increasing the incentives for states to develop ASAT capabilities. Evidence of this shift in incentives in favor of ASAT capability development in the post–Cold War period can be traced back at least to the George W. Bush administration. President Bush unilaterally withdrew from the anti–ballistic missile treaty in 2001 to develop a national ballistic missile defense system designed to counter North Korean and Iranian threats. The Bush administration then funded development of ASAT jammers and missile defense systems based on potentially dual-use technologies like hit-to-kill interceptors.[28] While these developments may have been an earnest shift to protect the United States against rogue threats, it is also possible that they signaled to aspiring regional powers like China and Russia that the United States would increasingly leverage its military advantage in space against them as well.[29]

Indeed, one might trace this shift in incentive structures even farther back to the 1991 Gulf War. Often considered the "first space war," the Gulf War operationally demonstrated the value of GPS-enabled guidance and satellite-generated warnings of Iraqi tactical Scud missile launches.[30] In the aftermath of that war, U.S. investment in space-based C4ISR capabilities surged, and the role of space services in theater commands grew substantially, building on their traditional strategic-level role. This shift made space assets more tactically useful to U.S. forces; yielded a U.S. force

---

[27] Andrew F. Krepinevich, "The Military-Technical Revolution: A Preliminary Assessment," Center for Strategic and Budgetary Assessments, 2 October 2002, accessed 31 January 2018, http://csbaonline.org/research/publications/the-military-technical-revolution-a-preliminary-assessment/publication.

[28] Grego, "A History of Anti-satellite Programs," 8–11.

[29] Baohui Zhang, "Security Dilemma in the U.S.-China Military Space Relationship," *Asian Survey* 51, no. 2 (March–April 2011): 311–332, http://doi.org/10.1525/AS.2011.51.2.311.

[30] Barry D. Watts, "The Military Use of Space: A Diagnostic Assessment," Center for Strategic and Budgetary Assessments, February 2001, accessed 31 January 2018, http://large.stanford.edu/courses/2010/ph240/riley1/docs/2001.02.01-Military-Use-of-Space.pdf; Ellen Pawlikowski, Doug Loverro, and Tom Cristler, "Space: Disruptive Challenges, New Opportunities, and New Strategies," *Strategic Studies Quarterly* 6, no. 1 (Spring 2012): 27–54, http://www.airuniversity.af.mil/Portals/10/SSQ/documents/Volume-06_Issue-1/Pawlikowski.pdf.

of smaller, more mobile, better-connected units; and rendered those forces increasingly reliant on space assets.[31] In short, the United States proved the utility of space-enabled conventional warfare on the battlefield, but at the same time, an increased reliance on these systems opened up new doors of vulnerability for forces engaged in conventional military operations.

Tempted by the advantages conferred by integrated space support for conventional forces, other states—including both U.S. allies and potential adversaries—have been working to follow the United States' lead in space. This includes the development and use of space-based C4ISR; position, navigation, and timing (PNT) systems like GPS; and satellite early warning systems (SEWS). Today, space services are arguably fundamental to the conduct of advanced conventional warfare for all advanced powers (see table 6.1 for an overview of the military-related space capabilities of leading states). This integration has opened new windows of opportunity and vulnerability for the United States and its allies and potential adversaries alike.

Indeed, the operational military vulnerability from this increased dependence on space systems is widely recognized by leading U.S. competitors. Russian thinkers, for example, have argued that "information-space support is acquiring decisive significance in contemporary wars."[32] This logic is also evident in China, where analysts now argue that information supremacy is a precondition for victory, and as such, China considers access to space imperative for its national security.[33] As China's 2015 national defense white paper argues,

> the world revolution in military affairs (RMA) is proceeding to a new stage. Long-range, precise, smart, stealthy and unmanned weapons and equipment are becoming increasingly sophisticated. Outer space and cyber space have become new commanding heights in strategic competition among all parties. . . . Countries are developing their space forces and instruments, and the first signs of weaponization of outer space have appeared. China has all along advocated the peaceful use of outer space, opposed the weaponization of an arms race in outer space, and taken an active part in international space cooperation. China will keep abreast of the dynamics of outer space, deal with security threats and challenges in

---

[31] Ibid.

[32] Igor Morozov, Sergey Baushev, and Oleg Kaminskiy, "Space and the Character of Modern Military Activities," *Vozdushno-Kosmicheskaya I Oborona*, no. 4 (2009).

[33] Kevin Pollpeter, "PLA Space Doctrine," in *Chinese Aerospace Power, Evolving Maritime Roles*, edited by Andrew Erickson and Avery Goldstein (Annapolis: China Maritime Studies Institute, Naval Institute Press, 2011), 53–56; Xianqi Chang, *Military Astronautics* (Beijing: National Defense Industry Press, 2002), 147–148.

Table 6.1 **Military space capabilities of key space-enabled states**

	Orbiting objects[1]	Orbiting and deorbited objects[1]	Real-time ISR capable	Military communications capable	SEWS capable	Indigenous GPS	ASAT testing
Russia	1506	3516	Maybe	Yes	Yes	Yes	Yes
China	309	380	Maybe	Yes	Maybe[2]	Yes[3]	Yes
Japan	176	231	No[4]	Yes[5]	Yes[6]	No	No
India	84	95	No	Yes[7]	No	In dev[8]	No
USA	1778	2800	Yes[9]	Yes	Yes	Yes	Unknown

¹ Numbers taken from the Online Index of Objects Launched into Outer Space, maintained by the UN Office for Outer Space Affairs. Though this office attempts to track both announced and unannounced launches, the dataset may not be complete. The information represented in this table is in a constant state of change; the table was current as of 2 January 2018. Up-to-date information can be found at the Office's website, accessed 31 January 2018, http://www.unoosa.org/oosa/osoindex/search-ng.jspx.

² "China Seen Readying Space-Based Warning Sensor," Nuclear Threat Initiative, 25 July 2013, accessed 31 January 2018, http://www.nti.org/gsn/article/china-seen-readying-space-based-warning-sensor; Rui C. Barbosa, "Long March 3B Conducts Another Secretive Launch," NASA Space Flight, 12 September 2015, accessed 31 January 2018, http://www.nasaspaceflight.com/2015/09/long-march-3b-conducts-another-secretive-launch; "Chinese Ballistic Missile Early Warning," GlobalSecurity.org, accessed 31 January 2018, http://www.globalsecurity.org/space/world/china/warning.htm.

³ China's GPS network (Beidou) has not yet achieved persistent global coverage, but rollout of this capability began in 2015. China's latest launch of two third-generation Beidou GPS satellites into medium Earth orbit in November 2017 was part of a new constellation that will establish a persistent global posture for China. Zhao Lei, "China's Beidou Satellite System Upgraded for Global Reach," Telegraph, 4 December 2017, accessed 31 January 2018, http://www.telegraph.co.uk/news/world/china-watch/technology/new-china-satellite-system/.

⁴ Stephen Clark, "Japan Launches Radar Reconnaissance Satellite," Space.com, 12 December 2011, accessed 31 January 2018, http://www.space.com/13900-japan-reconnaissance-satellite-launch.html; Stephen Clark, "Japan Launches Spy Satellites into Orbit," Space.com, 28 January 2013, http://www.space.com/19503-japan-spy-satellites-launch.html.

⁵ "Japan Military Satellite Communications," Globalsecurity.org, accessed 31 January 2018, http://www.globalsecurity.org/space/world/japan/milsatcom.htm.

⁶ Chris Bergin, "Japanese H-2A Launches with New IGS Military Satellite," NASA Space Flight, 22 September 2011, accessed 31 January 2018, http://www.nasaspaceflight.com/2011/09/japanese-h-2a-launches-new-igs-military-satellite.

⁷ "GSAT-7," Department of Space, Indian Space Research Organisation, 30 August 2013, accessed 31 January 2018, http://www.isro.gov.in/Spacecraft/gsat-7.

⁸ K. Raghu, "India to Build Constellation of 7 Navigation Satellites by 2012," LiveMint.com, 5 September 2007, accessed 31 January 2018, http://www.livemint.com/Industry/Goaf3BXSo1qfrjnx6DTgTO/India-to-build-a-constellation-of-7-navigation-satellites-by.html; "Indian PSLV Successfully Launches IRNSS-1A Navigation Satellite," ZeeNews, 2 July 2013, accessed 31 January 2018, http://zeenews.india.com/news/space/indian-pslv-successfully-launches-irnss-1a-navigation-satellite_859281.html.

⁹ "National Reconnaissance Office: The Nation's Eyes and Ears in Space," United States National Reconnaissance Office, accessed 31 January 2018, http://www.nro.gov/about/nro/NRO_Fact_Sheet.pdf.

that domain, and secure its space assets to serve its national economic and social development, and maintain outer space security.[34]

The Reemergence of Geopolitics and the Growing Threat to Space Security

This view of space as critical for successfully conducting advanced conventional conflict continues today to make space systems a tempting target for any state facing a space-enabled adversary and, in turn, continues to increase the incentives for states to develop ASAT capabilities. For instance, after a long hiatus, Russia today has renewed its development and testing of ASAT capabilities. Russia's development of these capabilities may be influenced by concerns about its ability to prevail in potential future regional contingencies if it finds itself in conflict with the United States and its allies.[35] Russia's contemporary efforts reportedly include a "satellite catcher," which could be an evolution of Soviet-era hunter-killer satellites, and a reintroduction of the Soviet-era Kontakt program, which was a MiG-31[36] air-launched hit-to-kill ASAT interceptor.[37] Some analysts have also noted recent Russian military activity surrounding a Soviet-era airborne laser weapon, positing that it, too, may have future ASAT capabilities.[38] These developments have not gone unnoticed in Washington; Director of National Intelligence Clapper in January 2014 highlighted Russia's open claim to have counter-space capabilities, including

---

[34] State Council Information Office. "China's Military Strategy." Beijing: The State Council Information Office of the People's Republic of China, May 2015. http://www.chinadaily.com.cn/china/2015-05/26/content_20820628.htm

[35] James Clapper, "Statement for the Record, Worldwide Threat Assessment of the US Intelligence Community."

[36] The Mikoyan MiG-31 is a supersonic interceptor aircraft, developed for the Soviet Air Forces, that is used by the Russian Air Force.

[37] Paul Rincon, "Russia Tests 'Satellite Catcher,'" *BBC News*, 20 November 2014, accessed 31 January 2018, http://www.bbc.com/news/science-environment-30097643; Laura Grego, "Russia's Small Maneuvering Satellites: Inspectors or ASATs?," Union of Concerned Scientists, 1 December 2014, accessed 31 January 2018, http://allthingsnuclear.org/russias-small-maneuvering-satellites-inspectors-or-asats; Terrence McCoy, "A Mysterious Russian Space Object Could Be the Return of the 'Satellite Killer,'" *Washington Post*, 18 November 2014, accessed 31 January 2018, http://www.washingtonpost.com/news/morning-mix/wp/2014/11/18/a-mysterious-russian-space-object-revives-speculation-about-satellite-killer; "MiG-31 Will Shoot Down Enemy Satellites," NewsRbk.ru, 13 December 2013, accessed 31 January 2018, http://all-rss.com/item-1182600-mig-31-will-shoot-down-enemy-satellites.

[38] "Is Russia Reviving an Old Laser ASAT Project?," *Russian Strategic Nuclear Forces*, 27 May 2015, accessed 31 January 2018, http://russianforces.org/blog/2011/05/is_russia_reviving_an_old_lase.shtml.

jammers and hit-to-kill weapons, as well as Russia's continued research and development of ASAT systems.[39]

According to U.S. space security analysts and military officials, the Chinese military has also been pursuing ASAT technology, conducting direct ascent hit-to-kill tests to lower orbits in 2007, 2010, and 2014, as well as a test of a possible new hit-to-kill system that possibly went as high as geostationary orbit in 2013.[40] For China, development of ASAT capabilities like direct-ascent hit-to-kill interceptors and coorbital satellites comports with the broader trends in Beijing's anti-access/area-denial and its asymmetry doctrine.[41] Moreover, given China's potentially increasing reliance on space assets for conventional military operations, and to the extent that Beijing depends on such systems for military success and believes that the United States could strike its space systems, China's apparent development of ASAT capabilities to threaten strikes against Washington may be part of a broader strategy of deterrence-by-punishment or mutual vulnerability.

In short, officials in both China and Russia today see space not only as a key military enabler but also as a Clausewitzian "center of gravity" for space-enabled powers like the United States. Thus they see space assets as a tempting target to strike in order to disrupt U.S. C4ISR, which enables its long-range precision strike and missile defense capabilities. The development of ASAT weapon capabilities—be they reversible weapons like jammers or permanent destruction weapons like direct ascent hit-to-kill interceptors—are a natural consequence of these views.

But such thinking is not limited to Russia and China. Analysts have written about a great Asian space race, for example, pitting China against India and Japan.[42] To that end, it is worth noting that India, like Russia and China, also seems to have commenced a nascent exploration of counter-space contingencies, almost certainly driven by perceptions of a degrading regional security environment in the face of

---

[39] Clapper, "Statement for the Record, Worldwide Threat Assessment of the U.S. Intelligence Community."

[40] Brian C. Weeden, "Through a Glass Darkly: Chinese, American and Russian Anti-satellite Testing in Space," *Space Review*, 17 March 2014, accessed 31 January 2018, http://thespacereview.com/article/2473/3; Colin Clark, "Chinese ASAT Test Was 'Successful': Lt. Gen. Raymond," *Breaking Defense*, 14 April 2015, accessed 31 January 2018, https://breakingdefense.com/2015/04/chinese-asat-test-was-successful-lt-gen-raymond.

[41] Brian C. Weeden, "*Dancing in the Dark: The Orbital Rendezvous of SJ-12 and SJ-06F*," *Space Review*, 30 August 2010, accessed 31 January 2018, http://thespacereview.com/article/1689/1; David Axe, "Chinese Laser vs. U.S. Sats?," *Defensetech*, 25 September 2006, accessed 31 January 2018, https://www.military.com/defensetech/2006/09/25/chinese-laser-vs-u-s-sats; Michael Pillsbury, *Chinese Views of Future Warfare* (Washington, DC: National Defense University Press, 1998); Ashley J. Tellis, "China's Military Space Strategy," *Survival* 49, no. 3 (2007): 41–72, https://doi.org/10.1080/00396330701564752.

[42] James C. Moltz, *Asia's Space Race: National Motivations, Regional Rivalries, and International Risks* (New York: Columbia University Press, 2011).

China's rise as a regional power rather than perceived threats from Washington. In 2010 the director general of India's Defense Research and Development Organization announced the development of a hit-to-kill ASAT system with a laser tracker that was initially conceived for missile defense purposes. Following the successful 2012 test of the Agni-V intermediate-range ballistic missile, the director of the Defense Research and Development Organization stated: "we have developed all the building blocks for an ASAT capability"—though Indian officials since then have been reluctant to announce an explicit ASAT program or the development of complementary space situational awareness, which is necessary for fielding a fully operational ASAT capability.[43] The at least minimal commitment by India to ASAT latency, while aggressively funding missile defense programs that may have significant ASAT dual-use aspects, shows no signs of abating. To the contrary, one might venture that India's statements are almost certainly designed to demonstrate a latent ASAT capacity without incurring the diplomatic costs of declaring an active program.

The Logic and Growing Threat of Conflict in Space

This growth in the reliance on space systems for conventional military operations by military powers, and their concomitant development of ASAT capabilities, suggests that space may be a growing component of strategic stability. Barry Posen's concept of "command of the commons"[44] provides an elegant device for elaborating this point. As Posen argues, Washington's post–Cold War ability to militarily engage and dominate other states has fundamentally relied on its command of the sea, air, and space commons.

Without this command of the commons, argues Posen, the United States would be forced to fight in a "contested zone" where the value of its technological superiority to dominate conventional military conflicts with other states would quickly diminish. While the United States could still prevail in a conventional ground war absent its command of the commons, a "contested zone" victory would be far more costly and time-consuming. By extension, states seeking to challenge the United States in a conventional military conflict would be strongly incentivized to deny Washington its command of the commons. Accordingly, U.S. adversaries are

---

[43] Sandeep Unnithan, "India Takes on China: India Attains the Capability to Target, Destroy Space Satellites in Orbit," *Indiatoday*, 28 April 2012, accessed 31 January 2018, http://indiatoday.intoday.in/story/agni-v-launch-india-takes-on-china-drdo-vijay-saraswat/1/186367.html; Brett Biddington, "India, ASATs and the Regional Balance: An Australian Perspective," *India Review* 10 (2011): 406–421, https://doi.org/10.1080/14736489.2011.624031.

[44] Barry Posen, "Command of the Commons: The Military Foundation of U.S. Hegemony," *International Security* 28, no. 1 (Summer 2003): 5–46, https://doi.org/10.1162/016228803322427965.

strongly incentivized not only to develop ASAT capabilities but also possibly to use them in future military crises or conflicts with Washington.

But this observation is not limited to Washington's potential adversaries. To the contrary, a similar observation will probably hold in the future for any state facing a space-enabled power in a military conflict, especially if that power is trying to project force over great distances. The key role of military space systems is to generate or transmit data over the horizon, when terrestrial systems cannot do so. Thus, logic dictates that striking the military space systems of a space-enabled opponent can be a useful—and perhaps critical—tool for leveling the military playing field. At a minimum, ASAT strikes or threats to employ ASAT weapons could deter a space-enabled adversary from entering or escalating a conflict because doing so might entail paying far greater costs than would otherwise be necessary. At a maximum, ASAT strikes could increase the likelihood of battlefield success. Indeed, finely tailored employment of ASAT threats and strikes could enable an aggressor to achieve limited aims against a militarily superior but asymmetrically vulnerable opponent.

The United States is currently the most powerful space-enabled state in the world, one that frequently projects military power in the service of its national interests or those of its allies. Consequently, Washington may currently be the state most threatened by the development of ASAT capabilities around the world. Space is a critical enabler for both Washington's defensive (e.g., missile defense) and offensive (e.g., targeting of mobile forces at a distance) military operations though PNT services, military C4ISR, missile warning, and secure communications.[45] The salience of space-based ISR is likely to only increase in the coming years, for instance, as sophisticated integrated air defense systems make the collection and dissemination of intelligence from air-breathing platforms against a near peer adversary increasingly tenuous, especially if a military contingency were to arise.[46] Yet as other states increase their military reliance on space systems, they too will grow more vulnerable to ASAT strikes, and their adversaries will likely seek to target these vulnerabilities. In select future contingencies, the most powerful space-enabled states, like the United States, may actually face even stronger incentives to launch ASAT attacks, including early in a conflict, than will their relatively weaker adversaries, due to the potential risk to their forward deployed forces that are sent in to project power.

While we expect ASAT weapons to grow dramatically in number over the next decade, an "arms race in space" analogous to the nuclear-focused Cold War–era arms race is unlikely to unfold according to the same script. For instance, it is difficult to imagine a state developing ASATs solely because another is doing so.

---

[45] Pawlikowski et al., "Space"; Ashton B. Carter, "Satellites and Anti-satellites: The Limits of the Possible," *International Security* 10, no. 4 (Spring 1986), 46–98, https://doi.org/10.2307/2538950.

[46] "Russia Confirms Arms Deal to Supply China with S-400 Air Defense Systems," *Sputnik News*, 13 April 2015, accessed 31 January 2018, https://sputniknews.com/world/201504131020809219/.

Instead, the number of fielded ASAT weapons will likely be driven by the numbers of military satellites that competing states have and the extent to which those satellites enable either key offensive or defensive capabilities. This vicious cycle may be inescapable, particularly given the possibility of major powers like Russia, China, or the United States successfully harnessing the ongoing commercial revolution in space to field larger numbers of capable small satellites. However, the number of weapons developed may only loosely track the number of satellites on orbit, particularly if states develop various options for targeting adversary satellites (i.e., a variety of jamming and destructive weapon systems) and if defensive measures include both larger numbers of satellites and more resilient individual satellite systems.

We also expect that "first strike stability"[47] is likely to be weak at all stages of escalation between space-enabled states and those with ASAT capabilities.[48] Here, one might note the emphasis in Chinese writings on gaining "mastery by striking first" and the apparent Russian and Chinese fear that U.S. military operations may neuter a state's ability to conduct space strikes once a conflict has begun.[49] Indeed, contrary to popular wisdom, even major space-enabled powers like the United States may have strong incentives to strike first in space and, potentially, early in a conflict. While observers often assume that the United States would have greater incentives to avoid space warfare than weaker regional aspirants less dependent on space systems, as it has relatively more to lose than most hypothetical adversaries if a conflict escalates into space, one should consider that in principle, ASAT attacks can enhance military force survivability for power-projecting states, particularly if an adversary's defenses are space-enabled.

Yet the growing logic of conflict extending into space, and the precarious nature of first-strike stability, is more than just a consequence of growing vulnerabilities—it is also a consequence of increasing target distinguishability and increasingly sophisticated ASAT strike technologies. First, it is becoming increasingly possible to strike the C4ISR satellites of an opponent that support conventional military capabilities without threatening the opponent's nuclear C2 infrastructure, ability to detect nuclear missile launches,[50] or commercial or other interdependent satellite capabilities (e.g., weather satellites).[51] This is a marked difference from the past, when space systems were much fewer in number and military-related systems were

---

[47] First-strike stability is defined as the condition that exists when no state perceives another as motivated by the posture of strategic forces to launch the *first strike* in a crisis.

[48] Morgan, *Deterrence and First-Strike Stability in Space, A Preliminary Assessment*; Zhang, "Security Dilemma in the U.S.-China Military Space Relationship," 311–332.

[49] Pollpeter, "PLA Space Doctrine," 55–57; Morozov et al., "Space and the Character of Modern Military Activities."

[50] Carter, "Satellites and Anti-satellites."

[51] Morgan, *Deterrence and First-Strike Stability in Space, A Preliminary Assessment*.

tightly coupled to strategic nuclear stability. Since space threats in the future will not necessarily pose risks to nuclear escalation, as past strikes would have,[52] ASAT strikes will be a more credible option for coercing opponents at all levels of crisis escalation.

Second, technological developments—particularly the development of non- or minimal debris-producing ASAT options, as well as reversible ASAT options like jamming—will also strengthen the logic of ASAT strikes against space-enabled opponents. For example, there are several ways to theoretically attack satellites, either kinetically or nonkinetically, to minimize debris production, including jamming, coorbital attacks, cyberattacks, and directed energy attacks.[53] Even when using direct ascent hit-to-kill interceptors, attacks in space do not necessarily entail a debris-induced catastrophe for all space systems.[54]

Put differently, future ASAT threats are likely to be perceived as consistent with limited war constructs rather than as precursors to nuclear escalation. The ability to conduct limited and discrete strikes against an adversary's space systems without risking massive retaliation may make these strikes more likely. Former U.S. secretary of defense Ashton Carter recognized that such strategic developments were under way as early as 1986, when as an academic he published a seminal article presaging the current age of space-enabled warfare and the logic of ASAT weapons.[55] While the collapse of the Soviet Union put great-power politics and ASAT competition on hold for well over a decade, Carter's predictions now seem to be very much coming true.

To be sure, arms control proponents are today advocating treaty-based prohibitions on space weapons. In particular, China and Russia have proposed that the gridlocked Conference on Disarmament in Geneva negotiate an outer space arms control agreement, the "Prevention of the Placement of Weapons in Outer Space Treaty." But such proposals are fundamentally unverifiable and provide very limited utility for bolstering strategic stability.[56] Indeed, this treaty would technically limit the placement of weapon systems in orbit but would place no controls on ground-based ASAT weapons and contains only oblique calls for future transparency and confidence building measures to address the most complex problems of all: compliance and verification.[57] Others are advocating a space "code of conduct,"

---

[52] Carter, "Satellites and Anti-satellites."

[53] Wright et al., *The Physics of Space Security*.

[54] Bruce M. DeBlois, Richard L. Garwin, R. Scott Kemp, and Jeremy C. Marwell, "Space Weapons: Crossing the U.S. Rubicon," *International Security* 29, no. 2 (Fall 2004): 64–65, https://doi.org/10.1162/0162288042879922.

[55] Carter, "Satellites and Anti-satellites."

[56] DeBlois et al., "Space Weapons."

[57] "Treaty on the Prevention of the Placement of Weapons in Outer Space, the Threat or Use of Force against Outer Space Objects," Reaching Critical Will, accessed 31 January 2018, http://www.reachingcriticalwill.org/images/documents/Disarmament-fora/cd/2014/documents/PPWT2014.pdf.

which while well-intentioned will neither solve the verification problem nor constrain belligerents during a conflict. Without effective verification, there can be no meaningful arms control, on the ground or in space. It is unsurprising, therefore, that key spacefaring states continue to develop and test ASAT capabilities.

The Cross-Domain Character of Threats to Military Space Systems

To reiterate, the threat of attacks against military-related space systems is likely to be an inherent feature of future competition between space-enabled powers, because these systems are key enablers of advanced conventional warfare. These space capabilities will advance broader military-political goals, including deterring an adversary's intervention in a conflict, deterring escalation, and even increasing the likelihood of battlefield victory.[58] Military planners will be tempted to leverage such threats for tactical ends, and a technological trend toward more discriminate strike options could lower the risk somewhat that these strikes will trigger runaway conflict escalation.

Threats to military-related space systems can be based in all military domains, including land, sea, air, space, and cyberspace. Moreover, the ends these threats serve are likely to be cross-domain in nature. Space systems will be such attractive targets, after all, because they facilitate the systems and operational integration that undergirds advanced conventional warfare. The combination of these factors requires that credible deterrence against space attacks be considered in the context of cross-domain deterrence.

Less certain is whether it will be possible for states to deter attacks on their space systems, because of the strong incentives to strike first and because situational awareness and defense is extremely challenging. Nonetheless, it is imperative that policymakers and strategists work through these conceptual and technical difficulties, for as Forrest Morgan has argued, the stability of deterrence in space will be highly consequential for general conventional deterrence relationships. A failure of deterrence in space could prompt cascading deterrence failures across other domains, resulting in crisis escalation, even if the threat of nuclear escalation from space strikes is relatively less than that during the Cold War. By contrast, successful deterrence of space attacks could strengthen crisis stability.[59]

Since space is an inherently cross-domain environment and since competition in space ultimately serves terrestrial, geopolitical goals, aggression against space systems and the deterrence of this aggression will be an extension of activities in traditional

---

[58] Morgan, *Deterrence and First-Strike Stability in Space, A Preliminary Assessment*.
[59] Ibid.

strategic domains. The 2011 U.S. National Security Space Strategy recognizes these links when it cites cross-domain solutions as a means for enhancing space system resilience and leaves open the possibility that a "multilayered deterrence approach" might include cross-domain solutions.[60] Notably, in an article published during the same time frame as the 2011 National Security Space Strategy, James Finch and Shawn Steene, at the time director and deputy director of Space Policy and Strategy Development in the Office of the U.S. Undersecretary of Defense for Policy, argued that "the credible ability to carry out retaliation [for attacks against space systems] . . . includes all elements of national power in any domain. It need not, and should not, be limited to military actions in the space domain."[61]

Thus, deterring attacks against space systems, at least by threat of punishment, will probably require the development of credible cross-domain options to hold assets other than an opponent's space systems at risk. Deterrence-by-denial strategies will probably also benefit from attempts to leverage assets in multiple domains. For instance, the resiliency of space-based C4ISR capabilities could be bolstered not only by developing declared space systems held in reserve that are ready for quick launch but also by developing nonspace backups for space services, such as point-to-point forward communications and high altitude airborne ISR. Moreover, since the primary role of space systems is to collect and deliver information where it is otherwise impossible to do so, some form of cyber or electronic warfare may actually be the most attractive first-strike option against them (or to defend assets under attack).

Challenges of a Cross-Domain Deterrence Strategy for Space

Deterrence-by-punishment strategies aim to prevent an adversary from taking an undesired action by threatening costly retaliation for that action. Deterrence-by-denial strategies aim to prevent an adversary from taking an action by reducing or eliminating the adversary's ability to achieve its intended goals through that action. As outlined in table 6.2, states may use a variety of capabilities to support space deterrence—by which we mean deterrence of attacks against space systems in their own right, as well as the use of ASAT capabilities to manipulate broader cost calculations and thus support general deterrence goals in all domains.

---

[60] U.S. Department of Defense and Office of the Director of National Intelligence, "National Security Space Strategy."

[61] James P. Finch and Shawn Steene, "Finding Space in Deterrence: Toward a General Framework for 'Space Deterrence,'" *Strategic Studies Quarterly* 5, no. 4 (Winter 2011): 14, http://www.airuniversity.af.mil/Portals/10/SSQ/documents/Volume-05_Issue-4/FinchSteene.pdf.

Table 6.2 **Space-related capabilities supporting deterrence by punishment and by denial**

Space-related capabilities supporting deterrence

By punishment	By denial
Kinetic weapons (orbital, ground/sea/air-based)	Jamming (orbital, ground/sea/air-based)
Directed energy weapons (orbital, ground/sea/air-based)	Directed energy weapons (orbital, ground/sea/air-based)
Attacks on satellite ground stations	Disaggregation
Cyberattacks	Reconstitution
Economic sanctions	Active/passive protection
Space situational awareness (enabling offensive space control)	Space situational awareness (enabling defensive space control operations)
Behavioral/international norms	Behavioral/international norms

In a deterrence framework, the capabilities outlined in table 6.2 would support one of four missions: (1) offensive space control, (2) defensive space control, (3) space resiliency, and (4) space situational awareness. Offensive space control missions would seek to deter or defeat an attack in or from a variety of domains by denying an adversary's ability to use space and space systems for hostile purposes.[62] Defensive space control missions would seek to actively or passively deter or defeat attacks by blunting or denying an adversary's ability to damage or destroy one's own space systems.[63] Space resiliency would help bolster deterrence by denying the effects of space control attacks or ensuring that an adversary's gains via such attacks would be small or short-lived. Space situational awareness missions would strengthen deterrence by enhancing real-time knowledge of the threat environment and therefore the ability to anticipate and respond to threats.

Still, there is a significant difference between observing that deterrence of space attacks requires consideration of cross-domain dynamics and opportunities, and actually crafting a cross-domain deterrence strategy that incorporates space. Crafting a cross-domain deterrence strategy for space will be difficult, and a state seeking to deter attacks against space systems will face a number of key challenges in doing so, including the following.

---

[62] "Joint Publication 3-14, Space Operations," U.S. Joint Chiefs of Staff, 29 May 2013, accessed 31 January 2018, II-8–II-10, https://info.publicintelligence.net/JCS-SpaceOps.pdf.
[63] Ibid.

Determining what types of cross-domain threats will be credible. For example, terrestrial retaliation may not be credible against limited ASAT strikes, particularly against a near-peer competitor or nuclear-armed state or during the early stages of a conflict. Indeed, the threat to strike an adversary's homeland, which might also result in civilian or military casualties, in response to a counter-space attack in which nobody dies, might not be credible because such strikes could be sharply escalatory. This challenge would be particularly acute in the aftermath of an ASAT strike if one's adversary had few space systems against which to launch retaliatory strikes.

Determining what demonstrated capabilities are needed. Some ballistic missile defense systems may have the potential to destroy satellites, for example, but is simply possessing these capabilities enough to assert a credible ASAT capability or is it necessary to demonstrate such capabilities to establish credibility? A similar conundrum holds with space-based or ground-based nonkinetic capabilities; namely, in both cases it may be difficult to credibly communicate deterrence threats without some form of demonstration. Put differently, a vague cross-domain declaratory policy may be insufficient for communicating one's intentions and capabilities to an adversary without a demonstration of one's capabilities, which could itself be destabilizing.[64]

Understanding the operational requirements of communicating cross-domain deterrence messages and signaling resolve, credibility, and resiliency in real-time. What force posture and operational capabilities, demonstrated or not, will states need to credibly issue deterrence threats in real time? How can states effectively signal resolve and resiliency before and during a crisis? More research is needed in this area, perhaps drawing from historical case studies on cross-domain crises and using conflict scenarios to elucidate challenges and opportunities.

Clearly defining variables. Deterrence of space attacks is not simply a question of deterring attacks against space systems but is a challenge of deterring specific actors from conducting attacks against specific space systems using specific weapons. Consequently, the requirements for deterring near-peer competitors may be different from those for deterring a weaker regional power; the requirements for deterring destructive ASAT attacks may be different from those for deterring reversible attacks; the requirements for deterring debris-generating attacks may be different from those for deterring non-debris-generating attacks; and there may be very different requirements for deterring attacks against ISR, GPS, or NC2 systems or for using threats against space systems to support deterrence of terrestrial actions. In short, deterrence challenges are likely to vary greatly depending on whom one is trying to deter, what one is trying to deter, the tools one hopes to use

---

[64] James Lewis, "Reconsidering Deterrence for Space and Cyberspace," in Krepon and Thompson, *Anti-satellite Weapons, Deterrence and Sino-American Space Relations*, 61–80.

for deterrence, and the price one is willing to pay to ensure the credibility of one's deterrent threats.

Such questions highlight that many of the dynamics of space deterrence are still poorly understood. To begin with, satellites, much like drones, are inanimate objects, raising again the question of whether out-of-domain deterrence threats that endanger human life are credible. A related question is whether retaliatory attacks against the sovereign territory of an aggressor in space would risk further conflict escalation.[65] How escalatory would reversible space attacks like jamming be, as opposed to nonreversible ones like hit-to-kill? Leaders may claim that they will retaliate for attacks on their space systems, but what would be credible methods of retaliation for specific types of attacks? What would be the implications of deterrence failure for horizontal and vertical escalation?

Signaling issues are also poorly understood, including how signaling will function in space and for space assets. What types of signaling—both on the ground and on-orbit—will be stabilizing or destabilizing? This question is critical, because even capabilities like space situational awareness, which will likely be unevenly distributed between potential belligerents, could be potentially destabilizing. On the one hand space situational awareness capabilities can strengthen deterrence by denial by providing the ability to respond to events in real time, but theoretically they can also be exploited to manipulate uncertainty and target adversary systems, and so the development of certain space situational awareness capabilities might actually increase a state's paranoia about the space threat environment.

Another poorly understood issue is the impact of asymmetries in capabilities, goals, and interests on the success or failure of space deterrence. The variety of possible asymmetries here does not lend itself to easy prediction, and much will depend on each side's risk tolerance and willingness to escalate. For example, as discussed earlier, though it is commonly assumed that space-enabled power-projecting states would have the most to lose from an ASAT exchange and so would avoid being the first to launch such strikes, powerful, space-enabled states might actually have strong incentives in certain contingencies to strike first in order to protect forward-deployed forces and their command of the commons. However, while power projectors are more likely to fight farther away from home for ends other than national survival, regional defenders are more likely to fight closer to home, increasing the likelihood that losing a conflict could risk national sovereignty and regime survival, potentially impacting each of their relative risk tolerance and escalation propensities.

Moreover, although a weaker regional power might be relatively limited in its ability to execute space deterrence strategies as compared to a power projector, its space deterrence requirements might also be relatively less severe because it has

---

[65] Morgan, *Deterrence and First-Strike Stability in Space, A Preliminary Assessment.*

fewer or less capable on-orbit assets to protect and because its primary deterrence goal—preventing regional intervention by a stronger power projector—might depend only minimally on space systems for success. Although this scenario may at first suggest that the regional power, being least vulnerable, would be more likely to attack a powerful adversary's space systems first in a conflict, the implications of such asymmetries are actually far from clear. If the weaker power were to launch limited ASAT strikes early in a conflict to deter a power projector's intervention but fail to halt the power projector's advances, its only remaining options could be to launch a highly escalatory out-of-domain strike that gives the power projector a pretext and motivation to demonstrate its escalation dominance, notwithstanding the costs of doing so.

Even enhanced resilience of space systems and space architectures might not have straightforward implications for space deterrence scenarios. Resilience, though often touted as a stabilizing factor that enhances space security, might be destabilizing in some cases. Power projectors with highly resilient ISR and PNT systems, for example, might feel emboldened to conduct aggressive actions because they believe that they could operate through a limited ASAT attack at reduced cost. Consequently, increased resilience might actually increase the likelihood that powerful, space-enabled states will choose to strike first against an adversary's space systems, even though such states are commonly believed today to have the most to lose during an ASAT exchange. Thus, future studies should examine whether resiliency in some space capabilities (e.g., NC2) or orbital regimes (geostationary orbit instead of low-earth orbit) should be promoted while resiliency in others could be counterproductive.

We should also make a broader, final point about the cross-domain nature of space deterrence and space war. While this article has focused on deterrence of attacks against space assets, space-related systems play a vital role in deterring attacks in other domains. For instance, a space power's ISR capabilities may deter a potential adversary from taking action in other domains, such as air, sea, or land, for fear of being observed in the act and potentially thwarted or facing retaliation. This link between space deterrence and deterrence in other realms is also ill understood and should be addressed as part of the cross-domain deterrence challenge.[66]

In conclusion, incentives for launching limited attacks against space systems are on the rise, and states around the world are developing the capabilities to conduct such attacks. Since space is an inherently cross-domain environment—enabling operations in every other domain—threats to space systems and the deterrence of such attacks are likely to be tightly coupled with strategies and actions in other domains. A failure to deter attacks against space systems could precede and be an indication

[66] Ibid.

of general deterrence failures. Since the current state of space stability is fragile, and given the dependence of modern militaries on space systems and the increasing number of these systems being put on orbit, future studies on cross-domain deterrence must incorporate the space domain and address the many conceptual and operational challenges that operations in this domain present.

7

Air Power versus Ground Forces

Deterrence at the Operational Level of War

PHIL HAUN

After the introduction of atomic weapons at the end of World War II, Bernard Brodie noted: "thus far the chief purpose of our military establishment has been to win wars. From now on its chief purpose must be to avert them."[1] Since then, international security scholars have been interested in understanding how threats of violence could be used to prevent war. Deterrence introduces a selection effect into the study of war, as the threat of force causes a nation to reconsider whether to take military action; as a result, an avoided war remains unobserved. But even in the wars that do occur, the dynamics of deterrence apply once the fighting commences.

Military strategists have long understood the role coercion plays in war. Threats and acts of violence can either deter an opponent from taking an action it otherwise would or compel an opponent to stop or reverse an action. Carl von Clausewitz defined war in coercive terms: "an act of force to compel the enemy to do our will."[2] Not quite as obvious, yet worth examining, is how in war the threat or use of force can deter the enemy from its preferred course of action. In war, coercive force can be applied either within the same domain (i.e. land-to-land, air-to-air, etc.) or across domains (i.e., air-to-land, land-to-air, etc.). This chapter explains how an asymmetric advantage in power across domains may at times be so significant and place the enemy at such a disadvantage as to deter it from employing its otherwise favored strategy.

This chapter considers cross-domain deterrence (CDD), specifically how air forces can deter ground forces in a war.[3] The cross-domain advantage of air power

---

[1] Bernard Brodie, *The Absolute Weapon: Atomic Power and World Order* (New York: Harcourt, 1946), 76.

[2] Carl Von Clausewitz, *On War* (Princeton, NJ: Princeton University Press, 1976), 75.

[3] The asymmetric advantage of one domain over another is not limited to air forces against armies. The advantage that surface-to-air weapon systems hold against aircraft has long deterred air forces from employing air-to-ground weapons in the heart of weapons engagement envelopes, compelling combat

lies in its lethality against concentrated and maneuvering armies, as the North Vietnamese Army (NVA) discovered in the Easter Offensive and the Iraqi army encountered on the road to Al Khafji. While air attacks are most lethal against large mechanized formations in the open and on the move, such encounters are rare, as ground forces foresee the air threat and take measures to avoid catastrophic loss. It is, however, through the anticipation of what an air force can do that CDD works, by convincing the enemy not to employ two essential principles of war, mass and maneuver, denying its army the ability to mount an effective campaign.

There are limits, however, to an air force's ability to deter armies. Attacks are usually less effective in air-only offensives (absent friendly ground force) against an army that can conceal and disperse. The Serbian army deployed in Kosovo responded to air strikes by hiding its armor from view. For transportation, they used civilian vehicles largely immune from air strikes according to the rules of engagement of the North Atlantic Treaty Organization (NATO). Alternatively, an army may be able to fortify its positions to neutralize the effects of air strikes. In the final two years of the Korean War, the Chinese army took refuge in tunnels dug to avoid detection and provide cover from U.S. air strikes.

This chapter identifies the conditions under which air power is most lethal and therefore most likely to have the greatest CDD effect against ground forces. The thesis is that command of the air over the battlefield deters ground forces from massing and maneuvering, but the degree to which an air force can deter depends on the offensive or defensive posture of enemy forces, as well as four additional operational factors and four environmental factors. Operational factors that impact the projection of air power onto land include: the degree of air superiority achieved over the battlefield; the capability of an air force to locate, identify, target, and assess air strikes against ground forces; the composition of enemy's ground forces; and the presence and capability of friendly ground forces. Environmental factors include weather, lighting, terrain, and cover.

The chapter proceeds in five sections. First examined are the operational and environmental factors that detract or enhance air power against land forces. Second, a summary of coercion and military theory grounds the examination of air-to-ground CDD in war. Third, the Battle of Britain and the Easter Offensive are examined to demonstrate the success of air power in deterring armies on the offensive. Counter-examples of the Battle of the Bulge and the Battle of Quang Tri demonstrate limits imposed on air power by operational and environmental factors. Fourth, Germany's defense at Normandy and Iraq's defense in 2003 demonstrate how air forces, under

---

aircraft to fly at high altitude and to limit their time over target. Likewise, across the ground-to-sea domains it has been acknowledged that shore defenses tend to have the advantage over fleets. Lord Nelson's observation that "a ship's a fool to fight a fort" highlights the way the protection and firepower advantage of fortified positions can deter navies from projecting power ashore.

certain conditions, can deter an army from its preferred defensive strategy. Finally, the conclusion draws relevant lessons for CDD in war.

Operational Factors Affecting Cross-Domain Deterrence

Air Superiority

The threat to strike aircraft has a direct impact on the ability of an air force to project power onto land. The threat can come from enemy aircraft, from radar- and infrared-guided surface-to-air missile systems, and from antiaircraft artillery and small arms. The threat is multiplied if the enemy coordinates its weaponry with early-warning radars in an integrated air defense system. Air superiority over the battlefield, gained by neutralizing enemy air defenses, is prerequisite for effective air-to-ground operations and therefore also for CDD. An enemy is not likely to be deterred if it believes it can defend itself against air attack.

Since the Vietnam War, air-to-air engagements have been rare. Over the past twenty-five years, the air forces of the United States have quickly swept the skies clear of enemy fighters.[4] Although the destruction of surface-to-air missile systems has proven more difficult, the combination of electronic jammers and antiradiation homing missiles has neutralized the threat of all but the most sophisticated radar-guided surface-to-air missiles.[5] Defending against infrared-guided surface-to-air missiles, unguided antiaircraft artillery, and small arms has proven more difficult, as these weapons are cheap, easy to operate, and widely dispersed and pose a threat to aircraft operating at low altitude. To counter this threat, aircraft are flown above the threat envelope at medium altitude, a trade-off between aircraft survivability and lethality in air-to-ground attacks.[6]

Air-to-Ground Capability

Air superiority over the battlefield is only a prerequisite for effective cross-domain operations. To project power onto land, an air force must have the capability to locate, identify, engage, and assess strikes against ground targets. For this, it must have

---

[4] The U.S. air forces include those of the U.S. Air Force, the U.S. Navy, and the U.S. Marines.

[5] Russian double-digit surface-to-air missiles, the SA-10 and SA-12, introduced in the late 1970s, led to the development of stealth aircraft by the U.S. Air Force. The United States has yet to face these missiles in battle, but the development, at great expense, of fifty-generation aircraft with stealth capability is an indication of the lethality of the modern surface-to-air threat to air forces.

[6] For good discussion, see: Barry Posen, "Command of the Commons: The Military Foundation of U.S. Hegemony," *International Security* 28, no. 1 (Summer 2003): 5–46, https://doi.org/10.1162/016228803322427965.

integrated intelligence, surveillance, and reconnaissance assets, and aircraft outfitted with appropriate air-to-ground sensors, accurate weapons delivery systems, and a proper assortment of munitions. Equally important, an air force requires personnel well versed in "counter-land" doctrine, i.e., experienced with the unique challenges of attacking armies from the air.

Composition of Enemy Ground Forces

Another factor that determines how effective air operations are against armies is the composition of the enemy's ground forces. Armored units have a large footprint, with heavy weaponry and mechanized supply lines, both relatively easy to identify and attack from the air. By contrast, infantry units, guerrilla forces, and insurgency groups are much more difficult to locate, identify, and attack.

Stephen Biddle in his book *Military Power* argues that the increased lethality of the battlefield has become the dominant factor in warfare, and he discusses the importance of the composition of ground forces and how they operate. He identifies the *modern system* as a type of ground force employment that is a "tightly interrelated complex of cover, concealment, dispersion, suppression, small-unit independent maneuver, and combined arms at the tactical level, and depth, reserves, and differential concentration at the operational level of war. Taken together, these techniques sharply reduce vulnerability to even twenty-first century weapons and sensors."[7] The degree to which enemy ground forces are capable of utilizing such tactics to minimize exposure adversely affects the ability of air forces to project power on to land.

Friendly Ground Force Capability

The final operational factor for effective air-to-ground operations is the presence of a competent friendly ground force. Credible air and ground forces place the enemy army on the horns of a dilemma: whether to concentrate against an approaching army or to disperse and conceal its position against the threat of air attack. The lethality of an air force is multiplied when attacks are coordinated with a friendly army through a tactical air control system. Intelligence on enemy positions and the use of air force liaison officers to coordinate air and ground operations can vastly improve air-to-ground operations, as demonstrated by the South Vietnamese Army's dependence on U.S. air power to repel a superior NVA during the Easter Offensive of 1972.[8]

---

[7] Stephen Biddle, *Military Power: Explaining Victory and Defeat in Modern Battle* (Princeton, NJ: Princeton University Press, 2004), 2–3.

[8] Phil Haun and Colin Jackson, "Breakers of Armies: The Easter Offensive and the Myths of Linebacker I and II," *International Security* 40, no. 3 (Winter 2015-16): 139–178, https://doi.org/10.1162/ISEC_a_00226.

Environmental Factors

Weather

In addition to operational factors, one of the most significant variables affecting air operations is weather, particularly cloud cover and inflight visibility. Airmen early on developed instrument flying and navigational aids to conduct flight operations in adverse weather. Being able to fly under such conditions, however, and being able to locate and engage targets on the battleground are two entirely different matters. Effective air-to-ground operations require visual flight conditions. Low-level clouds and fog provide refuge for ground forces to operate immune from the threat of air attack. For example, low-level cloud cover over Germany during the winter months of World War II and over North Vietnam during the monsoon season largely negated the ability of the U.S. air forces to perform precision attacks. By contrast, clear skies and good visibility enhance an air force's ability to attack ground forces. The desert climates of Kuwait, Iraq, Afghanistan, Libya, and Syria have proven more conducive for air-to-ground operations than tropical or temperate environs. This does not mean that air-to-ground operations cannot be employed in inclement weather, however. In Vietnam, B-52s vectored by ground-based radar sites were able to deliver bombs onto North Vietnamese positions, and GPS-guided weapons now allow modern aircraft to accurately deliver through the weather. Still, such all-weather weapons have their limitations, as those who deliver them rely on others to identify targets, and subsequent strikes are only as lethal as the timeliness of the intelligence and the accuracy of coordinates allow.

Lighting: Day versus Night

Nighttime air operations have historically been less effective than daytime missions. So long as the enemy maintains light discipline, it is more challenging to locate, identify, and target enemy forces at night. Still, advancements in such technologies as night vision devices, low light sensors, infrared targeting systems, and air-to-ground radar and moving targeting indicators have enhanced nighttime air operations. One of the most successful aircraft for night operations has been the AC-130 gunship, a modified transport aircraft that utilizes an array of sensors to identify and engage ground targets with laterally mounted guns. In the past two decades, tactical air forces have also improved night operations by mounting infrared targeting pods on fighter aircraft flown by pilots utilizing night vision goggles. One advantage of night operations is that just as it is more difficult to find ground targets at night, it is more difficult for the enemy to locate and engage aircraft with unguided surface-to-air weapons. Yet even with improvements in sensors and a reduced surface-to-air threat, nighttime operations are still less effective than daytime ones under visual flight conditions, as it remains relatively more difficult to locate, identify, and attack an army in the dark.⁹

Terrain and Cover

In addition to weather and lighting, terrain plays a significant role in the attack of ground forces. Ideal terrain is flat, open, and featureless. Vertical changes in terrain have a pronounced impact on surface-to-surface operations by reducing line of sight visibility, but so too can it diminish air operations, as airmen do not operate directly overhead targets. Aircraft are instead offset to avoid threats and to be in a position to employ weapons. As a result, even minor changes in elevation degrade air operations, as such changes can break line of sight and thus mask enemy positions.

In addition to rapid changes in elevation, ground cover also affects the ability of an air force to engage an enemy army. Heavily vegetated or urban terrain provides cover for armies. By contrast, open deserts are better suited for air-to-ground operations, and it is not a coincidence that the United States premiere air-to-ground training ranges are in the Nevada and Mojave Deserts.¹⁰

The foregoing discussion underscores the fact that the degree to which power can be projected across the air and land domains depends on a number of operational and environmental factors. Any claim that air power will be able to deter ground forces must first account for these factors. Making generalizable, deterministic claims on the dominance of one domain over another is therefore inappropriate.

Coercion and Deterrence

Before proceeding to examine cases of CDD in war, it is first advisable to review the relationship between coercion and deterrence. Coercion is the threat or restricted use of force to compel an opponent to concede to demands.¹¹ Coercive demands seek to convince an enemy to stop or reverse what it is currently doing: to halt or withdraw its invading force.¹² By contrast, deterrent demands exhort an opponent

---

⁹ Interestingly, one of the least effective times for air operations is at dawn and dusk, where it is difficult to see targets on the ground, though not vice versa, and where there is too much light to operate night sensors.

¹⁰ The U. S. Air Force's Nellis Test and Training Range is in Nevada and the U.S. Navy's Naval Air Weapons Station China Lake is in California.

¹¹ Restricted uses of force are combat operations short of major ground operations (which are better understood as part of a brute force strategy) or unconstrained air campaigns against civilian populations, economic infrastructure, or national leadership. Restricted force can still be quite lethal, such as the thirty-four days of air strikes against Iraqi forces prior to the ground invasion of Kuwait or the seventy-eight days of air strikes in the Kosovo campaign in 1999.

¹² For further discussion see Robert Pape, *Bombing to Win* (Ithaca, NY: Cornell University Press, 1996), 4; Robert Art, "To What Ends Military Power?," *International Security* 4, no. 4 (Spring

not to change its current behavior: not to invade a neighbor or not to launch its nuclear arsenal. Though the cases considered in this chapter have been chosen to assess CDD, the logic also applies to cases of coercion.

For deterrence or coercion to work, threats of force must be credible. A military must have, and at times demonstrate, either the ability to defeat the enemy's military and thus deny it any hope of victory or the ability to punish the enemy by targeting what it values and thus increase its costs of war.[13] Air power deters when it threatens to deny the enemy army victory or to punish the enemy should its army take action.

Military Strategy—Command of the Heights

This chapter examines CDD during war, in particular how an air force can deter an army from its preferred strategy, thus placing the enemy at a disadvantage that reduces its likelihood of winning or increases its cost of continuing to fight. In *On War*, Clausewitz provides a good starting point for considering the advantage air forces have over ground forces in his brief chapter "The Command of the Heights."[14] Though Clausewitz is writing specifically about the advantages of ground forces on high terrain, his insights remain relevant for the air domain.[15]

Clausewitz asserts that the "high ground offers three strategic assets: *greater tactical strength, protection from access, and a wider view.*"[16] "Greater tactical strength" refers to the advantage accrued to the side that has gravity working for it. Not only does having gravity as an ally lend greater kinetic energy to one's weapons but also an attack from above improves the accuracy of weapons delivery, as it reduces the flashlight effect on weapons patterns.[17] Aircraft rely on a combination of gravity and

---

1980): 3–35, http://doi.org/10.2307/2626666; Thomas Schelling, *Arms and Influence* (New Haven, CT: Yale University Press, 1966), 69–91.

[13] For denial threats see: Pape, *Bombing to Win*. For punishment threats see: Schelling, *Arms and Influence*. Clausewitz identified these two coercive mechanisms of denial and punishment when he asserted that the [inability to carry on the struggle can, in practice, be replaced by two other grounds for making peace: the first is the improbability of victory; the second is its unacceptable cost." Clausewitz, On War, 91.

[14] Ibid., 352–355.

[15] Clausewitz was personally made aware of one of the earliest employments of air power in military operations. At the age of fourteen, he was in the Prussian army at the Siege of Maine in 1795 when the French Aerostatic Corps employed an observation balloon. Napoleon would disband the unit in 1799. Clausewitz does not, however, make any reference to observation balloons in On War.

[16] Clausewitz, *On War*, 353.

[17] Ibid., 352. The flashlight effect can be illustrated by taking a flashlight and shining it straight down at the ground. The light pattern is round, and the area covered is smaller than when holding the flashlight parallel to the ground. Likewise, bombs dropped from a level delivery have a greater bomb dispersal pattern than those dropped from a vertical delivery.

aircraft forward velocity to impart the energy required to get a bomb to the target. To overcome inaccuracies of level bombing, tactical air forces developed dive-bombing techniques, combining gravity with the downward vector of a diving aircraft to decrease the dimensions of the bomb dispersal pattern as well as reduce the errors associated with wind drift and bombardier aim point error. The development of precision weapons has further improved air-to-ground accuracy, particularly for aircraft operating from high altitude to avoid surface-to-air threats.[18]

The second advantage of commanding the heights is *protection from access*. The combination of *greater tactical strength* and *a wider view*, discussed next, gives air forces the ability to locate, identify, and strike attacking armies. Maneuvering armies are exposed, and their movements stand out in comparison to static surroundings. Movement of enemy forces solves the most difficult tactical challenge facing an air force: that of locating and identifying valid targets. Armies on the move have proven to be exceptionally vulnerable to air attack, for example the columns of Iraqi armor that were confronted en route to Al Khafji during the 1991 Gulf War.[19] Sun Tzu concurs with Clausewitz on the advantage of the heights in providing protection when he warns: "therefore, the art of employing troops is that when the enemy occupies high ground, do not confront him; with his back resting on hills, do not oppose him."[20]

The third advantage, *a wider view*, is perhaps the most obvious. Viewing the battlefield from above eliminates vertical obstructions that restrict the line of sight to surface forces. As a result, the cavalry, once the only eyes and ears of the army, has long been replaced by air- and space-borne platforms to provide integrated intelligence, surveillance, and reconnaissance (ISR). Even in Clausewitz's day, observation balloons were being experimented with to gain access above the terrain and deliver intelligence on the enemy's location and movement.

Clausewitz warns, however, against making too much of observation, as "the advantage of a wider view also has definite limitations. It will do no good where the lower ground is wooded."[21] Ground cover can obscure the view from directly

---

[18] For an examination of precision weapons directed by radio, electro-optical (TV), laser, and GPS guidance see: Paul Gillespie, *Weapons of Choice: The Development of Precision Guided Munitions* (Tuscaloosa: University of Alabama Press, 2009). For surface-to-air defenses, gravity restricts the ceiling for effective weapons employment. A firing solution for antiaircraft artillery against maneuvering aircraft is notoriously challenging, as a valid solution depends on aircraft altitude and airspeed and predicting the aircraft's flight path. Surface-to-air weapon's technology has, over the decades, been adapted to solve this problem through the development of rocket-powered missiles to increase range and altitude and the incorporation of radar and infrared guidance systems to improve accuracy with inflight target tracking. Antiaircraft artillery has also long relied on barrage and curtain fire to saturate the skies in an effort to overcome inaccuracies in its firing solutions.

[19] Phil Haun, *Coercion, Survival, and War: Why Weak States Resist the United States* (Palo Alto, CA: Stanford University Press, 2015), 61.

[20] Sun Tzu, *The Art of War*, trans. Samuel B. Griffith (London: Oxford University Press, 1963), 109.

[21] Clausewitz, *On War*, 352–353.

above. Armies take advantage of natural and artificial obscurants and employ concealment techniques to deny detection. For example, even though NATO had air superiority over Kosovo and reconnaissance drones flew persistently overhead, the Serbian Army was able to camouflage and conceal its armor using vegetation and humanmade structures.

Despite the limitations of observing from above, Clausewitz underscores the true value in gaining command of the heights: "in reality, the occupation is nothing but a raised arm, and the position itself only a lifeless tool, a mere potentiality that needs an object for its realization, a simple plus or minus sign without a value attached. The real thrust and blow, the object, the value is *victory in battle*. It is the only thing that really counts and can be counted on, and one must always bear it in mind, whether it be in passing judgment in books or in taking action in the field."[22] In the case of CDD, gaining air superiority is a necessary but insufficient condition. It is an air force's ability to then exploit the advantage in battle and the recognition by the enemy that it will be defeated that deters an army from massing and maneuvering, the subject considered next.

Mass and Maneuver

In *The Art of War* Sun Tzu observes the importance of the mass and maneuver of ground forces when he writes: "war is based on deception. Move when it is advantageous and create changes in the situation by dispersal and concentration of forces."[23] Mass and maneuver have long been requisite principles of war for successful military operations.[24] Mass allows an army to bring firepower to bear at the decisive point of the battlefield. Maneuver can produce mass with the concentration of forces and can project power with the movement of those forces.

The greatest asymmetric advantage of an air force with command of the skies over a battlefield is its ability to locate, identify, and attack concentrating and moving ground forces. This deters the mass and maneuver of troops and places an army at an enormous disadvantage in offensive operations and, under some conditions, in defensive operations, as considered in the next two sections.

---

[22] Ibid., 354.
[23] Sun Tzu, *The Art of War*, 109.
[24] *U.S. Army Doctrine Publication 3-90: Offense and Defense* (Washington, DC: HQ Department of the Army, August 2012), 5, accessed 8 February 2018, https://armypubs.army.mil/epubs/DR_pubs/DR_a/pdf/web/adp3_90.pdf.

Air Force Deterrence of Enemy Ground Offensives
The Battle of Britain

Gaining command of the air can create such adverse asymmetric conditions for an army that it may be deterred from taking action—for example, from launching a ground offensive. In the case of the Battle of Britain in 1940, the Royal Air Force (RAF) Fighter Command engaged and defeated the Luftwaffe in an epic air-to-air campaign. Though it never defeated the German army in battle, the RAF did deny the Germans air superiority over the English Channel and southeast England, as well as the secure sea lines of communication required to launch an invasion of England. It was a stunning aerial victory to be sure, yet its most important outcome was the deterrence of battle, an invasion that did not take place, as the Germans perceived that without air superiority they could not succeed against British air and naval power.[25] It is easy to dismiss the outcome of battles not fought. Clausewitz reminds us, however, that "possible engagements are to be regarded as real ones because of their consequences."[26] Just because the engagement of German troops by the RAF never took place does not mean that the battle was immaterial to the outcome of the war. Though the Battle of Britain did not end World War II for the British, it changed the nature of the war, as the British Isles were no longer threatened with invasion.

Commando Hunt and the Easter Offensive

Unlike the Battle of Britain, where command of the air deterred the German invasion, in other cases having air superiority may be insufficient to deter an army from launching an offensive, but having an asymmetric advantage in air power may still deter an enemy army from adopting its preferred strategy. This was the case with the North Vietnamese in the Easter Offensive of 1972.

In the Tet Offensive of 1968, the Viet Cong were decimated as an insurgent group. The U.S. Army then turned its attention from conventional warfighting to implementing policies known as "pacification" and "Vietnamization."[27] The defeat of the Viet Cong provided space for pacification to take hold, and by 1971

---

[25] Air power alone did not deter the German invasion of England. The Royal Navy, which had for centuries defended the British Isles, was a "fleet-in-being" that threatened sea lines of communication across the Channel. Obtaining air superiority was a prerequisite for the Germans to be able to defeat or deter the Royal Navy prior to an invasion. This case illustrates the interaction of CDD among air, land, and sea powers.

[26] Clausewitz, *On War*, 181.

[27] "Pacification" was a series of security and infrastructure improvement measures meant to garner support from the South Vietnamese population. Vietnamization was the policy of training and arming indigenous forces to take over the duties of the U.S. ground forces being withdrawn from South Vietnam.

these efforts had expanded the control of President Nguyen Van Thieu's government beyond Saigon. It was anticipated that by the end of 1972 the handover of both domestic and external defense duties would be complete. In 1971, the South Vietnamese conducted an interdiction campaign into Laos, codenamed Lam Song 719. Initially, the offensive worked well, as the South Vietnamese were able to cut off the Ho Chi Minh Trail. Soon however, significant numbers of North Vietnamese forces engaged the South Vietnamese. In the subsequent action, U.S. air power did not deter the North Vietnamese Army (NVA) from attacking the South Vietnamese Army (Army of the Republic of Vietnam; ARVN).[28] As a result, the ARVN forces took heavy losses as they were forced to withdraw from Laos. Following Lam Song 719, which the NVA considered a victory despite their own heavy losses, North Vietnam decided on a large-scale invasion of South Vietnam.

The judgment to invade in 1972 not only was based on the belief that the ARVN could be easily defeated but also arose out of a concern that Thieu's government was growing daily in power and gaining greater control over the countryside. North Vietnam's leaders believed they could not afford to wait until the United States had withdrawn. They decided to launch an offensive during the Tet holidays in January 1972, but due to difficulties in deploying forces, they delayed the start until the end of March, which coincided with Easter. Importantly, the emphasis for the planned three-pronged offensive shifted away from Saigon.

The North Vietnamese committed fourteen of its fifteen army divisions to the Easter Offensive. The primary attack had been planned to be deep in the south, in Military Region III, with the objective of taking Saigon. A second attack would take place in the Central Highlands of Military Region II, with the objective of cutting South Vietnam in half. A third attack would be in the north, just across the Demilitarized Zone in Military Region I in Quang Tri province. The North Vietnamese were deterred from this preferred strategy, however, by the impact of the U.S. air interdiction campaign along the Ho Chi Minh Trail.

United States air forces had been restricted from bombing North Vietnam following the Tet Offensive in 1968. With a decrease in Viet Cong and NVA activity in South Vietnam, the emphasis of air operations shifted to a series of seasonal air campaigns, codenamed Commando Hunt, against North Vietnamese operations along the Ho Chi Minh Trail in Laos and Cambodia. Commando Hunt could not completely stop the flow of supplies, however, and the inability of the U.S. Air Force to do so had necessitated ground incursions in Cambodia in 1970 and Laos in 1971. Still, the air interdiction campaign had hampered the movement of the NVA, deterring the North Vietnamese from commencing their invasion for several

---

[28] Friendly ground forces were not effective in integrating air power, as there were no U.S. military advisers or air liaison officers alongside South Vietnamese Army leadership. This was a result of the 1970 U.S. Army operation in eastern Cambodia to deny the NVA sanctuary. Once word of the operation reached Congress, further cross-border excursions by U.S. ground personnel were outlawed.

months and convincing them to shift the emphasis of their attack away from Saigon. They instead chose to make their primary attack along the Demilitarized Zone.

When the North Vietnamese launched the Easter Offensive, they met with success on the prioritized front, the attack on Quang Tri province (considered in the next section), but not in the central and southern military regions, where U.S. air strikes proved decisive. Had the NVA been able to place the weight of its effort in the south and had the same level of success as at Quang Tri, Saigon would likely have fallen and the war ended in 1972 instead of 1975.

As the Battle of Britain and Easter Offensive demonstrate, CDD by air forces against armies can not only deter the commencement of a ground offensive but also deter an army from its preferred strategy. In the Battle of Britain, the RAF's attainment of air superiority deterred the German Army from invading England. In the Vietnam War, although U.S. air superiority did not deter the North Vietnamese from carrying out the Easter Offensive, the Commando Hunt air interdiction campaign did deter the NVA from adopting their preferred strategy of placing their primary effort along the southern front aimed at Saigon.[29]

The next section considers two cases in which operational and environmental factors precluded air power from deterring an enemy's ground offensive.

When Air Forces Do Not Deter in War

As the cases in the previous section demonstrate, gaining command of the air or interdicting lines of communication can deter armies from launching an offensive or from following a preferred strategy. There are occasions, however, when operational and environmental factors can neutralize an air force's ability to project power onto land. In this section, two cases are analyzed in which CDD failed and an overwhelming advantage in air power did not deter ground forces from launching an offensive: the German counteroffensive in the Battle of the Bulge and North Vietnam's seizure of Quang Tri. Adverse flying weather, the enemy's utilization of terrain and cover, the composition of enemy ground forces, and effective enemy air defenses all contributed to the failure of CDD. The lessons from these cases help refine the contingencies for which air forces can deter enemy ground offensives by pinpointing the conditions under which aerial attack is less likely to be effective.

The Battle of the Bulge

The Battle of the Bulge, the December 1944 counteroffensive by the Germans to halt the Allied invasion, drove four German armies, totaling 200,000 soldiers, deep

---

[29] Ngo Quang Truong, *The Easter Offensive of 1972* (Washington, DC: U.S. Army Center of Military History, 1977), 13.

into the Ardennes in an effort to split the American and British armies, a combined force of 600,000. Superiority of the Allied air and ground forces did not deter the Germans from launching their ground offensive. Outnumbered, low on fuel, and facing Allied air superiority, the Germans relied on the element of surprise to gain an advantage. Operating from their homeland, the Germans employed telephone and telegraph communications instead of radio broadcasts, thus robbing the Allies of their Enigma intelligence. In addition, they concealed their positions during the day and moved only by night in order to avoid Allied aerial observation. The timing of the offensive, December 16, was chosen to coincide with predicted fog and poor flying weather, so that Allied air forces would likely be grounded.[30] The plan initially worked. Fog and low clouds prevented Allied aircraft from operating for nearly a week as the Germans pushed westward. When the weather did lift on 23 December, General Dwight Eisenhower ordered a counterattack. Air strikes targeted supply lines and attacked German troops on the move and caught out in the open. By the next day, the German offensive had ground to a halt.[31]

Cross-domain deterrence failed to prevent the Battle of the Bulge, as the Germans initially conceived of a way to negate the asymmetric advantage the Allies enjoyed in the air domain. Once the skies cleared, however, the advancing German Army again found itself vulnerable to the air attacks it feared.[32]

The Fall of Quang Tri

A second example of the failure of CDD comes from the Easter Offensive of 1972, when Quang Tri, the northernmost province of South Vietnam, fell to the NVA. The South Vietnamese leadership knew that the NVA were preparing for an offensive but were surprised when the NVA chose to invade across the Demilitarized Zone, open terrain where their armor would be exposed to U.S. air attack and South Vietnamese artillery fire. As with the Germans in the Battle of the Bulge, the NVA planned on launching the offensive under poor flying conditions in order to negate the effectiveness of air strikes. In addition, two operational factors contributed to the United States' inability to employ its air forces effectively: incapable South Vietnamese ground forces who were unable to integrate U.S. air strikes and only

---

[30] Danny Parker, ed., *The Battle of the Bulge: The German View: Perspectives from Hitler's High Command* (London, UK: Greenhill Books, 1999), 55.

[31] In addition to air superiority, several other factors contributed to stalling the German offensive. The Allied armies enjoyed a three-to-one numerical advantage; the Germans had a severe shortage of fuel; and the German offensive bogged down in the Ardennes with limited roads and overall terrain that favored the Allies' defensive positions.

[32] Peter Caddick-Adams, *Snow and Steel: The Battle of the Bulge* (Oxford: Oxford University Press, 2015), 260.

partial command of the air in the face of the potent threat from North Vietnamese surface-to-air weapons.

By March 1972, the United States had completed its policy of Vietnamization in Military Region I along the Demilitarized Zone. Freshly minted ARVN units, totaling 25,000 soldiers, now defended the region previously manned by 80,000 U.S. soldiers and marines.[33] These were up against two divisions of more than 40,000 NVA mechanized forces massed along the border. In addition to the removal of U.S. combat troops, the tactical air control system for Military Region I had also been handed over to South Vietnamese control. Vietnamization had brought a rapid expansion of the South Vietnamese air force, such that not enough qualified airmen were available to coordinate air strikes, particularly when a large number of U.S. tactical aircraft quickly deployed to support the South Vietnamese. When North Vietnam launched its offensive across the Demilitarized Zone into Quang Tri province, South Vietnamese forward bases along the border were quickly overrun. Bad weather and the loss of observation posts blinded the South Vietnamese, a limitation that combined with the inept indigenous tactical air control system to render U.S. air power incapable of stopping the NVA's tanks or silencing its artillery.

A second operational factor that neutralized U.S. air forces over Quang Tri was the lethality of the NVA's air defenses. Soviet-built SA-2 radar-guided surface-to-air missiles, previously used to defend Hanoi and other high-value targets in the north, were sent south. These were especially effective against the B-52 bomber. In high demand by U.S. Army commanders, B-52 Arc Light missions, controlled by U.S. ground-to-air radar stations, could drop massive amounts of bombs accurately through clouds and at night. This capability was withdrawn from Military Region I because the presence of the sophisticated Soviet missile system posed too great a threat. In addition to the SA-2s, the North Vietnamese deployed for the first time the SA-7, a shoulder-fired, infrared-guided, surface-to-air missile, which proved lethal to slow, fixed-wing observation aircraft, helicopters, and AC-130 gunships. The combination of SA-2s, SA-7s, antiaircraft artillery, and small arms negated the employment of the U.S. aircraft that were most capable of operating in marginal weather. Without U.S. air support, the ARVN quickly fell back, leaving Quang Tri to be overrun by the North.

As these two failed cases of CDD illustrate, a combination of environmental and operational factors can neutralize the advantage in air superiority even when enemy ground forces mass and maneuver and are the most vulnerable to air attack. In the case of the Battle of the Bulge, weather was the most significant factor in undermining the asymmetric advantage enjoyed by the Allies. While weather played a key role in the fall of Quang Tri, so did the strong composition of enemy air defenses and the inability of friendly ground troops to integrate air strikes.

---

[33] Ngo Quang, *The Easter Offensive of 1972*, 16.

Deterring Armies on the Defense

The previous two sections highlighted cases in which an asymmetric advantage in the air domain deterred or failed to deter an enemy army on the offensive. The Battle of Britain and the Easter Offensive demonstrate deterrence success: air superiority deterring an invasion and air interdiction deterring the enemy from its preferred invasion strategy. The Battle of the Bulge and the fall of Quang Tri illustrate the limits of air power for deterring ground offensives by highlighting the operational and environmental factors that negated an air force's ability to engage land forces.

This section switches gears to consider how an asymmetric advantage in air power can deter ground forces from conducting effective defensive operations. Of the operational factors, the one of most concern here is the presence of a friendly army capable of conducting combined arms operations that integrate air forces with the ground scheme of maneuver. An effective combined arms approach places the enemy on the horns of a dilemma, forcing it to choose between defending against air or surface attack. The preferred defense against air attack is to disperse and conceal ground forces, but against a land offensive, the conventional wisdom is to maintain a strategic reserve capable of concentrating and maneuvering wherever the enemy attacks. Air forces capable of directly attacking fielded forces deter the enemy from employing such a strategic reserve. The German defense of France in 1944 and the Iraqi defense of its own territory in 2003 illustrate the degree to which the domination of the air can, or should, deter an enemy's preferred defensive strategy.

Normandy and the Rommel versus Rundstedt Debate

In 1944, the Germans anticipated a combined British and American invasion of France. As such, the predominant question on the minds of German Army leadership was how best to defend against the Allied offensive. The conventional view, held by the commander in chief of the West, General Karl Rudolf Gerd von Rundstedt, was to hold a strategic reserve of panzer units that could be quickly brought forward to reinforce German troops wherever the Allies broke through. Rundstedt did not want to disperse all his forces along the coast, where a concentrated Allied offensive could overpower the Germans at any given point.[34]

Rundstedt's strategy only made sense, however, if the Allies did not control the air over France and their aircraft were not capable of delaying or destroying his reserves. General Erwin Rommel disagreed with Rundstedt and lobbied instead for a forward defense. Rommel had learned from the North African campaign that the Germans would not be able to mass and maneuver their armored units under the

---

[34] Dieter Ose, "Rommel and Rundstedt: The 1944 Panzer Controversy," *Military Affairs* 5, no. 1 (January 1986): 7–11, http://doi.org/10.2307/1988527.

threat of Allied air attack. He unsuccessfully lobbied for the leadership to decide that the Germans' best chance was to use all the ground forces available to fortify the coast. Rommel labored to build the Atlantic Wall, but he was unable to convince Hitler to overrule Rundstedt and forward deploy the panzer units held in reserve.

The case of the German defense of France demonstrates the degree to which command of the air can impact the ability of a defensive ground force to mass and maneuver. The German reserves, under constant air bombardment, were never employed as envisioned by Rundstedt, and the German Army failed to keep the Allies from establishing their beachhead on the Continent. This case is not an example of successful CDD, however, as Rundstedt still followed his preferred defensive strategy of maintaining an armored reserve. Under the circumstances, the strategy was flawed, as he, unlike Rommel, did not understand that Allied air superiority would render his reserve useless.[35]

Saddam Hussein's 2003 Defense of Iraq

A second case of an air force deterring an army from conducting effective defensive operations can be found in the 2003 Iraq War. Despite U.S. preparations for a ground war, Saddam Hussein refused to allow the Iraqi Army to prepare defensive positions at strategic choke points to protect against an invasion or to destroy key bridges or set fire to oil fields to delay the U.S. advance. Instead, Hussein adopted a ringed defense around Baghdad, aimed primarily at protecting his regime from domestic threats, including elements of his own Republican Guard. Only his loyal Special Republican Guard, a separate elite military organization, was allowed to enter the city.[36]

As for the threat from the United States, Saddam expected his cooperation with UN weapons inspectors to prevent U.S. military action. When this failed, he still expected the United States to initiate an air-only campaign and instructed the Iraqi Army to disperse, conceal, and dig in its equipment.[37] Instead, the United States launched a ground invasion on 20 March, and Iraqi conventional forces suddenly found themselves unable to concentrate; when their divisions did attempt to maneuver, they were destroyed by air strikes, or, out of fear of air strikes, entire units evaporated when soldiers abandoned their armored vehicles.[38] Hussein's strategy,

---

[35] Interestingly, had Rommel had his way and the Germans been deterred from maintaining an armored reserve and instead deployed these forces along the coast, this would have made the Normandy invasion even more difficult and costly for the Allies.

[36] Kevin M. Woods, Michael R. Pease, Mark E. Stout, Williamson Murray, and James G. Lacey, "Iraqi Perspectives Project: A View of Operation Iraqi Freedom from Saddam's Senior Leadership," United States Joint Forces Command: Joint Center for Operational Analysis, 2006, 27, accessed 8 February 2018, http://www.dtic.mil/dtic/tr/fulltext/u2/a446305.pdf.

[37] Woods et al., "Iraqi Perspectives Project," 110, 125.

[38] Ibid., 126.

which focused on defending against domestic threats and air strikes, left Iraqi forces ill prepared for the U.S. ground invasion.

Deterrence Failure against Defensive Forces

The defense of France by Germany and the defense of Iraq illustrate the ability of an air force to destroy, delay, and dissolve a conventional ground force that is attempting to concentrate and maneuver in defensive action. The key to both successful air operations, however, was the presence of a credible friendly ground force. Had the Allies not landed at Normandy, or had U.S. forces not invaded Iraq, the air forces would have been able to attrit, but not independently defeat, the enemy army. The presence of a capable friendly ground force has proven to be a critical factor in effective air attacks of fielded forces. Absent friendly ground forces, air power can be negated, as was the case in the Kosovo air campaign in 1999. In March 1999, NATO launched air strikes against Serbia, including attacks against Serbian forces deployed in Kosovo. In response, the Serbian forces conducted Operation Horseshoe, the massed expulsion of hundreds of thousands of Kosovar Albanians from their homes. Initially, poor flying weather precluded air strikes directed against Serbian fielded forces. When the weather did clear and U.S. airmen began to attack Serbian armored vehicles, the Serbs hid their mechanized weapons, exchanging tanks for civilian automobiles, and continued with their ethnic cleansing campaign. Indeed, the U.S. strategy had already ruled out the use of combat troops on the ground, thus leaving the Serbians to conduct their business with near impunity. When they finally were coerced into withdrawing from Kosovo, it was the rising costs imposed on the Serbian economy for continuing the war, rather than any military threat to Serbian forces operating in Kosovo, that brought them to accept a peace agreement.[39]

The NATO air forces failed to deter the Serbian Army in part because there was not a capable friendly ground force in Kosovo. The Kosovo Liberation Army (KLA), a brave but motley collection of Kosovar Albanian resistance fighters, never posed a serious threat to Serbian forces. In the one effort by the KLA to mount an offensive along the Kosovo-Albanian border, Serbian forces crushed the KLA attack even as U.S. attack aircraft circled overhead. The KLA and NATO were never able to coordinate air strikes in the manner that U.S. Special Forces would later do by embedding tactical air controllers with the Northern Alliance army in the defeat of the Taliban in Afghanistan in 2001.

[39] Haun, *Coercion, Survival, and War*, 130.

Though air forces can deter ground forces from concentrating in defensive positions, it is more difficult than deterring an army from taking the offensive and requires the presence of competent friendly ground forces.

Conclusion

This chapter has argued that the dynamics of CDD are relevant in the context of war and that an asymmetric advantage in air power can deter a ground force from taking actions it otherwise would, thus reducing an opponent's probability of victory. An air force is most potent when it can gain command of the air over the battlefield, its personnel are well trained and equipped in air-to-ground operations, and friendly ground forces are present to coordinate air attacks through a tactical air control system. A conventionally armed, mechanized army is most vulnerable to air attack when concentrated and maneuvering across flat, open terrain during the day and in the clear. Under such circumstances, air attacks can be devastating, prompting the enemy to disperse and conceal its army. As the actual destruction of an army by air strikes alone is rare, an air force more often affects the battlefield by deterring ground forces from taking offensive or defensive action. In certain cases, the air power advantage may be such that an enemy army suspends a planned offensive, as the Germans did in the Battle of Britain, or deviates from a preferred offensive strategy, as the North Vietnamese did in the Easter Offensive. In a defensive posture, as well, an army may be deterred from keeping its forces in reserve, as Rommel argued for in the German defense of Normandy. Or an enemy army may prioritize its defense against air attack over the threat of a ground invasion, as Saddam did by dispersing the Iraqi Army in 2003.

As this chapter has highlighted through numerous examples, the ability to deter ground forces from the air depends on whether operational and environmental factors dilute or negate an air force's ability to project power onto land. The relevance of CDD in warfare today and the future will thus be the result of the ability of air forces to mitigate, where possible, such operational and environmental constraints through the development of technology and doctrine, and through realistic training.

The U.S. air strikes over Syria and Iraq since 2014 illustrate the degree to which CDD has affected Islamic State of Iraq and Syria (ISIS) operations. Environmental and operational factors have been conducive for air operations. Under clear skies and over an arid desert terrain, U.S. air strikes quickly stopped the advance of ISIS forces across northern Iraq. With a permissive surface-to-air threat environment, experienced U.S. aviators with over a decade of combat experience in Iraq and Afghanistan expertly employed their advanced targeting pods and precision-guided weapons in lethal attacks against ISIS convoys. In response, ISIS halted its offensive, dispersed its forces, and retreated in order to constrict overly exposed lines of communication. It further morphed by abandoning its conventional, mechanized units and converting back into an irregular force. Without a capable friendly ground force, U.S. air power deterred ISIS from further expanding its control into Iraq.[40] As expected, however, air strikes alone were far less effective in offensive operations, as ISIS, absent a serious threat of ground attack, was free to disperse and conceal its movements. It was not until Kurdish Peshmerga forces launched their offensive in 2016 that U.S. air power again had success.[41]

Advances in technology may further enhance the ability of air forces to project power onto land. The development of remotely piloted aircraft has added persistence as one of the defining characteristics of the twenty-first-century air force. The ability to operate armed drones 24/7 simultaneously across multiple theaters throughout the Middle East has expanded the capacity of the U.S. Air Force to deter not only conventional armies but also insurgent and terrorist groups. This does not mean that air power alone will defeat or destroy these groups, but a consistent air presence has had a significant impact in the attrition and deterrence of Al Qaeda in Yemen, Afghanistan, Pakistan, and Somalia.

The effect of an asymmetric advantage in air power against ground forces goes beyond the physical damage of air strikes, restricting the options available to an army that must operate under the constant threat of air attack. Though dispersing and concealing forces may preserve an army from the direst consequences of air strikes, doing so deters it from concentrating and maneuvering, conducting offensive operations, and defending against ground attack.

---

[40] Nolan Peterson, "Waging the Tangled Air War over Syria and Iraq," *Newsweek*, 30 September 2015, accessed 8 February 2018, http://www.newsweek.com/waging-tangled-air-war-over-syria-and-iraq-378166.

[41] Even with integrated air operations, it still took nearly a year to dislodge ISIS from Mosul, and the western half of the city was left devastated.

8

Sea Power versus Land Power

Cross-Domain Deterrence in the Peloponnesian War

JOSHUA ROVNER

Cross-domain deterrence (CDD) describes efforts to dissuade a rival from action in one warfighting domain by threatening action in another. States may possess comparative advantages in one area—land, sea, air, space, or cyberspace—that they use to secure their interests and coerce their rivals. Comparative advantages in one domain may also help them make up for their own relative weaknesses in another. For instance, a maritime state without much of an army may deter a stronger land power if it can threaten to strangle its economy through blockade, or if it can raise the potential costs of action by using its control of sea lines of communication to transport and resupply its own allies on land. Conversely, continental powers may deter their maritime rivals from encroaching on their own interests and threatening their security by building formidable defenses and consolidating control on land.[1]

The most stable CDD obtains when rival powers do not need to make explicit threats. Bluster is unnecessary when asymmetric advantages are clear and overwhelming and crises are rare because mutual deterrence by denial acts as a constraint on both sides.[2] At other times, status quo powers may resort to explicit cross-domain threats in order to warn off potential challengers.[3] States may be tempted to indulge in revisionism when the asymmetric balance is murky or if they believe they have the ability to rapidly change the cross-domain balance. Status quo

---

[1] On the use of sea power to extract costs from continental powers see Julian S. Corbett, *Some Principals of Maritime Strategy* (London: Longmans, Green and Co., 1911). The early debate on the value of maritime versus land power is summarized in Paul Kennedy, *The Rise and Fall of British Naval Mastery* (London: MacMillan, 1976), ch. 7.

[2] Robert S. Ross, "The Geography of the Peace: East Asia in the Twenty-First Century," *International Security* 23, no. 4 (Spring 1999): 81–118, https://doi.org/10.1162/isec.23.4.81.

[3] Nuclear theorists have referred to this as the distinction between general and immediate deterrence. Patrick M. Morgan, *Deterrence Now* (Cambridge: Cambridge University Press, 2003).

powers may take steps to remind challengers of the dangers of pushing too hard, either by publicizing their superior capabilities or by warning of violence.[4]

Interest in CDD is part of a broader intellectual movement to revive the study of geopolitics, which treats strategy and international relations as a function of geography.[5] Geopolitical analysts assume that geography compels different kinds of behavior. States blessed with long coastlines and deepwater ports have incentives to invest in large navies, for example, while states with long and vulnerable land borders must focus on armies first. Not everyone agrees about the consequences of geography on strategy. States with opportunities for maritime expansion may develop stronger industrial and merchant communities who demand political accountability. Thus they tend to be more democratic, but they also push for grand strategies favoring aggressive expansion in order to capture foreign markets. Continental powers, on the other hand, tend toward autocracy and conservative grand strategies. Others argue that maritime powers are inherently less threatening; they have smaller armies, fewer resources for conquest, and little incentive to undertake it.[6] This debate indicates a growing interest in exploring the strategic interaction between states with forces designed to operate in different domains.

Traditional geopolitics thrived before and after World War I, a conflict preceded by a long peacetime competition between the leading maritime power and its aspiring rival on land. Germany's rise was characterized by ambition and fear. While it famously sought a "place in the sun" alongside the other imperial powers, it recognized that its rise as a major trading state made it vulnerable to economic warfare, especially because it had no way of stopping Great Britain from crippling its economy though blockade. Germany spent almost two decades trying to cut into Britain's naval lead through an ambitious battleship buildup. It did not seek to overwhelm British naval power; it simply wanted a strong enough navy to deter London from obstructing its own imperial project. Some observers worried that the Anglo-German naval arms race was a prelude to open conflict: as Germany grew its fleet, it feared less about British offshore balancing. Because the arms race threatened

---

[4] Saudi Arabia's recent spending spree on air power and missile defense is an unsubtle signal to Iran, which possesses a much larger population and army. As one analyst concluded, "the Saudi aim is to send a message especially to the Iranians—that we have complete aerial superiority over them." Roula Khalaf and James Drummond, "Gulf States in $123bn US Arms Spree," *Financial Times*, 20 September 2010, https://www.ft.com/content/ffd73210-c4ef-11df-9134-00144feab49a.

[5] Examples include Walter Russell Mead, "The Return of Geopolitics," *Foreign Affairs* 93, no. 3 (May–June 2014): 69–79, https://www.foreignaffairs.com/articles/china/2014-04-17/return-geopolitics; Sarah C. M. Paine, *The Wars for Asia, 1911–1949* (Oxford: Oxford University Press, 2012).

[6] Jack S. Levy and William R. Thompson, "Balancing on Land and Sea: Do States Ally against the Leading Global Power?," *International Security* 35, no. 1 (Summer 2010): 7–43, https://doi.org/10.1162/ISEC_a_00001.

to upset the previously stable cross-domain status quo, leaders in both countries attempted to stop it. Their efforts failed.[7]

Current interest in CDD is also fueled by the rise of China and the U.S. response. For many years the balance of capabilities was clear, and geography and technology combined to dampen the ideological rivalry between Beijing and Washington. China enjoyed the advantage of numbers and vast strategic depth on land, while the United States easily maintained maritime dominance in East Asia, buttressed by a network of offshore bases that helped project U.S. power and constrained Chinese ambitions. The United States would not risk a large war on the Chinese mainland, and China could not afford a blue-water navy. Since the 1990s, however, China has invested heavily in capabilities designed to reduce the United States' maritime position and make it more difficult for naval vessels to operate in the South and East China Seas. China's booming economy has enabled the kind of acquisitions—especially submarines and antiship ballistic missiles—that raise the cost of the United States' naval intervention in defense of its allies and partners in the region. This "anti-access" effort has subsequently led Washington to develop new operational concepts in order to ensure access and reinforce the land-sea balance that underwrote the postwar peace for decades. The fact that both sides possess nuclear weapons complicates the evolving military balance, and some analysts fear that nuclear escalation is possible if one or both sides decide to put CDD to the test.[8]

Fears about China spurred Pentagon interest in CDD. China's acquisition priorities appeared to threaten U.S. maritime dominance, which in turn called the regional balance into question. New technologies, particularly long-range precision missiles that could put U.S. warships at risk, were especially concerning. Other novelties potentially threatened the reliability of command and control networks the United States relies on to organize multiservice operations over vast spaces in maritime East Asia. Exotic tools like antisatellite missiles and offensive cyberweapons

---

[7] John H. Maurer, "Arms Control and the Anglo-German Naval Arms Race before World War I: Lessons for Today?," *Political Science Quarterly* 112, no. 2 (Summer 1997): 285–306, https://doi.org/10.2307/2657942. On German fears of blockade, see John H. Maurer, "A Rising Power and the Coming of a Great War," *Orbis* 58, no. 4 (Fall 2014): 504–507, https://doi.org/10.1016/j.orbis.2014.08.004.

[8] Caitlin Talmadge, "Would China Go Nuclear? Assessing the Risk of Chinese Nuclear Escalation in a Conventional War with the United States," *International Security* 41, no. 4 (Spring 2017): 50–92, https://doi.org/10.1162/ISEC_a_00274; Thomas J. Christensen, "The Meaning of the Nuclear Evolution: China's Strategic Modernization and US-China Security Relations," *Journal of Strategic Studies* 35, no. 4 (2012): 447–487, https://doi.org/10.1080/01402390.2012.714710; Joshua Rovner, "AirSea Battle and Escalation Risks," *Policy Brief* 12 (January 2012), https://escholarship.org/uc/item/08m367zt; Thomas G. Mahnken, "Future Scenarios of Limited Nuclear Conflict," in *On Limited War in the 21st Century*, edited by Jeffrey A. Larsen and Kerry M. Kartchner (Stanford, CA: Stanford University Press, 2014), 138–140; Paul I. Bernstein, "The Emerging Nuclear Landscape," in Larsen and Kartchner, *On Limited War in the 21st Century*, 111–117.

potentially compromised the intelligence and communications infrastructure that underwrote U.S. military power in the region. Innovative technologies seemed to be changing the balance.

Chinese military doctrine complemented its new capabilities. New Chinese thinking mirrored U.S. ideas about seizing the initiative and disrupting adversary communications. Early operational success in a conflict would help to overcome China's disadvantages by forcing its adversaries onto the horns of a dilemma: whether to try to recover from a crippling attack on command and control and put precious assets at risk in an effort to restore access and freedom of action in the Chinese littoral, or abandon the fight and accept China's terms. Such an approach held out the prospect of defeating the U.S. Navy without having to engage U.S. warships directly. In so doing, it would create uncertainty about cross-domain stability.[9]

This perspective may exaggerate the importance of modern technologies, however, because cross-domain competitions have gone on for centuries. Indeed, the paradigmatic case is the Peloponnesian War (431–404 BCE), which pitted the dominant maritime power against the dominant land power in the Greek world. As I discuss below, this ancient conflict is relevant for the U.S.-China standoff, suggesting that the underlying characteristics of the domains are more important than the vintage of the technology at work. If this is true, then CDD theory is more than a faddish reflection of contemporary policy debates. It may shed new light on very old cases in ways that open the aperture on current problems.

The cross-domain balance in ancient Greece was clear. No one really questioned Athens's naval mastery or Sparta's dominance on land. This was no accident. Both sides had spent decades concentrating on combat in their preferred domains and crafted grand strategies reflecting their comparative advantages. Athens built a naval empire that allowed it to extract revenue from distant colonies and tributary allies that it then used to build more and better warships. The need to patrol over vast distances also put a premium on skilled rowers and captains, which reinforced Athens's lead in technology and numbers. At the start of the war, Athens had about 300 seaworthy triremes—elaborate and expensive three-tiered rowing galleys that were the ships of the line in the Greek world—as well as many others that were capable of repair. This was more than twice the number of the second strongest naval power in Greece, Corcyra, which had about 120. In theory, the Athenian treasury could be used to build thousands more, though it faced a familiar budgetary trade-off between procurement and readiness: the high cost of paying for rowers meant that Athens would struggle to simultaneously fight a war and increase the size of its navy. Its annual imperial revenue plus its existing war chest gave it the ability to fight for about three years, assuming that it made no changes in what it demanded from

---

[9] For an excellent recent survey of Chinese doctrine, see: Joe McReynolds, ed., *China's Evolving Military Strategy* (Washington DC: Jamestown Foundation, 2016).

allies or what sacrifices it was willing to make at home. The war went on for much longer, of course, and in fact Athens did have to increase its requirements from tributary allies, levy new taxes, and even melt down gold statues to cover ship losses and pay crews. It was also able to call on private citizens to sponsor new triremes, as it did in the massive and rapid fleet buildup before the ill-fated Sicilian Campaign (415–413 BCE).[10]

Despite these problems, Athens was far superior to any other naval power. The nearest possible competitors were Corcyra and Corinth, both of which maintained 100–120 triremes.[11] (In fact, Corcyra was richer and stronger at sea than Corinth, and when it joined Athens at the beginning of the war, it only increased Athens's overall naval lead.)[12] Sparta could muster about 100 ships but possessed few competent ship captains, rowers, or steersman.[13] It only had one serviceable port, Gythium, which was more than thirty miles from Sparta itself. Few Spartan leaders understood the relationship between money and maritime power, and the peculiarities of their political economy blocked their efforts to build navy. For example, Sparta used heavy iron spits rather than coins for its currency, based on its belief that coinage was corrupting. This made it difficult to attract mercenary crewmen.[14]

There were good reasons why Sparta never invested much time or effort in building the kind of navy that could challenge Athens. Sparta's economy relied on a large slave population that allowed the Spartans to devote themselves to military training and service. Unlike the Athenians, however, the Spartans had very little interest in projecting power outside the Peloponnese, fearing that the prolonged absence of Spartan soldiers would inspire slave uprisings. So Sparta's military was focused almost exclusively on heavy infantry and perfecting the art of phalanx tactics. Spartans drilled from an early age and learned to obey orders efficiently, which helped commanders to choreograph rapid maneuvers even in the confusion of battle. As a result, Spartan hoplites gained a reputation for extraordinary courage and ruthlessness. And because Sparta never took its own navy seriously, it could spend the bulk of its resources fielding the largest army in Greece, which was at least two to three times the size of Athens's ground force. Plutarch estimates that the army that invaded Attica in 431 BCE was 60,000 strong, while Athens could only

---

[10] Lisa Kallet-Marx, *Money, Expense, and Naval Power in Thucydides' History 1–5.24* (Berkeley: University of California Press, 1993); Donald Kagan, *The Peloponnesian War* (New York: Penguin, 2003), 60–62, 452; Victor Davis Hanson, *A War Like No Other: How the Athenians and Spartans Fought the Peloponnesian War* (New York: Random House, 2005), 27.

[11] Robert B. Strassler, ed., *The Landmark Thucydides* (New York: Free Press, 1996), 17; Kagan, *Peloponnesian War*, 27.

[12] Kallet-Marx, *Money, Expense, and Power*, 74.

[13] Kagan, *Peloponnesian War*, 59.

[14] Later in the war, Sparta loosened up this practice and, in the last years of the war, made inroads against the Athenian navy by buying its rowers with promises of better pay. Hanson, *War Like No Other*, 23. On Spartan ignorance, see: Kallet-Marx, *Money, Expense, and Power*, 85–87.

mobilize about 10,000 soldiers at any time during the war.[15] Though this number is probably high, it does reflect the consensus at the time that Sparta's army was bigger and more powerful than any other city-state by a wide margin. Boeotia had the next best army in terms of training, equipment, and size (7,000–12,000 soldiers) and was Sparta's ally.[16]

These cross-domain asymmetries were clear to all when the fighting began. Athens was dominant at sea but disadvantaged on land. Sparta's army could beat the whole of Greece in a single battle, as the Athenian leader Pericles admitted, but it had a small navy led by inexperienced captains and unskilled crews.[17] If cross-domain theory tells us anything new about deterrence, it should tell us something about the Peloponnesian War. A close examination of the war might also say something new about the theory.

The following analysis explores the causes and conduct of the war in terms of CDD. I find that deterrence failed when both sides wanted it to succeed; and succeeded when both sides wanted it to fail. Cross-domain deterrence failed to prevent the war because the two sides believed they could overcome their asymmetric disadvantages through alliances and arms racing. The disastrous first few years of the war proved these beliefs to be wrong, and both sides grudgingly admitted that cross-domain asymmetries were facts of life. Because neither side was willing to challenge the other on its favored domain, however, a decisive battlefield victory became impossible. Athens repeatedly tried to lure Sparta into fleet-on-fleet engagements, and Sparta repeatedly tried to bait Athens into pitched battle. Both were frustrated. Cross-domain asymmetries deterred each side from attacking the other's center of gravity, that is, neithermeaning they could not engineer the kind of confrontation that might have forced the other to capitulate.

Cross-Domain Deterrence before the War

The Peloponnesian War, as Thucydides describes it, was the second major conflict between Athens and Sparta in the fifth century BCE. The first ended in 445 after fifteen years of fighting. That war was essentially a draw, and the peace treaty reflected military realities. Decisive victory was impossible, writes Donald Kagan, because "the sea power had been unable to sustain its triumphs on land, and the land power had been unable to prevail at sea."[18] Why did the peace break down, given that these same asymmetries were in place in 431? Why did Athens and Sparta go back to war?

---

[15] Kagan, *Peloponnesian War*, 57–60.

[16] Boeotia defeated Athens soundly at Delium in 424. See: Strassler, *Landmark Thucydides*, 272–278. For an estimate of the size of the Boeotian infantry see: Hanson, *War Like No Other*, 22.

[17] Kagan, *Peloponnesian War*, 57–58.

[18] Ibid., 19.

Thucydides famously said that the answer lay in Sparta's fear of growing Athenian power. The dominance of Athens over the Delian League—the association of Athens and its allies—created new dangers for Sparta during the tail end of the Pentecontaetia (479–431), a period that began with a Greek alliance against the invading Persian Empire and ended with war among the Greek great powers. Athens invested revenue from its maritime trading empire into its growing navy, creating a virtuous circle of economic and military might. It also bolstered its relative power in the Delian League by offering naval protection in return for annual tribute. This was tolerable to the Spartans, writes Thucydides, until "their own confederacy became the object of its encroachments."[19] The Spartans were concerned that there was no obvious end to the Athenians' ambitions, however much they claimed to be interested in peace. The proximate causes of the war were simply the pretext for Sparta's efforts to break out of the Athenian trap. Failure to act would leave Sparta permanently encircled and vulnerable.

This argument is plausible, although Spartan hawks did not spell out their own logic in detail. Corinth, not Sparta, made the clearest explication of this kind of preventive war logic, and the Corinthians had obvious reasons to exaggerate the threat in order to convince Sparta to come to their rescue. Nonetheless, their arguments were convincing. The Spartans went to war on a voice vote following a short statement from one of their political leaders, who simply argued that the Athenians were "injuring our allies and the Peloponnesus." Since the long-ago war with the Persians, they had changed from loyal Greeks into self-aggrandizing tyrants.[20]

If Thucydides is right that fear motivated Sparta's decision to fight, then left unexplained is why Spartan hawks were so confident that they could win a quick victory. They should have been less confident. If anything, Athens had solidified its maritime dominance, and the long walls around Athens made the city invulnerable to the Spartan infantry. If Sparta chose to fight under these conditions, it risked hastening its own demise. And even though Athens enjoyed clear economic advantages, war with Sparta appeared to violate the basic precepts of Athenian grand strategy, which was based on growing its navy and expanding its maritime reach. Defeating Sparta meant undermining its land power, but the Athenians had neither the desire nor the capability to fight the Spartan phalanx. Why, then, did both sides take the risk of war in 431? Why were they both confident of a quick decisive victory, despite their comparative weaknesses?

Cross-domain deterrence theory suggests an answer. While the Spartans certainly worried about Athens's increasing reach, the proximate cause of the war was Athens's concern about the breakdown in cross-domain stability. Athens feared a sudden shift in the naval balance that would erode its maritime mastery, and Spartan

---

[19] Strassler, *Landmark Thucydides*, 65.
[20] Ibid., 48.

hawks convinced themselves that they could muster a sufficient fleet through alliance diplomacy and arms racing, all the while forcing Athens to fight on land.

The prelude to the war was a crisis between Corcyra and Corinth, two medium-sized powers whose combined navies equaled about 75 percent of the Athenian fleet. In the wake of a rapid Corinthian naval buildup in 433–432, neutral Corcyra turned to Athens for assistance and a place in the Athenian alliance. Corcyra promised that a combined fleet would represent the union of the two dominant navies in the Greek world, which would be extraordinarily important if Sparta chose to make war. But Corcyra also warned Athens that if it lost the war, Corinth would bring the combined Corcyran-Corinthian fleet to the Spartan-led Peloponnesian League, which could then challenge Athenian naval mastery.[21]

Not surprisingly, Corinth attempted to block the alliance between Corcyra and Athens while simultaneously appealing to Sparta for assistance. Playing on Spartans' fears that Athens was implementing "a program of universal empire," Corinth warned Sparta that if it did not ally with a strong naval power, then Sparta would be "weaker and less terrifying to a strengthened enemy." At the same time, the Corinthians offered a number of ways the Spartans could overcome their disadvantages. These included the opportunity to encourage uprisings in Athens's restive colonies and allies, an approach that held out the promise of reducing Athens's resources. Corinth also promised that a combined Peloponnesian League fleet could challenge Athens at sea. This would force Athens to think twice, because its grand strategy relied on unquestioned naval mastery and, as the Corinthians put it, "a single defeat at sea is in all likelihood their ruin."[22] In short, both Corcyra and Corinth were playing on each of the great powers' fears that its security, which had been based on overwhelming command of a single domain, might disappear.

Not all observers believed that the balance was fragile or that war made much sense. Corinth had obvious reasons to exaggerate the danger to Sparta, leading some Spartans to reassess the balance for themselves.[23] Chief among these was King Archidamus, who provided a thorough and prescient net assessment during the Spartan assembly's debate before the war. He stressed that Athens was wealthy and dominant at sea. Its naval mastery would allow it to open up new theaters of its choosing, which would make it well-nigh impossible for Sparta to force a decisive

---

[21] Thucydides, *History*, 1.32–1.36.

[22] Strassler, *Landmark Thucydides*, 69, 24, 67. Compare this to Winston Churchill's description of Admiral John Jellicoe in World War I: "the only man on either side who could lose the war in an afternoon." Winston S. Churchill, *The World Crisis, 1911–1918* (1931; reprint, New York: Free Press, 1993), 602.

[23] To compel Sparta into the war, Corinthian ambassadors warned Sparta that Athenian naval power would be unbeatable and that Spartan credibility would evaporate. To deter Athens from entering the war, the Corinthian ambassadors blustered that even a combined Athenian/Corcyran navy would only provide a temporary advantage.

victory. In addition, Sparta's army could not overcome the long defensive walls that protected Athens and its route to the port of Piraeus. He also reminded his colleagues of Sparta's advantages, especially its army, which was the ultimate guarantor of its sovereignty. For those reasons, Archidamus believed that a war would be a costly stalemate at best, and he encouraged patience and restraint and recommended that Sparta slowly build up its own resources rather than rushing into a conflict that was neither necessary nor wise.[24]

His colleagues were not persuaded. Thucydides does not spend much time explaining why not, except to reiterate that they were simply frightened of growing Athenian power. This is certainly plausible, given that by this point Athens had mastered the art of translating naval expertise into commercial expansion. Athenian revenue was growing alongside its fleet, and if the Spartans believed that the next war would resemble the last one—a protracted war of attrition—then it made sense to fight now rather than later. But the Spartans did not make this case. At best, they hinted at it before they voted by acclamation to go to war. A more complete explanation, based on the speeches and commentary in Thucydides's text, is that they were simultaneously fearful and hopeful about the end of cross-domain stability. If Athens helped Corcyra destroy Corinth, it would have no naval challengers, and in that case there would be nothing to stop it from isolating Sparta on the Peloponnese and cutting off its grain supply. Nor would Sparta be able to stop Athens from going on a genuine imperial mission. From 445 to 431 BCE, Athens had not acquired any new territory, and its one quasi-colonial project was the establishment of a pan-Hellenic colony at Thurii. Spartan leaders may have been concerned that an unfettered Athens, having disposed of Corinth, would dispense with the fiction that it was anything other than an empire. The Spartans also seem to have believed that the Athenians' ruthless suppression of revolts in the Delian League foreshadowed similar efforts against their own allies.

Yet Sparta also seem to have believed that it could tilt the cross-domain balance in its favor. First, if Corinth could overcome Corcyra, the result would be a Peloponnesian navy not terribly smaller than Athens's own. Spartan leaders seem to have been extraordinarily naïve about the requirements for naval warfare. They failed not only to understand the financial requirements of building and maintaining a fleet, but also to appreciate the demands of recruiting able and skilled seamen, while developing the operational skills and command and control arrangements needed to maintain order and discipline during chaotic naval melees. The Sparta had spent decades cultivating these skills on land but practically no time thinking about what it would take to fight effectively at sea. In the first few years of the war, Athens demonstrated that it could beat Sparta even when it was fighting with fewer triremes, but Sparta had not yet learned this lesson. Second, Sparta hoped to secure

---

[24] Strassler, *Landmark Thucydides*, 45–47.

an alliance with Persia, which could provide the resources for a rapid buildup of triremes. The fact that the balance seemed increasingly precarious opened up new possibilities for Sparta's security, including some kind of preventive naval deployment to insulate itself against future Athenian aggression. The logic of Sparta's grand strategy was not exactly clear on this point, but it did seem to be driven by a kind of zero-sum logic: any relative decrease in Athenian naval power meant that much more security for Sparta.

Corcyra's appeal to Athens also played on a combination of fear and greed. Doubts about cross-domain stability created new dangers and new opportunities. The danger, of course, was that Athens stood to lose its wide margin of superiority at sea, which was the foundation of its grand strategy and its economy. The opportunity was the chance to strengthen its lead by allying with a medium-sized fleet, thus ensuring its security and prosperity indefinitely. Corcyra's envoys understood the Athenians' naval fixation and urged them to focus on their comparative advantage instead of wasting time and resources trying to challenge the Peloponnesian League on land. "There is a wide difference between declaring the alliance of an inland and of a maritime power," they declared. "Your first endeavor should be to prevent, if possible, the existence of any naval power except your own; failing this, to secure the friendship of the strongest that does exist."[25]

The Athenians ultimately decided to form a defensive alliance with Corcyra, which called for mutual support in the case that one or the other was attacked. The Athenians also took steps to alleviate Spartan concerns, sending only a token fleet to assist Corcyra and putting it under the command of Lacedaemonius, whose father was the famously pro-Sparta Cimon and whose name meant "Spartan." These steps seemed to reinforce the basic cross-domain asymmetry that had dominated Greek politics for decades, while also assuaging Sparta concerns about Athenian intentions. The Athenian leaders hoped that combining implicit threats and explicit reassurances would encourage Sparta to back down.

Why did CDD fail? Thucydides does not provide a full explanation, but some have argued that the Athenians' decision made matters worse.[26] According to this logic, any kind of alliance with Corcyra was bound to cause fear in Sparta. But while the alliance certainly did so, the defensive conditions of the agreement and the Athenians' tepid follow-through meant that the alliance didn't cause *enough* fear. Indeed, the alliance deterred neither of its adversaries. Corinth sponsored a revolt by Potidea in 432, which caused the Athenians to worry that other colonies might also defect. The Sparta agreed to attack Attica over land if the Athenians attacked

---

[25] Ibid., 24.

[26] For background and an explanation of Athens's decision, see: Donald Kagan, *The Outbreak of the Peloponnesian War* (Ithaca, NY: Cornell University Press, 1969), 222–250. Kagan ultimately criticized this decision and treated it as a cautionary tale about the dangers of "minimal deterrence." Donald Kagan, *On the Origins of War and the Preservation of Peace* (New York: Doubleday, 1995), 41–48.

Potidea; the Athenians decided to lay siege anyway, and Sparta invaded Attica the next year.

All of this suggests that the balance of capabilities in a crisis may not be sufficient for CDD to hold without explicit threats. There are two related possible reasons why. One is that implicit cross-domain signals carry too little information to be persuasive to the target.[27] It may be unclear, for example, *how* a rival army can overcome its relative disadvantages and threaten the core interests of a naval power, especially if that naval power believes that it can work around its rival's comparative advantages. In addition, a selection effect might be at work, because states are more likely to provoke a crisis if the cross-domain balance seems to have already started breaking down. Unambiguous threats may be necessary, if not sufficient, in these cases.

Neither Sparta nor Athens was eager for war, and both needed to be cajoled by smaller allies to start fighting. Leaders on both sides were also well aware of their weaknesses. Yet they convinced themselves that cross-domain asymmetries were not insurmountable. As noted, the Sparta believed that new allies could deliver critical resources and that efforts to provoke rebellions could undermine the Athenian empire without having to stare down the Athenian fleet. Likewise, the Athenians were tempted by the possibility of open-ended naval mastery through an alliance with Corcyra, which would allow them to coerce Sparta without having to face a Spartan phalanx. Pericles based his strategy on the belief that naval advantages trumped land advantages. A dominant fleet would allow Athens to find new resources, while Sparta, which could hardly project power, faced the risk of starvation and could not fight a long war. Finally, a navy could do more than simply fight other navies, because it could deliver and resupply land forces for raiding Sparta's allies and stir up insurrection among the slaves of the Peloponnese. As he put it, "our naval skill is of more use to us for service on land, than their military skill for service at sea."[28]

Cross-domain deterrence failed even though Athens and Sparta both wanted it to succeed. Neither was clamoring for conflict, and presumably each would have been satisfied if its rival had been deterred by superior asymmetric capabilities. But key leaders worried that shifting alliances made the balance tenuous, and by 431 both were convinced that war was inevitable. Indeed, one of the most striking aspects of the prewar speeches is the growing sense that deterrence was increasingly irrelevant, despite the fact that all agreed about the basic cross-domain balance.[29]

Shifting alliances, however, also convinced each side that finding new coalition partners could help it overcome its rival's comparative advantages. The Spartans believed that they could engage in a naval arms race if they had Persian resources;

---

[27] I thank Barry Posen for making this point.
[28] Strassler, *Landmark Thucydides*, 82.
[29] Ibid., 22–23, 27–28, and 41–43.

the Athenians believed that if they had Corcyra's support they could deny Sparta basic resources. Finally, each side thought that it could craft strategies that would force its enemy to fight in its preferred domain. The Athenians' strategy was to stay behind their city walls and use their navy to harass the Peloponnese, instigate a slave rebellion, undermine the Spartan economy, discredit the Spartan war party, and force Sparta to admit the impossibility of winning. The Sparta's' strategy was to invade Attica and ravage the land, baiting the inferior Athenian infantry to come out from behind its city walls and fight a pitched battle.

These strategies failed. Neither Athens nor Sparta took the bait. Both were extremely cautious when it came to facing the enemy on its own terms, and both sides routinely fled rather than fight in an unfamiliar domain. Cross-domain deterrence took hold early in the war, causing political and military leaders to avoid the kind of battles that might have ended it.

Cross-Domain Deterrence during the War

Prewar hopes of a roundabout victory did not last long. The Athenians and Sparta learned painful lessons in the early years of the conflict that demolished their belief that they could win without confronting their enemy's center of gravity. Both attempted something like what Liddell Hart called the "indirect approach," with disappointing results.[30]

Athens's strategy was based on evacuating Athenians from the countryside and sheltering them behind the city walls, while the Athenian navy pressured Sparta by raiding the Peloponnese in the hope of provoking a slave revolt. One problem with this strategy was that it transformed the city of Athens into a crowded, oppressive, disease-ridden place full of distraught citizens who had been forced to leave their farms open to the Spartan invaders. Sparta hoped that public pressure would compel Athens's leaders to mobilize an army for battle outside the city walls. In other words, Sparta hoped to bait the Athenian leader Pericles into abandoning his conservative strategy and fight on Spartan terms. But Pericles had ways of relieving public pressure without taking the bait. In order to satisfy public desire for action without challenging the Spartans directly, he mobilized a large army—the largest in Athens's history—in a campaign to ravage the land around Megara, Sparta's ally. The sight of 10,000 Athenian hoplites in action seems to have inspired his fellow citizens and bought their continued support, but the campaign itself achieved very little.[31]

Sparta suffered the same fate the next year, when it launched a hopeful but ill-conceived naval expedition. Like the Athenians when they marched to Megara,

---

[30] B. H. Liddell Hart, *The Strategy of the Indirect Approach* (London: Faber and Faber, 1941).
[31] Strassler, *Landmark Thucydides*, 109–110.

the Spartans sought to attack Athens's allies without confronting its main source of power, and the expedition was predictably futile. Things went from bad to worse for Sparta's fledgling navy in 429, when a combined Spartan/Corinthian fleet was routed at Naupactus, despite enjoying a large local advantage. The Peloponnesians brought forty-seven ships to battle against twenty Athenian triremes, but the Athenian captains were vastly more experienced and skilled, and the Peloponnesian force fell into disarray at the first sign of trouble. The Sparta may have believed that a dramatic naval victory would destroy the image of Athenian naval dominance and convince Persia to enter the war on Sparta's side, but Athens's victory reinforced the its reputation of Athens. Sparta also hoped to partner with Corinth and build a force capable of large amphibious offensives, but "the first major Peloponnesian effort at an amphibious offensive had ended in humiliating failure."[32]

Sparta's naval incompetence affected its strategy in other ways. In 430 Sparta attempted to contact Persia for assistance in building a 500-ship fleet. The idea itself was delusional, given that Sparta lacked the port facilities, knowledge, and manpower necessary to maintain such a fleet. But this became a moot point after Sparta's negotiators were captured at sea and killed.

Mutual caution set in after these disappointments, and neither side was eager to launch major expeditions after the first few years of the war. Nor was either eager to fight in the other's domain. Sparta settled for small naval raids harassing Athenian commercial shipping, and Athens conducted a series of small amphibious landings to encourage slave rebellions. The great powers fought no significant land battles for the first seven years of the war. They fought no significant naval battles for eighteen years after Naupactus. Athens and Sparta had their first major fleet-on-fleet engagement in 411, some twenty years into the war.[33]

Instead of looking for creative ways to break the balance, both sides retreated to familiar operations, which enabled thboth sidesem to continue fighting but prevented either from winning. The Athenians continued to pin their hopes on small raids along the Peloponnesian coast, and the Spartans continued their ritual invasions of Attica. The problem for the Athenians was that while they added many more targets starting in 430, coastal raiding failed to really threaten the Spartan army, which could easily return to the Peloponnese in the event of a serious slave uprising and whose officers were generally disinclined to project power in the first place. The problem for Sparta was that their strategy failed to target any of the three main sources of the Athenians' power: their navy, their alliances, and their long walls.[34]

---

[32] Kagan, *Peloponnesian War*, 94.

[33] As I discuss below, the first sign that Athens was vulnerable at sea came two years earlier, when Syracuse destroyed the Athenian fleet at the culmination of the Athenians' disastrous Sicily campaign (415–413).

[34] Sparta's strategy had been more successful in the first Peloponnesian War (460–445), but in the decades that followed Athens had grown wealthy, its navy had grown in size and sophistication, and it had extended and fortified its defensive walls.

Both sides were also cautious in tactics. Athenian land commanders and Spartan captains repeatedly passed up opportunities for decisive battle on hearing that the enemy was nearby. Tactical retreat became the default position when operating on the other's domain. Spartan captains, for instance, abandoned an uncharacteristically ambitious plan for a surprise naval attack on in the winter of 429–428. The attack was timed to occur outside the normal sailing season, and Spartan planners were counting on lax Athenian security at its main port. But the Spartans got cold feet and attacked the island of Salamis instead. When Athens heard of the campaign it immediately mobilized a fleet. When Spartan captains heard that Athens was mobilizing, they returned to the Peloponnese rather than risking fleet-on-fleet battle. The Spartans were well aware of Athens's tactical superiority and feared the worst. They were also disheartened because their allies, who were similarly nervous about challenging the Athenian navy, did not honor their promise to support the invasion.

In 428, another Spartan fleet reached Mytilene as part of a joint land and sea invasion of Attica. The Mytileneans, who wished to use the Spartans' power to help them capture the whole island of Lesbos, had lured the Spartan's into joining the undertaking by arguing that their independence would deprive Athens of additional tribute it needed to sustain naval operations. In other words, it was exactly the kind of operation that could strike at the heart of Athens's strategy. The Mytileneans also reported that Athens's fleet was overrated and its strength flagging. To dispel any illusions and deter Sparta, Athens quickly organized a fleet of 100 triremes to sail around Mytilene in a show of strength. On hearing this news, the Spartans turned tail and rowed. While The Spartan hawks continued to push for amphibious operations, but ship captains simply would not take the risk.[35]

In 427, Corcyra had fallen into civil war, and Sparta had the opportunity to tip the balance of it in favor of a group of oligarchs. Had they won, Corcyra would likely have joined the Peloponnesian League or at least defected from Athens. Sparta launched a modest intervention and had some early success against a disorganized Corcyran trireme squadron, but the Spartan fleet fled when news arrived that the Athenians were sending substantial reinforcements.[36] Thucydides reports that in 424 the Spartans "reached the highest peak of hesitation ever, having to deal with what was beyond the scope of their existing kind of preparation, namely, a naval contest, and that against the Athenians, people for whom not attempting an attack was always viewed as a failure to gain an achievement."[37]

The Athenians tactical decisions followed the same pattern. Their occasional land campaigns relied on stealth and trickery: rather than staring down Spartan

---

[35] Strassler, *Landmark Thucydides*, 166–167; Kallet-Marx, *Money, Expense, and Naval Power*, 128–130, 139; and Kagan, *Peloponnesian War*, 96, and 102–104.

[36] Strassler, *Landmark Thucydides*, 196–198.

[37] Thucydides, *History*, 4.55.1–4.55.2.

infantry, Athenian commanders hoped to gain entry into defended cities through bribery and surprise. These plots generally amounted to nothing, however, and Athenian leaders usually withdrew when they heard that Spartans were nearby. In 425, for example, the Athenian leader Nicias conducted an amphibious landing at Corinth and had initial success but retreated after receiving intelligence that Spartan reinforcements were coming. In 424, Athens launched another invasion of the Megarid with the hope of convincing the local population to betray the city, but the Athenians fled when Spartan and Boeotian hoplites appeared.[38]

Athens's best shot at decisive victory came in 418 at the Battle of Mantinea, when Sparta fought Argos in the largest land battle of the war. Argos and its allies fielded about 12,000 troops on the Peloponnese, while Sparta mobilized as many as 18,000.[39] Argos benefited from several tactical advantages, including the fact that it was fighting on home terrain, and enjoyed early success in the battle. But Athens was reluctant to send more than a token force, which arrived too late to help Argos. Had the Athenians been more aggressive, they might have been able to help Argos defeat the Spartan army, which was led by a young and inexperienced commander. A Spartan loss, moreover, would have left Sparta isolated on the southern half of the peninsula and without a large army to suppress a slave revolt. Again, however, CDD prevented Athens from intervening more quickly and aggressively.[40]

Cross-domain deterrence also meant that bold commanders were hard to find. Most Athenians would not pursue campaigns that risked significant conflict with Spartan or Boeotian land forces. The major exceptions to the rule were Demosthenes and Cleon. Demosthenes, disobeying orders, tried but failed to engineer a complicated coalition offensive against Boeotia in 426. He had more success in 425, when along with Cleon he captured over 100 Spartans at Pylos and Sphacteria. Interestingly, no one in Athens expected such a victory, and in fact the Athenian assembly had only agreed to Cleon's expedition in order to get rid of a man they considered a dangerous, rabble-rousing hawk. They had assumed that he would fail. Moreover, even the occasionally daring Athenians had their limits. Small amphibious operations were one thing, but a pitched battle against the Spartan army was another. Demosthenes, for example, "never intended to risk a battle against an army of comparable size."[41]

---

[38] Kagan, *Peloponnesian War*, 153, 163–165. In the meantime, the Athenians overindulged in maritime operations that went far beyond the requirements of Pericles's original strategy. Kallet-Marx, *Money, Expense, and Naval Power*, 153–154. Kagan, *Peloponnesian War*, 163–165.

[39] Thucydides calculates a somewhat smaller Spartan force. Compare Hanson, *War Like No Other*, 155, and Strassler, *Landmark Thucydides*, 342.

[40] Athenian leaders were mindful of the fact that the battle occurred while Athens and Sparta were under a truce. But the so-called Peace of Nicias of 421 was never much more than a useful fiction, and the peace itself started to break down less than a year after it was signed.

[41] Kagan, *Peloponnesian War*, 128–132, 149–150, 166.

Spartan commanders, who were cautious by nature, were even more risk-averse after they found themselves fighting in a maritime context.[42] Brasidas, Sparta's most aggressive and creative strategist in the first half of the war, continually faced resistance from other officers. In 427, he advised the admiral Alcidas to follow up on his temporary success at Corcyra by attacking the city before the arrival of the Athenian fleet, but Alcidas demurred.[43] In 425, while commanding a trireme off the coast of Pylos, Brasidas urged his fellow captains to be bold in their efforts to dislodge the Athenian garrison there. But, in the words of one account of the battle, "the Peloponnesian ships were . . . not fully committing themselves to the attack for fear of causing damage to their vessels."[44]

Like Demosthenes, Brasidas deliberately ignored orders when he went on the offensive. In 424, he launched an audacious northern campaign toward Thrace that culminated in the victory at Amphipolis. Sparta was initially reluctant to engage in this campaign, owing to their traditional conservatism, but at the time they were especially fearful of a slave revolt and used the expedition to get rid of several hundred of their boldest helots. (The slaves were promised freedom as their payment. The rest of the army was made up of Peloponnesian mercenaries. No Spartiates participated, which says something about Sparta's enthusiasm for the campaign.)[45] Along the way, Brasidas mixed threats and promises of self-government to persuade a number of cities to break from Athens and support his offensive. He also made an alliance with the king of Macedonia, Perdiccas, who provided much-needed resources. The campaign was fraught with danger, given the distance involved and the need to march through potentially hostile areas, but the potential benefits were high. Stripping Athens of its allies meant reducing the revenue that underwrote its navy. In 423, however, Sparta and Athens agreed to a one-year truce, depriving Brasidas of a decisive victory. In direct contravention of Spartan policy, he engineered a false pretext for keeping the fight alive and prepared his armies. While he succeeded in undermining the truce, the next year's battles were indecisive.[46]

Some historians believe that Amphipolis was a missed opportunity for Sparta. Decisive victory in the northern campaign would have deprived Athens of revenue, and the areas surrounding Amphipolis were rich with timber that could have

---

[42] Strassler, *Landmark Thucydides*, 253–254.

[43] Alcidas also chose caution when he was presented with the opportunity to support the rebellion on Lesbos and to attack unfortified cities along the Ionian coast at a time when Athens's war chest was depleted and their ability to defend these cities was in doubt. Donald Kagan, *The Archidamian War* (Ithaca, NY: Cornell University Press, 1974), 148–152; Kallet-Marx, *Money, Expense, and Naval Power*, 139–143.

[44] Godfrey Hutchinson, *Attrition: Aspects of Command in the Peloponnesian War* (Gloucestershire, UK: Spellmount, 2006), 70–71.

[45] Kagan, *Archidamian War*, 287–290.

[46] On the origins of the expedition, see: Thucydides, *History*, 4.80–4.81. On Brasidas's efforts to undermine the truce, see: Kagan, *Peloponnesian War*, 178–180.

been used to build a much larger Spartan fleet. More important, the campaign represented the first truly successful effort to weaken the Delian League along the Aegean littoral. Consolidating that victory would have allowed Sparta to use central Greece as a launchpad to inspire rebellions in Athenian colonies.[47] None of this would have been easy, of course, and Sparta's leaders had legitimate reasons to oppose Brasidas's effort. His strategy required large reinforcements that would be at risk as long as Athens dominated the sea and its allies harassed Sparta's lines of communication on land. Nonetheless, his offensive hinted at a plausible theory of victory, at a time when Sparta was in desperate straits. Brasidas himself was killed at Amphipolis in 422, and another decade passed before Sparta produced a comparable military leader.[48]

Athens and Sparta each tried repeatedly to win without challenging the other's strategic center of gravity. They attempted arms racing, deception, stealth, and roundabout operations designed to break the deadlock. They both also hoped to find new allies who would be able or at least willing to challenge the enemy on its domain, but these attempts failed. Athens half-heartedly supported Argos but was unwilling to do so fully if that meant risking a substantial number of Athenian hoplites in battle, as was the case at Mantinea. Sparta did not secure meaningful Persian support until the tail end of the war, and by that time it was so exhausted that its ultimate triumph over Athens was fleeting.[49]

Cross-domain deterrence produced a stalemate that did not start to break down until the Sicilian Expedition, nearly two decades into the war. Sicily was a disaster for Athens, of course, but even that catastrophe did not end its naval dominance, and it was able to rapidly rebuild the fleet and score convincing victories at Cynocessma in the Hellespont (412), Cyzicus (411), and Argonusae (406). Still, the loss at Sicily was the first clear sign that Athens could be beaten at sea, and Sparta and its allies started chipping away at the cross-domain balance. Syracuse won the naval battle at the end of the Sicilian campaign in part through new technologies and tactics. The Syracusans strengthened the fronts of their triremes to permit head-on ramming; Athenian commanders trying to operate in close quarters were not prepared for this maneuver and were defeated in detail. Later, Sparta took advantage of Athens's financial troubles by luring Athenian rowers to defect through promises of better pay. The experience of battle, along with efforts to buy more experienced crews, allowed Sparta to finally challenge Athens on the sea. The war ended for all practical purposes when Sparta defeated the Athenian fleet at Aegospotami in 404.

---

[47] Hutchinson, *Attrition*, 77.

[48] Kagan, *Peloponnesian War*, 179–188; Hutchinson, *Attrition*, 65–94.

[49] Spartan hegemony in Greece was brief, and Sparta was eventually defeated by Thebes and Macedon.

Implications

What does all this suggest about CDD theory? First, clear asymmetries may increase stability, as was the case in the decade after the first Peloponnesian War (445–435). During this time, Athens and Sparta watched one another warily, but both crafted grand strategies to ensure long-term security without having to fight again. At the same time, CDD is fragile if states believe that they can overcome their disadvantages through arms racing or new alliances. Even though they recognize their own relative weaknesses, they may be able to convince themselves that that these are only temporary. They may also assume that because CDD is unstable, war is inevitable. This will accelerate the process of breakdown as each side rapidly builds arms and searches for allies. Hawkish leaders will also find it easier to marginalize their political opponents.

Second, explicit signaling may be required to backstop the regional balance of capabilities. Cross-domain asymmetries may be less obvious than differences in aggregate power. That is, the cross-domain balance may be relatively complex, especially as more domains come into play, and clever or delusional strategists may become convinced that they can change it without having to fully upend the overall balance. Leaders are likely to indulge in wishful thinking under these conditions. Threats in one domain may not be persuasive to a rival who is dominant in another, especially if the target believes that there are plausible ways to work around its own disadvantages. A failure to send clear deterrent signals that reinforce CDD may compound the problem.

Third, while asymmetries do not necessarily prevent war, they can prolong it. The experience of battle demolishes prewar fantasies, leads to strategic and tactical caution, and makes it difficult for audacious commanders to influence strategic decisions. Painful learning experiences in the early stages of war serve as stark reminders of the underlying balance. This means that while neither side can easily win, neither is at grave risk of decisive defeat. In the Peloponnesian War, CDD failed when Athens and Sparta wanted it to succeed and succeeded when both wanted it to fail. The result was a long war that proved catastrophic to both sides.

Finally, efforts to reduce the costs and risks of war may backfire. Both sides may prove reluctant to challenge the opponent on its preferred domain for fear of disastrous escalation. The last thing Athens sought was a pitched battle on land, in which Sparta could rally the bulk of its infantry, and the last thing Sparta wanted was a fleet-on-fleet engagement against far superior triremes from the Delian League. Both sides sought to keep the fighting at a relatively low level, unless they were able to bait the adversary into foolish engagement where its weaknesses would be exposed. This strategy was perfectly rational in the short term. It reduced the risk of catastrophe while creating a small chance of taking advantage of enemy blunders. But neither side made such blunders, and over time both discovered that it was safe to fight a limited war. Neither Athens nor Sparta was paying high enough costs to give up. Of course, neither could figure out how to convince its enemy to take new risks, which meant that neither of them could compel surrender.

This chain of events is somewhat similar to the stability-instability paradox. Developed in the Cold War, the basic idea was that two nuclear-armed powers were more likely to fight at the conventional level if they were confident that neither would risk escalation. The paradox was that stability at one level of violence would create instability and encourage violence at another.[50] Perversely, the existence of genuine nuclear stability might increase the risk of conventional war. In this case, the existence of cross-domain stability, which was revealed after prewar illusions were destroyed, taught Athens and Sparta that they could safely continue the fight as long as they took few risks. This went on for nearly three decades, and the accumulated costs broke them both.

A twist on this pattern might define a U.S.-China conflict today. Beijing and Washington have been investing in capabilities designed to help them overcome their cross-domain weaknesses. China's antiaccess weapons might blunt U.S. naval power by increasing risks to surface vessels operating in defense of local allies and partners. Long-range precision munitions are particularly worrisome, given that the United States has placed its maritime bets on a decreasing number of warships. Rather than building many vessels to accomplish a range of tasks, the United States has invested in very expensive multimission platforms. Adversaries with more lethal and accurate antiweapons thus face a smaller target set and can conceivably reduce the U.S. margin for error. Chinese strategists may reasonably believe that U.S. leaders will be reluctant to put their pricey fleet at risk in the event of a crisis, and China can threaten the American fleet without sacrificing Chinese advantages on land.

Over the last decade, U.S. strategists have provided a glimpse into their thinking about how to overcome China's new suite of antiaccess weapons. The ideas originally centered on what U.S. strategists called "AirSea Battle." Though the name has since changed, the broad outlines have not. At the outset of a conflict, U.S. forces will quickly move against command and control networks to force China into operational sclerosis. Such "blinding attacks" will also target Chinese intelligence capabilities in order to obscure China's ability to monitor events. The United States' vessels and bases will remain relatively secure in the resulting confusion, and U.S. leaders will have the luxury of sending reinforcements at their leisure. Blocking China from using its antiaccess weapons effectively will allow U.S. forces to seize the initiative and control the scope and pace of the war. Critically, none of this will require challenging the Chinese army.

---

[50] For a concise discussion, see: Robert Jervis, *The Illogic of American Nuclear Strategy* (Ithaca, NY: Cornell University Press, 1984), 31.

This all makes sense in terms of conventional operations and is consistent with the style of warfare the United States has practiced over the last three decades. The problem, of course, is that this scenario has not been tested against a nuclear-armed adversary. Analysts have warned that blinding strikes might encourage nuclear escalation. Attacks on command and control deliberately increase confusion, which might lead to misperception about U.S. intentions. If Chinese leaders believe the United States intends to conduct a disarming strike against its nuclear complex, it may feel placed in a terrible use-it-or-lose-it dilemma. The pressure to escalate will also increase if Chinese leaders believe that their regime's survival is tied to the outcome of the war. A successful U.S. campaign would be humiliating, with blinded Chinese forces unable to coordinate any meaningful response while the United States able to slowly marshal overwhelming force offshore. Rather than accepting such an ignominious end to their regime, Chinese leaders might gamble for resurrection by unleashing their country's nuclear arsenal.

On the other hand concerns about escalation might lead to caution on both sides in the early days of a conflict. Leaders have gotten cold feet about actually crossing the nuclear threshold in the past. Leaders in a hypothetical U.S.-China conflict might deliberately scale back their plans in order to reduce the risk. A watered-down version of AirSea Battle, for instance, would conspicuously avoid targets on the Chinese mainland and would deliberately leave channels of communication open in order to reduce the chance of misperceptions.

It is also possible that both sides might be frustrated in their early efforts. China's hope of seizing the initiative and controlling the modern "informationized" battle space might prove to be a techno-fantasy.[51] So, too, might the U.S. desire to guarantee access by forcing China into a state of operational sclerosis after a rapid blinding attack. Like Sparta and Athens, both sides may be disappointed after the first volley but perfectly able to continue skirmishing. The United States can fall back to its blue water refuge, confident that its durable advantages in power projection and undersea warfare allow it to continue operations indefinitely. China enjoys a vast land refuge of its own, of course, and has built a large arsenal of ballistic missiles it can use to harass U.S. allies and U.S. bases in a protracted campaign. Even though China's naval power attenuates the further it operates from the coastline, China can lay mines and use its growing maritime militia to complicate U.S. operations and threaten commercial shipping. None of these operations would be likely to lead to

---

[51] On "informationized" wars, see: M. Taylor Fravel, "China's New Military Strategy: 'Winning Informationized Local Wars,'" *China Brief* 15, no. 13 (June 2015), accessed 14 February 2018, https://jamestown.org/program/chinas-new-military-strategy-winning-informationized-local-wars/. On the importance of seizing the initiative, see: Aaron L. Friedberg, *Beyond Air–Sea Battle: The Debate over US Military Strategy in Asia* (London: International Institute for Strategic Studies, 2014).

a quick resolution of the war, but the cumulative effects could be disastrous, especially given the centrality of Asian trade to the global economy.[52]

Leaders in Beijing and Washington seem to understand the economic risks, namely , meaning that the political stakes would have to be very high in a hypothetical U.S.-China conflict, or they would not take the risk of fighting in the first place. War termination is a knotty problem in any war, but it will be particularly difficult if both sides believe that everything, including national security and regime survival, is on the line. The strategic problem will be finding a mutually acceptable settlement before, as happened in the Peloponnesian War, the costs overwhelm them both.

---

[52] For analyses of protracted war, see: Joshua Rovner, "Two Kinds of Catastrophe: Nuclear Escalation and Protracted War in Asia," *Journal of Strategic Studies* 40, no. 5 (2017): 696–730, https://doi.org/10.1080/01402390.2017.1293532; David C. Gompert, Astrid Smith Cevalious, and Cristina L. Garafola, *War with China: Thinking through the Unthinkable* (Santa Monica, CA: Rand, 2017), accessed 14 February 2018, https://www.rand.org/pubs/research_reports/RR1140.html.

COMMUNICATION AND CREDIBILITY ACROSS DOMAINS

9

International Law and the Common Knowledge Requirements of Cross-Domain Deterrence

JAMES D. MORROW

Cross-domain deterrence (CDD) seeks to deter violations in one domain, say outer space, by threatening retaliation in another, say cyberspace. Cross-domain deterrence promises to restore deterrence for issues wherein the United States lacks the ability to respond with a sufficiently large threat to deter or where retaliation within the domain of the attack would be so costly as to make the threat incredible.[1] The domain of the response could be chosen to make the deterrent threat more effective by increasing the damage it does to the party to be deterred or by reducing the cost of carrying out the threat and thereby raising the credibility of the deterrent. The system of CDD should be designed to ensure that the threats of retaliation across domains are sufficient to discourage violations.

The anticipations of all parties involved are key to an effective system of CDD. It is not enough for one side to know how it will respond to what acts it deems to be provocations; the parties to be deterred must also know what acts will be considered provocations and what the response to those violations will be. If the target of deterrence does not know what acts are considered provocations, it might trigger a response without realizing that it crossed a line. It could then deem the deterrent response to be a provocation rather than retaliation. Such a provocation, in turn, might be seen as necessitating a retaliatory response by the party that had in fact triggered that response. Both parties might thus, tragically, see themselves as justified and the other as the transgressor. In sum, if the party to be deterred does

---

[1] Deterrence of attacks on satellites could be an example of the latter, because the consequences of adding to space debris, by attacking a satellite of a country that has destroyed a U.S. satellite, could damage other satellites.

not know what the retaliatory response will be, it might proceed and trigger a response that both parties would have preferred to avoid.

For a system of CDD to work as intended, all the parties need to share common understandings of what acts will trigger a response, what that response can be, and the fact that the responding party is willing to carry out that response. Such a system is more complex than the understandings behind conventional or nuclear deterrence during the Cold War. Standards of acceptable conduct need to be set in each domain, appropriate responses established, and the links among the domains that show how and when the parties can respond to a violation in one domain by retaliating in another created. The complexity of the system increases by the magnitude of the square of the number of domains in the system compared to deterrence solely within each domain separately. Because the number of such systems is very large, creating that shared understanding is necessary and difficult. International law provides a way to create shared understandings of unacceptable conduct and appropriate responses to that conflict that is stronger than declarations of intent by individual actors.

Further, any system of CDD will be less robust than nuclear and conventional deterrence was during the Cold War. Several of the areas that CDD seeks to address suffer from the additional problem that violations are not open and public, most notably those in cyberspace. Both sides could reveal parts of their capabilities during the Cold War, allowing the other side to know that retaliation would be devastating. Deterrence was foremost a concern between the superpowers, while CDD might have to target many states that could pose a threat. In some domains, acts that could be considered violations will occur because those acts fall below the level of triggering a response. It may be unclear whether those carrying out attacks are operating under the control of a state or acting on their own.

International humanitarian law—the body of treaties that seek to regulate conduct during wartime—provide a better analogy to build on than nuclear deterrence. These treaties have a mixed record of outcomes, with some notable successes as well as failures. But this body of international law has confronted many of the same issues facing CDD throughout its long development in the twentieth century. Many standards were possible, and states needed to coordinate on one, so they could anticipate how one another would act during wartime. Not all violations rose to the level that required a response. Control of state agents is a central concern, because soldiers have the ability to commit atrocities in violation of state policy on many issues. The law relied on principles that states could use to reach a common understanding of whether novel acts were violations or not.

I begin by explaining how shared understanding makes deterrence possible, and then I consider the strategic requirements of deterrence given a shared understanding. International law seeks to create such shared understandings of acceptable conduct and appropriate responses to unacceptable conduct. Treaties, however, matter only to the extent that they fit with the incentives of the parties to comply, with deterrence as one such incentive. I lay out the weaknesses of the nuclear analogy and how the analogy to law of war is superior. I consider whether the parties could negotiate law to make CDD work, primarily their willingness to reveal their capabilities and concerns. The full range of these complications makes me pessimistic about whether all states can agree to create an effective system of CDD across all domains. More limited agreements might be feasible.

How Shared Understandings Underpin Deterrence

Deterrence is often thought of as a situation of opposed interests; the deterring party seeks to discourage the other party from doing something that it would like to do by the threat of retaliation. But the parties also share a common interest in avoiding a conflict that neither would seek. The party to be deterred might misjudge what acts would trigger a response, perhaps because the deterring party was vague about what values it would act to defend. How can they avoid such conflicts in the face of their opposed interests over the issues that the deterring party seeks to defend?

Deterrence is a reciprocal threat, where the party attempting deterrence threatens to respond in kind to acts it views as violations. But what acts trigger a response? There are many ways to set the line between what the deterring power can accept and what it must respond to. Further, the deterring party may obscure the exact triggers in an effort to deter violations it could tolerate but would like to discourage. The other side might test those limits when they are unclear. Deterrence shares these properties with other issues in world politics where reciprocal threats are used to deter certain acts and allow the parties to realize a common interest. In trade, reciprocal sanctions limit the extent of barriers to trade to create a more open world economy. In the laws of war, the prospect of retaliation in kind, sometimes carried out on the battlefield by soldiers acting against state policy, produces better compliance with that law and a more restrained battlefield.[2] For both of these issues, treaty law supports these systems of reciprocity.

The logic of how reciprocity can allow parties to realize mutual gain in the face of individual interests to act against those gains and the factors that complicate its practice have been examined thoroughly in game theory. The folk theorem (more accurately, theorems) in game theory shows that if the reciprocity can support shared gains, then many such systems are possible where the parties realize different benefits. These systems of reciprocity differ in what conduct they judge as acceptable and what the responses to unacceptable behavior are. In the language of game theory, there are multiple equilibria, where each equilibrium is an internally consistent and self-enforcing system of reciprocal deterrent threats that enforces

---

[2] James D. Morrow, *Order within Anarchy: The Laws of War as an International Institution* (New York: Cambridge University Press, 2014).

a standard of acceptable conduct.[3] The concept of equilibrium in game theory entails two requirements: first, the strategies are mutual best replies, and second, the players share a common conjecture that all players will play their equilibrium strategies. Most studies of deterrence focus on the first requirement; when do deterrent threats discourage challenges? The second requirement addresses the ways each of the players anticipates how the other will act; what acts trigger what response? When both requirements hold, the strategies are self-enforcing and in the interest of all the players, in the sense that none can better itself by deviating to another strategy. When multiple equilibria exist in a game, the common conjecture allows the players to form strategic expectations about how each player will act, so each will know that its own strategy is best.

The range of possible equilibria can be immense; iterated prisoners' dilemma has an infinite number of reciprocal equilibria, which vary in how the players divide the benefits of cooperation and the length of reciprocal punishments and how they make those costly punishments credible. Which equilibrium the players play depends on the common conjecture they hold, and the common conjecture then shapes how they act. Common conjectures have to be common knowledge (something everyone knows, everyone knows that everyone knows it, ad infinitum through all the levels of knowledge), and as they include the equilibrium strategies, they also explain how the players will play (up to the uncertainty captured in mixed strategies) in all possible situations in the game, including those that are off the equilibrium path, that is, those moves that will not happen if the players play according to the candidate equilibrium. Creating this common knowledge about when and how CDD will be used is a fundamental challenge for its effective implementation.

The Strategic Requirements of Effective Deterrence

For CDD to work the parties need to share an understanding of what behavior is acceptable and what is not. For example, what sorts of cyber activities are seen as acceptable and what are not? A common standard of behavior allows the parties to know what acts trigger a response and so allows them to avoid those acts if they deem the response more costly than the benefits of the act. In nuclear deterrence, all eventually accepted that nuclear retaliation was appropriate in response to a nuclear attack or conventional attack on the homeland but not for military actions against client states in the developing world. A common standard also helps to avoid inadvertent escalation, where one party takes actions it thinks are acceptable while the other sees them as unacceptable violations.

---

[3] Ibid., ch. 2.

A common standard also helps the parties distinguish between violations and acceptable retaliation. In many cases, the acts in the deterrent threat are the same as those ruled out as unacceptable behavior. In trade law, tariffs are the appropriate reciprocal responses to violations of trade law that the violating party refuses to remedy, but those same tariffs would be violations if they were not authorized in the context of a trade dispute ruled on by the World Trade Organization. With a common standard and public actions, violations become common knowledge when they occur. This shared understanding allows the parties to then interpret the retaliation as acceptable; this common interpretation prevents a chain of retaliatory responses from escalating.

Arriving at a common understanding of a possible violation and the acceptability of any retaliation is easier when all acts are public. When violations are not, the problem of misattribution arises. One side might claim that the other has violated it in order to justify its intended violations as acceptable retaliation. This concern looms very large in domains like cybersecurity, where there is no public demonstration of a violation, only the claim by the damaged party.[4] This problem is not insoluble; the dispute resolution procedure in the World Trade Organization creates a single, public judgment on the claim of a disputant that a particular policy of one of its trading partners violated trade law. The side that loses a dispute may disagree with the judgment, but that judgment is now a social fact on which others can and will condition their behavior. Deterrence through reciprocity requires a return address.

The parties also need to share an understanding of what responses are appropriate for what violations. This avoids a party using a violation as a justification of a disproportionate response to its own benefit. Imagine if one act of cyber espionage triggered widespread cyberattacks to acquire industrial secrets from the firms of the violating power, justified as retaliation for the initial act. The shared understanding has to be precise, as even a small disagreement as to the magnitude of appropriate response could lead to unintended escalation of retaliation. What should the rules of proportionality be? Reciprocal responses need to be significant enough to deter opportunistic violations but not so large as to trigger further responses.

Finally, the parties need to understand that all of them will carry out the reciprocal responses needed to deter. In some cases, this is not an issue because the retaliatory act benefits the party carrying it out. When retaliation is costly, however, credibility becomes a problem; it becomes a larger problem when third parties rather than the damaged party are called on to retaliate. The system could compel retaliation by invoking sanctions against those who refuse to carry out their responsibility to enforce the system.[5] Alternatively, they could be rewarded for their costly

---

[4] See Jacqueline Schneider, chapter 5 here.

[5] Robert Axelrod, "An Evolutionary Approach to Norms," *American Political Science Review* 80, no. 4 (1986): 1095–1111, https://doi.org/10.1017/S0003055400185016.

task; trade law effectively does this by allowing the damaged party to impose tariffs that will shift an amount of trade determined by the panel in its ruling. In other cases, a period of degraded relations could be self-enforcing.

Creating Common Knowledge through International Law

Game theorists argue that common conjectures can arise through a shared experience of play, common culture, focal points, and preplay negotiation.[6] In the nuclear realm, constructivists have argued that elites in the United States and the Soviet Union came to a common understanding of the very limited circumstances under which nuclear weapons could be used,[7] and that arms control could be used to limit the nuclear arms race[8]—examples of a shared experience of play creating common knowledge. But this process could take substantial time to lead to common knowledge, and it might settle on an inferior equilibrium in the short run or might fail to converge at all.[9] Negotiation to create a shared understanding is a more attractive option.

Unilateral declarations of intent are unlikely to establish the common knowledge needed for CDD to work. Parties may seek to deceive the other side to gain an advantage, making unilateral declaration of benign intent ineffective to signal that intent credibly. On the laws of war, not all parties have the incentive to reveal their interest in limiting violence during war at its outbreak.[10] Others may discount such declarations of intent to use CDD, undermining its efficacy to deter.

International law addresses this concern by creating a single text that multiple states accept through ratification. The single text clarifies what the standards of acceptable conduct are and lays out responses to inappropriate conduct, where reciprocity is often assumed, if not spelled out. The parties may later disagree about the interpretation of the law in a specific case, but they have to base those claims on the law rather than their discretion. Ratification as a public act signals acceptance of that treaty and the standards it encodes. As a public act, it creates common knowledge about which parties have accepted the standard and those that wish to remain

---

[6] Thomas C. Schelling, *The Strategy of Conflict* (Cambridge, MA: Harvard University Press, 1960); David M. Kreps, *Game Theory and Economic Modelling* (New York: Oxford University Press, 1990).

[7] Nina Tannenwald, "The Nuclear Taboo: The United States and the Normative Basis of Nuclear Non-use," *International Organization* 53, no. 3 (1999): 433–468.

[8] Emanuel Adler, "The Emergence of Cooperation: National Epistemic Communities and the International Evolution of the Idea of Nuclear Arms Control," *International Organization* 46, no. 1 (1992): 101–145, https://doi.org/10.1017/S0020818300001466.

[9] Morrow, *Order within Anarchy*, ch. 7.

[10] Ibid., ch. 3.

outside it. In the laws of war, joint ratification—when both sides in a conflict have ratified the most recent treaty on the issue—leads to stronger reciprocity and better compliance.[11]

But ratification of a treaty is not the meaningful signal; nonratification is. When a state chooses to stay out of a treaty, it signals its intent to violate the standards of the treaty. This happens in both the law of war and human rights.[12] Creating an international treaty on CDD would help to clarify what the standards of appropriate conduct are in the domains it covers, to specify what cross-domain retaliation would be, and to identify those parties that are unwilling to live under that system.

Finally, international law is incomplete compared to a common conjecture, in four important ways. First, international law cannot specify exactly what should be done in all possible events. Law seeks to deal with this incompleteness by creating principles that the parties can use to reach common judgments about the acceptability of specific cases. Second, multiple principles might conflict in a specific case, leading the parties to disagree about whether a particular act violated the relevant standards because they disagree about which principle applies. Third, the parties might disagree about the application of the principles to a specific case. Fourth, the parties might be unsure whether the others fully accept the standard, as ratification is not a definitive signal of intent to comply. All of these fall under the idea of law as an incomplete contract. Even with these limitations, international law will be a necessary part of an effective system of CDD.

How Treaties and Deterrence Work Together

Law works together with capabilities to make deterrence work; it is not a substitute for deterrence. Law can clarify what acts are unacceptable and so to be deterred. Transgressions become apparent to all parties, which allows the parties to comprehend when a deterrent response is legal instead of a violation of their agreement. Because reciprocal responses are often the same acts as violations, this shared understanding of when these acts are legal and acceptable responses, as opposed to violations, is necessary to avoid retaliatory spirals. The strategic logic of deterrence provides the incentives that can make a legal system effective in reducing the frequency of violations, even if it cannot eliminate them.

Because there are many legal agreements that could be enforced through deterrence, the content of the specific agreement matters. Agreements that seek to limit more behavior either require stronger punishments or accept less compliance. Even

---

[11] Ibid., ch. 4.

[12] James Vreeland, "Political Institutions and Human Rights: Why Dictatorships Enter into the United Nations Convention against Torture," *International Organization* 62, no. 1 (2008): 65–101; Morrow, *Order within Anarchy*, chs. 4 and 5.

agreements with the strongest sanctions will fail to deter some violations. The management of violations becomes a key part of the design of an agreement. What level of violations are required before a response is triggered? Should some violations, particularly low-level ones, be ignored in the interest of reducing conflict and concentrating on major ones? Deterrent threats do not need to respond to every possible violation to maintain general compliance with the underlying agreement. Irregular responses in turn need larger responses to keep the full deterrent effect. Systems of irregular and disproportionate deterrent responses lead to less than full compliance, so we should expect that a successful system does not induce a perfect record of compliance with the limits sought in the treaty standard. Competition among states across and within the domains will continue even after the negotiation of an agreement to define and deter violations for the domains covered by that agreement.

Treaties do not end strategic competition by outlawing it; they redirect it into forms that the parties see as acceptable or tolerable. The first Strategic Arms Limitation Treaty of 1972 (SALT I) exemplifies how an agreement redirects strategic competition. The United States and the Soviet Union agreed to cap the total number of nuclear-armed missiles and bombers that each side had and to limit the deployment of antiballistic missiles while not limiting the deployment of multiple independently targetable reentry vehicles (MIRVs). Consequently, both sides turned their weapons development toward the conversion of their ballistic missiles to MIRVs and reduced their investments in antiballistic missiles, with the United States choosing not to create the antiballistic missile system it was allowed under the treaty. SALT I did not end the competition over nuclear arms; it redirected it. Even with the agreement and the move away from antiballistic missiles, there were still disagreements over whether particular installations and improvements violated the treaty, most notably the Soviet radar installation at Abalakova. There were also disagreements about whether novel developments violated the treaty, such as the legal interpretation by the United States that its research into its Strategic Defense Initiative did not violate its treaty obligations. Despite these disagreements, both sides generally kept to the deal and built their nuclear forces in the direction embodied in the principles underlying the treaty. It may be that this direction reduced the stability of the nuclear balance by increasing the number of warheads that could be delivered from a fixed number of missiles; however, both sides countered the increase in warheads through other means that also did not violate their agreement, such as mobile intercontinental ballistic missiles, instead of breaching the agreement openly.[13] The strategic incentives that a treaty creates

---

[13] Because the Reagan-era Strategic Defense Initiative never reached the deployment stage during the Cold War, the question of whether deployment of a system of defense based on it would violate the treaty was never forced.

matter as much as the abstract principles that underlie them. Cross-domain deterrence requires the matching of the principles defining violations and prescribing possible responses with the ability and willingness of the parties to carry them out. Those incentives are unlikely in practice to compel complete compliance.

The Weakness of the Nuclear Analogy

Are treaty law and the negotiations to produce agreement on that law necessary to the development of the shared understanding required for CDD to work? The emergence of agreement about the appropriate role of nuclear weapons during the Cold War did not rely on treaty law; the nuclear powers came to understand that nuclear weapons should be reserved for the deterrence of strategic nuclear war and the preservation of national existence. The experience of nuclear crises and limited war undermined the arguments of those who wished to leverage strategic nuclear forces for extended deterrence or to use tactical nuclear weapons in limited wars. Not that the advocates of either of those views disappeared completely in either superpower, but their views never prevailed as a general view of how nuclear weapons should be used. Can the world grope toward a similar understanding about how and when CDD should be used, or are negotiations necessary?

Unfortunately, the domains where CDD might be used lack a number of the properties of the domain of nuclear weapons that reduced the difficulty of reaching a shared understanding about their appropriate use and of producing effective deterrence of their inappropriate use. Some of the domains do not have any of these properties, but all of them lack some of them.[14] These properties made nuclear deterrence more likely to hold even if and when the shared understanding was weak. Deterrence was sufficiently robust that it could hold even when some of the key elements of a system of deterrence were not common knowledge, which otherwise could possibly lead to misunderstandings between the parties about when and how deterrence should work.

First, the parties could know when a violation took place. Nuclear detonations over valued targets could not be hidden.[15] A side under attack might not have advance warning, but once both sides had secure second-strike capabilities, they could ride out an attack and then retaliate. In several of the domains, the only evidence of a violation might be the failure of key capabilities, such as satellite communications, where there could be plausible alternative explanations of that failure. Alternative explanations create the possibility that an attacker could dissemble about what it

[14] See Jacqueline Schneider, chapter 5 here, on cyberspace, and Benjamin Bahney, Jonathan Pearl, and Michael Markey, chapter 6 here, on space.

[15] Nuclear tests were a different matter, although the superpowers developed ways to monitor the tests of the other side.

had done. The clear public nature of a nuclear attack provided the public trigger that the nonuse of nuclear weapons had been breached.

Second, the two superpowers each understood that the other was the most likely source of an attack. In the event of a strategic nuclear strike, both would know what party had committed it. Intercontinental ballistic missiles effectively had return addresses during the Cold War. The lesser nuclear powers lacked the ability to launch the massive nuclear attacks that the superpowers could. The attribution of the source of a strategic nuclear war would not have been problematic. An attacker could not hope that its target would retaliate against someone else because of misattribution.

Third, the superpowers had only one other party to worry about. There was no need to produce a multilateral understanding of how and when nuclear weapons could be used. The two sides could work toward their own shared understanding without having to worry about whether the lesser nuclear powers would accept the same limits and prescribe the same responses to breaches of those limits. Because the capabilities to inflict damage in new domains today are more widespread among countries, more parties must be part of the evolution of a shared understanding of how to handle CDD. Alternatively, every pair of countries could have its own agreement, which would lead to a huge number of bilateral negotiations, with greater associated transaction costs.[16]

Fourth, no third parties outside the control of either actor possessed the capability to carry out attacks that might be identified as coming from one of the superpowers. Both superpowers undertook steps to ensure command and control over their nuclear weapons, in part to prevent unauthorized launches. Nonstate actors lacked access to nuclear weapons and their delivery systems. In some of the new domains, most notably cyberspace, there are numerous nonstate actors with capabilities similar to those that might be used in violations or retaliation. In the Cold War, the lack of the possibility of attack from outside the control of either actor reduced the chance of an actor outside national control triggering a retaliatory spiral that produced a wider conflict (e.g., the General Ripper scenario in *Dr. Strangelove*). The small number of relevant nuclear superpowers (two) also eliminated another source of misattribution.

Fifth, the certainty of the level and speed of devastation were very high once both superpowers developed secure second-strike capabilities. Nuclear threats did not require a high probability of being carried out to be effective deterrents. Although some in both countries argued for warfighting strategies such that a party could imagine that a nuclear war could be contained and so might be willing to initiate a

---

[16] The lack of a multilateral agreement regulating international investments is an example of the latter. The proliferation of bilateral investment treaties provides legal agreements on how investments from one country to another should be protected. I note that many bilateral investment treaties have essentially identical language, which simplifies the negotiation of a large number of them.

limited nuclear war, doctrine never fully embraced such ideas. In contrast, attacks in many of the new domains start small, where the threat of escalation to high levels of damage seems small. A party could believe that an attack in these areas would be unlikely to trigger catastrophe.

Sixth, both sides had the ability to monitor the capabilities of the other side, so they knew roughly what the other side was capable of. This knowledge of capabilities grew over time; it was most limited in the early days of intercontinental ballistic missiles, when they were rare, expensive, and less than reliable. As both sides increased their national means of verification and intelligence, and as their confidence in the importance of revealing the broad outlines of their capabilities to one another grew, both understood the broad outlines of the other's nuclear arsenal. Each superpower also came to see the value of revealing some of their capabilities in ways that the other could verify, in order to improve the other's confidence in its knowledge of what one could do. In contrast, some capabilities in new domains, particularly cyberspace, will be rendered ineffective if they are revealed, so the parties work to keep them secret.

Seventh, the lines to be enforced were well established and clear. If the use of nuclear weapons was limited to deterrence of strategic nuclear war and the protection of national sovereignty, the magnitude of nuclear war and the publicly accepted location of national borders provided clear lines. A primary problem with using nuclear weapons for coercion or deterrence in limited wars was the difficulty of determining what triggers were sufficient for their use.[17] If the deterring party could not determine where those lines were, how could the party to be deterred know not to cross them?

Finally, there were few cross-domain questions to consider in nuclear deterrence. Efforts to use nuclear weapons to deter nonnuclear transgressions was the primary example of CDD during the Cold War, and it was seen as credible only for the most obvious transgressions, such as a Soviet ground invasion of Western Europe. As the number of domains linked in CDD increases, the number of understandings about how they are linked—what is inappropriate conduct in each domain and what cross-domain responses are allowed—increases as the square of the number of domains.

Nuclear competition during the Cold War and the emergence of shared restraint over how and when nuclear weapons could be used seems an attractive analogy to the problems of CDD. But these new domains lack some of the features that made nuclear deterrence overdetermined during the Cold War. Given these features that complicate a system of CDD, groping toward a common understanding of how and when such deterrent responses will be used seems likely to lead to

---

[17] This is one of the primary themes in Thomas C. Schelling, *Arms and Influence* (New Haven, CT: Yale University Press, 1966), ch. 4.

misunderstandings, failures of deterrence, and unnecessary responses to imagined breaches.

The Law of War Analogy

The law of war provides an alternative analogy for the development of shared understandings needed to make CDD work. The Hague and Geneva Conventions and other international treaties that seek to regulate conduct during wartime operate in ways that fit with the problem of making CDD work. They are a good parallel for what an agreement to produce a shared understanding on CDD would look like.[18]

First, the law of war creates a common standard of appropriate conduct in areas where states disagree about what that standard should be. Many standards to limit conduct during war are possible and sustainable; the treaties and their application to cases create a common idea of which standard should be used. Those standards result from the combination of multilateral negotiation and practical experience in applying standards during wartime.

Second, treaty language creates common knowledge of what the standards are. Treaties are public knowledge, with agreed-on versions in multiple languages in some cases. When a state ratifies a treaty, it publicly accepts that standard. These public acts differ from statements of intent, where the party could dissemble, and from private agreements, where third parties may not know the precise terms of the agreement even if they know of its existence. In addition, treaties legalize some acts that violate humanitarian norms; the law of war is not just a broad presumption against all acts that harm protected people and property or that employ proscribed methods of war.

Third, ratification acts as a screen of the intentions of states for their conduct in the future. Nothing in treaty ratification compels states to comply with the treaty. However, the parties that reject a treaty by refusing to ratify identify themselves as parties that will not live up to the standards of the treaty if war comes. Failure to ratify, not ratification, is the meaningful signal of a state's intentions.

Fourth, although the presumption is that states that ratify intend to comply, it is understood that compliance varies across issues and types of violations. In some cases, both sides will descend into unrestricted violence even when both have ratified. In others, the parties will not retaliate fully to some violations, providing

---

[18] Michael M. Schmidt, "Cyber Operations in International Law: The Use of Force, Collective Security, Self-Defense, and Armed Conflicts," in National Research Council, *Proceedings of a Workshop on Deterring CyberAttacks: Informing Strategies and Developing Options for U.S. Policy* (Washington, DC: National Academies Press, 2010), 151–178.

a cap on escalatory spirals of violence. Even partial limitation on violence is preferable to none.

Fifth, the law embodies principles—proportionality and military necessity, to name two—that parties can use to judge the law's application to novel and unanticipated cases. The possibility of reaching agreement on how to apply those principles to such cases exists, even if achieving such agreement in a particular case is difficult. The law can grow and respond to changes in the future.

Sixth, the law of war creates obligations and rights for the agents of states, most commonly soldiers, in addition to states themselves. It seeks to induce states to train, control, and discipline their agents if those states wish to comply. Achieving internal control of soldiers on the battlefield is not easy, as even the best disciplined militaries have soldiers who violate the law. Still, the law of war seeks to produce a system such that agents as well as states bear responsibility for their acts.

Even with these strengths, there are limitations to the analogy between the law of war and an effective system of CDD. First, the law of war has been less successful at controlling violence by nonstate actors.[19] For the domains where acts by nonstate actors create problems of attribution because of others' inability to determine whether those carrying out violations are in the control of another state, the difficulty of controlling nonstate actors produces a concern that the parallel with the law of war does not help.

Second, the law of war has not been systematically enforced with retaliation across issues covered by the law.[20] Cross-issue retaliation has occurred in some cases, but these instances are not evidence of a shared understanding that cross-issue retaliation is appropriate and should be used systematically. Firewalls among the issues help to prevent the spread of violations on one issue leading to a deterioration of conduct in others. But this historical experience suggests that systems of CDD are particularly demanding to create and that actors fear that issue linkage is prone to spreading bad conduct from one domain to another.

The Difficulties of Honest Signaling and Information Sharing during Negotiations

The analogy to the law of war does not mean that negotiating a system of CDD will be easy.[21] These negotiations are likely to be difficult because the parties may

---

[19] For evidence on how and when rebel groups follow law of war, see: Hyeran Jo, *Compliant Rebels: Rebel Groups and International Law in World Politics* (New York: Cambridge University Press, 2015).

[20] Morrow, Order within Anarchy, 134–136, 183.

[21] For a review of the parallels between existing international agreements and issues in cybersecurity, see: Abraham D. Sofaer, David Clark, and Whitfield Diffie, "Cyber Security and International

be reluctant to share key information about their capabilities even though doing so is necessary to reach an agreement on how a system of CDD should work. During negotiations on the law of war, capabilities and the damage they could do were generally well understood by all parties. When states sought to address weapons whose effects were uncertain or existed only in the minds of weapons designers, they floundered.[22] How do you develop rules of proper conduct for something whose effects are not well known? Some want sweeping restrictions—most commonly those who fear that they will be the targets of such weapons—while others are hesitant to limit what might be the source of their military advantage in the future.

The shared understanding supporting a system of CDD needs to outline what conduct will be considered violations and what will be considered acceptable, allowing for a gray area between the two. The scope of violations could include all acts that are significant enough to require a response—for example, those that kill someone will trigger a response—while those that are acceptable will not. The scope of acceptable acts could cover everything from those acts where a party suffers damage that is not viewed as significant enough to trigger a response to those acts that fall into the realm of "fair game" in interstate relations even if they cause significant damage. The gray area in between, which might cover a wide range of possible acts, might trigger a response based on the consequences of a particular act and the political situation between the parties. Those in the gray area face probabilistic deterrence; parties engaged in these acts would then run a risk of some response but not the certainty of one.

Probable responses also need to be clarified in order to produce an effective deterrent. First, the magnitude of the response to a given level of violation must be clarified. Deterrence requires that the probability of response combined with the magnitude of response must exceed what the violator gains from its violation. Otherwise, the deterrent response is not large enough to dissuade the violator from transgressing. For those acts agreed to be significant enough to require a response, the damage of the response need only match the infringement. The same is not true for acts in the gray area that face probabilistic deterrence. Disproportionate responses are needed to make a system of irregular deterrent responses work. The parallel during the Cold War was the doctrine of Massive Retaliation, by which the United States threatened large-scale nuclear war in response to Soviet aggression. Responses that are larger than the initial violation risk escalatory spirals if both sides do not understand that responses must be larger than the violation when the harmed party does not respond to every violation in the gray area. Gray areas then

---

Agreements," in National Research Council, *Proceedings of a Workshop on Deterring CyberAttacks*, 179–206.

[22] The exception here is the ban on blinding laser weapons: Protocol on Blinding Laser Weapons (Protocol IV to the 1980 Convention), negotiated and signed in 1995. Although such weapons did not exist, states were beginning to use lasers for military purposes, such as target identification and aiming.

create risks of escalation—risks that can be controlled if both sides understand the logic of irregular and disproportionate deterrence.

Second, the likelihood that responses will be carried out in response to violations in a system of CDD must be clarified.[23] Even if violations in the obviously unacceptable category are deterred, violations in the gray area are still likely to occur, because a violating party suspects that there may be no response to such a violation. In turn, the party suffering the violation still has some chance of responding with some sort of retaliatory response. Unlike the nuclear deterrence parallel from the Cold War, CDD is likely to lead to both violations in the gray area as well as disproportionate responses to those violations in some cases. This prospect also limits the size of disproportionate responses: they cannot be massive retaliation.

Because CDD seeks to link conduct across domains together, the demands of the system increase as the square of the number of domains, as noted. One way to reduce this complexity would be to designate one domain as the domain of retaliation. Standards of conduct could be set in the other domains, with the understanding that the responses to violations would all occur in the domain of retaliation, reducing the complexity of the resulting agreement. Conventional kinetic responses are one obvious domain for retaliation. But proportionality rears its head here. Is a kinetic attack appropriate after violations that do not kill people or destroy property? A second obvious domain for retaliation would be economic sanctions. This possibility confronts the concern that economic sanctions might not be a strong enough sanction to deter the worst breaches of agreed conduct. Designating a domain of retaliation simplifies the complexity of the understanding needed to support a system of CDD, but the obvious candidate domains of retaliation might not be sufficient to create effective deterrence.

Some of the acts covered in the domains fall into the realm of intelligence activities rather than violations or responses. In the cyber domain, many states use cyber capabilities to collect information from foreign governments or to test their capabilities. Intelligence collection and counterintelligence have been areas of interstate competition where states have engaged in and tolerated acts that they would not accept outside those areas, such as espionage, kidnapping, blackmail, and the killing of operatives, provided that only those involved in intelligence activities are the targets of such acts. If intelligence is recognized as a walled-off "Wild West" compared to regular state relations, and will occur in some of the most salient domains of CDD, such as space and cyberspace, then the parties will need to agree on what constitutes intelligence and how to judge when acts fall into that rule-free zone. Intelligence also increases the likelihood that the parties will engage in acts that some would consider violations and so requiring a retaliatory response.

---

[23] This is why Massive Retaliation was not a good doctrine.

Because technology is changing rapidly in some domains, those changes compound this problem. States and their agents will produce novel capabilities that they may wish to conceal for future use or develop new vulnerabilities that they wish to protect through CDD. The parties will need to revise their understanding of where the lines between acceptable and unacceptable conduct will be, along with what responses are appropriate. In contrast, those domains where technology is well known and unlikely to change dramatically in the future, such as kinetic attacks, do not require frequent revisions in the understanding. Dramatic changes could enable one to attack new targets, penetrate defenses that were invulnerable before, or improve the efficacy of attacks on targets that are known to be vulnerable. Any of these changes raise the possibility of a surprise attack using behavior that falls outside the range of whatever behavior is agreed to be acceptable but not within the range of those agreed to be unacceptable. Such an attack would likely provoke a retaliatory response and the possibility of an escalatory spiral, exactly what a shared understanding over acceptable conduct is designed to prevent.

Revisions of the shared understanding will be difficult to make, because the parties lack incentives to reveal new capabilities and vulnerabilities. During the Cold War, the superpowers could reveal their strategic capabilities through weapons testing and displays of weapons systems, such as displays of aircraft at air shows. While these tests did not seek to reveal all of the details of these capabilities, both sides could determine the likely damage the other could do. In the cyber domain, however, vulnerabilities can be closed if the parties become aware that they exist, meaning that those who find such vulnerabilities may wish to keep them secret. In the space domain, the testing of antisatellite weapons causes undesirable debris, threatening collateral damage to satellites in the relevant orbits. Because public demonstrations of novel capabilities are difficult, the parties would have to voluntarily reveal those capabilities during negotiations to revise the limits on conduct. They might do so if they thought the other side would reciprocate by revealing some of its own secret capabilities; both could be better off either by placing the use of some secret capabilities off limits or by revealing them and allowing the other to take measures to render them impotent. The parties would have stronger interests in revealing such vulnerabilities if nonstate actors could also find and exploit them, as they could share an interest in forestalling attacks by nonstate actors.

Even when a party is willing to reveal its own capability or a weakness of the other, will the other believe it? Effective signaling depends on both the willingness of the sender to transmit information and whether the receiver believes that signal to be credible. If a party reveals a previously unknown capability, the other may conclude that the former does not view that capability as useful. In the light of the difficulty of demonstrating new capabilities, the receiver might interpret the revelation as a bluff, a capability that the sender is willing to give up because it does not have it. Negotiations to define acceptable conduct as capabilities change require both parties—those revealing capabilities and those receiving that claim—to engage in the revision of that understanding. Receivers who doubt the veracity or value of revelations are unlikely to respond with concessions of their own in turn.

These difficulties in credibly revealing information pose serious issues for understanding the limits of acceptable behavior in the face of changing technology and capabilities. A shift of focus away from capabilities and toward general principles of conduct might remedy these issues. Instead of identifying violations by capability, they could be identified by effect. For instance, any act that kills nonmilitary personnel seems clearly unacceptable from a parallel to the laws of war. A party might breach this line inadvertently, a form of collateral damage, which might deter some attacks designed not to kill but with unpredictable effects. Any principle could legalize some acts that the target might see as unacceptable after the fact. A state-led cyberattack that drained the financial assets of many people or major corporations would not breach the "no dead bodies" line but would provoke substantial outrage and calls for a response from the targets.[24] Still, it should be easier to agree on general principles of what outcomes are unacceptable and what areas are fair game than on limits on specific capabilities. Government targets might be deemed acceptable while private ones are not.

These problems are not unique to CDD; they are common across almost any area where states compete and cooperate, although the mix of them varies across those areas. There is an essential tension between distribution and information when states decide how to cooperate.[25] Cooperation, where states agree on the limits between appropriate and inappropriate conduct, poses combinations of these problems, as there are many ways states could cooperate. Distributional issues arise because the parties disagree about which solution is best; settling on a solution means that some will be content with it while others prefer an alternative solution. Informational issues occur because no party knows the complete and true value of any of the available solutions, but each has some partial knowledge of their values. All parties would be better off if they freely shared what each knew on its own. For CDD, competition between states and the acceptance of the use of some acts in certain domains creates the distributional problem. Each would like to limit its own vulnerabilities while retaining capabilities against the others, even if it would only use such capabilities in an extreme case.[26] The information problems stem from changing technology and the role of third parties. States might wish to obscure new capabilities and links to nonstate actors to preserve an advantage rather than openly

---

[24] An example might be the WannaCry cyberattack in 2017.

[25] James D. Morrow, "Modeling the Forms of International Cooperation: Distribution versus Information," *International Organization* 48, no. 3 (1994): 387–423, https://doi.org/10.1017/S0020818300028241.

[26] As an example of this issue, see the discussion in Bahney et al., chapter 6 here, of the self-interested proposals advanced by China and Russia for limiting weapons in space but not ground-based antisatellite weapons.

sharing them, and others might suspect that any disclosure is less than full and complete. The chances for cooperation are higher as the players believe that their shared interests loom larger than their divergent, distributional ones. Focusing on common interests in preventing nonstate actors from using the capabilities in these domains for their own purposes and in maintaining an open, global commons in the Internet and in geosynchronous orbits could help.

Conclusion

I am not optimistic about the ability of states to reach the shared understanding needed to make CDD work. The complexity of that understanding—what conduct is acceptable in each domain, what are the triggers for retaliatory responses, and how those responses are linked across domains—is substantially greater than in other areas of international cooperation. States do not seem to emphasize their common interests in domains such as cyberspace, or they seem only to see those common interests in the most general terms. The technology in some of the domains is changing rapidly, requiring agile revision of the shared understanding. Some acts covered in these domains will be used by all parties and considered to be acceptable intelligence work, breaking down a clear line of no use. Because many of these capabilities are untested, and they could prove to have more destructive consequences than those who use them anticipate. A party making a unilateral declaration of intent—both what acts are unacceptable to it and what action it will take in response to a breach—is unlikely to convince other governments to take that declaration as a clear guide as to how that state will act. The employment of CDD entails an acceptance that under a system of CDD, low-level violations will occur and some retaliatory responses will happen.

What is to be done then? Discussions on possible limits in individual domains have occurred, as Jacquelyn Schneider discusses (chapter 5 here) for cyberspace, and Benjamin Bahney, Jonathan Pearl, and Michael Markey discuss (chapter 6 here) for space weapons. Such discussions should focus on general principles of what sort of damage is unacceptable rather than on what sorts of attacks should be banned. The bounds of areas that are open for intelligence purposes should be clarified. Advancing directly to treaties in the absence of common agreement on the proper standards is premature. Increasing contacts among the personnel who deal with these domains across countries is desirable, provided that all recognize that they may be reluctant to share information on capabilities and vulnerabilities freely and honestly.

10

Signaling with Secrets

Evidence on Soviet Perceptions and Counterforce Developments in the Late Cold War

BRENDAN RITTENHOUSE GREEN AND AUSTIN G. LONG

A central challenge for deterrence today is the increasing complexity and uncertainty of the modern political-military environment. This complexity and uncertainty is driven in large part by rapidly changing technology. Warfighting capabilities now depend on utilizing military instruments from multiple domains, combining the traditional forces of land, sea, and air with newer elements of power in space and cyberspace. Sensors that exploit every aspect of the electromagnetic spectrum have proliferated across land, sea, air, and space. They are integrated in real time by computer networks defended by cyber capabilities and directed by sophisticated command, control, and communications (C3). A variety of new capabilities, including offensive cyber and counter-space systems, hold these new C3 systems at risk, compounding complexity and uncertainty.

In recent years, U.S. military thought has grappled with the implications of the changing technological environment. On the one hand there is a real fear that cross-domain complexity could pose a major challenge to U.S. military primacy, through anti-access/area-denial capabilities (A2/AD), offensive cyber operations, and attempts to deny U.S. forces the use of space.[1] On the other hand the United States also appears well positioned to dominate cross-domain operations like no one else: initiatives like the new Joint Concept for Access and Maneuver in the Global Commons (JAM-GC)—the concept formerly known as AirSea Battle— emphasize rapid blinding attacks on enemy C3 and the use of information dominance from U.S. C3; the history of the Stuxnet worm and the catalogue of low-earth

---

[1] See: Robert Work, "The Third U.S. Offset Strategy and Its Implications for Partners and Allies: As Delivered by Deputy Secretary of Defense Bob Work, Willard Hotel, Washington, D.C.," Department of Defense, 28 January 2015, accessed 25 March 2018, http://www.defense.gov/News/Speeches/Speech-View/Article/606641/the-third-us-offset-strategy-and-its-implications-for-partners-and-allies.

orbit (LEO) satellites shows that the United States, as yet, has no equal in either space or cyberspace.[2]

As this book underscores, cross-domain military interactions might be rising in salience, but they are not new. Many of the very same technological capabilities and "novel" links between domains that dominate today's debate—the integration of target intelligence across sensor platforms, including space; the importance of command and control (C2); the rise of computer and electronic warfare—first arose more than three decades ago in a different context: the Cold War nuclear competition. During the latter part of the Cold War, the United States made a concerted effort to hold Soviet nuclear forces at risk. Importantly, this meant building capabilities to track Soviet ballistic missile submarines (SSBNs) from under the sea; target Soviet mobile intercontinental ballistic missiles (ICBMs) from space; and disrupt Soviet C3 in order to prevent its fixed site ICBMs from launching under attack (LUA).

In short, U.S. nuclear strategy during the later Cold War depended on executing complex cross-domain operations in a conflict and outcompeting potential Soviet countermeasures during peacetime. Indeed, insofar as many of CDD's core concepts are predicated on the complexity of the political and operational environment, it is worth pointing out that contemporary military competition has yet to equal the Cold War's rivalry in its complexity. Pace Lehman's otherwise excellent chapter here, Cold War competitors also had to account for multiple theatres of battle, multiple potential combatants, global geographic scope, and threats of vertical and horizontal escalation. The Cold War struggle therefore represents an ideal case for exploring the dynamics of CDD. In this chapter, we elaborate two groups of loosely connected hypotheses about how a technologically complex cross-domain military environment might impact deterrence, and we compare expectations to evidence from the late Cold War nuclear competition.

The first group of hypotheses might be broadly grouped under the heading of "bad news" for deterrence and U.S. military primacy. Many of the cross-domain capabilities sketched above depend on secrecy for their effectiveness; but how can secret capabilities be leveraged for political gain when revealing them will allow the enemy to take countermeasures that vitiate them? The bargaining theory of war has long stressed that such "private" information about the balance of power is a major cause of war, and if so, it would appear that increasing technological complexity is bad for deterrence.[3]

---

[2] Austin Long, "A New Wary Titan: US Defence Policy in an Era of Military Change, Asian Growth and European Austerity," in *Security, Strategy and Military Change in the 21st Century: Cross-regional Perspectives*, edited by Jo Inge Bekkevold, Ian Bowers, and Michael Raska (London: Routledge, 2015), pp. 241–265.

[3] The urfather of the bargaining model of war is Geoffrey Blainey, *The Causes of War* (New York: Macmillan Co. of Australia, 1988). For a succinct overview, see: Dan Reiter, "Exploring the Bargaining Model of War," *Perspectives on Politics* 1, no. 1 (March 2003): 27–43, https://doi.org/10.1017/S1537592703000033.

Similarly, the complexity of cross-domain operations might be bad for U.S. conventional superiority, if it allows weaker powers to apply their asymmetric strengths against weak points in tightly integrated multi-domain U.S. operations. Technological change might allow the weak to throw well-timed wrenches into the plans of the strong. Finally, and in a completely different vein, it might be that the nuclear revolution (the advent and proliferation of nuclear weapons in international politics) simply overwhelms the strategic dynamics of any new technology. However complex new cross-domain interactions might be, there is something clarifying about the logic of extinction. This would be good for deterrence but bad for U.S. primacy, since nuclear arms are the ultimate weapons of the weak.

A second group of hypotheses might be grouped under the heading of "good news" for deterrence and U.S. military primacy. It might be that there are ways to signal the efficacy of clandestine capabilities that do not obviously supply the enemy with the necessary means to counter them. If changing cross-domain capabilities can be shown to exist without revealing the mechanism of their operation, perhaps military strength can be converted into bargaining advantage without war. Moreover, one might also suppose that rising technological complexity is subject to increasing returns, rather than burdened by multiple failure modes. That is, cross-domain interactions might strengthen the strong rather than empowering the weak. And the nuclear revolution, for all its intellectual popularity, has not universally captured the minds of political leaders. If political leaders perceive exceptions to its pacifying logic, then there will be greater scope for conventional competition across technological domains.

The undeveloped state of cross-domain theory makes this exercise more useful for developing and refining hypotheses than for rigorously testing them or generalizing widely across space and time. Nevertheless, our findings are suggestive: the late Cold War nuclear case appears to confirm the second group of hypotheses much more strongly that the first. The United States found ways to signal its capabilities; the Soviets appeared to at least partially get the message; they attempted to adjust their policies both symmetrically and asymmetrically; and they had little success with either. Neither the nuclear revolution, asymmetric Soviet responses, nor the clandestine nature of military technology prevented the United States from integrating military capabilities across multiple domains so as to put tremendous political pressure on the Soviet Union. At the same time, the story is not one of unalloyed triumph either. United States policy came with many dangers, and those seeking lessons from the case must pay careful attention to its Cold War context.

We begin by briefly sketching the nature of U.S. cross-domain nuclear initiatives during the late Cold War. Next, we elaborate two groups of hypotheses concerning how changing technology in a cross-domain environment might impact deterrence outcomes, with regard to the impact of military secrecy, asymmetric power relationships, and the nuclear revolution. We then examine whether the United States attempted to signal the secret cross-domain military capabilities it had built from changing technology; whether the Soviets got the message and perceived a threat; and how Moscow adjusted its policy in response. Our conclusion discusses the implications of our findings for CDD theory and contemporary debates in U.S. defense policy.

Late Cold War United States Nuclear Strategy

The United States had a nuclear counterforce strategy during the late Cold War that was designed to hold Soviet nuclear forces at risk. However, potential U.S. capabilities against fixed targets depended on cross-domain technological enablers. It was crucial to prevent ICBM LUA after a U.S. attack had started but before the target set had been destroyed, perhaps by deploying hard-target systems, like the Pershing-II intermediate-range ballistic missile (IRBM) and the Gryphon ground launched cruise missile (GLCM) close to Russian borders, where they could plausibly target Soviet early warning. Attacks on Soviet C2, from land, sea, air, or with electronic warfare, were an important part of U.S. doctrine.

Technological innovation was also necessary to find relocatable Soviet nuclear targets, particularly SSBNs and mobile ICBMs. The United States' antisubmarine warfare (ASW) operations were enhanced with increasingly sophisticated sonar equipment, including enhanced bow sonars on attack submarines (SSNs), more sensitive towed arrays, and signal processing of greater computational power. These innovations allowed U.S. ASW to overcome the quieting of Soviet SSBNs and follow them into their new deployment areas in "bastions" close to Soviet home waters. Meanwhile, signals intelligence (SIGINT) from space-based sensors, when combined with direction finding and cryptography, could potentially intercept routine status communications from mobile ICBMs. This intelligence, when combined with other sources, could be used to "map" the peacetime patrol patterns of missile platforms and potentially find them in a crisis.[4]

This is not to argue that the United States achieved anything like a disarming capability against the Soviet nuclear force during the late Cold War but that real damage limitation might have been within the realm of possibility and, since possible, perhaps on the minds of political leaders. Moreover, the shadow of the future, with a potentially even more favorable combination of cross-domain capabilities,

---

[4] On U.S. intelligence capabilities against Soviet mobile targets, see: Austin Long and Brendan Rittenhouse Green, "Stalking the Secure Second Strike: Intelligence, Counterforce, and Nuclear Strategy," *Journal of Strategic Studies* 38, nos. 1–2 (February 2015): 47–56, https://doi.org/10.1080/01402390.2014.958150.

loomed large. The late Cold War nuclear case is therefore of great interest, as past leaders had to grapple with three key issues that characterize technological change across military domains today: the role of military secrecy, the dynamics of power asymmetries, and the influence of nuclear weapons.

Hypotheses on Cross-Domain Deterrence

Here we develop two groups of hypotheses about these issues and derive predictions from them about U.S. signaling concerning its nuclear capabilities, Soviet perceptions of the nuclear competition, and Soviet adjustments to U.S. nuclear policies. Again, the exercise is more one of theory elaboration and refinement than testing. The hypotheses in each group, summarized in table 10.1, are only loosely connected to each other and have been placed together based on whether they have pessimistic implications for deterrence and U.S. conventional military primacy or whether they present a more complicated picture.

We have derived these propositions from a mix of sources. The hypotheses on the impact of clandestine military capabilities stem from the bargaining literature in political science; the alternative views concerning power asymmetries represent our renditions of "folk theories" that we see as implicit in many contemporary defense policy debates; the deductions about the nuclear revolution come from both academic and policy literatures.

Bad News for Deterrence and United States Military Primacy

Standard deterrence theory is underwritten by a logic of rational expectations often referred to as the "bargaining theory of war."[5] In this school of thought, deterrence can fail when two sides disagree about the balance of military power, which prevents them from reaching a mutually agreeable peaceful bargain that reflects that balance. Clandestine military capabilities therefore represent a kind of "private information" that could be a major cause of war.

Increasing technological complexity in a densely integrated cross-domain military environment, one might conjecture, might undercut deterrence by increasing the salience of private information about military capabilities. For example, how could political benefits be gained from the U.S. Cold War antisubmarine warfare advantage without giving away the secrets that would allow the Soviets to reduce their vulnerability? Telling the Soviets "we listen

---

[5] See Reiter, "Exploring the Bargaining Model of War"; James Fearon, "Rationalist Explanations for War," *International Organization* 49, no. 3 (Summer 1995): 379–414, https://doi.org/10.1017/S0020818300033324; Erik Gartzke, "War Is in the Error Term," *International Organization* 53, no. 3 (Summer 1999): 567–587, https://doi.org/10.1162/002081899550995.

Table 10.1 **Summary of hypotheses**

	Signaling	Perceptions	Adjustments
"Bad news"			
Clandestine capabilities	No signals or failed signals	Depends on signals	Quick and successful adjustments to any perceived vulnerabilities
Power asymmetries	N/A	Not overly concerned about any perceived vulnerabilities	Successful, cheap, and asymmetric adjustments to perceived vulnerabilities
Nuclear revolution	N/A	Perceptions of a stalemated nuclear balance; few concerns about vulnerability	Adjustments are few, minor, and successful
"Better news"			
Clandestine capabilities	Attempts to signal clandestine capabilities; attempts to use mechanisms that preserve the advantages of those capabilities where possible	Perceptions of specific vulnerabilities in early warning, C3, and mobile nuclear platforms; perceptions of vulnerability in long-term ability to run arms race	Symmetric and asymmetric adjustments that are challenging and difficult
Power asymmetries	N/A	Concerns over specific vulnerabilities and long term competitiveness should be serious	Neither symmetric nor asymmetric adjustments are likely to be very successful
Nuclear revolution	N/A	Perceptions that the nuclear balance has meaning even when nuclear weapons are plentiful	Symmetric and asymmetric adjustments that are challenging and difficult

for XYZ mechanical blade rate tonals" might quickly send Soviet subs back to the machine shop; while simply telling them "we can hear your SSBNs" could simply be laughed off as an incentive to misrepresent. At the same time, disaster might have resulted if Moscow had rested its diplomacy on the mistaken belief that it possessed totally invulnerable SSBNs. Similar problems might arise today in the context of U.S. cyber or electronic warfare capabilities that assist kinetic operations; adversaries cannot exactly be told that they need to concede at the negotiating table because Washington has really potent plans for disabling the air defenses and C3 they were depending on.

This pessimistic view of clandestine military capabilities implies that in the late Cold War case, the United States should have been unable to successfully convert its military capabilities into political advantage. In this scenario, either it will recognize that its military capabilities have only warfighting utility and make no attempt to signal them, or it will unsuccessfully signal their existence and see them ignored or attenuated. Soviet perceptions of the nuclear competition will depend on U.S. signals, but if Moscow perceives a threat, it ought to adjust efficiently to meet it.

Another pessimistic hypothesis can be seen in defense policy writing about the emerging cross-domain military environment. Implicit in many contemporary worries is the idea that changing technology and rising complexity in military operations is allowing weaker actors to exploit asymmetric advantages that undermine U.S. military power. Perhaps surprise disruption in the space or cyber domains of tightly coupled, complex operations can rapidly degrade vaunted U.S. technological advantages. Others are concerned that the proliferation of relatively cheap anti-access/area-denial technologies threatens to neuter decades of U.S. investment in sophisticated hardware and cross-domain capabilities.[6]

This hypothesis makes no predictions about U.S. signaling but expects that, in this scenario, Soviet leaders will not be overly concerned with U.S. capabilities. After all, the increasingly cross-domain nature of military interaction and the corresponding increase in technological complexity and uncertainty should leave the weaker Soviet Union with a number of cheap, asymmetric responses. The Soviet Union should therefore eschew technological competition in the nuclear arena, looking instead for other domains where it can compensate, particularly those where it holds the comparative advantage. Moreover, it should have achieved a fair amount of success with these kinds of asymmetric adjustments.

A different but equally dour proposition would dismiss the importance of technological complexity and CDD altogether. According to classic theories of the nuclear revolution, once states obtain nuclear forces that can survive an adversary's

---

[6] See for example Evan Braden Montgomery, "Contested Primacy in the Western Pacific: China's Rise and the Future of U.S. Power Projection," *International Security* 38, no. 4 (Spring 2014): 115–149, https://doi.org/10.1162/ISEC_a_00160.

first strike, the military balance loses its meaning. Additional increments of nuclear strength cannot protect one's cities and therefore cannot provide meaningful political leverage, which derives from resolve rather than military power.[7] Cold War nuclear competition, whatever its interesting cross-domain flourishes, was thus, under this interpretation, a largely meaningless sideshow, and so such competition remains today. While the nuclear revolution might be good for deterrence moreover, it bodes ill for U.S. conventional superiority, which faces a trump card when other states gain nuclear weapons. This kind of argument can be seen most clearly in policy discourse that prioritizes counter-proliferation goals on the assumption that U.S. conventional influence diminishes as the nuclear club increases.[8]

The nuclear revolution hypothesis predicts that signaling about nuclear capabilities will be of little relevance. The Soviets should certainly not have perceived much of a threat from U.S. nuclear initiatives, since the nuclear balance was permanently stalemated and no political leverage could accrue from technological innovation. The nuclear balance is just not meaningful. Likewise, there will be little need for military or political adjustments to U.S. policies, symmetrical or otherwise. Such adjustments as occur will be small, cheap, and very successful.

Better News for Deterrence and United States Military Primacy

A second set of hypotheses presents a more optimistic, or at least more complex, picture for U.S. military primacy. This view begins with the observation that there might be some circumstances under which clandestine military capabilities could have political value short of war. To the extent that a measure-countermeasure competition in a given domain—or across a combination of emerging domains—favors the initiating state, that state might be able to tolerate some secret capabilities being discovered. Deterrence, especially in a technologically complex cross-domain environment, might be as much about long-term competition and the pressures of strategic adjustment as about crisis behavior. Bargaining can occur tacitly in peacetime just as it occurs explicitly in crisis or war. In this scenario, if the United States expected to dominate a long-term antisubmarine warfare competition with the Soviet Union, perhaps it was willing to risk temporarily ceding some military advantage to signal that fact; likewise with U.S. space and cyberspace dominance today.

Moreover, in some cases there might be mechanisms that allow a state to reveal the existence of clandestine capabilities while concealing information necessary to

---

[7] Charles L. Glaser, *Analyzing Strategic Nuclear Policy* (Princeton, NJ: Princeton University Press, 1990); Robert Jervis, *The Meaning of the Nuclear Revolution: Statecraft and the Prospect of Armageddon* (Ithaca, NY: Cornell University Press, 1989).

[8] Office of the Secretary of Defense, "Proliferation: Threat and Response," Department of Defense, 2001, accessed 25 March 2018, https://fas.org/irp/threat/prolif00.pdf.

counter them. Military exercises might demonstrate potential operational capacity to enemy eyes without revealing how the results are to be achieved. Another possibility is the careful use of counterintelligence channels: feeding selective information to the adversary's most trusted intelligence sources could leverage clandestine capabilities without attenuating them. Finally, in a highly competitive environment, information operations, military propaganda, leaks, or simple public statements could paint a picture of military capabilities for enemy intelligence that is incomplete or mistaken. Especially if long-term competition has made the adversary sensitive to information about the military balance, enemy intelligence will be prone to a variety of perceptual and inferential errors, and it might prove possible to provide deceptive accounts of capabilities that defeat countermeasures.[9]

It could also be that a world of increasing cross-domain interactions and technological complexity favors the strong rather than the weak. Complexity in economic interactions often features increasing returns to scale. It is possible that a similar phenomenon might be at work in military affairs. It might require very large fixed investments to even compete in a world of intense cross-domain interactions, and these might present serious barriers to entry for weaker powers. Few states are better poised to disrupt in the space or cyber domains, or to degrade adversary C3, than the United States.[10] In short, rather than providing multiple failure modes for the weak to exploit, cross-domain interactions might strengthen the strong.

Finally, the logic of the nuclear revolution is only ironclad if mutually assured destruction (MAD) is permanently entrenched against any conceivable technological change. But if cross-domain interactions and technological complexity are on the rise, they might well increase uncertainty among political leaders about the future persistence of MAD, even if nuclear stalemate remains for the present circumstances. In this situation, not just the current nuclear balance but also trends in each of its emerging components could start to take on pressing relevance and might carry political weight. Furthermore, the competition would also highlight

---

[9] For thoughts on the role of deception in deterrence, see Erik Gartzke and Jon R. Lindsay, "Weaving Tangled Webs: Offense, Defense, and Deception in Cyberspace," *Security Studies* 24, no. 2 (2015): 316–348, https://doi.org/10.1080/09636412.2015.1038188; Huw Dylan, "Super-weapons and Subversion: British Deterrence by Deception Operations in the Early Cold War," *Journal of Strategic Studies* 38, no. 5 (2015): 704–728, https://doi.org/10.1080/01402390.2015.1029120.

[10] On U.S. offensive cyber capabilities, former commander of U.S. Cyber Command General Keith Alexander noted in 2013: "we believe our offense is the best in the world." See: "H.A.S.C. No. 113-17: Information Technology and Cyber Operations: Modernization and Policy Issues to Support the Future Force," House Committee on Armed Services hearing, Intelligence, Emerging Threats and Capabilities Subcommittee, 13 March 2013, 87, https://www.hsdl.org/?view&did=742663. On other commons see Barry R. Posen, "Command of the Commons: The Military Foundation of U.S. Hegemony," *International Security* 28, no. 1 (Summer 2003): 5–46, https://doi.org/10.1162/016228803322427965.

information about each side's relative capability to carry on the arms race over the long haul, which might weigh in the political scales as well.

Unlike the more pessimistic propositions, these hypotheses generate similar predictions. Washington will have every incentive to signal its clandestine cross-domain capabilities in the nuclear realm, and should search for mechanisms that will allow it to do so without destroying their military value. Moscow should get the message: it should perceive its specific weaknesses in the areas of C3, early warning (EW), and mobile nuclear platforms. Because the nuclear revolution is not an absolute solution, these problems should be perceived as real and pressing. In addition, the Soviets should be concerned about their long-term competitiveness in a nuclear arms race with the United States. After all, in a world with high barriers to entry and increasing returns, they will not be able to ignore traditional symmetric adjustments and will need to compete economically, technologically, and politically with the superpower. Finally, given Soviet weakness at the end of the Cold War, neither contemporary Russia's symmetric nor asymmetric adjustments should be especially successful.

Signaling Clandestine Cross-Domain Capabilities

The United States' behavior is consistent with an ability to signal clandestine military capabilities, at least in a limited manner. Washington used selective leaks, public propaganda, and military demonstrations to draw Russia's attention to the vulnerability of its C3, early warning, and SSBNs.

To begin with, both the Carter and Reagan administrations made sure the press was aware of nuclear planning that emphasized the United States' C3 advantages. The so-called Hines report (1995) concludes that "the essence of Presidential Directive 59 (PD-59) was leaked in order to let Soviet leaders know that ... the Soviet leadership's highest political priorities were selectively targeted by U.S. missiles."[11] The U.S. government report "Fiscal Year 1984–1988 Defense Guidance," which was leaked to the *New York Times*, called for strategic strikes against "the [Soviet] political and military leadership based on decapitation" and rendering "ineffective the total Soviet (and Soviet-allied) military and political power structure."[12]

---

[11] John G. Hines, Ellis M. Mishulovich, and John F. Shull, *Soviet Intentions 1965–1985*, vol. 1, *An Analytical Comparison of U.S.-Soviet Assessments during the Cold War*, BDM Federal, Inc., 22 September 1995, unclassified, excised copy, 15, accessed 25 March 2018, https://nsarchive2.gwu.edu/nukevault/ebb285/doc02_I_ch2.pdf.

[12] Benjamin B. Fischer, "CANOPY WING: The U.S. War Plan That Gave the East Germans Goose Bumps," *International Journal of Intelligence and CounterIntelligence* 27, no. 3 (2014): 444, https://doi.org/10.1080/08850607.2014.900290.

These leaks did not go unnoticed in Moscow, where they started a furious public debate among nuclear policymakers. Optimists argued that U.S. efforts were part of a strategy to "pressure the other side politically" in a crisis and "economically exhaust" the Soviet Union in a long-term arms race. Pessimists, including Marshal Nikolai Ogarkov, head of the Soviet General Staff, argued that U.S. plans were aimed at achieving enough "strategic superiority" to "change in its favor the approximate military balance" and ultimately were intended to "keep the world on the brink of war."[13]

Deliberate leaks were quickly combined in the Soviet mind with openly announced North Atlantic Treaty Organization (NATO) policy. The most prominent East-West military issue at the cusp of the 1980s was NATO's decision to deploy Pershing II ballistic missiles and Gryphon ground launched cruise missiles to central Europe in order to counter Moscow's deployment of the mobile intermediate range SS-20. Though the sources of this decision were multifaceted, the purported technical capabilities of the missiles were deeply worrisome to Soviet strategists. As Colonel General Andrian Danilevich put it, "both types of weapons were perceived as a very serious threat, since their [Pershing-II] time of flight was only [six] minutes to vitally important regions. . . . Also, our air defense systems were not designed to detect such missiles. And [the Pershing-IIs] pushed us to such a quick response. . . . They were considered to be a great threat to our administrative-political centers, and the possibility of a surprise attack was very threatening."[14] An operational general in charge of detecting incoming missiles and generating the Soviet response was more blunt: the missiles were "a cocked pistol aimed at Moscow's head."[15]

Another mechanism by which cross-domain technological innovations were revealed was revelations from Hauptverwaltung Aufklärung (HVA), East Germany's foreign intelligence service, which had obtained documents from their U.S. spy, James W. Hall III, that revealed the existence of a highly compartmentalized "black" program code-named CANOPY WING. The program was a well-funded research effort to produce a suite of electronic warfare capabilities for a decapitation strike aimed at Soviet C3. It was built on a vulnerability in Russian high-frequency communications, discovered in the late 1970s, that "could be exploited to shut down . . . orders from the high command to its strategic missile forces, submarine fleet, and air forces." According to Hauptverwaltung Aufklärung, CANOPY WING aimed to develop additional methods of "short-circuiting communications and weapons

---

[13] Benjamin B. Fischer, "The Soviet–American War Scare of the 1980s," *International Journal of Intelligence and CounterIntelligence* 19, no. 3 (2006): 493–494, https://doi.org/10.1080/08850600600656400.

[14] Danilevich interview in Hines et al., *Soviet Intentions 1965–1985*, vol. 1, 34, https://nsarchive2.gwu.edu/nukevault/ebb285/doc02_I_ch3.pdf.

[15] Fischer, "The Soviet–American War Scare of the 1980s," 487.

systems," including the use of "microscopic carbon-fiber particles and chemical weapons," as well as deception based on "computer-simulated voices to override and substitute false commands from ground-control stations to aircraft and from regional command centers to the Soviet submarine fleet." Another East German agent, Jeffrey Carney, revealed the existence of a U.S. National Security Agency (NSA)-Air Force database of just such voiceprints, created by lengthy periods of eavesdropping on Soviet ground controllers.[16]

These plans, and the kind of capabilities they revealed, were alarming. Hauptverwaltung Aufklärung operatives have claimed that the plan gave them "goosebumps" and "sent ice-cold shivers down our spines." It seemed to confirm that earlier reports of NATO briefings about decapitation attacks that were being prepared with the latest technology. The Soviet reaction to CANOPY WING is not available, but according to a senior Soviet diplomat, the earlier NATO briefings produced a "top secret/eyes only KGB report in 1983 stating that the [U.S.] had prepared everything for a first-strike, might resort to a surgical strike against command centers in the Soviet Union, and had the capability to incapacitate command centers."[17]

It is not clear whether the revelation of NATO decapitation planning was completely unknown to the West or whether it was (or became) part of the larger set of nuclear signaling policies. In any case, the Soviets took the information seriously and fixed the underlying vulnerability that CANOPY WING exploited.[18]

Finally, and most important, the Reagan administration, shortly after entering office, launched a series of psy-ops shortly after entering office, which signaled both potential U.S. capabilities and Soviet technological inferiority. These were primarily Air Force and Navy exercises close to Soviet borders. The psychological operations initially began as a targeted effort to deter Soviet forces exercising within and just across the Polish border from intervening to suppress the Solidarity movement in Poland but quickly expanded. Strategic Air Command (SAC) commander General John T. Chain, Jr., subsequently recounted: "[sometimes] we would send bombers over the North Pole and their radars would click on"; in other instances, forward based fighter-bombers in Asia and Europe would probe the air defenses along the Soviet periphery. According to Schweizer, "during peak times, the operation would include several maneuvers in a week. They would come at irregular intervals to make the effect all the more unsettling. Then, as quickly as the unannounced flights began, they would stop, only to begin again a few weeks later."[19] These probes frequently threw the Soviet Air Defense into a state of high alert and sometimes disarray.[20]

---

[16] Fischer, "CANOPY WING," 439, 442, 443.

[17] Ibid., 439, 451. Internal quotation marks have been removed.

[18] Ibid., 442.

[19] Peter Schweizer, *Victory: The Reagan Administration's Secret Strategy That Hastened the Collapse of the Soviet Union* (New York: Atlantic Monthly Press, 1994), 8–9.

[20] Ibid., 8–9.

Even more threatening was a series of naval operations launched along Soviet coastlines. In August and September 1981, a NATO fleet of eighty-three ships managed to transit the Greenland-Iceland-United Kingdom (GIUK) gap without initial detection, using a variety of both active and passive measures. This gap was a key chokepoint in any naval campaign between NATO and the Warsaw Pact and was thus the target of the Soviet Union's massive ocean surveillance system. The NATO fleet was not positively identified until it was well within operating range of Soviet reconnaissance aircraft—defeating a satellite launched explicitly to find it—which were unable to track the NATO ships. As the Soviet planes were refueling, they were buzzed by U.S. F-14s, which were operating from more than a 1,000-mile distance from their aircraft carrier and had avoided Soviet radars.[21]

Meanwhile, four ships split off from the rest of the fleet and sailed into the Barents Sea, the heart of Soviet naval power and home to the submarine "bastions" whence SSBNs would launch their weapons. These ships operated off the coast of the Kola Peninsula and the city of Murmansk for nine days without being identified. They were only detected once by a patrol of Soviet planes that happened across them by chance; failed Soviet attempts to reacquire them by putting two new satellites into orbit revealed glaring weaknesses in Moscow's space programs.[22] Gordon Barrass, a former British intelligence official, reports that as the ships were headed home, "about [twenty kilometers] from the main Soviet naval base at Murmansk[,] they switched on all their electronic equipment. The message was loud and clear—'We can run rings around you.'"[23]

In 1983, the U.S. Navy ran a multicarrier battle group exercise in the Pacific Ocean with similar purposes. This time, the ships openly approached the Kamchatka peninsula in the Soviet Far East, home to the only Russian naval base with access to the open ocean, and another SSBN bastion. The U.S. armada ran twenty-four-hour air operations, probing for weaknesses and forcing Soviet air defenses to react, and ran aggressive antisubmarine warfare exercises near the Soviet bastions. During one part of the exercise, an aircraft carrier repeated the 1981 trick of sneaking away from the rest of the fleet; it steamed toward Soviet home waters without being detected and violated Soviet airspace with its flight operations.[24]

Interestingly, there was a key difference between the Atlantic and Pacific exercises. In the 1981 North Atlantic exercise, the orders and planning for the exercise were changed after they had been sent out over naval communications, and new

---

[21] Gregory Vistica, *Fall from Glory: The Men Who Sank the U.S. Navy* (New York: Touchstone, 1997), 129–133.

[22] Fischer, "The Soviet–American War Scare of the 1980s," 485.

[23] Gordon Barrass, *The Great Cold War: A Journey through the Hall of Mirrors* (Stanford, CA: Stanford Security Studies, 2009), 280.

[24] David E. Hoffman, *The Dead Hand: The Untold Story of the Cold War Arms Race and Its Dangerous Legacy* (New York: Anchor, 2010), 64–65.

plans were delivered by hand. High-ranking figures in the Navy—including Admiral Bobby Inman, the commander of the Atlantic exercise and the director of the National Security Agency, already suspected that Soviet espionage had penetrated naval communications. Inman's suspicions were correct, as the Soviet penetration was later revealed to be the Walker family spy ring.[25] In the 1983 exercise, whether intentionally (i.e., as a counterintelligence effort to shape the perceptions of Soviet intelligence) or not, normal naval communications were used. John Walker later turned much of this traffic over to the Russians.[26]

In total, these exercises demonstrated a number of U.S. capabilities. The U.S. Navy showed that it could defeat Soviet ocean surveillance from land, air, and space; that it could deny the Soviet military tactical warning; could probe, confuse, penetrate, and exploit Soviet air defenses; t could conduct surprise operations in submarine Soviet bastions; and perhaps could even evade Soviet espionage.[27] As the chief of naval operations later testified to Congress about the effects of the 1983 exercise, "our feeling is that an aggressive defense . . . is the greatest deterrent we can have. And the Soviets really understand that. We can get their attention with that concept. . . . Kamchatka is a difficult peninsula. They have no railroads to it. They have to resupply it by air. It is a very important spot for them, and they are as naked as a jaybird there, and they know it."[28]

But the exact technological sources of U.S. capabilities, which in the case of the 1981 exercise were quite sophisticated and complex, were not immediately apparent from the operations themselves.[29]

The Soviet Union reacted to the Reagan psy-ops with alarm. Vigorous protests were made to the U.S. naval attaché in Moscow as well as the U.S. ambassador. Soviet pilots were chastised for allowing the 1983 violation of Soviet airspace, and new aggressive procedures were put in place. These probably caused the downing of Korean Airlines Flight 007 on 1 September 1983 after it strayed into Soviet airspace. That downing further revealed the dissolute state of air defenses in the critical Kamchatka region, where eight of the eleven tracking radars on the peninsula were not operational. The KGB interpreted this incident, in line with the psy-ops that had preceded it, as "political provocation carefully organized by the US special services." One purpose of the provocation "was to use the incursions of the intruder aircraft

---

[25] Vistica, *Fall from Glory*, 108.

[26] Hoffman, *The Dead Hand*, 66–68.

[27] Benjamin B. Fischer, *A Cold War Conundrum: The 1983 Soviet War Scare* (Washington, DC: Central Intelligence Agency, September 1997), 10, accessed 25 March 2018, https://www.cia.gov/library/center-for-the-study-of-intelligence/csi-publications/books-and-monographs/a-cold-war-conundrum/source.htm.

[28] Hoffman, *The Dead Hand*, 64–65.

[29] It is worth noting that during the same time period, the U.S. Navy ran a number of other forward exercises, including carrier operations out of the Norwegian fjords and trailing Soviet SSBNs stationed under the polar ice caps. Fischer, *Cold War Conundrum*, 10.

into Soviet airspace to create a favorable situation for the gathering of defense data on our air defense in the Far East, involving the most diverse systems, including the Ferret satellite."[30] Many Soviet officials never abandoned the position that Korean Airlines Flight 007 was actually an U.S. spy plane.[31]

Soviet Perceptions of Vulnerability

Soviet policymakers appeared to "get the message" about the nuclear balance in three different ways. First, top political-military leaders believed that the nuclear balance could matter even in a world of nuclear plenty. Second, they perceived specific vulnerabilities in Soviet nuclear posture, including in those areas of emerging cross-domain technological complexity that the United States had been emphasizing: C3 and mobile targets. Third, they were concerned about their country's prospects in a long-term nuclear competition because of Soviet technological, economic, and political weakness relative to the United States. This evidence is consistent with a less restrictive version of the nuclear revolution, a world where cross-domain interactions impose symmetrical requirements and where clandestine capabilities can be communicated effectively.

The Meaning of the Nuclear Balance

Soviet nuclear strategists perceived two basic problems that might undermine MAD, even in a world of nuclear plenty. Their perceptions generated pressures for competitive arms racing. First, there was no guarantee that Soviet nuclear forces would succeed in effective retaliation under Clausewitzian conditions of fog and friction—uncertainties that are likely to become ubiquitous as cross-domain technological complexity increases. As General Danilevich put it, even the best analysis of the nuclear balance could not "capture effectively the art (or luck) of the commander who might make or fail to make the 'critical' decision that will tend to dominate all other factors in determining the outcome of a given operation." In theory, he argued, "we may have the possibility to totally destroy the U.S. and vice versa. But in practice . . . the result could be completely unexpected. Because perhaps not all of these forces you have would be used. Because in the end you might not find the man who will press that button. That depends on many, many things." Explicitly comparing a nuclear campaign to the command and intelligence catastrophes of Cannae and Barbarossa, he emphasized that despite well-laid plans, "in practice, things may go otherwise. And it is the fear of that 'otherwise' that forces

---

[30] Ibid., 21, 23.
[31] Hoffman, *The Dead Hand*, 65–66.

us to modernize nuclear weapons, the control systems, to develop various options for their use, etc."[32]

Second, the political leadership might falter at the critical moment, hesitating long enough for hard-target systems to do their deadly work. The Hines report suggests that Soviet leadership was resistant to facing up to the realities of nuclear war. The only time the Politburo was integrated into a serious nuclear exercise, in 1972, General Secretary Leonid Brezhnev was "visibly shaken and pale and his hand trembled" as he asked several times "for assurances that the action would not have any real-world consequences."[33] High-level involvement in strategy for nuclear operations was thereafter curtailed; "after that [1972 exercise], the political leadership did not participate in any of these events even once."[34]

This dissociation extended to issues of nuclear policy more broadly. Danilevich reported that "[General Secretary Yuri] Andropov did not get involved," that "[General Secretary Konstantin] Chernenko did not touch these matters at all," and that "[as] for [General Secretary Mikhail] Gorbachev, he was involved, but in an incompetent and perfunctory manner."[35] Moreover, accurate information on nuclear operations was actively suppressed. The study that had precipitated the 1972 exercise was "buried" because its "message was judged too psychologically detrimental to morale and resolve. . . . For subsequent studies, coefficients were introduced into the models which artificially reduced the level of destruction." Unsurprisingly, Russian strategists felt that "looking back, there was a certain unseriousness about" nuclear weapons among Soviet political leadership: "the thinking was, 'we've got nuclear weapons and will use them if we need to.'"[36] Given the importance of quick and informed decisionmaking during a nuclear crisis, this attitude provided little comfort that mutually assured destruction would hold. The United States' programs exacerbated a critical preexisting C3 weakness at the very top of the Soviet chain of command.

Independent of worries about whether Soviet capabilities would actually perform retaliatory missions effectively, Soviet nuclear policymakers felt that falling behind in the arms race had political meaning. The Hines report concluded that Moscow believed it could not allow "U.S. leaders to feel such a sense of security and superiority that they would try to exercise their will in Europe with impunity"

---

[32] Hines interview with Andrian A. Danilevich, in John G. Hines, Ellis M. Mishulovich, and John F. Shull, *Soviet Intentions 1965–1985*, vol. 2, *Soviet Post–Cold War Testimonial Evidence*, BDM Federal, Inc., 22 September 1995, unclassified, excised copy, 25, 30, accessed 25 March 2018, https://NSARCHIVE2.gwu.edu/nukevault/ebb285/vol%20iI%20Danilevich.pdf.

[33] Ibid., 27. Brezhnev apparently kept inquiring whether the defense minister was "sure this is just an exercise?"

[34] Ibid., 43.

[35] Apparently, Gorbachev once attended an exercise in Minsk where he gave a prepared speech and departed before the exercise commenced. All quotations from ibid., 43.

[36] Ibid., 28, 2, 62.

or "pursue adventurist policies in the Third World."[37] As Danilevich put it, both superpowers knew that "if there were a [technological] breakthrough, it would take a certain amount of time to develop the means to counteract it, and that every such [breakthrough] gave a temporary technological superiority, and that technological superiority allowed political pressure to be brought to bear, and all of this was linked into a single chain." These realities meant that "there were technological, strategic, and political reasons for further development" of the strategic arms race.[38]

Specific Nuclear Vulnerabilities

Soviet strategists perceived specific vulnerabilities in their relocatable targets and C3, as well as the cross-domain sources of such vulnerabilities. Danilevich recounted that "you had an advanced system of passive detection and antisubmarine warfare ... this made our subs very vulnerable .... Plus, we were blocked in by your anti-sub barriers, both in the east and in the west, which made our access to open seas very difficult." Moreover, "you had better hydro-acoustics. So when there is anti-submarine surveillance you can hear us, but we cannot hear you. This worried and continues to worry us." The problem was so worrisome that the Soviet Navy even considered launching its submarines' missiles (SLBMs) from their home bases, even though this would vitiate nearly the entire purpose of submarines as a nuclear launch platform.[39]

Soviet strategists also recognized the problem of mobile missile vulnerability. As the Cold War was ending, Vitalii Kataev, a senior advisor to the defense policymaking body of the Communist Party Central Committee, circulated a memo on "Mobile Missile Basing" to the defense department of the committee. He argued: "in the period up to [the year] 2000 ... the use of mobile missile complexes is the only course that provides the necessary level of retaliatory force in the Strategic Rocket Forces." But given U.S. counterforce advantages, Soviet retaliatory capability was under pressure: "existing Strategic Rocket Forces are capable of hitting [eighty] enemy rear area targets in retaliation, by 1995 100 targets and by 2000 150 targets, slightly below the calculated level of retaliation required—200 targets." Furthermore, the memo stated, "a definite impact on the survivability and combat effectiveness of mobile rocket complexes is the possibility that the United States can improve its space surveillance and create systems to defeat the mobile targets."[40]

---

[37] Hines et al., *Soviet Intentions 1965–1985*, vol. 1, 16.
[38] Danilevich interview, Hines et al., *Soviet Intentions 1965–1985*, vol. 2, 33.
[39] Ibid., 46.
[40] Vitalii Kataev, "Mobile Missile Basing," trans. Austin Long, Vitalii Leonidovich Kataev Papers, Hoover Institution Archive, Stanford University. The memorandum is undated, but based on context it is from the late 1980s or early 1990s.

The Russians understood the basic outline of what these capabilities looked like. The earlier memo, authored by one N. A. Brunitsyn, had explained that "eight satellites in stationary orbit of the 'Chalet' and 'Rhyolite' type" could "exercise detection and interception of radio relay trunks of the national [communications] network." At the same time, "[two] new generation satellites 'Aquacade'/'Magnum' in stationary orbit are intercepting radio and radio-technical emissions and eavesdropping on radio channels in an extended frequency range," and the former satellite "has a very high sensitivity and accuracy for locating radiating objects."[41]

Perhaps the greatest area of Soviet fear, though, was the vulnerability of the Soviet C3 systems, which would enable a retaliatory strike. According to Lieutenant-General Mikhail Kalashnikov, C3 was the Soviet Union's "Achilles heel": Moscow was never able "to create a sophisticated, survivable, [and] integrated command, control, and communications system." He described a marked contrast with U.S. C3, which contained eight command centers that were "absolutely protected" and an entire computerized network of command nodes linked together with long-wave communications, elements of which could be bypassed quickly if they were damaged. For the Soviets on the other hand "a major difficulty was the lack of an adequate communications infrastructure," with, for example, "only one military communications cable linking Moscow with the Far East." In a related vein, Kalashnikov had to fight "titanic battles" just to "[introduce] scrambling devices into Soviet naval communications," having become convinced that they were necessary after an admiral "described shadowing a U.S. fleet on maneuvers and not hearing any radio traffic."[42]

Several other Soviet nuclear strategists perceived similar problems with Soviet C3 and made the assessment that they would make LUA impossible. General Igor Illarinov, special assistant to Soviet defense minister Dmitry Ustinov, recalled that during the early 1970s, "we came to the conclusion that . . . we did not have the capability to conduct a retaliatory launch before the enemy's warheads hit our missiles. There were many debates and calculations, but the doctrine [of launch on warning] was not worked out." He also worried that the political "taking of decisions would require not minutes and seconds, as would be required by the time of flight of a missile, but hours."[43] Iurii A. Mozzhorin, director of the missile industry's think tank, similarly emphasized that "no launches could be made without a political decision"

---

[41] N. A. Brunitsyn, "Monitoring and Intelligence," Kataev Papers, Hoover Institution Archive, Stanford University.

[42] Kalashnikov interview, Hines et al., *Soviet Intentions 1965–1985*, vol. 2, 90, 94, accessed 25 March 2018, https://nsarchive2.gwu.edu/nukevault/ebb285/vol%20II%20Kalashnikov.PDF.

[43] Institute for Defense Studies interview with General-Colonel Igor V. Illarionov, Hines et al., *Soviet Intentions 1965–1985*, vol. 2, 80, accessed 25 March 2018, https://nsarchive2.gwu.edu/nukevault/ebb285/vol%20II%20Illarionov.PDF.

and thus "argued in favor of giving the SRF [Strategic Rocket Forces] [a] physical quick reaction capability" as that much more important.[44]

But it was not at all clear how effective such retaliation might be. Kalashnikov believed that "the situation regarding EW [early warning] protection against a surprise attack was quite serious"; and he served on a commission formed only in 1975 to begin work on the problem. And the C3 challenges were even worse. At some point, Kalashnikov produced a report calculating "that after sustaining an all-out nuclear strike," the Soviets "would be able to launch only [2 percent] of their [remaining] missiles."[45]

The Pressures of Long-Term Competition

Moscow not only perceived specific vulnerabilities in its nuclear posture to U.S. cross-domain innovations but also felt compelled to respond and worried that it might not withstand the pressures of a long-term arms race. As Danilevich reported, "the Soviet General Staff believed that there were a great number of areas where the Soviets were not only behind, but where the U.S. advantage continued to grow." Indeed, "serious resumption of [strategic] force building [was] stimulated above all by the desire to get ahead of," or at least keep up with, "the U.S. competition."[46]

The root cause of Soviet weakness was the United States' qualitative technological advantage, which Soviet analysts "never did understand very well." "Because of qualitative deficiencies," Danilevich thought, "one side could have a tenfold quantitative advantage and still be behind." This feature of the arms race was especially troubling, given the Soviet focus on quantitative production. While "on a large scale over a long time period, [total force] numbers do matter," qualitative advantages and Clausewitzian factors tend to drive outcomes in "operations of limited duration." Danilevich noted that a purely "mathematical analysis would have predicted other outcomes for the Russian-German conflict in World War I and for the Pakistan-Bangladesh conflict."[47]

The result was an overpowering sense of a weaker Soviet Union hard-pressed by U.S. technological developments. Danilevich recounted that "the technological policies of the U.S., the breakthroughs that you achieved, the struggles that went on there—all of this was taken into consideration. Take the intelligence data. You confused us terribly.... We had to investigate it all." Even when U.S. moves appeared irrational, the Soviets felt compelled to respond: "[sometimes] your scientists were in

---

[44] Hines interview with Iurii A. Mozzhorin, Hines et al., *Soviet Intentions 1965–1985*, vol. 2, 125, accessed 25 March 2018, https://nsarchive2.gwu.edu/nukevault/ebb285/vol%20II%20Mozzhorin.PDF.

[45] Kalashnikov interview, Hines et al., *Soviet Intentions 1965–1985*, vol. 2, 88, 90.

[46] Danilevich interview, Hines et al., *Soviet Intentions 1965–1985*, vol. 2, 22–23.

[47] Ibid., 25.

a rush and even though the necessary conditions did not yet exist you would adopt the corresponding concepts or postures. This baffled us; we could not see why you took such steps. We denounced them, then we would begin ourselves to look for solutions, and thus you would push us to further improvements and developments."

The need to wage a technological competition, however, did not equate to the ability to prosecute it successfully. Soviet strategists feared that they lacked the technological, economic, and political flexibility to keep pace with the United States. Kalashnikov, a rocketry expert in charge of missile and warhead testing, believed that much "economic over-extension was driven by the arms race and by the growing complexity and sophistication of modern weapons," estimating that 60–70 percent of Soviet "industrial plants, which under normal conditions would be non-defense, were deliberately and systematically drawn into defense production." The result was a "vast industrial base devoted to the production of missiles [that] destroyed the national economy and pauperized the people."[48]

Dr. Vitalli Tsygichko agreed, explaining that his own modeling effort confirmed forecasts of "a bleak future for the Soviet economy because of significant distortions, maldistribution of investment, and excessive nonproductive expenditures such as those devoted to defense."[49] Such poor "inter-sector balance within the Soviet economy," compared to the economies of the West, meant that the gap in "output was widening at a nonlinear rate." At the same time, if Moscow conceded the race, "[the] Soviet economy would be forced to undergo radical adjustments which few were able or willing to contemplate."[50] Who knew where such a political upheaval might lead? The arms race meant the Soviet Union was economically damned if it did and politically damned if it didn't. Not by accident, the KGB work plan for 1984 was "a reorientation of intelligence collection requirements away from advanced Western technology applicable to the ailing Soviet economy, and to new U.S. weapon systems and military technologies."[51]

Such trade-offs between long-term economic health and a desperate need for short-term technological competitiveness filtered all the way to the top, especially under General Secretary Yuri Andropov. Andropov, according to a KGB officer who served on his staff, "had an unusual fascination with things American and marveled at US human and materiel potential, especially in military matters." Unusually technologically sophisticated for the political leadership—he could apparently hold his own with the professional military—he once "exploded when he realized that

---

[48] Kalashnikov interview, Hines et al., *Soviet Intentions 1965–1985*, vol. 2, 37, 42, 92.

[49] Hines interviews with Vitalli Nikolaevich Tsygichko, Hines et al., *Soviet Intentions 1965–1985*, vol. 2, 152, accessed 25 March 2018, https://nsarchive2.gwu.edu/nukevault/ebb285/vol%20II%20Tysgichko.PDF.

[50] Tsygichko interview, Hines et al., *Soviet Intentions 1965–1985*, vol. 2, 153, 138.

[51] Fischer, "The Soviet–American War Scare of the 1980s," 491.

Soviet labs were incapable of producing spy gear comparable to a small transmitter the counterintelligence service had taken from a US agent."[52]

In short, the political and military leadership of the Soviet Union saw a series of connections between technological backwardness, economic weakness, and political inflexibility. They were therefore pessimistic about the Soviet ability to compete in a high-tech nuclear arms race.

Soviet Policy Adjustments

As predicted by the more optimistic group of hypotheses, increasing technological complexity and cross-domain operations benefited the stronger rather than the weaker superpower. Soviet policymakers could not afford to ignore traditional U.S. strengths in a cross-domain competition and felt obliged to engage in symmetric technological responses, as well as asymmetric innovations, as they strove to fix their nuclear vulnerabilities. Moreover, neither sort of response was especially successful. Soviet policymakers were correct to perceive their long-term technological and economic weaknesses, and their haphazard attempts at asymmetric substitutes were largely failures.

Symmetric Technological Responses

The Soviet Union adjusted symmetrically to U.S. cross-domain technological superiority with a technological push of its own—Moscow made a major attempt to fix its early warning and C3 vulnerabilities during the last part of the Cold War. The early warning modernization effort consisted of three projects: an effort to improve the ground radar network with cutting-edge Daryal large phased array radars(LPAR); the development of over-the-horizon (OTH) radars; and the construction of a satellite constellation of "Oko" satellites in highly elliptical orbits (HEO). Together, the three elements of the early warning system were to be mutually reinforcing, providing multiple sources of launch confirmation and therefore the confidence to order LUA.[53]

Soviet technologists also worked toward corresponding improvements in nuclear C3. Two versions of the "Signal" nuclear command system, "M" and "A," were deployed in 1982 and 1985, respectively. These systems aimed to connect launch crews to all levels of command and enable simultaneous status reporting up and down the chain of command—critical for ensuring and coordinating retaliation after an attack. Several nuclear sanctioning systems were also developed, including

---

[52] Fischer, *A Cold War Conundrum*, 18, n. 71.

[53] Pavel Podvig, "History and the Current Status of the Russian Early-Warning System," *Science and Global Security* 10, no. 1 (2002): 21–60, https://doi.org/10.1080/08929880212328.

the nuclear "briefcase" (*cheget*), to connect the top leadership and communicate their decisions down the chain of command.[54]

The Soviet Union's revitalized early warning programs were mostly failures. Technological problems abounded: "designers faced serious interface problems and had to rework combat algorithms and computer programs so that the various components [of the early warning system] could exchange data." The program was ultimately scrapped, with its radars being derided as "virtually useless": they could reliably detect the simultaneous launch of thousands of missiles but not the smaller launch numbers that would be associated with a preemptive attack on Soviet C3. The program did manage to produce one innovation, the Daryal large phased array radars, two of which were deployed in 1984–1985—six years late and billions of rubles over budget. Even here, in this case of innovation, there had been big problems. "The biggest problem," Fischer argues, "came in the one area where the Soviets were weakest, namely computers and algorithm software. The Daryal program was a microcosm of the Soviet system on the eve of its collapse. The USSR could still build mammoth Stalin-era projects (though not well) but could not cope well with microelectronic engineering."[55]

The Soviet Union also had large problems with its satellite program. The Oko satellites used thermal imaging to detect boost phase rocket plumes coming from U.S. ICBM fields, giving Soviet C3 a crucial extra ten minutes to react. However, they had no capability to detect submarine missile launches. After a number of problems associated with "working out an algorithm for its on board computer," the first Oko deployed in 1978, and the full constellation of the satellites was operating by 1982, four years behind schedule. However, a series of terrifying false alarms shortly after the downing of Korean Airlines Flight 007 revealed that the Oko was "extremely unreliable," according to a Soviet commission investigating the incident. The satellites' hardware and software were both "far from perfect," and Soviet ground radar performance also laid bare "many disappointing details." The commission found that the Oko constellation had been deployed before testing and evaluation could be completed and was "horrified" by the overall performance of Soviet early warning.[56]

Soviet C3 efforts were not much better. Signal-M contained vulnerabilities that permitted exploitation by NATO's CANOPY WING electronic warfare techniques; after a decade in development it had to be hastily replaced by Signal-A.[57] The *cheget*, meanwhile, could connect surviving members of the high command but could not issue orders directly. Moreover, Moscow did not consider these systems sufficient to assure retaliation, let alone LUA. In 1979, the Soviets relaunched a program for

---

[54] See: Valery E. Yarynich, *C3: Nuclear Command, Control Cooperation* (Washington, DC: Center for Defense Information, 2003).

[55] Fischer, "The Soviet–American War Scare of the 1980s," 501, 502.

[56] Ibid., 504. For a dramatic account of the false alarms, see: Hoffman, *The Dead Hand*, 6–11.

[57] Fischer, "CANOPY WING," 448–449.

a system known as Perimitr, designed to ensure automatic retaliation even if the Soviet leadership had been decapitated. Evoking Dr. Strangelove's doomsday machine, one variant of Perimitr was referred to as "the Dead Hand," and as in the case of the fictional doomsday machine, no version of Perimitr was ever revealed to the West, vitiating any deterrent capability it might have had.[58] In the event, according to the Hines interviews, a highly automatic system was probably never deployed and may not have advanced very far in development.[59]

Asymmetric Cross-Domain Responses

The Soviet Union also tried to respond to U.S. nuclear policy asymmetrically in other domains. One domain where the Eastern Bloc traditionally held an advantage was human intelligence, which became the focus of a multiyear program called RYaN—a Russian acronym for "nuclear missile attack." In May 1981, shortly after the Reagan psy-ops began in earnest, then KGB chief Andropov made a surprise announcement at a secret KGB conference: "the new American administration, he declared, was preparing for nuclear war."[60] He then explained that the Politburo had decided on a massive intelligence-gathering operation aimed at producing warning of any Western nuclear attack. RYaN would also be a joint operation: for the first time ever, the KGB would collaborate with the Soviet military intelligence organization (the GRU). The operation was to be global in scope: all foreign intelligence residencies were to report RYaN data every two weeks.[61]

However, RYaN was neither cheap nor effective. It "required an inordinate amount of time," according to an officer in the KGB's Washington residency. It was not officially canceled until 1991, and even then "the chief of foreign intelligence noted that . . . by that late date the alert still 'involved huge material and human resources' and required biweekly reports from KGB residencies."[62] In 1985, East German intelligence (HVA) organized an even more massive RYaN effort, greatly aided by the fact that the HVA was a much more effective intelligence agency than the KGB. The effort was the "absolute priority" for East German intelligence and included a "gigantic" command center to monitor NATO and U.S. exercises, with a "special communications link" to Moscow Center; a new organizational headquarters to manage the incoming intelligence; special training for HVA intelligence officers; annual exercises that simulated the intelligence situation before a surprise attack; a massive signals intelligence apparatus; and intensive recruitment

---

[58] One suspects that late Cold War Soviet leadership must have loved surprises.
[59] Hines et al., *Soviet Intentions 1965–1985*, vol. 1, 19–21.
[60] Christopher Andrew and Oleg Gordievsky, eds., *Comrade Kryuchkov's Instructions: Top Secret Files on KGB Foreign Operations, 1975–1985* (Stanford, CA: Stanford University Press, 1994), 67–69.
[61] Ibid.
[62] Fischer, *A Cold War Conundrum*, 5, 31, n. 115

of Western spies. In the end, the effort collected precious little intelligence of real value.[63]

The Soviet Union also tried to shift to traditional diplomacy in order to relieve some of the pressure from the nuclear competition. Andropov had a meeting earlier in 1983 with Averell Harriman, who had been U.S. ambassador to the Soviet Union during World War II and was presently posing as a "private citizen" unconnected with the U.S. government. Harriman reported that Andropov alluded four separate times to the threat of nuclear war and to the alarm the aggressive U.S. policies, which were moving toward "the dangerous red line," were causing in Moscow. Harriman offered that Moscow realized that "taking into account the military situation and the growing number of explosive problems, we cannot afford the luxury of destructive rivalry." Problems in the superpower relationship, though, were the result of a U.S. policy aimed at "military preponderance and economic and other kinds of harm." The Soviets would be willing to cooperate but would not accept Reagan's implicit proposal of a "unilateral laying down of [Soviet] arms."[64]

On the other hand the Soviets also tried diplomatic maneuvers to indicate their willingness to be reasonable. In October 1983, Jack Matlock, the U.S. National Security Council (NSC) senior director of European and Soviet affairs, took a meeting with Sergei Vishnevsky. As Matlock described him, "he clearly has sound party and (almost certainly) KGB credentials. . . . We must assume that, in general, he was conveying a series of messages someone in the regime wants us to hear." Indeed, "he was so intent on getting his comments off his chest that he carefully avoided debating me on any points I made, either agreeing with them or letting them pass." While there was a real possibility of "disinformation," the back-channel communication appeared genuine.[65]

The message was simple: "the economy was a 'total mess, and getting worse.' " The Politburo understood that they "need a decrease in tension to concentrate on economic reform." Vishnevsky emphasized: "the domestic economy remains the priority issue for them." However, the Soviet leadership was completely frustrated by the failure of their own policies and the string of military, economic, and political successes the Reagan administration was having at home and abroad. The Politburo was "frustrated because they feel beleaguered and simply do not know how to proceed" in the face of signs that "the Reagan administration is out to get them and will

---

[63] Fischer, "The Soviet–American War Scare of the 1980s," 486–487.

[64] Andropov-Harriman meeting on 2 June 1983, Memorandum of Conversation between General Secretary Yuri Andropov and Averell Harriman, 3:00 PM, June 2, 1983, CPSU Central Committee Headquarters, Moscow "The 1983 War Scare: 'The Last Paroxysm' of the Cold War Part I," W. Averell Harriman Papers, Library of Congress, Manuscript Division, Box 655 National Security Archive, 16 May 2013, 3, 4, 10, accessed 25 March 2018, http://www2.gwu.edu/~nsarchiv/NSAEBB/NSAEBB426/.

[65] Ibid., 2.

give no quarter." They worried that they might have "no choice but to hunker down and fight back."[66]

Conclusion

The historical record gives reasonably strong support to the more optimistic set of hypotheses about the impact of increasing cross-domain technological complexity on deterrence and U.S. military primacy. Despite the clandestine nature of U.S. cross-domain capabilities against Soviet SSBNs, mobile ICBMs, early warning systems, and C3 networks, Washington made a number of efforts to signal its military advantages without giving away crucial information necessary for countermeasures. These efforts relied on military demonstrations, selective leaks, possible counterintelligence operations, and, probably, the fact that compromising a few select capabilities was not as significant in a long-term competition.

Furthermore, consistent with optimistic views on signaling and a weaker version of the nuclear view of the nuclear revolution, Moscow apparently "got the message." Soviet political-military leaders perceived specific weaknesses in their mobile nuclear platforms and C3 generated by U.S. technological innovations and believed that these vulnerabilities could generate political liabilities even in an era of nuclear plenty. They were also greatly concerned about the potential implications of the arms race that would be necessary to remedy their nuclear failings, as it would be waged against a more technologically, economically, and politically flexible superpower.

Finally, as these worries indicate, increasing cross-domain technological complexity, rather than serving as a weapon of the weak, helped the stronger superpower get even stronger during the later Cold War. Soviet policymakers felt compelled toward symmetrical technological responses to U.S. innovations, as they attempted to improve their early warning and C3 systems for LUA or post-ride-out retaliation. But they lacked the technological, economic, and political capabilities to execute these projects over long periods of time at the high levels of effectiveness necessary for them to work. Likewise, their asymmetric innovations, even in areas of strength like human intelligence, absorbed massive resources while yielding few results.

What are the implications of this study for U.S. defense policy in the emerging era of cross-domain interactions? On the one hand this study offers a qualified vote for good news. Whatever problems enemy anti-access/area-denial, cyber, antispace, and hybrid warfare capabilities might cause for U.S. cross-domain operations, increasingly complex terms for military competition can probably only redound to Washington's benefit. Some have criticized U.S. responses to these threats as setting

[66] Ibid.

goals that are unnecessarily challenging, as is arguably the case for the U.S. Joint Concept for Access and Maneuver in the Global Commons response to the Chinese anti-access/area-denial threat.[67] But, even accepting this critique for a moment, the late Cold War case shows the possibilities that become available to a technologically and economically advanced superpower.

Holding Soviet strategic nuclear forces at risk was a *very* challenging task indeed, but the U.S. military achieved a fair measure of success and in the process put quite a bit of economic, military, and political pressure on its chief rival. The strong can, if they choose, compete on an adversary's turf in a world of cross-domain complexity. But the reverse is not true. It is hard to imagine that U.S. adversaries with the potential to mount a multidomain challenge would fare much better than the late Cold War Soviet Union, which had already overcome substantial barriers to entry.

On the other hand we must be cautious about drawing policy lessons from the case divorced from potentially limiting context. In what respects does the Cold War nuclear competition provide a good or bad analogy for contemporary CDD, where both the technology and the identity of the adversary have changed?

In some respects, adding cyber capabilities might cause modern military competition to depart from the Cold War example. Cyberweapons would appear to produce military advantages that are especially difficult to signal. They tend to rely on highly specific vulnerabilities that are easy to repair once discovered. The rapid deterioration of Stuxnet's effectiveness, once the worm escaped into the wild and came to the attention of private cybersecurity firms, testifies to the potentially fleeting nature of a cyber advantage.[68] Similarly, the despair and horror in the national security community at the exposure of hacking tools belonging to the National Security Agency's Tailored Access Operations division suggests that many cyberweapons have a short half-life once they are discovered.[69] Best-of-both-worlds signaling mechanisms that demonstrate capability without compromising technique might be few and far between in the cyber domain.

Moreover, states might also be less inclined to risk a loss of military effectiveness by engaging in signaling with cyber capabilities. Many of the most attractive cyber weapons will exploit enemy coding vulnerabilities to produce one-use, "kill shot"–type capabilities, such as interfering with C3, air defenses, or other points of maximum leverage in modern military organizations. If the United States could turn off an adversary's nuclear command and control networks, it is hard to imagine anyone

---

[67] For a summary of much of the debate, see: Aaron Friedberg, *Beyond Air–Sea Battle: The Debate over US Military Strategy in Asia* (London: International Institute for Strategic Studies, 2014).

[68] For the definitive account of Stuxnet, see: Jon R. Lindsay, "Stuxnet and the Limits of Cyber Warfare," *Security Studies* 22, no. 3 (2013): 365–404, https://doi.org/10.1080/09636412.2013.816122.

[69] See, e.g., Scott Shane, Nicole Perlroth, and David E. Sanger, "Security Breach and Spilled Secrets Have Shaken the N.S.A. to Its Core," *New York Times*, 12 November 2017, accessed 25 March 2018, https://www.nytimes.com/2017/11/12/us/nsa-shadow-brokers.html.

breathing a word about it before the fateful moment, even if Washington believed some sort of political advantage might be obtained by signaling. To the extent that cyberspace favors the creation of military capabilities that are unique and irreplaceable, we will probably witness a greater premium on concealment, compared to the emphasis on signaling in the case of the Cold War.[70]

However, not all features of cyberweapons cut against signaling. One feature of the capabilities that might tend to favor signaling is the responsiveness of the adversary in devising countermeasures. It is, after all, less costly to signal a capability if the adversary does not seem likely to implement the correct response should key secrets be discovered. The United States' own appalling lack of good cyber hygiene demonstrates that knowing about a cyber vulnerability and remedying it are very far from being the same thing.[71] This kind of problem has a direct analogy in the Cold War nuclear competition: one of the reasons that the United States became willing to signal its advantages in antisubmarine warfare was policymakers' realization that the Soviet Union's stormy relationship with its naval yards and increasing financial problems made it unlikely that it would implement efficacious fleet-wide countermeasures in response to any new information.[72] The peculiar characteristics of individual adversaries might contribute to their responsiveness and, in turn, the United States' willingness to signal with its cyber capabilities.

Consider, for example, the difference in Washington's response to the North Korean hack on the Sony Corporation and Russia's attempts to influence the 2016 U.S. presidential election. In the former case, the United States made a presidential-level decision to reveal penetrations of North Korean networks in order to attribute the hack to Pyongyang.[73] Meanwhile, U.S. policy on the Russian hacks was debated furiously throughout the summer and autumn, and the final public attribution did not contain any reference to U.S. cyber sources and methods.[74] There are numerous

---

[70] For a fuller set of hypotheses about state decisions about clandestine capabilities and the causes of their success and failure, see Brendan Rittenhouse Green and Austin Long, "The Role of Clandestine Capabilities in Deterrence: Theory and Practice," U.S. Naval Postgraduate School, Project on Advanced Systems and Concepts for Countering WMD (PASCC), Grant N00244-16-1-0032: Final Report, 2016.

[71] Joe Gould, "Official Warns of DoD's Sloppy Cyber Hygiene," *Defense News*, 24 June 2015, accessed 25 March 2018, https://www.defensenews.com/2015/06/24/official-warns-of-dod-s-sloppy-cyber-hygiene/.

[72] Green and Long, "The Role of Clandestine Capabilities in Deterrence," contains a detailed reconstruction of antisubmarine warfare signals during the Cold War.

[73] Shane Harris, "U.S. Spies Say They Tracked 'Sony Hackers' for Years," *Daily Beast*, 2 January 2015, accessed 25 March 2018, https://www.thedailybeast.com/us-spies-say-they-tracked-sony-hackers-for-years.

[74] "Background to "'Assessing Russian Activities and Intentions in Recent US Elections': The Analytic Process and Cyber Incident Attribution," Office of the Director of National Intelligence, 6 January 2017, accessed 25 March 2017, https://www.dni.gov/files/documents/ICA_2017_01.pdf.

factors that might help explain the difference, with the Trump campaign's allegations of electoral tampering only the most obvious. But one plausible explanation for divergence in case outcomes is the likely judgment that North Korean networks could be reinfiltrated after the initial North Korean response, while Russian networks would be difficult to penetrate a second time.

As this example demonstrates, the applicability of our findings to contemporary CDD depends as much on the character of the adversary as on technology. How far might Cold War lessons extend to the possible great power rivalry between China and the United States?

The similarities between the cases are potentially legion. Like the Cold War, a serious military rivalry in the Pacific would be a multitheater affair with potential contemporary flashpoints all along the Chinese littoral: from disputed islands in the South China Sea to Taiwan and to the Senkakus and the Korean peninsula. The struggle would also be a multidomain one. Ground combat in Korea, combined with air and naval campaigns in other hot spots, would be supplemented from space and cyberspace on both sides. Nuclear weapons would loom behind any outbreak of conventional violence, and there would be exposed allies on both sides. Such a military competition would therefore see the same pressures for horizontal and vertical escalation the Cold War saw, as well as the similarly bracing dynamics of N-player games.

On the other hand the two cases also have differences that might cut toward opposite results. The Soviet-American case took place at the end of the most intense geopolitical competition in world history, a multidecade endeavor that spanned the globe and ate resources like nothing before or since. For structural, historical, psychological, and political reasons, both sides may have seen the competition in purely zero-sum terms that are not as likely to obtain in the future. The foregoing analysis is thus heavily biased toward a competitive environment. Though the Sino-American relationship has experienced increasing tensions over the past decade, it has not yet reached the point where either side dismisses opportunities for real cooperation. For instance, some have suggested that the interest of presidents Xi Jinping and Donald Trump in infrastructure investment present real opportunities for joint gains.[75] Likewise, with the relationship more ambiguous than between the Cold War superpowers, competitive behavior might have serious political repercussions—reasons some have offered for tamping down U.S. military efforts, especially in the nuclear field.[76]

---

[75] Gal Luft, "A New Way to Hold the U.S.-China Relationship Together," 10 January 2017, *Foreign Policy*, accessed 25 March 2018, http://foreignpolicy.com/2017/01/10/a-new-way-to-hold-the-us-china-relationship-together-infrastructure-cooperation-not-climate-aiib-end-of-kumbaya/.

[76] Charles L. Glaser and Steve Fetter, "Should the US Reject MAD? Damage Limitation and US Nuclear Strategy toward China," *International Security* 41, no. 1 (Summer 2016): 49–98, https://doi.org/10.1162/ISEC_a_00248.

In some ways, the two cases are different without clear implications for our findings here. The Soviet–American technological competition took place mainly at the nuclear level, and the primacy of the nuclear competition during the broader Cold War period was widely acknowledged by both superpowers. However, it is by no means a given that future cross-domain military complexity will imply nuclear competition. Rising potential rivals to the United States, such as China, might simply think about nuclear weapons differently from the Soviet Union; or it might be that the conditions of geography and extended deterrence commitments that made nuclear weapons supreme in Europe will not govern a Pacific rivalry.[77] At the same time, though, differences in the Pacific context might actually give more scope for the use of clandestine military capabilities and signals about their existence. It opens up the Sino-American rivalry to the influence of a wider set of military capabilities and potential secret changes to local military balance.

These important uncertainties aside, the picture presented here gives some cause for optimism about future U.S. defense policy. It does not seem likely that there are easy disruptive innovations that will shatter U.S. technological dominance, that the United States will be wholly unable to communicate that dominance without attenuating it, or that nuclear weapons will be a trump card. David can have his slingshot, but in a cross-domain world, it is good to be Goliath.

---

[77] Fiona S. Cunningham and M. Taylor Fravel, "Assuring Assured Retaliation: China's Nuclear Posture and U.S.-China Strategic Stability," *International Security* 40, no. 2 (Fall 2015): 7–50, https://doi.org/10.1162/ISEC_a_00215; Richard C. Bush, "The U.S. Policy of Extended Deterrence in East Asia: History, Current Views, and Implications," Brookings Institution, February 2011, accessed 25 March 2018, https://www.brookings.edu/wp-content/uploads/2016/06/02_arms_control_bush.pdf.

11

Extended Deterrence and Assurance in Multiple Domains

RUPAL N. MEHTA

With the advent of new capabilities for combat, the nature of international relations has become increasingly complex and intertwined. Conflicts and crises are no longer fought in isolation, and states often must rely on friends and allies to assist in warfighting. In today's international environment, a few capable states have the ability to project power and deploy troops, resources, and sophisticated technologies to distant allies with relative ease. While in previous eras of history it would have seemed impossible to deploy and maintain an active military presence more than 6,000 miles away, the United States now has the technological capacity to sustain multiple competing commitments simultaneously, using a variety of advanced capabilities.

The creation and extension of the U.S. nuclear umbrella and defense commitments to allies throughout the international system, for instance, remains at the center of U.S. foreign policy and broader grand strategy debates. While scholars' and policymakers' emphases oscillate between strengthening alliance commitments (and the degree to which U.S. forces are involved in the defense of an ally's territory) and slowly shifting to a more restrained and narrow international presence, existing allies and interested states curiously watch to see which side will win out and how these decisions impact their long-term security interests. Allies like Japan, South Korea, Australia, and Israel are experiencing similar foreign policy debates surrounding the future of their own defenses in response to U.S. extended deterrence policy. Observing Japan, scholars contend: "Japan also has seen America's attention shift from the Asia-Pacific region in the years following 9/11. As a result of these and other factors, there is greater acceptance in Japan today of open discussion of nuclear issues, including discussion of America's ability to provide an effective extended nuclear deterrent. The political stalemate in Washington on the future of America's nuclear weapons infrastructure and program has been visible in Japan."[1]

These concerns are unsurprising, considering that the long history of external deterrence agreements similarly raised questions of uncertainty and commitment to allies in the face of increasing threats from new adversaries. In the midst of the Cold War, as the United States and the Soviet Union began to establish informal/formal agreements to provide defense and security against foreign threats, allies have questioned the strength of these commitments and the likelihood that a patron state would actually come to their defense in a time of crisis. Fears of entrapment and escalation, together with the costs of security guarantees, generated uncertainty about the reliability of the extended deterrent, demands for more formalized agreements codifying defense commitments, and discussions regarding the need for enhancing the capabilities of client states. For the most part, these debates have also made one key hopeful assumption about the future of defense commitments. The public discourse in the United States and among its allies, for example, assumes that U.S. extended deterrence commitments will remain the same in a world of increasing complexity. Despite an increasing number of threats to security and a broader range of capabilities that pose challenges to allies, the nuclear umbrella will be well suited to manage these threats to key allies. Indeed, some analysts argue that even in some instances, the use of emerging technologies that intersect multiple domains may have the added benefit of simultaneously assuring allies and deterring adversaries.[2] Consider the case of Stuxnet, a cyber tool that was used to disrupt Iranian nuclear development. The use of this cyber weapon in the nuclear domain, in addition to deterring and delaying Iran's nuclear progression without resorting to the use of military force, was intended to reassure and restrain Israel from taking action.

Yet is this always the case? Should we assume that the manner in which the United States manages its defensive alliance commitments in the twenty-first century will rely on the same set of capabilities and means that it employed in the twentieth century, yielding similar outcomes? Further, should we expect that as patron states develop new technologies, concerns over credibility and assurance will be assuaged? This chapter engages this discussion by posing a crucial question: how does the development and proliferation (among both patrons and adversaries) of new capabilities

---

[1] Michael O. Wheeler, "The Changing Requirements of Assurance and Extended Deterrence," Institute for Defense Analyses, Paper P-4562/ (2010), 43, accessed 23 February 2018, https://www.hsdl.org/?abstract&did=716312; Keith Payne, Thomas Scheber, and Kurt Guthe, *US Extended Deterrence and Assurance for Allies in Northeast Asia* (Fairfax, VA: National Institute Press, 2010), accessed 23 February 2018, http://www.nipp.org/wp-content/uploads/2014/12/US-Extend-Deter-for-print.pdf.

[2] See Michael Nacht, Patricia Schuster, and Eva Uribe, chapter 2 here; Jon R. Lindsay, "Stuxnet and the Limits of Cyber Warfare," *Security Studies* 22, no. 3 (2013): 365–404, https://doi.org/10.1080/09636412.2013.816122.

that cross the kinetic and nonkinetic spectrum alter extended deterrence dynamics? Indeed, in their introduction, Jon Lindsay and Erik Gartzke have started this endeavor by further dissecting the ways increasing complexities across technologies and the market of new actors intersect with political and economic dynamics.[3]

To get at these questions, I briefly describe a logic for the ways some forms of military advancements may exacerbate concerns over assurance. I then explore extended deterrence dynamics, specifically how patrons and protégés view the question of adequate deterrence and assurance, at the onset of the nuclear triad era. I develop an argument that issues of credibility and resolve (to defend) may be exacerbated in areas of increased technical, economic, and political complexities in cross-domain deterrence. Specifically, I analyze whether extended deterrence agreements face the same (or a growing) set of deterrence and assurance challenges in a cross-domain environment, among a potentially new set of adversarial actors or the emergence of new capabilities in other military domains provides an opportunity to better assure and deter allies against foreign aggressors. This analysis yields some degree of pessimism: existing concerns over assurance and credibility are likely to be exacerbated in the cross-domain context.

To delve into these dynamics, I explore credibility in two distinct eras that saw significant technological transitions. I first examine historical U.S. commitments to assure and protect allied partners and to deter aggression, and how these policies have evolved since World War II with increased investment and development of new kinetic capabilities, including the enhancement of the United States' nuclear arsenal with the introduction of long-range and sea-based capabilities. The initial wave of force structure development throughout the Cold War, including the introduction of mobile air- and sea-based missile technology, presents a useful analogy to examine the future of extended deterrent capabilities moving forward. Unsurprisingly, the United States' deterrence commitments to its allies in East Asia and Western Europe were dramatically altered by the development of intercontinental ballistic missiles and submarine-launched ballistic missile technology. Theoretically, if the United States could deploy submarines and carriers in East Asia while simultaneously leveraging air- and land-based capabilities in defense of its North Atlantic Treaty Organization (NATO) allies, it would be better able to assure and defend multiple allies on multiple fronts. Yet the introduction of the nuclear triad, and a diversified nuclear portfolio, similarly created increasing demands on the U.S. nuclear arsenal that inadvertently created uncertainty among both allies and adversaries about the strength of the U.S. security guarantee. As the United States increasingly extended its power-projection capabilities, it began to develop more commitments than it could physically uphold. The relative inability to provide sufficient commitments to all its allies created opportunities for challenges and threats from new and existing adversaries that were similarly developing their own capabilities.

---

[3] See Jon R. Lindsay and Erik Gartzke, chapter 1 here.

This historical analysis provides a useful backdrop and context for assessing modern-day extended deterrence in a cross-domain system and what we may expect for the future of the U.S. nuclear umbrella in the twenty-first century. This is particularly useful in light of the emergence of new kinetic and nonkinetic capabilities that might ease the demands on the United States to assure (and perhaps restrain) its friends and allies across the world or serve to further exacerbate concerns over credibility and resolve. Within this analogous framework, I engage a broader discussion—tied to other chapters here on credibility, particularly regarding the pivot to East Asia and commitment signaling[4] —so as to better understand the implications of how strategies of extended deterrence, and the market for capabilities-based alliances, will continue to shift and evolve in an increasingly cross-domain system. I argue that despite advances in cross-domain capability and the means by which patron states, like the United States, are able to provide extended deterrence to their clients, questions of assurance and credible commitment are likely to persist and challenge the United States and its alliances.

This argument is driven by two key observations: first, existing adversaries similarly have the opportunity to acquire new capabilities to threaten allies, potentially fueling a cross-domain arms race, and second, the emergence of new capabilities with lower barriers to entry might facilitate the introduction of a new cadre of actors who challenge or target allies in extended deterrence agreements. These changing dynamics make it difficult for the United States, or other patron states, to adequately provide assurances about the credibility of their commitments to provide security. Without these assurances, allies may be willing to engage in riskier behavior to provide their own defense. In addition, as existing and new adversaries continue to introduce and develop new capabilities that create intersections between existing military domains and emerging arenas of nonkinetic conflict in cyber or space, it may become increasingly challenging and costly for the United States to continue to provide a sufficient nuclear umbrella for all of its allies. Coupled with other challenges to credibility and concerns over resolve, providing assurance to allies could become increasingly difficult in a cross-domain environment. The chapter concludes with a discussion of these implications for U.S. alliance policy in the twenty-first century.

Dynamics of Extended Nuclear Deterrence

Defining Deterrence and Assurance

To better understand the dynamics of extended nuclear deterrence, it is first necessary to get a clear picture of the scope of deterrence and extended deterrence alliances—also conceived broadly as security guarantees—the United States has

---

[4] See Chin-Hao Huang and David Kang, chapter 14 here.

granted to allied states. While the consideration of the concept of deterrence has usually been reserved for dyadic disputes between the United States and an adversary, doctrine provides for the extension of U.S. deterrent capabilities to include the protection of allies and partners abroad. Given this objective of protecting allies in the event of external aggression, U.S. policy also aims to provide assurances to allies that adversaries will not succeed in their goals if they choose to attack a U.S. ally or partner. As stated in a U.S. Air Force Occasional Paper, "as a strategic concept, extended deterrence involves the United States using all the tools of state power, to include the use of military force, to deter a foreign actor from undertaking hostile actions against *a third party* . . . the United States may also extend deterrence to prevent harm against neutral or even adversarial states."[5]

Development of extended deterrence as a focal point of U.S. nuclear doctrine and foreign policy helped form the increasingly expansive academic scholarship on how extended deterrence alliances actually operate in the international system. Specifically, this literature examines how these agreements are useful in defending allies against foreign aggressors and the mechanisms by which patrons can credibly signal their commitment to assist allies without tying their hands to costly conflict. This literature focused on the specific characteristics of a nuclear commitment (rather than a solely conventional commitment) and the altered relationship between patron, protégé and adversary—specifically, how best to prevent an adversary from initiating a crisis or aggressing upon the ally. According to Fuhrmann and Sechser, "several studies had already explored the theoretical mechanics of alliance signaling, . . . and others have investigated the empirical effects of alliance commitments."[6] That research was primarily aimed at assessing how alliances helped to strengthen deterrence and prevent external aggression or help to settle disputes with a third party.[7]

---

[5] "Deterrence Operations Joint Operating Concept (Version 2.0)," Department of Defense (2006), accessed 23 February 2018, http://www.dtic.mil/dtic/tr/fulltext/u2/a490279.pdf; Justin V. Anderson, Jeffrey Larsen, and Polly Holdorf, "Extended Deterrence and Allied Assurance: Key Concepts and Current Challenges for U.S. Policy," INSS occasional paper 69, United States Air Force Institute for National Security Studies, 2013, http://www.dtic.mil/dtic/tr/fulltext/u2/a584552.pdf.

[6] Matthew Fuhrmann and Todd S. Sechser, "Signaling Alliance Commitments: Hand-Tying and Sunk Costs in Extended Nuclear Deterrence," *American Journal of Political Science* 58, no. 4 (October 1, 2014): 919–935. https://doi.org/10.1111/ajps.12082.

[7] Glenn H. Snyder, *Alliance Politics* (Ithaca, NY: Cornell University Press, 1997); James Fearon, "Bargaining, Enforcement, and International Cooperation," *International Organization* 52, no. 2 (1998): 269–305, https://doi.org/10.1162/002081898753162820; Amy Yuen, "Target Concessions in the Shadow of Intervention," *Journal of Conflict Resolution* 53, no. 5 (2009): 727–744, https://doi.org/10.1177/0022002709339046; Brett V. Benson, Adam Meirowitz, and Kris Ramsay, "Inducing Deterrence through Moral Hazard in Alliance Contracts," *Journal of Conflict Resolution* 58, no. 2 (2014): 307–335, https://doi.org/10.1177/0022002712467936; Brett Ashley Leeds, "Do Alliances Deter Aggression? The Influence of Military Alliances on the Initiation of Militarized Interstate Disputes," *American Journal of Political Science* 47, no. 3 (2003): 427–439, https://doi.org/10.1111/

However, as many scholars have highlighted in the extended deterrence scholarship, these alliances work best when allies and adversaries believe in their strength. For patron states, like the United States, this is often incredibly difficult to demonstrate, given the high costs of providing a credible commitment to their allies. As Hunzeker and Lanozska state, "although the United States can promise to intervene on an ally's behalf in a crisis, the ally knows no international court, police force, or coalition has enough power to force the United States to fulfill its pledges. Especially because it is so powerful, the United States always has the option to renege if it changes its mind. For example, the US president might decide not to defend an ally if an imminent war appears more costly than the United States anticipated when it entered into the alliance."[8]

Given these trade-offs and diverse domestic and international demands on U.S. forces, it is not surprising, then, that allies might feel "unassured" by the United States' commitment to provide defense and security in the event of a foreign threat. Furthermore, attempts at providing assurances to one set of allies (and their adversaries) might create uncertainty among others. Thus, it is not difficult to see how this dynamic could conceivably produce some types of negative consequences (i.e., crisis initiation, escalation, full-scale conflict) for one or both parties. Given this, scholars began to identify two primary perspectives on the international consequences of extended nuclear deterrence agreements: the first argues that these agreements can produce unnecessary and unforeseen risks to the patron state (primarily the United States) because of uncertainty and noncredible commitments, and the second argues that these alliances actually help to induce stability in the international system.

While this literature focused on the consequences of extended deterrence in the international system, a next wave of scholarship and policy discussions seeks to identify and assess how new means and capabilities have provided defense and security to allies abroad and have potentially impacted the extended deterrence

---

1540-5907.00031; Vipin Narang, "What Does It Take to Deter? Regional Power Nuclear Postures and International Conflict," *Journal of Conflict Resolution* 57, no. 3 (2013): 478–508, https://doi.org/10.1177/0022002712448909; George Perkovich, "Extended Deterrence on the Way to a Nuclear-Free World," International Commission on Nuclear Nonproliferation and Disarmament, (Canberra, July 2009); Steven Pifer, Richard C. Bush, Vanda Felbab-Brown, Martin S. Indyk, Michael O'Hanlon, and Kenneth M. Pollack, "US Nuclear and Extended Deterrence: Considerations and Challenges," paper 3, Brookings Arms Control Series, Brookings Institution, May 2010, accessed 23 February 2018, https://www.brookings.edu/wp-content/uploads/2016/06/06_nuclear_deterrence.pdf; Brad Roberts, "Extended Deterrence and Strategic Stability in Northeast Asia," NIDS Visiting Scholar Paper Series 1, National Institute for Defense Studies, 9 August 2013, accessed 23 February 2018, http://www.nids.mod.go.jp/english/publication/visiting/pdf/01.pdf.

[8] Michael Allen Hunzeker and Alexander Lanoszka, "The Efficacy of Landpower: Landpower and American Credibility," *Parameters* 45, no. 4 (2015-16): 17–26, accessed 23 February 2018, http://ssi.armywarcollege.edu/pubs/parameters/issues/Winter_2015-16/5_Hunzeker.pdf.

equation as the United States has established the nuclear umbrella. The next section develops a logic that addresses how increasing complexities impact concerns about credibility and resolve.

Theory: The Search for Credibility in the Nuclear Age

In the aftermath of World War II, the United States saw the establishment of broad alliance networks, and more narrow bilateral alliances, that shifted the United States from being a previously isolationist member of the international community to being one heavily involved in the protection of friends and allies. In a natural evolution from the multinational military alliances of the war and the growing Soviet threat in Europe, the United States took on the mantle of leading a collective defense organization that was meant to credibly assure states of their protection and deter foreign aggression from proximate adversaries. The emergence of the United States as a global power during World War II helped to solidify its image as a credible alliance partner, and potential patron, to states across the international system. Since that time, some scholars argue, the United States has been focused on sustaining that credibility. According to Steve Walt, "as anyone who's studied the history of U.S. foreign relations knows, American leaders have been obsessed with credibility ever since World War II. If other states ever doubted U.S. power or resolve, so the argument ran, communists would be emboldened, deterrence would weaken, and America's allies would be intimidated and neutralized, leaving the United States isolated and friendless in a hostile world. This concern led American leaders to constantly reiterate their pledges to defend allies all over the world."[9] Yet, during the Cold War, the introduction of missiles capable of delivering nuclear weapons from one continent to another without requiring forward basing on allied territory, changed the way allies and the United States viewed the credibility of assurances to protect allied territory. As Kegley and Raymond argue, "European members of NATO in particular began to question whether the United States would, as it had pledged, protect Paris or Bonn by sacrificing New York. Under what conditions might Washington or Moscow be willing to risk a nuclear holocaust? The uncertainty became pronounced while the pledge to protect allies through extended deterrence seemed increasingly insincere."[10]

Despite rhetoric to the contrary, it was challenging to convince allies in Europe and East Asia that the United States would be willing to undertake action that could potentially risk the security of the U.S. homeland. The ready ability to deploy, and redeploy, troops and assets raised several important questions: Would the

---

[9] Stephen M. Walt, "The Credibility Addiction." Foreign Policy (blog), January 6, 2015, https://foreignpolicy.com/2015/01/06/the-credibility-addiction-us-iraq-afghanistan-unwinnable-war/.

[10] Charles W. Kegley and Gregory A. Raymond, *The Global Future: A Brief Introduction to World Politics* (Boston, MA: Wadsworth, Cengage Learning, 2011), 240.

United States be willing to enter into a conflict in defense of an ally that endangered U.S. national security? How could an ally be assured that the United States would provide protection, even through the use of nuclear weapons, to counter foreign aggression? And how did shifting geopolitics, or domestic politics, influence these commitments? While allies want a generous interpretation of provocation to encourage action from the United States, traditional defensive agreements do not codify the extent to which the United States may be willing to "risk New York for Paris" in most circumstances, especially those in which the rules of engagement and combat are not spelled out. If the threshold or "redline" for a U.S. military response is uncertain in the most traditional of security environments, where known enemies can use physical weapons against a discrete set of U.S. or allied targets, the ways security umbrellas are likely to manifest in the multitheater, cross-capability environment are likely to be even more complex. I argue that two characteristics of the modern military (and the future of cross-domain deterrence and assurance) might make allies less assured about U.S. commitments in the current (and anticipated future) climate than in previous eras of military modernization.

First, concerns over credibility and assurance are likely to be even more pressing with the development and inclusion of new forms of capabilities that can be easily moved and used elsewhere. Allies may previously have been assured of physical commitments like the establishment of military bases, military personnel who form actual tripwires, and billions of dollars in military hardware. With technologies that allow missiles to be deployed out of theater or carriers that can be moved to other conflict hotspots or the use of force to be conducted in cyberspace or actual space, allies may not see these commitments as continuing to be as strong or robust.[11] And with multiple allies seeking assurances simultaneously, already burdened systems may become more exhausted. As with existing military technologies, costly trade-offs may complicate cross-domain strategies of extended deterrence that may perversely destabilize already tense regional environments.

Second, some states have begun to mirror investment in similar new types of technology to counteract the emergence of cross-domain capabilities that can be used between patrons and their client states. By pinpointing weaknesses in defensive alliance commitments, some states have started to develop "puncture" capabilities that are low-cost, high-technology, and highly effective means of countering advances in extended deterrent capabilities. Further, as the barriers to entry for the capability market decrease, more states may be able to challenge alliances and threaten client states. In a cross-domain environment where more nefarious actors can flood the system and pose additional burdens to patron states committed to providing protection to their allies, the credibility of these defense pacts may start to decline. If the United States is not willing to "risk Paris for New York," this may be especially

---

[11] See Brendan Rittenhouse Green and Austin Long, chapter 10 here.

salient if Paris is facing nonkinetic challenges from new adversaries, including nonstate actors. Unfortunately, with these pressures, even conventional dominance (as the United States enjoys and other nuclear powers may enjoy regionally) is unlikely to satiate assurance demands or improve issues of credibility.

This logic may yield some important implications for the future of alliance commitments, especially with regard to U.S. assurances. First, concerns over a credible commitment to defend may actually discourage some allies from seeking alliances at the outset. If the introduction of emerging technologies (like cyberweapons) or military innovations that produce uncertainty as to a patron's actual commitment to defend an ally might drive down demand for alliances or alter ally behavior, especially as some have begun to question the utility of alliances in particular regions.[12] Further, potential allies might seek commitments from other patrons seen to be more reliable—new patrons that still rely on hard military power. This uncertainty might result in a variety of other second- and third-order effects. Potential clients might seek other forms of assurance or seek to challenge adversaries on their own—engaging in moral hazard. Clients might even begin to develop counterbalancing technology that allows them independence from their patrons and a means to challenge adversaries. Indeed, a cross-domain environment (even in the context of conventional superiority) that introduces new capabilities, new actors, and new threats might have serious negative repercussions for U.S. defensive commitments and its position as a credible nuclear patron.

The next section explores these dynamics in the context of U.S. foreign policy throughout the twentieth century. The emergence of the nuclear triad serves as a useful analogy for (and precursor to) understanding how these dynamics might influence assurance and deterrence.

Assurance and Credibility in the Twentieth Century: A Case Illustration of the Nuclear Triad

To examine this logic, I first trace the intersection of assurance and emerging technologies in the context of the twentieth century—namely the introduction of new capabilities (including the nuclear triad) that significantly impacted the evolving relationships between patrons and protégés. Analysis of this case yields important contributions. The introduction of the nuclear triad represents a signification shift in the conduct of U.S. military operations, national deterrence, and extended deterrent protections over friends and allies. Understanding how changes in warfighting, as a result of the triad, impacted credibility will result in important

---

[12] See Huang and Kang, chapter 14.

lessons. Next I examine the changes in the ways that wars are conducted, as a result of cross-domain capabilities.

Throughout World War I and the interwar era, the United States' grand strategy was based on isolationism and neutrality. Despite the massive and unprecedented expansion of U.S. military capabilities, the development of policy to involve and commit U.S. troops abroad was severely constrained by congressional legislation and public opinion.[13] In the early 1930s, the United States' initial response to growing German and Japanese aggression was the imposition of economic sanctions and a legislatively mandated arms embargo in the event of a large-scale, multinational conflict.[14] Throughout this time, however, President Franklin Roosevelt was simultaneously trying to assure the United Kingdom that the United States would provide limited support in the event of full-scale war. To the British ambassador, Ronald Lindsay, this signal loosely translated into a personal promise from President Roosevelt to provide everything except troops and loans.

Indeed, it was the outbreak of full-scale war in Europe in September 1939 that fundamentally altered the nature of U.S. grand strategy and commitments to the defense and protection of allies and friends abroad. In response to attacks on western Europe, Roosevelt began by asking for revisions in U.S. neutrality laws and significant increases in the U.S. military arsenal (for transfer or sale to the Allies), without committing the U.S. military to combat until the attack on Pearl Harbor. The United States' grand strategy and alliance policy during the initial stages of World War II suggest that while the United States had clearly developed a military production capability that outpaced Germany and Japan (and saw unprecedented growth in naval and air power that could be projected overseas easily), it was not willing to make or uphold credible alliance commitments.

The remainder of World War II and the official entrance of the United States into the conflict alongside the Allies fundamentally reshaped how it engaged in alliances and its willingness to commit and project air power overseas. It had become rapidly apparent that the United States had developed and consequently needed to maintain military commitments throughout western Europe and parts of East Asia that would require significant financial and military capabilities. These commitments were further entrenched in response to the threat of Soviet expansion and the desire to prevent another disastrous global conflict.

The culmination of World War II resulted in two significant developments in warfighting: (1) large-scale use of strategic air power and flight-based weapon delivery systems across multiple theaters, and (2) an emphasis of defensive alliance commitments that necessitated a power-projecting, global U.S. military presence.

---

[13] Arthur A. Stein, "Domestic Constraints, Extended Deterrence, and the Incoherence of Grand Strategy: The United States, 1938–1950," in *Domestic Bases of Grand Strategy*, edited by Richard Rosecrance and Arthur Stein (Ithaca, NY: Cornell University Press, 1993), 96–123.

[14] Ibid.

These changes were further entrenched in the ethos of U.S. warfighting with the introduction of nuclear capability at the end of World War II: the need for overseas commitments and military forces was reinforced by new technical challenges that also shaped U.S. grand strategy. No longer could the nation rely on its relative geographic isolation and its allies to give it time to mobilize for war. Rather, the nature of new weapons—missiles and atomic bombs—mandated overseas bases and a forward military posture.

The use of atomic weapons over Japanese territory had highlighted the very real possibility of using strategic air power, such as bombers, to deploy, deliver, and use a variety of kinetic weapons across huge distances and multiple theaters. Early scholarship on the development of U.S. force structure, both advances in conventional weaponry and the development of a U.S. nuclear capability, suggested myriad motivations and explanations for the U.S. nuclear triad. These arguments ranged from the power of organization and bureaucratic inertia and fears of arms racing to challenges arising in the security environment and the desire to match the capabilities of rivals and adversaries.[15]

Yet this literature also outlined the important, though not sole, role that alliance commitments had historically played in motivating the U.S. military to develop a far-reaching, diverse nuclear portfolio. While this was certainly not the only factor that influenced the development and increases in U.S. force structure, an enhanced ability to power-project and defend allies abroad became a positive externality of these decisions. After World War II and with the emergence of global alliance commitments, especially in light of bureaucratic pressures to advance and modernize, the U.S. nuclear umbrella required a diversified force structure that could be deployed to distant areas and was capable of coming to the aid of U.S. allies.[16] To reach distant allies, the United States needed to develop mobile and deliverable weapons systems that could be relevant in any type of conflict and in multiple theaters and could meet the increasing demands for U.S. military superiority.

---

[15] Charles Perrow, "Economic Theories of Organization," *Theory and Society* 15, no. 1 (January 1986): 11–45, http://www.jstor.org/stable/657174; Scott D. Sagan, "The Perils of Proliferation: Organization Theory, Deterrence Theory, and the Spread of Nuclear Weapons," *International Security* 18, no. 4 (March 1994): 66–107, https://doi.org/10.2307/2539178; Kenneth N. Waltz, "Nuclear Myths and Political Realities," *American Political Science Review* 84, no. 3 (September 1990), https://doi.org/10.2307/1962764; Alain C. Enthoven and K. Wayne Smith, *How Much Is Enough? Shaping the Defense Program, 1961–1969* (Santa Monica, CA: RAND Corporation, 1971); Muhammet A. Bas and Andrew J. Coe, "Arms Diffusion and War," *Journal of Conflict Resolution* 56, no. 4 (May 2012): 651–674, https://doi.org/10.1177/0022002712445740; Todd S. Sechser and Elizabeth N. Saunders, "The Army You Have: The Determinants of Military Mechanization, 1979–2001," *International Studies Quarterly* 54, no. 2 (2010): 481–511, https://www.jstor.org/stable/40664176.

[16] Erik Gartzke, Jeffrey Kaplow, and Rupal N. Mehta, "The Determinants of Nuclear Force Structure," *Journal of Conflict Resolution* 58, no. 2 (April 2014): 481–508, http://www.jstor.org/stable/24545649.

The Evolution of the Nuclear Triad and Alliance Commitments

At the onset of the Cold War, the United States was facing a new set of logistical challenges and constraints that necessitated innovative thinking about how to ensure the territorial defense of a broader set of allies in the international community. The United States now faced new threats from a broader range of adversaries in various regions and a more extensive assurance to defend allies from conventional and nuclear threats of conflict. This necessitated a commitment from the United States to a defense posture that included regularly forward-deployed forces on permanent bases throughout Europe and East Asia, while also maintaining some military presence in other key regions. In addition to demonstrating the United States' willingness to bear the costs of the defense of an ally, the U.S. military presence in multiple parts of the world was meant to deter potential adversaries from threatening U.S. or allied interests globally.

To do this effectively, the United States began to produce and heavily rely on a combination of conventional and nuclear forces, tactical and strategic, permanently deployed abroad that leveraged the growing comparative advantage the United States had developed in air power throughout the two world wars.[17] The development of nuclear weapons and the first set of mobile delivery platforms, namely the use of strategic air power, allowed the United States to significantly extend the scope of its power-projection capabilities and establish an expansive U.S. military presence. Yet, with growing demands for increasing extended deterrence assurances to allies and the emergence of new threats from the Soviet Union and its proxies during the Cold War, the United States needed to develop new capabilities and postures within the existing conventional and nuclear domains that would mitigate these additional logistical challenges. It was under these conditions that the nuclear triad was able to significantly alter the nature of defensive commitments and the United States' ability to assure its allies.

This is not to say that the nuclear triad was established as a result of alliance demands or the challenges associated with maintaining extended deterrence commitments. In another work, my coauthors and I examine the evolution and drivers of U.S. nuclear force structure.[18] We build on the foundation work of conventional and nuclear force structure that assesses the role of bureaucratic politics and arms racing as the primary drivers of nuclear posture decisionmaking, and we create a new dataset that examines the universe of nuclear force structure by examining

---

[17] Anderson et al., "Extended Deterrence and Allied Assurance."
[18] Gartzke et al., "The Determinants of Nuclear Force Structure."

every nuclear weapons state from its initial development of nuclear forces to the present.[19]

To assess patterns, and potential trade-offs, over time, we advanced a portfolio theory of nuclear force structure that looks at the impact of various domestic and international determinants and constraints on the diversification of nuclear force structure in nuclear weapons states. Primarily, this work argues that diversification— or the relevant weight placed on particular land-, sea-, or air-based weapons delivery systems—of nuclear force structure represents an important, strategic decision by policymakers when determining which capabilities to emphasize in their arsenal. A diversified nuclear portfolio provides a unique defensive advantage in preventing the crippling of all three legs of the nuclear triad simultaneously as well as tangible offensive advantages such as the reduction of platform vulnerability and an ability to compensate for another weapons system's weakness. These findings, unsurprisingly, yield important implications for deterrence and extended deterrence. While the concept of cross-domain deterrence did not emerge in the post–World War II, nuclear age, several of the key concepts integral to nuclear (and extended) nuclear deterrence were introduced with the advent of sea and air power and an emphasis on having a diversified, mobile, and survivable force structure.[20] Throughout the Cold War, policymakers and military strategists were focused on creating a force posture that enhanced both defensive and offensive advantages. No doubt, U.S. conventional and nuclear force structure was focused on adjusting to the needs of defending U.S. territory from external aggressors, including growing threats from the Soviet Union. Yet these decisions had a significant impact on defensive alliance commitments. The following sections highlight the role of the U.S. nuclear triad in shaping assurances to its allies.

Affecting Deterrence Dynamics

At the time, the United States was already effectively employing capabilities in one domain to deter against attacks or threats to allies in another. Introducing multiple

---

[19] Graham T. Allison and Frederic A. Morris, "Armaments and Arms Control: Exploring the Determinants of Military Weapons," *Daedalus* 104, no. 3 (1975): 99–129, http://www.jstor.org/stable/20024348; Morton Halperin, *Bureaucratic Politics and Foreign Policy* (Washington, DC: Brookings Institution, 1974); Perrow, "Economic Theories of Organization"; Sagan, "The Perils of Proliferation"; Waltz, "Nuclear Myths and Political Realities"; P. R. Chari, "Nuclear Crisis, Escalation Control, and Deterrence in South Asia," Henry L. Stimson Center, August 2003, https://pdfs.semanticscholar.org/b52d/2a2d54117826d94be58d12b6e2860cbcbd21.pdf; Vipin Narang, "Posturing for Peace? Pakistan's Nuclear Postures and South Asian Stability," *International Security* 34, no. 3 (2010): 38–78, https://doi.org/10.1162/isec.2010.34.3.38.

[20] R. J. Vince, "Cross-Domain Deterrence Seminar Summary Notes," Lawrence Livermore National Laboratory, 1 May 2015, https://cgsr.llnl.gov/content/assets/docs/SummaryNotes.pdf; Gartzke et al., "The Determinants of Nuclear Force Structure."

platforms into the United States' force structure theoretically allowed the U.S. military to better defend multiple theaters from attack across myriad domains. This was primarily accomplished by pursuing a diverse force structure whereby platforms varied in terms of range, effectiveness against adversaries, vulnerability to attack, and mobility and ultimately an ability for one type of weapons system to complement and compensate for another.[21] For example, the introduction of sea-based platforms, such as submarine-launched systems, into conventional and nuclear forces allowed the United States to forward-deploy and maintain a strong U.S. nuclear presence in East Asia against a rise in conventional threats from regional adversaries, while allowing the United States to maintain its commitment to defend NATO from a superior conventional Soviet force through nuclear-capable strategic delivery systems, including F-16 warplanes.[22]

Introducing different types of conventional and nuclear platforms had the added, though unintended, benefit of better defending distant allies threatened by different types of enemy forces in a given theater. What was needed to defend NATO territory from a conventional Soviet threat was likely to be different from the needs in South Korea for deterring North Korean ground aggression during the Korean War and after. With the threat of Soviet conventional forces as part of the Warsaw Pact's Eastern bloc at the borders of NATO territory, the United States committed to forward-deploying nearly 435,000 U.S. forces (including some nuclear-capable platforms) during the peak of the Cold War. The 1999 NATO "Strategic Concept" reiterated that the presence of U.S. nuclear forces on European territory was critical to more effective deterrence against external threat, whether conventional or nuclear, in response to a growing threat of escalation and use, despite the demise of the Soviet threat: "nuclear forces based in Europe and committed to NATO provide an essential political and military link between the European and the North American members of the Alliance. The Alliance will therefore maintain adequate nuclear forces in Europe. These forces need to have the necessary characteristics and appropriate flexibility and survivability, to be perceived as a credible and effective element of the Allies' strategy in preventing war. They will be maintained at the minimum level sufficient to preserve peace and security."[23]

---

[21] Richard Burt, "Reducing Strategic Arms at SALT: How Difficult, How Important?," Adelphi Papers 18, no. 141 (1978): 4–14, https://doi.org/10.1080/05679327808448503; John F. McCarthy, "The Case for the B-1 Bomber," International Security 1, no. 2 (1976): 78–97, https://muse.jhu.edu/article/446084/pdf; Donald M. Snow, "Current Nuclear Deterrence Thinking: An Overview and Review," International Studies Quarterly 23, no. 3 (1979): 445–486, https://doi.org/10.2307/2600176; Gartzke et al., "The Determinants of Force Structure."

[22] Vince, "Cross-Domain Deterrence Seminar Summary Notes"; Wheeler, "The Changing Requirements of Assurance and Extended Deterrence," 43.

[23] "The Alliance's Strategic Concept," Press Release NAC-S(99) 65, North Atlantic Treaty Organization, 24 April 1999, accessed 23 February 2018, http://www.nato.int/cps/en/natolive/official_texts_27433.htm.

Similarly, in the aftermath of the Korean War, the signing of the Mutual Defense Treaty between the United States and South Korea created a security relationship that guaranteed 28,500 United States Forces Korea troops on the ground in the demilitarized zone, in addition to forward-deployed conventional weapons, with the option for the temporary deployment of strategic B-2 and B-52 bombers, to defend the Republic of Korea from both conventional ground aggression and a nascent nuclear North Korea. In addition to these two alliance commitments, throughout this time, the United States simultaneously established and sustained defense pacts with Japan, Taiwan, and Israel that leveraged emerging new sea- and air-based nuclear and conventional capabilities to defend an ever-expanding set of allies, with different deterrent needs, across multiple theaters.

Indeed, the introduction of the nuclear triad yielded several advantages for the United States' ability to provide deterrence to allies in multiple regions. First, it worked to reduce the demands and costs on any one type of deterrent platform. If the U.S. military could be deployed to multiple regions to defend multiple allies at the same time, no one type of platform or capability was overused or exhausted and thus vulnerable to attack. Second, the ability to simultaneously extend the reach of the U.S. military to various regions using a mix of land-, sea-, and air-based capabilities provided not only strong power-projecting capabilities for the protection of allies but similarly ensured the survivability of U.S. forces through a secure second strike: the diversification of U.S. nuclear forces virtually ensured that the United States could withstand conventional, nuclear, and other types of aggression from its adversaries.[24] The introduction of the nuclear triad simultaneously reduced the burden of U.S. nuclear forces aimed at extended deterrence while also attempting to decrease the likelihood of provoking retaliatory escalation against the United States.

Affecting Assurance Dynamics

How did the development of the nuclear triad impact the way *allies* viewed the strength of the U.S. commitment to provided extended deterrence? The evolution of U.S. force structure to include other technological means, specifically the introduction of sea-based, mobile capabilities, theoretically allowed for a more vigorous and "ready" posture that signaled to both allies and adversaries and, ideally, assured them of the United States' unwavering commitment to its alliances. The deployment of troops and the stationing of costly assets in allies' neighborhoods was intended to "tie the hands" of the United States to protecting its clients and

---

[24] Erik Gartzke, Jeffrey Kaplow, and Rupal N. Mehta, *Nuclear Deterrence and the Structure of Nuclear Forces* (San Diego: University of California, 2018).

deterring foreign aggression on their territory or regional environment.[25] Indeed, throughout the Cold War, with an ever-evolving mix of multidomain threats to a growing list of friends and clients, the United States' ability to deter and assure anxious allies was fundamentally restructured with the emergence of the nuclear triad and the unprecedented growth of the "nuclear umbrella." While the United States still heavily relied on conventional forces (as it continues to today), the option to deploy nuclear assets to multiple theaters was a costly but potentially effective signal of commitment.

However, analysis of empirical evidence suggests that the introduction of cross-domain capabilities, in the form of the nuclear triad, may not have been as effective at enhancing U.S. assurances to its allies. First, contrary to the conventional wisdom that suggests that military mobilizations (made easier with the nuclear triad) are an effective strategy for the "tying of hands" of the defender, the higher costs and fear of escalation associated with military mobilization also increased a defender's desire to use its influence to settle disputes peacefully—potentially without fully meeting the demands of or satisfying the ally. Such a lackluster response, driven by patrons' fears about how forward deployment made feasible by the triad's power-projecting capabilities, could weaken the way allies view the reputation and credibility of a patron's commitment to provide defense and security in the event of a crisis in the future.

Second, and perhaps more important, the very nature of mobile forces—an element that is integral to the survival and success of the nuclear triad—raises concerns about the credibility of an assurance. In the pre–nuclear triad era, extended deterrence generally involved the use of ground troops, whose redeployment was prohibitively costly. The ability to reposition or "pivot" submarines and aircraft carriers, two cornerstones of the nuclear umbrella, is beneficial to the United States but presents it with a significant challenge as to how it can effectively assure its allies that those forces will be available and present in the event of a crisis or conflict.[26]

Thus, while it may have been predicted that the nuclear triad would be a side benefit of developing a cross-domain-capable force structure, the nuclear triad did not assist the United States in providing a more compelling and effective assurance to its allies. The prioritization of sea- and air-based power and a deemphasis on ground power may have inadvertently weakened the symbol of a U.S. *resolve* to defend allies and raised doubts among potential adversaries of the United States' *ability* to adequately deter aggressors in the event of a dispute.[27]

---

[25] Thomas Schelling, Arms and Influence (New Haven, CT: Yale University Press, 1966); Fearon, "Bargaining, Enforcement, and International Cooperation"; Erik Gartzke and Koji Kagotani, "Trust in Tripwires: Deployments, Costly Signaling and Extended General Deterrence," unpublished paper.

[26] Gartzke et al., "The Determinants of Nuclear Force Structure."

[27] Hunzeker and Lanoszka, "The Efficacy of Landpower"; Neil Narang and Rupal Mehta, "The Unforeseen Consequences of Extended Deterrence: Moral Hazard in a Nuclear Protégé," *Journal of Conflict Resolution* (2017), https://doi.org/10.1177/0022002717729025.

Given the deterrence and assurance challenges intrinsic to extended deterrence, a new discussion has emerged about how the United States can best employ its technological advantages to protect the U.S. homeland and its allies and friends as they continue to face a growing number of adversaries that threaten stability and aggression in a range of arenas. First, the historical trend of deterring aggression or fighting wars on the battleground has shifted dramatically to include combat zones in space and cyberspace. In addition, and perhaps of more concern, the movement of disputes and the potential for conflict escalation from discrete physical targets to these new domains has also reduced the barriers to entry: the emergence of new domains of warfighting has allowed a new range of players, both state and nonstate, to present a realistic and potentially costly threat to U.S. national and international security. These developments raise questions about the future of extended deterrence: what precisely does this mean for the United States' ability to effectively assure its allies that it will protect them and deter their adversaries from initiating aggression if the available options now include such things as the use of space technology to disrupt terrestrial military operations or anonymous, nonattributable cyberattacks. In the remainder of the chapter, I examine how the emergence of multiple, often intersecting domains of combat impacts the ability of patrons, such as the United States, to adequately assure their allies that it will protect them, given the possibility of attacks in a much broader range of theaters and adversaries.

Assurance and Credibility in a Cross-Domain World: The Role of Emerging Technology

Unsurprisingly, the state of interstate relations has evolved dramatically since the end of the Cold War. Changes in the number and nature of superpowers, theaters of operation and combat, alliances and adversaries, posture, and doctrines have all influenced the way the United States sees its commitments to other states in the international system. I have already analyzed how these changes, specifically the evolution of U.S. military forces during the Cold War, provide a useful backdrop and foundation for assessing how newly emerging, kinetic and nonkinetic capabilities may impact the way the United States can work to deter and assure its allies in the international community. Specifically, I have examined how cross-domain capabilities might alter the dynamic between nuclear patrons, such as the United States and its protégés, using the example of the nuclear triad. The analogy of the diversification of the nuclear triad might seem to suggest that diversified cross-domain capabilities might allow for more efficient and less costly power projection while still creating uncertainty among allies about the credibility of the assurance; however, the inherent vulnerabilities of a multidomain security umbrella may actually pose a challenge to the United States' ability to effectively deter interstate conflict for its protégés.

Using this backdrop, it is similarly important to assess how increasing technical and political complexities changes the dynamics of assurance and credibility between patron states and their protégés. The current state of the United States' extended deterrence commitments to NATO/western Europe has been significantly impacted by a new set of costly challenges (namely recent Russian behavior) and the U.S. conventional and nuclear "pivot to East Asia." Given these challenges, the United States has had increasing difficulty assuring its NATO allies (and subsequently its allies in East Asia) about its capacity to adequately defend both regions against their adversaries. The United States faces competing demands to project hard military power in two distinct regions simultaneously has only prompted both sets of allies to become less persuaded of the United States' capacity to actually defend them in the event of external aggression (sometimes opting to take matters into their own hands by pursuing advances in their own military power). While Chin-Hau Huang and David C. Kang argue in chapter 14 that there is little evidence that East Asian states will engage in an arms race as a result of dueling U.S. and Chinese presences in the region, these states may still question the extent of U.S. credibility and resolve. Indeed, it could be the case that adversaries themselves are increasingly less convinced of the United States' commitment to defend its allies—potentially motivating some aggressors to use this opportunity to provoke allies into disputes when the extent of U.S. ability to provide adequate defense is uncertain or to seek an indigenous nuclear deterrent (especially if seen as condoned by the United States).[28] Primarily, I have focused on assessing these dynamics for the United States and its allies, and today's adversaries, in the context of an existing force structure and a static set of capabilities. Yet it is simultaneously necessary to assess how the introduction of cross-domain capabilities influences a broader set of patron/protégé relations in the future.

The Future of Cross-Domain Assurance: Space and Cyber

Recall that the logic described earlier highlights two factors—mobility/ease of redeployment and reduced barriers to entry for new adversaries—that place constraints on U.S. assurance and deterrence. As the emergence of the nuclear triad demonstrates, military modernization or advances—or in this case, a cross-domain environment—may exacerbate these concerns. Indeed, the development of new technologies—including capabilities in the space and cyber domains, drones or

---

[28] Matthew Fuhrmann and Todd Sechser, "Moral Hazard or Prescription for Peace? Nuclear Alliance Commitments and the Conflict Behavior of Protégés," paper presented at annual meeting of the Peace Science Society, Philadelphia, October 10–11, 2014; Narang and Mehta, "The Unforeseen Consequences of Extended Deterrence."

unmanned aerial vehicles, and precision global strike—have raised a whole host of new questions about the credibility of the United States' commitment to fight wars in new theaters against different adversaries in response to emerging capabilities.[29] Recently, for example, the United States has increasingly been facing concerns regarding the militarization of space and how it will impact the United States' relationships with its allies and with space-dominant actors, such as China.[30]

As multiple actors, including India, China, Brazil, and Japan, previously absent from the "traditional space race" of the twentieth century, join the ranks of states that have a variety of space assets in positions and are developing antisatellite weaponry, new questions arise about how threats emerge and develop in space will provoke responses on the ground. If, for example, China continues to engage in controversial activities, such as the January 2007 antisatellite test and the potential threat to U.S. space assets or allied assets in low-earth orbit, how might this impact U.S.-China cooperation in other military domains, for example regarding competition over the modernization and development of conventional and nuclear forces?[31]

These concerns are also present in the concern over the strength of the United States' own deterrent capability against new threats, such as Russian territorial and cyber challenges to actors in Europe and the Middle East. Furthermore, simultaneously, the United States is beginning to experience new security risks to cybersecurity from a new generation of nonstate actors—self-identified hackers often affiliated with larger, politically violent nonstate organizations. For example, recent attempts by the Islamic State Hacking Division (the cyber unit of the Islamic State of Iraq and Syria) to reveal personal identifying information about U.S. military personnel based in the United States and abroad has highlighted potential security concerns in the cyber domain and the way cyber operations indeed intersect with the more traditional theaters of U.S. warfighting. Even if, as Gartzke states, "war is a fundamentally political process ... the internet is generally an inferior substitute for terrestrial force in performing the functions of coercion or conquest,"[32] how these technologies can be employed in conjunction with other domains (such as the international economy or multilateral trade) remains an

---

[29] Julia Macdonald and Jacquelyn Schneider, "Presidential Risk Orientation and Force Employment Decisions: The Case of Unmanned Weaponry," *Journal of Conflict Resolution* 61, no. 3 (2017): 511–536, https://doi.org/10.1177/0022002715590874.

[30] Michael Krepon and Julia Thompson, "Anti-satellite Weapons, Deterrence, and Sino-American Space Relations," Stimson Center, 2013, accessed 23 February 2018, https://www.stimson.org/content/anti-satellite-weapons-deterrence-and-sino-american-space-relations.

[31] Jeffrey Logan, "China's Space Program: Options for US-China Cooperation," Congressional Research Service Report RS22777, Library of Congress, 29 September 2008, accessed 23 February 2018, https://fas.org/sgp/crs/row/RS22777.pdf.

[32] Erik Gartzke, "The Myth of Cyberwar: Bringing War in Cyberspace Back Down to Earth," *International Security* 38, no. 2 (Fall 2013): 41–73, https://doi.org/10.1162/ISEC_a_00136.

important factor in U.S. security.[33] Indeed, these new technologies challenge our theoretical understanding and historical record of effective deterrence, prompting a new set of questions about what counts as deterrence across and between these new domains.

Theoretically, if the United States is able to leverage the natural intersection between new domains and traditional military domains, such as the interdependence between cyber and drone technology and hard military power, it is possible that it could increase the credibility of its commitments to its allies. However, new capabilities that allow the United States to expand its global presence without continuing to strain its conventional and nuclear forces may provide an opportunity for it to extend the security umbrella. If the United States can deploy complementary space, cyber, and drone technologies that reduce the emphasis on hard military power, it could theoretically provide more compelling assurances to a broader set of allies, and their adversaries, without dramatically increasing the cost of doing so.

However, if the past is any indicator of the future, it could also be that the emergence of cross-domain capabilities might also differentially undermine some alliance commitments or otherwise present challenges certain sets of allies in the international system. An increasing reliance on mobile assets, such as intercontinental ballistic missiles, that didn't require the same degree of infrastructure as forward-deployed conventional forces or military personnel raised concerns about how credible the U.S. commitment was to defend another territory, potentially at the risk of inadvertently creating vulnerabilities in the U.S. national defense.[34]

Second, these concerns are likely to be even more salient if emerging deterrent capabilities can be easily relocated. As Gartzke et al. note, "being able to shift the local balance of power in more places raises questions about where power will actually be applied, or concentrated, and where mobility tends to undermine signals of commitment.... Submarines—emblematic of stealth—should be better at projecting power than at exerting influence, also leading to increased uncertainty about the intensity or permanence of national interests."[35] If the dilution of credibility is a likely consequence of the positioning of submarines, aircraft carriers, or other mobile but discrete assets, it is then difficult to assess how the "deployment" of cyber or drone technology, which is easier to redeploy to different theaters, in

---

[33] Jon R. Lindsay, "Stuxnet and the Limits of Cyber Warfare," *Security Studies* 22, no. 3 (2013): 365–404, https://doi.org/10.1080/09636412.2013.816122; Jon R. Lindsay and Lucas Kello, "Correspondence: A Cyber Disagreement," *International Security* 39, no. 2 (Fall 2014): 181–192, https://doi.org/10.1162/ISEC_c_00169.

[34] Hunzeker and Lanoszka, "The Efficacy of Landpower."

[35] Gartzke et al., "The Influence of Seapower on Politics."

defense of an ally will impact its perception of the permanence of U.S. forward deployed forces and the U.S. commitment to deterring foreign aggressors. As with existing military technologies, costly trade-offs may complicate cross-domain strategies of extended deterrence, so as to perversely destabilize already tense regional environments.

Finally, some states have begun to mirror investment in similar, new types of technology to counteract the emergence of cross-domain capabilities that can be used between patrons and their client states. By pinpointing weaknesses in defensive alliance commitments, some states have started to develop "puncture" capabilities that are low-cost, high-technology, and highly effective means of countering advances in extended deterrent capabilities. In the case of China, for example, the People's Liberation Army is beginning to establish "new-type combat forces" that merge naval aviation, cyber, and special forces to adapt to changing demands for combat readiness and military doctrine.[36] In addition, China has begun to use "low-intensity coercion" to advance its maritime objectives in the East and South China Seas—often threatening U.S. allies in the region, including the Philippines and Japan. While these moves are made in order to incrementally increase China's presence and control over these disputed islands, Chinese aims and means of escalation control—and avoiding conflict with the United States—remain unknown.

This type of technological "arms racing" beyond the kinetic realm—especially as adversaries develop new capabilities to counteract innovations in the U.S. security umbrella—may produce some unforeseen and potentially destabilizing consequences. It could be that extended deterrence in a cross-domain world operates similarly: adversaries are still hesitant to escalate conflicts that may require the involvement of the patron, and clients are more likely to avoid conflict but gain some political benefits or concessions by the presence of their patron.[37] Alternatively, it could be that the vulnerabilities increasing in a cross-domain world may undermine the attempt to adequately deter adversaries from attacking client states, similar to dynamics seen during the Cold War with the emergence of the nuclear triad. Rather, it could be that concerns over credibility and vulnerability will prompt more allies to seek to proliferate their own indigenous nuclear deterrents in

---

[36] Office of the Secretary of Defense, "Military and Security Developments Involving the People's Republic of China 2015," Annual Report to Congress, RefID: D-117FA69, 7 April 2015, accessed 23 February 2018, https://www.defense.gov/Portals/1/Documents/pubs/2015_China_Military_Power_Report.pdf.

[37] Fuhrmann and Sechser, "Moral Hazard or Prescription for Peace?"; Narang and Mehta, "The Unforeseen Consequences of Extended Deterrence"; Benson et al., "Inducing Deterrence through Moral Hazard in Alliance Contracts"; Brett V. Benson, *Constructing International Security: Alliances, Deterrence, and Moral Hazard* (Cambridge: Cambridge University Press, 2012); Jeffrey Knopf, ed., *Security Assurances and Nuclear Nonproliferation* (Stanford, CA: Stanford University Press, 2012).

order to revise the status quo. Given these various possibilities, how the inclusion of multiple, intersecting capabilities will actually more efficiently or effectively defend a protégé from attack remains a critical question for the future of cross-domain deterrence.

Ultimately, the discussion of extended deterrence in a cross-domain environment raises more questions than answers. For example, do new forms of nonkinetic deterrent capabilities suggest that more actors, whether conventionally superior or nuclear-capable, may serve as patrons of extended deterrence? Will the creation and use of new technologies in the twenty-first century reduce the barriers to entry in the security umbrella market (thus increasing the potential supply of patrons) or just reduce the demand for nuclear patrons in general if more states are able to acquire their own capabilities to use for their own deterrence? Does this suggest that new regional powers like China and India might take on a greater share of the protection of states in their regions by pursuing the development of the necessary capabilities and force posture to adequately do so?

Second, this discussion suggests that there are likely to be some critical implications for defensive alliance commitments themselves. One might logically conclude that the addition of more capabilities that allow the United States to increase its global presence and project power to multiple theaters credibly may continue to increase the nature of the demands that allies place on the United States. Japan, South Korea, and NATO states in western Europe may see the potential spread of U.S. kinetic and nonkinetic capabilities as a way to alter the status quo more efficiently and promptly; allies may seek to alter the arrangement between themselves and the United States in order to reflect their increasing reliance on the U.S. security umbrella. Similarly, the existing alliances may serve as precedents for other nonsecure states to seek the benefits of the U.S. alliance. If the full force of the U.S. military establishment can be "in multiple places at once," new states may seek to move from informal alliance commitments to formal and legal defense pacts that demand a U.S. conventional, and potentially nuclear, presence if attacked.

This suggests that the United States will have to carefully attune its foreign policy to these changing demands. If allies favor some emerging cross-domain capabilities over others, the United States may need to consider adapting its force structure to accommodate alliance concerns. Yet U.S. extended deterrence policy must also conform with formal treaty obligations that require further reductions in nuclear force structure. As the United States and Russia continue to draw down their nuclear stockpiles—necessitating a change in the distribution of the U.S. kinetic and nonkinetic arsenals—the United States will no doubt alter the way it responds to allies' demands for reassurance and broader foreign policy pressures.

Indeed, a survey of the political landscape highlights these concerns. Alliances are predicated on the ability of actors to credibly signal their intentions to abide by the negotiated settlement. In an era where carefully crafted political statements are easily replaced with off-the-cuff political bluster, credibility, especially in with regard to the sanctity of alliance agreements, matters more than ever.[38] To ensure that both patrons and clients are upholding their ends of the agreement—defense in the face of aggression and a commitment to forgo an indigenous deterrent, respectively—leaders must demonstrate their resolve and leadership.[39] A shift in foreign policy that demotes these principles, especially in a shifting geostrategic environment, will have severe consequences for the United States and its allies.

---

[38] Frank P. Harvey and John Mitton, *Fighting for Credibility: US Reputation and International Politics* (Toronto: University of Toronto Press, 2016).

[39] Rupal N. Mehta, *The Politics of Nuclear Reversal*, Revise and Resubmit (Oxford University Press, 2018).

INTERACTIONS ACROSS MILITARY AND NONMILITARY DOMAINS

12

Asymmetric Advantage

Weaponizing People as Nonmilitary Instruments of Cross-Domain Coercion

KELLY M. GREENHILL

In the introduction, Jon R. Lindsay and Erik Gartzke pithily define "cross-domain deterrence" as "the use of unlike . . . means for the political ends of deterrence." In practice, this means the employment of capabilities and resources drawn from one domain or environment with the aim of preventing or forestalling actions in another. While CDD as a term of art is new, the behaviors it describes are not. Domain crossing, hopping, and swapping to effect deterrence have long been common practices. The same is true of the flip side of the coercion coin: cross-domain compellence. In this realm, too, means/domains have long been crossed, hopped, and swapped (as well as employed in tandem) in times of war as well as peace.[1]

Indeed, states and nonstate actors have long employed a varied portfolio of coercive means when attempting to influence others both to take actions (compellence) as well as to refrain from doing so (deterrence). On the face of it, that this should be the case seems self-evident: since actors in the international system vary significantly in relative power and comparative advantage(s) across a range of kinetic and nonkinetic capabilities, it is unsurprising that these selfsame actors would seek to leverage the available tools and domains that promise the most highly remunerative ratio of potential benefits to recognized risks and costs. Moreover, in our contemporary, highly interconnected and globalized world, it is no longer just economies that are interdependent but also governments and the people in them. This interconnectivity opens up new pathways for cross-domain manipulation and exploitation—in political, social, economic, virtual, and physical domains.[2]

---

[1] "Combined arms operations" is a commonly employed term for a reason.

[2] See, for instance, Mark Leonard, ed., *Connectivity Wars: An Essay Collection* (London: European Council on Foreign Relations, January 2016).

Yet despite concomitant growing recognition of the complexity of the twenty-first-century threat environment and of the multifaceted and multidimensional nature of the capabilities that states and nonstates bring to bear, most analyses of cross-domain influence still focus narrowly and squarely on the traditional big five operational environments (land, sea, air, space, and more recently cyber). This is a mistake and a missed opportunity. To concentrate only or largely on the big five and kinetic means gives myopically short shrift to a range of other means and milieus that play key roles in contemporary coercion, and in relations between states more generally.[3] Since U.S. adversaries and competitors are themselves clearly thinking outside the traditional box of five environments, it is incumbent on American analysts and policymakers to expand their analytical aperture as well and, ideally, to do so with alacrity.[4]

With such a mission in mind, this chapter expands the study of CDD beyond traditional, principally military-focused domains by examining a very particular kind of nonkinetic cross-domain influence: the coercive weaponization of migration flows, real or threatened. In examining migration-driven coercion, this chapter also extends the analysis of cross-domain influence beyond deterrence to also encompass compellence, which appears to be the most common manifestation of this kind of cross-domain coercion.

Although long underappreciated by scholars of security studies, the employment of real or threatened cross-border population movements as a means of state-level coercion has had a lengthy and sordid history as a largely, but not exclusively, asymmetric instrument of state-level influence.[5] Indeed, since the advent of the 1951 Refugee Convention alone, there have been more than seventy-five confirmed cases of this unorthodox brand of nonmilitary coercion, well over half of which have been successful in achieving their stated military, political, or economic

---

[3] On the importance of embracing a broader perspective when analyzing and evaluating cross-domain influence, see, for instance, Chin-Hao Huang and David Kang, chapter 14 here.

[4] For a sample of Chinese strategists' views of multidomain influence, see, for instance, Qiao Liang and Wang Xiangsui, *Unrestricted Warfare* (Beijing: PLA Literature and Arts Publishing House, 1999). The CIA's Foreign Broadcast Information Service produced an English translation available at, accessed 29 March 2018, http://www.c4i.org/unrestricted.pdf; for one Russian general's widely cited views, see, for instance: Valery Gerasimov, "The Value of Science Is in the Foresight: New Challenges Demand Rethinking the Forms and Methods of Carrying Out Combat Operations," *Voyenno-Promyshlennyy Kurier*, 26 February 2013; for one (nonunique) nonstate take on these issues, see, for instance, Charlie Winter, "Media Jihad: The Islamic State's Doctrine for Information Warfare," *ICSR* (February 2017), accessed 29 March 2018, http://icsr.info/wp-content/uploads/2017/02/Media-jihad_web.pdf.

[5] The March 2016 deal forged between the EU and Turkey is only one recent example, albeit a very widely publicized, high-profile one. See: Kelly M. Greenhill, "Open Arms behind Barred Doors: Fear, Hypocrisy and Policy Schizophrenia in the European Migration Crisis," *European Law Journal* 22, no. 3 (May 2016): 279–294, https://doi.org/10.1111/eulj.12179.

objectives.⁶ This record of success suggests that when we step outside traditional operational domains and deterrence scenarios, our understanding of what does and does not work in coercion may bear some rethinking. At a minimum, it suggests that some conventional wisdom about the efficacy and relative facility of deterrence and compellence writ large might actually be domain- or context-specific. If this is true, then—as we move into an arguably still more complex and cross-domain-laden threat environment—we require a more nuanced and fine-grained understanding of a wider array of coercive means and operational domains. A study of the coercive use of migration and refugee flows offers an evidence-rich and potentially analytically fruitful step in this direction. This is because, unlike some other cross-domain tools, such as cyber, there is a long history of the use of this tool on which we can draw for potentially useful lessons that can be applied to arenas without such histories.⁷ At the same time, the coercive weaponization of migration shares some key similarities with the domain of cyberspace (and some other nontraditional domains), strongly suggesting that lessons from this particular domain may bear fruit in an array of others—for example, although nonkinetic, both cyber- and migration-driven coercion can both be very persuasive tools; their natures permit coercers to more easily engage in plausible deniability than is true for some other domains; their natures also permit the often secret (as opposed to public) issuance of threats and demands; and their users often experience difficulties conveying the credibility of their threats to powerful targets in early stages of bargaining games/crises.

In the pages that follow, I first offer definitions, and I introduce and briefly explicate the key theoretical propositions and causal mechanisms that undergird this unconventional cross-domain tool. I also detail the ways it comports with, and differs from, traditional military coercion; these identified distinctions are noteworthy as they carry relevance for other nonkinetic forms of cross-domain influence. I then discuss why turning people into "demographic bombs" has been an attractive and relatively successful instrument of cross-domain persuasion for those state and nonstate actors who are willing to employ it, despite the obvious moral and legal impediments to its use. I further identify a range of implications this specific tool

---

⁶ This means that CEM is markedly more prevalent than both intrastate wars (around 0.7 cases/year) and extended intermediate deterrence crises (around 0.6 cases/year). See: Kelly M. Greenhill, introduction to *Weapons of Mass Migration: Forced Displacement, Coercion and Foreign Policy* (Ithaca, NY: Cornell University Press, 2010). The existence of additional cases has been asserted—one prominent example is General Philip Breedlove's assertion in March 2016 that the Russians were using this tool against NATO in Syria—but as of this writing, I have not as yet been able to independently corroborate that case or some others whose existence has been asserted. See, for instance: Geoff Dyer, "NATO Accuses Russia of Weaponizing Immigrants," *Financial Times*, 1 March 2016, accessed 29 March 2019, https://www.ft.com/content/76a52430-dfe1-11e5-b67f-a61732c1d025.

⁷ For detailed specific and more general discussions of how these factors have played out in the migration realm over the last seventy-plus years, see: Greenhill, *Weapons of Mass Migration*.

holds for our understanding of contemporary coercion more broadly, and I identify some areas that require further research. By examining a "domain" of coercion that is radically different from the traditional five typically discussed, I highlight the importance of understanding how differing political characteristics vary across disparate means of influence and why actors might choose to make threats that vary rather significantly in kind from whatever they are attempting to prevent or to achieve.

Defining Coercive Engineered Migration

Coercion comes in two basic forms: deterrence and compellence. Deterrence is a coercive strategy designed to discourage a target from taking an undesirable action, that is, from changing its behavior and altering the status quo. Deterrence can be effected through the threat of painful retaliation (deterrence by punishment) or by denying the opponent its political or military aims (deterrence by denial). Deterrence can be pursued for one's own state (direct deterrence) or for one's allies (extended deterrence).

In contrast, compellence is a coercive strategy designed to get a target to change its behavior and alter the status quo.[8] The desired end-state may be a return to an earlier status quo, for example, prior to a deterrence failure, or to a new state of affairs. Like deterrence, compellence can be undertaken in the interest of one's own state (direct compellence) or for one's allies (extended compellence). Compellence by denial is achieved by attacking or undermining a target's military forces, while compellence via punishment is achieved by attacking a target's population and civilian infrastructure and by inflicting unacceptable risks and pain on the target. Compellence, either through threat or action, is a form of coercion because the target's preference is not to change its behavior and it is being forced to do so. Compellence can also be employed directly, on a target, or indirectly, on a target's state and nonstate allies. Deterrence is a coercive strategy, based on threat of retaliation, to keep a target from changing its behavior, whereas compellence is a coercive strategy, based on inflicting pain on the target (or threatening to do so), to force the target to change its behavior. In both cases, the target is pressured to do something it does not want to do.[9]

Coercive engineered migrations (CEMs) are, by extension, those real or threatened cross-border population movements that are deliberately created or manipulated, as instruments of deterrence and/or compellence, to prevent or

---

[8] Thomas C. Schelling, *Arms and Influence* (New Haven, CT: Yale University Press, 1966), 71.

[9] Robert J. Art and Kelly M. Greenhill, "Coercion: An Analytical Overview," in *Coercion: The Power to Hurt in Theory and in Practice,* edited by Kelly M. Greenhill and Peter Krause (Oxford: Oxford University Press, 2018), 3–32; ; Robert J. Art and Kelly M. Greenhill, "The Power and Limits of Compellence," *Political Science* 133, no. 1 *Quarterly* (Spring 2018): 77–97..

induce changes in political behavior and/or to extract political, military, and economic concessions from a target state or states. Like traditional military coercion, CEM can be employed in times of war as well as peace. An example of the former is threats by the regime of Syria's president Bashar al-Assad against Syria's neighbors during the early stages of the post-2011 civil war; an example of the latter is the use of CEM by several ASEAN states against the United Kingdom and the United States in the late 1970s and early 1990s, wherein Indochinese boat people were used as the victims/pawns.[10]

Like traditional, kinetic coercion, CEM can be direct or extended. It can be employed directly against a target (as Cuba's Fidel Castro successfully used it against the United States at least three times between 1965 and 1995). And it can be employed indirectly against a target's allies (as Slobodan Milosevic, Yugoslavia's president, attempted unsuccessfully to use it against Italy to try to pressure the United States and other North Atlantic Treaty Organization (NATO) allies during the Kosovo conflict in 1999, and as Libya's leader Muammar Gaddafi used it rather more successfully against Italy to pressure the broader European Union in the 2000s).[11] The instruments used to effect CEM have ranged from compulsory to permissive, from the employment of hostile threats and the use of military force through the offer of positive inducements and provision of financial incentives to the straightforward opening of normally sealed borders. In all cases, however, this kind of coercion has been unambiguously cross-domain—the means of real or threatened outflows (or their prevention) is threatened in the service of achieving objectives in other realms and policy arenas.

In traditional military coercion, the aim is to achieve political goals "on the cheap."[12] In CEM, the *spirit* of the enterprise is the same—achieving a political benefit at a more attractive cost than all-out war—but the specifics are perforce different. In the majority of cases thus far identified, weak state and nonstate actors employ CEM with the aim of achieving political goals that would be utterly unattainable through military means. For instance, the idea that states such as Cuba, Haiti, and Mexico could successfully coerce their neighbor the United States with the threat of military force is absurd. But successfully threatening them via the tacit or explicit threat of demographic bombs is a different story. (Indeed, as noted, Cuba's

---

[10] See, for instance: Courtland Robinson, *Terms of Refuge: The Indochinese Exodus and the International Response* (London: Zed Books, 1998).

[11] For details, see Greenhill, *Weapons of Mass Migration*, chs. 2, 3, and 6, on Cuba, Kosovo, and conclusions and policy implications, respectively. On Libya: Kelly M. Greenhill, "Migration as a Coercive Weapon: New Evidence from the Middle East," in Greenhill and Krause, *Coercion*, 204–227; Emanuela Paoletti, *The Migration of Power and North-South Inequalities: The Case of Italy and Libya* (London: Palgrave MacMillan, 2011).

[12] Robert Pape, *Bombing to Win: Air Power and Coercion in War* (Ithaca, NY: Cornell University Press, 1996), 19.

president Fidel Castro successfully coerced the United States to the negotiating table on three occasions, most famously during the 1980 Mariel boatlift, but also in 1965 and, most significantly, in 1994–1995. (It has been further argued that Raoul Castro's regime was gearing up to do the same thing in early 2016 in the midst of the subsequently stalled normalization process with the United States.)[13]

In a more limited number of known cases, more powerful states have resorted to CEM to achieve aims wherein the use of military force was viewed as being too costly or potentially escalatory and hence dangerous.[14] Some in the first George W. Bush administration, for instance, hoped to catalyze regime change in North Korea by provoking a massive outflow into China.[15]

Who Engages in It, and to What End?

Three distinct types of challengers employ CEM: generators, *agents provocateurs*, and opportunists.[16] As a rule, generators and *agents provocateurs* actively create and manipulate migration crises, while opportunists exploit crises initiated and created by others. Generators are those actors who directly instigate, or threaten to instigate, cross-border population movements unless targets concede to their demands. Historically, the majority of identified generators (like Castro and Milosevic) have been weak (at least relative to their targets), undemocratic actors who lack effective recourse to more conventional methods of influence.[17] *Agents provocateurs*, in contrast, do not create crises directly but deliberately act in ways designed to incite the generation of outflows by others. One prominent historical example is that of the Algerian National Liberation Front insurgents who undertook actions during the course of the 1954–1962 French-Algerian War that they fully anticipated would

---

[13] See, e.g.: Ian Smith, "Raul Castro Is Launching a 'Weapon of Mass Migration' against the U.S.," *National Review*, 28 January 2016, accessed 29 March 2018, http://www.nationalreview.com/article/430385/cuban-refugee-crisis-fabricated-win-sanctions-repeal.

[14] For example, while John F. Kennedy's administration was understandably reluctant to use force to influence Soviet behavior vis-à-vis Berlin in the early 1960s, U.S. officials—at the very least—entertained the idea of using CEM to "encourage" greater cooperation from Moscow. See, for instance, the partially declassified "(Secret) US Department of State Telegram, from US Embassy Berlin (Deputy Commandant Allen Lightner) to US Secretary of State, 'Refugee Problem May Deter Soviets from Going Ahead with Treaty,'" 24 July 1961, no. 87, control no. 15686, and "(Secret) Memo 'Discontent in East Germany,'" 18 July 1961, 3, both available through the Digital National Security Archive https://nsarchive2.gwu.edu/NSAEBB/NSAEBB354/7-24-61%20Moscow%20cable.pdf and https://nsarchive2.gwu.edu/NSAEBB/NSAEBB354/7-18-61%20Ausland%20memo%20on%20GDR.pdf.

[15] China quickly put the kibosh on this proposed and piloted operation, however. See, for instance, Greenhill, *Weapons of Mass Migration*, ch. 5.

[16] These types are identified as G, AP, and O in table 12.1.

[17] However, on the difficulty of defining what exactly constitutes a "weak state," see: David Handel, *Weak States in the International System* (London: Frank Cass, 1981), ch. 1.

provoke brutal, refugee-generating responses by the French military.[18] A more recent example of insurgents engaged in similar tactics is the Kosovo Liberation Army in the late 1990s.[19] Opportunists play no direct role in the creation of migration crises but simply exploit for their own gain the existence of outflows generated or catalyzed by others. Opportunists might threaten to close their borders and thereby create humanitarian emergencies, unless targets take desired actions and/or proffer side payments. Opportunists might also offer to alleviate existing crises in exchange for a political and/or financial payoffs, as Turkey did in March 2016 and as Libya has repeatedly done, both during Gaddafi's long reign and in the years since he was deposed in 2011.

Just as is the case with traditional military coercion, cross-domain and otherwise, demands issued using this coercive tool have been highly varied in scope, content, and magnitude. Demands have been both concrete and symbolic and have made entreaties both to undertake actions and to cease undertaking them. (See table 13.1 for capsule descriptions of articulated objectives for all identified potential cases of CEM up to December 2016.) Demands have run the gamut from the simple provision of financial aid to the termination of insurgent funding and to full-scale military intervention and even regime change.

Broadly speaking, these myriad coercive objectives can be divided into political goals, military goals, and economic goals. More than 60 percent of heretofore identified coercive attempts have been undertaken in pursuit of political objectives, just over 30 percent in pursuit of military objectives, and approximately 50 percent in pursuit of economic objectives.[20] Thus, as noted, CEM is by definition an archetype of cross-domain coercion: both the means and the goals of the states and nonstate actors who employ CEM tend to be distinct from the means used to achieve those goals. As is the case with other forms of cross-domain coercion, moreover, CEM may be employed discretely or in conjunction with other means, but CEM is virtually always employed in the service of one or more cross-domain objectives, be they economic, political, or military.

Coercive engineered migration has been used to achieve myriad diverse objectives that have thus far ranged from the simple and straightforward provision of financial and/or military aid to full-blown military operations in support of regime change. An example of the former is that of Turkey's president, Recep Tayyip Erdoğan, who threatened to overwhelm Europe with (mostly Syrian) refugees if

---

[18] See, for instance, Yahia H. Zoubir, "US and Soviet Policies towards France's Struggle with Anticolonial Nationalism in North Africa," *Canadian Journal of History* 30, no. 3 (Winter 1995): 439–466, https://doi.org/10.3138/cjh.30.3.439.

[19] See, for instance, Greenhill, *Weapons of Mass Migration*, ch. 3.

[20] That the sum of these three sets of objectives is greater than 100 percent makes it clear that numerous coercers have sought multiple, often disparate objectives. See also: Greenhill, *Weapons of Mass Migration*.

Table 12.1 Cases of coercively engineered migration, 1953–2016

Year	Challenger/coercer	Principal target(s)	Principal objective(s)	Deterrence, compellence or both?	Outcome
1953	West Germany (O)	United States	Financial aid, political support	Compellence	Partial success
1954–55	South Vietnam, United States (G)	North Vietnam	Defer/cancel reunification elections	Deterrence	Failure
1954–60	Algerian insurgents (AP)	French allies, esp. United States	Convince allies to pressure France to relinquish Algeria; political-military intervention	Compellence	Partial success
1956	Austria (O)	United States	Aid and resettlement	Compellence	Success
1961	United States (AP/O)	Soviet Union	Deterrence re: Berlin	Deterrence	Indeterminate
1965	Cuba (G)	United States	Regularized immigration	Compellence	Partial success
1967–70	Biafran insurgents (G)	United States	Aid; intervention; political and diplomatic support	Both	Partial success
1967	Israel (G)	Jordan	Bilateral negotiations/peace talks	Compellence	Indeterminate
1967	Jordan (O)	United States	Pressure Israel re: Palestinian return	Compellence	SR success; LR failure**
1971	Pakistan (G)	India	Cease support for Bengali rebels	Compellence	Failure
1972	Uganda (G)	United Kingdom	Rescind decision re: military assistance	Compellence	Failure

Year	Challenger/coercer	Principal target(s)	Principal objective(s)	Deterrence, compellence or both?	Outcome
1978–82	Bangladesh (G/O)	Burma	Halt outflow of Burmese Muslims	Compellence	Success
1978–82	ASEAN, Hong Kong (O)	Western great powers, esp. United States	Resettlement and financial aid	Compellence	Success
1979	Vietnam (G/O)	European Community, United States	Aid, diplomatic recognition, credit	Compellence	Indeterminate
1979–1980s	Thailand (O)	United States; China	An alliance; political-military support	Compellence	Success
1979–81	Haiti (G)	United States	Financial and military aid	Compellence	Success
1979–81	NGO activists	United States; Haiti	End support for regime; undermine it	Compellence	Failure
1980s	Pakistan (O)	United States	Alliance; political-military support	Compellence	Success
1979–1980s	Soviet Union (G)	Pakistan	Cease support for insurgents	Compellence	Failure
1979–1980s	Exiled insurgents (O)	Pakistan	Control over peace settlement	Compellence	Success
1980	Cuba (G)	United States	End hijacking; normalize migration; etc.	Compellence	Partial success
1981–82	Austria (O)	Western Europe, United States	Refugee resettlement and aid	Compellence	Success

(continued)

Table 12.1 Continued

Year	Challenger/coercer	Principal target(s)	Principal objective(s)	Deterrence, compellence or both?	Outcome
1982	Thailand (O)	United States, France	Financial aid	Compellence	Success
Early 1980s	Honduras (O)	United States	Military aid, training; security pact	Compellence	Success
1980s–1997	Bangladesh (G)	India	End Shanti Bahini (insurgent) funding	Compellence	Indeterminate
1983–86	East Germany (AP)	West Germany	Aid; tech assistance; border fixity	Compellence	Success
1984–85	East Germany (AP)	Sweden	Financial aid	Compellence	Success
1985	Libya (G)	Tunisia, Egypt, and Mauritania	Shift diplomatic alliances/positions	Compellence	Indeterminate
Late 1980s	Hong Kong, ASEAN (O)	United States, Western Europe	Aid and resettlement	Compellence	Success
1989–1990s	Vietnam (O)	European Community, United States	Political-diplomatic recognition; aid	Compellence	Success
1989–92	Bangladesh (G)	Burma	Halt outflow of Burmese Muslims	Compellence	Success
1990–92	Saudi Arabia (G)	Yemen	Change position on Gulf War/Iraq	Compellence	Failure

Year	Challenger/coercer	Principal target(s)	Principal objective(s)	Deterrence, compellence or both?	Outcome
1990s–	Israel (AP/O)	Palestinians	Relinquish claims on Jerusalem	Compellence	Failure
1991–92	United States (O)	Israel	Stop settlements in Occupied Territories	Compellence	Partial success
1990–91	Albania (G)	Italy	Food aid, financial credits, other assistance	Compellence	Success
1991	Albania (G)	Italy, European Community	Financial aid	Compellence	Success
1990–94	Albania (G)	Greece	Financial aid	Compellence	Success
1991	Poland (G,/AP)	European Community, United States	Debt relief; financial aid	Compellence	Indeterminate
1990	Ethiopia (G)	Israel	Monetary payoff	Compellence	Success
1991	Turkey (O)	United States	Humanitarian-military intervention	Compellence	Success
1992–94	Jean-Bertrand Aristide (AP)	United States	Return to power; U.S. military intervention	Compellence	Success
1992–95	Bosniaks (G/AP)	UN Security Council	Troop presence; air evacuation	Compellence	Partial success
1994	Poland (O)	Germany	Monetary payoff	Compellence	Success
1994	Cuba (G)	United States	Regularized immigration, etc.	Compellence	Success

(*continued*)

Table 12.1 Continued

Year	Challenger/coercer	Principal target(s)	Principal objective(s)	Deterrence, compellence or both?	Outcome
Mid-1990s	Zaire (O)	Largely United States, France, Belgium	Political-diplomatic recognition, aid	Compellence	Success
1995	Libya (AP/O)	Egypt	Lifting of sanctions; shift in policy toward Palestinians	Compellence	Failure
Mid-1990s	North Korea (G)	China	Financial aid, political support	Both	Success
1997	Albania (G)	Italy	Military intervention	Compellence	Success
1998	Turkey (G)	Italy	Support/punishment re: EU bid	Compellence	Indeterminate
1998–99	Kosovar Albanians (AP)	NATO	Military aid; intervention	Compellence	Success
1998–99	FRY (G)	NATO, esp. Germany, Greece, Italy	Deterrence, then compellence	Both	Failure
1998–99	Macedonia I (O)	NATO	Financial aid	Compellence	Success
1999	Macedonia II (O)	NATO	Financial aid	Compellence	Success
2001–3	Nauru (O)	Australia	Financial aid	Compellence	Success
2002	Belarus (AP)	EU	Diplomatic recognition; aid	Compellence	Failure
2002–5	Activists/NGO network (AP)	China	Policy shift on North Korea; regime collapse	Compellence	Failure
2002–5	Activists/NGO network (AP)	South Korea	Policy shift on North Korea; regime collapse	Compellence	Failure

2002–	North Korea (NK) (G)	China	Continued diplomatic support, aid	Both	Success
2004	Nauru (O)	Australia	Financial aid	Compellence	Success
2004	Haiti (G)	United States	Military assistance	Compellence	Failure
2004	Belarus (AP)	EU	Financial aid	Compellence	Failure
2004	Libya (AP)	EU	Lifting of sanctions	Compellence	Success
2004–5	Chad (G)	UN Security Council	Military-political intervention	Compellence	Indeterminate
2006	Libya (AP/O)	EU	Financial and other aid	Compellence	Partial success
2007	Malta (O)	EU	Burden-sharing assistance	Compellence	Indeterminate
2008	Libya (AP/O)	EU	Financial and other aid	Compellence	Success
2008	Iran (G)	Afghanistan	Deterrence	Deterrence	Partial success**
2010	Libya (AP/O)	EU	Financial and other aid; EU-Libya treaty	Compellence	Partial success
2010	Turkey (G)	UK	Deterrence re: 1915 genocide finding	Deterrence	Indeterminate
2011	Syria (O)	Neighboring states, including Israel, Jordan, Lebanon	Deterrence re: support of protesters/insurgents	Deterrence	SR success; LR failure
2011	Libya (G/AP/O)	EU	Deterrence, then compellence	Both	Failure
2011	Italy (AP)	EU, esp. France	Burden-sharing assistance	Compellence	SR failure; LR partial success

(*continued*)

Table 12.1 Continued

Year	Challenger/coercer	Principal target(s)	Principal objective(s)	Deterrence, compellence or both?	Outcome
2011	France (O)	Italy	Compellence re: North African policy/actions	Compellence	Partial success
2012	Turkey (O)	UN Security Council	Financial aid	Compellence	Success
2012	Pakistan (G)	UN donor countries, esp. Australia	Financial aid	Compellence	Success
2012	Iran (O)	Afghanistan	Deterrence re: treaty with United States	Deterrence	Failure
2014	Russia (G)	Central Asian states, esp. Kyrgyzstan, Tajikistan, Moldova	Deterrence re: support of UN resolution	Deterrence	Success
2014	Libya (O)	EU	Financial assistance, logistical support	Compellence	Success
2014	Turkey (O)	NATO allies	No-fly zone; financial and other aid	Compellence	Partial success
2014	France with help from mayor of Calais (O)	United Kingdom	Financial and in-kind assistance	Compellence	Success
2014	Islamic State in Libya (G)	EU/NATO	Deterrence	Deterrence	Indeterminate (but possibly a failure)

2015	Italy (O)	Fellow EU states	Aid	Compellence	Partial success
2015	Turkey (O)	EU	Financial aid; visa-free travel; EU membership talks; no-fly zone	Compellence	Partial success
2015	Libyan government faction (G, O)	EU	Diplomatic recognition; aid	Compellence	Indeterminate
2015	Islamic State in Libya (G)	EU/NATO	Compellence/cease attacks	Compellence	Indeterminate
2016	Turkey (O)	EU	Financial aid; visa-free travel; EU membership talks; reduced pressure re: human rights issues	Compellence	SR success, but implementation still ongoing
2016	Egypt (O)	Italy	Reversal of decision to draw down military aid	Compellence	Indeterminate as of this writing but likely failure

Key: AP = agent(s) provocateurs; G = generator; LR = long run; O = opportunists; SR = short run
* The more powerful actor (challenger or target), if discernable
** Existing data are suggestive, but finding is only provisional as of this writing

not granted a wide range of military and, later, political and economic concessions. An example of the latter is that of Haiti's former president Jean-Bertrand Aristide, who threatened to encourage Haitians to decamp to Florida by boat and raft if the Bill Clinton administration did not facilitate his return to power in Haiti in 1994.[21] Erdoğan's threats gave rise to the much-criticized 2016 EU-Turkey deal, while Aristide's resulted in the also unpopular 1994–1995 U.S.-led military intervention Operation Uphold Democracy.

How Does Coercive Engineered Migration Work?

In practice, CEM functions much like more traditional forms of coercion. Operationally, it is generally a punishment strategy, rather than a denial strategy, that can be used in exercises of coercion and of counter-coercion—sometimes simultaneously—although, to be sure, mass migrations can also be used to undermine and impede the achievement of military aims.[22] As is the case with other punishment strategies, such as terrorism and strategic bombing, the principal targets of this kind of coercion, states, tend not to be synonymous with the principal victims, the displaced themselves. Coercers aim to create domestic conflict or public dissatisfaction in the target state in an attempt to convince the target's leadership to concede to the challenger's demands rather than incur the anticipated (domestic or international) political costs of resistance.[23]

There are two distinct but non–mutually exclusive pathways by which CEM can be effected using punishment strategies: capacity swamping and political agitating. Capacity swamping focuses on manipulating the target's *ability* to accept, accommodate, or assimilate a given group of migrants or refugees. Political agitating focuses on manipulating the target's *willingness* to do so. In both swamping and agitating, coercion is effectively a dynamic, two-level game in which the target's international-level responses to the coercer's threats or actions tend to be driven by simultaneous (or subsequent) actions taken by actors in the target state.[24]

---

[21] For details, see ibid., ch. 4, on the Haitian case; Greenhill, "Open Arms behind Barred Doors," on the Turkish case.

[22] See, e.g.: Kelly M. Greenhill, "Strategic Engineered Migration as a Weapon of War," *Civil Wars* 10, no. 1 (Spring 2008): 6–21, https://doi.org/10.1080/13698240701835425.

[23] "The hope is that the government will concede or the population will revolt." Pape, *Bombing to Win*, 21.

[24] See: Robert Putnam, "Diplomacy and Domestic Politics: The Logic of Two-Level Games," *International Organization* 42, no. 3 (Summer 1988): 427–460, https://doi.org/10.1017/S0020818300027697.

Coercive engineered migration is one manifestation of what Jonathan Shimshoni and Ari Levite refer to as "societal warfare."[25] As is the case with other two-level, dynamic bargaining games, the lynchpin of CEM's success depends on coercers being able to impose unacceptable costs (short- and long-term); to create seemingly irreconcilable differences among segments of the target society—since, for instance, leaders cannot simultaneously accept and reject a particular group of refugees or migrants; and to make the prospect of continued resistance less palatable than that of acquiescence.

Thus, in short, challengers aim to influence targets by what is known in traditional coercion literature as force majeure, that is, a choice dictated by overwhelming circumstances. Targets, of course, always have a choice, but one that is skewed if they believe the consequences of noncompliance will be a denial of future choice.[26] Thus coercers seek to narrow a target's set of domestic policy responses to an outflow—or, in game theory terms, narrow the target's "win-set"—such that concession begins to appear more attractive, at least relative to the possibility that the future will hold fewer, even less auspicious choices.[27] Under such conditions, concession can become increasingly appealing, which is exactly the coercer's intent. This is not to suggest that concession is cost free, only that in the face of a threatened or mounting crisis, the anticipation of future pain and mounting costs has to be weighed against the costs and opportunities associated with ending the crisis immediately by conceding to the challenger's demands. These dynamics are not unique to CEM. However, they are fundamental to its elevated rates of success relative to more traditional intra- and cross-domain means.

Most coercers who utilize CEM appear to favor risk strategies, that is, they prefer to inflict costs at a gradually increasing rate, threatening bigger punishment later for noncompliance.[28] Because the punishment is not inflicted all at once, the coercer "may interrupt operations temporarily in order to provide time for reflection or negotiation or to reward the target state for concessions, thus encouraging minor demonstrations or willingness to accommodate the demands as well as major

---

[25] Ariel E. Levite and Jonathan Shimshoni, "The Strategic Challenge of Society-centric Warfare," *Survival* 60, no. 6 (December 2018–January 2019): 91–118.

[26] Lawrence Freedman, "Strategic Coercion," in *Strategic Coercion: Concepts and Cases*, edited by Lawrence Freedman (Oxford: Oxford University Press, 1998), 29.

[27] See: Kenneth A. Shepsle and Barry R. Weingast, "Uncovered Sets and Sophisticated Voting Outcomes with Implications for Agenda Institutions," *American Journal of Political Science* 28, no. 1 (1984): 49–74, http://www.jstor.org/stable/2110787.

[28] Risk strategies are likely preferred, for two reasons. First, too large an outflow may itself destabilize a regime. Second, at least recently, massive outflows have increased the probability of military interventions undertaken to stop or reverse them. However, coercers, frequently perpetrators, do not have the luxury of pursuing such strategies and often find themselves generating larger outflows than they strictly speaking view as desirable.

concessions."[29] Whether one makes a threat once or serially, risk is a cheap form of punishment and, even if administered indirectly, can be quite effective at changing the decisionmaking calculations of both states and nonstate actors, as I discuss further below.

However, three factors tend to impede the successful employment of risk strategies in exercises of CEM: principal-agent problems; the migrants themselves; and the nature of risk strategies. With regard to principal-agent problems, as Schelling argued, "the ideal compellent action would be one that, once initiated, causes minimal harm if compliance is forthcoming and great harm if compliance is not forthcoming."[30] The problem is that once an outflow has been initiated, coercers often lose at least some degree of control over it. Those who conduct ethnic cleansing may be irregulars or even simply "bands of thugs" who lack discipline and may even pursue their own self-serving strategies, which may run contrary to or even undermine the coercive strategy.[31] Likewise, the displaced—the real victims of this kind of coercion—have agendas of their own. Once outside the sending state, refugees and migrants are capable of autonomous actions that are not necessarily compatible with the coercers' goals.

Such loss-of-control-related situations—whether driven by the actions of the cleansers or the victims of cleansing—are analogous to complications inherent in using cyber weapons, such as worms and viruses, which also can take on lives of their own and disperse and wreak havoc in ways inconsistent with the objectives and interests of their creators.[32] A prominent example of this kind of loss of control is what happened with the Stuxnet worm in the aftermath of the successful execution of Operation Olympic Games.[33] Thus, in CEM, cyber, and potentially other cross-domain operations, promises to inflict no future harm if concessions are forthcoming may ring hollow and undermine the efficacy of coercion.

Furthermore, just as is the case with traditional military coercion, CEM-focused risk strategies are often viewed as incredible by targets. According to Robert Pape, "instead of being convinced of the perpetrator's resolve to inflict maximum damage if demands are not met, the opponent is more likely to be convinced that the

---

[29] Shepsle and Weingast, "Uncovered Sets and Sophisticated Voting Outcomes with Implications for Agenda Institutions," 19.

[30] Schelling, *Arms and Influence*, 89.

[31] See, e.g.: John Mueller, "The Banality of 'Ethnic War,'" *International Security* 25, no. 1 (Summer 2000): 42–70, https://doi.org/10.1162/016228800560381.

[32] On limitations and constraints of using cyberweapons, see, for instance: Jacquelyn Schneider, chapter 5 here.

[33] On Olympic Games, see: Michael Nacht, Patricia Schuster, and Eva Uribe, chapter 2 here; Jon R. Lindsay, "Stuxnet and the Limits of Cyber Warfare," *Security Studies* 22, no. 3 (2013): 365–404, https://doi.org/10.1080/09636412.2013.816122. On how the worm got lose and its wielders lost control of it, see: Lindsay, "Stuxnet and the Limits of Cyber Warfare"; David E. Sanger, *Confront and Conceal: Obama's Secret Wars and Surprising Use of American Power* (New York: Crown, 2012).

coercer will never escalate far above current restrained levels."[34] This can happen for two reasons, neither of which are unique to CEM: one is the difficulty of signaling one's intentions, resolve, and capabilities to one's potential adversaries and targets;[35] a second is the fact that targets, especially powerful ones, frequently calculate that the costs for challengers of following through on their threats would be so high that they will be self-deterred from escalating and will back down rather than follow through. This is a refrain heard time and time again throughout history, both in the CEM realm and in more traditional military domains. However, coercers who have opted to make threats, especially against more powerful targets, are often highly resolved and not bluffing at all. Threats and demands have quite often been followed by demonstrative coercive actions and more often than not are at least partially successful.

From a bargaining perspective, this represents something of a puzzle. Both game theoretic logic and common sense suggests there should be a bargain that coercer and target are willing to strike before the coercer is forced to launch an outflow (that is potentially costly and/or uncontrollable) and before the target has to bear at least some (and possibly very significant and long-term) costs of absorbing an influx itself or assisting an ally or allies in doing so. Yet, historically, such bargains are rarely struck before threats become reality and threatened outflows materialize. There are a number of potential explanations to account for this fact—including hubris of the powerful, information asymmetries, and bureaucratic pathologies—but what is most germane for the study of cross-domain compellence is not why targets fail to strike preoutflow deals but how and why coercers are able to use CEM relatively successfully, and what this might mean for other coercive domains.[36]

Indeed, CEM's record as a punishment strategy is especially striking because it has long been asserted that denial strategies are superior to punishment strategies, particularly in the realm of compellence.[37] However, what is frequently treated as a blanket conclusion about the superiority of denial over punishment rests largely on findings from a single means/domain, air power, and from cases wherein punishment was constrained to a very particular set of targets—civilians and cities—and only during wartime. However, if one expands one's analytical focus to include wider ranges not only of (kinetic and unconventional) means/domains and targets but also of methods by which to inflict pain, risks, and costs, and if one includes

---

[34] Pape, *Bombing to Win*, 28.

[35] For a discussion of the difficulties of signaling and potentially effective strategies for overcoming them, see, for instance: Brendan Rittenhouse Green and Austin G. Long, chapter 10 here.

[36] For a discussion of these potential explanations, as well as the particular problem of information asymmetries, see: Greenhill, *Weapons of Mass Migration*, ch. 6.

[37] Pape, *Bombing to Win*.

coercion in times of both peace and war, conclusions are less cut and dried and require more nuance.[38]

Thus it is more defensible to assert that the relative efficacy of denial as opposed to punishment strategies likely depends on a combination of the context, targets, and chosen means of coercive influence, whether cross-domain or otherwise. More specifically, when a coercer employs air power against a target's military forces or civilian population in war, military denial appears to work better than punishment.[39] However, when military force (or other coercive instruments) are utilized not to kill the target's civilians but to produce (or threaten to produce) large population movements across state borders, then punishment can be quite effective.[40]

In short, this amendment to our understanding of the efficacy of coercion may carry significant implications for a broad array of contexts and additional domains. It raises the question, however, of what makes this rather unconventional tool so effective and attractive to coercers, especially given the myriad material, ethical, and legal impediments to its use, as well as the aforementioned risks associated with its use for coercers themselves? And what do these factors tell us about the use of asymmetric instruments of influence, more broadly?

What Makes Coercive Engineered Migration an Attractive (Asymmetric) Means of Influence?

It is a widely accepted axiom in international politics that, to paraphrase Thucydides's Melian Dialogue, the strong do what they can; the weak endure what they must. Yet, as Dwight D. Eisenhower also famously noted, "it's not the size of the dog in the fight. It's the size of the fight in the dog." In other words, with a well-chosen strategy, the right domain, and a favorable set of circumstances, highly motivated and resolute weak actors can triumph over more powerful ones. From the perspective of traditional international relations theory, such coercive challenges, cross-domain or otherwise, represent something of a puzzle. Yet a resort to unconventional, asymmetric means and domains may be eminently rational and very attractive for several distinct, and wholly rational, cost-benefit-driven reasons.

---

[38] See e.g., Karl Mueller, "Strategies of Coercion: Denial, Punishment, and the Future of Air Power," *Security Studies* 7, no. 3 (1997): 90–136, https://doi.org/10.1080/09636419808429354; James R. Cody, "Coercive Airpower in the Global War on Terror: Testing Validity of Courses of Action" (PhD diss., School of Advanced Military Studies, Ft. Leavenworth, Kansas, 2003), accessed 29 March 2018, http://www.au.af.mil/au/awc/awcgate/army/sams_cody.pdf; and Art and Greenhill, "Coercion."

[39] Pape has shown that when the compeller's air power is applied directly against the target, it is more effective when used for military denial than for civilian punishment. Pape located forty cases of coercive air power campaigns from 1917–1991 that involved military denial, civilian punishment, or both. The denial theory predicts accurately thirty-seven out of forty cases, or 92.5 percent.

[40] Art and Greenhill, "Coercion"; Art and Greenhill, "Power and Limits of Compellence."

Bargaining Leverage

Research on negotiating strategies of the (relatively) weak has revealed that such actors often view crisis generation—using a variety of means across multiple domains—as a necessary precursor to negotiations with their more powerful counterparts. This is because the powerful, who generally anticipate that their superior strength and capabilities will carry the day, tend to be reluctant to yield concessions and even to negotiate with weaker challengers absent crisis-generating incentives.[41] As Schelling put it: "if I say, 'Row, or I'll tip the boat over and drown us both,' you'll say you don't believe me. But if I rock the boat so that it may tip over, you'll be more impressed.... To make it work, I must really put the boat in jeopardy; just saying that I may turn us both over is unconvincing."[42]

Crisis generation offers relatively weak actors a tried-and-true cross-domain strategy for both overcoming powerful actors' reluctance to negotiate and leveling the playing field. It is one of the few areas where weak, even internationally illegitimate, actors may possess relative strength vis-à-vis more powerful target states, and certainly—in the case of migration crises—also vis-à-vis their even weaker domestic victims.[43] After intentionally generating crises, weak actors can offer to make them disappear in exchange for military, financial, or political payoffs. Indeed, international negotiators routinely report recognizable patterns of "drama and catastrophe" when dealing with particular international actors.[44]

In the face of such catastrophes, overlapping bargaining space may develop rapidly where before there was none. Indeed, strong actors, previously unwilling to even talk to, much less negotiate with, their weaker counterparts will often abruptly temper or reverse positions in the face of clear and present crises. As migration scholar Christopher Mitchell bluntly put it, "sending nations can sometimes structure emigration so that receiving states are very likely to respond with inconsistent administrative action," which can then be used as a lever against those who had "in effect brushed [them] off" previously.[45]

Consequently, migration, like other forms of crisis generation, can help enhance weak actors' credibility, increase the potency of their threats, and improve their

---

[41] For an examination of an analogous phenomenon in the nuclear arena, see: Scott Snyder, *Negotiating on the Edge: North Korean Negotiating Behavior* (Washington, DC: US Institute of Peace, 1999), ch. 3.

[42] Thomas Schelling, *The Strategy of Conflict* (Cambridge, MA: Harvard University Press, 1960), 196.

[43] Mark Habeeb, *Power and Tactics in International Negotiation: How Weak Nations Bargain with Strong Nations* (Baltimore: Johns Hopkins University Press, 1988).

[44] Habeeb, *Power and Tactics in International Negotiation*; Snyder, *Negotiating on the Edge*, 71, 43.

[45] Christopher Mitchell, "Implications," in *Western Hemisphere Immigration and United States Foreign Policy*, edited by Christopher Mitchell (University Park: Pennsylvania State University Press, 1992).

coercive capabilities in several different ways.[46] First, and arguably most important from a cross-domain perspective, because in-kind retaliation is rarely an option for targets—and alternate responses may also be problematic—coercers using CEM may achieve a kind of escalation dominance over potential targets.[47] For instance, launching a war to counter outflows may be an option in certain circumstances, but often the expected costs associated with escalation to that level far exceed the expected costs of conceding in whole or in part. For instance, as disconcerting as West German leaders found the periodic inflows of large numbers of Eastern bloc refugees, neither they nor their NATO allies were ever going to be willing to risk starting World War III by taking retaliatory military action against East Germany.[48] Russian interference in the 2016 U.S. presidential election comes to mind as a contemporary analogous example in another nonkinetic and nontraditional domain of influence.

Likewise, if a coercer is already internationally isolated, methods short of war that powerful states may employ in response to CEM may be slow-acting—for example, economic sanctions—and thus inappropriate as a method of counter-coercion during a crisis. And war itself can be a risky option, since armed conflicts are bloody and often costly and their outcomes and ultimate duration are uncertain. Indeed, targets who engage in foreign-imposed regime change often inadvertently create conditions even more conducive to the employment of CEM after they have intervened to change the incumbent regime, as the U.S. involvement in Afghanistan, Iraq, and Libya in recent years makes clear.

Simply put, in traditional military coercion, potential adversaries tend to be deterred from even attempting coercion unless they possess superior military capabilities that can protect them from retaliation. However, in the case of CEM, coercers are frequently undeterred by their targets' military superiority, because retaliation is only rarely a politically feasible option. This is due to the fact that targets generally value the issues at hand less than do the coercers, who as a rule tend to be

---

[46] This can be particularly important because powerful actors tend to dismiss weaker actors' threats, for two distinct reasons. First, they frequently have trouble believing their weaker counterparts would initiate crises or conflicts they seem destined to lose, based on relative capabilities. This tendency may be further exacerbated by the fact that targets may also underestimate the magnitude of the threats facing weak challengers when the issues at stake seem trivial to them, thus leading them to further discount the probability of crisis initiation. Second, because the majority of targets would not themselves initiate migration crises, they tend to dismiss threats to do so as "irrational" and "crazy" and, consequently, incredible.

[47] See Daniel Byman and Matthew Waxman, *The Dynamics of Coercion: American Foreign Policy and the Limits of Military Might* (Oxford: Oxford University Press, 2002).

[48] See, for instance: Valur Ingimundarson, "Cold War Misperceptions: The Communist and Western Responses to the East German Refugee Crisis in 1953," *Journal of Contemporary History* 29, no. 3 (July 1994): 463–481, http://www.jstor.org/stable/260769; Dean G. Pruitt, *Negotiation Behavior* (New York: Academic Press, 1981).

highly dissatisfied with the status quo and more highly resolved than their targets. This makes sense in that coercers are often fighting for their very political survival, whereas for targets the stakes at hand tend to be lower.

Indeed, although more research is necessary to properly explore this proposition, it is possible that in some contemporary conflict dyads, CEM may create a bastardized kind of stability-instability paradox, whereby certain coercers may be more willing to use this tool because they know that targets will be reluctant to escalate to war in response. In fact, this *may* be even more likely after Odyssey Dawn, the 2011 NATO-backed operation in Libya that led to the ouster and death of Gaddafi, did not mark the end of Libya's attempts to coerce its European neighbors through the threat of mass migration.[49] Indeed, if anything, circumstantial evidence suggests that Odyssey Dawn *may* have led others to "get in on" this profitable game.[50] Again, more research is needed.

Second, under certain conditions, migration crises may permit weak challengers to inflict punishment on targets that is disproportionate to the costs of compliance. Although targets may be understandably reluctant to concede ex ante, quite often demands that were unacceptable at the outset may begin to appear nominal compared with the costs of managing sustained, large-scale outflows into the indefinite future or the long-term assimilation costs of even more limited inflows. Consider that a migration crisis, unlike a bombing sortie, which may be profoundly damaging but is perforce finite, can be, as noted, "a gift that keeps on giving," to paraphrase the chestnut from the classic Hallmark greeting card campaign. This fact alone should arguably encourage targets to strike deals before outflows have commenced; but, as noted, it appears that this rarely occurs. What this finding might mean for other domains of influence bears further attention and requires additional research.

Finally, because of the widespread belief that liberal democracies possess particular characteristics that make them and their leaders behave differently from other types of regimes and leaders, "fellow liberals benefit from a presumption of amity; non-liberals suffer from a presumption of enmity."[51] Hence, illiberal actors—already generally viewed with suspicion and contempt by the most powerful members of the international community—have little left to lose should they choose to abrogate the norms

---

[49] See, for instance: Greenhill, "Open Arms behind Barred Doors"; and Kelly M. Greenhill, "Demographic Bombing: People as Weapons in Syria and Beyond," *Foreign Affairs*, 17 December 2015, accessed 29 March 2018, https://www.foreignaffairs.com/articles/2015-12-17/demographic-bombing.

[50] See, for instance: Kelly M. Greenhill, "Migration as a Weapon in Theory and in Practice," *Military Review* 96, no. 6 (November–December 2016): 23–36, http://www.armyupress.army.mil/Portals/7/military-review/Archives/English/MilitaryReview_20161231_art007.pdf.

[51] Michael W. Doyle, "Liberalism and World Politics," *American Political Science Review* 80, no. 4 (1986): 1151–1169, https://doi.org/10.1017/S0003055400185041; Bruce Russett, "Why Democratic Peace?," in *Debating the Democratic Peace*, edited by Michael Brown (Cambridge, MA: MIT Press, 1996), 93.

associated with the generation of migration crises. In short, nondemocratic, "illegitimate" states and nonstate actors face a double whammy: few are strong enough to impel their strong counterparts to take them seriously under normal conditions, and still fewer are likely to be trusted to negotiate in an aboveboard manner. Therefore, not only are the reputational barriers to resorting to such norms-violating tactics lower but also the bargaining advantages of doing so are far greater.[52]

Operational Advantages

Compared with more conventional military operations, catalyzing outmigrations is usually relatively cheap, particularly as the number of troops required is frequently small and the manpower necessary to effect population displacement need not be highly trained or well equipped.[53] Inducing mass migration does not rely on direct combat but on the expectations associated with the demonstrative capacity of the violence that can be brought to bear. Sometimes no force needs to be used at all; the fear of future violence may be sufficient to cause people to flee.[54]

Unsurprisingly, perhaps, in light of the aforementioned factors, more than 80 percent of coercers have been measurably weaker than their targets (detailed in table 13.1). Yet, despite their relative weakness, these cross-domain coercers have also been relatively successful on their own terms and in comparison to their more powerful targets.[55] Coercers who employed CEM between 1951 and 2016 achieved at least some of their stated objectives, cases I code as "partial successes,"

---

[52] For a discussion of how absence of agreement on shared norms and standards of behavior may directly impede CDD, see James Morrow, chapter 9 here. The direct implications for his argument on informational asymmetries and the (often unexpected) efficacy of cross-domain compellence using CEM are clear.

[53] In fact, the use of regular troops is often not even necessary; it can also be done with paramilitary "shock troops" and even bands of thugs, as the 1990s wars of imperial dissolution in the Balkans demonstrate. See, for instance, Mueller, "The Banality of Ethnic War," and Morrow, "International Law and the Common Knowledge Requirements of Cross-Domain Deterrence."

[54] See, for instance: James Gow, "Coercive Cadences: Yugoslav War," in Freedman, *Strategic Coercion: Concepts and Cases*, ch. 11.

[55] Success in this context is defined as persuading a target to change a previously articulated policy, to stop or reverse an action already undertaken, or to disburse side-payments, in line with a challenger's demands; in other words, most of a challenger's demands were met. A case is coded as a "success" if most or all of the challenger's known objectives were achieved and as a "partial success" if the challenger achieved a significant fraction, but not all, of its aims. If few or none of the challenger's objectives were achieved—or were achieved for what appear to be exogenous reasons—the case is coded as a "failure." Finally, a case is coded as "indeterminate" if (1) the challenger achieved at least some of its objectives, but causality is unclear; (2) there is insufficient evidence to conclude that coercion was in the end attempted; or (3) threats were issued, but a crisis never materialized, and it remains, as of this writing, unclear whether or not the challenger's demands were met. (Indeterminate cases are excluded from aggregate assessments of coercive success and failure, as is the currently ongoing case.)

or 73 percent of the time (in fifty-four of seventy-four heretofore identified cases). If one imposes a stricter measure of success and excludes partial successes, coercers have still achieved more or less everything they have reportedly sought 54 percent of the time (in forty of seventy-four cases), instances I code as "successes." While rather more modest, this more restrictive rate is comparable to some of the best-case estimates of deterrence success (around 57 percent) and substantially greater than best estimates of the success of economic sanctions (around 33 percent) or U.S. coercive diplomacy efforts, whose estimates of success range from 19 to 40 percent.[56]

Unpacking Coercive Engineered Migration: Disaggregating Deterrence and Compellence

Disaggregating CEM into exercises of compellence and deterrence reveals that the vast majority of the seventy-four to eighty-six heretofore documented cases of CEM have been exercises in cross-domain compellence (sixty-four determinate/ seventy-five determinate plus indeterminate cases); the remaining cases have consisted of episodes combining crisis deterrence and compellence (five, all determinate) and crisis deterrence alone (five determinate and one indeterminate). Given the nature and function of this unconventional brand of coercion, it makes sense that actors' attempts at compellence appear to dwarf complementary attempts at deterrence. Among other things, CEM is most frequently only threatened once actors have self-selected into—or have been thrust into—crisis bargaining situations.

That being said, however, it is of course also possible that there have been a large number of actual but as yet unidentified cases of CEM-driven deterrence, because if general deterrence succeeds, nothing happens. It is generally believed, for instance, that Chinese fears of both the direct and indirect anticipated costs and potentially destabilizing effects of a mass migration of North Koreans onto Chinese territory has long deterred the Chinese from exerting greater pressure on the Hermit Kingdom on a variety of fronts, including its nuclear weapons and ballistic missile program(s) and its occasional acts of aggression in the region.[57] How many other such cases might invisibly exist (or have done so previously) is an open and, at least as of this writing, unanswerable question.

---

[56] See, e.g.: Paul K. Huth, "Deterrence and International Conflict: Empirical Findings and Theoretical Debates," *Annual Review of Political Science* 2 (June 1999): 25–48, https://doi.org/10.1146/annurev.polisci.2.1.25; Gary Clyde Hufbauer, Jeffrey J. Schott, Kimberly Ann Elliott, and Barbara Oegg, *Economic Sanctions Reconsidered*, 3rd ed. (Washington, DC: Peterson Institute, 2008).

[57] For an argument that this factor no longer plays a role in Chinese thinking on North Korea, however, see Oriana Skylar Mastro, "Why China Won't Rescue North Korea," *Foreign Affairs* (January–February 2018), accessed 29 March 2018, https://www.foreignaffairs.com/articles/asia/2017-12-12/why-china-wont-rescue-north-korea.

While CDD attempts are in the aggregate successful at rates akin to those of U.S. coercive diplomacy (40 percent partial plus complete success; 20 percent complete success), cross-domain-compellence-only attempts have, on average, yielded rates significantly higher than CEM as a whole (78 percent partial plus complete success; 63 percent complete success). On their face, these findings may seem puzzling, since compellence is widely understood to be harder than deterrence, for four reasons.[58]

First, successful compellence generally requires that the target publicly give way to a coercer's demands, whereas in a successful general deterrent situation, the target can claim that it never intended to do what the coercer was trying to deter. Concession to a compeller involves public humiliation and damage to the target's reputation, things that do not happen in a general deterrent situation when a target merely continues doing what it has been doing.[59] In a general deterrent situation, the target has plausible deniability—"I never intended to do that"; in a compellent situation, it does not—"I had to change my behavior because you forced me to do so."[60] Concessions may also be viewed as signals of weakness by others—allies and adversaries alike—making a willingness to publicly concede still less desirable.

Second, for a variety of psychological and material reasons, defenders of the status quo are hypothesized to be more highly motivated—their resolve is greater—than challengers of the status quo. Challengers demand that targets relinquish something by altering their behavior. Targets are therefore the defenders of the status quo, while compellers are the challengers of the status quo. If defenders of the status quo are willing to take greater risks to keep what they have, and if challengers to the status quo are less willing to take risks to overturn it and gain more, then defenders should generally prevail over compellers.

Third, when a target concedes to a compeller, the act of doing so carries costs not just to its reputation but also to its power. Conceding once can weaken a target sufficiently militarily that it becomes harder to resist the compeller if it later comes back and demands further concessions. Consequently, the argument goes, targets are more likely to dig in at the outset, resist conceding to compellers' demands, and hope compellers turn out to be less resolved regarding the issues under dispute.[61]

---

[58] These four reasons may also be found in Art and Greenhill, "Coercion."

[59] Robert J. Art, "To What Ends Military Power?," *International Security* 4, no. 4 (Spring 1980): 9.

[60] Schelling was the first to argue that compellence is harder than deterrence. He argued that compellent threats tend to be vaguer in what they ask of a target. As he put it: "'do nothing' is simple. 'Do something' is ambiguous." Schelling, *Arms and Influence*, 72–73.

[61] Robert J. Art and Patrick M. Cronin, *The United States and Coercive Diplomacy* (US Institute of Peace Press, 2003), 366–367.

Fourth, and relatedly, when compellers are considerably more powerful than their targets, compellers cannot credibly commit not to come back in the future and demand further concessions. The inability of powerful compellers to make believable commitments about future behavior derives from the capability-intention dilemma, which, in turn, arises out of the anarchy of the international system. State intentions can change swiftly; capabilities, however, change much more slowly. Moreover, this problem becomes greater as the asymmetry in power between compeller and target increases.[62]

However, in some key respects, CEM is *unlike* traditional military compellence, and thus some of the conditions that theoretically make compellence especially difficult do not necessarily apply—intuition and recent research suggests that the same may be true of some other nontraditional coercive domains. First, with respect to signaling and humiliation, many coercers issue their threats only privately, making concession potentially more palatable both from a signaling and reputational perspective. Unless the coercer or target publicly discloses the fact of coercion, such bargains can be struck discreetly. As few leaders want to acknowledge being coerced unless they have to, such disclosures are rare.[63] This same condition might logically be expected to obtain in future in some other nontraditional domains of influence, such as cyberspace, as Lindsay and Gartze note in the introduction.

Moreover, because CEM is most often cross-domain in nature, publicly observable behavioral changes and concessions made in response to coercive demands may be harder for observers to recognize as coercive concessions than would be the case in traditional intradomain coercion; this camouflage offers plausible deniability and may aid both coercers and targets in reaching deals that would otherwise be (more strenuously) resisted. On the other side, this same camouflage may also permit coercers to unilaterally back down and still save face while doing so by claiming that their threats were never meant to be taken seriously.[64] Here again, potential cyber analogies and applications come readily to mind.

Second, once migration outflows or inflows have commenced, the status quo ante has already been upended. For reasons already discussed with regard to risk strategies, a return to the status quo ante tends to be more difficult to achieve than is the case for some other kinds of coercive exercises. Thus acquiescence before the

---

[62] See: Todd S. Sechser, "Goliath's Curse: Coercive Threats and Asymmetric Power," *International Organization* 64, no. 4 (2010): 627–660, https://doi.org/10.1017/S0020818310000214.

[63] Indeed, this is one reason why this phenomenon has been hiding in plain sight for so long, and past cases are often not identified until archives are opened or the relevant actors have left power and are willing to talk (or are no longer members of their administrations). For a discussion of how CEM tends to be a self-hiding phenomenon, see: Greenhill, *Weapons of Mass Migration*, ch. 1.

[64] See, for instance: Noura Ali, "Egypt's Implied Threat to Flood Italy with Migrants Isn't an Idle One," *Middle East Observer*, 3 August 2016, accessed 29 March 2018, https://www.middleeastobserver.org/2016/08/03/egypts-implied-threat-to-flood-italy-with-migrants-isnt-an-idle-one/.

situation on the ground becomes further indelibly altered might grow more attractive. Coercive engineered migration might be a unique domain in this regard, but my intuition suggests that it is not, as both nuclear weapons and some biological weapons could and surely would have far more devastating, far-reaching, and irreversible effects. In any case, research is needed to evaluate the cross-domain validity and applicability of this CEM-derived observation.

Third, because of the two-level nature of this kind of coercion, local actors on the ground inside target states (or inside supranational entities, like the EU) can independently defect and refuse to aid targets in their bids to resist coercion—for example, by threatening to seal internal borders, as Lawton Chiles, then governor of Florida, did in 1994, or by actually sealing internal borders, as Hungary's president, Victor Orbán, did in 2015.[65] The possibility of such behaviors complicates decisionmaking and further heightens some targets' incentives to concede. Obviously, the precision targeting that modern kinetic weapons (e.g., precision-guided missiles, drone strikes) and nonkinetic options (e.g., sanctions) enable makes the potential for defection potentially germane across a wide array of environments and domains.

Fourth, while the demands of coercers who employ CEM may be and, about a third of the time, *are* military in nature, such demands rarely threaten to materially undermine the target's military power. Conversely, however, a failure to concede to credible threats to swamp one's state with unwanted refugees and migrants can, if inflows do transpire, impose significant political, economic, and military costs on targets. So while concession to compellent threats may be highly undesirable, the costs of resistance may be far greater—and far more enduring.

Finally, since, as noted, about 80 percent of identified coercers have been weaker than their targets in terms of capabilities, concerns about salami tactics and future predation by powerful coercers are less germane than is often the case for other means and domains of coercion.[66]

The previous discussion notwithstanding, it is possible that CEM's impressive track record may simply be a reflection of strong selection effects. Whereas more conventional means of coercion are more broadly and rather less discriminately applied by more powerful actors against weaker, but more highly resolved, targets,[67] CEM might only be used by highly resolved challengers and only when they believe there is a relatively high probability of success. Put another way, CEM might only be used against carefully chosen vulnerable targets or where the stakes are high for the coercer but far

---

[65] See: Greenhill, *Weapons of Mass Migration*, chs. 2–5 (regarding Cuba, Kosovo, Haiti, and North Korea), and Greenhill, "Open Arms behind Barred Doors," regarding the EU migration crisis.

[66] Concerns about recidivism may on the other hand be quite relevant.

[67] See, e.g.: Phil Haun, *Coercion, Survival and War: Why Weak States Resist the United States* (Stanford, CA: Stanford University Press, 2015).

less so to the target(s).⁶⁸ We cannot know, for instance, how often the use of this tool is contemplated but ultimately eschewed because of low expectations of success.

Consider, for instance, the difference between general and immediate deterrence. The latter only comes into play if the former has failed. If a challenger has in fact selected itself into such a crisis, the challenger has either deemed the defender's/target's deterrent threats noncredible or is resolved to escalate/fight. Analogously, if a coercer has elected to employ CEM, it has opted into a high-stakes bargaining game. We might surmise that challengers who do so have correspondingly high resolve, because CEM is a blunt instrument, which is rarely a weapon of first resort, for several distinct reasons.

First, the political and military risks associated with CEM's employment can be enormously high, even fatal, as, for instance, Gaddafi discovered in 2011 when he overplayed his hand after an earlier set of successful uses of CEM throughout the 2000s.⁶⁹ Relatedly, challengers may ultimately catalyze larger crises than they anticipate or desire, and massive outflows can destabilize the states of both origin and destination.⁷⁰ Fears of just such a collapse, for instance, led to the construction of the Berlin Wall in the early 1960s.⁷¹ Second, as noted, once a crisis has been initiated, challengers often lose (some degree of) control over it. When this happens, an outflow can become more like an unguided missile than a smart bomb, thus making it more difficult to coerce a particular target. Third, the potential for blowback can be great, and the unintended consequences thereof can be quite costly. For instance, the U.S.-instigated mass migration of North Vietnamese southward following the First Indochina War not only failed to achieve its objective of deterring Ho Chi Minh from pushing for reunification elections but also, as an unintended result, further weakened the incumbent regime in South Vietnam while simultaneously increasing the United States' commitment to propping it up.⁷² The reputational costs of weaponizing innocent people to effect state-level coercion can also be great, as can be the international opprobrium incurred following such uses.

---

⁶⁸ See: James Fearon, "Selection Effects and Deterrence," *International Interactions* 28, no. 2 (2000): 5–29, https://doi.org/10.1080/03050620210390.

⁶⁹ See, e.g., Greenhill, "Migration as a Coercive Weapon." Some might say the same is true of Milosevic, although he was not removed from power until more than sixteen months after the conclusion of the Kosovo conflict and then only because the military revolted after he demanded that they fire on those protesting his unwillingness to cede power after he lost. See: Jonathan Steele, "An Outrage Too Far: How Milosevic Was Ousted," *Guardian*, 8 October 2000, accessed 29 March 2018, https://www.theguardian.com/world/2000/oct/08/warcrimes.balkans1.

⁷⁰ While just such an outcome will be seen as a good thing if the challenger is, for instance, an NGO trying to bring down a dictatorship, it is a highly undesirable outcome in most cases.

⁷¹ "The Construction of the Berlin Wall," Berlin.de, accessed 29 March 2018, http://www.berlin.de/mauer/geschichte/bau-der-mauer/.

⁷² See, e.g.: Ronald B. Frankum, Jr., *Operation Passage to Freedom: The United States Navy in Vietnam, 1954–1955* (Lubbock: Texas Tech University Press, 2007), 207.

Conclusions, Broader Implications, and Avenues for Further Research

When one refers to "asymmetric" instruments of influence, one may be referring to significant power disparities between coercer and target. One may alternatively be referring to qualitative differences in the sophistication or costs of the means used to coerce, resist, or counter-coerce. The term "asymmetric strategy" may also be used in relation to, or in comparison with, another strategy where the return on investment relative to the costs of engaging in coercion is measurably different—wherein, for instance, a significant amount of economic, social, and political damage might be imposed on targets without a correspondingly large investment. All of these definitions apply to the weaponization of people, which makes it unusual, if not unique, among instruments of coercion.

The means of CEM differ significantly from military means of coercion and achieve impressive results that overturn conventional wisdom about the difficulty of successful coercion. This is especially true given what may be accomplished with a limited investment. The analysis herein supports Lindsay and Gartzke's claims in the introduction that means matter, and that *how* actors deter affects the quality of the deterrence achieved. The findings of this chapter allow one to go further and say that these claims hold for compellence as well as deterrence, and that the *contexts* in which coercion takes place and *who and what* are targeted also affect the efficacy of coercion. It should perhaps be self-evident that effective coercion is not a one-size-fits-all exercise, yet the U.S. military's particular affinity for opting for bombing as a tool of choice under a rather wide array of circumstances suggests that it is a point worth reinforcing.

Asymmetric and hybrid means and strategies remain the exception in interstate conflicts, but this is arguably changing and will continue to do so, perhaps even at an accelerating rate, as power (potentially) diffuses globally in the decades to come. The strengths of symmetric strategies, such as conventional military operations, are understood and have a proven track record in warfighting. These five domains are unsurprisingly, therefore, the U.S. military's sweet spot and comfort zone but, when used in exercises of influence short of warfare, have a track record that is, at best, mixed. In such circumstances, one can effectively deploy instruments other than force alongside more conventional capabilities, in order to enhance those capabilities' overall effectiveness and to provide more choices for policymakers who are facing increasingly complex and fast-changing security environments.

Moreover, force is simply not always a practicable option. Indeed, as Lindsay and Gartzke note in the introduction, using force can even be suicidal in some contexts. Alternative, asymmetric means may be the only feasible ones. They may also be preferable and even more highly efficacious. As David Gompert and Hans

Binnendjik recently observed, coercive power is "an underrated, inchoate, yet increasingly useful category of power in-between making war and making nice."[73]

Coercive engineered migration is a *truly* cross-domain tool of influence, perhaps uniquely so, whose success rate and particular features make it a useful exemplar of how domain switching can help level the playing field, enable relatively weak actors to punch above their weight, and offer more powerful actors a broader array of policy tools than is commonly recognized. This tool bears greater analytical scrutiny for other reasons as well, including the fact that mass migrations may also be strategically weaponized in pursuit of political-military objectives other than coercion; but detailed examination of such alternative uses is beyond the scope of this chapter.[74]

---

[73] David Gompert and Hans Binnendjik, "The Power to Coerce," *US News and World Report*, 9 July 2014, accessed 29 March 2018, http://www.usnews.com/opinion/blogs/world-report/2014/07/09/how-the-us-can-use-its-non-military-power.

[74] See, for instance: Greenhill, "Strategic Engineered Migration as a Weapon of War."

13

Linkage Politics

Managing the End of the Cold War

JOSHUA R. ITZKOWITZ SHIFRINSON

Cross-domain deterrence (CDD) relies on a basic relationship. Seeking to achieve specified coercive ends against a target, CDD combines the various military means at a state's disposal to achieve these objectives. In this, it represents a subset of a larger phenomenon that analysts often refer to as *linkage*, that is, the notion that pooling together different capabilities across interest areas can help offset weakness in any particular arena in pursuit of one's objectives. Linkage has long been important to statecraft and grand strategy.[1] Diplomatic envoys, for instance, routinely threaten aggressors with economic sanctions if opponents engage in aggressive behavior. Similarly, the threat of force routinely makes diplomacy more credible and a more palatable alternative than fighting.[2] This situation is analogous to what CDD seeks to achieve in military affairs.

Existing research on CDD has largely ignored its relationship to linkage politics writ large. At the same time, existing studies (including other chapters here) have also tended to focus on the dynamics of linkage/CDD in scenarios where states are acquiring new tools of military power—largely as a result of rapid technological innovation—to affect deterrent relationships. This is problematic since, although deterrent relationships can be affected whenever states acquire new *means* to attain their political objectives, other deterrent relationships emerge when states seek *new objectives* (presumably reflecting new interests) in and of themselves. Indeed, recent years have seen the United States pursuing unexpected objectives in limiting Russian action in Ukraine, forestalling chemical weapons use in the

---

[1] A good discussion is Robert S. Litwak, *Détente and the Nixon Doctrine: American Foreign Policy and the Pursuit of Stability* (New York: Cambridge University Press, 1984).

[2] Rose Gottemoeller, "The Evolution of Sanctions in Theory and Practice," *Survival* 49, no. 4 (2007): 99–110, https://doi.org/10.1080/00396330701733902.

Syrian Civil War, and hindering unilateral Chinese maritime gains in the western Pacific; in each, the United States sought to deploy existing tools of statecraft to deter challenges to these evolving objectives. Current studies thus miss the possibility that linkage politics might be as (or more) relevant to coercive and deterrent relationships not when new means are coming online but when old means are repackaged for new ends.

Accordingly, this chapter serves two purposes. First, I situate CDD in broader research on linkage politics, highlighting the similarity between underlying concepts in each discussion, as well as the connection between military operations and the broader portfolio of national capabilities. Second, I develop and illustrate the logic and dynamics of linkage politics and CDD when a state's interests change while the tools to pursue those objectives remain fixed. In doing so, I focus on two interrelated questions. First, can existing tools used in a linkage relationship be repurposed to achieve new policy objectives, or do states need to acquire new tools to attain new ends? Equally important, how can policymakers best navigate periods when the ends and/or means in CDD change—what are the risks involved, and what options exist for strategists to address these problems? Addressing these questions while drawing out the connection between CDD and linkage politics constitutes a necessary step in developing a theory to account for when and why CDD—and any form of linkage—yields its desired effect, alongside the problems policymakers might encounter along the way.

The remainder of this chapter proceeds in several sections. First, it further relates CDD to diplomatic efforts linking the different means at a state's disposal to achieve foreign policy outcomes. Second, I hypothesize how shifts in either a state's desired ends or available means carry different strategic risks. This effort is particularly valuable given that analysts generally lack theories to explain the course of linkage politics and, since no plan survives first contact with an enemy, analysts can expect the means and/or ends of policy to change during a standoff; understanding the potential dynamics of such changes can help policymakers cope with the inevitable.

Third, I offer an initial test of these arguments by focusing on a notable case where the ends of policy changed while the means available to pursue policy remained constant, namely, U.S. efforts to deter a Soviet crackdown in Eastern Europe in the runup to the Revolutions of 1989. This case study is useful on both theoretical and empirical grounds. Theoretically, insofar as U.S. means remained broadly fixed, and given the narrow time frames involved, the case is intrinsically useful for theorizing and elaborating on linkage dynamics. Empirically, much of the evidence needed to reconstruct U.S. deterrent efforts during the case has been disclosed only recently, allowing us to shed new light on one of the most important diplomatic dialogues to occur in the shadow of a superpower nuclear confrontation. Finally, I conclude with lessons from the case for CDD, highlight avenues for future research, and briefly discuss applicability to current policy debates.

Security, Competition, and Resources: The Logic of Linkage

As analysts have long known, states looking to survive in an anarchic international system seek to create security for themselves.[3] To do so, they develop the military, economic, and political tools at their disposal in order to defend their vital interests and to promote a range of nonvital interests that nevertheless make the international system more conducive to their well-being.[4] This process introduces a baseline level of competitiveness into international politics: because each state faces similar incentives to secure and promote its interests, states cannot rest on their laurels without losing out relative to other actors.[5]

This dynamic also highlights one of the core problems inherent in strategy. Although competition is constant and threats numerous, resources are finite: resources are limited in an absolute sense compared to the nearly infinite array of possible challenges, while the need to allocate some share of a state's wealth to domestic consumption limits the capabilities states can realistically develop for the pursuit of foreign objectives.[6] States are therefore forced to make choices among both the interests they seek to protect or promote and the means developed to do so. These issues go hand in hand, as states generally seek a wider range of means to protect their vital interests than they do with nonvital interests.

Linkage—of which cross-domain relations are one type focused specifically on the military realm—enters this picture when the means a state develops to protect its interests are designed to offset the means another state acquires to promote its own, by threatening to move a diplomatic or military conflict into arenas where the former has an advantage over the latter. Seeking, for instance, to deter a Soviet conventional attack in Central Europe, the Truman and Eisenhower administrations were prepared to launch a nuclear attack against the Soviet homeland and made this threat clear.[7] Similarly, analysts today discuss deterring

---

[3] Kenneth N. Waltz, *Theory of International Politics* (Reading, MA: Addison-Wesley, 1979).

[4] On the different types of interests a state might have, see: Robert J. Art, *A Grand Strategy for America* (Ithaca, NY: Cornell University Press, 2003).

[5] John J. Mearsheimer, *The Tragedy of Great Power Politics* (New York: Norton, 2001).

[6] The trade-off between current military consumption and domestic growth is unclear, but the need to choose between "guns versus butter" is well understood in strategic discussions; on these dynamics, see: Paul Kennedy, *The Rise and Fall of the Great Powers* (New York: Random House, 1987); Robert Powell, "Guns, Butter, and Anarchy," *American Political Science Review* 87, no. 1 (March 1993): 115–132, https://doi.org/10.2307/2938960; Francis J. Gavin, *Gold, Dollars, and Power: The Politics of International Monetary Relations, 1958–1971* (Chapel Hill: University of North Carolina Press, 2007).

[7] Marc Trachtenberg, "A 'Wasting Asset': American Strategy and the Shifting Nuclear Balance, 1949–1954," *International Security* 13, no. 3 (Winter 1988–89): 5–49, https://muse.jhu.edu/article/446783/pdf; also Marc Trachtenberg, *History and Strategy* (Princeton, NJ: Princeton University Press, 1991), ch. 4.

possible cyberattacks against the United States with conventional retaliation, economic sanctions, and so on.[8]

Linkage politics in general, and cross-domain politics in particular, are strategically attractive for two reasons. First, moving a conflict into an area where one's state has an advantage over another allows one's state to play to its strengths. Rather than devoting scarce resources to competing where an opponent is strong, states attempt to generate political influence by focusing on things they already do well. Thus, in lieu of competing with numerically superior Soviet conventional forces, the United States under Eisenhower looked to exploit its nuclear monopoly; similarly, rather than developing a mass army for deployment to Europe, pre-1914 Great Britain planned on using its economic advantages to bring the German capacity for war to collapse if conflict erupted.[9] In theory, these approaches minimize a state's expenditures by reinforcing existing strengths and avoiding the costs of developing any new tool of statecraft. Accordingly, this approach can leave a state holding developed and tested tools with which to defend its interests rather than having to acquire a full spectrum of capabilities—some of which might not be effective or cost-efficient.

Second, and owing to the efficiency gains in moving a conflict into areas where a state has an advantage, a state has additional marginal resources with which to advance other interests. The Eisenhower administration, for example, was able to take the savings incurred from concentrating on the nuclear mission (avoiding matching the Soviets quantitatively) and use them to promote U.S. economic growth; similarly, Israel's ability to deter existential threats to its security by being the Middle East's only nuclear-armed power likely allows it to devote proportionally greater resources to counter-terrorism and similar operations than would otherwise be possible.[10] These freed-up resources form a kind of subsidy that helps a state protect a broader set of interests than would otherwise be the case.

Change in Linkage Politics and Cross-Domain Relationships

Treating CDD as part of state efforts to use strengths in one arena to offset weaknesses in another refocuses the analysis in several ways. First, it grounds the

---

[8] David Sanger, "U.S. Decides to Retaliate against China's Hacking," *New York Times*, 31 July 2015, https://www.nytimes.com/2015/08/01/world/asia/us-decides-to-retaliate-against-chinas-hacking.html.

[9] Nicholas A. Lambert, *Planning Armageddon: British Economic Warfare and the First World War* (Cambridge, MA: Harvard University Press, 2012).

[10] Israeli analysts hint at this issue, with Israel's former deputy national security advisor writing that a nuclear deal with Iran—which would leave Israel the only nuclear power in the Middle East—"will enable Israel to divert precious resources to more immediate threats, like Hezbollah's more than 130,000 rockets, Hamas and the Islamic State." Chuck Freilich, "A Good Deal for Israel," *New York Times*, 19 July 2015, https://www.nytimes.com/2015/07/20/opinion/a-good-deal-for-israel.html.

Table 13.1 **Change in linkage/cross-domain relationships**

Type	Mechanism	Results	Potential risks
Means-based change	State acquires or loses tools it relied on to attain strategic goals	Arms races	Spirals of insecurity
		Windows of opportunity/vulnerability	Preventive conflict
Interest-based change	State develops new interests it seeks to pursue or protect	Uncertain prioritization of interests	Miscalculation over interests and power
		Means poorly suited to ends sought	

idea of CDD in long-standing interactions at the heart of international relations. In fact, given this approach, war itself is related to dynamics highlighted by CDD: if, as Geoffrey Blainey argues, wars occur when states disagree over their relative power, then the decision to use force reflects a failure of military power to yield payoffs in the diplomatic realm.[11] Seen in this light, CDD is less a new and novel feature of world politics and more a particular manifestation of the process through which states use the tools at their disposal to prevent harm or to further specific interests in world politics. Simply put, CDD is part of a broader effort in which states combine multiple means for particular coercive effects. Cross-domain deterrence might focus on the military piece of this puzzle, but the distinction is one of form rather than substance.

Second, treating CDD as part of a larger process by which states relate available means to specified ends helps identify processes by which change in linkage and cross-domain relationships can occur. Two pathways are readily apparent: changes in the *means* states can employ in pursuit of their interests and change in the *interests* pursued per se (see table 13.1).

Means-Based Change

As technology diffuses, economic patterns shift, and states compete, the capabilities at states' disposal change as well. States can gain or lose means to seek particular ends as changes in technology, economics, and context give one actor new deterrent or coercive options. As a result, the advantages that enable State A to engage in cross-domain actions at Time 1 against State B might not exist at Time 2 as State B comes to match State A's capabilities.[12] This type of *means-based change* is discussed

---

[11] Geoffrey Blainey, *The Causes of War*, 3rd ed. (London: Macmillan, 1988).

[12] This could also work in the opposite direction as states gain new capabilities.

in several chapters here. It also has a long historical pedigree. After all, the growth of the Soviet nuclear arsenal by the mid- to late 1960s eliminated the United States' prior cross-domain nuclear advantage,[13] just as the first cavemen to discover how to control fire, once the secret was out, could probably no longer credibly threaten neighboring tribes on the basis of that discovery. More directly, means-based change is prominent in contemporary policy discussions as analysts debate whether, for example, China's acquisition of antiship ballistic missiles and economic inroads in traditional U.S. markets will deter U.S. adventurism in East Asia, or whether Iran might retaliate against Persian Gulf oil exports if the United States were to strike the Iranian nuclear program.[14]

In theory, means-based change can both exacerbate international competition and generate dangerous conflict spirals. On the one hand, as states lose a prior strategic advantage, they might cast about for new tools to gain a cross-domain advantage. Other states might then respond in kind, priming the international system for arms races as states gain and lose advantages over one another.[15] Conversely, states with a waning cross-domain advantage might worry that they will be unable to succeed in a competition for new tools. Thus, rather than trying to deter conflict, they might opt to use their advantages while they can in a preventive action.[16] It is not impossible, for instance, that a state that feels it is on the verge of permanently losing an offensive cyber capability as another state develops the ability to attack in kind will use its waning advantages to try to set back an opponent's cyber systems.

Interest-Based Change

As noted, analysts have long been interested in means-based change in linkage relationships. Less studied, however, is the second pathway to change, or what I term *interest-based change*. As the name implies, interest-based change occurs when a state

---

[13] For a discussion, see: Francis J. Gavin, *Nuclear Statecraft: History and Strategy in America's Atomic Age* (Ithaca, NY: Cornell University Press, 2012).

[14] Caitlin Talmadge, "Closing Time: Assessing the Iranian Threat to the Strait of Hormuz," *International Security* 33, no. 1 (Summer 2008): 82–117, https://doi.org/10.1162/isec.2008.33.1.82; Joshua R. Itzkowitz Shifrinson and Miranda Priebe, "A Crude Threat: The Limits of an Iranian Missile Campaign against Saudi Arabian Oil," *International Security* 36, no. 1 (Summer 2011): 167–201, https://doi.org/10.1162/ISEC_a_00048; Joshua Rovner, "Air-Sea Battle and Escalation Risks," Study of Innovation and Technology in China Policy Brief #12, (La Jolla, CA: Institute for Global Conflict and Cooperation, University of San Diego, January 2012); Leon Whyte, "China's Elegant, Flawed, Grand Strategy," *Diplomat*, 25 July 2015, accessed 20 March 2018, http://thediplomat.com/2015/07/chinas-elegant-flawed-grand-strategy/.

[15] The canonical example is the Anglo-German naval race before 1914, but arms races were also central to the deterrence and coercion strategies of states such as Japan and the U.S.; see: Paul Kennedy, *The Rise of the Anglo-German Antagonism, 1860–1914* (London: Allen and Unwin, 1980); William Braisted, *The United States Navy in the Pacific, 1909–1922* (Austin: University of Texas Press, 1971).

[16] Dale C. Copeland, *The Origins of Major War* (Ithaca, NY: Cornell University Press, 2000), 35–55.

identifies new or newly salient interests it wishes to advance and uses preexisting means not necessarily tailored to these interests to pursue them. Although subject to less attention, interest-based change is no less important than means-based change is to linkage and, by extension, cross-domain relationships. In fact, states often seek to utilize the capabilities developed in one arena to influence actions in another. For example, the conventional military developed by the United States to deter the Soviet Union was repurposed in the 1990s to deter smaller, regional actors from local aggression. Similarly, some analysts today fear that China is attempting to use the capabilities developed to deter action around the Chinese mainland to secure a broader Chinese perimeter in Asia.[17]

Interest-based change suggests different pitfalls from those of means-based change. First, interest-based change increases the risk of conflict from miscalculation and deterrence failures. As scholars such as Thomas Schelling suggest, deterrence requires a state to threaten retaliation if another state acts in ways that contravene its interests.[18] To make this threat credible, a state must convince a target that the interest is so important that it is willing to risk diplomatic or military conflict.[19] For this reason, analysts and policymakers have often looked to make a state's focus on particular issues clear and explicit, partly by lavishing them with attention and partly by developing retaliatory tools tightly coupled to the interests in question and presumably less likely to be questioned by an opponent.[20] Combined, these approaches allow a state to focus on maintaining a known status quo—retaliation is less subject to ambiguity.[21]

---

[17] Alexander Sullivan and Andrew S. Erickson, "The Big Story behind China's New Military Strategy," *Diplomat*, 5 June 2015, accessed 20 March 2018, https://thediplomat.com/2015/06/the-big-story-behind-chinas-new-military-strategy; Jeremy Page, "China Sees Itself at Center of New Asian Order," *Wall Street Journal*, 9 November 2014, accessed 20 March 2018, https://www.wsj.com/articles/chinas-new-trade-routes-center-it-on-geopolitical-map-1415559290.

[18] Thomas C. Schelling, *Arms and Influence* (New Haven, CT: Yale, 2008).

[19] For discussions of credibility, see Daryl Press, *Calculating Credibility: How Leaders Assess Military Threats* (Ithaca, NY: Cornell University Press, 2005), 8–31.

[20] Thus Schelling's discussion of "throwing the steering wheel out the window" when trying to convince an opponent that one is willing to act in a seemingly irrational way. On sinking costs and lavishing attention on an issue, see: James Fearon, "Signaling Foreign Policy Interests: Tying Hands versus Sinking Costs," *Journal of Conflict Resolution* 41, no. 1 (1997): 68–90, https://doi.org/10.1177/0022002797041001004. My thinking on lavishing attention has benefited from conversations with Barry Posen and Daryl Press on postwar U.S. strategy in Europe.

[21] Analysts often consider military means when thinking of automatic retaliation, in part due to the emergence of deterrence theory in Cold War nuclear strategy debates. In the U.S. context, however, policymakers have also looked for automatic nonmilitary tools with which to influence an opponent. In trying to deter Iranian aggrandizement, for instance, Congress has repeatedly passed laws posing automatic economic penalties on any state or business engaged in trade with Iran. This is partly designed to make ongoing U.S. sanctions on Iran credible.

Interest-based change upsets these calculations. As states fix on new interests, their ability to signal their focus on these interests may diminish as they lose prior investments of time and energy, and a gap opens up between the means at their disposal and their interests at hand. Put differently, interest-based change alters the status quo in terms of a state's hierarchy of priorities. It might thus raise questions in an opponent's mind over whether one's efforts are credible.[22] Uncertainty can increase as targets are unsure whether and how far a state is willing to go in defense of a certain issue. Moreover, because a state is using mismatched means to gain new ends, the target might question whether the costs the state threatens to impose outweigh the benefits it hopes to gain. In such situations, blunders and missteps can accrue, and a breakdown in deterrent relationships can emerge.

This relationship is not one-sided, with a target simply questioning another's credibility. For states trying to advance their interests, interest-based change can present difficult questions of prioritization. Policymakers used to thinking of certain issues as those worth fighting over, for instance, might be uncertain how new interests compare to old ones when debating whether to tilt with an opponent.[23] They might likewise face difficulties in identifying appropriate tools to attain these new interests, a task that could be compounded if they are uncertain how these interests compare in value to old ones and they recognize that any target is likely to ask itself the same question.[24] This situation introduces conflicting incentives into one's decisionmaking calculus: uncertainty over the value of the interest might lead policymakers to exercise caution, while the incentive to address any ambiguities in the eyes of a target might lead to steps that antagonize it.

Ultimately, if means-based change risks insecurity spirals and preventive conflict, then interest-based change risks a meeting engagement as states interact—attempting to deter and compete—on unfamiliar political ground with poorly understood tools and interests. States seeking to defend or advance new interests might be uncertain as to how far they are willing to go for these issues and might question whether they have the right tools to do so. States on the receiving end of this effort might ask themselves the same set of questions. Unlike means-based change, this process therefore appears paradoxically prone to both miscalculation and caution as states both feel their ways forward and uncertainty increases along

---

[22] As Press points out, credibility relies on an opponent's perception that the stakes are worth fighting over. Thus, anything that changes the perception of one's interests and the means one has to fight over them risks upsetting this relationship.

[23] This is analogous to Walt's discussion of the difficulties that states encounter in identifying the interests of other states undergoing fundamental domestic political unrest; see Stephen M. Walt, *Revolution and War* (Ithaca, NY: Cornell University Press, 1996), 30–37.

[24] For example, U.S. policymakers in the emerging Cold War felt that U.S. efforts to deter Soviet aggression in Europe were undermined by the limited tools the United States had both to fight in Europe and to threaten attacks on the Soviet Union directly. These problems are detailed in Steven T. Ross, *American War Plans: 1945–1950* (Portland, OR: Frank Cass, 1996).

the way. Deterrence might appear stable as policymakers proceed cautiously, but be fraught with risks of sudden missteps and crises.

Interest-Based Change at the End of the Cold War

Though both sources of change are difficult to study, it is especially difficult to examine whether changing interests affect linkage and cross-domain relationships. State interests generally do not change significantly or rapidly, meaning states often have time to develop means, plans, and concepts to secure these objectives. This does not vitiate the importance of examining interest-based change, however: under certain circumstances, state interests *do* change dramatically, and it might be those moments that are most prone to conflict. After all, the onset of World War I followed the emergence of an Anglo-German rivalry for global influence as Germany decided it had new overseas interests; today, the search for cross-domain options is driven in part by concerns that states such as China will expand the range of issues over which they seek influence in world affairs at a faster clip than others can develop deterrent options.

Accordingly, one way to address the dynamics of interest-based change is to examine critical moments in the past when state interests changed unexpectedly and rapidly. By focusing on such moments, one can better establish the link between changing interests; at the same time, one can analyze the ways states look to bring preexisting capabilities to bear in a cross-domain relationship—given the short time frames involved, states are pushed into cross-domain action as there is no time to acquire new means. These moments are therefore as "pure" a test of interest-based change as one is likely to find in the empirical record.

United States efforts to deter a Soviet crackdown in Eastern Europe in 1989–1990 represent a fruitful case. As elaborated below, the United States' decision to become overtly and directly involved in Eastern Europe represented a departure from prior U.S. policy and reflected new-found U.S. interests in Eastern Europe. Equally important, the rapidity of the case—covering roughly twelve months in 1989–1990—left U.S. policymakers reliant on linkage to influence Soviet action; although the United States retained both an extensive conventional presence in Western Europe and a range of nuclear options, strategic considerations meant that policymakers were not going to use military force to deter Soviet action within the Warsaw Pact. Instead, members of the George H. W. Bush administration turned to economic and diplomatic levers to shape Soviet behavior.[25] Given that most deterrence theories assume that the threat of force is needed to deter or compel change in the use of force—such that economic or diplomatic tools are suboptimal

---

[25] Robert A. Pape, "Why Economic Sanctions Do Not Work," *International Security* 22, no. 2 (1997): 90–136, https://muse.jhu.edu/article/446841; Kimberly Ann Elliott, "The Sanctions Glass: Half Full or Completely Empty?," *International Security* 23, no. 1 (1998): 50–65, https://doi.org/10.1162/isec.23.1.50.

solutions—the Bush administration's effort to link U.S. economic and diplomatic levers to Soviet policy both illustrates cross-domain efforts in action, and highlights the relationship between deterrence and foreign policy writ large.[26] To demonstrate the debates, difficulties, and opportunities involved in establishing CDD as interests change, the case of the end of the Cold War provides a valuable area of study.

Diplomatic Drama and Deterrence: Setting the Strategic Context for the Case

Through the end of the 1980s, the United States focused heavily on competing for power and influence with the Soviet Union while developing the means to deter a Soviet attack on vital regions in Eurasia. This effort represented a traditional deterrence relationship, as the United States emphasized acquiring the conventional and nuclear means to deter or defeat Soviet and Warsaw Pact military assets.[27] As Brendan Green and Austin Long demonstrate (chapter 10 here), the United States' efforts increasingly turned toward shifting the military balance in its favor, moving away from mutually assured destruction as the locus of strategic planning and toward pursuing counterforce options against Soviet nuclear assets.[28] Arms control negotiations that began to bear fruit after the 1985 arrival of Mikhail Gorbachev as new general secretary of the Communist Party of the Soviet Union also contributed to this effort by lowering the nuclear ceiling and helping bring a stability to the U.S.-Soviet arms race within which U.S. counterforce options could develop. United States policy, in short, was oriented toward gradually moving the military balance in its favor, with the underlying goal of affording U.S. policymakers military options to deter or coerce a change in Soviet behavior in a crisis.[29]

---

[26] The literature on deterrence is vast. Standard accounts include John J. Mearsheimer, *Conventional Deterrence* (Ithaca, NY: Cornell University Press, 1983); Press, *Calculating Credibility*; Schelling, *Arms and Influence*; Samuel Huntington, "Conventional Deterrence and Conventional Retaliation in Europe," *International Security* 8, no. 3 (Winter 1983–1984): 32–56, http://www.jstor.org/stable/2538699; Paul Huth and Bruce Russett, "General Deterrence between Enduring Rivals: Testing Three Competing Models," *American Political Science Review* 87, no. 1 (March 1993): 61–73, http://www.jstor.org/stable/2938956; on the difficulties of using diplomatic and economic levers, see Pape, "Why Economic Sanctions Do Not Work"; Elliott, "The Sanctions Glass."

[27] These efforts are discussed at length in James Wilson, *The Triumph of Improvisation: Gorbachev's Adaptability, Reagan's Engagement, and the End of the Cold War* (Ithaca, NY: Cornell University Press, 2014), 9–36; George Pratt Shultz, *Turmoil and Triumph: My Years as Secretary of State* (New York: Scribner's, 1993); Hal Brands, *What Good Is Grand Strategy? Power and Purpose in American Foreign Policy from Harry S. Truman to George W. Bush* (Ithaca, NY: Cornell University Press, 2014), ch. 3.

[28] See also: Austin Long and Brendan Rittenhouse Green, "Stalking the Secure Second Strike: Intelligence, Counterforce, and Nuclear Strategy," *Journal of Strategic Studies* 38, nos. 1–2 (January 2015): 38–73, https://doi.org/10.1080/01402390.2014.958150.

[29] For elaboration, see Joshua R. Itzkowitz Shifrinson, *Rising Titans, Falling Giants: How Great Powers Exploit Power Shifts* (Ithaca, NY: Cornell University Press, 2018), ch. 5.

In this environment, the United States paid only limited attention to political developments in Eastern Europe. To be clear, change in the region was accorded attention early in the Reagan years as the Solidarity movement gained traction in Poland. Similarly, the Reagan administration—working through nongovernment and quasi-nongovernment organizations—encouraged select groups in the region to challenge the authority of ruling Communist regimes while seeking long-term liberalization in the region.[30] Relative to the attention paid to the U.S.-Soviet military balance, however, these issues were of decidedly lower priority. By the mid-1980s, Eastern Europe was rarely discussed by the National Security Council or the National Security Planning Group.[31] Through the end of President Reagan's tenure in office, he, Secretary of State George Shultz, and other senior advisors focused on improving the U.S.-Soviet relationship, leaving Eastern Europe to the purview of sub-Cabinet officials such as Deputy Secretary of State John C. Whitehead.[32]

George H. W. Bush's victory in the 1988 presidential election, coupled with developments in Eastern Europe, precipitated a change in U.S. priorities. Bush came to office having served as Reagan's vice president for eight years and appreciated that the warming of U.S.-Soviet relations opened a broader range of possible bilateral outcomes. Nevertheless, Bush and his advisors, such as Secretary of State James Baker and National Security Advisor Brent Scowcroft, took office convinced that Reagan had focused too heavily on the arms race and spent too little time addressing the underlying "causes" of the Cold War.[33] Particularly important in their estimate was the Soviet military presence in Eastern Europe and the dominance of Communist regimes in the area. By enabling the Soviet Union to attack Western Europe on short notice,[34] these features of Europe's political geography gave the U.S.-Soviet competition and the nuclear arms race momentum by presenting the

---

[30] Gregory F. Domber, *Empowering Revolution: America, Poland, and the End of the Cold War* (Chapel Hill: University of North Carolina Press, 2014), 11–133. I have also benefited from conversations with Katherine Geohegan on U.S. efforts to challenge the status quo in Eastern Europe in the 1980s. For illustration of U.S. plans, see: George Shultz to President, "Poland: Next Steps," 28 March 1983, box 8, Clark Files; William P. Clark to President, "Poland: Next Steps," c. 28 March 1983, box 8, Clark Files; William P. Clark to President, "NSPG Meeting on Poland in the Situation Room (Friday, April 8, 1983—11:00–11:30 a.m.)," and enclosed options paper and talking points, box 91306, Executive Secretariat: National Security Planning Group Records, all in Ronald Reagan Presidential Library, Simi Valley, CA.

[31] See also the repeated meetings on Poland in 1981–1983 and the paucity of meetings to be found thereafter in Executive Secretariat, NSC: National Security Planning Group (NSPG): Records, 1981–1987, https://www.reaganlibrary.gov/sites/default/files/archives/textual/smof/nsexnspg.pdf, and Executive Secretariat, NSC: NSC Meeting Files: Records, 1981-88, https://www.reaganlibrary.gov/sites/default/files/archives/textual/smof/nsexmeet.pdf.

[32] Author's interview with John C. Whitehead, August 2011.

[33] George H. W. Bush and Brent Scowcroft, *A World Transformed* (New York: Knopf, 1998), 36–49.

[34] Robert L. Hutchings, *American Diplomacy and the End of the Cold War: An Insider's Account of United States Policy in Europe, 1989–1992* (Washington, DC: Woodrow Wilson Center Press, 1997), 36–37.

Soviet Union with compellence options vis-à-vis Western Europe while requiring intensive efforts to deter Soviet aggression.

The net effect of this rethink was to solidify the importance of Eastern Europe in U.S. calculations and generate a search for short-term options that would allow the United States to pursue its new-found interests in the area. Of course, the Bush administration was not the first to seek a reduction of Soviet influence in Eastern Europe; both presidents Franklin Roosevelt and Harry Truman, for example, had worried what Soviet dominance in Eastern Europe would mean for European security, while the Eisenhower administration had made the "rollback" of Soviet influence a component of its foreign policy.[35] That said, the George H. W. Bush administration was the first since the early Cold War to make limiting or undoing Soviet influence a cornerstone of the United States' efforts. If, as the administration's logic went, one removed or limited the Soviet and Communist presence in the area, then the U.S.-Soviet competition would abate as the need to deter the Soviet Union and its allies waned. Change in this direction, however, required U.S. action to simultaneously pressure the Soviet Union to allow change in Eastern Europe and deter a Soviet crackdown that could unwind such changes. Put differently, the United States' new focus on interests in Eastern Europe required the United States to coerce and deter Soviet actions that could harm those interests and to creatively package existing capabilities so as to shape Soviet policy within the narrow time frame at hand.

The Bush administration's gambit was possible because of shifts in the U.S.-Soviet distribution of power and the Soviet response to these changes.[36] Starting in 1987, the Soviet Union had enacted a series of liberalizing political and economic reforms, while Gorbachev encouraged had leaders in Eastern Europe to follow suit.[37] The underlying Soviet goal—as U.S. analysts at the time suggested—was to help sustain Soviet influence in the region by heading off popular discontent while improving economic conditions in Eastern Europe. Gorbachev coupled this pressure with a subtle threat that if Soviet client states refused to reform, then the Soviet Union might not intervene to shore up Communist regimes if their domestic

---

[35] John Lewis Gaddis, *The Cold War: A New History* (New York: Penguin, 2005), Kindle ed., 357–383; Lindsey O'Rourke, "Secrecy and Security: U.S.-Orchestrated Regime Change during the Cold War" (PhD diss., University of Chicago, 2013); László Borhi, "Rollback, Liberation, Containment, or Inaction? U.S. and Eastern Europe in the 1950s," *Journal of Cold War Studies* 1, no. 3 (1999): 68–71, https://doi.org/10.1162/152039799316976814.

[36] William C. Wohlforth, "Realism and the End of the Cold War," *International Security* 19, no. 3 (Winter 1994–1995): 91–129.

[37] A good overview of Soviet reforms is in Mark L. Haas, "The United States and the End of the Cold War: Reactions to Shifts in Soviet Power, Policies, or Domestic Politics?," *International Organization* 61, no. 1 (Winter 2007): 162–172, https://doi.org/10.1017/S002081830707004X. For Gorbachev and Eastern European reforms, see: Mark Kramer, "The Collapse of East European Communism and the Repercussions within the Soviet Union (Part I)," *Journal of Cold War Studies* 5, no. 4 (Fall 2003): 181–205, https://doi.org/10.1162/152039703322483783.

conditions unraveled. Still, Gorbachev's calls for reform led to mixed results. With economic problems and political discontent mounting, Polish and Hungarian leaders responded to Gorbachev's calls and began reforming; by February 1989, Hungary had moved to relax the Communist Party's hold on power, while Polish leaders launched roundtable discussions with non-Communist opposition groups. Other Soviet clients, such as East Germany and Romania, however, were less forthcoming. Opposing Gorbachev's message, these more conservative regimes sought to induce the Soviet Union to shift course by supporting internal crackdowns to arrest popular calls for reform that might threaten Communist control. Increasingly, the question became whether the Soviet leadership would resist calls to use force in Eastern Europe if events accelerated and Soviet influence in the area was directly challenged.[38]

Combined, the U.S. and Soviet interests and plans began to intersect at the start of 1989 in such a way that deterrence and coercion failures were a growing possibility. Just as it seemed that U.S. military power could deter Soviet aggrandizement in Western Europe, changing U.S. priorities in Eastern Europe raised a new set of interests in the U.S.-Soviet relationship. Successfully pursuing these interests through *some* means promised to yield large payoffs for the United States, but doing so also held significant peril. After all, while Soviet leaders sought to spur change in the Eastern bloc, not even Gorbachev and his advisors wanted to create conditions that would risk the wholesale loss of the region or to appear to allow change in the area in response to U.S.-led pressure. Despite the Soviet desire to see the region reform, it was distinctly possible that U.S. activism could trigger a hostile Soviet response, roil U.S.-Soviet relations, and perhaps risk war itself.[39]

The Deterrence Dance of 1989

Within this context, the United States moved to deter a crackdown in Eastern Europe at two main points in 1989. The first came during the spring and early summer as the Polish Socialist Workers Party, Poland's Communist party, was evicted from office due to popular unrest and elections held as part of the April 1989 Roundtable Agreement with Polish opposition groups. The second episode came in the fall and early winter of 1989, as citizens in East Germany (the German Democratic Republic; GDR) demanded reforms while the GDR leadership, unwilling to concede, sought Soviet backing for a crackdown. Watching the situations unfold, U.S. policymakers were forced to improvise, seeking ways to pressure the Soviet Union to allow change to unfold and to deter a crackdown yet to avoid so

---

[38] The preceding is drawn from the collection of primary documents in Svetlana Savranskaya, Thomas S. Blanton, and V. M. Zubok, eds., *Masterpieces of History: The Peaceful End of the Cold War in Europe, 1989* (Budapest: Central European University Press, 2010).

[39] Shifrinson, *Rising Titans*, ch. 5.

direct an investment that a crackdown would irrevocably harm U.S.-Soviet relations and risk a direct U.S.-Soviet confrontation.

Ironically, the U.S. deterrent effort was likely one-sided. In retrospect, evidence from Soviet and East European sources indicates that the Soviet leadership was disinclined to allow a crackdown to occur; even as U.S. interests were expanding to include Eastern Europe, Soviet interests were contracting to the detriment of Soviet clients in Eastern Europe.[40] Still, and as elaborated below, the Soviet leadership was less than transparent on this central point at the time. Moreover, the large number of Soviet forces and the history of Soviet interventionism gave U.S. policymakers ground to question Soviet intentions. Though retrospectively it looks like the United States prepared to deter a crackdown that was unlikely to occur, U.S. policymakers could not have been confident in Soviet forbearance at the time. Given the shift in both U.S. and Soviet interests, the decisionmaking process of 1989 is all the more important for understanding cross-domain relationships.

Deterring Action in Poland: January–July 1989

Poland led all the Warsaw Pact states in pursuing political and military reforms. By February 1989, Poland's Communist government had agreed to talks with Polish opposition groups—the labor union Solidarity being the most prominent among them—as part of a plan to head off mounting political unrest and strengthen the Polish economy. These talks culminated in the April 1989 Roundtable Agreement, committing Poland to hold free elections in June.[41] Undergirding the Roundtable accords was a calculation, as the U.S. ambassador to Poland explained, by Poland's Communist leaders that Poland was moving toward a "democratic neo-socialism" that "seems to have more in common with modern Sweden than with Stalinist Russia."[42] The Polish government also expected that Polish Communist leader Wojciech Jaruzelski would be selected as president regardless of the results of the June election, reinforcing the government's willingness to accept the Roundtable Agreement by suggesting that the Polish Socialist Workers Party would maintain significant political influence even if it shared power with non-Communist groups.

---

[40] For the evolution of Soviet policy, see Mark Kramer, "The Collapse of the Soviet Union (Part I): Introduction," *Journal of Cold War Studies* 5, no. 1 (2003): 3–16, https://muse.jhu.edu/article/38255; Vladislav Zubok, "With His Back against the Wall: Gorbachev, Soviet Demise, and German Reunification," *Cold War History* 14, no. 4 (Fall 2014): 619–645, https://doi.org/10.1080/14682745.2014.950251.

[41] Gregory F. Domber, "Skepticism and Stability: Reevaluating U.S. Policy during Poland's Democratic Transformation in 1989," *Journal of Cold War Studies* 13, no. 3 (2011): 54–56, https://doi.org/10.1162/JCWS_a_00142.

[42] American Embassy Warsaw, "When the Roundtable Ends: The U.S. Response" 7 March 1989, box 35, Soviet Flashpoints, National Security Archive, George Washington University, Washington, DC (hereafter NSA).

The Bush administration was pushed into a corner by Polish developments. Events in Poland suggested to policymakers that they faced a "historic opportunity" to expedite change in the Soviet bloc. United States policy in Poland would therefore "be taken as a signal throughout Eastern Europe . . . of a new U.S. approach to the region."[43] However, Polish developments also raised the prospect of hardliner pushback, precipitating debate over whether change in Poland (and the rest of Eastern Europe) "would lead to catastrophe or liberation." As the National Security Council concluded in April, "instability and repression in Eastern Europe would have dire consequences for East-West relations and, arguably, for the course of reform in the Soviet Union itself."[44] Still, the United States had limited interest and few means of responding militarily if a crackdown occurred. United States strategists thus needed to find a way, as secretary of state Baker later recalled, of "maneuvering so that we supported reform without triggering a backlash."[45]

Quid Pro Quo Deterrence: January–March 1989

To deter a crackdown and ensure Soviet quiescence, U.S. policymakers gradually escalated the diplomatic and economic tools the United States deployed as Polish conditions edged closer to assumed Communist redlines. The first move to deter a crackdown began in January 1989, as the United States played to Gorbachev's desire for political and diplomatic support from the United States as the Soviet Union reformed. Even before the Roundtable Agreement was signed, former secretary of state Henry Kissinger was dispatched to Moscow to explore Soviet interest in a quid pro quo.[46] In exchange for U.S. pledges not to exploit unrest in Eastern Europe and to continue backing Gorbachev's reforms, the Soviet Union would promise to exercise "restraint" as change occurred in the area. In effect, Soviet forbearance would be met by the U.S. in kind; given the absence of U.S. tools with which to deter a Soviet crackdown, the United States attempted to substitute political understandings and diplomatic engagement for material capabilities.[47]

---

[43] Brent Scowcroft, "Meeting with the National Security Council," 4 April 1989, NSC Meeting Files, George Bush Presidential Library (hereafter GBPL), College Station TX.

[44] Hutchings, *American Diplomacy*, 8; Robert Hutchings, "National Security Council Meeting on Western Europe and Eastern Europe," 3 April 1989, NSC Meeting Files, GBPL.

[45] James Baker, *The Politics of Diplomacy* (New York: Putnam, 1995), 64.

[46] Igor Lukes, "Central Europe Has Joined NATO: The Continuing Search for a More Perfect Habsburg Empire," *SAIS Review* 19, no. 2 (Summer-Fall 1999): 53–54, https://muse.jhu.edu/article/30447.

[47] See "Record of Conversation between Aleksandr Yakovlev and Henry Kissinger, January 16, 1989," "Record of Conversation between Mikhail Gorbachev and Henry Kissinger, January 17, 1989, and "Letter from George H.W. Bush to Mikhail Gorbachev, January 17, 1989," all in Savranskaya et al., *Masterpieces of History*, 341–348.

Both the Soviet Union and the United States were interested in the Kissinger plan as a seeming way for each side to deter the other while pursuing their broader objectives.[48] However, as the Roundtable looked more and more likely to yield a power-sharing arrangement, opposition to the Kissinger approach mounted within the U.S. government.[49] In the changing East European environment, concern grew that Kissinger's plan would tie the United States' hands prematurely: as the National Security Council concluded in early April, "events in Poland and Hungary are moving so fast that Moscow cannot control them anyway, and we should not be seen as the ones imposing limits on Eastern Europe's evolution."[50] Instead, the United States sought ways to "buy in" to Eastern European events so as to ensure that the U.S. interest in the "political and economic structural reform" continued.[51] More important, the use of political agreements to keep military action in check was not credible in U.S. eyes. United States and Soviet understandings were well and good, but in the final analysis, "no Soviet commitment not to intervene in Eastern Europe would mean anything in the event of a real crisis."[52] If Soviet interests so dictated, the tanks would roll, and prior understandings would fall by the wayside. Deterrence and coercion via quid pro quo understandings would not suffice in the face of a pressing strategic need.

Deterrence as Reassurance and Engagement: Spring–Summer 1989

United States officials perceived a growing risk of a crackdown or Soviet intervention in the spring and summer of 1989 as Polish Communist authority was challenged after the Roundtable Agreement was formalized. This issue reached a head in June and July, as Polish elections went forward and delivered the Communist Party a significant political defeat. As U.S. ambassador John Davis cabled Washington shortly before the election itself, a Communist political defeat might upend the heretofore peaceful pace of change—"military responses could not be ruled out."[53] Soviet statements after the first round of Polish voting reinforced this potential, with Gorbachev himself suggesting that challenges to Soviet authority by seeking

---

[48] [No author; likely Henry Kissinger], "Details of first meeting with Gorbachev in the Kremlin," 17 January 1989, box 8, Baker Papers, Seeley Mudd Manuscript Library, Princeton University; Peter Rodman, "'Kissinger Plan' for Central Europe," 14 March 1989, box 91124, Scowcroft Files, GBPL; Michael R. Gordon, "U.S. Isn't Planning East Europe Talks," New York Times, 7 May 1989, https://www.nytimes.com/1989/05/07/world/usisn-t-planning-east-europe-talks.html.

[49] Condoleezza Rice, "DC Meeting on U.S. Policy Options If the Polish Roundtable Succeeds," 29 March 1989, document provided by GBPL.

[50] Hutchings, "National Security Council Meeting," 3 April 1989.

[51] Rice, "DC Meeting on U.S. Policy Options If the Polish Roundtable Succeeds," 29 March 1989.

[52] Hutchings, "National Security Council Meeting," 3 April 1989.

[53] American Embassy Warsaw to Secretary of State, "Election '89: Solidarity's Coming Victory: Big or Too Big?," 2 June 1989, box 34, NSA.

the overthrow of Communist regimes would be "a course toward confrontation, if not worse."[54] Past Soviet tolerance aside, U.S. officials worried—as National Security Council counselor Peter Rodman described—"that, somewhere out there, there is still a limit to that tolerance." After all, there remained "room for speculation about how the Soviet leadership would react to a new challenge ... say, a bloc country's attempt to go neutral, or to vote the Communist Party out of office."[55] When Solidarity won ninety-nine out of one hundred seats in the Polish Senate after the June elections and thereafter prepared to form a non-Communist government, this potential challenge became a reality.[56] Still, as the prospect of a major Soviet ally moving away from Soviet influence increased, the United States' interest in seeing liberalization continue expanded as well: paradoxically, U.S. interest in Poland grew parallel with concerns of a backlash.[57]

To deter Soviet action and facilitate continued liberalization, the United States proceeded along two parallel tracks. The first track consisted of diplomatic efforts to deter Soviet action by lowering Soviet threat perceptions and claiming that the Soviet Union had nothing to fear from change in Poland. This approach had two components. First, the United States tried to reassure the Soviet Union that neither events in Poland nor U.S. policy should necessarily be taken as indicative of Eastern Europe's future. For instance, the administration resisted pressure to use the signing of the Roundtable Agreement to call for change in Eastern Europe's status quo, instead releasing a simpler announcement welcoming the "historic step towards pluralism and freedom" in Poland.[58] Similarly, when explaining U.S. policy following the Roundtable Agreement, Bush narrowly argued that "if Poland's experiment succeeds, other countries *may* follow [emphasis added]."[59] Second, officials tried to convince Communist leaders that the United States did not intend to manipulate events in Poland for U.S. gain—in effect, signaling that the United States

---

[54] Bush and Scowcroft, *A World Transformed*, 115; see also Memorandum of Conversation (hereafter Memcon), "Telephone Call from Helmut Kohl, Chancellor of the Federal Republic of Germany," 15 June 1989, https://bush41library.tamu.edu/archives/memcons-telcons. Unless otherwise noted, all Memcons cited hereafter are available at this site.

[55] Brent Scowcroft, "Repudiating the Brezhnev Doctrine," 20 June 1989, box 91117, Rodman Files, GBPL. Bush's notes on the document indicate agreement with the analysis.

[56] American Embassy Warsaw, "Solidarity's Coming Victory: Big or Too Big?," 2 June 1989, and American Embassy Warsaw, "Solidarity's Victory Raises Questions," 6 June 1989, both in box 35, NSA.

[57] US Mission NATO, "Presentation by DAS Simons at April 13 NAC on Poland," 14 April 1989, box 35, NSA.

[58] George H. W. Bush, "Statement by Press Secretary Fitzwater on the Polish Roundtable Accords," 5 April 1989, in Gerhard Peters and John T. Woolley, *The American Presidency Project*, accessed 20 March 2018, http://www.presidency.ucsb.edu/ws/index.php?pid=16884&st=Poland&st1.

[59] George H. W. Bush, "Remarks to Citizens in Hamtramck, Michigan," 17 April 1989, in Peters and John Woolley, *The American Presidency Project*, accessed 20 March 2018, http://www.presidency.ucsb.edu/ws/index.php?pid=16935&st=&st1=.

prioritized stable change over rapid gains against the Soviet Union.[60] In April, for instance, Bush emphasized that the U.S. approach was intended to "have no anti-Soviet cast,"[61] while deputy assistant secretary of state Thomas Simons told North Atlantic Treaty Organization (NATO) leaders that "we recognize the risks of instability and have no interest in encouraging it."[62] And, as East European reforms proceeded, the United States tried to ensure that its rhetoric "didn't threaten the Soviet Union, ... didn't say that it's them or us."[63] To lend credence to these claims, meanwhile, the United States capped the economic and political support it afforded Solidarity following Poland's elections.[64] In short, and as Bush told Jaruzelski in July, the United States sought to avoid sticking "a finger in Gorbachev's eye."[65]

The second track to deter Soviet action and facilitate continued liberalization saw the United States reinforce deterrence by coercively linking the U.S.-Soviet relationship to developments in Poland. Meeting with Soviet foreign minister Eduard Shevardnadze that summer, Secretary of State Baker highlighted the importance of ensuring "that movement toward greater openness will continue in both the Soviet Union and Eastern Europe." Accordingly, "avoiding the use of force would be important ... to avoid an emotional outburst in the U.S. that might well be triggered by those who do not want to see [Soviet reforms] succeed." Insofar as the Soviet Union sought cooperation "from the United States, Europe, and Asia," the tacit threat was clear: a crackdown in Poland would threaten the broader U.S.-Soviet relationship. A subsequent meeting with Shevardnadze in September returned to these themes, as Baker acknowledged that the United States "did not desire to stir things up or foment unrest, but that we were going to help the Eastern Europeans."[66] Encapsulating the deterrent effort, the National Security Council pushed Bush to note that changes in Eastern Europe marked "a turning point in East-West relations. Poland and Hungary are leading the way in a process of democratic change that could transform and overcome the postwar division of Europe."[67]

Prima facie, the U.S. effort to reassure and engage the Soviet Union does not look like deterrence. By addressing Soviet concerns in Poland and circumscribing U.S. policy, one might argue that the United States was itself deterred by fear of

---

[60] Bush and Scowcroft, *A World Transformed*, 52.

[61] Memcon, "The President's Meeting with Berlin Governing Mayor Walter," 19 April 1989.

[62] "Presentation by DAS Simons at April 13 NAC on Poland," 14 April 1989.

[63] Author's interview with National Security Council official, 12 July 2012.

[64] Domber, *Empowering Revolution*, 227–229; Bush and Scowcroft, *A World Transformed*, 121–122. On the symbolic and political nature of U.S. assistance, see Robert Blackwill, "Strategy toward Poland and Hungary," 19 September 1989, box 91124, Scowcroft Files, GBPL.

[65] Memcon, "Bilateral Meeting with Wojciech Jaruzelski, Chairman of Poland," 10 July 1989. See also the conversation between Bush and Gorbachev's military adviser Sergei Akhromeyev, "Akhromeyev Memcon" (c. August 1989), box CF00721, Rice Files, GBPL.

[66] Baker, *Politics of Diplomacy*, 137–139, 148.

[67] "Draft Presidential Statement on Poland," 22 September 1989, CF01410, Hutchings Files, GBPL.

Soviet blowback. To be sure, there are elements of such calculations in the case.⁶⁸ That said, U.S. policymakers intended reassurance and engagement to deter reciprocal Soviet action. They also hoped that soft-peddling Poland would create incentives for continued Soviet cooperation and help Poland liberalize. Giving the Soviet Union space allowed the United States to use Gorbachev's desire to create a cooperative East-West relationship to box in the Soviet Union: by linking change in Poland to U.S.-Soviet relations, the United States held a core tenet of Soviet strategy at risk, forcing the Soviet Union to anticipate a problematic U.S. response if the Soviet Union acted in Poland.⁶⁹ In short, a web of Soviet-U.S. interactions outside the military realm would help keep Soviet military action in check.

The Polish Puzzle

By the fall of 1989, Poland was led by a non-Communist prime minister, was moving the system away from a command economy, and had not seen any outbreaks of violence sponsored or encouraged by the Soviet Union. Equally important, events in Eastern Europe were leaving Poland behind; by October, unrest had spread to other Soviet client states, including—significantly—East Germany. This diverted Soviet attention elsewhere and drew the United States into new deterrent relationships.

Deterring Action in the German Democratic Republic: October 1989–January 1990

Like Poland, events in the GDR escalated rapidly and, owing to Soviet interests and means for intervention, represented a difficult arena in which to deter Soviet action. After all, East Germany was what the State Department termed the "jewel in the [Soviet] imperial crown" and the cornerstone of the Soviet Union's alliance system; the Soviet Union would likely be hypersensitive to any indications that the GDR might

---

⁶⁸ Bush and Scowcroft, *A World Transformed*, 114–124; Peter Rodman, "Eastern Europe: Why Is Gorbachev Permitting This?," 28 July 1989, box 91124, Scowcroft Files, GBPL.

⁶⁹ Bush himself suggested the logic of the approach during a July press conference, telling reporters before a trip to Poland and Hungary that the visit "is not to try to—through this statement or anything else—drive wedges between the Soviet Union and Eastern Europe.... [Gorbachev is] talking about a European home [i.e., a Europe no longer divided between East and West and increasingly interconnected]. And I'm saying that's a good concept, but let's be sure a guy can move from room to room. Let's be sure it's open. Let's be sure people can move around in this home;" George H. W. Bush, "The President's New Conference with Journalists from the Economic Summit Countries," 6 July 1989, in Peters and Woolley, *The American Presidency Project,* accessed 20 March 2018, http://www.presidency.ucsb.edu/ws/index.php?pid=17246. In a preview of Bush's logic, Rodman had similarly emphasized the need to "keep the heat on the Soviets" with regard to Poland in a June memo; see: Scowcroft, "Repudiating the Brezhnev Doctrine."

be lost as an ally.[70] The stakes were simply too high for the Soviet Union to be complacent.[71] Coupled with an expansive Soviet military presence in East Germany that could implement a crackdown, the Soviet Union had both motive and opportunity to prevent East German unrest from getting out of control.[72] If the United States wanted to ensure Soviet inaction in Eastern Europe and deter a crackdown in the Warsaw Pact's keystone member, it needed to be creative in finding the means to do so.

As protests grew in the GDR and West Germany (the Federal Republic of Germany; FRG) began exploring options for German reunification, risks to U.S.-Soviet relations mounted.[73] It was not implausible that popular protests would threaten the GDR's ability to maintain domestic control and/or entice the West Germans to encourage their fellow German nationals in order to expedite reunification. The Soviet Union would then face the unpalatable choice of either accepting the loss of the GDR or risking a direct confrontation with a member of NATO. The potential dangers were manifest.[74] As an interagency study completed in early November argued: "in the event of severe internal unrest in the GDR, our overriding objective should be to prevent a Soviet military intervention, which could and probably would reverse the positive course of East-West relations for many years to come. More than that, it would raise the risk of direct U.S.-Soviet military confrontation [as Soviet intervention in the GDR was] among the World War III scenarios for which U.S. and NATO planners have been preparing for decades."[75]

Deterrence as Engagement: November–December 1989

The fall of the Berlin Wall on 9 November 1989 brought these issues to a head, raising the question of how the United States could deter intervention and address the return of the German Problem.[76] As in Poland, U.S. strategists were forced to walk a fine line that signaled interest in seeing GDR reforms proceed yet deterred a Soviet reaction that could threaten U.S. security.[77]

---

[70] Raymond Seitz, "The Future of Germany in a Fast Changing Europe," 10 October 1989, box 38, NSA.

[71] Central Intelligence Agency, "Germany Reunification: What Would Have to Happen?," 11 October 1989, box 38, NSA.

[72] Ibid.

[73] Robert Hutchings, "Berlin," 3 November 1989, GBPL.

[74] Bush and Scowcroft, *A World Transformed*, 147–149.

[75] Robert Blackwill, "GDR Contingency Planning," 7 November 1989, and enclosure, "GDR Crisis Contingencies," 6 November 1989, CF00182, Blackwill Files, GBPL. This perspective was reinforced in conversations between the author and former policymakers.

[76] For U.S. uncertainty, see: "Interview of the Honorable James A. Baker III by Dan Rather on CBS News Special," 9 November 1989, Department of State Press Release, PR no. 220, 10 November 1989; Bush and Scowcroft, *A World Transformed*, 148–150.

[77] See, for instance, Brent Scowcroft, "The Soviets and the German Question," 29 November 1989, 91116 Scowcroft Files, GBPL.

To this end, the United States initially followed the Polish model, seeking to prevent Soviet action through reassurance and engagement.[78] More assertive means were unpalatable and infeasible—declaring reunification a vital U.S. interest, for example, would invite Soviet retaliation that the United States, with limited ability to project military power into Eastern Europe, would find difficult to address.[79] Instead, a quieter approach that soft-peddled GDR developments and limited overt challenges to Soviet interests was preferable. United States strategists therefore emphasized the need for stability, caution, and prudence. For instance, as the United States debated how to react to GDR developments in mid-November, Bush's advisors presented him with three options. First, the United States could support a Four Power initiative by the United States, the Soviet Union, Britain, and France to control the situation. Second, the United States could defer to events on the ground and let the FRG set the pace. Finally, it could simply advocate German self-determination. Of the three approaches, the first approach would be most conducive to Soviet security but would "legitimize a Soviet role and veto" when trends were moving in the United States' favor.[80] Conversely, the second approach would be most problematic for the Soviets by excluding them from the decisionmaking process. Instead, Bush selected the third approach, deemed acceptable because it neither accelerated nor slowed the course of events.[81]

This approach reinforced U.S. deterrent efforts in the GDR by holding the U.S.-Soviet relationship hostage to Soviet quiescence. The policy came to the fore as Soviet and U.S. leaders prepared to meet at the December 1989 Malta Summit. As Bush told the National Security Council before departing: "I will explain that we are not trying to take unilateral advantage of the Soviet Union in Eastern Europe but that the peoples of the region must be allowed to determine their own political and economic futures."[82] The counterfactual was stark: if the Soviet Union tried to hinder East German self-determination, the United States would retaliate.[83] This

---

[78] This approach was outlined in Bush's initial letter to Gorbachev following the opening of the Berlin Wall. See: George H. W. Bush, "To Mr. General Secretary," 15 November 1989, box 91127, Scowcroft Files, GBPL.

[79] Bush and Scowcroft, *A World Transformed*, 148–150; Blackwill, "GDR Contingency Planning," and "GDR Crisis Contingencies."

[80] This echoed a State Department recommendation that the United States should avoid "Four Power intervention . . . [to] avoid a Soviet veto"; Philip Zelikow and Condoleezza Rice, *Germany Unified and Europe Transformed: A Study in Statecraft* (Cambridge, MA: Harvard University Press, 1995), 405 n. 32.

[81] Robert Hutchings, "The German Question," 20 November 1989, and enclosure, "Handling the German Question at Malta and Beyond," CF00717, Rice Files, GBPL.

[82] "Points to Be Made in NSC on Your Discussions with Gorbachev" (c. 30 November 1989), CF00718, Rice Files, GBPL.

[83] James A. Baker III, "Your December Meeting with Gorbachev," 29 November 1989, document provided by GBPL.

effort elaborated on plans, first floated in early November, that called for "warning [Moscow] against unilateral intervention" in the event of GDR unrest. Now, instead of basic diplomatic threats, the United States turned to the same policy that had developed in Poland and threatened to sanction the entirety of U.S.-Soviet relations if the Soviets crossed the U.S. redline.[84]

The United States communicated these latent deterrent efforts directly to the Soviet Union. At Malta, for example, Bush underscored both U.S. circumspection and the threat to respond if the Soviet Union changed directions, telling Gorbachev: "I hope you have noticed that as dynamic change has accelerated in recent months, we have not responded with flamboyance or arrogance that would complicate USSR relations [sic].... I have been called cautious and timid. I am cautious but not timid. But I have conducted myself in ways not to complicate your life. That's why I have not jumped up and down on the Berlin Wall."[85] Subsequently, Bush, Baker, and other members of the U.S. delegation clarified the U.S. position on European developments, calling on the Soviet Union to embrace self-determination for Eastern Europe. As Bush put it, "self-determination is a value. We endorse it and it is openness that permits self-determination. [It] does not mean the imposition of our system on Czechoslovakia, the GDR, or Romania." Coming after Bush also warned the Soviet Union that "if we can stick with the notion of peaceful change, better relations will occur between the Soviet Union and the United States." The message was clear: allow events to unfold in Eastern Europe, or the United States might penalize U.S.-Soviet relations.[86] Conversely, and as Bush elaborated at a NATO meeting immediately after the Malta discussions, peaceful change would facilitate the construction of a new, increasingly integrated, and cooperative Europe; if the Soviet Union did not intervene, then the United States would continue cooperating with Soviet initiatives.[87]

Deterrence as Exit: December 1989–February 1990

Ongoing events in the GDR and FRG, however, threatened to overtake U.S. linkage.[88] Even before Malta, FRG chancellor Helmut Kohl began floating plans to reunify the two German states, making the Soviet nightmare—a united Germany in the

---

[84] Blackwill, "GDR Contingency Planning" and "GDR Crisis Contingencies."

[85] Memcon, "First Expanded Bilateral with Chairman Gorbachev of the Soviet Union," 2 December 1989, CF00718, Rice Files, GBPL.

[86] Memcon, "Second Expanded Bilateral with Chairman Gorbachev of the Soviet Union," 3 December 1989, Rice Files, GBPL, CF00718; Memcon, "First Restricted Bilateral with Chairman Gorbachev of the Soviet Union," 2 December 1989, CF00769, Kanter Files, GBPL.

[87] George Bush, "Outline of Remarks at the North Atlantic Treaty Organization Headquarters in Brussels," 4 December 1989, in Peters and Woolley, *The American Presidency Project*, accessed 20 March 2018, http://www.presidency.ucsb.edu/ws/?pid=17906.

[88] See: Zelikow and Rice, *Germany Unified*, 102–125, 142–164.

heart of Europe—a realistic concern.[89] United States officials again feared that Soviet redlines were about to be crossed.[90] Paradoxically, the FRG's efforts also led to American worries that the Soviet Union might reverse course and, instead of opposing change in the GDR, agree to cooperate with the FRG on reunification in exchange for German concessions—especially a West German exit from NATO—that would aid the Soviet Union and harm the United States.[91]

Facing these pressures, U.S. policymakers struggled to prevent Soviet intervention while maintaining incentives for the Soviet Union to allow East German liberalization.[92] Deterring the Soviet Union seemed to require that the United States play for time and ignore the demands of a major U.S. ally. On the other hand this policy could fall victim to its own success and push the Soviet Union and the FRG into alignment, in which case deterrence would have succeeded for no clear strategic benefit.[93] A solution only emerged in January 1990.[94] With pressure to expedite reunification increasing, U.S. strategists decided to use the FRG's interest in reunification and the GDR's ongoing difficulties as leverage. Now, rather than simply calling for German self-determination, the United States upped its desired end-state and backed the FRG's efforts to reunify Germany.[95] However, the United States would also use the prospect of letting the Germans (meaning, in practice, the West Germans) decide the pace and form of reunification alone—a process that promised to sidestep Soviet concerns altogether—as a threat to keep Soviet pressure at bay.[96] In other words, U.S. policymakers hit upon the idea of using the pressure for German reunification and the Soviet fear of the result as a way of constraining Soviet behavior.

---

[89] Mary E. Sarotte, *1989: The Struggle to Create Post–Cold War Europe* (Princeton, NJ: Princeton University Press, 2009), 72–81.

[90] Joshua R. Itzkowitz Shifrinson, "The Malta Summit and US-Soviet Relations: Testing the Waters Amidst Stormy Seas New Insights from United States Archives," *Cold War International History Project e-Dossier*, no. 40, Woodrow Wilson International Center for Scholars, Washington, D.C., July 2013, accessed 20 March 2018, https://www.wilsoncenter.org/publication/the-malta-summit-and-us-soviet-relations-testing-the-waters-amidst-stormy-seas.

[91] Robert Hutchings, "Responding to Soviet Calls for a Peace Conference" (c. 15 January 1990), and enclosure to the President, "Responding to a Soviet Call for a German Peace Conference," CF01414, Hutchings Files, GBPL.

[92] Brent Scowcroft, "U.S. Diplomacy for the New Europe," 22 December 1989, box 91115, Scowcroft Files, GBPL.

[93] Robert Blackwill, "1990," 19 January 1990, CF00182, Blackwill Files, GBPL.

[94] Brent Scowcroft, "Objectives for U.S.-Soviet Relations in 1990," 13 January 1990, box 91127, Scowcroft Files, GBPL.

[95] Robert Blackwill, "Germany," and enclosure to the President, "A Strategy for German Unification," 30 January 1990, NSC PA Files, doc. No. 9000922, GBPL.

[96] For elaboration on this perspective, see Condoleezza Rice, "Preparing for the German Peace Conference," 14 February 1990, and enclosure to the President, "Preparing for the Six Power German Peace Conference," CF00716, Rice Files, GBPL; no author [likely Robert Zoellick], "Two Plus Four: Advantages, Possible Concerns, and Rebuttal Points," 21 February 1990, box 35, NSA.

To this end, the United States positioned itself as the honest broker in the reunification process and the best conduit for the Soviet Union to influence decisions surrounding reunification. This compelled the Soviet Union to confront a different counterfactual: if the Soviet Union responded with force, then the United States could abandon the Soviet Union and force it to address a German situation that it had already proven unable to control; needless to say, such a Soviet move would also squander Soviet hopes for a broader East-West rapprochement.[97] This strategy was not necessarily credible—as noted, the United States itself feared a German-led reunification process—but it was still embraced. As Robert Hutchings and Robert Blackwill of the National Security Council concluded on 26 January, built into this strategy was a stark U.S. reminder that even if Gorbachev opposed the turn toward reunification, "we could remind Gorbachev that his troops are fast being pushed out of the region anyway and offer to work with him to create [a] new European security structure that actually addresses Soviet security concerns."[98] Soviet power was waning; in the interim, the United States would use the threat of an isolated Soviet Union to block a last-chance Soviet grasp at imposing a solution in Germany. Diplomatic enmeshment would deter the Soviet use of force.

Conclusion: Grinding Away on Germany

By February 1990, the United States no longer needed to deter a Soviet crackdown. With Soviet forces being evicted from Poland, Hungary, and Czechoslovakia, the Soviet Union could not reliably maintain a security presence in the GDR that could impose a military solution. As in Poland, U.S. strategy nominally yielded payoffs as diplomatic maneuvering seemed to deter military action. From February onward, therefore, the United States turned its attention to reunifying Germany within NATO without fear of Soviet blowback.[99]

Summary and Implications

This chapter argued that U.S. strategy looked to deter a Soviet crackdown during the Eastern European Revolutions of 1989 at two major points: as events

---

[97] In addition to the documents in note 96, see also Scowcroft, "Objectives for U.S.-Soviet Relations in 1990."

[98] Robert Hutchings and Robert Blackwill, "Your Breakfast with Kissinger: Managing the German Question," 26 January 1990, CF00182, Blackwill Files, GBPL.

[99] This process is described in Mary Elise Sarotte, "Perpetuating U.S. Preeminence: The 1990 Deals to 'Bribe the Soviets Out' and Move NATO In," *International Security* 35, no. 1 (Summer 2010): 110–137, https://doi.org/10.1162/ISEC_a_00005; Sarotte, *1989: The Struggle to Create Post–Cold War Europe*, chs. 4–5. For U.S. efforts to nominally reassure the Soviet Union after February, see Joshua R. Itzkowitz Shifrinson, "Deal or No Deal? The End of the Cold War and the U.S. Offer to Limit NATO Expansion," *International Security* 40, no. 4 (Spring 2016): 7–44, https://doi.org/10.1162/ISEC_a_00236.

developed first in Poland, and then in East Germany. In both episodes, the United States utilized nonmilitary means in a cross-domain fashion to deter Soviet military action while helping the U.S. pursue new-found interests in Eastern Europe (see table 13.2). The United States gradually escalated the means employed in these efforts as it became more engaged in Eastern Europe, yet never committed to using force to advance its objectives. Instead, and as one expects when deterrence relationships change because underlying interests shift, U.S. policymakers repackaged preexisting means—many of which were not ideal for the interests at hand—to compel the Soviet Union to accede to U.S. demands. United States policymakers used linkage politics and cross-domain options at the strategic level to obtain the desired operational effects.

United States policy in 1989 and early 1990 illustrates three lessons about what to do when grappling with interest-based change and linkage/cross-domain relationships. First is the importance of proceeding with caution. As U.S. policymakers realized in 1989–1990, uncertainty over where Soviet redlines fell compounded U.S. deterrence problems and made linkage politics attractive—cross-domain action allowed the United States to test the waters with the Soviet Union while interests clarified. This suggests an underappreciated feature of CDD: cross-domain actions, applied in circumstances where interests are ambiguous, can let actors probe intentions, assess sensitivities, and adjudicate the risk of further escalation. As interests change, proceeding judiciously helps policymakers ensure that the effort to extend deterrence to new interests is actually a game worth playing. Equally important, playing for time enables policymakers to more carefully define the objective they are trying to secure and to more carefully link means—which might be poorly structured to secure this interest—to the interest at hand. Linkage and cross-domain options do not eliminate uncertainty and possible escalation; given fluid interests, they also run the risk of injecting additional complexity into an already fraught environment. Compared to a headlong rush with

Table 13.2 **Linkage politics in 1989–1990: Deterring Soviet intervention in Eastern Europe**

Case	U.S. means
Poland I, early 1989	Political promises of mutual restraint
Poland II, spring–summer 1989	Reassurance and engagement to create economic and diplomatic costs to Soviet intervention
East Germany I, fall 1989	Reassurance and engagement to raise broader economic and diplomatic stakes for the Soviet Union
East Germany II, winter 1990	Tacit threat to isolate the Soviet Union if it contravened U.S. interests

poorly scoped means into an uncertain arena, however, proceeding cautiously in complex environments limits the risks and prospective costs. This suggests the need for additional research on the strategic utility of time in linkage and cross-domain operations—counterintuitively, speed might not always be of the essence.

Second, the U.S. policy during this period reveals how changing interests can make different means relevant to cross-domain relationships. Throughout the 1980s, the United States sought to deter Soviet aggrandizement through the military means at its disposal. Eastern European events, however, saw the United States newly invested in political rather than military developments inside the Soviet empire. This led to a search for new concepts and means (especially nonmilitary means) that could influence events. For policymakers today seeking to understand cross-domain dynamics as new powers emerge on the international scene, the implication is that military means might not always be the most efficacious or viable when it comes to engaging in CDD. Political, strategic, financial, or other considerations might simply take military options off the table and render them unattractive.

Despite the contemporary focus on cross-domain military options, therefore, strategists would do well to cast a broad net when considering options that might be useful in future operational scenarios. And here, particular consideration should be given to diplomatic and economic options. Thus, when seeking to deter Russian aggrandizement in Ukraine or Chinese action in the Western Pacific, attention could be paid to developing sufficient nonmilitary links with those states so that broader political and economic relationships can be held at risk should the situation require. To be sure, the United States has engaged in elements of this strategy in the past, for example by embedding China in global financial institutions and hinting at broader engagement with Russia in European security affairs after the Cold War. Still, these relationships were never fully developed and have largely waned in recent years. Instead, it might be necessary to find ways of *deepening* economic and political relationships with potential trouble states and to *sustain* core elements of these relationships even amid tensions so as to retain flexible and graduated nonmilitary deterrent options. In sum, cross-domain operations should be broadly defined to encompass political, economic, and other nonmilitary statecraft tools.

Finally, policymakers must recognize that cross-domain activities amid changing interests might be prone to failure owing to a mismatch between ends and means. Deterrence is challenging enough when states try to link different-but-known issue areas together for deterrent effect. Change what the opponent knows of one's interests, however, and the problem is magnified. United States strategists in 1989–1990 were aware of this problem and struggled to overcome it; thankfully, the Soviet Union never forced a test of the United States' solution. Future work, however, needs to examine what happens when cross-domain efforts amid changing objectives *are* called into question—we need to know more about the risk of failure and the trade-offs that result. These cases would nominally represent instances of deterrence failure but, through examination of the decisionmaking involved, should provide insight into why such failures occurred and whether a different ends-means chain would have resolved the problem. Ultimately, because cross-domain relationships are influenced both by the ends sought and the means employed, we need to better understand whether and how deterrence, defense, diplomacy, and strategy are influenced as each factor changes across time and space.

14

Beyond Military Deterrence

The Multidimensionality of International Relations in East Asia

CHIN-HAO HUANG AND DAVID C. KANG

Introduction and Puzzle

The chapters in this book articulate a wide range of possible applications of cross-domain deterrence (CDD) in both theoretical and empirical settings. Thus, chapters address issues such as whether it is possible to deter cyber espionage through conventional military means or whether naval forces can deter a land-based infantry attack. In the abstract, these are all important issues to be raised, and the collection as it stands makes a number of important theoretical and empirical contributions to our thinking about deterrence in general, as well as how deterrence might work in its actual application.

This chapter provides a somewhat cautionary perspective on the question of *when* to apply CDD. After all, many of our theories of war, crisis bargaining, and conflict begin with one major—and key—assumption: that two states are *already* in competition. For example, the bargaining theory of war begins with the assumption that two states disagree about the status quo and are actively bargaining to revise it. Although in theory, states can negotiate over any issue that involves revising the status quo, Robert Powell notes that it is "usually about territory."[1] Yet in the real world, the vast majority of states are not in bargaining situations about revising the territorial status quo and have deeply stable relations with each other. In the same way, many states are not actively attempting to deter another state.

Moreover, deterrence theory is particularly concerned about the issuance of threats and punishments to induce change in an adversary's behavior. This perspective generally assumes high-level conflict as a constant feature in international politics and underemphasizes the importance of rewards and compromises as effective

---

[1] Robert Powell, "Bargaining Theory and International Conflict," *Annual Review of Political Science* 5 (June 2002): 8, https://doi.org/10.1146/annurev.polisci.5.092601.141138.

alternatives to threats. Deterrence, in other words, may be helpful in explaining conflictual relations and state behavior in international politics but is rather limited in helping us understand the diminution of conflict and the long stretches of peaceful and stable relations, particularly in Asia. Thus, beginning with the idea that deterrence—either conventional or cross-domain—is the only possible strategy already biases analysis toward one particular conception of the state of the world. While in some cases this may be correct, there are other important cases in which it might be important to attempt to avoid predetermining the outcome.

The application of CDD in actual contexts highlights the even more complex manner in which a state's grand strategy must be explored. Situating the security domain alongside economic and social domains of interaction among countries is important for creating a full analysis of a state's priorities in a particular region or with a particular other state. Put simply, the emphasis behind an effective CDD strategy should extend beyond different military modalities to include the full range of statecraft, such as diplomacy, political dialogue, trade, soft power, and cultural influence. As Jon R. Lindsay and Erik Gartzke point out in the introduction, strategic diversification across these different domains allows states to better manage the increasing complexity of the security landscape and can actually produce stabilizing effects. On the other hand policy and theoretical scholarship that begin with the assumption that another state must be deterred militarily and that security deterrence of another country is the only possible course of action unnecessarily restrict the full range of possible strategies a state might take and could result in potentially misleading analysis. When applied in the real world, overemphasizing military deterrence presupposes the enduring, zero-sum nature of international security. This can have the effect of determining the outcome before even starting the analysis: if one deters, then the other state is a threat and must be deterred.

Empirically, this chapter will use the U.S.-China relationship as an example of the potentially insalubrious effects of beginning too quickly with the idea that a course of deterrence must be pursued. There is increasing discussion of the idea that East Asia is experiencing an arms race, the regional security dilemma is intensifying, and balancing against China is in the offing; in the light of the current muscular U.S. rebalancing effort toward the Pacific, many observers see the region as ripe for rivalry.[2] Furthermore, the distributions of capabilities and of wealth have changed

---

[2] Adam Liff and John Ikenberry, "Racing toward Tragedy?: China's Rise, Military Competition in the Asia Pacific, and the Security Dilemma," *International Security* 39, no. 2 (2014): 52–91, https://doi.org/10.1162/ISEC_a_00176; John J. Mearsheimer, "The Gathering Storm: China's Challenge to U.S. Power in Asia," *Chinese Journal of International Politics* 3, no. 4 (December 2010): 381–396, https://doi.org/10.1093/cjip/poq016; Aaron Friedberg, *Contest for Supremacy: China, America, and the Struggle for Mastery in Asia* (New York: Norton, 2011); Avery Goldstein, "First Things First: The Pressing Danger of Crisis Instability in US-China Relations," *International Security* 37, no. 4 (Spring 2013): 49–89, https://doi.org/10.1162/ISEC_a_00114.

rapidly in East Asia over the past generation. By many measures, China has already completed a regional power transition. For example, China's share of regional GDP grew from 7 percent in 1988 to 46 percent in 2014, while Japan's has fallen from 72 percent of regional GDP in 1988 to 24 percent today.[3] Indeed, the debate over whether China's rise will provoke fear in its East Asian neighbors and concomitant balancing behavior has been raging for at least two decades.[4]

China has already risen to regional dominance and without provoking war. The only question is how much larger the gap between China and its neighbors will become. While "just wait" for East Asian balancing might have been a reasonable prediction in the mid-1980s or even the 1990s, if East Asian states were going to compete with China, they should have started long ago. Those who expect a counterbalancing coalition to arise against China in the future need to explain why this has not yet occurred, despite three decades of transparent and rapid Chinese economic and military growth. The calls to deter or balance China's rise are perhaps more reflective of the United States' strategic priorities to preserve its own interests and primacy in the region than of the region's multifaceted concerns and priorities, which extend beyond the military domain of deterrence and include a broadening array of mutual gains achieved through nonmilitary interactions that are producing more stability than a purely military focus might suggest.

Commenting on deterrence theory's ethnocentric tendencies, Robert Jervis opines that, "like most theories of international relations developed by Americans and West Europeans, it is grounded in the experience, culture, and values of the West; deterrence theorists usually assume that while countries differ in the goals they seek, they see the world in the same way. Others may hold a strategic doctrine

---

[3] "World Development Indicators," World Bank, 11 June 2010, accessed 2 April 2018, https://datacatalog.worldbank.org/dataset/world-development-indicators.

[4] Richard K. Betts, "Wealth, Power, and Instability: East Asia and the United States after the Cold War," *International Security* 18, no. 3 (1993): 34–77; Aaron L. Friedberg, "Ripe for Rivalry: Prospects for Peace in a Multipolar Asia," *International Security* 18, no. 3 (Winter 1993): 5–33, http://www.jstor.org/stable/2539204; Brantly Womack, *China among Unequals: Asymmetric Foreign Relationships in Asia* (Singapore: World Scientific, 2010); Alastair Iain Johnston, "How New and Assertive Is China's New Assertiveness?," *International Security* 37, no. 4 (Spring 2013): 7–48, https://doi.org/10.1162/ISEC_a_00115; Amitav Acharya, "The Emerging Regional Architecture of World Politics," *World Politics* 59, no. 4 (July 2007): 629–652, https://www.jstor.org/stable/40060175?seq=1#metadata_info_tab_contents; Amitav Acharya, "Power Shift or Paradigm Shift? China's Rise and Asia's Emerging Security Order," *International Studies Quarterly* 58, no. 1 (2013): 158–173, https://doi.org/10.1111/isqu.12084; M. Taylor Fravel, "All Quiet in the South China Sea: Why China Is Playing Nice (For Now)," *Foreign Affairs*, 22 March 2012, accessed 2 April 2018, https://www.foreignaffairs.com/articles/china/2012-03-22/all-quiet-south-china-sea; Brendan Taylor, "The South China Sea Is Not a Flashpoint," *Washington Quarterly* 37, no. 1 (2014): 99–111, https://doi.org/10.1080/0163660X.2014.893176; Michael D. Swaine and M. Taylor Fravel, "China's Assertive Behavior, Part Two: The Maritime Periphery," *China Leadership Monitor* 35 (2011): 1–29, http://hdl.handle.net/1721.1/71259.

that lags behind that of the United States, but they will eventually come around to the 'correct' way of seeing things."[5] Perhaps, more pointedly, he warns that "although deterrence theory leads us to see that it is sometimes in a state's interest to pretend to reject a doctrine whose validity it actually accepts, it does not consider that people from other cultures might develop quite different analyses."[6] Deterrence as a policy may thus make sense for Washington, but for policymakers in Hanoi or Jakarta, a confrontational policy based on threats and punishments may not. To assume that regional actors share threat perceptions about China identical to those of the United States reveals the most obvious and problematic assumption of military deterrence that makes Asia seem like a powder keg: it obscures the understanding that two neighboring states in the same region may hold very different views on the efficacy of the use of force and threats.

This chapter argues that there is little evidence that East Asian states are engaged in an arms race and that the explanation for continued low military expenditures and a peaceful power transition in East Asia is actually quite simple: few states fear for their survival, so most are not arming as if they do. Competing maritime claims in the South China Sea do not deny the right of any state in the region to exist. While China's claims are expansive, they are not new, nor are they increasing.[7] The United States and China may be facing off over regional hegemony, but few other states feel it necessary to choose sides. As Jeffrey Bader observes, "our security, and that of our partners, will not be aided, however, by a strategy that suggests we have decided that China is, or inevitably will be, an adversary. Our allies and partners in Asia certainly welcome our presence, security and otherwise, in the face of a rising and more assertive China, but they do not welcome hostility toward China."[8] Given that the stakes are fairly low, it is not surprising that few states appear willing to expend the domestic and economic costs that major, sustained military investment requires.

The U.S. Pivot to East Asia: Many Dimensions, Including Deterrence

Accurately understanding regional stability and military spending is central to understanding U.S. policy in East Asia. The key debate over U.S. policy in the region is whether priority should be given to diplomatic/economic or military concerns.

---

[5] Robert Jervis, "Deterrence Theory Revisited," 296.
[6] Ibid.
[7] Swaine and Fravel, "China's Assertive Behavior."
[8] Jeffrey Bader, "Changing China Policy: Are We in Search of Enemies?," Brookings Institution, June 2015, accessed 2 April 2018, https://www.brookings.edu/wp-content/uploads/2016/06/Changing-China-policy-Are-we-in-search-of-enemies.pdf.

The Obama administration's "rebalance" to Asia has been widely misunderstood as a primarily military project to balance China. The policy was framed by the administration, first and foremost, in terms of the "soft" elements of U.S. power. Secretary of State Hillary Clinton argued that "it starts with forward deployed diplomacy,"[9] a second dimension involves economic and business engagement, such as the ill-fated Trans-Pacific Partnership, while the third and final dimension is military.[10] As Brad Glosserman has noted, "that order matters. Framing the rebalance is the recognition that US engagement of the Asia-Pacific region has been too narrow and the military has borne a disproportionately large burden."[11]

Yet the rebalance is often seen simply as a military response to China's rise. However, if East Asian states have limited defense spending because they see few direct threats to their survival and because they prefer to use institutions and diplomacy to deal with issues that arise, then the U.S. rebalance to that reality must emphasize nonmilitary engagement with the region. Asia is in sync with the United States' desire to share burdens—the result of fiscal constraints in the United States, concerns in some domestic political parties in the United States about "getting our own house in order," and a desire to strengthen regional architecture in East Asia. In this way, regional attitudes about defense spending are critical to the rebalance. Research on the threat perceptions of East Asian states and their military spending priorities reveals that the region may be more stable than popularly believed, and that the U.S. rebalance to Asia should remain focused on diplomatic and economic initiatives and not be sidetracked too much by military issues. If there is no arms race in Asia and if states are not planning on using militaries to contest their claims, then worries about war and the need for a muscular U.S. military role are perhaps exaggerated.

How closely does a narrative of increasing fear of China track with the actual rise of Chinese power relative to the region and to the United States? Data on East Asian defense spending over twenty-five years appears to present a puzzle: by many measures, East Asian military expenditures have declined fairly significantly over the past quarter century. By focusing on what East Asian states are doing rather than what they are saying, we have one lens with which to view how these states view their own security situation and the relative rise of China. The picture becomes more complex when one adds in economic relations: all states in the region are actively

---

[9] "Clinton Emphasizes U.S. Engagement in Asia Pacific," East-West Center, accessed 2 April 2018, http://www.eastwestcenter.org/news-center/east-west-wire/clinton-emphasizes-us-engagement-in-asia-pacific.

[10] "National Security Strategy of the United States," White House, May 2010, accessed 2 April 2018, https://www.hsdl.org/?abstract&did=24251

[11] Brad Glosserman, "The U.S. 'Rebalance' and the U.S.-Japan Alliance," Istituto Per Gli Studi Di Politica Internazionale, 16 July 2013, accessed 2 April 2018, http://www.ispionline.it/pubblicazione/us-rebalance-and-us-japan-alliance.

increasing their economic interactions with China. Many U.S. allies are even joining China-led international institutions that some see as a rival to U.S. ones, such as the Asian Infrastructure Investment Bank, despite specific U.S. pressure not to join. The region's receptivity toward China's Belt and Road Initiative further highlights regional preferences for economic modes of engagement and interdependence with China that are inducing mutual restraint.

The situation in East Asia involves numerous factors that many pundits and scholars identify as dangerous for rivalry and war. If East Asian states are not, in fact, arming themselves as much as is widely believed, and if they are thus not in fact balancing China, then major contours of the debate about China's rise and East Asian security need to be abandoned or rethought. China has been growing economically and militarily for three decades without triggering war or significant balancing against it. A comparison of East Asian and Latin American defense spending over the past quarter century presents a puzzle. Latin America is generally considered to be relatively more peaceful but less wealthy than East Asia. Conversely, East Asia is widely considered to be less stable but richer. Yet by the widely used measure of "defense effort,"—military expenditures as a share of GDP—East Asian military expenditures have steadily declined over the past twenty-five years and are now more similar to those of Latin America than different (see fig. 14.1). Specifically, the defense expenditures of eleven main East Asian states declined from an average of 3.35 percent of GDP in 1988 to an average of 1.86 percent in 2013.

The standard way security scholars measure a country's militarization is to measure the "defense effort" or the "defense burden": the ratio of defense expenditures to GDP.[12] The defense effort serves as a proxy for both balancing behavior and domestic politics. The share of its economy that a nation devotes to the military reflects a nation's priorities and is a proxy measure for the trade-offs the country chooses to make. When countries perceive a significant external threat, military priorities take precedence over domestic priorities, such as education or social services. In times of relative peace, countries are more willing to devote a greater share of their economies to domestic priorities; perhaps the best example of this was the ephemeral "peace dividend" following the Cold War.

Perhaps these long-term trends mask more recent concerns about China. Yet even when measured in absolute terms, China's most likely rivals appear not to have responded with greater increases in defense spending between 2002 and 2013 (see fig. 14.2).

Over three decades, leaders in East Asia have seen China's military and economic growth and have decided year after year not to contest that growth and not

---

[12] Benjamin E. Goldsmith, "Defense Effort and Institutional Theories of Democratic Peace and Victory," *Security Studies* 16, no. 2 (2007): 189–222, https://doi.org/10.1080/09636410701399432; Dan Reiter and Allan C. Stam III, Democracies at War (Princeton, NJ: Princeton University Press, 2002).

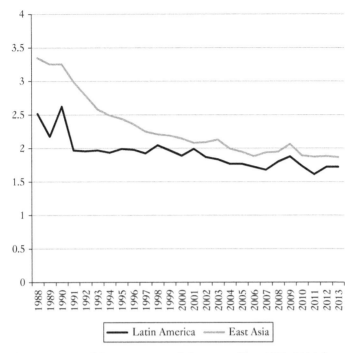

Figure 14.1 East Asian and Latin American defense spending, 1988–2013 (percent of GDP). Data from: SIPRI Military Expenditure Database, Stockholm International Peace Research Institute, 2014, accessed 2 April 2018, http://www.sipri.org/databases/milex; Countries, East Asia: China, Japan, South Korea, Taiwan, Vietnam, Philippines, Singapore, Malaysia, Indonesia, Thailand, Australia. Latin America: Argentina, Bolivia, Brazil, Chile, Columbia, Ecuador, Peru, Uruguay, Venezuela, Mexico. Created by author.

to prepare their militaries for war. It is probably unrealistic to argue that the United States and East Asian governments have been so myopic that a generation of their foreign policy, political, and military leaders have been unable to see China's growth as a potential challenger to the United States and as a dominant East Asian actor.

Economics and Regional Relations outside Military Issues

Looking only at security relations in East Asia will often mask, or obfuscate, the reality of strategic cross-domain interactions in the region. Focusing on larger diplomatic and economic initiatives contextualizes regional security issues. In many areas, such as trade and investment, Asian countries are rapidly increasing their ties with China rather than limiting them. China, for example, is the largest trade partner in the Association of Southeast Asian Nations (ASEAN), with two-way trade standing at

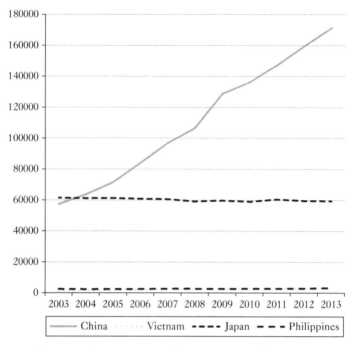

Figure 14.2 Defense spending, 2003–2013 (constant US$2011). Data from: SIPRI Military Expenditure Database, Stockholm International Peace Research Institute, 2014, accessed 2 April 2018, http://www.sipri.org/databases/milex. Created by author.

$350 billion in 2013, or 14 percent of Southeast Asia's total trade volume.[13] Between 2012 and 2014, Chinese investment flows to ASEAN countries grew by nearly 6 percent, and China has been the only country, besides Australia and South Korea, to increase foreign direct investment in Southeast Asia for each of the last three years.[14]

As has been shown by the response of countries to the founding of the Asian Infrastructure Investment Bank, many countries are even ignoring direct pressure from the United States and actively joining the China-sponsored bank. Key U.S. allies, including Australia, South Korea, the Philippines, and Thailand, have all agreed to join, as have India, Indonesia, and Malaysia.[15] This is because countries forge security policy woven together with economic and diplomatic policies. Surveying the changes in economic and trade relations will highlight

---

[13] "Top Ten ASEAN Trade Partner Countries/Regions, 2013," ASEAN, 4 December 2014, accessed 2 April 2018, http://www.asean.org/storage/images/2015/January/external_trade_statistic/table20_asof04Dec14.pdf.

[14] "Top Ten Sources of Foreign Direct Investment Inflows in ASEAN," ASEAN, 4 December 2014, 2 April 2018, http://asean.org/storage/2015/09/Table-27_oct2016.pdf.

[15] Malaysia, the Philippines, and Thailand have signed the founding charter of the Asian Infrastructure Investment Bank but have yet to join the bank.

that the region has continued to evolve and morph over the past two decades in ways that make it more focused on itself and less focused simply on the United States. For instance, Australia's decision to join the Asian Infrastructure Investment Bank came from the recognition that there is an estimated infrastructure financing gap of nearly $8 trillion in the region over the decade and that participating in the bank's projects would provide a significant opportunity for Australia to boost its exports of raw commodities and minerals, agriculture, and services to the region.

Likewise, the Belt and Road Initiative has emerged as another important means through which the region is diversifying and increasing its strategic ties with China. Launched in 2013, the initiative was formally rolled out in May 2017 to invest in infrastructure investment connecting maritime and continental Asia to its neighboring continents. The Chinese government intends to spend nearly $150 billion a year in partner countries to facilitate trade, establish transport and logistical hubs, and ease the movement of goods across borders. That it mirror-images a trans-Atlantic economic bloc is a welcome idea and reflects regional priorities for increasing multilateral trade and investment opportunities. Nearly seventy countries stand to benefit from this massive investment in regional infrastructure and in critical industries like electricity, communications, construction, and mining. With global manufacturing shifting to Southeast Asia, such investments provide the necessary means for transporting goods more efficiently, attract more foreign investment in the region, and accelerate regional connectivity, all of which complement ASEAN's long-standing prioritization of a more cohesive and integrated economic community.

The widening of Asia's diplomatic, economic, and institutional order to include the United States but to also move beyond it began in earnest in the wake of the Asian financial crisis of 1997. Following that crisis, two mutually exclusive viewpoints about the role of U.S.-dominated international institutions (such as the International Monetary Fund, the World Bank, and the Asian Development Bank) emerged. One, largely centered in the United States, sees these institutions as more transparent, careful, and reliable. The second view, largely centered in East Asia, sees these institutions as promoting U.S. power and pushing a particular ideological perspective. As Evan Feigenbaum has pointed out, "the crisis of 1997–98 . . . left a particularly searing legacy on many Asian countries. The US was perceived to be disconnected and aloof."[16] The roots of searching for alternative or complementary institutional means and relations by which to deal with their economic and security situations is thus not new and is not a function of China's rise. Rather, East Asian

---

[16] Evan Feigenbaum, "The U.S. Must Adapt to Asia's New Order," *East Asia Forum*, 22 March 2015, accessed 2 April 2018, http://www.eastasiaforum.org/2015/03/22/the-us-must-adapt-to-asias-new-order/.

states have always engaged in what Evelyn Goh calls "complicity and resistance" to the United States.[17]

In fact, the United States has not pursued a consistent or particularly compelling policy toward economic and diplomatic engagement in the region. From the abandonment of the Trans-Pacific Partnership to the waffling over the Asian Infrastructure Investment Bank, the United States has at times appeared unsure about its goals and role in the region. As the Senate Foreign Relations Committee recently concluded, the United States "should make clear that [U.S.] policy is about broadening U.S. engagement, not containing China; the re-balance seeks to expand economic growth, ensure regional security, and improve human welfare for the benefit of all, not the detriment of one." Former Singaporean foreign minister Kasiviswanathan Shanmugam made an even more pointed argument during his visit to Washington in 2015, commenting on declining U.S. influence in an increasingly important economic region should the Trans-Pacific Partnership (TPP) negotiations fail to progress:

> if you don't do this TPP deal, what are your levers of power? How integrated are you into the Asian economies? . . . So the choice is a very stark one: Do you want to be part of the region or do you want to be out of the region? And if you are out of the region . . . [and] not playing a useful role, your only lever to shape the architecture, to influence events is the Seventh Fleet and that is not the lever you want to use. Trade is strategy and you're either in or you're out.[18]

Furthermore, as the United States grapples with a rapidly changing regional institutional and economic environment in which many countries see their economic futures tied to that of China, the dilemma of how countries will manage their relationships with the United States, China, and each other intensifies. The cases of two key emerging U.S. security partners in Southeast Asia illustrate how the region is managing this unfolding dilemma. Indonesia has maintained a general preference for no single dominant external power in Southeast Asia. This preference is consistent with the core and long-standing principle of a "free and active" foreign policy, where Jakarta refrains from joining alliances with major powers and instead strives to carve out its own niche diplomacy and activism in regional and international affairs. Indonesia's president, Joko Widodo, has recently highlighted Indonesia's strategic opportunity to emerge as a key actor in maintaining the delicate security balance in

---

[17] Evelyn Goh, *The Struggle for Order: Hegemony, Hierarchy, and Transition in Post–Cold War East Asia* (Oxford: Oxford University Press, 2013).

[18] Jeremy Au Yong, "With Free Trade, US Faces Stark Decision on Asia: Is It In or Out?," *Straits Times*, 16 June 2015, accessed 2 April 2018, http://www.straitstimes.com/world/united-states/with-free-trade-us-faces-stark-decision-on-asia-is-it-in-or-out-minister.

the region, such that Indonesia would serve as a "global maritime fulcrum" through which global trade, commerce, and maritime traffic would pass, linking the Pacific and Indian Oceans. Rather than siding exclusively with the United States or China, Indonesia perceives a strategic opportunity for regional littoral states to increase access to all of the major powers' markets, all the while benefiting from military assistance, reassurances, and training from any combination of these powers.

Vietnam is another interesting case in point. It sits next to an economic giant and has had close, albeit complicated, ties with China.[19] With the United States, bilateral relations have grown closer in recent years, starting with normalization in 1995 and leading to the historic meeting at the White House in July 2015 between Nguyễn Phú Trọng, general secretary of the Communist Party of Vietnam (CPV), and President Obama. Human rights, lingering suspicion over the legacy of the Vietnam War, and the only partially lifted U.S. arms embargo continue to be persistent challenges to any further deepening of bilateral ties. Guided by pragmatism, the CPV leadership consciously avoids being co-opted into the U.S. agenda of actively deterring China—in any way that would cause any unnecessary complication for Hanoi's multidimensional engagement with Beijing. At a CPV Central Committee meeting in July 2003, senior Vietnamese officials outlined the country's basic strategy toward major external powers, emphasizing such key concepts as *doi tac* (cooperation) and *doi tuong* (struggle). In other words, Vietnamese leaders understand that any future engagement they have with Beijing and Washington will be shaped by elements of both cooperation and contention. As Vietnam foreign affairs specialist Bill Hayton opines, "ultimately the CPV leadership wants Beijing to see it as a bulwark against United States interference in the region and the United States to see it as a potential partner in its strategic competition with China."[20]

Given the delicate balance in its foreign policy approach, Vietnam has been cautious about developing overreliance on any major power on the security front. This is evident in the case of its Cam Ranh Bay port facilities: the United States, increasingly concerned about Chinese naval activity, became interested in making use of Vietnamese ports, and U.S. warships began making port visits to Vietnam in November 2003, but Vietnam has limited these visits to Ho Chi Minh City, Da Nang, and Haiphong.[21] The United States has been eager to gain access to Cam Ranh Bay, arguably Vietnam's most strategic deepwater harbor. There was

---

[19] David Elliott, *Changing Worlds: Vietnam's Transition from Cold War to Globalization* (New York: Oxford University Press, 2012).

[20] Bill Hayton, "Vietnam and the United States: An Emerging Security Partnership," United States Studies Centre, University of Sydney, November 2015, accessed 2 April 2018, https://assets.ussc.edu.au/view/47/c4/52/19/25/d3/d4/5c/a8/0a/fd/c2/e4/5a/40/84/original/959a3d253927020b0ed1a1bd671e65306f29b4f4/MacArthur-Vietnam-ONLINE.pdf.

[21] J. D. Gordon, "USS Vandegrift Concludes Historic Port Visit to Vietnam," U.S. Navy News Service, 27 November 2003, accessed 2 April 2018, http://www.navy.mil/submit/display.asp?story_id=10767.

speculation that Vietnam might provide authorization, but in October 2010, at the closing of the seventeenth ASEAN summit in Hanoi, Vietnamese senior officials made it clear that Vietnam would continue to be solely responsible for developing Cam Ranh Port. Vietnam would, however, rent out its services to foreign navies on a commercial basis rather than granting any single country all-access usage of the port facilities.[22] In August 2011, the first U.S. ship docked at the port for repairs, but they were logistics vessels—part of U.S. Military Sealift Command—not warships.[23] It appears that Vietnam has declined to accommodate the United States' interest in securing basing rights, storage, or even logistical arrangements at Cam Ranh Bay.

Vietnam, consistent with its underlying foreign policy approach, has been diversifying its economic ties with external major powers. With the United States, for instance, as Hoàng Bình Quân, chair of the CPV's Commission for External Relations, puts it, "we look to the United States for a lot of things: cooperation in education, science and technology, investment, markets, health care and culture."[24] Hoang is particularly keen to see the United States grant market economy status to Vietnam so as to boost bilateral trade and investment. At the same time, Vietnam is making continued progress in the Trans-Pacific Partnership negotiations, even without U.S. involvement in the pact. If successful, the Trans-Pacific Partnership will give Vietnam low-tariff access to nearly 40 percent of the world's economy, providing an excellent opportunity for Vietnam to further increase its exports, attract foreign investment, create jobs, and grow its economy. Among other implications, the prospect of the Trans-Pacific Partnership is encouraging Chinese foreign direct investment in Vietnam's textiles and clothing industries and is reducing Vietnam's trade imbalance with China.[25]

For now, it appears that beyond military- and security-related issues, a much more integrated, interactive region is emerging, one that wants U.S. engagement

---

[22] "PM Says Cam Ranh Port to Be Solely Managed by Vietnam," *Thanhnien News*, 31 October 2010, accessed 2 April 2018, http://www.thanhniennews.com/politics/pm-says-cam-ranh-port-to-be-solely-managed-by-vietnam-14520.html.

[23] "Press Release: MSC Ship Completes First U.S. Navy Ship Visit to Vietnam Port in 38 Years," U.S. Navy's Military Sealift Command, 23 August 2011, accessed 2 April 2018, http://www.msc.navy.mil/publications/pressrel/press11/press40.htm.

[24] Hoang Binh Quan, "A Milestone Visit to Washington by Vietnam's Communist Party," *Washington Post*, 3 July 2015, accessed 2 April 2018, https://www.washingtonpost.com/opinions/the-flourishing-us-vietnam-relationship/2015/07/03/43a0cfca-20de-11e5-84d5-eb37ee8eaa61_story.html.

[25] Nguyen Duc Thanh and Ngo Quoc Thai, "Impacts of the Incident of Oil Rig 981 on the Vietnamese Economy in 2014 and Beyond," Vietnam Institute for Economic and Policy Research, 7 August 2014, accessed 2 April 2018, http://vepr.org.vn/upload/533/20141231/HD981%20 20140826%20eng55.pdf.

but is also increasingly searching for alternative, complementary, institutional, and diplomatic arrangements.

The United States as Deterrent?

A key issue is the United States' role in Asia. A common explanation for low military expenditures and threat perceptions in East Asia emphasizes the reassuring character of the U.S. security presence in the region. It is widely held that the U.S. military presence in the Pacific dampens regional conflicts, reassures allies, and deters regional states from seeking hegemony. For example, Stephen Brooks, John Ikenberry, and William Wohlforth argue that U.S. retrenchment would lead to greater regional insecurity, which "could well feed proliferation cascades, as states such as Egypt, Jordan, South Korea, Taiwan, and Saudi Arabia all choose to create nuclear forces."[26] Stephen Walt argues for less U.S. commitment abroad precisely because he believes that U.S. allies are spending less than they would otherwise.[27]

The United States as normative leader, role model, and market of last resort is critical to East Asian states. But few of them appear to rely on the United States as security guarantor. This section explores the role of the United States from the perspective of the United States itself, as well as the enduring debates about U.S. grand strategy regarding East Asia.

It is certainly the conventional wisdom—indeed, in the United States it approaches the quality of an unquestioned assumption—that the U.S. military alliance system in East Asia is the key and primary factor preserving stability there. The argument put forth here challenges this conventional wisdom, not by overturning or ignoring it but by modifying and delimiting it. There is no question that the United States is important for leadership and stability in East Asia. Rather, the question is "How much does the United States matter, and when and where?"

The evidence for the importance of the U.S. alliance system is, perhaps, not as clear as some might believe. There are actually a number of logical and empirical reasons to avoid assigning too much weight to the United States' part in keeping the peace in East Asia. Logically, the U.S. military presence is clearly not a public good that is available to all. Thus, one cannot simply say that all countries shelter under a U.S. military umbrella and therefore have lower defense spending than might be expected.

---

[26] Stephen G. Brooks, G. John Ikenberry, and William C. Wohlforth, "Don't Come Home, America: The Case against Retrenchment," *International Security* 37, no. 2 (Winter 2012–13): 37, https://doi.org/10.1162/ISEC_a_00107.

[27] Stephen M. Walt, *Taming American Power: The Global Response to U.S. Primacy* (New York: Norton, 2006).

A second logical problem is the issue of moral hazard: too clear a U.S. commitment to its allies might embolden them to take risky actions because they believe the United States will support them, drawing the United States into a war that it does not want to fight. While it is plausible that the United States would defend its treaty allies from direct threats to their national survival, it is far less clear that the United States would engage in a major war with China over maritime disputes in which it has no direct stake. This became clear during recent oral arguments at the Philippine Supreme Court over the constitutionality and implications of the U.S.-Philippine Enhanced Defense Cooperation Agreement. The Philippines' solicitor general, Florin Hilbay, conceded that the Agreement does not amount to a blanket guarantee of military assistance from the United States to the Philippines in the event of an attack in the South China Sea.[28] In addition to the Enhanced Defense Cooperation Agreement, the U.S.-Philippine Mutual Defense Treaty, the Visiting Forces Agreement, and the Mutual Logistics Support Agreement were all meant to support but not replace the Philippines' national defense, and any U.S. involvement in response to the invocation of any of these bilateral military defense pacts would be more circumspect and limited in scope than is commonly assumed.

The United States is thus careful about clarifying or extending its security guarantees to its alliance partners. From the perspective of East Asian states, the U.S. alliance system may be reassuring about national survival, but it is unlikely to ever be a complete military guarantee against all contingencies. It is also clear from the perspective of U.S. allies that some issues may receive less U.S. support than others.

There is also a third logical problem with arguing that the only strategy East Asian states are pursuing is "external balancing": East Asian states have almost no measurable internal balancing (i.e., defense spending). To have what is essentially no measurable internal balancing is to rely completely on external balancing. It is fairly clear to many leaders in the region that U.S. military priorities are actually in the Middle East, and the United States' domestic politics—for example, the 2011 Budget Control Act—have led these leaders to fear U.S. actions, such as sequestration, that might render it unclear how robust the U.S. commitment to Asia will be. Indeed, despite a U.S. commitment to increase the ratio of naval forces deployed in East Asia from 50 to 60 percent, the overall U.S. fleet appears set to decline from the current 275 ships to between 208 and 251, according to a the Congressional Budget Office report from March 2015.[29] Thus, a relative increase could very likely be an

---

[28] Carmela Fonbuena, "SolGen: EDCA No Guarantee US Will Aid PH in Sea Dispute," *Rappler*, 25 November 2014, accessed 1 April 2018, http://www.rappler.com/nation/76069-edca-no-guarantee-west-philippine-sea; Jay L. Batongbacal, "EDCA and the West Philippine Sea," *Rappler*, 12 December 2014, accessed 2 April 2018, http://www.rappler.com/thought-leaders/77823-edca-west-philippine-sea-america.

[29] "Preserving the Navy's Forward Presence with a Smaller Fleet," Congressional Budget Office, 13 March 2015, accessed 2 April 2018, https://www.cbo.gov/publication/49989.

absolute decrease in U.S. naval deployments to the Pacific. It would be somewhat irresponsible of East Asian leaders to simply hope that the United States will be there when they need it. This is perhaps exacerbated by inconsistent messaging from the Trump administration on the future state of the U.S. naval fleet and assets. While the administration has indicated that it seeks to reverse the recent decline in the U.S. Navy's shipbuilding capacity and has pledged a 350-ship fleet, its 2018 budget proposal to Congress called for a mere 3 percent increase in core defense operations and did not add a single new warship to the U.S. Navy for 2018.[30] Put differently, if East Asian states do fear China, and if they are relying totally on the United States to defend them, this would seem to be a fairly risky strategy.

Countries in East Asia are, in fact, pursuing a multifaceted approach to achieving adequate security. The U.S. deployment of the Terminal High Altitude Area Defense (THAAD), a new missile-defense and deterrence system based in South Korea, for instance, has raised mixed reactions among South Korean decisionmakers. Further expanding THAAD deployment risks undermining South Korea's improved ties with China, and South Korea's president, Moon Jae-in, suspended further expansion of the controversial military program shortly after taking office in mid-2017. Even in light of the intercontinental ballistic missile test from North Korea in November 2017, South Korea's response has been carefully calibrated to include a mix of diplomatic and security responses with the United States and its regional partners. South Korea took part in a bilateral military drill with the United States that involved some 230 aircraft and 12,000 personnel, followed by a subsequent two-day joint exercise with the United States and Japan that involved destroyers engaging in a computer-simulated training to track and respond to potential submarine missile launchings by North Korea. The military exercises complemented Moon's state visit to China in December 2017, which was aimed at aligning approaches and interests of Seoul and Beijing in order to help restrain North Korea's bellicose, unpredictable behavior and to restore overall bilateral ties between South Korea and China. China's Ministry of Foreign Affairs has voiced concerns about the actual purpose of the THAAD, suspecting that the deployment is targeted against China. South Korean officials had previously clarified that the existing THAAD deployment would not be withdrawn but impending ones would be subject to further review and assessment, which could take up to a year.[31] The debate in South Korea on the THAAD reflects the larger ongoing

---

[30] Zachary Fryer-Biggs, "The U.S. Military Was Supposed to Get Much Bigger under Trump. Here's Why It Hasn't," *Newsweek*, 24 October 2017, accessed 2 April 2018, http://www.newsweek.com/gop-budget-deal-doesnt-help-military-689605.

[31] Thomas Maresca, "South Korean President Moon Jae-in Suspends Further THAAD Deployment," *USA Today*, 7 June 2017, accessed 2 April 2018, https://www.usatoday.com/story/news/world/2017/06/07/south-korean-president-moon-jae-suspends-thaad-deployment/102582572/.

discussion about national security and how the country should best defend itself beyond the confines of military deterrence against North Korea. The THAAD controversy points to the observation that South Korea is taking into account a broader portfolio of domains beyond strictly military domains in crafting its overall foreign policy strategy and in managing a delicate balance between forging closer economic and diplomatic ties with China and maintaining U.S. security assistance in the country at the same time.

Taiwan's military expenditure in recent years is perhaps even more telling. In spite of China's threat to unify the island by force if necessary and notwithstanding the continued strategic ambiguity of the U.S. defense commitment, Taiwan's defense spending has actually declined nearly every year since 1990. In addition, the move toward eliminating mandatory military conscription has received bipartisan support in Taiwan, and public opinion shows increasing confidence and support for maintaining the status quo in cross-Strait relations.[32] For Taiwan's decisionmakers, managing relations with a long-standing, potential adversary is thus broader and more complex than a strategy of armament and deterrence.[33]

On top of these logical issues, is there any empirical evidence that U.S. allies are underspending because a U.S. security umbrella allows them a free ride on defense? If this were the case, we would expect that non-U.S. allies would spend more on their militaries than U.S. allies because of being unable to count on the United States to defend them in a contingency. However, East Asian countries with U.S. alliances and those lacking U.S. alliances have similar military expenditures (see fig. 14.3). While there was a notable difference in defense spending at the end of the Cold War in the late 1980s, defense expenditures then converged over a short period of time.

Instead of simply positing the U.S. military presence as a reason for East Asian stability, it is more meaningful to consider where, when, and under what circumstances that is the case. Our argument is that the United States is important for regional stability but perhaps not as important as some believe. This argument is a provocative one that will not be popular in the United States, but it is an argument backed by both theory and considerable evidence. Both the scholarly and policy-oriented literature must strive to be more logically careful and empirically precise about how to describe and explain the impact of the U.S. alliance system in East Asia.

---

[32] "News Release: MAC: Over 70 Percent of the Public Approve the Orderly Operation of Institutionalized Cross-Strait Negotiation Mechanisms," Mainland Affairs Council, Republic of China (Taiwan), 7 January 2011, accessed 2 April 2018, http://www.mac.gov.tw/ct.asp?xItem=92766&ctNode=6337&mp=3.

[33] Chin-Hao Huang and Patrick James, "Blue, Green or Aquamarine? Taiwan and the Status Quo Preference in Cross-Strait Relations," *China Quarterly* 219 (September 2014): 670–692, https://doi.org/10.1017/S0305741014000745.

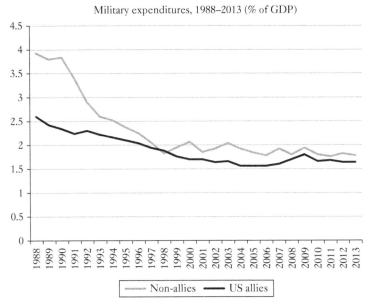

Figure 14.3 U.S. allies and nonallies in East Asia. Data from: SIPRI Military Expenditure Database, Stockholm International Peace Research Institute, 2014, accessed 2 April 2018, http://www.sipri.org/databases/milex. U.S. allies are: Japan, Korea, Philippines, Thailand, Australia. Nonallies are: China, Indonesia, Malaysia, Vietnam, Taiwan. Created by author.

Conclusion: A Cautionary Note about Cross-Domain Deterrence

In some circumstances, it may be prudent to be aware of the multiplicity of domains in which a state may interact with another state, and to explore economic dimensions along with security dimensions. This is not to conclude that the concept of CDD is never useful; but rather to caution that examining only the security dimensions of a relationship may not provide a complete picture of one country's relationship with another.

In particular, the United States and other countries in the Asia-Pacific region would benefit from considering the whole spectrum of the political, economic, and security domains when evaluating the potential risks China poses to the region. An accurate assessment of China's capabilities and intentions cannot be measured solely through the military domain. In fact, doing so exaggerates threat perceptions and leads to an inefficient use of finite political, military, and economic assets and resources. Most problematic, it risks inviting counterproductive confirmation of each other's worst-case assumptions, intentions, and attribution errors.

Forging effective U.S. policy to East Asia starts with understanding the region from the inside out. Only with deep knowledge of the goals, perceptions, hopes, and intentions of the East Asian countries themselves can the United States craft policies that further its national interests and that help stabilize the region and continue the peace and prosperity that has characterized the region for the past thirty years.

15

Conclusion

The Analytic Potential of Cross-Domain Deterrence

JON R. LINDSAY AND ERIK GARTZKE

Deterrence in practice is an ancient political problem, but deterrence theory emerged in response to modern technology. The nuclear revolution dramatically increased the upper bound of political violence and concentrated its use in the hands of civilian decisionmakers. Deterrence theory emerged to help political leaders and military planners navigate the fundamental paradox of the nuclear age, namely how to credibly threaten to initiate a war that was too costly to fight. Theory and policy often diverged in practice, notably in the United States' sustained pursuit of nuclear counterforce and counterproliferation doctrines in the face of sage advice about the stability of mutually assured destruction. Moreover, the parsimonious framework of rational deterrence theory elided the political, cultural, and technological complexities that constrained and enabled actual policy. Political and military competition did not end with the advent of nuclear weapons, of course, but conflict and coercion in the nuclear age was constrained to posturing, intelligence activity, and limited war in the shadow of annihilation.[1]

---

[1] On the development of counterforce strategy during and after the Cold War, see: Austin Long and Brendan Rittenhouse Green, "Stalking the Secure Second Strike: Intelligence, Counterforce, and Nuclear Strategy," *Journal of Strategic Studies* 38, nos. 1–2 (2014): 38–73, https://doi.org/10.1080/01402390.2014.958150; Keir A. Lieber and Daryl G. Press, "The New Era of Counterforce: Technological Change and the Future of Nuclear Deterrence," *International Security* 41, no. 4 (Spring 2017): 9–49, https://doi.org/10.1162/ISEC_a_00273; Matthew Kroenig, *The Logic of American Nuclear Strategy: Why Strategic Superiority Matters* (New York: Oxford University Press, 2018). For the classic arguments against counterforce, see: Robert Jervis, *The Illogic Of American Nuclear Strategy* (Ithaca, NY: Cornell University Press, 1984); Charles L. Glaser, *Analyzing Strategic Nuclear Policy* (Princeton, NJ: Princeton University Press, 1990). Questioning the rationality assumption of deterrence, see: Robert Jervis, Richard Ned Lebow, and Janice Gross Stein, *Psychology and Deterrence* (Baltimore: Johns Hopkins University Press, 1985); Janice Gross Stein, "The Micro-foundations of International Relations Theory: Psychology and Behavioral Economics," *International Organization*

Yet as the nuclear revolution made large-scale warfare unattractive, the information revolution multiplied the possibilities for transactions in the gray zone between peace and war. The ability to gather, process, and transmit data—over terrestrial networks, on the airwaves, under the waves, and in orbit—expanded the scope and efficiency of administration, commerce, and entertainment in civil society. The political-military consequences, however, were much less clear. The information revolution increased the range, lethality, and precision of power projection, but it also created new vulnerabilities and management challenges. It enabled new reconnaissance and precision strike capabilities to hold both conventional and nuclear arsenals at risk, but it also created many new options for influence below the threshold of credible retaliation. New actors have been empowered to disrupt the status quo, but they have also been entangled in familiar political dynamics. Just as the technological innovation of nuclear weaponry gave rise to deterrence theory in the first place, the profusion of sociotechnical innovation in the twenty-first century creates many new challenges for deterrence.

Deterrence was not a new phenomenon at the dawn of the nuclear age, but the demand for an explicit understanding about it was new. Similarly, cross-domain deterrence is not new today, but its relevance is increasing. Strategic actors have long combined capabilities or shifted domains to make coercive threats or design around them. The siege of Troy was a stalemate of symmetric armies that ended with the asymmetric ruse of the Trojan Horse. Sun Tzu highlighted the role of deception in war long before Chinese hackers began phishing American defense contractors. The British sank the French fleet in the Battle of the Nile rather than confronting Napoleon's army in Egypt. Over a century later, the British used midget submarines and airpower to sink Hitler's largest battleship in a Norwegian fjord, rather than sending out the surface combatants of the world's most capable navy. The United States combined a naval blockade with the threat of nuclear escalation to compel the Soviet Union to redeploy missiles from Cuba. Indeed, leaders and commanders have long made intuitive choices about how to choose between different means to shift competition onto more favorable terms, just as the use of deterrent threats by statesmen (or parents) was intuitive long before the articulation of deterrence theory. Intuition may no longer be sufficient, however, given that technological innovation has increased the difficulty of selecting among available options and multiplied the number of potential combinations and interactions. As a larger and more diverse portfolio of tools available for coercion complicates strategic choices,

---

71, no. S1 (April 2017): S249–S263, https://doi.org/10.1017/S0020818316000436. On the gap between theory and practice during the Cold War, see: Francis J. Gavin, *Nuclear Statecraft: History and Strategy in America's Atomic Age* (Ithaca, NY: Cornell University Press, 2012); Robert Powell, "Nuclear Brinkmanship, Limited War, and Military Power," *International Organization* 69, no. 3 (2015): 589–626, https://doi.org/10.1017/S0020818315000028.

a better understanding of CDD becomes a critical enabler for effective national security strategy.

As explained in our introduction and by Nacht et al. in chapter 2, the notion of CDD emerged in American strategic thought in the context of technological challenges in space and cyberspace and political challenges from a rising China and resentful Russia, Iran, North Korea, and others. This book has attempted go beyond this historically contingent beginning to assess the general analytic potential of CDD. In this concluding chapter, we provide a structured review of the insights that have emerged in the process. The following sections present several stylized claims about CDD supported by arguments and evidence from the previous chapters. We first discuss the usefulness of CDD as a general analytic concept. Next, we highlight the ways in which the differential characteristics of particular domains affect bargaining behavior. We then address the problem of complexity and the challenges it creates for integration and credible communication across domains. We close by sketching out tentative implications for policy and research. The chapters herein provide encouragement that a future research agenda in this direction would be worthwhile.

The Promise of Cross-Domain Deterrence as a Concept

By and large, the authors in this book find CDD to be a useful, though challenging, concept. CDD is predicated on the idea that means matter for deterrence; to paraphrase Marshall McLuhan, the medium of coercion is the message. The chapters show how different means have different, or sometimes complementary, strengths and weaknesses for coercion and warfighting. These differences are more or less useful in pursuing a range of objectives in different geopolitical contexts. In short, actors' choices of means, and combinations of means, affect the credibility and effectiveness of deterrence (or compellence) that they can achieve.

The case studies in the chapters also show that choices to vary or combine domains have been consequential in history, from the Peloponnesian War to the Cold War and beyond. Rovner's application of CDD in chapter 8 to one of the most ancient and famous of cases in all of international relations is perhaps the strongest endorsement for the concept's general relevance. Rovner advances a novel explanation for both the outbreak of the war and its protraction: CDD failure and CDD success, respectively. He posits that his findings are likely relevant for understanding future cases as well (i.e., a war between the United States and China) because "the underlying characteristics of the domains are more important than the vintage of the technology at work. If this is true, then CDD theory is more than a faddish reflection of contemporary policy debates. It may shed new light on very old cases in ways that open the aperture on current problems." Several other chapters (e.g., chapters 2, 10, 11, and 13) similarly find the concept useful for revisiting key episodes in the Cold War. It turns out that the moment of maximal danger in the Cold War was also an exemplary case for CDD; as Nacht et al. explain: "[the] Cuban missile crisis was the most complex and stressful for U.S. policymakers, as it called on them to use naval assets to *compel* withdrawal of the Soviet missiles, nuclear threats to *deter* their use, and extensive and subtle diplomatic maneuvering to resolve the crisis peacefully." They point out that "many of the hard problems in CDD—new means, multiple means, ambiguous means, surprising actors—have appeared before." According to Green and Long, "U.S. nuclear strategy during the later Cold War depended on executing complex cross-domain operations in a conflict and outcompeting potential Soviet countermeasures during peacetime."

Cross-domain interactions are so prevalent in military history, in fact, that we conjecture that CDD is a more general rather than specific form of deterrence. Nuclear deterrence, from this perspective, is really a subset (or lesser included case) of CDD that only considers the peculiar, and frighteningly unique, characteristics of the nuclear domain, namely prominence of existential costs and unreliable defenses. Lehman (chapter 4) cites a 2014 National Research Council study that states: "there does appear to be agreement within DoD and within the Air Force that *strategic* deterrence is *cross-domain* deterrence." Indeed, as Green and Long note, the venerable Clausewitzian formula—war as politics by other means—is inherently cross-domain because war is conceived an instrument that states use to impose their will in lieu of peaceful diplomacy. Yet war is a peculiar kind of political instrument that combines the "paradoxical trinity" of reason, violence, and chance; these properties make war difficult to control, terrifying, and therefore useful for coercion. The particular nature of "other means" matters. There are now many different military and nonmilitary means available for the various ends of competitive politics than in Clausewitz's day. Lehman notes that while CDD itself is not new, "[what] is new is the sense of urgency in dealing with these complex interactions with nuclear deterrence even at lower levels of escalation."

CDD is politics by many other means. If the basic stylized problem of coercive diplomacy is to confront an adversary with a choice of "war" or "not-war" to achieve one's political aims, then it is reasonable to suspect that the availability of further choices about the type of war or conflicts other-than-war should further complicate the logic of coercion. "Deterrence" policy in practice may seek to preserve the status quo, to advance cherished interests, to achieve influence without resort to violence, to shift the costs of defense to other actors, or to avoid the costs of war or commitment to war. Different means may serve these different ends, for better or worse, and there will inevitably be trade-offs across them. A general theory of deterrence should thus explain how actors make trade-offs across the portfolio of means or domains that they have available and that they confront. In sum, deterrence in practice has always been cross-domain, but deterrence theory has not.

The bricks and mortar for a theoretical account of CDD are within reach. Classical deterrence theory rests on a notion of strategic interaction between broadly rational actors.[2] Rational bargaining models of politics conceive of social institutions as a type of bargaining equilibrium between agents in a political system and war as a type of bargaining failure. Rational actors would prefer to negotiate a peaceful deal to fighting a costly war, but their desire to get a better deal in peace or reduce their costs in war can lead them to exaggerate their power (to bluff) or, alternately, to hide their capabilities. Miscalculation about power and resolve make deterrence failure more likely. Most of the chapters explicitly leverage the rational bargaining model of war to analyze CDD. Bahney et al. (chapter 6) argue that new cross-domain applications of space technologies and improving antisatellite technologies are eroding first-strike stability. Schneider (chapter 5) examines the role of uncertainty in deterrence of and by cyber operations. Morrow (chapter 9) considers common knowledge criteria in repeated coordination games. Mehta (chapter 11) explores the credibility of extended deterrence commitments to allies under CDD conditions. Greenhill (chapter 12) develops the rationalist logic of compellence in a nontraditional domain (refugees and forced emigration).

The assumption of rationality in international relations can be and has been contested. There is a significant literature in behavioral economics and psychology about the deviation of human decisionmaking from rationalist ideals.[3] Both Morgan (chapter 3) and Lehman (chapter 4) offer some reasons to suspect that the technological and cross-cultural complexity of CDD might make these deviations more salient. At the same time, it is desirable to first capture the logic of optimal choice given a portfolio of different means and strategic interaction across different domains. We still do not have a solid understanding of what rational expectations of a multimeans-based system of deterrence might be. Furthermore, apparent irrationality may at times simply reflect the effects on decisionmaking of the complex dynamics of CDD. Seemingly "bad" decisions can emerge from complex environments when a given aspect of strategy is understood operationally but has not clearly been distinguished from other levels of analysis or confounding factors. It is, therefore, helpful to first develop a rational baseline for CDD strategy before

---

[2] For exposition see, inter alia: Geoffrey Blainey, *Causes of War*, 3rd ed. (New York: Simon and Schuster, 1988); James D. Fearon, "Rationalist Explanations for War," *International Organization* 49, no. 3 (1995): 379–414, https://doi.org/10.1017/S0020818300033324; Robert Powell, "Bargaining Theory and International Conflict," *Annual Review of Political Science* 5, no. 1 (2002): 1–30, https://doi.org/10.1146/annurev.polisci.5.092601.141138; Dan Reiter, "Exploring the Bargaining Model of War," *Perspectives on Politics* 1, no. 01 (2003): 27–43, https://doi.org/10.1017/S1537592703000033; Charles L. Glaser, *Rational Theory of International Politics: The Logic of Competition and Cooperation* (Princeton, NJ: Princeton University Press, 2010).

[3] Stein, "The Micro-foundations of International Relations Theory."

considering the effects of nonrational deviations or decision heuristics on strategic dynamics.[4]

The Bargaining Characteristics of Different Domains

A theory of CDD can and should look to familiar deterrence principles. What differs is the technological and political context. Traditional deterrence theory is agnostic about means (usually assuming the means are nuclear), but choice among means is essential for CDD. These considerations lead us to posit that different domains have different implications for political bargaining. Technologies do not simply determine politics, but they often do create constraints that channel political interaction.[5]

In this section, we briefly summarize findings from seven different domains examined in this book. Domains might vary in *barriers to entry* for would-be coercers, to include the financial and technical requirements of acquiring a technology or the organizational and social requirements of operationalizing it.[6] Some capabilities thus will only be available to strong states who have the resources and ability to field them; others will be more widely available to many types of actors. Different domains also have different informational characteristics, depending in particular on the stealth and mobility of operational platforms. The clear observability or deceptive obfuscation of means, in turn, can facilitate or undermine, respectively, the *credible communication* of threats and assurances to use tools in that domain. The inverse of credible communication is *plausible deniability* or the potential difficulty of the attribution problem. Plausible deniability can be useful for intelligence collection or covert action to subtly shift costs and benefits, and it can also be used to preclude embarrassing public reversals or capitulations. One important distinction in CDD is between deterrence signaling and warfighting performance, or more pithily between "warning" and "winning." The win-warn tradeoff is a major problem in CDD. Whereas credibility and deniability are political informational characteristics, other characteristics affect military potency. They may or may not be able to be revealed; indeed, revelation may undermine the utility of some warfighting tools. Some kinds of means offer important advantages in *warfighting potential*,

---

[4] On the distinction between a rational baseline for a theory of international relations and subrational deviations rooted in domestic politics or cognitive heuristics see Glaser, *Rational Theory of International Politics*, ch. 2.

[5] Allan Dafoe, "On Technological Determinism: A Typology, Scope Conditions, and a Mechanism," *Science, Technology, & Human Values* 40, no. 6 (November 1, 2015): 1047–1076.

[6] Michael C. Horowitz, *The Diffusion of Military Power: Causes and Consequences for International Politics* (Princeton, NJ: Princeton University Press, 2010); Andrea Gilli and Mauro Gilli, "Why China Hasn't Caught Up Yet: Military-Technological Superiority and the Limits of Imitation, Reverse Engineering, and Cyber-Espionage," *International Security*, 2019.

which increases the likelihood that an actor will be able to win a military contest, should one occur. "Contests of strength" over resources or territory that only require "brute force" military operations to change the distribution of power and benefits may not worry much about communicating with the enemy. Denial strategies that seek to physically prevent such changes may also require very little communication, although the possibility of denial must be somehow credibly advertised if it is to be used for deterrence. The ability to deny the effective exercise of the adversary's warfighting potential, or the feasibility of defense, can be described as *counterforce potential*. These are not necessarily the same things, as some means may enhance offensive military operations without, however, improving defense against them. Other means may be less useful for denial and more useful for imposing *punishment costs* that heighten the consequences of deterrence failure. Domains might also vary in the types of targets exposed to coercive punishment in a given domain or in the targets in other domains for which capabilities in that domain are best suited.

Table 15.1 highlights some of the relative strengths and weaknesses of different domains along the six dimensions just discussed to provide a sense of how means can differentially affect deterrence. The "mixed" coding indicates that different aspects of the same domain behave differently in various circumstances, often as a result of diversity within the domain. For example, while it is difficult to disguise large formations of troops, a special operations detachment may infiltrate undetected. Submarines and aircraft carriers differ markedly in their speed, stealth, and power projection capability. Haun (chapter 7) points out that strategic bombing is often ineffective for strategic communication but close air support can effectively deter the concentration of land forces in war. Table 15.1 merely codes the "systemic"

Table 15.1 **Bargaining Characteristics of Domains**

	Nuclear	Land	Sea	Air	Space	Cyber	Migration
Barriers to entry	Higher	Mixed	Higher	Higher	Higher	Lower	Lower
Credible communication	Higher	Higher	Mixed	Mixed	Mixed	Lower	Higher
Plausible deniability	Lower	Mixed	Mixed	Mixed	Mixed	Higher	Mixed
Warfighting potential	Lower	Mixed	Higher	Higher	Higher	Mixed	Negligible
Counterforce potential	Lower	Mixed	Mixed	Mixed	Lower	Mixed	Lower
Punishment costs	Extreme	Mixed	Higher	Higher	Lower	Mixed	Higher

tendencies of different domains. Yet we might expect the attributes of domain-specific capabilities to be further sensitive to variation in "dyadic" pairings between specific states in specific regions. Green and Long (chapter 10), for instance, raise the possibility that the warfighting and counterforce potential of nuclear forces in the Cold War may not have been as low as nuclear deterrence theorists have traditionally assumed. Land forces that might be successful in major combat operations against similar forces might run into problems against irregular adversaries hidden in the civilian population. Further research is needed to refine, explicate, and test these codings, develop hypotheses about their effects on CDD in particular circumstances, and to consider other domains or variations within domains. Table 15.1 also omits domains for nonmilitary cooperation that may be quite important for CDD, as both Shifrinson (chapter 13) and Huang and Kang (chapter 14) stress. This summary is not meant to be the final word on CDD but a set of conjectures about the ways in which means vary across characteristics that are salient for political-military bargaining.

Even so, at this gross level of generalization we already begin to see that there are some significant tradeoffs across domains in different politically salient characteristics of deterrence. Means differ, and those differences matter. CDD works by combining, offsetting, substituting, or complementing the bargaining properties of different domains that produce a competitive advantage. Different means can thus serve different ends in deterrence. Sometimes different means work together to create synergies. In other circumstances, there are difficult trade-offs across them. The chapters highlight many of these differences and trade-offs.

Nuclear Weapons

Deterrence theory grew out of the nuclear revolution of the mid-twentieth century, and as Lehman and other authors in this book emphasize, nuclear weapons retain pride of place for deterrence in "the second nuclear age" of the twenty-first. The chapters by Mehta and by Green and Long point out that nuclear deterrence in the Cold War was already a thoroughly cross-domain affair exemplified by the nuclear triad of aerial bombers, land-based missiles, and ballistic missile submarines, as well as interactions between nuclear and conventional forces. Bahney et al. argue that the space domain improved the stability of nuclear deterrence by reducing information asymmetries: "[attacking] early warning or NC2 systems that served to underpin the nuclear deterrent in both nations could have potentially been interpreted by either side as a preparatory move for a nuclear strike. Consequently, the United States and the Soviet Union had a strong mutual disincentive during much of this period to develop broad counter-space capabilities or doctrine, except to hedge against the possibility of escalation to general nuclear war." While cross-domain changes during and after the Cold War have perhaps been destabilizing, as we will discuss further, a few key characteristics of nuclear weapons still have special salience for deterrence. Some authors dispute the use of the term "domain" to refer to nuclear weapons, preferring to restrict the term to the geographical arena in which weapons are deployed. But from the perspective of a political theory of CDD that highlights and focuses on salient political differences across means, it often makes sense to talk about a distinct nuclear domain. As Green and Long put it, "[however] complex new cross-domain interactions might be, there is something clarifying about the logic of extinction."

Nuclear weapons produce horrific destruction and are difficult to defend against.[7] Together these properties enhance mutual information about the consequences of war. Morrow enumerates several properties of nuclear deterrence during the Cold War that helped to stabilize superpower relations, several of which remain relevant today. First, "the parties could know when a violation took place" because "[nuclear] detonations over valued targets could not be hidden" and "both sides had the ability to monitor the capabilities of the other side, so they knew roughly what the other side was capable of." Thus nuclear parties were more likely to have a mutual understanding of the balance of power. Second, "the certainty of the level and speed of devastation were very high once both superpowers developed secure second-strike capabilities." Thus they had a mutual understanding of the probable, and prohibitively high, costs of war. Third, "the superpowers had only one other party to worry about" and they "undertook steps to ensure command and control over their nuclear weapons, in part to prevent unauthorized launches. Nonstate actors lacked access to nuclear weapons and their delivery systems." Even in the more multilateral second nuclear age, states still guard their deterrents dearly and work to counter proliferation. Thus, the attribution problem remains comparatively easy to solve, especially in the context of a militarized crisis.[8] Fourth, and as a result of the preceding points, "the lines to be enforced were well established and clear." Nuclear weapons are excellent deterrents to protect a state's vital existential interests. Nacht et al. point out that they are less useful for compellence.[9] The cost of nuclear war against an ally resolved enough to become the subject of a nuclear contest (more likely when a state fears for its existence) is generally greater than any offsetting political benefit for the coercer. Difficulties in credibility emerge when less-than-vital interests are at stake in conventional/subconventional conflicts or when counterforce capabilities have muddied perceptions of the nuclear balance of power. Both of these exceptions,

---

[7] Damage limitation is possible, as Green and Long point out, but the punishment inflicted by even a single enemy weapon that gets through would be quite severe. On improvements in nuclear defense see Lieber and Press, "The New Era of Counterforce."

[8] Keir A. Lieber and Daryl G. Press, "Why States Won't Give Nuclear Weapons to Terrorists," *International Security* 38, no. 1 (Summer 2013): 80–104, https://doi.org/10.1162/ISEC_a_00127.

[9] This finding is consistent with Todd S. Sechser and Matthew Fuhrmann, *Nuclear Weapons and Coercive Diplomacy* (New York: Cambridge University Press, 2017).

interestingly, involve cross-domain interactions. As a general rule, the nuclear domain has strongly stabilizing informational characteristics.[10]

Land Power

Another domain that has strong informational characteristics for deterrence is land. Mehta highlights this trait in her analysis of the effects of the U.S. adoption of the sea-based deterrent during the Cold War:

> it is the very nature of mobile forces—an element that is integral to the survival and success of the nuclear triad—that raises concerns about the credibility of an assurance. In the pre–nuclear triad era, extended deterrence generally involved the use of ground troops, whose redeployment was prohibitively costly. The ability to reposition or "pivot" submarines and aircraft carriers, two cornerstones of the nuclear umbrella, is beneficial to the United States but presents it with a significant challenge as to how it can effectively assure its allies that those forces will be available and present in the event of a crisis or conflict.... The prioritization of sea- and air-based power, and a deemphasis on ground power may have inadvertently weakened the symbol of a U.S. *resolve* to defend allies.[11]

The fundamental problem of credibility in U.S. extended deterrence commitments to allies during the Cold War was pithily summed up by questioning whether the United States would be willing to trade Washington, DC for a European capital. One way that the United States addressed this credibility problem was by deploying ground forces to Europe. Schelling comments on the purpose of these forces with characteristic flair: "bluntly, they can die. They can die heroically, dramatically, and in a manner that guarantees that the action cannot stop there."[12] The purpose of tripwire forces, whether in Central Europe during the Cold War or in the Baltic region today, is not to successfully defend but rather to fail, and thereby to generate the use of more force. The expense and public nature of deploying troops and investing in their maintenance on foreign soil, together with the difficulty of moving them

---

[10] An additional feature of nuclear capabilities that make it easier for adversaries to assess the balance of power is that their effectiveness as military weapons is not much affected by enemy knowledge of their existence. For a discussion, see: Erik Gartzke and Jon R. Lindsay, "Thermonuclear Cyberwar," *Journal of Cybersecurity* 3, no. 1 (February 2017): 37–48, http://doi.org/10.1093/cybsec/tyw017.

[11] Mehta draws on arguments about the deterrence characteristics of land power in Michael Allen Hunzeker and Alexander Lanoszka, "Landpower and American Credibility," *Parameters* 45, no. 4 (2015): pp. 17–26, http://strategicstudiesinstitute.army.mil/pubs/parameters/issues/Winter_2015-16/5_Hunzeker.pdf.

[12] Thomas C. Schelling, *Arms and Influence: With a New Preface and Afterword* (New Haven, CT: Yale University Press, 2008), 47.

out of the way in the event of hostilities to avoid a very public loss of life, makes a ground force deployment a costly and credible signal of intent to defend an ongoing interest.

Modern land warfare is also itself a highly cross-domain affair. Combined arms warfare works by using the advantages of one category of force to cover the weaknesses of another. Armor can provide fires and protection, even as it is vulnerable to other arms, such as artillery and tactical aviation. The emergence of modern combined arms warfare (or what Stephen Biddle calls "the modern system"), beginning in World War I, enabled military organizations to restore movement to an increasingly lethal and static battlefield.[13] This method of force employment has repeatedly proved is usefulness in battle; however, mastering its inherent complexity and accumulating the human and organizational capital required is beyond the reach of many states. There are also civil-military constraints, insofar as the modern system requires empowering junior military leaders, which may increase the risk of insubordination or coups.[14] There are thus steep barriers to entry for the modern system. At the same time, it is possible for militarily weak but politically resolved actors to oppose the modern system at relatively low material cost (if high human cost) through irregular warfare. Weaker guerrillas can complicate a stronger army's ability to discriminate valid targets by hiding in rough terrain and among the civilian population. As Haun notes, ground forces, especially irregular forces, can take advantage of factors like these to defeat aerial targeting, thus limiting the coercive effectiveness of air power in particular and the modern system in general.[15]

If relative immobility and public observability make ground forces an effective deterrent at the grand strategic level, relative variation on these factors in the composition of ground forces should affect deterrence at the operational level. Some ground forces are more mobile than others. Armored tanks are highly mobile and lethal but are also relatively costly to replace compared to foot soldiers; armor is also vulnerable to antitank weapons deployed on the ground or from the air. Haun points out: "[while] air attacks are most lethal against large mechanized formations in the open and on the move, such encounters are rare, as ground forces foresee the air threat and take measures to avoid catastrophic loss." Armored warfare is somewhat like naval warfare in this respect. Fleet-on-fleet naval battle is relatively rare

---

[13] Stephen D. Biddle, *Military Power: Explaining Victory and Defeat in Modern Battle* (Princeton, NJ: Princeton University Press, 2004).

[14] Risa Brooks, "Civil-Military Relations in the Middle East," in *The Future Security Environment in the Middle East: Conflict, Stability, and Political Change*, edited by Nora Bensahel and Daniel L. Byman (Santa Monica, CA: RAND Corporation, 2005), 129–162, http://www.rand.org/content/dam/rand/pubs/monograph_reports/2005/MR1640.pdf; Caitlin Talmadge, *The Dictator's Army: Battlefield Effectiveness in Authoritarian Regimes* (Ithaca, NY: Cornell University Press, 2015).

[15] See also: Barry R. Posen, "Command of the Commons: The Military Foundation of U.S. Hegemony," *International Security* 28, no. 1 (2003): 5–46, https://doi.org/10.1162/016228803322427965.

in history, precisely because the loss of the entire fleet, and thus of the protection of supply lines and power projection that a fleet provides, has the potential to be decisive for the entire war. Corinth thus observed of Athens that "a single defeat at sea is in all likelihood their ruin," a statement that Rovner compares to Winston Churchill's portrayal of Admiral Jellicoe in World War I as "the only man on either side who could lose the war in an afternoon." Actors may hesitate to use an asset that is too valuable to lose.

Sea Power

The distinction between land and sea power is the most ancient distinction between military domains. There is much scholarship on the political and economic differences between land powers and sea powers, for instance, their varying propensity for authoritarian control at home or imperial expansion abroad.[16] Maritime strategy in the tradition of Alfred Thayer Mahan and Julian Corbett is also inherently about the differential implications for strategy of these venerable domains. It is notable that the great naval theorists started writing just as sea power was completing its technological transformation from sail to steam. Some eternal political aspects of strategy are only recognized historically when technological innovation makes them salient. As Rovner notes, "[interest] in CDD is part of a broader intellectual movement to revive the study of geopolitics, which treats strategy and international relations as a function of geography." Modern technology makes geographical characteristics of domains more, not less, salient.

Rovner describes a number of attributes of sea power that still have resonance today, despite all of the technological differences between aircraft carriers and rowed triremes. First, naval power is a cross-domain tool, which is to say that it provides influence ashore. Even in ancient Greece, "a navy could do more than simply fight other navies, because it could deliver and resupply land forces for raiding Sparta's allies and stir up insurrection among the slaves of the Peloponnese." Sparta thus feared Athens because Athenian "naval mastery would allow [Athens] to open up new theaters of its choosing, which would make it well-nigh impossible for Sparta to force a decisive victory." Second, naval power is a grand strategic tool, meaning that it facilitates the development and exercise of national instruments of power beyond the military domain. Navies protect commercial trade, and commercial expansion enhances wealth, which can then be used to purchase more warships and pay more soldiers, in a positive feedback loop. Conversely, without naval protection

---

[16] Inter alia, Eric Heginbotham, "The Fall and Rise of Navies in East Asia: Military Organizations, Domestic Politics, and Grand Strategy," *International Security* 27, no. 2 (Fall 2002): 86–125, https://doi.org/10.1162/016228802760987833; Etel Solingen, "Pax Asiatica versus Bella Levantina: The Foundations of War and Peace in East Asia and the Middle East," *American Political Science Review* 101, no. 4 (November 2007): 757–780, https://doi.org/10.1017/S0003055407070487.

an enemy fleet might impose a blockade. Sparta thus worried that if Athens faced no naval challengers, "there would be nothing to stop it from isolating Sparta on the Peloponnese and cutting off its grain supply." Such a blockade had the potential to both degrade Spartan military power (coercion by denial) and create pain for Sparta's population (coercion by punishment). Third, naval power is capital and skill intensive. Naval power is not acquired overnight and is about more than the number of warships: "Sparta's leaders seem to have been extraordinarily naïve about the requirements for naval warfare. They failed no only to understand the financial requirements of building and maintaining a fleet, but also to appreciate the demands of recruiting able and skilled seamen while developing the operational skills and command and control arrangements needed to maintain order and discipline during chaotic naval melees. The Spartans had spent decades cultivating these skills on land but practically no time to thinking about what it would take to fight effectively at sea."[17] The implication is that the barriers to entry for naval mastery are high indeed. Fourth, it follows from these other attributes that it is dangerous to risk a fleet that is both vital for national power and costly to replace. Therefore, as mentioned, major fleet battles are rare in naval history.

The implications for deterrence are ambiguous. On one hand the mobile power projection capability of navies enables a state to rapidly shift its focus along an enemy's coastline or open up a new theater of operation, which can *improve* deterrence. Because a navy can appear anywhere to bombard the shore and deploy expeditionary troops, an army must defend everywhere, which denies land forces' ability to concentrate where they might gain the most military advantage. In this respect, naval power acts in a manner similar to that of Haun's account of tactical air power, discussed below. Navies force armies to choose between being flanked by an enemy landing or being too weak at the decisive spot. Both the air and sea domains involve smaller numbers of more expensive, more mobile, and more lethal platforms, operating in relatively homogenous domains (compared to land) that facilitate strategic flanking maneuvers (horizontally along an enemy coast in the case of navies and vertically in the case of air forces). By a similar but inverted logic, Green and Long note that American naval power (specifically antisubmarine warfare) nearly converted some Soviet naval assets into ground forces as the Soviets tried to preserve the Soviet nuclear deterrent that the U.S. Navy held at risk: "[the] problem was so worrisome that the Soviet Navy even considered launching its submarines' missiles from their home bases, even though this would vitiate nearly the entire purpose of submarines as a nuclear launch platform."

---

[17] Sparta found out the hard way in an early naval skirmish that it is not preponderance but operational skill that makes the difference, as Rovner relates: "a combined Spartan/Corinthian fleet was routed at Naupactus, despite enjoying a large local advantage. The Peloponnesians brought forty-seven ships to battle against twenty Athenian triremes, but the Athenian captains were vastly more experienced and skilled, and the Peloponnesian force fell into disarray at the first sign of trouble."

On the other hand an increase of warfighting options can also *undermine* deterrence in different circumstances. The same mobility and firepower that makes naval power so useful for cross-domain coercion can also become a liability for credible commitment. Coercion, as Schelling points out, relies on the threat of force held in reserve. Navies have plenty of coercive power. Yet coercion also relies on the credibility of a commitment to exercise that force when a redline is crossed. What if the exercise of power puts the entire fleet and all the benefits it provides at risk? As Francis Bacon observed, "he that commands the sea is at great liberty, and may take as much and as little of the war as he will."[18] While the *expansion* of options is a major advantage of sea power (and of air and cyber power), this becomes problematic from the perspective of commitment, which involves *limiting* options. Mehta sees this logic at work in the Cold War: "analysis of empirical evidence suggests that the introduction of cross-domain capabilities, in the form of the nuclear triad, may not have been as effective at enhancing U.S. assurances to its allies." While the triad improved the survivability of the American deterrent by expanding retaliatory options, allies began to worry that the United States might be more inclined to settle disputes peacefully without defending the allies' interests, and, moreover, the mobility of the triad undermined the U.S. commitment to be there.[19] Naval missions to "show the flag," including port visits and freedom of navigation operations, can demonstrate an ability to move firepower into an area, which can enhance coercion and assurance. Navies can assume risk by sailing into a potential adversary's engagement envelope, which can signal commitment. Such a signal is weakened, however, by the inherent mobility of the naval domain; ships can also sail away.

Air Power

Air power is even more mobile than sea power, so we should expect similar problems to be encountered in attempting to signal deterrence commitments. Air power is further able to deliver long-range lethal firepower to places far inland where naval power cannot reach. We should thus expect some similar, perhaps even more pronounced, coercive advantages. Indeed, the historical rise of air power is closely associated with the rise of deterrence thought. While the nuclear revolution was the more salient technological development that created the demand for deterrence theory, early theorists generally assumed that nuclear bombs would be delivered through the air, first by bombers and later by missiles (transiting through both air and space). Nacht et al. point out that core deterrence notions of counter-value

---

[18] Francis Bacon, *Essays, Civil and Moral: And The New Atlantis* (New York: P. F. Collier & Son, 1909), 83.

[19] Erik Gartzke, Rex Douglass, and Jon R. Lindsay, "The Influence of Seapower on Politics: Domain- and Platform-Specific Attributes of Material Capabilities," working paper, October 2018, https://github.com/CenterForPeaceAndSecurityStudies/InfluenceOfSeapower.

punishment (i.e., bombing cities) and tactical offensive advantage (i.e., defensive vulnerability) emerged not with nuclear weapons but with "air power, which allowed a nation to inflict serious damage on an enemy's territory without having to defeat its land forces." Strategic bombing doctrine argues that an air force can win a war independently by destroying core targets that undermine an enemy's will or ability to resist. The historical performance of air power as an independent strategic instrument, however, casts doubt on this proposition.[20]

An important open research question is how much of what we think we know about deterrence in general is biased by the prevalence of the air instrument in modern cases of deterrence. Greenhill points out that the conventionally accepted pessimism about the relative efficacy of compellence versus deterrence is based largely on findings from studies of air power. She finds, by sharp contrast, that a different instrument—coercive engineered migration, discussed below—has a high success rate in compelling policy concessions from target states (i.e., 63 percent complete success and 78 percent partial or complete success).

While strategic bombing alone may not offer policymakers a reliable or effective coercive instrument, Haun argues that air power *does* make a real coercive impact through its integration with, and lethality against, ground forces during war: "[the] cross-domain advantage of air power lies in its lethality against concentrated and maneuvering armies." Nuclear deterrence theory was designed to prevent nuclear war, and thus the outbreak of war is construed as deterrence failure in most treatments. Yet deterrence continues to operate within war to moderate decisions to escalate or expand the conflict. Schelling describes this process as "the idiom of military action."[21] Haun goes further to show how the basic distinction between warfighting (brute force) and deterrence (coercion) is in fact more complicated because warfighting itself employs deterrence at the operational and tactical levels of war. For example, a machine gun can be used to supply suppressive fire that deters enemy troops from firing on or maneuvering against friendly forces. Haun argues that air power provides a similar function by denying the enemy's preferred use of ground forces. Precisely because air power provides a potent brute force capability by supporting troops in contact ("close air support") or destroying enemy forces prior to ground contact ("air interdiction"), it also provides an important deterrent or suppressive effect. Haun points out that the comparative advantage of air power is to counter the comparative advantage of land power: "mass and maneuver have long been requisite principles of war for successful military operations. Mass allows

---

[20] Robert Anthony Pape, *Bombing to Win: Air Power and Coercion in War* (Ithaca, NY: Cornell University Press, 1996); Tami Davis Biddle, *Rhetoric and Reality in Air Warfare: The Evolution of British and American Ideas about Strategic Bombing, 1914–1945* (Princeton, NJ: Princeton University Press, 2002); Phil M. Haun, *Coercion, Survival, and War: Why Weak States Resist the United States* (Stanford, CA: Stanford University Press, 2015).

[21] Schelling, *Arms and Influence*, ch. 4.

an army to bring firepower to bear at the decisive point of the battlefield. Maneuver can produce mass with the concentration of forces and can project power with the movement of those forces." The use of air forces to counter the advantages of ground forces exemplifies the "rock-paper-scissors" logic of CDD. By the same token, therefore, "[the] greatest asymmetric advantage of an air force with command of the skies over a battlefield is its ability to locate, identify, and attack concentrating and moving ground forces."

A finding shared by several other authors in this book is that effective deterrence is quite sensitive to context. In the case of air power, according to Haun, deterrence depends on "the degree of air superiority achieved over the battlefield; the capability of an air force to locate, identify, target, and assess air strikes against ground forces; the composition of enemy's ground forces; and the presence and capability of friendly ground forces" as well as favorable environmental factors such as "weather, lighting, terrain, and cover." Importantly, tactical air power is itself a cross-domain instrument. It depends on intelligence from sensors located in space and in the air, and it depends on friendly ground forces that can "place the enemy army on the horns of a dilemma: whether to concentrate against an approaching army or to disperse and conceal its position against the threat of air attack." Friendly troops, if they have the strength, can flush enemy forces out into the open, where air power can attack them or, if they are relatively weaker, they can gather intelligence on concealed enemy forces. Thus, argues Haun, "the presence of a capable friendly ground force has proven to be a critical factor in effective air attacks of fielded forces. Absent friendly ground forces, air power can be negated, as was the case in the Kosovo air campaign in 1999." Future research can propose similar conditions that constrain or alternately enable the effectiveness of intrawar deterrence by and across other domains.[22] What, for instances, are the infrastructural and operational characteristics of cyber operations that make them effective in amplifying or subverting other military and political capabilities?

Space Operations

Space is vital for the American way of war, supporting nuclear, conventional, and unconventional operations by land, sea, or air. Space is perhaps the most cross-domain of all the domains in this respect, insofar as what happens in space matters most not in space but on Earth. Therefore, as Nacht et al. explain, the 2007 antisatellite test by China put the threat to American space capabilities in sharp relief and began the policy conversation about CDD in earnest. Space exhibits a similar "capability-vulnerability paradox" to the one Schneider finds in the cyber domain. While space

---

[22] For example, is anonymity in cyberspace a necessary enabling condition for successful network exploitation?

is a potent force multiplier for global combat operations and American "command of the commons," for the same reason, fragile and hard to replace U.S. space assets become attractive targets for U.S. adversaries.

During the Cold War, space improved strategic stability because space assets were primarily used for early warning and command and control in support of nuclear deterrence. Space reinforced the informational advantages of the nuclear domain discussed above. This began to change, however, as space assets increasingly supported nonnuclear missions. The signaling *dis*advantages of other domains (such as air and maritime operations which depend on maneuver, stealth, and secrecy to deny information to the enemy) began to destabilize space. The information technology Revolution in Military Affairs (RMA), according to Bahney et al., "vastly deepened the cross-domain integration of space-based C4ISR technology with military operations in the land, sea, and air domains." Moreover, "the United States and partner nations developed high-cost and long-lifetime national security space systems, favoring exquisite capabilities over redundant and resilient ones that could survive military attack." At the same time, it has become "increasingly possible to strike the C4ISR satellites of an opponent that support conventional military capabilities without threatening the opponent's nuclear C2 infrastructure, ability to detect nuclear missile launches, or commercial or other interdependent satellite capabilities," such as weather satellites. Not only is it now technically easier to discriminate the functions of satellites so as to target those less likely to trigger retaliation but also "there are several ways to theoretically attack satellites, either kinetically or nonkinetically, to minimize debris production, including jamming, coorbital attacks, cyberattacks, and directed energy attacks. Even when using direct ascent hit-to-kill interceptors, attacks in space do not necessarily entail a debris-induced catastrophe for all space systems."

A deterrence relationship is said to be "first-strike stable" when neither side has an incentive to launch a preemptive strike. In the Cold War, space reinforced nuclear first-strike *stability* by clarifying the balance of power (i.e., by providing a sort of arm's-length weapons inspection) and reducing the probability of success of any surprise attack (since preparations and launches would be detected in advance). Today, however, according to Bahney et al., space is increasingly characterized by first-strike *instability*. Targets of U.S. military coercion have incentives to strike the orbital Achilles heel of U.S. power, and the United States has incentives to strike even earlier to avoid this. Thus the United States "may currently be the state most threatened by the development of ASAT capabilities around the world" because it is so dependent on a small set of vulnerable satellites, and because prospective adversaries have access to a range of kinetic and nonkinetic antisatellite technologies. As a result, they argue, "the most powerful space-enabled states, like the United States, may actually face even stronger incentives to launch ASAT attacks, including early in a conflict, than will their relatively weaker adversaries, due to the potential risk to their forward deployed forces that are sent in to project power." These are important claims, and further analytical and empirical work (together with computational simulations and war-gaming) should be used to evaluate these and alternative hypotheses. For instance, the very fragility of space assets and increasing interdependence in and through space, both across countries and across commercial, scientific, intelligence, and military applications of space, may incentivize a more circumspect approach to space-based conflict. Are the military gains of antisatellite use in a minor crisis worth risking the commercial benefits of space in possibly precipitating a longer war? Under what conditions does destabilizing military interdependence trump stabilizing economic interdependence in space? The increasingly multipolar aspect of orbital space that the Obama administration described as "congested, contested, and competitive" only adds to the complexity of CDD via the extraterrestrial domain.

Cyber Operations

Much ink has been spilled debating whether the "fifth domain" of warfighting is *really* a domain at all. Indeed, all information networks and devices are physically located in at least one of the other four environmental domains, and all types of operations rely on command and control technology. We prefer to sidestep the ontological question and, for the purposes of comparison in this chapter, treat cyberspace as a domain for the same reasons that it makes sense to treat nuclear weapons as a distinctive domain: cyberspace features interestingly different characteristics for political-military bargaining interactions. Two characteristics stand out: the barriers to entry are comparatively low (e.g., an Internet connection, some technical knowledge, and the ability to manage a team), and cyberspace operations essentially depend on secrecy and deception.[23] As Schneider explains, "[because] cyber accesses are mutable and easy to lose, states are more likely to use covert operations and to obscure their activity in order to retain these accesses." The resulting uncertainty about almost every aspect of security affairs in cyberspace tends to undermine credible communication and thus deterrence.

There is a close conceptual and historical relationship between CDD and cybersecurity for two reasons: functionally, cyber capabilities provide command and control and intelligence in and across all other domains; historically, worries about the vulnerability of this information infrastructure first prompted policy discussion of CDD.[24] As Schneider points out, "it is the difficulty of deterring

---

[23] Erik Gartzke and Jon R. Lindsay, "Weaving Tangled Webs: Offense, Defense, and Deception in Cyberspace," *Security Studies* 24, no. 2 (2015): 316–348, https://doi.org/10.1080/09636412.2015.1038188.

[24] Jon R. Lindsay and Erik Gartzke, "Cross-Domain Deterrence and Cybersecurity: The Consequences of Complexity," in *US National Cybersecurity: International Politics, Concepts and Organization*, edited by Damien van Puyvelde and Aaron F. Brantley (New York: Routledge, 2017).

cyber operations that has provided the catalyst for discussion about the role of cross-domain deterrence as a substitute for within-domain deterrence strategies." Uncertainty is pervasive in cyberspace, in large part because cyber operations are most useful for intelligence and covert action, which in turn depend fundamentally on deception for their effectiveness. Uncertainty also pervades discourse about cybersecurity. According to Schneider, "resounding theme in the existing debates about deterrence in and through cyberspace is the role that uncertainty will play in successful cyber deterrence; uncertainty about effects of cyberattacks, capabilities to create cyberattacks, actors conducting attacks, and responses to cyberattacks. The uncertainty is a technical characteristic of these operations but extends to the behavioral reaction to cyber operations."

Cyberspace notably does not meet Morrow's conditions for effective deterrence, which we listed above in the section on nuclear weapons. First, a successful cyber operation might never be detected, so there would be no knowledge that a violation of deterrence had even occurred. Second, when a cyber intrusion is discovered, it will often be unclear whether an initiator intends to use the computer network exploitation for intelligence or for preparation for an attack.[25] There are ongoing debates in the cybersecurity literature about whether and how cyber operations actually enhance or degrade military power or inflict coercive costs on organizations or societies, implying that the magnitude of the detected or potential harm is uncertain. Third, it may not be clear who bears responsibility for a cyberattack, especially when barriers to entry are low. As Schneider notes, "this question of actors in cyberspace represents one of the largest problems for cyberspace deterrence in general." Fourth, it is not yet clear what is and is not acceptable in cyberspace and what is and is not acceptable to do in response to cyber aggression. Nacht et al. note that when CDD concerns first became apparent to the Department of Defense, "a pressing concern at the time was to identify the characteristics of a cyberattack on the United States that would likely necessitate a kinetic U.S. response." As Schneider points out, U.S. officials participating in wargame scenarios have often approached uncertainty about escalation in contradictory ways, both fearing that U.S. use of cyber operations *before* a war would spark a spiral of escalation and yet *during* a war reaching for options other than cyber during a war that would enable them to more effectively escalate a conflict; that is, they perceived cyber as simultaneously too escalatory and not escalatory enough. She notes a surprising insensitivity to escalation, speculating that actors perceive cyber options as "qualitatively different—less harmful, less escalatory—than their physical, kinetic counterparts."

---

[25] Schneider quips: "the separation between CNE [cyber network exploitation] and attack can be a few seconds and a few keystrokes." See also: Ben Buchanan, *The Cybersecurity Dilemma: Hacking, Trust and Fear between Nations* (New York: Oxford University Press, 2017).

Coercive Engineered Migration

Both the CDD policy debate and this book have focused mainly on the domains of military action. Yet the concept of CDD is potentially much broader. Indeed, the utility of the concept really stands out when considering domains that are totally different from the Pentagon's big five. Greenhill's discussion of coercive engineered migration (CEM) advances our understanding of CDD by considering a radically different coercive instrument and its utility for compellence rather than deterrence. As she puts it, CEM "is a *truly* cross-domain tool of influence, perhaps uniquely so, whose success rate and particular features make it a useful exemplar of how domain switching can help level the playing field, enable relatively weak actors to punch above their weight, and offer more powerful actors a broader array of policy tools than is commonly recognized."

CEM is a type of two-level game that puts pressure on a target government by putting pressure on its domestic polity, either through "capacity swamping" its ability to accept foreign migrants or "agitation" that undermines its willingness to accept them. Interestingly, Rovner notes that both sides in the Peloponnesian War were also engaged in two-level games to manipulate foreign populations: Sparta attempted to foment uprisings in Athens' colonies, and Athens attempted to encourage Spartan slave revolts. CEM works more indirectly by channeling migrants or refugees into the target society to coerce some policy concession from the government.

Coercion generally and compellence in particular are thought to be difficult, but CEM is surprisingly effective. Why? First, the barriers to entry are low. In fact, this is the rare domain that appears to be more available to militarily weak actors than strong ones. Greenhill points out that CEM is especially attractive to "weak state and nonstate actors" who can use it to achieve "political goals that would be utterly unattainable through military means." The character of the regime also matters, and thus CEM is particularly attractive for weak, nondemocratic, or pariah actors. Illiberal actors have little left to lose by behaving unethically and generating a refugee crisis, while their democratic target societies, which tend to uphold norms of openness and human rights while balancing cosmopolitan and nativist constituencies, are particularly vulnerable to migration pressures. Second, migrations have interesting informational characteristics. Their existence and the pain they cause is obvious to all. Yet the plausible deniability of the responsibility for the crisis enables the coercer to back down if necessary and enables the target to make concessions without losing face publicly. Coercers usually make their demands in private, while imposing costs in public, for just this reason. Third, the explicitly nonmilitary aspect of CEM means that the target does not suffer a diminution in military power by capitulating to demands. In addition, the target, usually a liberal democracy, cannot retaliate in kind and is usually unwilling to use military force to counter CEM. The very fact that CEM does not affect military power at all makes it more likely that the target will give in without retaliation. Fourth, the punishment costs of CEM can be considerable, especially for a rich liberal democracy that will experience economic and social stress from the sudden influx of migrants. Greenhill points out that CEM is often used as part of a risk strategy that imposes "costs at a gradually increasing rate, threatening bigger punishment later for noncompliance." She finds that CEM has a great return on investment for weak states: "a significant amount of economic, social, and political damage might be imposed on targets without a correspondingly large investment."

Cross-domain deterrence helps to explain why CEM is, under the right circumstances, so much more effective for coercion than other means. Comparing across these means (see table 15.1), it is striking that some of them support the communication of credible threats, notably nuclear weapons and strategic deployments of ground forces. Others have very different properties, with sea power and air power contrasting with the land domain (but comparing similarly to one another) in their enhanced abilities to augment military power but questionable utility for credible communication. Space and cyberspace have quite different barriers to entry and implications for military power, despite usually being conceptually grouped together on the basis of their common "informational" qualities. Cyberspace is literally built of information technology, but it may not necessarily enhance the mutual information that stabilizes deterrence, given that cyber operations depend on deception. Weak actors have the ability to access tools in cyberspace and in the land domain to some extent, but their coercive potential in both is limited, whereas CEM is quite potent for weak actors. In sum, we conjecture that means matter because the sociotechnical affordances of different domains have differential impacts on key parameters of the bargaining model of war.

Complexity and Strategic Stability

We posit that increasing sociotechnical complexity is the very problem that gives rise to CDD. Complexity can be considered in terms of the types of systems, activities, and divisions of labor and the interdependencies between them. The variety of technologies and practices tends to increase in political economic history. Over the long run, industrialization unlocks new resources but also requires more complicated institutions to coordinate labor and resources at greater scope and scale.[26] Economic actors are able to do more, yet because they act in a political system of

---

[26] James R. Beniger, *The Control Revolution: Technological and Economic Origins of the Information Society* (Cambridge, MA: Harvard University Press, 1986); Douglass C. North, *Institutions, Institutional Change, and Economic Performance* (New York: Cambridge University Press, 1990); Joel Mokyr, *The Gifts of Athena: Historical Origins of the Knowledge Economy* (Princeton, NJ: Princeton University Press, 2002).

other actors with similar opportunities, they also face increasingly complicated constraints on their choices. Security competition, likewise, tends to ratchet up the complexity of weapons and military operations over time.[27] Battlefield networks and autonomous robotics that improve warfighting, from this perspective, are simply the most recent manifestations of a long-term aspiration for more sophisticated control in war. This complexity, moreover, is as much political as technological. Unfortunately, much of the discussion of CDD and associated challenges in cyberspace, space, or elsewhere tends to focus on the technological "cross-domain" problem rather than on the political "deterrence" problem. A sophisticated theory of CDD should be mindful of the particular historical circumstances of the policymakers and commanders who choose various technological means to advance their political ends as they understand them.

Almost every chapter in this book comments on the complexity of CDD. According to Lehman, "[deterrence], like disarmament, leans heavily on one big idea—fear should stimulate restraint. A credible approach to deterrence and arms restraint, however, requires attention to many ideas—different values, alternative priorities, conflicting interests, uneven strengths, unequal vulnerabilities, competing histories, diverse cultures, divergent norms, anomalous psychologies, asymmetrical strategies, and countervailing technologies. Geopolitical and technological changes continuously alter these factors." Lehman is cautiously optimistic that new strategic concepts and deeper understandings of the nuances of new technologies and actors can help policymakers deal with the protean nature of CDD: "[across] all domains, the United States should exploit more sophisticated technology, simulations, and gaming in support of analysis, training, planning, and evaluation of tactics, forces, weapons, networks, and systems."

Other authors question whether CDD strategies are even possible in the face of so much complexity and uncertainty. Morgan believes that "the United States and its friends and allies have apparently been experiencing sharp declines in results from deterrence efforts because they have either failed or achieved only limited success." The problem, according to Morgan, is that policymakers and analysts have overstretched the concept of deterrence to deal with too broad a range of provocations, too many crisis dynamics, and too many possible responses: "[the] concept and strategy of deterrence, originally and obviously meant to prevent attacks, now embraces a wide range of fighting, from real attacks involving extensive, perhaps very destructive, warfare to those primarily encompassing lesser threatening conflicts, some with no fighting at all." Morgan

---

[27] Langdon Winner, *Autonomous Technology: Technics-out-of-Control as a Theme in Political Thought* (Cambridge, MA: MIT Press, 1977); William H. McNeill, *The Pursuit of Power: Technology, Armed Force, and Society since A.D. 1000* (Chicago: University of Chicago Press, 1982); Allan Dafoe, "On Technological Determinism: A Typology, Scope Conditions, and a Mechanism," *Science, Technology, & Human Values* 40, no. 6 (2015): 1047–1076, https://doi.org/10.1177/0162243915579283.

observes that emerging complexities in practice have challenged established theoretical concepts, for example, "[we] have some experience in practice but no reliable theory on how to effectively manage an emerging shift from general to immediate deterrence, smoothly or safely and durably, and on then reorienting in the opposite direction.... [Thus] shifts from general to immediate deterrence situations can spring up almost instantly, as with 9/11. Moreover, the range and scale of possible attacks have been expanding." Morgan thus questions whether it is too ambitious a goal to develop an "analytically rigorous but not overly complex theory" about CDD.

Complexity makes it difficult to understand the nuances of domains and the implications of combining them. Just as important, complexity makes it difficult to credibly communicate threats and assurances about behavior in them (with allies and adversaries alike). Force is a blunt instrument, and the clever nuances of CDD signaling may be "too clever by half." Subtle signals may be lost in a militarized crisis where "the fog of war" might be pervasive. Communicative difficulties arise, firstly, because many cross-domain capabilities for warfighting and intelligence operations depend on secrecy, and secondly, because many actors lack shared understandings of what is appropriate or transgressive in each domain. Morrow notes that creating "common knowledge about when and how CDD will be used is a fundamental challenge for its effective implementation" and points out that the "complexity of the systems increases by the magnitude of the square of the number of domains in the system compared to deterrence solely within each domain separately."

When CDD emerged in U.S. defense policy discourse, the concept was more of a commentary on the complexity of the issue than a practical solution. It remains so to a substantial degree. Complexity is both a daunting theoretical challenge and a strong prima facie case for the utility of CDD. Nevertheless, understanding CDD may turn out to be more useful in theory than in practice. A theory of CDD might, for instance, explain why deterrence is so hard to reliably achieve in many real situations. It could also explain how apparent deterrence failures in some domains may actually result from deterrence successes in others, and how these relative successes and failures should be expected to evolve over time. For example, the prevalent low-intensity cyber aggression and "gray zone" warfare appear to be attempts to work around the implicit and explicit deterrence postures of militarily strong targets. Complexity is a formidable obstacle to understanding and employing CDD. Green and Long point out that "Clausewitzian conditions of fog and friction . . . are likely to become ubiquitous as cross-domain technological complexity increases." Nevertheless, success in conflict or influence (deterrence or compellence) is all about relative advantage. Green and Long also observe that the United States was relatively better at coping with the fog and friction of CDD than were the Soviets. Even a marginally better understanding of the coercive strengths and weaknesses of each domain can be practically useful.

Clandestine Capabilities Complicate but Do Not Preclude Signaling

Most authors point out that secrecy (or private information) is a big problem for CDD. While ambiguity and plausible deniability can sometimes aid coercion, especially where the target incurs audience costs for making concessions, private information also dilutes the signals that enable targets to discriminate resolved coercers from bluffers. Secrecy is especially salient in the space and cyber domains, as Bahney et al. and Schneider both emphasize, respectively. The problem, as Morgan observes, is that "deterrence requires that the necessary capabilities for retaliation and resistance not be overly hidden! A secret domain of combat or potent enhancements to it, so unfamiliar to the opponents that they have nothing comparable, may be fine for handicapping their next attack, but it does not help get them to avoid starting it." Morrow likewise notes that deterrence "through reciprocity requires a return address."

Green and Long sound a note of optimism here. They find that in the late Cold War, "The United States' behavior [was] consistent with an ability to signal clandestine military capabilities, at least in a limited manner. Washington used selective leaks, public propaganda, and military demonstrations to draw Russia's attention to the vulnerability of its C3, early warning, and SSBNs." The United States, without revealing its precise methods, was able to use military exercises to demonstrate a capability to penetrate Soviet defenses. The sudden appearance of a ship or a submarine in an area previously believed to be secure could highlight a change in the relative balance of power. Clandestine intelligence capabilities could be used to feed selective information to the adversary, while the adversary's own intelligence coups allowed access to credible information. The signal the United States intended to send, according to Green and Long, was that it had a viable counterforce deterrent against Soviet deterrence capabilities. Furthermore, they argue that Soviet leadership got the message, which frightened them. The Soviets reacted to the revelation through arms-racing, but adjustments to the information thus revealed were often slow, costly, and/or ineffective; "[the] Soviet Union's revitalized [early warning] programs were mostly failures."

Green and Long present alternative sets of "bad news" and "good news" claims about clandestine capabilities, power asymmetries, and the nuclear revolution drawn both from conventional wisdom about CDD complexity and from their own research on the late Cold War contest. The "bad news" expects secrecy to impair signaling, weaker actors to benefit from asymmetric cross-domain capabilities, and nuclear weapons to swamp the effects of other domains. The "good news" predicts that states will find ways to signal capabilities without revealing methods, stronger actors will become stronger through cross-domain innovation, and nuclear deterrence will be very sensitive to cross-domain developments. While Green and Long's chapter finds more evidence to support the latter scenario, further examination of other cases or phases of the Cold War might suggest that these alternative explanations actually depend on an additional set of technological or political factors. If so, then how one expects "good news" or "bad news" to obtain in a given situation will depend on whether it looks similar to or different from the U.S.-Soviet confrontation.

Future research, especially regarding cyber and space capabilities, should develop theory about what can be revealed and how fast or effectively different types of actors can react to the revelation. A standard shibboleth of the cyber literature is that vulnerabilities revealed are vulnerabilities lost. Yet in fact many penetrations actually rely on known vulnerabilities that the target has not bothered to close, either out of negligence or legitimate concerns about violating software certifications with new patches. Some vulnerabilities may be difficult to alter in a strategically meaningful timeline, for instance in modifying expensive deployed hardware rather than simple software settings. Furthermore, in a manner analogous to the long-term strategic competition in the Cold War, the revelation and loss of some vulnerabilities convey information about an actor's ability to generate and stockpile more. Thus, for example, Edward Snowden's unauthorized dissemination (leak) of documents from the National Security Agency provided credible evidence of the sophistication of U.S. cyber operations. While the public compromise of U.S. tradecraft undoubtedly resulted in the loss of particular technical sources and methods, the leaks were also suggestive of the expertise and will to find and employ other vulnerabilities not revealed. Indeed, the credibility of the Snowden signal was probably enhanced by the costliness of the revelation, a proposition that should be empirically tested once data on foreign perceptions become available.

Cross-Domain Deterrence Can Both Help and Hinder Assurance

The complexity of CDD is in part a matter of more, and more diverse, capabilities and in part a matter of more actors utilizing this growing number of tools in pursuit of power and influence. Such complexity has ambiguous consequences for communicating with allies and adversaries. Nacht et al. argue that the Stuxnet episode was not simply an interaction between two adversaries, the United States and Iran, but also, and perhaps more important, an interaction between two allies, the United States and Israel. The cyberattack "was an effort not to deter Iran from furthering its clandestine nuclear program but to deter Israel from launching what the United States viewed as a premature, preemptive strike on Iranian nuclear facilities, in order to allow diplomatic alternatives to succeed." In this case, CDD offered reassurance to, and restraint of, a key ally that might otherwise have unraveled U.S. policy. Nacht et al. find that "[leaders] want options and do not seek to be constrained by within-domain responses. Flexibility is a virtually universal aspiration before making decisions, even if responses are frequently within-domain."

Yet the increase in options in the name of flexibility can also undermine commitment. Mehta finds that CDD, "in the form of the nuclear triad, may not have been as effective at enhancing U.S. assurances to its allies" as the prior U.S. reliance on ground forces and infrastructure. While the United States was able to enjoy more autonomy as a result of its mobile and survivable forces, it also could settle disputes peacefully without satisfying the ally. Modern CDD might be even more problematic in this regard because it not only offers U.S. policymakers more options but also calls the effectiveness of U.S. forces dependent on space and cyberspace into question. As Mehta argues, "analogy of the diversification of the nuclear triad might seem to suggest that diversified cross-domain capabilities might allow for more efficient and less costly power projection while still creating uncertainty among allies about the credibility of the assurance; however, the inherent vulnerabilities of a multidomain security umbrella may actually pose a challenge to the United States' ability to effectively deter interstate conflict for its protégés."

Deterrence requires assurance of opponents, not only allies, about the consequences of violations of declaratory policy and of compliance. Morrow explains how "shared understanding makes deterrence possible." International law is one important source of information in this regard, where, counterintuitively, "ratification of a treaty is not the meaningful signal; nonratification is. When a state chooses to stay out of a treaty, it signals its intent to violate the standards of the treaty." Law can be considered to be a nonmilitary domain that complements the exercise of force in other domains: "[law] works together with capabilities to make deterrence work; it is not a substitute for deterrence.... Because reciprocal responses are often the same acts as violations, this shared understanding of when these acts are legal and acceptable responses, as opposed to violations, is necessary to avoid retaliatory spirals." The purpose of international law is not (or not always) to outlaw force; on the contrary, it sanctions its use under particular conditions.

Yet for some emerging domains, the presence of the law is most felt through its absence, particularly in those, like cyberspace, that enable new deceptive tradecraft. As Morrow explains, "[intelligence] collection and counterintelligence have been areas of interstate competition where states have engaged in and tolerated acts that they would not accept outside those areas, such as espionage, kidnapping, blackmail, and the killing of operatives, provided that only those involved in intelligence activities are the targets of such acts." States have been casting about for new norms in space and cyberspace for over a decade, but new, commonly accepted standards of behavior have been slow to emerge. There does exist an international convention on cybercrime and, recently, an agreement to restrict economic, but not national security, espionage. These have emerged slowly as states have probed the bounds of what is and is not acceptable in cyberspace. Morrow points out that any technological innovation has the potential to disrupt established common knowledge arrangements: "[dramatic] changes could enable one to attack new targets, penetrate defenses that were invulnerable before, or improve the efficacy of attacks on targets that are known to be vulnerable. Any of these changes raise the possibility of a surprise attack using behavior that falls outside the range of whatever behavior is agreed to be acceptable but not within the range of those agreed to be unacceptable. Such an attack would likely provoke a retaliatory response and the possibility of an escalatory spiral, exactly what a shared understanding over acceptable conduct is designed to prevent."

When novel technological and political developments alter participants' bargaining power, beneficiaries may be tempted to renegotiate, while others may try to resist change they take to be disadvantageous. Disagreements about the effects of change can lead to war or to escalation within war. The disruptive technologies of CDD, which differentially affect various capabilities, linkages, and actors, thus have the potential to precipitate bargaining failures. Alternatively, as the examples from Nacht et al. illustrate, these new disruptive technologies can expand the options available to actors to avoid bargaining failure. The case of Stuxnet shows that both of these dynamics can occur simultaneously: Iran did not deter use of cyber warfare because it did not know a cyberattack was even a possibility, yet the U.S. avoided conventional warfare with Iran by using cyber operations to reassure Israel and buy time for diplomatic negotiations.

Complexity Can Be Both Stabilizing and Destabilizing

A basic question underlying these efforts is whether CDD—and sociotechnical complexity more generally—is fundamentally stabilizing or destabilizing. Many people are convinced of the latter. Emerging technologies seem, by many accounts, to advantage opportunistic attackers, weaker actors, and important or rising challenges to the status quo. Interdependent infrastructures create grave vulnerabilities for all, especially the strongest and wealthiest states. The growing number of potential threats from ever more state and nonstate actors complicates the choice of strategy.

However, the opposite dynamic can also take place. Many asymmetric capabilities, often thought to advantage revisionists, are often used to reinforce the status quo. As Green and Long conclude in their chapter, "David can have his slingshot, but in a cross-domain world, it is good to be Goliath." Global economic interdependence, the signature form of complexity since the industrial era, is generally thought to be pacifying. More and more actors gain a stake in commercial and social transactions within the established norms of the liberal international order, increasing the opportunity costs and reducing the relative benefits of wars of conquest. This perspective undergirds the optimism about East Asian international relations expressed by Huang and Kang. Improved theory and policy perspectives should aim to resolve or at least clarify the direction of these controversies.

While strategic stability is usually equated with peace, Rovner cautions that stable CDD in a war can also result in protracted conflict. Rovner reviews both the deterrence failures that preceded the Peloponnesian War and the deterrence successes that prolonged it, arguing that "[tactical] retreat became the default position when operating on the other's domain." As Rovner explains, "[because] neither side was willing to challenge the other on its favored domain, however, a decisive battlefield victory became impossible. Athens repeatedly tried to lure Sparta into fleet-on-fleet engagements, and Sparta repeatedly tried to bait Athens into pitched battle. Both were frustrated. Cross-domain asymmetries deterred each side from attacking the other's center of gravity, that is, neither could engineer the kind of confrontation that might have forced the other to capitulate." Rovner's insights about the stalemating potential of CDD are ripe for testing in other historical conflicts. They have particularly troubling implications for future conflict between the United States (a sea power) and China (a land power).[28]

CDD may even provide a useful way for policymakers to manage the uncertainty that emerges with changed circumstances. As Morgan observes, "[even] the government or its leaders often do not know exactly what they will do until getting very close to doing it." The expansion of domains of interaction expands the sources of information available as bargaining actors probe and react to one another. As Shifrinson explains: "[as] U.S. policymakers realized in 1989–1990, uncertainty over where Soviet redlines fell compounded U.S. deterrence problems and made linkage politics attractive—cross-domain action allowed the United States to test the waters with the Soviet Union while interests clarified. This suggests an underappreciated feature of CDD: cross-domain actions, applied in circumstances where interests are ambiguous, can let actors probe intentions, assess sensitivities, and adjudicate the risk of further escalation." Shifrinson starts with the idea that CDD is a relationship between a portfolio of means *and* ends and deduces different consequences for changes on either side of this relationship. Means-based change, the acquisition or loss of particular tools of statecraft, may give rise to arms-racing and windows of vulnerability and opportunity, which in turn raise the risks of spirals of uncertainty and preventative motivations for conflict. Interest-based change, by contrast, which is the emergence of new strategic interests or a deemphasis on old ones, can create uncertainty about how to prioritize interests and how to repurpose potentially ill-suited means to the task; this in turn raises the risks of miscalculation about power and interests. Shifrinson's case studies of U.S.-Soviet relations in Eastern Europe in 1989 suggest that shrewd leadership and careful repurposing of national instruments of influence, both as tacit threats and overt inducements, can be used to mitigate the risks of sudden interest-based change. Thus, he writes, "the George H. W. Bush administration was the first since the early Cold War to make limiting or undoing Soviet influence a

---

[28] See also: Joshua Rovner, "Two Kinds of Catastrophe: Nuclear Escalation and Protracted War in Asia," *Journal of Strategic Studies* 40, no. 5 (2017): 696–730, https://doi.org/10.1080/01402390.2017.1293532.

cornerstone of the United States' efforts." The administration did this by leveraging "a web of Soviet-U.S. interactions outside the military realm [that] would help keep Soviet military action in check." He suggests that "linkage politics might be as (or more) relevant to coercive and deterrent relationships not when new means are coming online but when old means are repackaged for new ends." Cross-domain linkage is a rich area for further exploration and presents a number of analytical challenges for utility-maximizing bargaining models that assume that preferences and interests are exogenously fixed.

Shifting domains can open up options. As discussed above, this has ambiguous implications for credible communication. Shifting domains also has ambiguous implications for escalation. A threat that is not credible, because the actor making the threat has options available to avoid executing the threat, can lead to deterrence failure. Yet additional options may also enable an actor to control escalation, particularly in cases of coercion that also feature counter-coercion by the adversary. In the Cuban Missile Crisis, the Soviet Union tried to compel by fait accompli the United States to accept a change in the nuclear balance of power. In response, the United States tried to compel the Soviet Union to remove its missiles. Nacht et al. point out that "[the] naval quarantine (with the threat of subsequent air strikes and land invasion) alternative was chosen specifically because it was a clear military response that kept two alternatives open: that of military escalation to remove the missiles by force if the Soviets did not retreat, as well as that of deescalation to avoid fracturing of NATO should Khrushchev seize Berlin." Thus, CDD expanded the palette of options available to Kennedy to press U.S. interests without triggering Soviet retaliation. In the case of Stuxnet, similarly, the Bush administration opted for a cross-domain response to the threat of Iranian nuclearization in order to advance U.S. interests without prompting escalation. As Nacht et al. explain, "[the] main constraint was not to risk actions that would provoke an escalation leading to widespread armed conflict." Moreover, as mentioned, the option selected in this case was chosen precisely because it was *not* observable to the adversary but *was* observable to an ally: "Use of cyber offensive operations had different objectives from those of the employment of nuclear threats in the Cold War cases: to *delay* progress of the program rather than to compel its closure, and to engage Israel's participation in order to *reassure* Jerusalem of the seriousness of U.S. intent and thus obviate the need for an Israeli air strike on the Iranian facilities." A pressing research problem in studying CDD is to determine the conditions under which an expansion of domains in a conflict helps to limit escalation rather than increase the risks of miscalculation, and further military violence. Lehman introduces the intriguing notion of "escalation geometries"; these might range from single point thresholds (i.e., from conventional to nuclear war) to linear movement up the traditional "escalation ladder" of increasing conflict severity and to planar movement across an "escalation matrix" of options in different domains of different intensity, and so on with the additional dimensions of time, number of actors, and so on. Future research might further refine and leverage his descriptive concepts as independent or dependent variables in studying the dynamics of cross-domain crisis escalation.

The Stability-Instability Paradox in Cross-Domain Deterrence

We believe that these ambiguous implications are likely to be fundamental to the phenomena of CDD. That is, ambiguity is not probably not just a result of an incomplete understanding of CDD but an intentional result of strategic action by political actors seeking out new ways and means to gain bargaining leverage. As a result of the different bargaining characteristics of domains available to actors in different contexts, we should not expect a uniform distribution of conflict interaction. Above all, CDD is about expanding and limiting policy options. As a result, successful deterrence in one area limits options available to a would-be revisionist, but the commitment of the would-be defender to deterrence also limits options. Both sides then have incentives to seek more options for working around or bolstering deterrence, for pursuing political aims in new ways, and for countering the dynamics of provocation and escalation.

Put simply, deterrence success in one domain can lead to deterrence failure in another. Several authors find that the "stability-instability paradox" pioneered by Cold War deterrence theorists seems to be relevant for contemporary CDD.[29] In its original formulation, the stability-instability paradox tells a story about where contests will occur, not whether. Nuclear weapons provide a credible deterrent against nuclear war, but nuclear threats are not credible when used against lesser provocations, such as limited conventional conflict or unconventional proxy war. The costs of exercising the ultimate deterrent are simply too great for the limited stakes involved in minor conflicts. Yet this also makes minor conflicts below the nuclear threshold especially appealing for coercion and incremental conquest. The risk that major contests escalate to nuclear use implies that the threat of major war is remote when using lesser forms of political violence.

Rovner sees the stability-instability paradox at work in the Peloponnesian War: "[in] this case, the existence of cross-domain stability, which was revealed after prewar illusions were destroyed, taught Athens and Sparta that they could safely continue the fight as long as they took few risks." The problem in such an environment, as perhaps exists with endemic cyber espionage campaigns, is that antagonists may suffer "death by a thousand cuts" even as they avoid a knockout blow. Limited war in the Peloponnese "went on for nearly three decades, and the accumulated costs broke them both." Bahney et al. also see the stability-instability paradox at

---

[29] Glenn H. Snyder, "The Balance of Power and the Balance of Terror," in *The Balance of Power*, edited by Paul Seabury (San Francisco: Chandler, 1965); Robert Jervis, *The Meaning of the Nuclear Revolution: Statecraft and the Prospect of Armageddon* (Ithaca, NY: Cornell University Press, 1989).

work in space: "future ASAT threats are likely to be perceived as consistent with limited war constructs rather than as precursors to nuclear escalation. The ability to conduct limited and discrete strikes against an adversary's space systems without risking massive retaliation may make these strikes more likely." Greenhill identifies the paradox as a permissive enabler of coercive migrations: "CEM may create a bastardized kind of stability-instability paradox, whereby certain coercers may be more willing to use this tool because they know that targets will be reluctant to escalate to war in response." The stability-instability paradox appears to be especially relevant in cyberspace, which provides many new options for deceptive influence and exploitation for actors who wish to work around the deterrence posture of stronger targets by manipulating the cooperative protocols that enable mutually beneficial exchange.[30]

Morrow generalizes the stability-instability logic, beginning with the classic case: "[in] nuclear deterrence, all eventually accepted that nuclear retaliation was appropriate in response to a nuclear attack or conventional attack on the homeland but not for military actions against client states in the developing world." He then points out that any common knowledge regime implicitly creates an arena of low-intensity probes and provocations: "the deterring party may obscure the exact triggers in an effort to deter violations it could tolerate but would like to discourage. The other side might test those limits when they are unclear." This gives rise to the contemporary problem of "gray zone conflict" between peace and war, exemplified by Russian "little green men" in Ukraine and Chinese "little blue men" in the South China Sea (i.e., nonmilitary coast guard and civilian vessels performing state-sanctioned missions): "[those] in the gray area face probabilistic deterrence; parties engaged in these acts would then run a risk of some response but not the certainty of one." Thus "violations in the gray area are likely to occur, because a violating party suspects that there may be no response to such a violation."

Future Prospects

The ability to manage complexity has become critical in all aspects of modern life. Military affairs is no exception and may even be exemplary in this respect. Combined arms warfare is a form of operational complexity management, integrating different branches of the army into a coordinated fighting force. Joint Force operations extends this concept further with the integration of forces from all services, as

---

[30] Jon R. Lindsay and Erik Gartzke, "Coercion through Cyberspace: The Stability-Instability Paradox Revisited," in *Coercion: The Power to Hurt in International Politics*, edited by Kelly M. Greenhill and Peter Krause (New York: Oxford University Press, 2018), 179–203; Jon R. Lindsay, "Restrained by Design: The Political Economy of Cybersecurity," *Digital Policy, Regulation and Governance* 19, no. 6 (2017): 493–514, https://doi.org/10.1108/DPRG-05-2017-0023.

well as capabilities from the civilian intelligence community or other government agencies. The production of sophisticated weapons in the Joint Force "system of systems" relies on practices of engineering systems integration, a complementary form of complexity management focusing on coordinating different defense contractors and scientific disciplines. Each of these different complexity-management practices work together to field the panoply of weapons and organizations that enable the United States to realize, and China or Russia to contest, "command of the commons." This brings us back to the problem with which CDD began, namely whether U.S. cross-domain prowess is being undermined by developments in space, cyberspace, and other arenas by actors like China and Russia, and whether other U.S. advantages might be brought to bear to compensate.

One way to think about CDD is by analogy to the problem of combined arms warfare, but applied to the level of foreign policy or grand strategy. Mastering combined arms operations often produced winners in combat on twentieth-century battlefields and enabled the United States to wield an effective form of dominance as military hegemon.[31] In the same way, making sense of the different political properties of different coercive instruments and their combinations may enable some actors to exercise increased influence in the future by restoring the credibility of deterrence and assurance policies that have been undermined by the combination of political will and technological innovation. While difficult to anticipate in detail, technological changes will continue to create new threats in the future. Instead of reacting piecemeal to each new threat or capability, a strategic policy designed explicitly to address the problem of the ongoing rise in sociotechnical complexity would make it easier to accommodate, even anticipate, novel threats.

Policy Implications

The chapters in this book draw some conclusions of tentative policy relevance, all qualified by calls for future research. Schneider asks policymakers to consider whether the uncertainty of the cyber domain is a fixed fact or whether can it be manipulated through technological interventions or declaratory policy. If uncertainty is absolute, then states will have to settle for, or embrace, ambiguous deterrent policies. If instead uncertainty can be reduced or managed, for instance by means of new electromagnetic incursion technologies that are not as sensitive to revelation as many existing software weapons, then states can adopt more explicit declaratory policies.

---

[31] Biddle, *Military Power*; Ryan Grauer and Michael C. Horowitz, "What Determines Military Victory? Testing the Modern System," *Security Studies* 21, no. 1 (January 1, 2012): 83–112, https://doi.org/10.1080/09636412.2012.650594.

Morrow proposes an interesting application from his work on the common knowledge requirements of deterrence and the difficulty of meeting them, given the complexity of CDD:

> [because] CDD seeks to link conduct across domains together, the demands of the system increase as the square of the number of domains, as noted. One way to reduce this complexity would be to designate one domain as the domain of retaliation. Standards of conduct could be set in the other domains, with the understanding that the responses to violations would all occur in the domain of retaliation, reducing the complexity of the resulting agreement. Conventional kinetic responses are one obvious domain for retaliation. But proportionality rears its head here. Is a kinetic attack appropriate after violations that do not kill people or destroy property? A second obvious domain for retaliation would be economic sanctions. This possibility confronts the concern that economic sanctions might not be a strong enough sanction to deter the worst breaches of agreed conduct. Designating a domain of retaliation simplifies the complexity of the understanding needed to support a system of CDD, but the obvious candidate domains of retaliation might not be sufficient to create effective deterrence.

Indeed, economic sanctioning appears to be the go-to choice for retaliation by the United States in cybersecurity. Targeted sanctions have been applied in response to Chinese economic espionage, North Korean blackmail in the case of Sony, and Russian electoral interference. Perhaps precisely because of the ineffectiveness of low-cost sanctions that Morrow mentions, a number of NATO nations recently opted to expel Russian intelligence personnel and diplomats in retaliation for the alleged Russian poisoning of a double agent in Britain.

It is unsurprising that the conversation about appropriate responses to CDD provocation (bearing in mind that strategic and normative appropriateness may not be the same) recurs with each new act of aggression. The recurrence of similar problems may reflect the incentives an attacker has to expand options and take new actions that are not clearly covered by explicit or tacit existing deterrents. Morrow recommends in response: "[the] parties will need to revise their understanding of where the lines between acceptable and unacceptable conduct will be, along with what responses are appropriate." Unfortunately, this is in many ways a restatement of the problem of CDD rather than the solution. Indeed, governments that seek effective deterrence policies may ultimately have to make peace with the stability-instability paradox: "[the] employment of CDD entails an acceptance that under a system of CDD, low-level violations will occur and some retaliatory responses will happen."

Shifrinson raises an especially cogent policy implication of CDD, namely the importance of slowing down and leveraging the inherent complexity of CDD to generate information rather than rushing in with a half-formed understanding of the situation. This may be especially critical when one's own priorities and values are not yet fully fleshed out. As Shifrinson explains, "[as] interests change, proceeding judiciously helps policymakers ensure that the effort to extend deterrence to new interests is actually a game worth playing. Equally important, playing for time enables policymakers to more carefully define the objective they are trying to secure and to more carefully link means—which might be poorly structured to secure this interest—to the interest at hand." Rovner seems to agree with Shifrinson's admonition. If Athens and Sparta had taken the time to appreciate the stability of the ancient cross-domain balance, perhaps they would not have rushed into war: "counterintuitively, speed may not always be of the essence," Rovner writes. A pressing question is whether states relying on CDD can afford the luxury of waiting to make the second move, thereby allowing competitors to clarify their true interests.

The uncertainty of CDD can be very dangerous if both sides perceive there to be first-strike advantages, a situation that Bahney et al. argue is now manifesting in the space domain. It is particularly troubling that both the U.S. military and the Chinese People's Liberation Army appear to see just such advantages in the cyber and space domains. If strategic stability is the goal, then reducing uncertainty about the true balance of power should be a top priority. In the Peloponnesian War, both sides rushed into a war because they misunderstood key characteristics of the cross-domain balance, which was actually quite stable. Rovner posits that "the balance of capabilities in a crisis may not be sufficient for CDD to hold without explicit threats." Even with only two domains to contend with in ancient Greece, the level of uncertainty about their status and interaction undermined deterrence. The situation today is far more challenging in this respect, with at least five military domains and many other arenas of influence that can interact and combine. As Rovner points out, "the cross-domain balance may be relatively complex, especially as more domains come into play, and clever or delusional strategists may become convinced that they can change it without having to fully upend the overall balance. Leaders are likely to indulge in wishful thinking under these conditions. Threats in one domain may not be persuasive to a rival who is dominant in another, especially if the target believes that there are plausible ways to work around its own disadvantages. A failure to send clear deterrent signals that reinforce CDD may compound the problem." It is thus essential, if stable deterrence is the goal, to clarify the cross-domain balance of power to avoid disappointments from the first battles and protracted tragedies due to subsequent ones.

Huang and Kang, finally, question the very assumption of inevitable conflict between China and the United States, or between China and any other country in the Pacific region. They point out that the way this book has tackled the problem of CDD, namely as a complex military-strategic issue, may be overly simplistic: "deterrence theory is particularly concerned about the issuance of threats and punishments to induce change in an adversary's behavior. This generally assumes high-level conflict as a constant feature in international politics, and it underemphasizes the importance of rewards and compromises as effective alternatives to threats." Huang and Kang are struck by the absence of balancing against China, the depressed rates of arms-racing, and increasing economic integration in the region. Therefore, they recommend broadening the aperture of grand strategic thinking so as not to privilege military affairs: "the emphasis behind an effective cross-domain deterrence strategy should extend beyond different military modalities to include the full range of statecraft, such as diplomacy, political dialogue, trade, soft power, and cultural influence."

Research Potential

A theory of CDD has to navigate the combinatoric complexity of more kinds of capabilities in different domains, more linkages across domains and capabilities, and more actors with different access to capabilities. Complexity is the very problem that gives rise to CDD. Future research on CDD should break down and make sense of this complexity. Whereas traditional deterrence theory focuses on bilateral bargaining with nuclear threats, a theory of CDD will have to systematically relax classical assumptions. First, it should increase the range of available capabilities to make symmetric or asymmetric moves possible in the bargaining process. Second, it should increase the linkages between these capabilities, to include interdependence in their production and exchange, interconnection through shared infrastructure, and the combination of capabilities in a portfolio of options. Third, it should increase the number and types of actors so as to consider different networks of strategic relationships, to include a greater density of agents, more complicated balancing, alliance, and extended deterrence commitments, and challenges posed by principal-agency and other contracting relationships. Questions about capabilities, linkages, and actors are hardly new and, in many ways, are the conceptual core of political science. What is new is the integration of each concept and accompanying knowledge into a common scientific research program for CDD.

It is possible to summarize a number of the research questions identified in this book by distinguishing between problems at the technical or operational level of analysis and problems at the political or strategic level of analysis (see table 15.2). The former category considers problems of sociotechnical possibility; how does a given domain work? The latter considers problems of bargaining utility and strategic interaction; why is that domain useful for political or economic advantage? This framing attends to the interesting structural characteristics or attributes of each domain yet also avoids the pitfalls of technological determinism by emphasizing the political nature of interests and strategies. As with classical deterrence, we believe that any theory of CDD should link the technical ability to harm with the political utility of exercising an available form of aggression.

Table 15.2 **Research Questions by Attributes of Complexity and Levels of Analysis**

	Operational questions	*Strategic questions*
Capabilities	• What are the important characteristics of emerging threat technologies? • What are their resource and human capital requirements for design and use? • Does the diffusion of capabilities harmonize or separate actors?	• How do bargaining dynamics differ among various combinations of strong and weak actors? • How does crisis stability and instability vary with mixes of capabilities? • Are asymmetric capabilities escalatory or deescalatory?
Linkages	• What types of interdependencies create vulnerabilities or resilience? • Are resources fungible across domains (political, military, economic)? • Are interdependent systems fragile or resilient?	• How does interdependence promote or shift advantages of offense relative to defense? • Does interdependence create incentives to move first or show restraint? • How do actors shift their advantages across interdependent domains?
Actors	• Which actors have the doctrine and ability to exploit which asymmetries and interdependencies? • What stakeholder coordination challenges exist in cross-domain operations (public-private, domestic-international)? • How do competitors work by, with, and through third parties, and what principal-agent problems and solutions emerge?	• How effective are alliance and wedge strategies in a cross-domain world? • How do multipolar cross-domain interactions affect the frequency and intensity of war? • Where and when in a complex political geography should we expect cross-domain conflict to escalate, even to nuclear war?

Research into CDD should aim to develop analytically rigorous theory to answer these questions and to continue the process of empirical and computational evaluation. Systematic investigation could progressively increase the complexity of analysis by multiplying the capabilities available, the types of relationships connecting actors, and the number of actors engaged. Yet beyond a few actors and relationships, interactions become too complex and convoluted to deal with analytically. Indeed, one would not want to produce overly complex theory, particularly given that the complexity of subjects and relationships already constitutes an important problem for CDD. The object of theory, after all, is to clarify and make practical the application of key insights. At the same time, complexity implies an even greater need for careful empirical assessment to ensure that theory is externally valid and to assess the potency of predictions.

The human-built world and conflict within it is steadily growing more complex. Cross-domain deterrence is becoming more relevant in global politics. Because of increasing means for coercion and the uncertainty that the resulting complexity creates, the lack of a clear conceptual understanding of CDD limits the coherence of contemporary articulations of national security strategy. It is easier to fund technology for offense or defense than to understand incentives or even strategy. Yet the clear articulation of theory becomes critical for military performance and political success as the complexity of new technologies makes their strategic implications ever harder to comprehend. China's rise makes CDD particularly salient, but CDD also matters for relations with Russia, Iran, North Korea, and NATO, to say nothing of other states and nongovernmental organizations. If CDD is becoming harder to manage, the potential advantages of getting it right are growing, too.

CONTRIBUTOR BIOGRAPHIES

Editors

Erik Gartzke is Professor of Political Science and Director of the Center for Peace and Security Studies at the University of California, San Diego, where he has been a member of the research faculty since 2007. Professor Gartzke's research appears in leading academic journals, including the *American Political Science Review, American Journal of Political Science, British Journal of Political Science, International Organization, International Security, International Studies Quarterly, Journal of Conflict Resolution, Journal of Politics, Security Studies, World Politics*, and elsewhere.

Jon R. Lindsay is Assistant Professor at the Munk School of Global Affairs and Public Policy and the Department of Political Science at the University of Toronto. His publications include *China and Cybersecurity: Espionage, Strategy, and Politics in the Digital Domain* (Oxford University Press, 2015), with Tai Ming Cheung and Derek Reveron. He holds a PhD in Political Science from the Massachusetts Institute of Technology and an MS in Computer Science and BS in Symbolic Systems from Stanford University. He has served in the U.S. Navy with operational assignments in Europe, Latin America, and the Middle East.

Authors

Benjamin W. Bahney is a political scientist at Lawrence Livermore National Laboratory and a Senior Fellow at the Center for Global Security Research. His research focuses on how the new domains of space and cyber affect strategic stability, deterrence, and escalation management. Bahney has contributed to the opinion pages of the *New York Times, Foreign Policy* and *Foreign Affairs Magazine*. He was formerly an Analyst at the RAND Corporation and received an MA in International Affairs from University of California, San Diego.

Brendan Rittenhouse Green is Assistant Professor of Political Science at the University of Cincinnati.

Kelly M. Greenhill is Associate Professor at Tufts University and Research Fellow at Harvard University's Kennedy School. Greenhill is author of *Weapons of Mass Migration: Forced Displacement, Coercion and Foreign Policy*, winner of the 2011 International Studies Association's Best Book of the Year Award. She is coauthor and coeditor of *Coercion: The Power to Hurt in International Politics*; *Sex, Drugs and Body Counts: The Politics of Numbers in Global Crime and Conflict*; and *The Use of Force: Military Power and International Politics* (8th ed.). Greenhill has served as an analyst for the Department of Defense.

Phil Haun is Professor and Dean of Academics at the U.S. Naval War College. He is author of *Coercion, Survival and War: Why Weak States Resist the United States* (Stanford University Press, 2015) and *A-10s over Kosovo*, (Air University Press, 2003). His next book, *The Book of ACTS: The Lectures of the Air Corps Tactical School and American Strategic Bombing in World War II*, is forthcoming from the University Press of Kentucky.

Chin-Hao Huang is Assistant Professor of Political Science at Yale-NUS College. His research focuses on international relations of East Asia. He is the recipient of the American Political Science Association Foreign Policy Section Best Paper Award for his research on China's compliance behavior in multilateral security institutions. He was previously a researcher at the Stockholm International Peace Research Institute and the Center for Strategic and International Studies. He received his PhD in Political Science from the University of Southern California and BS (Hons) from Georgetown University.

David C. Kang is Professor of International Relations and Business, Director of USC Korean Studies Institute, and Director of USC Center for International Studies at the University of Southern California. Kang's latest book is *American Grand Strategy and East Asian Security in the 21st Century* (Cambridge University Press, 2017).

Ron Lehman chairs the Department of Defense Threat Reduction Advisory Committee and the Board of the International Science and Technology Center and is the Counselor at Lawrence Livermore National Laboratory. Lehman was Director of the U.S. Arms Control and Disarmament Agency, Assistant Secretary of Defense (International Security Policy), Ambassador and Chief Negotiator for START I, and Deputy Assistant to the President for National Security Affairs, and served on the Staff of the Senate Armed Services Committee and with the U.S. Army in Vietnam. Lehman was Postdoctoral Fellow at the Hoover Institution at Stanford University and Adjunct Professor at Georgetown University.

Austin G. Long is a Senior Political Scientist at the RAND Corporation. He was an analyst and adviser to the U.S. military in Iraq (2007–8) and Afghanistan (2011 and 2013). In 2014–15, Long was a Council on Foreign Relations International Affairs Fellow in Nuclear Security, serving in the Joint Staff J5 (Strategic Plans and Policy) Strategic Deterrence and Nuclear Policy Division. Long received a BS from the Sam Nunn School of International Affairs at the Georgia Institute of Technology and his PhD in Political Science from the Massachusetts Institute of Technology.

Michael Markey is a Political Scientist at Lawrence Livermore National Laboratory. He previously worked for several years in the U.S. government studying national security issues, with an emphasis on arms control monitoring. Markey's current research interests include extended deterrence and strategic stability with an emphasis on emerging domains of competition. Markey holds an MA in International Affairs from the University of California, San Diego.

Rupal N. Mehta is Assistant Professor in the Department of Political Science at the University of Nebraska-Lincoln. Previously, Mehta was Stanton Nuclear Security Postdoctoral Fellow in the Belfer Center's International Security Program and Project on Managing the Atom. Mehta's book, *The Politics of Nuclear Reversal*, explores conditions under which states that have started nuclear weapons programs stop their pursuit. Her work has appeared in the *Journal of Conflict Resolution*, *International Studies Quarterly*, and *Washington Quarterly*. Mehta received a PhD and MA in Political Science from the University of California, San Diego.

James D. Morrow is A. F. K. Organski Collegiate Professor of World Politics and Research Professor at the Center for Political Studies at the University of Michigan. He is the author of *Order within Anarchy*, *Game Theory for Political Scientists*, coauthor of *The Logic of Political Survival*, and author of over thirty articles in refereed journals and another thirty other publications. Morrow is a member of the American Academy of Arts and Sciences. He received the Karl Deutsch Award from the International Studies Association in 1994. He was President of the Peace Science Society in 2008–9.

Patrick M. Morgan is Professor Emeritus with the Political Science Department at the University of California, Irvine. He has published a number of books and many articles, primarily dealing with American foreign policy, national security affairs, and international politics. He has been an occasional consultant with RAND, Sandia Labs, the U.S. State Department, and the U.S. Air Force. He is a board member and recording secretary for the Council on U.S.-Korean Security Studies annual conference. He has held several Fulbright fellowships and two fellowships at the Woodrow Wilson Center.

Michael Nacht is Thomas and Alison Schneider Professor of Public Policy at the University of California, Berkeley. He served as Dean of the University's Goldman School of Public Policy (1998–2008). His most recent book is *Strategic Latency: Red,*

White, and Blue; Managing the National and International Security Consequences of Disruptive Technologies (Lawrence Livermore National Laboratory, 2018). His articles have appeared in *Foreign Affairs, Foreign Policy, International Organization, Daedalus, International Security,* and *Survival.* He has twice held U.S. Senate–confirmed positions, including Assistant Secretary of Defense for Global Strategic Affairs (2009–10), for which he received the Distinguished Public Service Medal.

Jonathan Pearl is a Senior Fellow at the Center for Global Security Research at Lawrence Livermore National Laboratory. His work examines the impact of space, nuclear, and advanced technologies on strategic stability and deterrence. He has previously held appointments as a Stanton Nuclear Security Fellow at the Council on Foreign Relations, as a Jennings Randolph Peace Scholar at the United States Institute of Peace, as an Adjunct Researcher and Summer Associate at the RAND Corporation, and as a Foreign Policy Advisor to former Senator Christopher J. Dodd. He holds a PhD and MA in Government and Politics from the University of Maryland.

Joshua Rovner is Associate Professor at the School of International Service at American University. He is the author of *Fixing the Facts: National Security and the Politics of Intelligence* (Cornell University Press, 2011) and coeditor of *Chaos in the Liberal Order: The Trump Presidency and International Politics in the 21st Century* (Columbia University Press, 2018).

Jacquelyn G. Schneider is Assistant Professor at the U.S. Naval War College. Her research focuses on the intersection of technology, national security, and political psychology with a special interest in cyber, unmanned technologies, and Northeast Asia. Her work has appeared in the *Journal of Conflict Resolution* and *Strategic Studies Quarterly* and online in publications that include *Foreign Affairs, War on the Rocks,* and the *Washington Post.* Schneider spent six years as a U.S. Air Force officer and is currently a reservist assigned to U.S. Cyber Command.

Patricia Schuster is a President's Postdoctoral Fellow at the University of Michigan in the Nuclear Engineering and Radiological Sciences Department and the recipient of a Glenn F. Knoll Postdoctoral Education Grant. Her research focuses on advanced scintillator radiation detector materials for applications in nuclear science, security, safeguards, and nonproliferation. Schuster earned a PhD in nuclear engineering at the University of California, Berkeley, during which time she pursued her dissertation research at Sandia National Laboratories and studied nuclear security policy as an affiliate of the Nuclear Science and Security Consortium.

Joshua R. Itzkowitz Shifrinson is Assistant Professor of International Relations at Boston University's Pardee School of Global Studies, where his work focuses on U.S. foreign policy, grand strategy, diplomatic history, and international relations theory. His first book, *Rising Titans, Falling Giants: Rising States and the Fate of Declining Great Powers,* was recently published by Cornell University Press and examines why some rising states variously prey on or support declining great powers. His other projects investigate how and why states are able to cultivate and maintain spheres of influence, as well as alliance relations in the nuclear age.

Eva C. Uribe is a Postdoctoral Scholar at the Center for International Security and Cooperation at Stanford University. Her current research focuses on proliferation concerns associated with the thorium fuel cycle. Eva has a PhD in Chemistry from the University of California, Berkeley, where she was affiliated with the Lawrence Livermore National Laboratory and the Nuclear Science and Security Consortium. Her dissertation research investigated the interaction between organically modified silica and aqueous actinide and lanthanide species using solid-state nuclear magnetic resonance spectroscopy. She has also held internships with the Nonproliferaton Division at Los Alamos National Laboratory.

INDEX

Page numbers followed by *t* indicate tables.

Afghanistan
   air-to-ground operations in, 148
   coercively engineered migration, 266*t*
   defeat of Taliban in, 160
   limited Western deterrence results in, 55
   limited Western successes in, 55
   US. combat operations in, 4, 28, 63, 64, 69, 79
   U.S. military commitments in, 28
Africa
   coercively engineered migration, 266*t*
   limited Western deterrence results in, 55
   UN Security Council Summit, 72
   U.S. efforts at deterrence with, 53
agent provocateurs, uses of coercively engineered migration, 263
air domain, 3. *See also* air power
   cyber domain integration with, 66–67, 98–99
   fragility of chokepoints in, 11–12
   ISR systems' impact on, 142
   space operations in, 66–67
Air Force Space Command (U.S.), 68–69
Air Force (U.S.)
   establishment of cyber warfare command, 6–7
   Occasional Paper, 237–38
   psy-ops exercises, 216
   strategic bombing doctrine, 6–7
   U.S. Joint Force role, 5
air forces
   air-to-air engagements, 146
   asymmetric advantages, 144–45
   deterrence failures against defensive forces, 160
   deterrence of ground forces by, 144–45
   deterring armies on the defense, 158
      Hussein's defense of Iraq, 159
      Normandy invasion/Rommel vs. Rundstedt debate, 145–46, 155, 158–59, 160
   deterring enemy ground offensives
      Battle of Britain, 145–46, 153, 155, 158, 161
      commando hunt and Easter Offensive, 153–55
      Tet Offensive, 153–55
   factors in deterrence capabilities, 18–19, 146–49
   failures at deterring war, 155
      Battle of the Bulge, 137–56, 157–58
      fall of Quang Tri, 156–57
   strategic bombing doctrine, 6–7
   surface-to-air threats to, 145, 149–50
   threat to strike aircraft impact, 146
air power
   air-to-ground operations, 144–46, 147–48, 149, 161
   armies-on-the-move, vulnerability of, 151
   Bush administration policy on, 9–10
   conditions of greatest lethality, 18–19, 144–45
   counter value strategies, 36
   cross-domain advantage of, 144–45
   Cuban Missile Crisis and, 44
   environmental factors, 148
      lighting: day versus night, 148–49
      terrain and cover, 149
      weather, 148
   flashlight effect, 150–51
   greater tactical strength advantage, 150–51
   land power comparison, 349–50
   limited ability to deter armies, 145
   NATO rules of engagement, 145
   offense advantage of, 37
   operational forces affecting CDD
      air superiority, 146
      air-to-ground capability, 146–47
      composition of enemy ground forces, 147
      friendly ground force capability, 147
   projection onto land, 145
   protection from access advantage, 151

379

air power (cont.)
  for retaliation against terrorism, 4
  strategies for cover from, 145
  strategies for cover on the ground, 145, 146
  wider view advantage, 151–52
air superiority, 146
air-to-ground capability, 146
air-to-ground operations, 144–46, 147–48, 149, 161
AirSea Battle, 11–12, 181, 182, 205–6
Al Qaeda in Yemen, 162
Al Qaeda terrorist network, vii, 27–28
Alexander, Keith, 7, 208
Algerian insurgents, coercively engineered migration, 266t
Algerian National Liberation Front, 264–65
alliance signaling, 238
alliances
  assurances in, 237
  cyber operations and, 48
  entrapment/escalation fears, 235
  influences of changing dynamics, 237–38
  Kissinger on, 47
  NATO alliances, 27–28, 41, 43
  Northern Alliance, Afghanistan, 79, 160
  nuclear triad and alliance commitments, 245–50
  Peloponnesian War and, 19, 169–73
  post-World War II, 240–42
  trade-offs and demands of, 239
  U.S. alliances, 234–35, 240–42
anarchist movements, 2
ancient Greece. *See also* Peloponnesian War
  cross-domain balance, 166–67
  deterrence issues, 368
  naval power, 346–47
  Sparta land power wars with, 19
Andropov, Yuri, 224–25, 227, 228
Anglo-German naval arms race, 164–65
Anonymous, 2
anti-access/area-denial (A2/AD) strategy (China), 27–28, 205–6
antisatellite (ASAT) weapons, 18
  asymmetric advantage of, 121–22
  Bush administration funding for, 128
  China's development of, 9–10, 28, 35–36, 121
  Cold War era and, 18, 123, 124, 126–27
  deterrent influence of, 134
  disincentives to strike using, 125
  expected growth of, 134
  first strike stability of, 135
  hit-to-kill system, 132–33
  jamming systems, 106, 115, 135, 136, 141
  non- or minimal debris-producing options, 136
  Rose's comment on, 121
  Russia's development of, 121
  Russia's discontinuance of, 127
  U.S. approved programs, 125–26
  U.S. fears of attack by, 121, 122–23, 134
  U.S. "mothballing" of programs, 127–28
antisubmarine warfare (ASW) operations, U.S., 208
Aristede, Jean-Bertrand, 265–74
armies-on-the-move, vulnerability to air power, 151
Army Air Corps, 67–68
The Art of War (Sun Tzu), 152
ASAT missile 135 (ASM-135) system, 125–26
ASAT Treaty, 127
ASD-GSA (assistant secretary of defense for global strategic affairs), 29
Asia-Pacific region, 234–35
Asian Development Bank, 325–26
Asian Infrastructure Investment Bank, 321–22, 326
Asian space race, 132–33
al-Assad, Bashar, 73, 262–63
"Assault Breaker" (U.S.), 125–26
Association of Southeast Asian Nations (ASEAN), 262–63, 266t, 323–24, 327–28
  China's investment in ASEAN countries, 323–24
  coercively engineered migration, 262–63, 266t
  Hanoi, Vietnam summit (2010), 327–28
assurance(s)
  advanced technology and concerns about, 241
  in alliances, 237
  alliances and, 237
  Brezhnev's request for, 220
  in Budapest Memorandum, 73
  CDD as both help and hindrance to, 359–61
  challenges of, 236
  definition, 237
  necessity in deterrence policy, 20
  nuclear triad and, 242–44, 248–50
  role of emerging technology, 250–51
  role of space and cyber domains, 251–55
  in U.S.-Russia-Ukraine Trilateral Statement, 73
asymmetric advantage
  ability to attack space assets as, 122–23
  of an air force (air power), 152, 153, 158, 161, 162, 349–50
  Battle of Britain and, 152
  Battle of the Bulge and, 156, 157
  Berlin Wall and, 41
  Easter Offensive and, 153
  of network warfare, 8
  nonmilitary coercion and, 260–61
  of one domain over another domain, 144–45
asymmetric strategies
  of coercively engineered migration, 288–87
  cross-domain responses, 74–75, 89, 90, 144–45, 227–28
  as exception in interstate conflicts, 288
  geopolitics/technologies impact on, 71
  nuclear weapons and, 77
  Peloponnesian War, 173

responses and blowbacks, 78
space domain attacks, 121–22
U.S. Cold War cross-domain nuclear initiatives, 208
U.S. "soft power" strategy, 79
atomic weapons, 68–69
Australia, 234–35, 324–25
Austria, coercively engineered migration, 266t
autonomous robotics, 2

Baker, James, 300–1
Bangladesh, coercively engineered migration, 266t
bargaining theory of war, 206, 209, 317
Barrass, Gordon, 217
Battle of Britain (1940), 145–46, 153, 155, 158, 161
Battle of the Bulge (1944), 137–56, 157–58
behavioral investigations, of of cyberspace, 119
Belarus, denuclearization by, 72
Belt and Road Initiative (China), 321–22, 325
Berlin Crisis (1961)
  construction of Berlin Wall, 41
  described, 47
  Eisenhower and, 41–42
  Kennedy, John F., and, 41–43
  McNamara and, 38, 41–42
  Soviet Union and, 41–42
  Stalin's role in, 41
Betts, Richard, vii–viii
Biafran insurgents, coercively engineered migration, 266t
Biddle, Stephen, 147
bilateral nuclear balance era (c. 1961-1991), 76
biotechnology, 2
Blainey, Geoffrey, 294–95
Brezhnev, Leonid, 45, 46, 220
Brodie, Bernard, 1–2
Brooks, Stephen, 329
Brunitsyn, N. A., 222
Buchman, Ben, 106–7
Buckshot Yankee (Russian cyber attack), 7–8
Budapest Memorandum (1994), 73
Budget Control Act (U.S.; 2010), 330–31
Bunn, Elaine, 28–29
Bush, George H.W. (and Bush administration), and ending of Cold War, 298–99, 300–1, 304, 307, 310–11
Bush, George W. (and Bush administration), 3, 5
  ASAT jammers/missile defense funding, 128
  recognition of international security complexities, 28
  space policy (2006), 9–10, 35–36
  studies of cross-domain deterrence, 13
  use of "Axis of Evil" term, 32
  use of military coercion strategy, 264
  withdrawal from anti-ballistic missile treaty, 128

C3. See command, control, and communications
"Can Deterrence Be Tailored" (Bunn), 28–29
CANOPY WING (U.S. "black" program), 215–16, 226–27
capabilities-based planning, 28, 29
capacity swamping, 21, 274, 354
Carney, Jeffrey, 215–16
Carson, Austin, 116–17
Carter, Ashton, 136
Carter, Jimmy, 125–26, 214
Castro, Fidel, 47, 263
Castro, Raoul, 263–64
CDD-D. See cross-domain deterrence and (national) defense
CDDI. See 21st Century Cross-Domain Deterrence Initiative
CEM. See coercively engineered migration
Central Europe
  NATO deployment of missiles to, 215
  purpose of tripwire forces in, 344–45
  U.S. protection of, from Soviet attack, 292–93
Central Intelligence Agency (CIA), 68–69
Chain, John T,, Jr., 216
chemical weapons, 73, 290–91
China. See also United States (U.S.)-China relations
  advocacy for space weapons ban, 9–10
  anti-access/area-denial strategy, East and South China Seas, 27–28
  antisatellite weapons development, testing, 9–10, 28, 35–36, 121, 132
  antisatellite weapons threats from, 122–23
  asymmetrical, cross-domain capabilities, 89
  Beijing's deterrence perspective, 55
  Belt and Road Initiative, 321–22, 325
  CDD history and, 4
  cyber espionage by, 8
  cyberspace deterrence needs against, 104–5
  cyberspace's role in warfighting doctrrine, 99
  East Asia regional dominance of, 319
  East Asia's economic interactions with, 321–22
  geopolitical challenges created by, 337
  hacking/cyber capability, 72
  harnessing of commercial revolution in space, 135
  ideological rivalry with U.S., 165
  integrated strategic deterrence of, 3
  investments in ASEAN countries, 323–24
  "limited war under conditions of informatization" doctrrine, 8
  maritime weapons investments, 165
  military doctrine, 166–67
  military modernization efforts, 5, 166
  opposition to Western deterrence policy, 59
  proposal of ASAT limits, 136–37

China (cont.)
    provocation of territorial disputes, 68–69
    regional dominance in East Asia, 319
    regional power transition in, 318–19
    sea domain aggressiveness, 11–12
    South China Sea, anti-access/area-denial strategy, 27–28, 165–66
    space domain's importance to, 129
    strategic challenges posed by, vii
    Strategic Support Force, 9
    threats against Taiwan, 332
    U.S. comments on militarization in, 11–12
    U.S. "third offset" strategy vs., 12–13
    use of low-intensity coercion, 254
    Vietnam's ties to, 327
    warnings about space domain conflicts, 124
China-U.S. conflict, maritime (sea) domain, 165, 181–83
C4ISR. *See* command, control, communication, computation, intelligence, surveillance, and reconnaissance
civilian/military CDD interaction, 57
Clapper, James, 121
Clausewitz, Carl von, 86, 132, 144, 148, 150
Clinton, Bill, 32, 265–74
Clinton, Hillary, 320–21
Coast Guard (U.S.), 5
coercion. *See also* coercively engineered migration
    CDD domains as pathways for, 16, 57
    coercive diplomacy, 30, 51
    covert military forms, 116–17
    cross-domain coercion, 260
    definition, 14
    deterrence's relation to, 149–50
    growing portfolio of tools of, 4
    kinetic coercion, 260, 263
    low-intensity coercion, 197
    nonmilitary coercion, 260–61
    nuclear weapons and, 197
    restricted use of force and, 147
    state-level coercion, 260–61
    U.S.-Cuba example, 14
    vulnerability of liberal democracies to, 21
    war-time role of, 144
coercively engineered migration (CEM), 21
    agent provocateurs' uses of, 263, 264–65
    asymmetric influence of, 278–87
    bargaining characteristics of, 354
    bargaining leverage, 279–81
    capacity swamping pathway, 21, 274, 354
    cases (examples) of, 266t
    compellence and, 262, 266, 277–78, 283–84, 285t, 354
    cross-domain influence of, 289
    description, 262–63, 265
    disaggregation into deterrence and compellence, 283–87

efficacy factors, 278
game theory and, 275, 277
generators' uses of, 264–65
kinetic coercion comparison, 263
loss-of-control-related situations in, 276
mechanics of, 274–78
military coercion comparison, 261–64, 276–77, 280–81, 288
non-mutually exclusive pathways of, 274
objectives of, 265–74
operational advantages, 282
opportunists' uses of, 264–65
political agitation pathway, 274
prevalence of, 261–62
as punishment strategy, 274, 277–78
risk strategies/impediments to risk strategies, 275–77, 278
signaling and, 276–77
as societal warfare, 275
Cold War. *See also* Berlin Crisis; Cold War, ending of; Cold War, post-Cold War era; Cuban Missile Crisis; Korean War; Yom Kippur War
    ASAT weapons and, 18, 123, 124, 126–27
    clandestine deterrence problems, 20
    counter-value strikes strategy, 36–37
    cross-domain strategies, 12–13
    deterrence challenges, strategies, 3–4, 15, 27
    efforts at holding Soviet nuclear forces at risk, 206
    focus on escalation of existing attacks, 57–58
    force posture focus during, 246
    Freedman on deterrence during, 2
    high-stakes bargaining, 1–2
    Massive Retaliation doctrine, U.S., 200–1
    nuclear deterrence during, 19–20, 37, 57–58
    nuclear policymaking vs. strategic precepts, 2
    offense advantage strategy, 36–37
    "one size fits all" approach, 28–29
    psy-ops, 216, 218–19, 227
    revival between U.S.-Russia, 64
    signaling, by the U.S., during, 207, 209–14
    Soviet repression in Poland, East Germany, 21
    technology and, 15
    U.S. nuclear strategy during, 206, 208
    U.S.-Soviet informal/formal agreements, 235
Cold War, ending of
    Bush, George H.W. and, 298–99, 300–1, 304, 307, 310–11
    deterrence as reassurance and engagement, 305–7
    deterring action in Poland, 303–8
    diplomatic drama and deterrence, 299–302
    Gorbachev and, 220, 299, 301–2, 304, 305–6, 307–8, 311, 313
    interest-based change and, 298–313
    Kissinger and, 304–5

Reagan and, 300
U.S. efforts at deterring Soviets in Eastern
    Europe, 291, 298–300, 301, 302–8
Cold War, post-Cold War era
    ASAT weapons employment, 18, 123,
        124, 126–27
    deterrence problems, 17–18
    international nonproliferation consensus, 72
    political/economic collapse, Russia, 127
    unipolar moment (1990s), 127–28
    weakness of Soviet Union, 214, 223–25
collective actor deterrence, 55
command, control, and communications (C3), 205
    computer network integration and, 205
    Soviet vulnerabilities in, 214
    U.S. advantages in, 214
    U.S. plans for disrupting Soviets, 206,
        209–11, 213
command, control, communication, computation,
    intelligence, surveillance, and
    reconnaissance (C4ISR), 8–9, 86, 88,
    125–26, 129
commitment signaling, 237
common conjecture
    game theory and, 189–90, 192
    international law's differences from, 193
common knowledge
    common conjectures and, 190
    common standards, public actions, violations,
        and, 191
    creation through international law, 188, 192–93
    game theory and, 192
    treaty ratification and, 192–93
    unilateral declarations of intent, 192
Communist Party Central Committee (Soviet
    Union), 221
Communist Party of Vietnam (CPV), 327, 328
compellence
    coercive diplomacy and, 47
    coercively engineered migration and, 262, 266,
        277–78, 283–84, 285t, 354
    Cuban Missile Crisis and, 44–45
    definition, 14, 29, 30
    deterrence comparison, 30, 259, 262
    disaggregation of CEM into, 283–87
    Korean War and, 47
    in nonmilitary CDD, 21
    nuclear war and, 1–2, 40, 343–44
    Schelling on, 21, 288
    U.S.-Soviet competition and, 300–1
complexity of cross-domain deterrence
    barriers created by, 19–20
    expanding/retreating of, 62
    fears created by, 3
    simplicity/complexity, of nuclear
        deterrence, 70–71
    sociotechnical complexity, 4

tractability of, 22
unavoidability of, 59
complications for cross-domain deterrence
    emerging, 61–62
    familiar, 58, 59–60
"Comprehensive National Cybersecurity Initiative"
    (U.S.), 95–96, 100
conceptual stretching in deterrence, 53–56, 63, 64
counter value strategies, 36
covert operation studies, cyberspace
    operations, 116–17
credibility
    advanced technology and concerns about, 241
    nuclear triad and, 242–44
    role of emerging technology, 250–51
    search for, in the nuclear age, 240
    technological transitions and, 236
    of U.S. in extended deterrence
        commitments, 344–45
"Cross-Domain Deterrence and Credible Threats"
    (Lewis), 29–30
cross-domain deterrence and (national) defense
    (CDD-D), 64–65
cross-domain deterrence (CDD)
    ambiguity factors, 18, 21, 59–60
    analytical potential of, 14
    asymmetrical responses, 19
    Athens vs. Greece context, 19
    as both help and hindrance to
        assurance, 359–61
    Bush/Obama studies of, 13
    cautionary note about, 333
    challenges of, 30, 62
    characteristics of cases of, 38t
    civilian/military CDD interactions, 57, 62
    complications, emerging, 61–62
    complications, familiar, 58, 59–60
    of cyberspace operations, 104
    cyberspace tools, 115
    definition/description, 3–4, 30, 57, 163, 187–88,
        290, 337
    domain concept, 16–17
    general vs. immediate, 164
    geopolitics and, 164
    historical context, 4, 69–70
    increasing relevance of, 336–37
    integration across multiple domains, 69
    linkage politics and, 293
    linkages to nuclear deterrence, 90–91
    national security connection, 57
    before the Peloponnesian War, 168–74
    during the Peloponnesian War, 174–79
    physical implementation factors, 60
    as priority, 77
    psychological considerations, 60
    "rock, paper, scissors" analogy, 16
    stability-instability paradox in, 15, 181, 364–65

cross-domain deterrence (CDD) (cont.)
  stabilizing/destabilizing influences of, 361–63
  STRATCOM's focus on, 7
  ultimate concern facing, 63–64
  in U.S. foreign policy, 27, 30
  use of terminology challenges, 29
cross-domain deterrence (CDD), analytical potential of
  bargaining characteristics of different domains, 340–55t
    air power, 348
    coercively engineered migration, 354
    cyber operations, 352
    land power, 344
    nuclear weapons, 342
    sea power, 346
    space operations, 350
  complexity and strategic stability, 355–65
  future prospects, 365
    policy implications, 366–68
    research potential, 369–71
  promise of CDD as a concept, 337–39
cross-domain nuclear age
  asymmetrical responses, blowback effects, 78
  attribution and accountability, 78
  collateral damage and proportionality, 79
  counterforce, countervalue, escalation, deescalation, 80
  damage assessment, certainty, uncertainty, sufficiency, 80
  decision cycles, response time, "fait accompli," 81
  deterrence priority, 77
  measure/countermeasure dynamics, defenses, 81
Cuba
  coercively engineered migration, 266t
  Mariel boatlift, 263–64
Cuban Missile Crisis (1962), 14, 17, 42, 336–37
  complexity for U.S. poilicymakers, 47
  Kennedy, John F., and, 43–44
  Kennedy, Robert, and, 44
  Khrushchev and, 43, 44
  McNamara and, 43
  naval quarantine strategy, 42–44
cyber attacks (cyber warfare). *See also* Iran, cyberattack on uranium centrifuges
  Air Force command, 6–7
  defaced websites as, 104
  Denning on, 108
  global expansion of, 50
  immediacy of initiation of, 65
  on Iranian uranium centrifuges, 31–35
  North Korea vs. Sony Corporation, 101–2, 114, 231–32, 367
  Petya ransomware incident, 104
  phishing, 112, 114, 336–37
  spread of, 50
  ties to geopolitical realities, 106–7
  of U.S. Office of Personnel Management, 108–9
  WannaCry ransomware incident, 104
Cyber Command (CYBERCOM), 5, 7
"The Cyber Creed" (U.S. Air Force Cyberspace Task Force), 6–7
cyber deterrence
  Buchman on, 106–7
  buzzword status for U.S. policymakers, 95–96
  "Comprehensive National Cybersecurity Initiative," 95–96
  covert operation studies findings, 116–17
  criticism of, 116–18
  definition, 99–100
  determining how to deter, 112
  determining what to deter, 108
  determining whom to deter, 105
  deterrence-by-denial strategies, 100, 102–5, 111, 112–13
  deterrence-by-punishment strategies, 100–3, 104–6, 111, 112, 113–14, 115, 116, 119–20
  Glaser on, 104–5
  Goodman on, 104–5
  Libicki on, 105–6
  Rid on, 106–7
  U.S. DoD Cyberspace Strategy, 95–96
  U.S. policies and practices, 100–4, 119–20
cyber espionage, 5, 8, 101, 191–92, 317, 360–61, 364–65
cyber network exploitation (CNE), 105–6, 108–11
Cyber Strategy (U.S. Department of Defense; 2015), 102–3
cyber technologies, 96, 97–98, 119–20
cyberspace domain, 5. *See also* space domain
  Air Force/Army/Navy cyber warfare units, 6–7
  ambiguity factors, 21
  ASD-GSA and, 29
  assurance and, 251–55
  authoritarian regimes use of, 73
  bargaining characteristics of, 352
  behavioral investigations of, 119
  CDD history and, 4
  cross-domain questions about, 68–69
  cross-domain with space domain, 8–9
  cyber/cyberspace, definitions, 96
  cyberspace tools, 115
  deterrence challenges, 15–16, 68–69
  differences from space domain, 9
  distributed denial of service attacks, 7–8, 28, 110, 118
  empowering/exploitation effects of, 75
  extended deterrence to allied nations, 100–1
  fragility of chokepoints in, 11–12
  identification of attack characteristics, 29
  link to other domains, 66–67, 98–99
  policymakers and, 35
  Russian penetrations of Pentagon systems, 7–8
  space domain integration with, 68–69

INDEX

U.S. Cyber Command, 68–69
U.S. Department of Defense on, 29–30
U.S. efforts at discouraging attacks, 5
vulnerability of, 7–8
as warfighting domain, 6–7
cyberspace operations. *See also* Iran, cyberattack on uranium centrifuges
   asymmetrical integration strategy, 78–79
   bargaining characteristics of, 352
   counterforce/countervalue impacts, 88
   covert operation studies, 116–17
   criticism of, 116–18
   cross-domain deterrence of, 104
   cyber/cyberspace, definitions, 96
   cyber, definitions, 96
   debates about definition of, 18
   decision to employ, 75
   definition, 101
   description, 95–96
   empowering/exploitation effects of, 75
   equalizing effect of, 79
   offensive effect on conventional warfare, 96
   ongoing developments, 2, 74
   pre-conflict deployment, benefits, 81
   retaliation strategies against, 4
   retaliatory uses of, 4
   signaling and secrecy tools, 116
Cyberspace Strategy (U.S. Department of Defense, 2015), 95–96
cyberspace tools, 115
   criticism of, 116
   escalation dominance and control, 118–19
   signaling and secrecy, 116–18
Czechoslovakia, 311, 313

Danilevich, Andrian, 219–21, 223
Daryal large phased array radar (LPAR) program (Soviet Union), 225, 226
Davis, John, 305–6
DDoS attacks. *See* distributed denial of service (DDoS) attacks
Defense Authorization Act (U.S.)(2015), 121–22
Defense Research and Development Organization (India), 132–33
Delian League, 169, 171, 178–79, 180–81
Demchak, Chris, 98–99
Denning, Dorothy, 108
deterrence. *See also* deterrence language; deterrence, pre-nuclear deterrence thinking; deterrence theory; extended nuclear deterrence; nuclear deterrence
   assurance challenges, 236
   bargaining theory of war and, 206, 209, 317
   coercion's relation to, 149–50
   coercive diplomacy and, 47
   Cold War paradigm features, 36
   collective actor deterrence, 55
   compellence vs., 30, 259, 262
   conceptual stretching in, 53–56, 63, 64
   credibility factors, 1–2, 10–11, 14–15, 19, 29, 55, 58, 60
   definition, 14, 67–68, 237
   disaggregation of CEM into, 283–87
   disarmament comparison, 71
   expanding complexity of, 71
   failures against defensive forces, 160
   game theory and, 75, 189–90, 192, 275
   general deterrence, 50–52, 56, 75, 112, 283
   immediate deterrence, 51–52, 54, 56, 58, 59, 164, 287, 356–57
   initial vs. present focus of, 53
   instigation via low-level threats, 54
   integrated strategic deterrence, 29
   lower levels of, 74
   modern problems facing, 15–16
   multidisciplinary perspectives on, 57–59
   need for common standards between parties, 190–91
   nonfatal, limited casualty interventions, 54
   as political problem, 14–15
   pre-nuclear deterrence thinking, 36
      air-power counter value strategies, 36
      offense advantage, 37
   reciprocity factors, 189, 191, 192–93, 358
   regional, state, domestic level interventions, 50–51
   revived 21st century interest in, 50–51
   role of assurances of allies/adversaries in, 20
   "second nuclear age" framework, 14–15
   shared understandings' underpinning of, 189–90
   space/cyberspace challenges, 15–16
   strategic requirements for effectiveness of, 190–91
   tailored deterrence, 28–29
   technology and, 15
   treaties working together with, 193–94
   UK's preoccupation with, 50
deterrence-by-denial strategies, cyber deterrence, 100, 102–5, 111, 112–13
deterrence-by-punishment strategies, cyber deterrence, 100–3, 104–6, 111, 112, 113–14, 115, 116, 119–20
deterrence language
   "conflict" versus "crisis," 84
   "countervalue" versus "counterforce," 86
   "deterrence" versus "warfighting," 85
   "homeland security" versus "over there," 88
deterrence theory
   application of lessons learned, 71
   bilateral nuclear bargaining envisioned by, 2
   on compellence vs. deterrence, 21
   escalation dynamics and, 82
   "fait accompli" preoccupation in, 81
   focus on the challenge of credibility, 14–15

deterrence theory (*cont.*)
  high-stakes crisis bargaining focus ("chicken games"), 18–19
  historical origins, 14–15
  information limits on particular instruments, 3–4, 14–15
  irrationality factors, 60
  Jervis on ethnocentric tendencies of, 319–20
  limited information on instruments used to impose costs, deny benefits, 3–4
  modern focus on political, cultural change, 55–56
  neglect of preventing escalation of existing attacks, 57–58
  nuclear deterrence theory, 107
  past and future of, 50–65
  relationship of offensive-defense forces, 81
  as specialized subset of CDD, 23
"Deterring Complex Threats" research program, vii
distributed denial of service (DDoS) attacks, 7–8, 28, 110, 118
domains. *See also* air domain; cyberspace domain; land domain; sea (maritime) domain; space domain
  advantages of one over another, 144–45, 163
  communication/credibility across, 19
  definitions, 5–6, 16, 29, 57, 66–67
  military/nonmilitary, interactions across, 21
Dombrowski, Peter, 98–99
Dulles, John Foster, 39–40
dynamics of extended nuclear deterrence, 237–42

early warning (EW) protection, 214, 223
East Asia. *See also* Japan
  arms race/regional security dilemma in, 318–19
  China's expanding influence in, 27–28, 165, 319
  defense spending data, 321–22
  engagement in "complicity and resistance" to the U.S., 325–26
  increasing economic interactions with China, 321–22
  pursuit of adequate security, 331–32
  pursuit of "external balancing," 330–31
  threat perception research findings, 321
  U.S. alliance with, 236, 240–41, 245, 320–22, 329–32
East Germany (German Democratic Republic)
  Berlin Crisis (1961), 41–42
  Berlin Wall, construction of, 41, 287
  Berlin Wall, fall of, 309
  coercively engineered migration and, 266, 279–80t
  cross-domain technological innovation revelations from, 215–16
  ending of Cold War and, 308–13
  obtaining of secret U.S. documents, 215–16
  opposition to Gorbachev's call for reforms, 301–2
  Soviet post-WW II presence in, 41
  Soviet repression in, 21
  U.S. deterrent efforts in, 310–11
  U.S. efforts at deterring Soviets in, 312–13
Easter Offensive, Vietnam War, 144–46, 147, 153–55, 156–57, 158, 161
Eastern Europe, 21, 22
  National Security Council concerns about, 304
  Revolutions of 1989, 291
  Russian hybrid warfare in, 78–79
  U.S. challenge to status quo in, 303
  U.S. efforts at deterring Soviets in, 291, 298–300, 301, 302–8
economic sanctions, 32–33
Egypt
  Six-Day War, 45
  Yom Kippur War and, 45
Eisenhower, Dwight D., 39, 278, 320
  Berlin Crisis and, 41–42
  considered use of atomic weapons in Korea, 39–40
  exploitation of U.S. nuclear monopoly, 293
  "rollback" of Soviet influence by, 301
Electronic Ocean Reconnaissance Satellites (EORSATs), 125–26
Enhanced Defense Cooperation Agreement (U.S.-Philippines), 330
Erdoğan, Recep Tayyip, 265–74
escalation dominance and control, cyberspace tools, 118–19
escalation (escalation dynamics)
  classical deterrence theory on, 57–58
  complexity and, 59
  Cuban Missile Crisis and, 43, 44–45
  cyber domain and, 30
  nuclear, deterrence of, 20, 49, 52, 53
  risk factor provocations, 15
  space warfare and, 18–19
  unintentionality of, 36–37
Estonia, 4, 7–8
ethnic cleansing, 160, 276
ethnic conflicts, 67
Europe. *See also* East Germany; Eastern Europe; Germany; United Kingdom; West Germany
  U.S. efforts at deterrence with, 53, 245
  U.S. post-WW II alliance with, 240–41
  warnings about space domain conflicts, 124
European Union-Turkey deal (2016), 265–74
extended nuclear deterrence
  Cold War and, 77
  Cuban Missile Crisis and, 44–45
  cyberspace extended deterrence, 100–1
  deescalation and, 44–45

dynamics of, 237–42
evolution of strategies, 20
geopolitics and, 240–41
as key CDD element, 88–89
name derivation, 77
nuclear weapons and, 195, 233
U.S. policy of, 234–55

Feigenbaum, Evan, 325–26
financial sanctions, 54
Finch, James, 137–38
first strike stability, defined, 135, 141
"Fiscal Year 1984-1988 Defense Guidance" (U.S. government report), 214
flashlight effect, 150–51
"Follow-on Forces Attack" (U.S.), 125–26
Ford, Gerald, 125–26
FOREIGN POLICY US United States (U.S.) foreign policy, cross-domain deterrence, 27, 30. *See also* Cold War
    Bush, George W., recognition of international security complexities, 28
    "Comprehensive National Cybersecurity Initiative," 95–96
    "Cross-Domain Deterrence and Credible Threats" (Lewis), 29–30
    cyberattack on Iranian uranium centrifuges, 31–35
    cyberspace and, 96, 104, 109–10, 119–20
    Defense Authorization Act, 121–22
    extended deterrence and, 234–35, 238, 242–44, 255
    linkage politics, ending of the Cold War, and, 290–315
    neutrality laws, 243
    "Nuclear Posture Review" (Rumsfeld), 28
    "Nuclear Posture Review" (Trump), 28–29
    "Quadrennial Defense Review Report," 28
    tailored deterrence, 28–29
France, 145–46, 155, 158–59, 160, 266t
French-Algerian War (1954-1962), 264–65
full-spectrum deterrence, 3
functional kills, 76, 80

Gaddafi, Muammar, 263
game theory, 75, 189–90, 192, 275
    coercively engineered migration and, 275, 277
Gannon, J. Andres, vii–viii
general deterrence, 50–52, 56, 75, 112, 283
generators, uses of coercively engineered migration, 263
Geohegan, Katherine, 303
geopolitics
    cyberspace attacks and, 106–7
    extended deterrent commitments and, 240–41
    geographic factors, 164

nuclear era geopolitics, 74, 76
sea domain and, 164
shaping forces, 123
Soviet-American conflict and, 232
space security and, 131–32
World War I and, 164–65
Georgia (Eurasian country), 4, 7–8
Germany. *See also* Berlin Crisis; East Germany; West Germany
    air domain, weather, and, 148
    Anglo-German rivalry, WW II, 298
    defense of France by, 160
    1930s, U.S. response to aggression by, 243
    post-WW I geopolitics and, 164–65
    WW II military production capability, 243
GIUK gap. *See* Greenland-Iceland-United Kingdom (GIUK) gap
Glaser, Charles, 104–5
global commons, 10
Global Positioning Systems (GPS), 8–9
Glosserman, Brad, 320–21
Goh, Evelyn, 325–26
Goodman, Will, 104–5
Gorbachev, Mikhail, role in ending Cold War, 220, 299, 301–2, 304, 305–6, 307–8, 311, 313
GPS-guidance systems, 128–29
"gray zone" provocations, 15
Great Britain, 36–37, 71, 164–65, 293, 310, 367. *See also* Battle of Britain
Great Recession (2008), 55
Greenert, Jonathan, 11–12
Greenland-Iceland-United Kingdom (GIUK) gap, 217
ground forces
    air forces deterrence of, 144–45, 147, 150–52
    lethality of air power against, 145
    massing and maneuvering of, 18–19, 152
    strategies for cover on the ground, 145, 146, 148, 149
    Sun Tzu on mass and maneuver of, 152
Gryphon ground-launched cruise missile (GLCM), 208, 215
guerilla warfare, 50
Gulf War (1991), 128–29, 144–45, 151

hacking, 72
Haiti, coercively engineered migration, 266t
Hall, James W. III, 215–16
Halperin, Morton, vii–viii
Harriman, Averell, 228
Hauptverwaltung Aufklärung (HVA), East Germany's foreign intelligence service, 215–16
Haynes, Bill, 327
Hines report (1995), 214, 220–21
Hiroshima, Japan, 1, 37

Hungary
  eviction of Soviet forces, 313
  response to Gorbachev's call for reforms, 301–2
Hussein, Saddam, 159
hybrid warfare, 71, 78–79
  emergence of, 69
  outcomes of, 81
  risk factors, 85
  by Russia, 3, 78–79, 89
  by U.S. Special Forces, 79
hypersonic cruise missiles, 2
Hyten, John, 122–23

Ikenberry, John, 329
Illarinov, Igor, 222–23
immediate deterrence, 51–52, 54, 56, 58, 59, 164, 287, 356–57
India, 72, 132–33, 324–25
Indonesia, 324–25, 326–27
information revolution, 8, 336
Inman, Bobby, 217–18
insurgent warfare, 50
integrated strategic deterrence (China), 3
intelligence, surveillance, and reconnaissance (ISR) systems, 121–22, 127, 151
  air- and space-borne platforms for, 151
  high-altitude/space-based, 134, 138
  impact on multiple domains, 142
  in power projectors, 142
  requirements for deterring attacks against, 140–41
  Russia's discontinuance of, 127
intercontinental ballistic missiles (ICBMs), 76–77, 206, 208, 226, 229
interest-based change
  at the end of the Cold War, 298–313
  linkage politics and, 295–97
  method of addressing dynamics of, 298
  U.S. efforts in deterring Soviets in Eastern Europe, 291, 298–300
intermediate range ballistic missiles (IRBM), 43, 208
international law. *See also* treaties
  common conjecture's differences from, 193
  creating common knowledge through, 188, 192–93
  deterrence-by-denial and, 100–1
  formal declaration of war and, 84
  law of war analogy, 198–99
  nuclear deterrence and, 188
  treaties and deterrence working together, 193–94
  weakness of nuclear analogy, 195–97
International Monetary Fund, 325–26
International Strategy for Cyberspace (U.S., 2011), 100–1
International Studies Association, vii–viii

Internet. *See also* Stuxnet operation, in Iran; Stuxnet (Operation Olympic Games) cyberattack
  cyberspace domain and, 5
  defaced websites, cyber attacks, 5
Iran
  cyberattack on uranium centrifuges (Operation Olympic Games), 31–35
    core idea of, 33–34
    Israel's role, 7–8, 32, 33, 34
    outcomes of, 34–35
    U.S.'s role, 7–8, 32–35
  cyberspace deterrence needs against, 104–5
  deterrence and, 14–15
  hacking/cyber capability, 72
  Hussein's defense of, 159
  nuclear proliferation efforts, 4
  nuclearization efforts, 27–28, 32, 50
  as part of Bush's "axis of evil," 32
  strategic challenges posed by, vii
  U.S.'s deteriorating relations with, 31
Iran-Iraq War, 31
Iran Sanctions Act (1996), 32
Iranian Atomic Energy Organization, 35
Iranian Revolution (1979), 31
Iraq, 2
  confrontations on road to Al Khafji, 144–45, 151
  Iran-Iraq War, 31
  as part of Bush's "axis of evil," 32
  Scud missiles, 128–29
  U.S. airstrikes over, 161–62
  US. combat operations in, 4
  U.S. military commitments in, 28
Islamic Republic of Iran, 31
Islamic State (Daesh), 2
  attacks by, 54
  suicide attacks strategy, 27–28
Islamic State of Iraq and Syria (ISIS), 157, 161–62
ISR systems. *See* intelligence, surveillance, and reconnaissance (ISR) systems
Israel
  coercively engineered migration, 266t
  cyberattack vs. Iran uranium enrichment facility, 32
  foreign policy debates in, 234–35
  incremental punishment practice, 54
  Six-Day War, 45
  Yom Kippur War and, 45
Istrebel Sputnikov (Soviet "Satellite Killer"), 125

Jae-in, Moon, 331–32
Jakarta, 326–27
jamming systems, 106, 115, 135, 136, 141
Japan
  declining GDP in, 318–19
  foreign policy debates in, 234–35
  1930s, U.S. response to aggression by, 243

openness to nuclear issue discussions, 234–35
space race in, 132–33
U.S. atomic bombing of, 244
Jervis, Robert, vii–viii, 319–20
Joint Concept for Access and Maneuver in the Global Commons (JAM-GC), 205–6
"Joint Publication 3-12: Cyberspace Operations" (U.S. Department of Defense), 97–98, 102–3
Jordan, coercively engineered migration, 266t

Kagan, Donald, 168
Kalashnikov, Mikhail, 222, 224
Kataev, Vitalii, 221
Kazakhstan, 72
Kennedy, John F., 265
 Berlin Crisis and, 41–43
 Cuban Missile Crisis and, 43–44
Kennedy, Robert, 44
Kerns, Christine, vii–viii
Keuhl, Daniel, 97–98
Keyhole-11 satellites, 125
KGB (Soviet Union), 216, 218–19, 224, 227
 collaboration with GRU, 227
 NATO report on, 216
 1984 work plan, 224
 reaction to U.S. psy-ops, 218–19
Khomeini, Ayatollah, 31
Khrushchev, Nikita, 43, 44
kinetic coercion, 263
Kissinger, Henry, 304–5
Kohl, Helmut, 311–12
Korean War (1953), 17, 38
 Chinese avoidance of air strikes in, 145
 Dulles and, 39–40
 Eisenhower and, 34, 39–40
 onset/description, 38
 U.S. contemplated use of atomic weapons, 39
 U.S. role, 38–40
Kosovo conflict, 263
Kosovo Liberation Army, 264–65

land domain, 3
 air power projection onto, 145
 cyber domain integration with, 66–67, 98–99
 ISR systems' impact on, 142
 space operations in, 66–67
land power
 air power comparison, 349–50
 bargaining characteristics of, 344
 naval power impact on, 347
 vs. sea power, Peloponnesian War, 163–83
laser weapons, 193–94
launching under attack (LUA), by ICBMs, 206, 208, 222–23, 225, 226–27
Lawrence Livermore National Laboratory, vii, 18

learning curves/forgetting curves, of deterrence, 75
Levite, Ari, 275
Lewis, James A., 29–30
Libicki, Martin, 105–6
Libya, 263
Lindsay, Ronald, 243
linkage
 importance to statecraft and grand strategy, 290
 logic of, 292–93
linkage politics
 change in CDD and, 293
 changes in cross-domain relationships, 294t
 interest-based change and, 295–97
 means-based change and, 294–95
 strategic attractiveness of, 293
Lopez, Jason, vii–viii
Los Alamos National Laboratory, vii
low-earth orbit (LEO) satellites, 9–10, 205–6

Major, John, 71
Malaysia, 324–25
Malenkov, Georgy, 40
Malta Summit, 310–11
Mariel boatlift, Cuba, 263–64
Marine Corps (U.S.), 5, 67–68
Massive Retaliation doctrine (U.S.), 200–1
Matlock, Jack, 228
Matsuo, Kinoaki, 37
McNamara, Robert, 41–42, 43
medium range ballistic missiles (MRBM), 43, 47
Melian Dialogue (Thucydides), 278
Middle East. See also Egypt; Iran; Iraq; Israel; Six-Day War; Syria; Yom Kippur War
 deterrence efforts vs. low-level threats, 54
 limited Western deterrence results in, 55
 U.S. efforts at deterrence with, 53
 U.S. efforts at stopping Soviet invasions, 45–46, 47
migration. See coercively engineered migration
Military Power (Biddle), 147
military space systems
 ASAT testing, 126–27
 capabilities of key space-enabled states, 130t
 capabilities supporting deterrence by punishment and by denial, 139t
 cross-domain character of threats fo, 137–38
 key role of, 134
Milosevic, Slobodan, 263
Minerva Initiative (U.S. Department of Defense), vii
mobile nuclear platforms, 205, 210, 214, 229
Moonlight Maze (Russian cyber attack), 7–8
Mozzhorin, Iurii A., 222–23
multidisciplinary perspectives on deterrence, 57–59

multiple independently targetable reentry vehicles (MIRVs), 76–77, 194–95
Mutual Defense Treaty (U.S.-Philippines), 330
Mutual Logistics Support Agreement (U.S.-Philippines), 330
mutually assured destruction (MAD), 213–14, 220, 299, 335

N-body problem, 75
Nacht, Michael, vii, 7–8, 13
Nagasaki, Japan, 37
National Defense Strategy (NDS)(U.S.), 11–12
National Security Act (1947), 68–69
National Security Agency (NSA), 7, 215–16, 217–18
National Security Council (U.S.), 125–26, 228, 300, 305–6, 310–11
National Security Planning Group (U.S.), 300
"National Security Presidential Directive/NSPD-54/Homeland Security Presidential Directive/HSPD-23," 99–100
National Security Space Strategy (U.S.), 122–23, 137–38
naval quarantine strategy, Cuban Missile Crisis, 42–44, 363–64
Navy (U.S.)
  Atlantic and Pacific battle group exercises, 217–18
  establishment of cyber unit, 6–7
  growing complexity, 67–68
  Pacific battle group exercise, 217
  psy-ops exercises, 216
  U.S. Joint Force role, 5
Nehru, Jawaharlal, 39–40
neutrality laws (U.S.), 243
"New Look" nuclear weapons policy (U.S.), 34
New Triad (Rumsfeld), 28–29
NGO activists, coercively engineered migration, 266t
Nguyễn Phú Trọng, 327
Nile, Battle of, 336–37
9/11 attacks, 54, 234–35
Nixon, Richard, 45, 48
non-kinetic cross-domain attacks, 75, 80
nonfatal, limited casualty interventions, 54
Normandy invasion, 145–46, 155, 158–59, 160
North Atlantic Treaty Organization (NATO)
  air strike rules of engagement, 145
  East-West military issue (1980s), 215
  ending of Cold War and, 306–7
  missile deployment decisions, 215
  passage of NATO ships through GIUK gap, 217
  Russian intimidation of members, 27–28
  "Strategic Concept" (1999), 247
  Warsaw Pact campaign with, 217
North Korea. *See also* Korean War

cyberattacks against Sony Corporation, 101–2, 114, 231–32, 367
cyberspace deterrence needs against, 104–5
deterrence and, 14–15
nuclearization efforts, 50, 72, 74–75
opposition to Western deterrence policy, 59
as part of Bush's "axis of evil," 32
strategic challenges posed by, vii
2016-2018 nuclear weapons tests, 68–69
U.S. post-2016 election tension with, 60
North-South Korean Denuclearization Agreement (1991), 72
North Vietnamese Army (NVA), Easter Offensive, 144–45, 147, 153–54, 156–57
Northeast Asia, 53
nuclear age. *See also* cross-domain nuclear age
  eras of, 76
  innovations of, 2
  "second nuclear age," 14–15
nuclear command and control (NC2) space systems, 124, 125
nuclear deterrence. *See also* extended nuclear deterrence
  classical deterrence theory and, 14–15
  Cold War and, 1–2, 18, 19–20
  game theory and, 192
  international humanitarian law and, 188
  limitations of CDD, 195–97
  pre-nuclear deterrence thinking, 36–37
  revived 21st century interest in, 50–51
  simplicity/complexity dichotomy, 70–71
  space domain and, 18
  treaties and, 195–97
  UK's study of, 50
  U.S.-Soviet Union treaties, 194–95
"Nuclear Posture Review" (Rumsfeld), 28
"Nuclear Posture Review" (Trump), 28–29
nuclear revolution
  "bad news" and "good news" claims about, 358–59
  classic theories of, 211–12
  deterrence theory and, 328, 342–43
  impact on U.S. conventional superiority, 211–12
  increased political violence and, 335
  influence on large-scale warfare, 336
  mutually assured destruction and, 213–14
  overwhelming aspects of, 207
  political leaders thoughts on, 207
  signaling and, 212, 229
  U.S.-Soviet relationship and, 207
nuclear strategy
  American counterforce strategy, 20
  anchoring by "foxes" and "hedgehogs," 70–71
  by U.S. during the Cold War, 76, 206, 208
nuclear triad
  affecting assurance dynamics, 248–50
  affecting deterrence dynamics, 246–48

alliance commitments and, 245–50
assurance, credibility, and, 242–44
nuclear war
    CDD concerns in preventing, 18–19
    Cold War concerns in deterring, 3–4, 15
    Cuban Missile Crisis and, 44
    fears of escalating to, 53
    McNamara's search for alternative, 41–42
    as suicidal proposition, 1
nuclear weapons (and programs)
    asymmetric responses to, 74–75
    bargaining characteristics of, 342
    continuing development of, 2
    cross-domain effects of, 67
    mobile nuclear platforms, 205, 210, 214, 229
    "multidomain" status of, 67
    Russia's modernization of, 4, 77
    U.S. development of, 236, 245
    use to attack satellites, 124–25

Obama, Barack (Obama administration), 5
    cyberspace deterrence policies, 100–4
    focus on defense for global strategic affairs, 29
    meeting with Nguyễn Phú Trọng, 327
    Operation Olympic Games, 32
    "rebalance" to Asia, 320–21
    studies of cross-domain deterrence, 13
Occasional Paper (U.S. Air Force), 237–38
offense-defense strategic relationship, 81
"offshore balancing" strategy (Posen), 10–11
Ogarkov, Marshal, 215
Oko satellites (Soviet Union), 225
On War (Clausewitz), 150
Operation Burnt Frost, 9–10
Operation Desert Storm, 87
Operation Horseshoe, 160
Operation Olympic Games (Stuxnet cyberattack), 32, 33, 34–35, 276
Operation Uphold Democracy, 265–74
opportunists, uses of coercively engineered migration, 263
Outer Space Treaty (1967), 37, 124, 126–27
over-the-horizon (OTH) radars (Soviet Union), 225
overreaction by opponents, to CDD implementation, 61

Pahlavi, Mohammad Reza, 31
Pakistan, 2, 72, 266t
peer and pariah asymmetrical challenge era (c. 2014–?), 76
Peloponnesian War (431-404 BCE)
    Athens naval superiority, 167
    Corcyra and, 166–90, 193–95
    Corinth and, 167, 169, 170–71, 172–73, 174–75, 176–77
    cross-domain asymmetries, 168, 173, 180
    cross-domain deterrence, during the war, 174–79

cross-domain deterrence, pre-war, 168–74
Delian League and, 169, 171, 178–79, 180–81
events leading up to, 170, 171–72
implications of CDD theory, 180–83
pre-war cross-domain deterrence, 168–74
sea power vs. land power, 163–83
Sparta's army's strength, limited naval abilities, 167–68
Thucydides and, 1, 168–74, 176
People's Liberation Army (PLA; China), 8, 12–13
Pershing II intermediate-range ballistic missiles (IRBMs), 208, 215
Persian Gulf War (1991), 128–29
Petya ransomware incident, 104
Philippines
    Enhanced Defense Cooperation Agreement with U.S., 330
    membership in Asian Infrastructure Investment Bank, 324–25
    U.S. agreements of support with, 330
phishing, 112, 114, 336–37
physical implementation factors, in CDD, 60
Poland
    coercively engineered migration from, 266t
    eviction of Soviet forces, 313
    leadership of Warsaw States in pursuing reforms, 303–4
    move toward "democratic neo-socialism" 303
    pursuit of political and military reforms, 303–8
    response to Gorbachev's call for reforms, 301–2
    Roundtable Agreement, 302–4, 305–6
    Solidarity movement, 216, 300, 305–6
    Soviet repression in, 21
    U.S. efforts at deterring Soviets in, 302–8
    Warsaw Pact, 217, 298–99
political agitation pathway, in CEM, 274
Posen, Barry, vii–viii, 10, 133
Presidential Directive 59 (PD-59), 214
Presidential Policy Directive 21 (cyberspace deterrence), 101
Prevention of the Placement of Weapons in Outer Space Treaty, 136–37
Protocol on Blinding Laser Weapons (Protocol IV, 1980 Geneva Convention), 193–94
Proznitz, Beth, vii–viii
psy-ops
    Soviet alarm at, 218–19
    U.S. Cold War launch, 216, 218–19, 227
psychological considerations, in CDD, 60
punishment strategy(ies). *See also* coercively engineered migration; terrorism
    cyberspace attacks and, 114
    deterrence-by-punishment strategies, 114–15, 116, 138
    strategic bombing as, 6–7, 274, 341–42, 348–50
    U.S. government articulation of, 103–4
Putin, Vladimir, 27–28, 54–55

"Quadrennial Defense Review Report" (Rumsfeld), 28
Quang Tri, fall of (Vietnam War), 156
Quester, George, vii–viii, 37

Radar Ocean Reconnaissance Satellites (RORSATs)(Soviet Union), 125–26
rational deterrence theory, 20, 335
Reagan, Ronald, 191, 214, 216, 300
  psy-ops launched by, 216, 218–19, 227
reciprocity, of deterrence, 189, 191, 192–93, 358
religious conflicts, challenges of deterring, containing, ending, 67
Revolution in Military Affairs (RMA), 127–28
Rid, Thomas, 106–7
robotics, 2, 12–13, 355–56
Rodman, Peter, 305–6
Romania, 301–2
Rommel, Erwin, 155, 158–59
Roosevelt, Franklin D., 243, 301
Roundtable Agreement (Poland; 1989), 302–4, 305–6
Royal Air Force (RAF) Fighter Command, 153
Rumsfeld, Donald, 28
Rundstedt, Karl Rudolf von, 155, 158–59
Russia
  advocacy for space weapons ban, 9–10
  aggression in Ukraine, 4, 27–28
  antisatellite weapons development, testing, 132
  antisatellite weapons threats from, 122–23
  asymmetrical, cross-domain capabilities, 89
  CDD history and, 4
  cyberspace deterrence needs against, 104–5
  cyberspace's role in warfighting doctrine, 99
  hacking/cyber capability, 72
  harnessing of commercial revolution in space, 135
  hybrid warfare, 78–79, 89
  invasion of South Ossetia, 7–8
  naval blockade of Abkhazia invasion of South Ossetia, 7–8
  nuclear threats by, 74–75
  occupation of Crimea, 73
  opposition to Western deterrence policy, 59
  penetrations of Pentagon systems, 7–8
  political/economic systems collapse, post-Cold War, 127
  present nuclear capabilities, 27–28
  proposal of ASAT limits, 136–37
  provocation of territorial disputes, 68–69
  revival of Cold War with U.S., 64
  SA-10/SA-12 surface-to-air missiles, 145
  strategic challenges posed by, vii
  strategic deterrence of, 3
  U.S. electoral hacking (2016), 103–4
  warnings about space domain conflicts, 124
  the West's perception of, 54–55
RYaN, nuclear missile attack program (Russia), 227

Sadat, Anwar, 45, 46
sanctions, 54
Sanger, David, 32–33
satellites. *See also* antisatellite (ASAT) weapons
  deterrence of attacks on, 187
  Keyhole-11 satellites, 125
  low-earth orbit satellites, 9–10, 205–6
  nuclear weapons attacks on, 124–25
  telecommunications satellite revolution, 124
Saudi Arabia, 164–65, 266t, 329
Schelling, Thomas, 21, 29, 288
Schwartz, Norton, 11–12
Scowcroft, Brent, 300–1
Scud missiles, 128–29
sea (maritime) domain
  Anglo-German naval arms race, 164–65
  antisubmarine warfare operations, U.S., 208
  Athens vs. Greece conflicts, 166–68
  China's "antiaccess" effort, 165
  China's South and China Sea operations, 11–12, 165
  cyber domain integration with, 66–67, 98–99
  fragility of chokepoints in, 11–12
  geopolitics and, 164
  ISR systems' impact on, 142
  passage of NATO ships through the GIUK gap, 217
  Soviet ballistic missile submarines, 206, 208, 209–11, 214, 217, 229, 358
  space operations in, 66–67
  STRATCOM focus on, 7
  threat levels, 164
  U.S. Navy Pacific battle group exercise, 217
sea power vs. land power, 163–83. *See also* Peloponnesian War
secrecy
  Chinese military modernization and, 12–13
  cyberspace domain and, 20, 116
  signaling and, 116–18, 214–18
  space domain and, 20
Serbian army (in Kosovo), 145
Shammugam, Kasiviswanathan, 326
Shevardnadze, Eduard, 307
Shimshoni, Jonathan, 275
"shock and awe" weapons, 79
Shultz, George, 300
signaling
  about space domain, 126–27, 141
  alliance signaling, 238
  of clandestine cross-domain capabilities, 214–18
  coercively engineered migration and, 276–77
  commitment signaling, 237
  commitment tensions, 29
  cross-domain challenges, 19–20
  cyberweapons and, 231–32
  cybespace and, 114
  of deterrent policies, successes, 106
  honest signaling in negotiations, 199

of nuclear escalation, 124–25
nuclear signaling, 47
optimistic views on, 229
political advantages gained by, 230–31
secrecy and, 116–18, 214–18
space signaling, 9–10
by the U.S., in the Cold War, 207, 209–14
signaling with secrets, 116–18, 205
Signals Intelligence (SIGINT; NSA), 7, 208
Simons, Thomas, 306–7
simplicity and complexity, of nuclear deterrence, 70–71
Six-Day War (1967), 45
SM-3 (Standard Missile-3), 9–10
social engineering techniques, 114. *See also* phishing
societal warfare, 275
sociotechnical complexity, 4
Solidarity movement (Independent Self-Governing Trade Union), Poland, 216, 300, 305–6
Sony Corporation, cyberattacks against, 101–2, 114, 231–32, 367
South Africa, 72
South Asia, 53
South China Sea
  China's anti-access/area-denial strategy in, 27–28
  China's maritime objectives in, 232, 254
  potential U.S.-China face-off, 320
South Korea
  foreign policy debates in, 234–35
  membership in Asian Infrastructure Investment Bank, 324–25
  U.S. deployment of THAAD missile system in, 331–32
South Vietnam, coercively engineered migration, 266t
South Vietnamese Army (Army of the Republic of Vietnam; ARVN), 153–54, 157
Southeast Asia, 323–24, 326–27
Soviet Air Defense, 216
Soviet ballistic missile submarines (SSBNs), 206, 208, 209–11, 214, 217, 229, 358
Soviet Radar Ocean Reconnaissance Satellites (RORSATs), 125–26
Soviet Union. *See also* KGB; Russia
  ability to attack Western Europe on short notice, 300–1
  alarm at U.S. psy-ops, 218–19
  antisatellite weapons programs, 125–26
  asymmetric cross-domain responses, 227–28
  ballistic missile submarines, 206
  C3 systems vulnerability, 222, 226–27
  downing of Korean Airlines flight, 218–19, 226
  eviction from Poland, Hungary, Czechoslovakia, 313
  GRU/military intelligence organization, 227
  human intelligence superiority, 227
  intercontinental ballistic missiles, 76–77, 206, 208, 226, 229
  intercontinental ballistic missiles (ICBMs), 76–77, 206, 208, 226, 229
  Istrebel Sputnikov ("Satellite Killer"), 125
  military arsenal of, 1
  nuclear balance, meaning of, 219–20
  nuclear command and control (NC2) space systems, 124
  nuclear vulnerabilities, 219–25
  policy adjustments, 225–28
  post-Cold War weakness, 214, 223–25
  post-Stalin foreign policy shift, 36
  pressures of long-term competition, 223–25
  reconnaissance satellites, 125–26
  repression in Poland and East Germany, 21
  sea domain weapons, 206
  space domain weapons, 206
  space systems, real-time warning, 124
  Strategic Arms Reduction Treaties with the U.S., 76–77, 194–95
  symmetric technological responses, to U.S., 225–26
  U.S. focus on competing for power and influence with, 299–302
  Yom Kippur War and, 46–47
space domain, 3, 8. *See also* space operations; space security; space warfare
  Asian space race, 132–33
  assurance and, 251–55
  CDD history and, 4
  challenges of cross-domain deterrence, 138–42
  China's threat to, 35–36
  Clapper's comments on, 121
  credibility factors, 18
  cross-domain with cyberspace, 8–9
  cyber domain integration with, 66–67, 68–69, 98–99
  description, 8–9
  deterrence challenges, 15–16
  differences from cyber domain, 9
  fragility of chokepoints in, 11–12
  growing threat of conflicts in, 133–36
  importance to China, 129
  as key U.S. domain, 10
  Outer Space Treaty, 37, 124
  reliance on cyberspace, 8–9
  space-based signals intelligence, 7, 208
  stable/stabilizing nature, Cold War era, 124
  Trump administration policy, 121–22
  U.S. dependence on, 18
  U.S. operational concepts, 125–26
  warnings about conflicts in, 124
space operations
  bargaining characteristics of, 350
  Bush administration policy on, 9–10, 35–36
  Bush, George W., space policy, 35–36
  Cold War, 75–76

space operations (*cont.*)
  cyber integration with, 68–69, 88–89
  dependencies and vulnerabilities, 75
  impact of ASAT technology on, 18
  in multiple domains, 66–67, 69
  nuclear warfare and, 124–25
  technocratic experts management of, 9
space security
  geopolitics and growing threat to, 131–32
  National Security Space Strategy, 122–23, 137–38
  renewed focus on, 122–23
  U.S DoD spending on, 121–22
space warfare. *See also* antisatellite (ASAT) weapons
  asymmetrical responses and, 74–75
  debris potential of, 9–10
  Gulf War as "first space war," 128–29
  impact on nuclear forces, 86
  inherent cross-domain problems, 18
  U.S. incentives for avoiding, 135
Sparta (ancient Greece). *See* Peloponnesian War
Sparta (ancient Sparta), 166–68
spearphishing, 112, 114
Special Operations Command (SOCOM), 5
Sputnik I, 68–69
stability-instability paradox, 15, 181, 364–65
Stalin, Joseph, 36, 39
Starfish Prime nuclear test (outer space, 1962), 67
status quo powers, 163–64
Steene, Shawn, 137–38
Strategic Air Command (SAC; U.S.), 216
Strategic Arms Reduction Treaty I (SALT I), 194–95
Strategic Arms Reduction Treaty II (SALT II), 76–77
strategic bombing (strategic bombing doctrine), 6–7, 274, 341–42, 348–50
Strategic Bombing Survey (U.S.), 87
"Strategic Concept" (NATO; 1999), 247
Strategic Defense Initiative (SDI), 191
strategic deterrence (Russia), 3
strategic regional complexity era (c. 2009-2013), 76
Strategic Rocket Forces (SRF; Soviet Union), 221, 222–23
Strategic Support Force (China), 9
Stuxnet operation, in Iran, 235
Stuxnet (Operation Olympic Games) cyberattack, 7–8, 17, 32, 33, 34–35, 48. *See also* Iran cyberattack on uranium centrifuges
suicide attacks strategy, 27–28
Sun Tzu, 151, 152, 336–37
Syria
  chemical weapons, 73
  U.S. airstrikes over, 161–62
  use of chemical weapons in, 73, 290–91
  Yom Kippur War and, 45
Syrian Civil War, 290–91

tailored deterrence, 28–29
technologies. *See also* antisatellite (ASAT) weapons; nuclear weapons
  anti-access/area-denial technologies, 211
  artificial intelligence, 12–13
  attribution technologies, 104, 120
  classical deterrence theory and, 15–16
  communication technology, 97–98
  contradictory expectations of, 3
  cross-domain technology, 4, 8–9, 56–57, 62, 80, 202–4, 206, 208–9, 212, 215–16, 219
  development of "puncture" capabilities, 241–42
  geopolitics and, 71
  GPS-guidance systems, 128–29
  increasing complexity of, 206
  information technology, 71, 81, 84, 97–98, 112
  jamming systems, 106, 115, 135, 136, 141
  military technologies, 17–18, 60, 69, 207, 208–9, 224, 241–42
  potentially disruptive effects of, 2
  "shock and awe" weapons, 79
  space/cyberspace technologies, 20, 48, 96, 97–98, 250–51
  strategic dual use of, 72
  symmetric technological response, 225
  technological singularity, 69
  telecommunications satellite revolution, 124
  U.S. advantage vs. Soviets, 206, 208–9, 212, 215–16, 219, 223–4
telecommunications satellite revolution (1970s-1980s), 124
Terminal High Altitude Area Defense (THAAD; U.S.), 331–32
terrorism
  air strike retaliation against, 4
  Bush's "Axis of Evil" description, 32
  challenges of deterring, containing, ending, 67
  global expansion of, 50, 66–67
  retaliatory measure against, 4
  terrorist groups, 2
Tet Offensive (1968), 153–54
Thailand, 266t, 324–25
The Three Power Alliance and a United States-Japanese War (Matsuo), 37
Thucydides, 1, 168–74, 176, 278. *See also* Peloponnesian War
Trans-Pacific Partnership (TPP), 320–21, 326, 328
treaties. *See also* North Atlantic Treaty Organization
  ASAT Treaty, 127
  common knowledge and ratification of, 192–93
  content specificity importance, 193–94
  mechanics of working with deterrence, 193–94
  negotiation challenges, 199–203
  nuclear deterrence and, 195–97
  Outer Space Treaty, 37, 124, 126–27, 136–37
  Peloponnesian War, 168
  probable responses discussions, 200–2
  ratification of, 192–93

reciprocity of deterrence and, 189
Strategic Arms Reduction Treaty I, 194–95
Strategic Arms Reduction Treaty II, 76–77
strategic incentives created by, 194–95
Trojan Horse, Greek mythology, 336–37
Truman, Harry S., 38, 301, 320
Trump, Donald (Trump administration)
  campaigns' allegations of electoral tampering, 231–32
  inconsistent messaging from, 330–31
  National Security Strategy, 121–22
  "Nuclear Posture Review" (2018), 49, 60
  tensions with North Korea, 60
Tsygichko, Vitalli, 224
21st Century Cross-Domain Deterrence Initiative (CDDI), vii, 13

Uganda, coercively engineered migration, 266t
Ukraine
  decision to give up nuclear weapons, 72
  Russian aggression in, 4, 27–28, 290–91
  U.S.-Russia-Ukraine Trilateral Statement, 73
UN Security Council, 50, 55, 66–67
UN Security Council Summit (1992), 72
unipolar moment (1990s), 127–28
United Kingdom (UK)
  ASEAN states use of CEM against, 262–63
  preoccupation with deterrence, 50
  role in overthrowing Mosaddegh, 31
  Roosevelt's assurance to, 243
United States-Russia-Ukraine Trilateral Statement, 73
United States (U.S.). *See also* Bush, George H.W.; Bush, George W.; Obama, Barack
  abandonment of Trans-Pacific Partnership, 326
  airstrikes over Iraq, Syria, 161–62
  alliance with East Asia, 236, 240–41, 245, 320–22, 329–32
  antisatellite weapons programs, 125–26
  ASAT test, 9–10
  ASEAN states use of CEM against, 262–63
  Budget Control Act (2010), 330–31
  C3 advantage of, 214
  CANOPY WING ("black" program), 215–16, 226–27
  cautiousness in domain shifting, 17
  challenges in conducting conflicts, 63–64
  China-U.S. conflict, sea domain, 165, 181–83
  China-U.S. maritime conflict, 165, 181–83
  China's focus on vulnerabilities of, 27–28
  on China's military modernization, 11–12
  China's threats to maritime dominance of, 165–66
  coercion example, 14
  coercively engineered migration, 266t
  Cold War nuclear strategy, 206, 208
  counter-force strikes focus, WW II, 36–37
  cyber deterrence policies, practices, 100–4
  cyberspace strategies, initiatives, 95–96, 99
  defensive alliance commitments, 235–36
  denuclearization efforts, 77
  dependence on space domain, 18
  deployment of THAAD missile system, 331–32
  economic sanctions imposed by, 32–33
  efforts at deterring Soviets in Eastern Europe, 291, 298–300, 301, 302–8
  extended nuclear deterrence policy, 234–55
  fear of ASAT attack on, 121, 122–23, 134
  first strike incentives, space domain, 135
  general deterrence activities, 67–68
  harnessing of commercial revolution in space, 135
  ideological rivalry with China, 165
  invasion of Iraq, 32
  Iran Sanctions Act, 32
  Iran's deteriorating relations with, 31
  Korean War, 38
  late Cold War nuclear strategy, 208
  Massive Retaliation doctrine, 200–1
  military arsenal of, 1
  military complexity, 67–68
  National Defense Strategy, 11–12
  National Security Act, 68–69
  National Security Council documents, 125–26
  National Security Space Strategy, 122–23, 137–38
  "New Look" nuclear weapons policy, 34
  9/11 attacks on, 28
  nuclear alert during Yom Kippur War, 47
  nuclear command and control (NC2) space systems, 124
  nuclear doctrine, 238
  "offshore balancing" strategy, 10–11
  Posen on U.S. military power, 10
  post-2016 election tension with North Korea, 60
  preparations for actions against national security space systems, 123
  Presidential Directive 59, 214
  reluctance to use cyber operations in the offense, 119
  revival of Cold War with Russia, 64
  role in attack on Iranian uranium centrifuges, 7–8, 32–35
  role in overthrowing Mosaddegh, 31
  SALT treaties with Soviet Union, 194–95
  signaling during the Cold War, 207, 209–14
  Soviet power/influence competition with, 299–302
  space domain operational concepts, 125–26
  space domain's importance, 10, 18
  space systems, real-time warning, 124
  Strategic Arms Reduction Treaties with Soviet Union, 76–77, 194–95
  Strategic Bombing Survey, 87
  support agreements with the Philippines, 330

United States (U.S.) (*cont.*)
  turn to training, special operations, protection, selective attacks, 63
  warnings about space domain conflicts, 124
  World War I isolationism, neutrality strategy, 243
United States (U.S.)-China relations
  China's East Asia dominance, 318–19
  China's South China Sea objectives, 14.P8, 27–28, 232, 254, 330
  China's threats against Taiwan, 332
  nonmilitary economic and regional relations, 323–49
  potential face-off over East Asia regional hegemony, 320
  U.S. alliance with East Asia, 236, 240–41, 245, 320–22, 329–32
  Vietnam's Cam Ranch Bay port facilities issue, 327–28
University of California San Diego (UCSD) Center for Peach and Security Studies (cPASS), vii–viii
U.S. Air Force Cyberspace Task Force, 6–7
U.S. Air Force Space Command, 122–23
U.S. Congressional Budget Office, 330–31
U.S. Cyber Command, 68–69, 97, 208
"U.S. Cyberspace Policy Review" (2009), 99–100
U.S. Department of Defense
  "Cross-Domain Deterrence and Credible Threats," 29–30
  Cyber Strategy (2015), 102–3
  "Joint Publication 3-12: Cyberspace Operations," 97–98, 102–3
  Minerva Initiative, vii
  National Security Space Strategy revision, 122–23
  role in Operation Olympic Games, 34
  space control review, 121–22
U.S. Department of Defense Cyberspace Strategy, 95–96
U.S. Department of Homeland Security, 101
U.S. Department of Justice, 103
U.S. Department of State, 68–69, 95–96, 101
U.S. Department of Treasury, 101, 103
U.S. Department of War, 68–69
U.S. Director of National Intelligence, 122–23
U.S. Joint Force, 5
U.S. Military Sealift Command, 327–28
U.S. military superiority era (c. 1992-1998), 76
U.S. National Reconnaissance Office, 125
U.S. nuclear monopoly era (c. 1945-1949), 76
U.S. nuclear superiority era (c.1950-1960), 76
U.S. Office of Personnel Management, 108–9
U.S. Senate Foreign Relations Committee, 326
U.S. Strategic Command, 29, 32–33
U.S. Strategic Command (STRATCOM), 7–8, 68–69
Ustinov, Dmitry, 222–23

Vietnam
  Cam Ranch Bay port facilities issue, 327–28
  coercively engineered migration, 266t
  diversification of economic ties, 328
  ties to China, 327
  Trans-Pacific Partnership negotiations, 328
Vietnam War
  air-to-air engagement in, 146
  Easter Offensive, 144–46, 147, 153–55, 156–57, 158, 161
  fall of Quang Tri, 156
  Tet Offensive, 153–54
Vishnevsky, Sergei, 228
Visiting Forces Agreement (U.S.-Philippines), 330

Walker, John, 217–18
WannaCry ransomware incident, 104
war. *See* bargaining theory of war; nuclear war; specifc wars
warfare
  CDD-D and, 64
  China's doctrine on, 8
  electronic warfare, 18
  guerilla/insurgent, 50
  "information" warfare, 6–7
  large-scale non-nuclear, 42
  space warfare, 9–10
  Western "hybrid" warfare, 3
warfighting domains. *See* air domain; cyberspace domain; land domain; sea (maritime) domain; space domain
Warsaw Pact, 217, 298–99, 303
weapons of mass destruction (WMD)
  cross-domain activities comparison, 90
  deterrent effects of, 71–72
  Libya's giving up of programs, 73
  Majors on the dangers of proliferation of, 71
  multidomain qualities of, 67, 69–70
  nonnuclear WMDs, 81
  types of, 90
the West
  backlash against values of, 74
  China's view of, 55
  domestic environments impact on deterrence, 55
  Middle East ethnic/religious anger at, 54
  negative perception of Russia, 54–55
  surprise at China's ASAT tests, 35–36
  use of nonfatal/limited casualty steps, 54
West Germany (Federal Republic of Germany)
  coercively engineered migration, 266t
  efforts at reuniting Germany, 309, 310, 311–12
Whitehead, John C., 300
Widodo, Joko, 326–27
Williams, Brett, 97
WMD. *See* weapons of mass destruction
Wohlforth, William, 329
World Bank, 325–26

World Trade Organization (WTO), 191
World War I (WW I), 243, 298
World War II (WW II), 36–37, 240–42, 243–44
World War III (WW III), 279–80

Yarhi-Milo, Keren, 116–17
Yom Kippur War (1973), 45
    Brezhnev and, 45, 46
    ceasefire/ceasefire violations, 45
    description, 45
    Nixon and, 45, 48
    Sadat and, 45, 46
    Soviet Union and, 46–47
    U.S. nuclear alert during, 47
Yugoslavia, 263

Zetter, Kim, 32
Zhou Enlai, 36

CPSIA information can be obtained
at www.ICGtesting.com
Printed in the USA
BVHW031453090120
569011BV00004B/10/P